DIRECTORY
ENABLED NETWORKS

John Strassner

MACMILLAN
TECHNICAL
PUBLISHING
U·S·A

Directory Enabled Networks

By John Strassner

Published by:
Macmillan Technical Publishing
201 West 103rd Street
Indianapolis, IN 46290 USA

International Standard Book Number: 1-57870-140-6

Library of Congress Catalog Card Number: 99-62126

03 02 01 00 99   7 6 5 4 3 2 1

Interpretation of the printing code: The rightmost double–digit number is the year of the book's printing; the rightmost single–digit number is the number of the book's printing. For example, the printing code 99-1 shows that the first printing of the book occurred in 1999.

Composed in Galliard and MCPdigital by Macmillan Computer Publishing

Printed in the United States of America

Trademark Acknowledgments

Warning and Disclaimer

Feedback Information

At Macmillan Technical Publishing, our goal is to create in–depth technical books of the highest quality and value. Each book is crafted with care and precision, undergoing rigorous development that involves the unique expertise of members from the professional technical community.

Readers' feedback is a natural continuation of this process. If you have any comments regarding how we could improve the quality of this book, or otherwise alter it to better suit your needs, you can contact us at networktech@mcp.com. Please make sure to include the book title and ISBN in your message.

We greatly appreciate your assistance.

PUBLISHER
David Dwyer

EXECUTIVE EDITOR
Linda Ratts Engelman

MANAGING EDITOR
Gina Brown

ACQUISITIONS EDITOR
Karen Wachs

DEVELOPMENT EDITOR
Lisa M. Thibault

PROJECT EDITOR
Theresa Wehrle

COPY EDITOR
Anne Owen

INDEXER
Cheryl Landis

AQUISITIONS COORDINATOR
Jennifer Garrett

MANUFACTURING COORDINATOR
Brook Farling

BOOK DESIGNER
Ann Jones

COVER DESIGNER
Karen Ruggles

LAYOUT TECHNICIANS
Steve Balle-Gifford
Amy Parker

About the Author

John Strassner, as a Cisco Fellow, drives the use of DEN and policy-based networking. The original inventor of DEN, he is responsible for the overall direction and strategy for the definition and development of directory services and directory enabled networking for Cisco Systems. He is a co-founder of the DEN Initiative, an open initiative that models network elements and services in the directory. John is instrumental in setting the direction for directory- and policy-enabled products and technologies within Cisco, as well as defining a new set of applications that will enable the creation of Intelligent Network products and services.

John is the Chair of the Networks Working Group of the DMTF (Distributed Management Task Force). This standards body oversees the development of the part of the Common Information Model (CIM) that models network elements and services and is responsible for the DEN effort and specification. John is a voting member of the CIM TDC, an architectural board that directs the overall development of the CIM, as well as an active member in several other DMTF working groups.

In addition, John is the co-chair of two IETF working groups: the LDUP (LDAP Duplication and Update Protocol) Working Group, which is tackling LDAP-based replication; and the Policy Framework Working Group, which is specifying a standard architecture for policy representation and communication, along with an accompanying Information Model, generalized schema (applicable to all disciplines), and specific schema for network QoS. John is an active member of several other IETF working groups.

John has an extensive background in distributed systems, directories, and directory-enabled applications. He speaks regularly on the topic of directory enabled networks and policy at Cisco customer meetings and conferences, such as Networld+Interop. He received a B.S. in Electrical Engineering from the University of Southern California.

About the Technical Reviewers

These reviewers contributed their considerable practical, hands-on expertise to the entire development process for *Directory Enabled Networks*. As the book was being written, these folks reviewed all the material for technical content, organization, and flow. Their feedback was critical to ensuring that *Directory Enabled Networks* fits our readers' need for the highest quality technical information.

Thomas McNeill is a Consulting Software Engineer for SwitchSoft Systems, Inc., a developer of network management software. He joined SwitchSoft Systems when it was the Utah Development Center of UB Networks. Prior to SwitchSoft Systems, he worked in the Advanced Technology Group of WordPerfect Corporation, later Novell. Thomas has been involved in the Directory Enabled Networks Initiative since its inception. He is an active member of the Networks Working Group of the DMTF, in which he has focused especially on the modeling of virtual LANs. Thomas is a member of the ACM and the IEEE Computer Society. He received a Ph.D. in Computer Science from Brigham Young University.

Chris Lowde graduated from the University of Warwick, UK, in 1977, and has worked in the information technology arena in a variety of roles. For the past 15 years, Chris worked for Texaco where he was the Data Center supervisor at their Pembroke Refinery in the UK before moving to Houston 10 years ago to work on a series of projects relating to the use and implementation of Open Systems at Texaco's Refineries. Chris was the principal architect of Texaco's migration to a unified messaging system and is currently working on re-architecting Texaco's client/server architecture to support Texaco's business into the next decade. Chris was a member of the DEN Customer Advisory Board that oversaw the development of the DEN specification and its hand over to the DMTF.

OVERVIEW

Contents

Dedication

For my wife, Kim, without whose love and support this book would not have been possible.

Acknowledgments

I would first like to thank my parents for their constant encouragement and support. I'd also like to thank Shari Daiuto and Carla Leal for also lending an ear and helping in their own ways.

Sincere thanks go to my management at Cisco Systems for encouraging me and supporting me in writing this book. I also would like to thank several key industry people for their thoughtful discussions concerning subjects discussed in this book: Fred Baker, Jim Turner, Keith McCloghrie, Silvano Gai, Andrea Westerinen, Ed Ellesson, Lee Rafalow, and Bob Moore.

Thanks in general to the Networks Working Group of the DMTF for doing a remarkable job of getting the Networks Model of CIM 2.2 out the door, especially Thomas McNeill, Al Grimstad, Walter Weiss, Lee Rafalow, and Marc Lavine. Thanks also to the many people in the Policy Framework Working Group of the IETF who provided valuable support and assistance in designing the architecture and enhancing the DEN Policy Model. Specifically, I would like to thank Steve Schleimer, Keith McCloghrie, Silvano Gai, Dave Durham, Francis Reichmeyer, Hugh Mahon, Shai Herzog, Mark Stevens, Andrea Westerinen, Ed Ellesson, Lee Rafalow, and Bob Moore.

I would especially like to thank Thomas McNeill and Chris Lowde, who provided valuable feedback and suggestions during the course of their review of this book.

Finally, I'd like to thank the incredible team at Macmillan Technical Publishing, especially Linda Engelman, Lisa Thibault, and Jennifer Garrett. Their guidance improved this book and made me a better writer in the process.

Foreword

Managing the Network

In 1990, I was involved in the development of a network management protocol in the Internet Engineering Task Force (IETF). One of the raging debates, at the time, considered the relative merits of three major contenders: ISO's Common Management Interface Protocol (CMIP), Craig Partridge's Hierarchical Entity Management Service (HEMS), and the Simple Network Management Protocol (SNMP). Each did approximately the same thing in its own way: enabled a central network management system to communicate with agents in managed systems about their configuration and status. Each had its merits and its shortcomings, and the level of debate varied from the pragmatic to the religious. Craig removed his proposal from the running with a statement that has haunted me ever since: "The interesting thing about network management is not the protocol used to communicate between the network management system and the managed device, but the artificial intelligence system you place on top of it."

Our problem in network management has been, in short, that we have never actually managed the network. What we have managed is the individual devices in the network. We understand reasonably well, at least in a static network, what it is to give an interface an IP Address, give a system a name, determine how much traffic has passed a certain way, or decide when something has become active or gone away. We even have an idea of how to do those things in a network composed of dynamic links, if the network is simple enough, and as long as real-time failure detection and recovery (apart from re-routing data) in an occasional access network is not a requirement. We have been less successful at managing configurations in a scalable manner. In networks of a decade ago, where there were thousands or tens of thousands of end systems but at most tens to hundreds of network elements like routers and switches, this was challenging but doable. Today's networks, however, contain thousands to tens of thousands of network elements, and device-centric management simply cannot cope. We must manage the network itself, or ultimately fail to manage anything at all.

Directory enabled networking, of which this book's author was one of the original designers, holds the promise of enabling us to cross this conceptual barrier. It enables us to tell the network, in some sense, that it should be configured in such a way as to achieve a specific business objective, and let it determine what individual device configuration is necessary to implement that. This step forward involves new concepts and new complexities, but in the end may systemically solve the problem of massive unorganized detail, or at least part of it. To do so, it marries sets of systems that have traditionally passed like ships in the night: Hosts, switches, and routers operate off a common configuration database, and business systems maintained by Human Resources directly affect minute network interactions. This change in paradigm, and casting into one bed of seemingly odd bedfellows, is not without its pain and requires an explanation comprehensible to all concerned in order to be achieved.

Seeking Intelligence in the Network

The 19th Century philosopher Hegel promoted a notion that political and economic systems progress through a series of revolutions, which he referred to as the "dialectic." First, some number of differing approaches exist that meet the needs of the people who use them; the agrarian society, for example, operates first by collecting food in the forest, and then by taming the forest in domesticated fields of livestock and grain. Changes happen in it that are incompatible with the overall paradigm—blacksmiths and bakers start specialized businesses, perhaps, that serve but do not participate in the production of food, perhaps—and the tension results in societal problems. These tensions are resolved as a new paradigm evolves that better meets the needs of the changing society.

I don't know if Hegel's notions are pervasively accurate; I certainly do not walk with the political theories of his pupil, Karl Marx. I do observe that this process of thesis, antithesis, and synthesis operate in the world of ideas, however. One of these changes is occurring today in the debate about the intelligence of the network.

For the past century, telephone networks have operated on the notion that the network edge device—the telephone—must be simple, cheap, and dedicated entirely to a single purpose. Because providing good telephone service requires a great deal of intelligence, this forces all intelligence into the network itself. Because telephone networks have been entirely proprietary by nature, it has not been difficult for telephone companies to specify to their suppliers the equipment they need and the management procedures they require. Vendors have vied for the business, producing equipment at their customer's bidding. The so-called "Intelligent Network" has not been without problems, however.

The fundamental problem with the existing Intelligent Network is that changing its application requires changing the network itself. Until about 1962, voice was the only application the telephone network catered to, and it did so by mimicking the energy in sound waves with electrical energy. When the digital networking hierarchy—T-1 and T-3 trunks connecting central offices—was developed, analog circuits were relegated to the last mile, and the core of the network was unceremoniously dumped and replaced. As a result, the network became capable of supporting digital applications—not only digitized voice, but digitized video and digital communication between computers. In this past decade, as the digital networking hierarchy has proven to not sufficiently scale, we have again relegated it to the edge (business last mile), introducing SONET/SDH and ATM to the backbone. It will soon change again, collapsing under the weight of its own complexity as the network core is replaced with photonic switches. Changing the network itself is a giant task.

The Internet was developed around the opposite principle, however. The End to End Principle, as it is called, is an argument for simplicity in the network, moving intelligence to the edge device. It suggests that reliability is not to be found in a battle-hardened network element, because in such a network a chain's strength is the strength of its weakest link. Instead, it is to be found by distributing redundant functionality, capitalizing on the fact that the strength of a web is the strength of the strongest path that a given stress tests. It also suggests that if intelligence is moved to the edge, it can be readily changed at the edge without affecting the substance of the network. In this model, the network provides its "best effort" to all traffic, and the application does what is necessary to effectively take advantage of that service.

The end to end design of the Internet has been notably successful by the measure of the deployability of new applications. It was originally designed for the movement of large files between research sites, for the replacement of ASCII terminal networks with virtual terminals, and for the relay of electronic mail. These served their designers well but never anticipated the deployment of the World Wide Web. Over the summer of 1992, however, Internet traffic quadrupled, and Internet growth has never looked back. The Web has become ubiquitous that is has changed the fundamental mathematics of the Internet and obsoleted ideas about its design and optimization that once were unquestioned. Today, my sister-in-law talks about at one time having "only electronic mail access" via Juno, and now having "Internet access," by which she means the use of the Web. To me, they are both applications that use the Internet, but I sometimes wonder if I am the one who is wrong. What is important in this is that over the past decade we have deployed a new application on the Internet, essentially in our sleep, and without infrastructure changes.

The deployment of voice and video on the Internet has not been as wildly successful, although business economics will bring it wide deployment over the coming decade. There are several reasons, including the immaturity of the technology, the lack of supporting policy enforcement infrastructure, and the fact that they do require certain guarantees from the network. In short, the Best Effort paradigm has not been sufficient for its purpose. The thinking that has gone into making multimedia applications work has moved a small amount of intelligence back into the network, because it makes both mathematical and business sense to move it there. This has forced some rethinking of the design paradigm. The "Intelligent Network" of telephony and the Best Effort paradigm of the Internet are similar in two respects: They promote intelligence in one sort of device at the expense of another, and presume that the entire problem can be solved by that kind of device. If these paradigms are what Hegel would call "thesis" and "antithesis," the resulting synthesis is the network of the future, which has several interesting attributes.

First, it enfranchises every device, host or network element, permitting it as much intelligence as it requires while limiting it to the intelligence it needs. For quality of service, this has been shown necessary mathematically; a packet network is predictable if and only if both the edge devices and the network elements operate in a predictable manner. For business policy, it is also necessary; enforcement of policy must occur where traffic that might violate it can be detected, which may be at a sensitive host, a firewall, or anywhere else.

Second, it forces the aggregation of information. The network can no longer worry about the requirements of a particular application or a particular user. The first device to know about these—the host or the first hop router—is normally the last, as it marks traffic with the salient attributes of that application or person: "This application qualifies for and needs low loss and low latency for a negotiated bit rate" or "This traffic is elastic in nature, and the person originating has the privileges of a corporate officer or a certain type of contract." By handling information in useful aggregates, the network can remain suitably unencumbered with limiting intelligence, and therefore flexible, and still provide the type of service guarantees—and access controls—that it is required to deliver.

Finally, it enables the Internet to remain flexible in application deployment, using best effort techniques, while providing flexible and predictable variation in service. Many different applications—voice, video, the Web, and new applications that we have not yet thought of—can be deployed in a controlled and scaleable manner without having to redeploy the entire network.

Why a Directory?

A directory is not the obvious choice for the storage of data for a network, at least as it is conceived at this time. Why? Simply, a directory is like a telephony directory in that the information it contains is found by providing the necessary search key but may be related only tenuously to the key itself. An address or a telephone number is associated with a person's name in the sense that he may usually be found by their use; however, if he is on a business trip, the telephone directory contains the wrong information— he is not there. A computer directory may similarly contain information that is normally useful but not always true. However, for the directory to be useful to the network, the information found in it must indeed always be useful. This means one of two things: Either the information it may contain is limited to that which is always true, or it must be dynamically updated as information changes, and those changes must take effect at the time they are made.

The successful deployment of directory enabled networking, therefore, depends on significant advances in directory technology. The directory must no longer be a write-once-read-many database of salient facts but an active participant in the network, whose entries have knowledge of who needs to know about them, and whose facilities are informed of a change as a natural side effect of the fact that it was made. These changes are reflected in the growing technology of DEN.

So, why a directory? Simply, because it is there and business already knows how to use it, and because it inherently provides information containment and therefore a certain kind of security and descriptive power. One of the challenges in DEN will be to effectively leverage the directory without losing these important attributes.

Value in Information Modeling

Information modeling is the soul of this book. One might ask, "Why do we need to think so much about that?" We need Information Models because they help us organize information and deal with it effectively. For example, when we select clothing, we might observe that one shirt is red, another is blue, and another is green. Those are useful attributes for us (or at least they are for those of us who have some sense of style), but in isolation they can be unwieldy. We really don't want to ask about a shirt, "Is it red, green, blue, chartreuse, off-white, pink, or ...?" We want to ask, "What color is it?" The shirt may be assumed to have an attribute that we call "color" and that may take a number of values taken from the set of "colors." Those values may have relationships: blue "goes with" red, green, or yellow, but not with, say, purple or violet. So we may choose sets of clothing to wear together that all have the attribute "color" and whose values for that attribute meet that relationship.

Similarly, in the Internet and in corporate intranets, systems and software have attributes. The attributes may have to do with capabilities, such as "It has a certain application loaded on it." They may relate to privileges, such as "It is used by a person who is a corporate officer." They may be related to locations: "It is located in an insecure place and is therefore not trusted absent a Kerberos Ticket." They may relate to temporary conditions, like "Its Kerberos ticket is _____" or "It is involved with a Voice on IP 'telephone' call."

Objects in the Internet also have methods for dealing with their attributes. "Methods" are nothing but ways of accessing, comparing, or manipulating objects and their attributes. For example, if the attribute under consideration is color, a method may exist to change an object's color. If the object is a shirt, changing its color may involve the use of dye or bleach. If the object is a house, the same method exists but involves the use of siding or paint. If the object is a leopard's spot, Kipling's method for changing them would simply inform us that it is not meaningful in the specific context. We can enumerate the methods by object type—we can discuss dying or painting something, and know that those are different activities—but if we look for a common way to refer to them, we find it easier, perhaps, to generalize their function.

Similarly, methods in the Internet vary from device to device but can be organized for utility. For example, there are many kinds of network interfaces: ethernets, serial links, ATM connections, and so on. We understand that each has some set of attributes that tell us how much traffic has crossed them and a method for reading the current value of those numbers. The method may vary, but for objects within a class, it can be usefully referred to in an abstract way regardless of the type of object it applies to.

The important thing in information modeling is to organize and enumerate kinds, or classes, of objects, and their associated methods and attributes in a way that enables the efficient and effective management of the network. The Common Information Model and DEN are designed to make the next generation management scheme cohesive, understandable, and usable.

So, Then, About This Book...

My mother used to tell me, when I came home from my technical jaunts and tried to tell her where I had been and what I had been doing, that she would know that I understood what I was talking about when I could explain it to her in such a way that she could understand it, too. I can think of none better to explain these concepts than the present author can. I think the reader will agree that he makes it understandable to all who need to understand—not only the technical wizard, but the technical middleman who must deploy it and the manager who must describe his policies in a manner that the network can implement.

—Fred Baker

INTRODUCTION

The Internet, whether in its original form or in variations like the corporate intranet and the private extranet, is becoming a ubiquitous way of providing connectivity and application services. New applications are being conceived that have their own special requirements but are being adapted to run on the Internet due to market demand. People are demanding more robust services for less cost, which may be able to be achieved by using Internet technologies. These three factors are primarily responsible for driving an increased demand for more intelligent networking.

Technology keeps evolving to meet these needs, which means networks are becoming increasingly complex. Network device vendors install more functions on different types of network devices to solve specific problems but, in so doing, complicate the interoperation of these devices with each other. The proliferation of protocols, along with the reliance on individual device management, exacerbates this problem and makes managing network devices even harder. What is required is a new way of thinking about providing network services. Intelligence needs to be distributed between the clients using the network, the network elements themselves, and additional infrastructural components that can decide what action to take when the needs of multiple applications conflict and/or the network becomes congested.

Directory Enabled Networking (DEN) was conceived as the foundation to building an intelligent network. It is a specification, as well as a way of thinking, that defines a means to store information describing the services that the client of the networks needs and the capabilities of the devices that make up the network. This information is stored in a common repository in an agreed-upon data format. This enables applications to be able to use and share data managed by other applications. This represents a fundamentally new way of thinking about network management applications.

DEN builds on and enhances the Common Information Model (CIM), which is defined by the DMTF. It adds the modeling and management of network elements and services, and seamlessly integrates this model into the rest of CIM. This enables entire systems to be abstracted into simpler management objects.

In addition, DEN defined a basic policy model for controlling network elements and services. The DMTF and the IETF have enhanced this work, producing a richer information model that can control network elements and services in a consistent and comprehensive manner. Intelligent networking can now be achieved through employing DEN as a means to model and manage the network, its capabilities, and its services. Policy-based networking will use DEN as its foundation to bind network clients to services that the network provides to optimize the use of network resources for each service being managed.

The goal of this book is to provide a solid understanding of DEN and how it is used in both directory-enabled applications and policy-based networking. To achieve this goal, this book first provides a brief background in object modeling and directory services. CIM is first described to provide a foundation of the philosophy and functions of the model. Then, DEN is described as an extension of CIM. Finally, a brief summary of the current use of DEN in the industry, along with specific emphasis on policy-based networking, is provided. Figures illustrate every major concept.

Audience

You can benefit from this book if you are responsible for planning, implementing, or supporting intelligent networks. Specifically, CIOs, network architects, network administrators, and developers of equipment who want to position their products within a managed network will benefit from reading this book. In addition, developers of network management applications, along with developers of applications that exploit network services, will want to read this book.

This book will provide ISVs and VARs, which are developing directory enabled applications, with technical and strategic insights into building an extensible network that can be better managed.

Consultants, systems engineers, and sales engineers who design corporate networks for clients also can benefit from the technical information in this book. The material in this book can also be used as a reference resource for personnel who are responsible for managing and implementing corporate and service provider networks and services.

Organization

The book is organized into three parts. The first part provides essential background information necessary to better understand the motivation behind DEN. The second part includes a detailed exposition of CIM and DEN. The third part describes applications of directory-enabled networks and policy enabled networks.

Part I: Background Information

This section provides essential background information on DEN, including motivation for DEN and theoretical background.

Chapter 1 discusses the DEN value proposition. It provides an overview of the major reasons that drove the creation of DEN, and then defines how intelligent networks can be realized using DEN. It concludes with a discussion of the benefits of DEN and how the IETF and the DMTF are involved in the continued development of DEN.

Chapter 2 provides a brief introduction to object-oriented modeling. It defines basic terms and types of object-oriented modeling, and the structure of CIM and DEN information models. It defines the six key axioms of object-oriented modeling, and then provides an overview of attribute, method, and relationship design. Finally, it provides insight into some advanced modeling techniques.

Chapter 3 describes recommendations for extending the CIM and DEN information models. Both class as well as relationship design extension principles are discussed. Finally, a checklist for extending the information model is provided.

Chapter 4 introduces the concept of a directory service. It defines what a directory service is, as well as what a directory has been used for traditionally. It then discusses why intelligent networking needs a directory service, and explains the difference between a directory service and other types of repositories. The characteristics of directory services are then discussed. Finally, good and bad uses of a directory service, as well as application and use of directory services in networking, are explained.

Chapter 5 discusses DEN in more detail. It discusses the role of directory services in intelligent networking and how to use DEN to facilitate the implementation of intelligent networks. Finally, DEN compliance is briefly discussed.

Part II: Inside DEN

DEN is an extension of CIM, the Common Information Model. This section provides a brief background of CIM, and then discusses in detail the physical, logical, and policy models of DEN.

Chapter 6 reviews the CIM specification. This includes the meta-model, the language MOF (used to define a management information model), naming, and the three layers of CIM. Benefits of CIM are described. Finally, this chapter concludes with XML, and the newly defined XML mapping and encoding of CIM.

Chapter 7 describes the key design principles of DEN, followed by the parts of the Core and Common models that are used in the DEN model.

Chapter 8 describes the DEN physical model and how this model was migrated into CIM. The result of this process was the CIM physical model. Future directions of the physical model are also discussed.

Chapters 9 discusses the DEN logical model, and its enhancement and transition to the CIM network model. As in Chapter 8, particular attention is paid to the status of DEN classes and their relation to the new CIM network model. In some cases, they were deleted; in others, they were either kept as is or enhanced.

Chapter 10 presents the original DEN policy model and its evolution to the current IETF/DMTF policy model. This transformation required an enhancement of the basic concepts of the DEN model as well as its associated LDAP mapping. The motives for the new LDAP mapping are discussed, along with additional design insight into its implementation.

Part III: Applications of DEN

Chapter 11 discusses policy-based networking. It starts with describing the motivation for using policy-based networking, and then defines the theory behind it. Intra- versus inter-domain issues, including a detailed discussion of the emerging policy architecture, is provided. QoS policies are then discussed in detail. The chapter concludes with a partial examination of Cisco's policy-based architecture, which serves as an example of the principles discussed in this chapter.

Chapter 12 describes how DEN is currently being used. It first discusses compliance, and then examines two of Cisco's products as examples. It concludes with a survey of DEN products and support from other industry vendors.

Chapter 13 discusses the future of directory-enabled networks and policy enabled networks. It discusses the direction that policy-based networking is taking and concludes with an update of the IETF and DMTF activities in this area.

PART

I

Background Information

1

The DEN Value Proposition

Directory Enabled Networks (DENs) describe a philosophy for transforming the network from a passive collection of devices that route and forward traffic to an active set of cooperating devices that intelligently provide services to the user. DEN can fundamentally change how applications, along with network elements and services, are developed and used.

This chapter provides an overview of the value of DEN and examines some of the benefits it can provide. It then describes how Intelligent Network can be more easily implemented with DEN, and concludes with which standards bodies are currently guiding the further development of DEN.

What Is DEN?

DEN is *not* a product, or even a technology. DEN is a specification that defines an information model. This prescribes an interoperable model of network elements and services, and how each interacts with other elements of a distributed system. As such, it is an extension of the *Common Information Model (CIM)* of the *Desktop Management Task Force (DMTF)*. An *information model* is a means of describing objects comprising a system, their inter-relationships and behavior, and how data flows within the system. *CIM* is an object-oriented extensible information model for managing systems and devices. We'll explore information models and CIM in much more depth in Chapters 2 and 6, respectively.

CIM defines specific devices and systems that are to be managed. DEN builds on CIM by defining network elements and services, along with the general concepts of profiles and policies, that can be used with CIM objects to model the functions and behavior of a system. The DEN information model can be viewed as an extensible template. The fixed parts of the template describe network elements and services. The variable parts are defined by the specific CIM models that are used, which define various devices and systems that interface with network elements and services. DEN, then, is a way to manage a system that uses network elements and services.

Motivation Behind DEN: Building Intelligent Network

Technology keeps evolving, and networks have become increasingly complex in an attempt to provide better service and to meet the needs of an increased number of users and more sophisticated applications. The increasing number of different types of network elements, each running a (potentially) different set of protocols and services over (possibly) different media, has resulted in an application model that is referred to as *stovepipe applications* for building network configuration and management applications. For example, in this model, individual applications store their own data needed to configure a device in their own private data stores. This means that the same object (for example, users and devices) may be stored in different ways (for example, named differently). Even if the same representation is used in the different data stores, applications can still only access their own data, and they cannot interoperate with each other.

Two of the promises of DEN are to define a means to store data in a common repository and to provide a way for applications to be able to take advantage of data managed by other applications. This represents a fundamentally new way of thinking about network management applications, along with applications that seek to leverage the power of the network. One example of this is to compare existing network management with directory-based network management that uses DEN. In a traditional network management system, each device in the network is represented once. However, each device has detailed configuration information that is stored not in the network management system, but in either the application itself or in another data store. The role of portraying the device in the network management system is to enable the user to launch a particular management application that is focused on one or more aspects of managing that device. Thus, the network management system provides a common place to represent the device, but not to store its information.

Note

This is very different than a directory-based approach that uses DEN. The fundamental purpose of DEN is to provide a common, unifying information repository that is used to store data and information about the data (that is, metadata) for multiple applications to share and use. This is examined more thoroughly in Chapters 4, 5, and 11.

Thankfully, there are measures that can be taken to alleviate these problems. These take the form of separate efforts that were united in the DEN Initiative and consist of

- Better utilizing the directory, which is discussed in Chapters 4 and 5

- Developing and using an information model for representing network element and service information, which is discussed in Chapters 2, 3, and 6 through 10

- Simplifying the implementation of Intelligent Network, which is discussed in Chapters 11 through 13

Note

The *DEN Initiative* refers to the formation of an industry-wide ad-hoc working group to develop the DEN specification. The DEN specification is now under the charter of DMTF.

Key to this effort is the transformation of the network from a "dumb" to a "smart" entity. Currently, the network consists of a set of devices that work semi-autonomously. This does not mean to say that there is no information exchanged between the devices. Rather, it means that there is a lack of cooperation between the devices in implementing a service on behalf of a client. The "intelligent" network is one that consists of a set of devices that work together, each delivering its own part to implement a service, and adjusting as appropriate to changes in the environment in order to continue to deliver that service. The intelligent network is one where devices have distinct embedded intelligence, as in the capability to configure themselves. This is the subject of Chapters 11 through 13.

The network must support the differentiation of traffic and application of different qualities of service to different users and applications. Services, not just traffic forwarding or bandwidth, are what is now important.

There are many factors driving the need for an intelligent network. These include customer demand for applications that provide greater productivity, the need of the service provider to support differentiated services, and the need of the enterprise to ensure that the various needs of its traffic are given the appropriate priority. For example, the delivery of mission-critical traffic must be protected from people casually browsing the Internet and downloading large graphics.

The Internet is alluring due to its greatly simplified interaction paradigm, which enables the user to simply click on an object to retrieve more information about that object, and is considerably simpler than even many GUI applications, let alone applications that use a character-based or command line interface. Consequently, application vendors are striving to "Internet-enable" their applications. However, there are many applications, such as intra- and inter-company collaboration (for example, shared white boards and video-conferencing) and electronic commerce tools, that have specialized needs that traditional "best-effort" services cannot support.

The preceding is exacerbated by the growth of private intranets and secure extranets. These require additional security and traffic conditioning options above and beyond the (public) Internet.

DEN was conceived in large part to satisfy these and other concerns. DEN addressed these concerns in two ways:

- DEN defined a specification to represent and share information. This is the first step in building an intelligent network.

- It was a method to link business processes and requirements to network elements and services. For example, a *service level agreement (SLA)* defines a service contract between a customer and a service provider that specifies the expected operational characteristics of their relationship (for example, how to treat different types of traffic). An SLA may be written in relatively high-level terms (for example, provide this subscriber access to his or her corporate intranet). The danger is that the translation of this high-level objective to low-level network commands may be difficult as well as non-standard in a heterogeneous network.

DEN provides specific mechanisms to form the basis of this association in the design of its network element and services classes along with its policy classes (see Chapters 9 and 10). An added benefit is that the users and applications that consume those services can also be linked to both the business processes as well as the network elements and services.

Principal Goals of DEN

DEN has four main objectives:

- To model network elements and services, and their interaction with other elements in a managed system

- To provide the means for interoperable network-enabled solutions to be built

- To enable applications to leverage the power of the network without requiring the user to know or set esoteric network-related information

- To define a way to manage the network, as opposed to an element within a network

These objectives are described more fully in the following sections.

Modeling Network Elements and Services

Before DEN, directories did not include objects for representing or managing network elements and services. Furthermore, directories were often used to support a single application or set of applications. This gave rise to conflicting schemata that were not compatible with each other. For example, a company might have an email directory and an HR directory. A user might be represented as johns in one and jstrassn in the other. There is no simple way to know that these are in fact the same objects, which means that data not only cannot be shared, but also must be *duplicated* in each directory. Furthermore, there is no easy method to determine which data is associated with which object (for example, mail settings are associated with johns, but salary and staff are associated with the jstrassn object). This, of course, increases the overall cost in managing the data and the applications that want to use the data. Management has two aspects here:

- *Consistency checking*—Each object must be checked for any changes each time a change to the data it represents changes.

- *Referential integrity*—Some objects refer to other objects (for example, the supervisor of a set of employees); when a new supervisor is added or deleted, changes to the employees that are under his or her supervision must also be made.

This segregation of data is referred to as creating *information islands*, which is the separation of what should be common data that lives in a single common repository into separate data stores. The problem is that data that should be shared is not and cannot be shared. Information islands have in part prevented the development of standard schemata to represent these objects. For example, there are several conflicting proposals for object classes that represent users—see, for example, the Internet Organizational Person proposal from Netscape [INTOPS] and the LIPS schema proposal from the Networks Application Consortium [LIPS]. Both of these are proposals for representing user attributes in a directory.

Schema Standardization

The worry over the lack of standard schemata was, in fact, one of the driving factors behind DEN. Specifically, there was concern that network elements and services were much more complex objects than the traditional objects that were contained in a directory (for example, user and printer objects). DEN therefore needed to propose a standard schema for describing network elements and services before multiple proposals that conflicted with each other (as was the case with person objects) were generated. If everyone could agree on a single standard schema, it would be much easier to build directory-enabled solutions. This was accomplished in the DEN Initiative through two open meetings and an active email list.

In summary, two related problems were addressed by DEN:

- Network elements and services must be modeled and represented by appropriate object classes in the directory.

- A standard set of object classes, or schema, must be created to prevent the generation of multiple conflicting proposals to model network elements and services.

When DEN was being designed, it was decided that just defining a set of object classes and attributes to represent network elements and services was not enough. Even if this set of classes was standardized, the result would not be good enough, because schemata don't capture behavior, object relationships, and other non-structural aspects of interacting with a system. This is especially important for a network, whose behavior changes dynamically as a function of the environment.

Instead, a standard *information model* for representing network elements and services had to be developed. This was especially important because of the increased complexity involved in modeling network elements and services and the different ways they interact with applications, users, and systems. The DEN Initiative stated this as an explicit goal, which was endorsed by more than 175 vendors and customers. The DEN information model has provided a strong foundation for modeling the physical and logical aspects of network elements and services. Furthermore, since it is designed to be an extensible schema, adding new functionality will not affect existing functionality. This, in fact, is what the Networks Working Group of the DMTF is currently doing.

What Is the DMTF?

The *Distributed Management Task Force (DMTF)* is an industry consortium founded in 1992. It is chartered with the development, support, and maintenance of management standards that simplify the burden of enterprise management. These include Desktop Management Interface (DMI), Common Information Model (CIM), and Web-Based Enterprise Management (WBEM).

The DMTF uses a collaborative, working-committee approach that involves its members in the development of its specifications. The DMTF also works closely with related industry organizations such as the IETF, The Open Group, and the Network Management Forum (NMF) to ensure that DMTF solutions thoroughly address customer issues and overall management needs.

The goal of the DMTF is to ease the burden of PC and enterprise system management, consequently reducing the total cost of ownership.

Building Interoperable Network-Enabled Solutions

The growth in complexity in network functionality has had several impacts. First, configuring an individual network device has become increasingly complicated. This makes configuring a set of network devices to cooperatively work with each other even more difficult. Second, managing a network device is becoming more complicated. This is exacerbated by the greatly increasing number of users who want to use networked devices. The Internet, the growing popularity of extranets for linking together business partners, and the increased features of applications and their network requirements have resulted in a dramatic increase in the number, as well as the complexity, of network devices required.

This trend will keep increasing as people embrace the simpler interface paradigms of the Internet and demand applications with greater functionality to increase their productivity. So how will the needs of these more advanced applications be met?

Fundamentally, applications require the capability to have their traffic differentiated from other traffic. This enables their traffic to receive preferential services. This also implies the need to be able to quickly reconfigure the network in response to an ever-changing environment. In addition, management must be improved so that it is easier to coordinate multiple devices in providing a service. Many technological hurdles must be overcome; the following are the most important of these:

- Interoperability within the network

- Interoperability among different networking vendors

- Interoperability among the different network management applications from different vendors that comprise a network management system

- Network model extensibility

- The capability to identify and use the same class of service across different networking technologies

- Managing the different services in a multi-service network

- Integrating networking concepts with directories

Interoperability Within the Network

Network design will optimize traffic along different layers. For example, if we consider a service provider architecture, Layer 1 and 2 networks supply traffic from various customers into the network of the Internet service provider (ISP). Different technologies, such as SONET, Dial, Frame Relay, xDSL, and ISDN, all route traffic to the network, which now has to figure out what to do with each type of traffic. The ISP network will use Layers 2 and 3 technologies to treat each traffic stream appropriately. This is illustrated in Figure 1.1.

Figure 1.1   Simplified service provider support architecture.

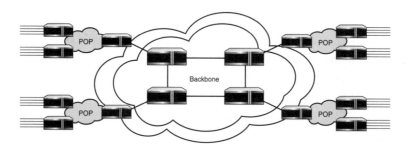

In the ISP's network, the network elements at the edge of the network perform a much different set of functions than those in the core of the network. Network elements at the edge are responsible for identifying, filtering, and controlling traffic, whereas network elements at the core of the network want to forward traffic as quickly and as efficiently as possible, along with managing congestion if it occurs. Network edge elements are where service policies are applied and where statistics on customer usage are gathered. Consequently, these devices require the highest intelligence to differentiate traffic and provide the flexibility to create new services.

This implies that to provide an end-to-end service, the edge and core devices must work together to condition the traffic appropriately. DEN is more than just a model that represents the functionality of a given network element; it contains metadata (for example, data describing the purpose and/or use of data) that enable the function or role of the modeled component to be described. This helps relate edge and core functions to the provisioning of a network service.

Interoperability Among Different Networking Vendors

Most service providers and enterprises want to use equipment from different network vendors. This helps them maintain their relative independence from networking vendors. This enables service providers and enterprises to use specialized equipment, provides a good balance between functionality and cost, and diminishes the chances of any one supplier from furnishing all their needs. However, it complicates matters because different network elements now must recognize the same service and play their parts in providing that service. This applies not just to network elements, but also to host devices and servers. For example, Figure 1.2 shows a route that electronic commerce traffic took from within Cisco to a vendor on the Internet.

Figure 1.2 The complexities in providing an end-to-end service.

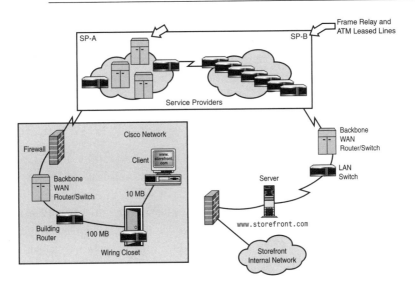

DEN provides an extensible information model to help achieve this interoperability between network elements, servers, applications, and other components of an end-to-end service. DEN models each of these components in a customizable amount of detail; then models their various inter-relationships. DEN provides a rich foundation for defining policies to control, manage, and share data between multiple components in a vendor-independent way.

The work of the Policy Framework Working Group of the IETF [PFWG] is also of great importance in solving this problem. This is discussed more thoroughly in Chapters 10 and 11. Note that the PFWG is using all the DEN policy classes as the basis for its work.

Network Model Extensibility

It is very important that the underlying network model be extensible by vendors in order to model their specific devices and mechanisms. This requires a way for the model to enable common information to be communicated in a vendor-independent fashion while providing a means for vendor-specific information to be represented and mapped to the vendor-independent information.

For example, the physical aspects of a network element are divided into a number of different DEN classes. `PhysicalPackage` is a class that represents physical elements that contain or host other physical elements. `Card` is a class that defines the characteristics of different types of cards that can be installed in a network device, such as system, networking, and memory cards. There are additional classes that model other physical aspects of a network device. This paradigm of partitioning functionality into separate, modular classes enables vendors to model common information using standard DEN classes and to model vendor-specific information using vendor-specific subclasses derived from the DEN standard classes.

As another example, assume that a `Gold` class of service is to be provided for streaming video traffic. Further suppose that this traffic will pass through the equipment of multiple network vendors. The parameters of this `Gold` class of services in high-level terms (for example, jitter, latency, and so on) must be able to be specified in a vendor-independent manner. Each vendor's network element must be able to recognize what is required of that device relative to the delivery of the traffic according to `Gold` service contract and configure the device appropriately. For example, one vendor might use one form of queuing to manage congestion, whereas another might use a different form of queuing for the same function. Furthermore, this must be equated to the proper filtering and shaping mechanisms used by other mechanisms.

This is accomplished by using DEN as the foundation to define what these services mean and how their corresponding mechanisms are used to implement these services. DEN can also be used to manage the configuration of these devices, and to model what would happen in the rest of the network if device configurations were changed.

Finally, DEN forms the basis of the work of the PFWG, which is defining

- An overall architecture in which multiple vendors can control heterogeneous devices within a specific policy domain

- A schema, based on the DEN policy classes, that defines a common representation of policy information and structure to be stored in a policy repository

- A vendor- and device-independent language to describe policies

Policy services can be provisioned and managed within this standard architecture by using the DEN policy schema. This is discussed further in Chapter 10.

In summary, DEN provides an information model to relate services to systems to hardware.

Mapping the Same Class of Service to Different Networking Technologies

This is a much more difficult problem than it sounds. In general, there are several problems in selecting and delivering a specific class of service or quality of service and communicating that selection between different technologies. This is because different technologies define different mechanisms for delivering these services, and as the packets flow across protocol boundaries, the class of service configuration information is lost because the two protocols do not communicate with each other. For example, the configuration information in Layer 2 signaling mechanisms (such as Frame Relay's Committed Information Rate) cannot be directly communicated to Layer 3 protocols.

This is where DEN can help. DEN can model protocols as well as specific mechanisms used at a given networking layer (for example, different types of queuing and traffic shaping). DEN can add metadata that equates Frame Relay Committed Information Rate to the appropriate Layer 3 mechanisms. This in turn helps the network designer deliver a comprehensive end-to-end strategy that uses the appropriate technology at each given point in the network.

Managing the Different Services in a Multi-Service Network

A *multi-service network* is defined as a single backbone that combines different technologies to produce a common platform for all offered services (see Figure 1.3).

Figure 1.3   A multi-service network.

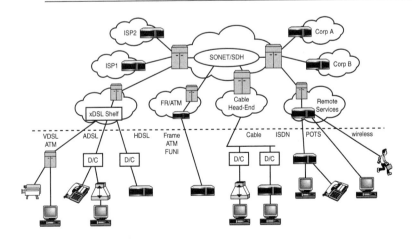

The advantage of using a multi-service network is that it provides more flexibility in deploying services: it allows differentiation by services, quality, or cost. An ATM/SONET backbone is scalable and reliable, and when integrated with IP services, provides easily configurable and customizable services. The problem with using a multi-service network is that a set of different services and technologies is brought together in a single offering.

DEN can make the advantages greater while mitigating the disadvantages. DEN provides a rich model to describe the design of the multi-service network and to plan its configuration. It also enables the many disparate services and technologies provided to be conceptually, logically, and physically modeled as a single cooperating platform.

Integrating Networking Concepts with Directories

Besides being a powerful mechanism to search, find, and retrieve information, directories are the de facto method for representing people, printers, and other common resources on the network. One of the goals of the DEN Initiative was to leverage this use of the directory so that services provided by the network could be associated with clients of the network. This is the first step toward making network devices more intelligent.

By modeling network elements and services and their interaction with other managed system components, DEN enables applications to leverage the power of the network without requiring the user to know or set esoteric system- and network-related information.

Leveraging the Network Using DEN

One of the most important aspects of DEN is that it provides an interoperable information model for exchanging management, as well as operational and functional information describing the network and the systems the network communicates with. This enables network-enabled solutions to be built.

A *network-enabled solution* is a set of cooperating products and technologies that transparently leverage the network to provide services for its clients. The key word here is *transparently*. Applications are getting more and more complex as a greater number of people want to use the Internet for an increasingly different set of tasks. Applications therefore *require* more from the network to provide the user with a good end-user experience as well as to be able to function properly.

Traditionally, this has come at the expense of the user. The user has been required to perform complicated application setup and configuration requirements, know special network and other system settings, and carry out other similarly difficult tasks. DEN offers the promise of embedding this required knowledge in the network and the systems in which the network resides. This enables the application to negotiate appropriate settings with the system to meet the needs of the user without requiring the user to get involved in this process.

DEN `Profile` classes can be used to personalize the end-user experience as well as customize and store these settings. DEN network element and service classes, as well as application and system classes, can be used to model the components providing the desired services to enable the application to negotiate appropriate settings with the network and the rest of the system.

Finally, DEN `Policy` classes can be used to control these settings and ensure that they don't conflict with other services the network provides.

Managing the Network Using DEN

There is a large body of work that defines how to manage individual network elements. Recent IETF working groups have started to address managing some network services (primarily to provide a prescribed quality of service [QoS]). However, the management and configuration of a network has yet to be addressed by anything other than DEN. This is what makes DEN different from other efforts. DEN has defined a way to manage the *network*, as opposed to *an element within* a network. Similarly, DEN provides a way to manage *all the services* provided by the network, as opposed to *one specific service* (that is not related to the other services) provided by the network. This is what makes DEN fundamentally different from SNMP, RMON, and other similar efforts.

Note

It is important to note the difference between how the Lightweight Directory Access Protocol (LDAP) and the Simple Network Management Protocol (SNMP) are used with respect to DEN and managing the network compared to an individual device. LDAP is a directory access protocol and is used to talk to the directory *about* devices. SNMP is a network management protocol and is used to talk *to* devices directly. New devices will have the capability to talk SNMP and LDAP.

So how does this fit together? DEN is an information model that unifies data; it defines how to use diverse information to completely describe an entity. As such, DEN unites information contained in directories with other information, such as that gathered from SNMP agents. This enables a more complete picture to be obtained about how the device is currently functioning (from SNMP data) compared to how it is supposed to function.

DEN does this in an extensible manner. All objects that are managed—whether network elements, network services, computers, or other components—are described in both physical as well as logical terms. Furthermore, DEN describes the function of the object as well as how it relates to other objects, and, in certain cases, how it may be used.

Realizing Intelligent Network with DEN

Historically, networks have treated the traffic from every user and application the same. This has often been referred to as a "best effort" service. Unfortunately, this is no longer good enough. For a variety of reasons, enterprises, service providers, and even small businesses are changing to a more intelligent, services-oriented model wherein the network can provide differentiated services to certain users and applications. This is referred to as the *intelligent network.*

The network gains its intelligence in several ways. These include

- A robust information model (DEN) for modeling the network and its interaction with the environment

- A directory as a unified information repository

- Unique data stores for supplying specific types of information

- Specialized system components (for example, Policy Servers) for managing and coordinating traffic

The interaction of users and applications with the intelligent network is represented conceptually in Figure 1.4.

Figure 1.4   Interaction with the intelligent network.

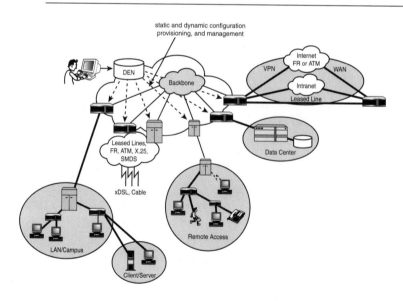

The Directory and DEN

Directories are used to store, identify, and retrieve various types of resources and information in a distributed computing environment. Resources represent objects, such as users, groups, file servers, and printers, which serve a defined purpose in the computing environment. Directory services also provide the foundation for adding, modifying, removing, renaming, and managing system components without disrupting the services provided by other system components.

The advantage of the directory is that it can be used as a single logical repository for storing and accessing information about services provided by the network and clients that want to use those services. The directory serves as the single source of information for the diverse components of a system from which to obtain information.

Policy Controlled Networking Using DEN

One of DEN's strengths is its definition of `Policy` classes. The successful wide-scale deployment of advanced networks and the services they offer depends on the capability to administer and distribute consistent network element and network service configurations and other types of information. This requires a set of policies that manage and configure the network elements appropriately based on the client of the network.

`Policy` is used to ensure that different network elements have the same interpretation of the business functions and services they are providing *as a group*. This requires a dedicated architecture to define, edit, and manage policies, as well as to detect conflicts between different policies and to resolve those conflicts. The DEN `Policy` class hierarchy plays an essential role in this architecture.

Using `Policy` to control networks and networked applications requires the following four elements:

- An extensible information model for network elements, network services, networks, and clients of the network

- A scalable framework for policy administration, management, conflict resolution, and distribution

- A policy specification, written in terms of a policy definition language, that can represent business requirements and functions in a vendor- and device-independent manner

- A scalable means to translate from the device- and vendor-independent policy specification to vendor- and device-specific configuration commands

DEN is the extensible information model referred to in the first point. The PFWG is providing an architecture that meets the second requirement. The PFWG is also defining a *Policy Definition Language* that has all the characteristics of the third requirement. The Policy Definition Language becomes the way to ensure that multiple vendors interpret the policy the same way while enabling vendors to provide value-added services. The fourth point is necessarily vendor-specific. Examples illustrating the power of these features working together are given in Chapter 11.

Intelligent Network Device Configuration Using DEN

The use of the directory in applications that administer or configure the network is a powerful configuration management paradigm. It is a way to manage the *network*, as opposed to individual systems or devices *in* the network. It is, therefore, inherently different from SNMP and better suited than SNMP to the task of expressing and distributing policy or other types of information that affects multiple devices.

So, where should the added intelligence reside? Simply put, in the network element itself. This will encourage a new era of network elements to be built, which have special capabilities to enable them to respond as managed system elements. Such capabilities will include

- Dedicated directory interfaces, such as LDAP

- Dedicated policy interfaces, such as those provided by the Common Open Policy Service (COPS) protocol

- Dedicated software and/or hardware to generate and respond to policy events

- Dedicated software and/or hardware to interpret policy requests and commands

This does not mean that functionality such as that offered by SNMP is no longer needed. In fact, it means almost the opposite. SNMP provides specialized information that plays a vital role in managing some system functions. Directories in general and DEN in particular provide a means to *integrate* information such as that provided by SNMP or RMON with other vital network and system information.

As an example, DEN and the Policy Definition Language provide the ability to define a business function or service ("Voice traffic should get the following class of service in this network") and then relate this directly to a set of device configurations that must be executed. Individual systems and devices will have to interpret this policy locally. For example, one instance may interpret this as

> Voice over IP (VoIP) traffic is marked with the Per Hop Behavior of 111000, and should be admitted using RSVP and placed into the EF queue on each interface.

> **Note**
> Per Hop Behavior and EF are defined in the Differentiated Services Architecture [DSARCH]. It defines externally observable forwarding behavior applied at a network device.

Another instance might instead use a different Per Hop Behavior that prescribes a different queuing mechanism. DEN enables these different queuing mechanisms to be recognized as being applicable to supplying the same business function.

Configuring network elements is becoming increasingly complicated. SNMP could be used to monitor and perform certain types of configuration, while the directory could manage other aspects of configuration, and manual configuration could be required perhaps for yet other kinds of configuration. DEN provides the framework for keeping these different, yet related, configuration tasks coordinated and applied to the appropriate devices.

More importantly, DEN provides the foundation for translating the business requirement into network device configuration commands. DEN can also represent the equating of the different Per Hop Behaviors, the different mechanisms that they imply, and the relation between signaled and provisioned network services. DEN provides a higher level of abstraction of modeling the network and its services than SNMP and other similar functions. By thinking in this more abstract way, DEN enables new solutions to be built by being able to integrate and use different types of information that are tailored to represent different aspects of network configuration.

Characteristics of a DEN-Based Intelligent Network

The best way to define the features and functions of an intelligent network is to see how it would be managed and function compared to the way existing networks are managed and function. Table 1.1 compares the old (non-DEN) and new (DEN) ways of developing and using applications.

Table 1.1   Comparison Between Current Networks and the Intelligent Network of the Future

Feature or Function	Existing Network Implementation	Intelligent Network Implementation
Configuration Approach	Focus is on configuring individual devices	Focus is on configuring the network and ensuring that all devices in the network work together.

continues

Table 1.1   Continued

Feature or Function	Existing Network Implementation	Intelligent Network Implementation
Configuration Process	Separate processes to configure people, applications, and devices	Links devices to people, applications, and other resources as part of the same process.
Management	A set of loosely related applications that are oriented towards managing individual devices	One or more *layered* applications that manage the network (with the ability to drill down into network components) as well as devices in the network (with the ability to abstract up into aggregations of devices and the network).
Policy	If present, used to control individual device configurations	Integral part of the system. Used to control the configuration of the system and its components.
Use of Directory	Isolated functionality, if used at all	Integral—it is a unifying information repository.
Use of an Information Model	Not Used	Integral—it models network elements, the network, network services, and how the network relates to the rest of the system.
Passive or Active System	Passive—network elements are assigned a role to play in providing network services	Active—network elements play a dynamically changing role in providing network services.
Modeling System Components	Treat applications, devices, services, and people as separate entities	Treat applications, devices, services, and people as an integral partnership.

The modeling of system components is especially important. The Intelligent Network binds clients of the network—whether they are users, applications, processes, or services—to the services they require of the network as a function of the application, location, job role, and other factors that belong to *both* the client and the network.

Transition from a Passive to an Active Network Model

The previous sections have described a transition from a "passive" network model to an "active, services-based intelligent" network model. This is one of the most important things the DEN Initiative started. DEN defined a new approach to building Intelligent Network by introducing the notion of a logically centralized common repository where network elements and services are represented in a common way. This enables applications of different types and functions to use and share information about network elements and services. The notion of a common repository in turn united the up-to-then separate worlds of networking and Object-Oriented Modeling.

This transition replaces the current practice of operating on a best-effort model with a set of dynamic, interoperable services. These services can be customized in a number of different dimensions:

• With respect to business requirements and processes through a service level agreement

• As a function of the individual user or application

• As a function of the group, organization, or other aggregate the client is a part of

• As a function of the role that the client plays in the group, organization, and so on

• As a function of the time of day or some other combination of statically defined parameters

• With respect to a unique event that occurred dynamically (for example, a stock market crash or a firewall breach)

The Intelligent Network unites different technologies, including network- and application-oriented technologies, with specialized services. These services include

• Standard network services, such as switching and routing

• Advanced network services (for example, class of service, quality of service, and address management)

• Other related services (for example, security, including access control and encryption)

The unification of these diverse services can be achieved because of the architecture proposed by standards organizations such as the PFWG and the Networks Working Group of the DMTF, the use of a common information model (DEN), and the use of the directory as a unifying information repository. The result is a unified architecture for managing complex distributed systems in an extensible, object-oriented way.

The Intelligent Network model provides a compelling set of benefits, including the following:

- Capability to personalize network services

- Capability to coordinate network services

- Support for more advanced applications that require specialized network services and treatment without requiring knowledge and interaction from the end user

- Capability to accommodate QoS and other dynamically changing network services

Personalization of Network Services

Providing value-added services that differentiate classes of users, especially if they offer the capability to be customized to suit the needs of a particular user, are of great importance to service providers. The following two examples describe two different ways in which DEN can help the application developer as well as the service provider and enterprise deliver a better, more compelling end-user experience.

Customizing an Application for Different Users

Consider an application that requires special treatment from the network (for example, NetMeeting, which must have a defined jitter and latency to operate correctly). Assume that there is congestion in the network and that the combination of parameters required for optimal delivery of the full-motion video (bandwidth, jitter, latency, and so on) is not simultaneously available. One user might be willing to sacrifice frame rate in order to view a full-motion video, while another user might instead want to adjust the window size or reduce the color palette, but keep the frame rate as fast as possible. What is required is the capability to

- Differentiate the different components of the NetMeeting traffic from the other traffic types in the network.

- Recognize that NetMeeting traffic is in fact comprised of data, audio, and video traffic that require different levels of QoS.

- Validate that a given client is authorized to have preferential treatment for its NetMeeting traffic, and then ensure that preferential treatment is in fact provided.

DEN helps solve these requirements because its information model can be used to associate the different needs of an application with users and ensure that the appropriate service level agreement is satisfied. DEN `Profile` classes can be associated with the user (or a higher-level aggregate, such as a group or `OrganizationalUnit`). DEN `Service` classes can be used to model the needs of NetMeeting. DEN `Policy` classes can be used to ensure that traffic differentiation, as defined by any service level agreements, are related to a user as well as a network and an application. It should be noted that either the native DEN classes or subclasses of these DEN classes can be used to incorporate application-specific information. For example, the DEN `Profile` classes may be subclasses so they can store application profile settings. *Subclassing*, as explained in Chapter 2, is a way of refining the definition of an existing class such that the new class inherits all the existing attributes and methods of the parent class but also adds new attributes and behavior.

Note
`OrganizationalUnit` is an X.500 term that refers to a unit of management of a company or organization.

Customizing an Application for Different Events

Most enterprises and service providers build their networks to support a pre-defined set of applications. This is done by mapping the needs of these applications into pre-defined, pre-provisioned service classes. For example, "best-effort" traffic may be assigned to FTP and Telnet applications, whereas certain types of users (for example, the CEO and CTO) may get preferential treatment, and business applications may get a different type of traffic conditioning.

What happens when an unusual event occurs? The CEO might require extra bandwidth for an important video conference, or a stock market crash might have just occurred. Such events cannot really be pre-planned, as they require an abnormally large expenditure of resources for their successful completion. Plus, there is really no way to anticipate *when* they will occur.

DEN, in combination with middleware solutions that provide, for example, a publish-subscribe event mechanism, can be used to plan for such situations. When these events are detected, the appropriate event(s) can be sent and detected by an entity that is responsible for controlling the configuration of the network (for example, the "Policy Server" described in the Policy Framework, Differentiated Services, and RAP working groups of the IETF). The Policy Server can then issue some emergency configuration changes that all or part of the network will respond to. The modeling of these changes is again made possible by the use of appropriate DEN classes. The advantage is that the network will not have to be engineered to meet these requests statically; it can *intelligently* react to the changing needs of its environment.

Coordination of Network Services

Sometimes, different network services need to be coordinated to satisfy a particular policy or service level agreement. For example, a video conference might use the *Resource Reservation Protocol* (*RSVP*, an explicit signaling mechanism) for reserving bandwidth necessary to conduct the video conference, and then use different mechanisms to ensure that the traffic is detected, prioritized properly, and given precedence. This might require different mechanisms to manage congestion it experiences or to rate-limit its input. All these are different "micro-services" that together implement the "macro-service" according to a prescribed service level agreement.

Note

RSVP is used by a host to request a specific QoS from the network for particular traffic. The network in turn passes these QoS requests to all nodes along the path(s) of the flow of traffic, and establishes and maintains state to provide the requested service. RSVP requests generally result in resources being reserved in each node along the data path.

When multiple services are used to realize a single function, it is imperative that they be properly coordinated. DEN `Policy` and `Service` classes (among others) can be used to do this.

Support for Advanced Applications

Certain types of applications require special treatment. For example, some applications use dynamic or negotiated application ports to communicate. A simple example is Telnet. When the Telnet session is opened, the TCP source port is chosen dynamically, while the TCP destination port is fixed (port 23). More complex examples include video-conferencing traffic, as well as many business applications (such as PeopleSoft or SAP), that use a special protocol to negotiate the ports they require. This presents particular problems for firewalls; if they don't know the port beforehand, they can't be configured to admit the traffic.

DEN can be used to model the requirements of these applications. Then, in combination with other techniques (such as *stateful inspection*), the appropriate action can be taken.

> **Note**
>
> *Stateful inspection* is a technique used to inspect the control flows associated with an application to determine the particular TCP or UDP port numbers currently in use by the application.

Support for Dynamically Changing Network Services

Consider a network that has different classes of service. Congestion occurs because too much traffic is generated. Policies can govern which clients continue to receive service and which get a degraded form of service. Within a particular service class, policies can even be used to differentiate clients that meet the general requirements of that class. But what happens when the CEO logs on and there isn't enough bandwidth available for him or her to work?

Fortunately, DEN can be used to help plan for such circumstances. In this case, we must find enough bandwidth to make the CEO happy. Since DEN models users and applications as well as services, we can make a detailed matrix that determines how to obtain the required bandwidth for the CEO. This matrix details what qualities (for example, bandwidth, latency, and so on) each application the CEO runs should be assigned. The matrix is then stored in a common (DEN) repository. This enables all applications and policy decision and enforcement devices (see Chapter 11) to ensure that the CEO obtains the desired services. For example, policy decision and enforcement devices can be used to detect traffic from the CEO. They follow the general guidelines of the different service classes defined in this common matrix, but are free to modify them to obtain their application- and/or user-specific goals. This may take the form of degrading or even logging out other users to retrieve the required bandwidth under severe conditions of network congestion. Without DEN, there is no *structured* way to do this because of the number of different types of objects (users, applications, SLAs, capabilities of certain devices in the network, and so on) that must concurrently be changed.

Benefits of Intelligent Network

As businesses increase their use of various forms of networking—the Internet, as well as corporate intranets and extranets—Intelligent Networks become more and more important. This enables two important benefits to be realized: differentiated services and more efficient sharing of networked resources between users and applications.

There are three main problems faced in building Intelligent Networks:

- Managing the increasing configuration complexity of devices

- Ensuring that consistent policies are applied to all elements of the system

- Enabling the needs of applications to be related to the services the network provides

This is shown conceptually in Figure 1.5.

Figure 1.5   Problems the Intelligent Network solves, and derived benefits.

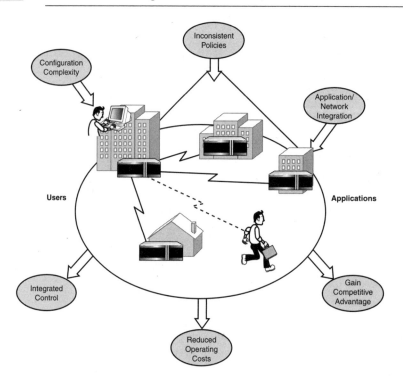

Key to all these is the capability to manage and maintain a comprehensive Information Model that enables each of these components to be related to each other. The *Information Model* presents a single mechanism to represent how network elements provide services, and how policies can be used to control them. It also links to existing models of users, applications, printers, and other resources, and associates their use with network services.

This results in a new philosophy that can be used to build Intelligent Networks: a *service-oriented* philosophy. Enterprises and service providers alike can use this.

Many specific benefits can be obtained from a directory-enabled network. The rest of this section provides a brief overview of some of them. These are all discussed more thoroughly in Chapters 11 through 13.

Enterprises

Enterprises can use DEN in many different ways. However, they are concerned mostly with its application to policy-controlled network services.

Enterprises can lose millions of dollars in a matter of hours if a mission-critical application becomes unavailable or does not run correctly, quickly, or completely. Mission-critical applications need special handling to ensure that delivery of their traffic will not be adversely affected by other applications using the network.

As important as mission-critical applications are, however, enterprises must also strive to satisfy the needs of the rest of their users. This includes accommodating the special needs of Web traffic (including push technology and dynamic Java applets) as well as multi-media and voice applications (including distance learning and training, audio- and video-conferencing, and collaborative applications). These application needs must be combined with the rest of the traffic, which should receive "best-effort" delivery.

Both of these require associating a given user or application with a number of different parameters (time of day, job role or function of the user, type of traffic being sent, and so on). The combination of a large number of parameters and a large number of objects mandates a robust information model. The directory is particularly well suited to represent users, applications, printers, and so on, and DEN defines additional objects that can be used to represent network elements and services. These diverse objects are then combined into a managed system through the use of relationships and other object-oriented tools of the DEN information model.

The association between user and service must be done independent of location and type of connection to as large an extent as possible. This requires intimate knowledge of the physical and logical topology of the network, which is provided by the DEN information model.

DEN provides a framework for associating all of these complex elements together through the coordinated modeling of each element in the system. It also provides a way for enterprises to define policy and use it to assign different levels of service to its users and applications.

Service Providers

Service providers need the ability to differentiate their service offerings based on providing added value. This added value is achieved through the delivery of end-to-end services that offer a wide variety of pricing options based on the type of service, quality of service, and usage. This is complicated by the desire of service providers to address many different market segments.

Therefore, service providers demand an open, standards-based solution that can be integrated with existing legacy systems while providing a minimum of, and preferably no, disruption to their currently deployed services. Many service providers are looking toward work being done in the IETF to standardize the protocols and APIs, and more recently schemata, used to build their infrastructure.

DEN is well-suited to meet these requirements. DEN is itself a standard and is being used now by several groups of the IETF. In addition, important IETF work, like the differentiated services [DIFSRV] and integrated services [INTSRV] efforts, along with the Policy Framework [PFWG] work, can all be modeled using DEN. The DEN framework is able to model these protocols and architectures and, more importantly, relate them to other managed systems and system elements.

Perhaps the most important benefit to service providers is the following: DEN enables service providers to sell services, as opposed to "just" connections.

Developers and Independent Software Vendors

Developers and independent software vendors (ISVs) are very excited about DEN. This is because the DEN information model enables the developer or ISV to represent the entire system and how each component communicates with each other. This in turn provides a means for applications to take advantage of the power of the network in a transparent fashion.

Consider a video-conferencing application. DEN provides the application developer with additional information that can be detected by the network and used to provide a more powerful and compelling end-user experience. This is illustrated by the following example.

Suppose that users log onto the network using dynamically assigned IP addresses (for example, using DHCP). Further suppose that software is in place that detects each logon and, through querying various DEN classes, determines if that user can run a video-conferencing application. If it is determined that the user can run a video-conferencing application, software can gather information defining how a user is currently logging onto the network (for example, through Ethernet in the corporate campus, or through a PPP analog modem). The type of connection, plus additional information (for example, which subnet the user is placed on) can then be used to determine default settings for the video-conferencing application (for example, don't send streaming video over a slow modem connection; instead, send text). Network information can be used to further supplement this (for example, a particular network policy is in place that restricts the services a user receives when that user logs on).

The advantage of DEN is the tight integration between the network and the application, and the capability to pass detailed information specific to the user (whether it is network- or system-related) to the application without requiring the user to do anything. This enables the application to appear "more intelligent" to the user and automatically adjust to different environmental conditions. This is achieved through access to common information represented through DEN that is stored in a common repository. This enables one application to use information in the repository by other applications as well as share its own information in that repository. In this example, the video-conferencing application can determine who the user is and the rights of that user from information in the DEN repository that was put there by other applications. The video-conferencing application can also put its own information in the common DEN repository that other applications can use. It is this capability for applications to share and use information from other applications that is so important to developers and ISVs.

End Users

Continuing the preceding example, note that additional information can be seamlessly integrated into the end user's experience. For example, as additional users log in, similar information can be gathered and displayed in a dialog. The end user can simply click on an entry in the dialog, as opposed to entering the IP address of a user to video-conference with. Furthermore, each user will already know the transmitting and receiving capabilities of each other.

Most importantly, the end user can concentrate on *using*, as opposed to *configuring*, the video-conferencing application.

DEN, the DMTF, and the IETF

This section provides a brief review of how DEN was created; then describes how its development is proceeding in the standards community.

How DEN Was Created

DEN started as an idea proposed by Cisco and Microsoft to leverage the power of the network using a directory. Cisco and Microsoft created the *DEN Ad-Hoc Working Group (AHWG)* to propose this as an open standard in which all vendors could participate. Because the purpose of DEN was ultimately to bind users and applications to services available from the network, the AHWG specifically solicited advice and guidance from end users and customers who would benefit from DEN. This group was termed the *DEN AHWG Customer Advisory Board (CAB)*. The DEN CAB was comprised of representatives from four different sectors to ensure that a wide set of interests was represented. The CAB members were from Sprint, Charles Schwab, Texaco, and the University of Washington.

After the general community endorsed the DEN effort, it was time to examine how its further development would take place. There were several directions that could have been taken with DEN. It could have remained an ad-hoc working group, or it could be given to an industry consortium. What the DEN AHWG decided was to select a standards organization that could adopt DEN and put its development under the formal methodology and procedures of that standards organization. The DMTF was selected because of its role in the development of CIM, the Common Information Model. At that time, the DEN specification was changed to embrace CIM and to become an extension of CIM. The Networks Working Group of the DMTF was selected as the particular subgroup that would own the continuing development of DEN.

The initial draft of the DEN specification was authored by Steven Judd of Microsoft and me. An email discussion list was then set up so that all interested parties could comment on the specification and add to it; this was hosted by Carnegie-Mellon University. Valuable input was received from many organizations as they embraced DEN and started to experiment with its use.

The draft went through three major revisions. It also tracked the continuing evolution of CIM. Indeed, DEN added to the richness of CIM, and CIM provided valuable knowledge and concepts that helped DEN immensely. A Last Call was issued, which then produced the final version of the DEN AHWG: DEN v3.0c5. This version was then approved by the DEN CAB for submission to the DMTF. The DMTF formally accepted ownership of the DEN specification on September 28, 1998.

DEN and the DMTF

The DMTF is the standards organization that now owns the development of DEN. Most of the work is done in the Networks Working Group of the DMTF. However, work that affects CIM in general or other technologies of interest to the DMTF as a whole is worked on by the Technical Development Committee [DMTF].

CIM is concerned about information modeling independent of the underlying implementation. This means that CIM can be implemented by a directory, by a relational or object database, or by other means. DEN extends CIM, but also defines optimizations that enable the object-oriented features of CIM to be mapped into a directory implementation (this is covered in more detail in Chapter 7).

DEN and the IETF

The IETF defines protocols, schema, and APIs. Protocols and APIs that are developed in the IETF, such as LDAP and SNMP, represent the standard way the industry uses to communicate with various system components. The DEN information model assumes the use of these protocols and APIs to access and transfer information between system components.

Recently, the IETF has chartered focused schema work. The work of most relevance to DEN is that done for directories that use LDAPv3 as their access protocol. There is now an excellent exchange of information between the DMTF and the IETF, as evidenced by several Internet drafts that are based on parts of DEN and the PFWG. The PFWG is chartered to standardize policy schemata for various IETF working groups and a policy definition language to communicate policy. The PFWG uses DEN as the basis for all its work.

All these efforts are discussed further in Chapters 8 through 11.

Summary

This chapter has provided an overview for what DEN is, the motivation for its creation, and how it can be used. DEN is a specification that describes how the network can be transformed from a passive collection of devices that route and forward traffic to an active set of cooperating devices that intelligently provide services to the user. It represents both a philosophy as well as part of the means to build service-oriented solutions. This is fundamentally a different way of thinking about how to build networks and applications.

The strength of DEN lies in its interoperable framework that describes how heretofore unrelated system components can work together to provide a service. DEN provides a uniform way to manage different network mechanisms, such as congestion avoidance and rate limiting, which can be used in conjunction to provide a network service (for example, quality of service). DEN also provides a uniform way to combine network services together (for example, quality of service, encryption, and compression) as directed by one or more applications on behalf of a user.

DEN provides many benefits for enterprises, service providers, and developers. These include being able to dynamically configure the network to provide personalized network services; providing the means for different services to be provided based on cost, quality, and other metrics on a per-user and/or per-application basis; and enabling applications to be built that transparently leverage the network without requiring end users to configure them (or the network). End users will benefit from applications that can take better advantage of the network.

DEN is now a recognized standard under the auspices of the DMTF. In addition, the IETF is basing more and more of its work under DEN.

Recommended Further Study and References

[COPS]: The RSVP Admission Policy (RAP) Working Group of the IETF is concerned with developing standards for enabling a scalable policy control model that can provide quality of service on the Internet using explicit signaling protocols like RSVP. Common Open Policy Service (COPS) defines a protocol to transmit policy requests and responses. More information on both can be found at

http://www.ietf.org/html.charters/rap-charter.html

[DIFSRV]: The Differentiated Services IETF Working Group is defining "relatively simple and coarse methods of providing differentiated classes of service for Internet traffic." Specifically, a small, well-defined set of building blocks is defined that enables quality of service to be defined on a "per-hop" basis. This work is described in

http://www.ietf.org/html.charters/diffserv-charter.html

[DMTF]: The Desktop Management Task Force (DMTF) is the industry consortium chartered with development, support, and maintenance of management standards for PC systems and products, including CIM and DEN. The following URLs will direct you to more information about the DMTF in general and DEN in particular:

`http://www.dmtf.org` (home page for the DMTF)

`http://www.dmtf.org/restricted/workgroup.html` (pointer for DMTF members to access various workgroups and subcommittees, such as the Networks Working Group)

`http://www.dmtf.org/members/tdc/wg-network/` (specific pointer for DMTF members to access the Networks Working Group)

`http://www.dmtf.org/spec/cims.html` (public pointer to access information about CIM, including downloading specs, viewing the tutorial, and so forth)

[DSARCH]: This Internet RFC defines an architecture for implementing scalable service differentiation in the Internet. This can be retrieved as

`ftp://ftp.isi.edu/in-notes/rfc2475.txt`

[INTOPS]: An Internet draft for defining a person object class based on X.521. See the Internet draft titled `draft-smith-ldap-inetorgperson-03.txt` (or the latest version thereof), retrievable from a number of different repositories, such as

`http://www.ietf.org/internet-drafts/draft-smith-ldap-inetorgperson-03.txt`

[INTSRV]: The Integrated Services Working Group of the IETF. Recent experiments demonstrate the capability of packet switching protocols to support Integrated Services: the transport of audio, video, real-time, and classical data traffic within a single network infrastructure. These experiments suggest that expanding the Internet service model would better meet the needs of these diverse applications. The purpose of this working group is to specify this enhanced service model and then to define and standardize certain interfaces and requirements necessary to implement the new service model.

The working group will focus on defining a minimal set of global requirements that transition the Internet into a robust integrated-service communications infrastructure. Enhancements to individual protocols (for example, adding additional routing information to routing protocols, or choosing IP queuing disciplines for routers) will be left to other working groups, except in those rare cases where detailed definitions of behavior are critical to the success of the enhanced architecture.

`http://www.ietf.org/html.charters/intserv-charter.html`

[LDAP]: The LDAP Extensions (LDAPEXT) Working Group of the IETF is chartered with continuing to develop an Internet directory service. The LDAPEXT Working Group defines and standardizes extensions to the LDAP version 3 protocol, extensions to the use of LDAP on the Internet, and the API to LDAP. More information can be obtained from

`http://www.ietf.org/html.charters/ldapext-charter.html`

[LIPS]: Another proposal for defining a person object class is called the Lightweight Internet Person Schema, available from the Network Application Consortium. Their URL is

`http://www.netapps.org/`

[PFWG]: The Policy Framework Working Group of the IETF. The charter is available from

`http://www.ietf.org/html.charters/policy-charter.html`

[RMON]: The Remote Network Monitoring Management Information Base is available in two versions. The following RFCs define it:

`http://info.internet.isi.edu/in-notes/rfc/files/rfc1757.txt`
(Remote Network Monitoring Management Information Base)
`http://info.internet.isi.edu/in-notes/rfc/files/rfc2021.txt`
(Remote Network Monitoring Management Information Base v2 using SMI v2)
`http://info.internet.isi.edu/in-notes/rfc/files/rfc2074.txt`
(Remote Network Monitoring MIB Protocol Identifiers)

[RSVP]: Several RFCs define RSVP. The ones most relevant to this book are listed later. Also check the RAP Working Group. Go to the following URL:

`http://info.internet.isi.edu/in-notes/rfc/files/`

Pull the following files:

rfc2205.txt—RSVP Functional Specification

rfc2206.txt—RSVP Management Information Base Using SMIv2

rfc2207.txt—RSVP Extensions for IPsec Data Flows

rfc2208.txt—RSVP Applicability Statement

rfc2209.txt—RSVP Message Processing Rules

rfc2210.txt—The Use of RSVP with IETF Integrated Services

[SNMP]: There are several IETF working groups that actively work on the development of Simple Network Management Protocol (SNMP). Two to examine are

```
http://www.ietf.org/html.charters/agentx-charter.html
http://www.ietf.org/html.charters/snmpv3-charter.html
```

The goal of the first working group is to make the SNMP Agent more extensible. The goal of the SNMPv3 Working Group is to define the next generation of SNMP.

CHAPTER 2

What Is Object-Oriented Modeling?

This chapter provides an introduction to Object-Oriented Modeling and examines some of the benefits it can provide. Then, this is related explicitly to the fundamental design principles behind the Common Information Model (CIM) and Directory Enabled Network (DEN). Finally, this chapter provides some insight as to how Object-Oriented Modeling can be applied to modeling network elements and services.

Object-Oriented Modeling is a design methodology that applies object-oriented analysis and design techniques to describe a system. A complete Object-Oriented Model will describe both the physical as well as the logical aspects of the system, and use these to characterize its static and dynamic properties.

Object-Oriented Modeling Defined

To define Object-Oriented Modeling, we first need to define some basic terminology. First, we'll define some basic concepts applicable to object-oriented thinking. Next, we'll describe what it means to be "object-oriented" and what is meant specifically by the terms *object-oriented analysis* and *object-oriented design*. Armed with these definitions, we can then define Object-Oriented Modeling and explain why it is of interest to DEN.

Defining Basic Object-Oriented Terminology

This section defines the basic terminology of object-oriented technology. These terms are used throughout the remainder of this book. Additional terms are defined as they are introduced. Refer to the references at the end of this chapter for more information about object-oriented technology in general and object-oriented analysis, design, and modeling in particular.

Object-oriented technology models the real world in terms of objects. An *object* is an abstraction of something that consists of a collection of related data and functions. This collection is treated by the system as a named entity that has state, behavior, identifiable properties, and a unique identity. Objects are used to represent certain characteristics of the system. They promote understanding of the system as well as provide a basis for implementation.

The structure and behavior of similar objects are defined by their common object class. A *class* is a description of one or more objects that have a uniform set of data, called *attributes*, and functions that manipulate and operate on the data, called *methods* (formal definitions of both attributes and methods are offered later in this section). Objects that are grouped into the same class can also share similar relationships between other objects, as well as share common semantics. A class can be thought of as a template that defines attributes, methods, and relationships that describe the class in a uniform way.

An *instance* refers to an actual object that belongs to a particular class. Each instance of a class has the same attributes and methods, but can contain different values for its attributes. The class defines the attributes, methods, and relationships the instance can possess; the instance defines and differentiates objects that belong to the same class.

An *attribute* (also called a *property*) is a data value that is retained by an object. An attribute represents the ability to store data that should be associated with a class. The data can be a simple data type (for example, integer), a complex data type that is comprised of simple data types, or a reference to another object. This is similar to a data member in C++.

Note

A directory implementation distinguishes between "must have" and "may have" attributes. *"Must have" attributes* are those that are required to be present in an object class. *"May have" attributes* are those that can optionally be present. The "must have" attributes are those that represent the minimum necessary to characterize the object. The "may have" attributes are those that help differentiate different instances of the same object but are not required to be present.

For example, some employees of an organization may have both a telephone and a fax number, while others may have only a telephone number, and still others may have neither. But, all employees would have a name. Thus, the name attribute is a "must have" attribute, whereas the telephone and fax numbers are "may have" attributes.

A *method* is a procedure that represents some behavior that characterizes the class. This behavior may represent the accessing, transformation, and sharing of data. Complex operations may also have side effects, which may also be modeled. More formally, the attributes of a class are read, written, and edited using the methods of the class. Methods may therefore be viewed as performing a transformation, or mapping, of the attribute(s). This is similar to a member function in C++.

Principles of Object-Oriented Thinking

The term *object-oriented* means many things to many people. However, there are some important characteristics associated with the implications of being object-oriented that are of critical importance for Object-Oriented Modeling in general and DEN in particular.

Object-oriented implies a particular way of organizing and using information to build software and systems. Specifically, it means that a system is thought of as comprised of a set of objects, each of which encapsulates data and behavior. The following six fundamental axioms are required by this type of thinking:

- Identity
- Abstraction
- Classification
- Encapsulation
- Inheritance
- Polymorphism

Systems are inherently complex, comprised of a multitude of diverse objects.

Identity means that each object can be uniquely identified within the system, and that two instances of the same class can be identified even if they have the exact same attribute values.

Abstraction is one of the fundamental ways humans use to cope with complexity. Formally defined, abstraction is the process of ignoring certain aspects of a subject to focus on a different set of essential characteristics of that subject. *Data abstraction* is the process of defining and manipulating attributes in terms of operations that apply to those attributes. Abstraction is most often implemented in two complementary ways, called generalization and specialization. *Generalization* is the process of identifying common attributes and behaviors in classes lower in the hierarchy and moving those common attributes and behaviors higher up the hierarchy (to a superclass). *Specialization* is the exact opposite: It is the process of refining generic concepts into more specific ones. These are also sometimes referred to as "bottom-up" and "top-down" thinking. Generalization and specialization are complementary because they can be used in a coordinated fashion to develop the model given different knowledge. This will be described in the sections "Generalization" and "Specialization," respectively, later in this chapter.

Classification means that objects having the same characteristics and behavior (for example, attributes and methods) are grouped into the same class. Classification further implies that there is a structured hierarchy for organizing all classes in a system. Most models represent this using "just" a class *inheritance hierarchy*. In addition, CIM and DEN define a *relationship hierarchy* to characterize the different types of relationships that exist between objects in the system. The relationship hierarchy defines how different objects interact with each other in the system through the use of relationships that have special semantics (for example, associations and aggregations, which are defined in the sections "Associations" and "Aggregations," respectively, later in this chapter. Also refer to the section "Association and Aggregation Hierarchies," which follows the sections on associations and aggregations). Both the inheritance and the classification hierarchies use the principle of abstraction to guide their formation. Classification can also be defined as the ordering (or structuring) of all the different abstractions that comprise a system. Abstraction and classification lead to the next principle: encapsulation.

Encapsulation is the process of separating the external characteristics of an object from its internal implementation. An object can be viewed as having a contract that specifies the behavior of the object. Other objects in the system can then depend on that behavior without having to know how the object is implemented. Encapsulation uses the concept of *information hiding* to conceal the structure and implementation of an object, and instead focuses on its externally visible characteristics and behavior. This process is critical, not just because it promotes reusability, but because it enables a complex object to be described in terms of a set of simpler objects that are themselves independent of each other. Encapsulation enables object classes to be added and removed from the system while isolating the effects of the addition or removal to a small part of the system. Encapsulation limits the changes to the classes that were added, removed, or modified. The rest of the system still operates the same way (for example, an object still executes the same method to perform a function). This is because encapsulation represents a contract between the objects in a system; functions are provided by methods that act on attributes. As long as this contract doesn't change, the system is invariant to class changes. This capability to isolate the implementation of an object from change is arguably one of the most powerful and compelling benefits of encapsulation.

Inheritance is a mechanism for expressing that two classes are related to each other. Specifically, a *subclass* inherits all the attributes and methods of its *superclass*. This enables common attributes and methods to be expressed once in a superclass. It also enables a subclass to represent a specific refined behavior of the superclass. Every instance of a subclass is also an instance of its superclass (note that the converse is not true).

Polymorphism means that several classes share the same type of functionality, but the same operation may behave differently in each of the classes. For example, consider a draw function that is used by two different shapes (a line and a circle). Both of these shapes need to utilize a draw function to render themselves, but the implementation of the draw function for each class is different. Furthermore, each of these functions may have different prerequisites and side effects. Consider a repair function that is applied to two different subclasses of a common vehicle superclass: a bicycle and a car. The repair function will need different types of materials, different repair people with different skill sets, and have different associated costs for each of these classes. Polymorphism disassociates the specification of common functionality from its implementation (in our case, both a bicycle and a vehicle need to be repaired). This simplifies system design because it enables the essential aspects of a function (for example, repair) to be identified and shared among different classes without getting distracted by implementation particulars.

Defining Object-Oriented Analysis, Design, and Modeling

Object-oriented analysis is the process of studying a problem domain that results in a specification of how the objects of that domain function and relate to each other. Implicit in this definition is the process of dividing a problem into smaller parts to better understand each part and the whole problem. *Object-oriented design* is the process of taking a specification and adding enough detail to enable it to be implemented. The implementation is developed using the object-oriented principles defined earlier.

Object-Oriented Modeling is a three-step process:

1. Analyze the problem using object-oriented concepts.

2. Build an Object-Oriented Model that is used to develop a solution to the problem.

3. Modify the model as required to better represent the additional detail discovered in the object-oriented design process.

Object-Oriented Modeling is by nature an iterative process. The model itself will grow and become more functional as more analysis of the problem domain is performed and a more detailed implementation evolves. DEN is an extension of the CIM defined by the Desktop Management Task Force (DMTF). CIM, and therefore DEN, use the concept of a *layered Object-Oriented Model*. CIM and DEN will be defined in more detail in Chapters 5 through 10. A layered model is defined in the section "What Is a Layered Model?" later in this chapter.

Modeling and DEN

Modeling network elements and services is fundamentally different than modeling other types of objects. This is because most objects are inherently simple objects that exist within well-defined, relatively static boundaries. For example, an object that models a user might have attributes added to or deleted from it, or it might be moved to another container. None of these actions change the fundamental purpose of the user object. We could say that the *ontological* purpose of the user object remains the same, even though the environment of the user changes.

This is not true for network elements and services. This is because they are inherently complex objects and exist in a constantly changing environment. For example, by removing a network card from a router and installing a different network card, the purpose of the router might be changed from an edge router to a core router. This is a dramatic change; new protocols are used, different media are used, and the fundamental purpose of the device (filtering versus forwarding traffic) has changed. Yet, the device remains outwardly the same. Furthermore, the environment the network element operates in can directly affect the functionality and services provided by the network element. This is not true of simpler objects, such as users, printers, and file servers.

In summary, class hierarchies, by themselves, are insufficient to model the complex functionality of network elements and services. Furthermore, networks interact with a large number of diverse objects, each of which has its own specialized extrinsic and intrinsic characteristics and behaviors. This results in a complex interconnected system in which different objects interact. Thus, what is required is the ability to model the objects in the system, as well as how they interact with each other.

Different Types of Models Are Required

The fundamental problem with modeling network elements and services is that many different information domains must be seamlessly integrated. Network elements and services are dynamic in nature and are directly related to the behavior of the systems with which they interact. This causes the services that network devices provide to change over time. What is required is to separate the different aspects of the systems that network devices interact with so that different types of models can be applied to describe them. This can be done by using object, behavioral, and functional models to model the structural, dynamic, and data flow aspects of the network and its surrounding environment.

It is also crucial to define these models in such a way so as to ensure that information can be shared and mapped between the different models as appropriate. This is illustrated conceptually in Figure 2.1.

Figure 2.1   Modeling network elements and services.

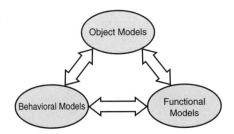

However, we need to be careful to use the right model at the right time. For example, consider a router that provides connectivity to different subnets based on the role of the user. Suppose that a system administrator wants to change the mapping of subnets to physical buildings. It is probably incorrect to equate physical location with IP subnet. And where does the poor user fit in? This problem requires the integration of three different models: one that describes the physical and spatial relationships of equipment, one that describes the services provided by network devices, and one that describes the users and what services a user is entitled to. The integration is achieved by using specific classes in each model to link to other models.

DEN recognizes the need for behavioral and functional models but currently has concentrated solely on the development of a robust object model.

Object Models

Object models serve two purposes. First, they describe the static structure of objects in a system. Second, they describe how objects in the system are related to each other. The structure of objects is represented by the attributes and methods of each object class. This takes the form of an *inheritance class hierarchy*.

The relationship between objects is modeled by a relationship class hierarchy. In CIM and DEN, classes are used to describe relationships and the structural characteristics of objects. However, a relationship class hierarchy is separate and different from an inheritance class hierarchy. A relationship class hierarchy is used to describe how objects are related to each other. Another way of thinking about this is that the relationship hierarchy shows potential relationships between *instances*, while the inheritance hierarchy shows the classification (for example, the subclass-superclass relationships) between *classes*.

A Network Object Model consists of four different types of information.

Intrinsic information are data that are essential in representing a particular element or service. There are two types of intrinsic data:

- Data that never changes (for example, the MAC address or the serial number of the device)

- Data that changes infrequently (for example, the device name or its IP address)

Intrinsic data are used to uniquely identify that device or service.

Configurable information are data that control the operation of a device or help determine how that device or service operates. These data remain static until the configuration of the device or service is explicitly changed (for example, a new interface processor is put into a router, giving it new capabilities, or a different routing algorithm is used). Furthermore, the values that data belonging to this category can take for devices are always chosen from a pre-defined list. Configurable data are used to define how the device or service will function.

Operational information controls how a device or service interacts with its surrounding environment. This information is derived from the operational environment of the device or service and changes as a result of operating conditions such as network load.

Contextual information defines how the device or service relates to other components in a larger, network-wide context. This information is used in conjunction with lower-level device information, especially intrinsic and operational data, to fine-tune services.

Directories currently store mostly intrinsic information and some configurable information. Other data stores are used to store configurable, operational, and contextual information.

Behavioral Models

Behavioral models represent the dynamic nature of the system. These are aspects of the system that change over time. A behavioral model represents the various *states* that the system takes. This is usually conveyed using *state diagrams*, where events are used to model interesting occurrences and stimuli, and states are defined that represent the time-dependent transition between events. A state diagram is a directed graph whose nodes are states and whose arcs represent events. A behavioral model consists of a set of state diagrams.

Behavioral models are concerned with modeling how elements in a system are controlled; that is, given an event, define the sequence of actions that will take place that are used to either maintain the current state of the system or transition the system to a new state. Note that in a behavioral model, the only items of concern are the sequence of operations that take place and the current and future states the system can take on. What each operation does, how each operation is implemented, is not modeled in a behavioral model.

Functional Models

Functional models describe how data flow within a system, without specifying how or when results are computed. They also describe data value changes within a system and the computations that are necessary to produce these changes. This is done by using *data flow diagrams*.

A functional model consists of a set of data flow diagrams. Each data flow diagram describes the functional flow of data with respect to input and output values, as well as internal intermediate values. A data flow diagram contains processes that transform data, flows that move data, actors that produce and consume data, and stores that persist data. A data flow diagram is a graph that represents how data flows from a source through intermediate stores to one or more destinations. The flow is governed by processes that either pass information along, gather additional information for further processing, or change the values of data. A data flow diagram does not show any control-related information, nor does it show how information is spread among different objects in the system; these are performed by behavioral and object models, respectively.

Relationship Between Object, Behavioral, and Functional Models

These three models are intimately related. The object model specifies what is being operated on, the behavioral model specifies when the operation occurs, and the functional model specifies what happens.

The structure of the object model defines the structure of the behavioral and functional models. That is, the data structure and methods of a class are defined in an object model; the behavioral and functional models augment these definitions with respect to modeling how objects change over time and what information flows through each object over time.

The behavior model defines the different states an object can have over time, as well as different events an object can respond to. These can be represented by a separate event hierarchy that can be related to the inheritance and relationship hierarchies defined in the object model. The events an object responds to help determine its methods and attributes.

The functional model is used to specify the meaning of the operations in the object model and the actions in the behavioral model. It also specifies the constraints in the object model. The functional model shows what must be done to a system to accomplish an action or actions. It uses the objects defined in the object model as the actors in the system. Each process defined in a data flow diagram corresponds to a method on an object. Each sequence of operations performed is defined by the behavioral model. The operations themselves correspond to methods of classes. High-level operations usually correspond to methods of objects that are higher in the class hierarchy, while low-level operations similarly correspond to methods of objects that are lower in the class hierarchy. Furthermore, operations act on objects and are persisted in data stores, both of which are specified as objects in the object model.

Information Modeling, CIM, and DEN

To properly model network elements and services, and their interaction with other objects in the system, two fundamental things have to occur. First, we must separate the structural, behavioral, and functional aspects of the system, while retaining the ability to relate each of these models to the other models. This requires a structured approach to modeling systems. Though this is somewhat outside the scope of the DEN initiative and effort, it was discussed in the DEN presentations and mailing lists during the review process. This book will concentrate just on the structural part of modeling network elements and services (for example, the object model).

Second, we must separate the modeling of network elements and services from the rest of the system. In particular, we must be able to represent the intrinsic capability of network elements and services to mutate and take on different roles. This can be accomplished by providing multiple sub-models that focus on particular aspects of the system and of network elements and services, while allowing both models to be easily traversed. Finally, a mechanism must be found that can integrate specialized models that are used to describe the characteristics and behavior of different objects and systems the network interacts with.

Therefore, what is required is to have a single-object model that can relate these different models to each other to properly model the interaction between network elements, the services they provide, and the objects they interact with. This is one of the underlying purposes of DEN. This single-object model is, in reality, a blend between an information model and an object model, and is called CIM. The mechanism by which the different models communicate with each other is predominantly through the use of shared classes. That is, a class is designed such that it acts as a "bridge" between different knowledge domains and/or different models. Both CIM and DEN use this design principle.

Information Modeling

Information modeling originated in the database community and concentrated on modeling the structure of data so that it could be properly managed using a database. The strength of information modeling is that it maps information in the domain being modeled directly to objects in the model. It also has well-developed techniques for defining object relationships and identifying redundant data. The traditional weaknesses with information modeling are its lack of defining and representing services and its lack of explicit representation of the encapsulation of attributes, behavior, and services as inheritance and relationship hierarchies. These deficiencies have been addressed in CIM and DEN.

An Overview of the Structure of CIM

The DMTF CIM is an object-oriented approach to the management of information and systems. It combines the classic concept of an information model with an object model to build a *layered* information model that combines the strengths of each. CIM uses object-oriented techniques to create system and component models that enable a robust object model to be developed. The resulting object model is independent of platforms and specific technologies (for example, relational databases, object databases, or directories). DEN extends this information model to ensure that it can be efficiently implemented on a directory. Thus, DEN serves two purposes. First, it is an extension of CIM. Second, it provides a methodology to map information to a specific type of repository: a directory. This is discussed in more detail in the section "DEN Approach to Modeling" later in this chapter, as well as in Chapter 5, "Motivation for DEN," and Chapter 7, "CIM: The Foundation of DEN."

What Is a Layered Model?

A *layered Object-Oriented Model* starts with a small basic model that is generic to all domains and then extends this model to represent derivatives of that domain or additional detail not present in the basic model. The extension is done as a series of layers that build upon each other. A layered model is inherently extensible.

CIM Defined

CIM is a blend between an information model and an object model. It supplements an object model with the ability to capture the information in a system using a set of classes. This is because CIM is concerned with managing the system and its components. Because the resulting information model is focused on common aspects, the DMTF refers to this information model as CIM, the Common Information Model.

The Three Layers of CIM

CIM defines three layers in its model. The *core model* is the topmost layer and must always be used in any CIM-compliant schema. This defines essential objects, like `System` and `ManagedSystemElement`, that are of use across all knowledge domains. This layer also defines refinements of these generic objects (for example, `ComputerSystem`, `PhysicalElement`, and `LogicalElement`) to represent more detailed behavior that is still generic in nature. For example, CIM defines a `ComputerSystem` class as the superclass to model functionality that represents the ability to compute a result and make a decision. As such, it serves as the superclass of not just laptop and desktop computers, but also for any object that possesses computing power. This includes network elements, such as routers and switches.

The second layer of CIM is a set of *common models* that define concepts specific to certain general areas. These areas, though still general in nature, represent more detailed knowledge than that used in the more generic core domain. At this time, CIM has defined the following common models:

- System
- Application
- Device
- Network
- Physical
- Distributed Application Performance (DAP)
- Support
- Service level agreement (SLA)
- User
- Database

All but the last two are immediately relevant to DEN and discussed further in Chapter 7. The combination of the core model and one or more common models provides a base CIM schema, consisting of inheritance and relationship class hierarchies, that models the structure and information of a domain.

The third layer of CIM is called an *extension model*. This represents technology-specific extensions of the common model that are specific to certain platforms and environments (for example, aimed at UNIX but not Windows NT) and/or are specific to certain implementations (for example, directories but not relational databases).

DEN Approach to Modeling

There are two approaches to modeling complex systems. One approach is to use a single monolithic complex model that attempts to model all aspects of the system. The second approach is to use a set of specialized models that target specific aspects of a system.

DEN uses the second approach. This enables specific aspects of one model to be fine-tuned without affecting the other models. DEN will eventually partition the modeling of a system into three cooperating models: an object model, a behavioral model, and a functional model. Currently, the DEN specification covers the object model only, with "hooks" to other models in the form of specialized classes (for example, the StatisticalInformation class, along with the Check and Action classes).

DEN is an extension model of CIM. It uses CIM's core model, all of CIM's network model, plus many concepts from CIM's device, physical, system, and application models, as a starting point. DEN then does two things:

- Adds additional network-specific information required for implementation using a directory that is not present in any of the sub-models that DEN uses

- Optimizes the resulting model so that it can be represented in a directory

Application of Object-Oriented Modeling to Networks

Object-Oriented Modeling is a paradigm, a way of thinking about specific ways to categorize knowledge using object-oriented tools and constructs. As previously stated, an object model captures both the static structure of objects comprising a system as well as how these objects are related to each other and (possibly) to other objects in other systems.

Therefore, there are three fundamental ways for classifying knowledge:

- The structure of an object
- The behavior of an object
- The relationships an object has with other objects

The structure and behavior of an object are captured by the class inheritance hierarchy, whereas the relationships an object has are captured in a separate relationship hierarchy. Note that classes are used to represent all three types of information.

> **Note**
>
> *Structure* refers to the arrangement of the parts of an object with respect to the whole. For a system component, we are concerned with the attributes and methods of an object, any particular semantics it has, and how it interacts with other objects. For a system, we are concerned with these same things but on a slightly different level. In particular, we are concerned with how the aggregation of all the components that comprise the system function together to make the system work, along with how the system as a whole interacts with other components and systems.

This is a very complex task. Network elements and services make this task even more difficult, due to their inherent complexity and the complexity involved in modeling their interaction with their environment. Formal object modeling is a proven methodology for dividing a large, complex problem into smaller, simpler problems. The principles defined earlier in this chapter, including abstraction, encapsulation, and inheritance, are of critical importance in designing object models. It is also very important to understand these concepts to understand the design of DEN. The rest of this chapter will relate the theory summarized earlier in the chapter to the modeling of network elements.

The Six Core Axioms of Object Orientation

The following sections will describe the six core principles of object orientation. These are fundamental to thinking and modeling in an object-oriented fashion.

Identity

Identity can be defined as the property of an object that is used to distinguish it from all other objects in the system. The identity of an object is implemented in a directory using one or more, but usually one, of the "must have" attributes of the object. Object identity is mandatory to enable the identification and sharing of objects through the use of pointers, aliases, and other programming constructs. It is also required for fundamental operations, such as copying and assignment. Finally, it is obligatory when it is necessary to determine if two objects are related in some fashion (for example, equal, greater than, less than, and so on).

Abstraction

As mentioned previously, abstraction enables the modeler to focus on a set of important aspects of an object while ignoring other aspects of the object. This is visually depicted in Figure 2.2.

Figure 2.2   The use of abstraction in Object-Oriented Modeling.

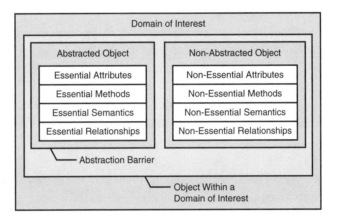

A system can be partitioned into one or more knowledge domains. For example, DEN defines four knowledge domains: physical and logical containment, and physical and logical connectivity. Each domain models a particular aspect of the system. In DEN, the physical containment domain describes the physical and spatial location of network devices, along with how devices are physically constructed (for example, a chassis contains a set of slots, and each slot contains a board). The DEN logical containment domain defines the users in a business organization that can log onto a device and change its settings (for example, the filtering performed on different traffic). Physical and logical connectivity model the physical and logical topology of networks. The overall DEN object model combines these and other domains that together are used to model network elements, network services, and how both interact with their environment.

Each domain is built using abstraction to isolate the essential characteristics of each object that are of interest to that domain. For example, in DEN, each network element has a physical and a logical aspect to it. Abstraction can be used to focus on the logical aspects of a network element while ignoring other attributes that do not belong to the domain governing those logical aspects. These are termed *"non-essential" attributes*. In this case, focus might be placed on the services that a network element performs (such as routing and forwarding traffic), while purely physical properties (such as the power consumption of a network board in the second slot of the chassis of the network element) are deemed "non-essential" and ignored in this domain. This is visually illustrated by the abstraction barrier that isolates the essential characteristics of an object from all other non-essential characteristics of the object within a given knowledge domain (refer to Figure 2.2).

Abstraction is important because it enables all unique objects that comprise a system to be identified. Each unique object class represents a set of characteristics that distinguish it from all other objects in the system. These characteristics are a combination of the attributes, methods, relationships to other objects, and any additional semantics the class may have. The other, non-essential, characteristics of the object do not disappear; they are just not relevant in this particular knowledge domain. They are instead part of other knowledge domains.

Note

Along these lines, it is important to note that no single abstraction will in general completely capture all the salient characteristics, behaviors, and semantics of a complex object. Rather, a *set* of abstractions, each focusing on a particular aspect of the object, is needed to completely model a complex object. For example, to model a router, we need to model its physical characteristics, the logical functions it provides, and which people of which organizations can log onto the router and change its configuration. These correspond to the physical containment, logical connectivity, and logical containment domains of DEN. These capabilities are integrated into a single object model but represent knowledge from different domains and possibly different abstraction levels.

Classification

Classification, in an object-oriented sense, is more than just a grouping of classes that share a common set of attributes and methods. Classification implies grouping together multiple classes that serve the same *purpose*. For example, a security object and a differentiated services object (one that provides a prescribed quality of service on a per-hop basis) might use the same protocol stack, be enabled by the same administrator, and even share other services. However, these two objects serve entirely different purposes and therefore belong to entirely different classes. This is illustrated in Figure 2.3, which shows a set of instances from two different classes: a user class and a network device class. We see that although there are differences between various instances of the user class (as shown by differences in the attributes of each instance), all instances of the user class exhibit a set of common characteristics. Furthermore, these characteristics make instances of the user class distinct from instances of the network device class.

Figure 2.3   Classifying object instances.

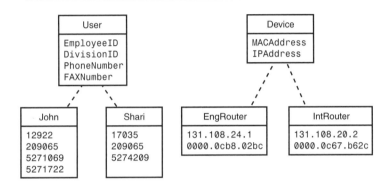

Categorization of object classes is key to building robust models. The development of inheritance and relationship class hierarchies is based on combining classification with different abstract models. Classification is used to recognize similarities between different object classes that belong to different abstract models. Generalization and specialization are then used to fine-tune each hierarchy.

There is, in general, no single correct way to classify different objects. Classification is a function of *how* the developer wants to structure information and knowledge. This is best understood by taking a brief look at how DEN applies the principles of classification and abstraction.

Classification and Abstraction in DEN

There are many different protocols that are used for many different purposes. Since DEN was focused on modeling network elements and services, the larger domain of protocols was abstracted into the smaller domain of network protocols (deliberately excluding protocols whose primary purpose was not networking, such as HTTP). Once this was done, classification was used to organize knowledge according to which layer of which reference model (for example, the network layer of the OSI reference model) the protocol operates in, and what the purpose of the protocol was in that layer. Note that other organizations of this knowledge are possible. However, this organization suits the purposes of DEN very well.

This illustrates a layering of knowledge, which corresponds to both a class inheritance hierarchy as well as a class relationship hierarchy. Abstraction enables us to focus on what a protocol does, as well as which protocols are supported, in which devices in a network. Classification enables us to combine these two different domains—protocols and devices—and derive a model that can relate protocols to devices. The information model therefore contains both an inheritance hierarchy as well as a relationship hierarchy. Neither of these hierarchies could have been designed without using the principles of abstraction and classification.

Encapsulation

Encapsulation in object-oriented design is defined as the separation of the external aspects of an object from its internal implementation. Encapsulation is usually associated almost exclusively with object-oriented programming, where it is used to prevent changes in program components from affecting other program components. However, encapsulation also has a critical role to play in Object-Oriented Modeling. It provides a methodology for combining data structure, behaviors that operate on and/or use those data structures, and relationships with other objects into a single entity.

Encapsulation, when used with abstraction and categorization, enables more robust classes to be designed. Encapsulation forces the class designer to think about *all* aspects of an object—attributes, methods, relationships to other classes, and any additional semantics of the class—as opposed to focusing on individual characteristics of a class. Encapsulation is complementary to abstraction; encapsulation describes how an object provides functionality, whereas abstraction describes the functionality provided by an object.

In CIM and DEN, encapsulation is particularly important. CIM explicitly does not define a specific type of data store to use. This requires the designer to map CIM data into the particular type of data store being used. The mapping is a transformation of concepts, data structures, and data from CIM to a specific type of data store. Encapsulation hides the implementation details of this transformation and enables the designer to focus on ensuring that the mapping itself is correct. This enables multiple interoperable solutions to be developed, each with its own (possibly proprietary) data store, that interoperate because the same information model is used and made accessible through a dedicated mapping.

Inheritance

Inheritance defines a structured relationship among classes, where a subclass shares the structure and behavior defined in its superclass. Inheritance defines a hierarchy of abstractions and encapsulated functionality.

> **Note**
>
> Technically, the preceding definition of *inheritance* should say that a subclass shares the structure and behavior defined in its superclasses. This covers the case of multiple inheritance. However, both CIM and DEN explicitly do not support multiple inheritance. Therefore, from this point on, we will consider only single inheritance.

In CIM and DEN, classes are used to define structure and behavior as well as relationships between objects. Thus, the CIM and DEN information models define both an inheritance class hierarchy and a relationship class hierarchy.

Semantically, inheritance denotes an *is-a* relationship. For example, a router *is-a* type of networking device, and its capability to forward traffic *is-a* type of networking service. Thus, inheritance describes a generalization/specialization hierarchy. We say that a subclass *specializes* or *refines* the structure and/or behavior of its superclasses, while a superclass *generalizes* the structure and/or behavior of its subclasses. In other words, the deeper we descend in a hierarchy, the more specialized the structure and behavior of the classes become; the higher we ascend in a hierarchy, the more generalized the structure and behavior of the classes become. For more information on different types of relationships, see the section "What Is a Relationship?" later in this chapter.

Generalization

Generalization is the process of finding common knowledge (specifically, data structures, behaviors, relationships, and any additional semantics of the class) among a set of classes and encapsulating that knowledge higher in the class hierarchy. Superclasses are more general, and their subclasses are more specific.

Specialization

Specialization is the opposite of generalization. Specialization is the process of refining the structure, behavior, relationships to other classes, and other semantics of a class to define knowledge that is encapsulated in one or more subclasses of a given class. Specialization refines the (more general) concepts of a superclass, focusing on particular added or enhanced functions and capabilities.

Tip

CIM implements associations (and aggregations, which are special types of associations) as classes. It is very important for the reader to think of relationships as classes and to realize that specialization and generalization can be applied to relationships also. For example, CIM_Dependency defines a generic association to define dependency relationships between two managed objects, such as a router and a routing card. The CIM_ServiceService Dependency association is a subclass of CIM_Dependency and defines an association between a service object and another Service object. Here, the association is used to indicate that the latter service (the "dependent" service) is required to have some relationship (for example, be present, be absent, or required to have completed) with the former Service (the "antecedent"). For example, Boot Services may be dependent upon underlying BIOS disk and initialization services.

Polymorphism

Polymorphism refers to the capability to characterize the same operation for many different classes, where the behavior of the operation depends on the class. For example, a Print method may be applied to a file. The specific behavior of the Print method is dependent on the type of file being printed. From an object-oriented viewpoint, one can describe the action of printing a file, without having to describe what type of file it is, what specific printing driver to use, how the file is to be printed, and other characteristics of the file and of the printer. This does not mean that such properties are not important. Rather, it means that the level of abstraction being described is not concerned with these properties.

If we define a method as having a certain *signature* (that is, the syntax and sequence of the parameters to a method, along with the return type of the method), we can extend the preceding definition to specify *signature polymorphism*. This is commonly called *function* or *method overloading*. It enables a different implementation of a function or method to be invoked based on the syntax of the parameters supplied to the function or method.

Polymorphism enables common operations to be specified for diverse classes without having to worry about differences in their implementation.

Classes and Directory Mappings

A class encapsulates unique types of information through its attributes, methods, relationships, and semantics. The attributes, methods, and relationships that comprise a class can be categorized into *distinguishing* and *non-distinguishing* attributes, methods, and relationships. The following discussion will use distinguishing attributes as an example but applies equally to distinguishing methods and relationships.

Distinguishing attributes are those that model the essential characteristics that distinguish this class from all other classes and are the basis for forming the class. Non-distinguishing attributes refine functionality represented in the class. They also provide flexibility in modeling other related functions and components by serving as the basis for subclasses.

There is a close correlation between distinguishing class attributes and the "must have" attributes in a directory class. (This will be covered more thoroughly in Chapter 4, "What Is a Directory?") Both must be present, or the class is not fully realized, nor are its capabilities, behavior, and relationships to other classes fully modeled. Similarly, there is a close correlation between non-distinguishing class attributes and the "may have" attributes of a directory class.

Directory classes do not have the means to represent methods and relationships directly. However, relationships can be mapped into directory classes. Therefore, distinguishing relationships often form the basis for directory classes or for "must have" attributes of directory classes.

Attribute Design

Specialization theory mandates that attributes and methods should not have functional dependencies on other attributes or functions. For example, attributes that can be derived from other attributes (for example, the average, maximum, and minimum count of a property) using one or more mathematical operations should *not* be modeled as independent attributes of a class.

There are two ways to use attributes to build subclasses. One is to add attributes that represent refined or additional functionality beyond the functionality of the superclass. This way corresponds to identifying new distinguishing attributes as the basis for refining a class. The other way is to restrict the value that attributes of a subclass can take. CIM and DEN use the first method almost exclusively. However, the second method is critical for extending the information model to represent vendor-specific functions and devices.

Adding Functionality through Adding New Attributes

This is the most common method of subclassing and is used heavily in CIM and DEN. In this method, new distinguishing attributes are used as the basis for refining existing functionality or behavior, or adding new functionality or behavior that is related to the functionality or behavior of the superclass.

For example, CIM defines a PhysicalFrame as a subclass of a PhysicalPackage. A PhysicalPackage models PhysicalElements that enclose or contain other components. Two examples of a PhysicalPackage are a Card and a Chassis. A Card can contain various PhysicalComponents, such as Chips. A Chassis provides a structure to contain Cards. However, other types of frame enclosures (for example, a Rack) exist. Hence, the PhysicalFrame serves as a base class for these enclosures.

Cards and PhysicalFrames in CIM have very different properties, even though they are descended from a common superclass (PhysicalPackage). For example, the CableManagementStrategy attribute contains information that describes how the cabling is connected and bundled in the PhysicalFrame. Cards have no such property. On the other hand, the RequiresDaughterBoard attribute of a Card is used to capture the fact that at least one additional Card is required to be attached to this Card in order for the functionality provided by the Card to work properly.

Other distinguishing attributes for the PhysicalFrame and Card classes exist. The CableManagementStrategy and RequiresDaughterBoard attributes are examples of two attributes that help define the functionality of their respective class and cannot be used by the other class.

Adding Functionality Through Restricting Existing Attributes

In an information model, specialization can be based on attributes, methods, or relationships. Attributes can serve as the basis of specialization either through restricting the values that an attribute ranges over or through restricting the set of enumerated values an attribute can possess. These are called *quantitative* and *qualitative attribute specialization*, respectively.

For example, suppose that the internal maximum bandwidth of a networking device (as defined by its internal backplane) was defined by an attribute called MaximumBackplaneBandwidth. Suppose that there were several types of related devices built that had different backplanes (for example, less than 1 Gbps and greater than 1 Gbps data transfer rate). One could then build two subclasses, MegabitDevice and GigabitDevice, based on restricting the value of the MaximumBackplaneBandwidth attribute to less than 1 Gbps and greater than 1 Gbps, respectively. Note that the superclass did not restrict the value of the MaximumBackplaneBandwidth attribute, but both subclasses did. This follows our intuition that a subclass provides refined behavior.

Alternatively, assume that a class specifies an attribute that has an enumerated set of values, called `RoleInterface`. For example, *roles* might be used to determine the configuration characteristics of device interfaces. An interface that is operating in an edge role cannot also assume a backbone role, because the two roles require different and conflicting functionality and are used for different purposes (note, however, that a device could have both edge and backbone interfaces). Thus, we could use this attribute as the basis for specialization, forming an `EdgeInterface` subclass and a `BackboneInterface` subclass that get associated with a particular device. Again, we note that the superclass did not restrict the value of the `RoleInterface` attribute, but that the `EdgeInterface` and `BackboneInterface` subclasses did.

We can combine these two methods to form a subclass. This effectively combines quantitative and qualitative specialization into a single level of the inheritance hierarchy. Alternatively, we can form multiple levels of inheritance, where one level uses quantitative specialization and another level uses qualitative specialization. Which of these two methods to use depends on what is being modeled as well as performance. Multiple levels of the hierarchy provide a narrow but deep hierarchy and require instantiating many classes. This can sometimes have performance penalties. On the other hand, while combining these methods leads to a wide but shallow hierarchy, it is sometimes harder to embed the desired amount of extensibility and flexibility.

Attribute Generalization

So far, we have talked about attribute specialization as the basis for subclassing. The reverse, using an attribute to generalize a superclass, is also possible. A useful technique is to define in detail the characteristics of a number of sibling classes, and then analyze their attributes (as well as methods, relationships, and semantics) to see if there are any common attributes. If there are, they can be consolidated into a single generic attribute in a superclass.

Again, there is no general guideline that can be given that defines whether we should generalize or specialize. It really depends on the system and components being modeled, the domains of knowledge that are being modeled, and the information that is available.

> ## Note
>
> I examine what is being modeled and what I know about the entities and functions being modeled to help me determine whether I should first generalize or specialize. I generally start with specialization, simply because I like to understand the overall framework first before I examine details.
>
> The important thing to remember is that you shouldn't stubbornly insist on using only one or the other. As more knowledge is gained that describes the entities being modeled, be alert to switch approaches to maximize the benefit gained from that new knowledge.

Method Design

The same general principles can be applied to method design. In particular, method parameters can be assigned different values corresponding to different domains. For example, a network device might specify a routing function that takes as one of its parameters an address. A subclass might then refine this function to take different *types* of addresses (for example, IP, IPX, and CLNP). Another subclass (of the first subclass) might differentiate between IPv4 and IPv6 addresses.

The preceding example showed how broadening the domain of a function parameter could serve as the basis for subclassing. A complementary approach is narrowing the domain of a function parameter as the basis of subclassing. This is analogous to restricting the domain of an attribute.

In each of these examples, we have refined the notion of an address and used that refinement as the basis for creating additional subclasses. Similarly, we could have started with more specific functions and then generalized them into a more general superclass. The point is to realize that methods play an equal role with attributes and relationships in defining a class, and the modeler must be alert to method refinements to develop a representative class inheritance hierarchy.

This is one of the inherent strengths of CIM and DEN. CIM and DEN are *more* than just a schema consisting of classes and attributes; they define an information model where attributes, methods, and relationships are used equally to determine class and relationship hierarchies.

Relationship Design

There is no single way of defining class and relationship hierarchies. Rather, the six fundamental principles previously described—identity, abstraction, classification, encapsulation, inheritance, and polymorphism—provide a means to classify knowledge within a given domain.

Each class or relationship should be associated with an entity, behavior, or function of the system being modeled. However, this does not mean that each class or relationship must correspond to a *physical* entity in the system. CIM and DEN both partition the functionality, structure, and behavior of a system into a physical and a logical hierarchy.

What Is a Relationship?

Relationships describe functionality that is provided by multiple objects. This functionality takes two general forms: sharing of common attributes and behaviors, and conveying special semantics that exist between the objects.

Technically, there are three types of relationships:

- The *"is-a" relationship* denotes a generalization or specialization relationship between two classes.

- The *"association" relationship* represents a semantic dependency between classes that are otherwise unrelated.

- The *"part-of"* (also called *whole-part*) *relationship*, which we refer to in this book as an *aggregation*, is a special type of association, and is used to describe a semantic relationship where one object is either physically or logically part of another object.

CIM and DEN refer to relationships as associations or aggregations, and call "is-a" relationships by the type of the relationship (either a generalization or a specialization). Therefore, for the rest of this book, we will use the term *relationship* to mean either an association or an aggregation.

There are two fundamental concepts that describe associations and aggregations. First, the connection between the objects is called a *link*. The type of link characterizes the semantic connection between the objects. Second, the term *multiplicity* is used to describe how many instances of one object can be related to how many instances of another object. These are described in the next two sections.

Links

A fundamental concept of a relationship is a *link*. A link describes either a physical or a conceptual connection between two objects. For example, consider an employee, Jane Doe, and an employer, Acme Corporation. The following example will lead us through the design of a relationship between Jane and her employer, illustrating the power of thinking of and implementing a relationship as a class.

We can describe the employment of Jane by Acme as a relationship, as in:

Jane Doe *is-employed-by* the Sales Department of Acme Corporation.

This expresses the fact that Jane Doe works for Acme Corporation (that is, from the point of view of the employee). Similarly, we could write:

The Sales Department of Acme Corporation *employs* Jane Doe.

This is the same relationship, but from the employer's point of view, not the employee's.

At this point, you might be wondering what the difference is between a relationship and an attribute. Can't we express this relationship as an attribute of the user class and simply fill in the appropriate department that a user works for? And can't we similarly have an attribute that represents all of the employees of a given department of Acme Corporation?

There are several problems with this. First, there is an inherent dependency between the *employs* and the *is-employed-by* relationships. That is, when one changes, the other needs to be updated. For a large corporation, this could be very difficult.

Second, remember that an attribute is a fixed characteristic of an object. Suppose that we want to extend this relationship and represent the fact that Jane, being very industrious, can work for multiple divisions of Acme. Or perhaps Acme is a holding company and assigns Jane to work for multiple companies it owns. Each of these cases cannot be represented by a single static attribute, because the employment relationship is really dependent on *both* the employer and the employee objects. Attributes cannot capture this dependency between multiple objects because they exist in only one object.

A relationship captures the very important fact that the function being modeled as a relationship is not dependent on either object by itself, but rather is dependent on both objects together. Using a relationship provides inherent flexibility, as is illustrated by the following example depicted in Figures 2.4, 2.5, and 2.6.

We want to add a salary attribute to the preceding example. So far, we know that Jane Doe works for Acme. We could, therefore, add an attribute called Salary to the employee object representing Jane to store her current salary. This is shown in Figure 2.4. Here, we have made the implicit assumption that Jane can only work for one employer (Acme). Thus, we can represent the multiplicity of the relationship by adding a 1 on the end of the relationship nearest the Company class and a * (which may zero or more—after all, Acme doesn't have to employ anyone!) on the end of the relationship nearest the Employee class.

Figure 2.4   Salary as an attribute of an employee.

However, what happens if Jane works for multiple companies, or even multiple divisions of the same company, that pay her different salaries? Where do we put the salary attribute? This problem is shown in Figure 2.5. Since there is now a many-to-many relationship between Employee and Company, we cannot attach the salary attribute on either the employee or the company. And, even if we did, we would be representing the same data with the same (or similar) attribute in two different classes. This would lead to synchronization problems.

Note also that we represent this added ability for Jane to work for multiple entities as a change on the Employee side of the relationship, from 1 to 1..n. This means "one or more." Thus, we have changed the multiplicity of the relationship from "one to zero-or-more" to "one-or-more to zero-or-more."

Figure 2.5   Trouble—who owns the Salary attribute?

The solution lies in realizing that the salary is an attribute of an association that links an employee to an employer. By making the salary an attribute of the association, we can model the individual differences between Jane's many employment relationships without having to bundle them into either the employer or the employee object. This is shown in Figure 2.6. We denote the addition of the Salary attribute to the relationship by adding it as a box attached to the relationship. Since there is now an attribute of the relationship, we represent its title (`Employs`) as a class.

Figure 2.6   Salary as an attribute of an association.

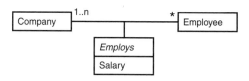

Multiplicity

Multiplicity specifies the number of components on each side of a relationship. It is used on both associations and aggregations.

It is common for multiplicity to specify an optional number of components as well as a specific number of components. The latter is especially useful in capturing the semantics of aggregations, which will be described in the section "Aggregations."

However, multiplicity can be explicitly quantified by several means. In CIM and DEN, the multiplicity of one side of a relationship is in general 0, 1, or *n* (for example, many). This is to ensure that the relationship can be kept as general as possible, so that many applications can use it. However, these are, in reality, specific examples of a *range*. Therefore, it is quite probable that vendors will subclass CIM and DEN relationships to restrict the multiplicity of a relationship to a range that has a lower and an upper limit. This allows more precise semantics to be expressed. For example, the range [1, 11] specifies that at least 1 but at most 11 of the components can be contained. This could be used to model the fact that at least 1 but at most 11 network cards can be installed in a Cisco 7513 router. (This example will get refined throughout the book.)

Associations

An *association* is a group of links that have a common structure and common semantics. Associations are inherently bidirectional. Convention uses a pair of descriptive names that are related to each other as labels for each of the directions of the associations (as *is-employed-by* and *employs* are in the preceding example).

Associations do not have to be bidirectional. Ternary associations are sometimes encountered. Associations that are more complex than ternary are rarely used because of their greatly increased complexity and lack of generality. This is because an association is an atomic unit. Therefore, a higher-order (for example, ternary) association cannot be represented as multiple lower-order associations (for example, two binary associations for a ternary association). This restricts the application of higher-order associations.

For example, suppose that a sales person works for several departments in a given year and works for the same company for several years. The company has many sales people, some work in multiple divisions and some do not. Each sales person has a sales record. To represent the sales record of each sales person as a function of division and year, a ternary association is required. More importantly, the relationships described here are atomic and cannot be represented by binary relationships without losing information.

Associations have an inherent multiplicity associated with each end of the relationship. This defines how many instances of one class may relate to another class. For example, in Figure 2.4, we saw that one company *employs* zero or more employees, and each employee *is employed by* one company. Figures 2.5 and 2.6 changed the multiplicity on the company side from one to one or more.

> ## Note
>
> CIM (and DEN) have also formalized the definition of a special type of association, called a *weak association*. This is a mechanism to name instances within the context of other object instances, meaning that the identity of the referenced class depends on the identity of the other participants in the association. Formally, this indicates that the keys (for example, distinguished values—see the sections, "A Directory as a Natural Publishing Medium," and "The Structure of Directory Information," in Chapter 4) of the referenced class include the keys of the other participants in the association.

Aggregations

An *aggregation* is a strong form of an association. It represents a "whole-part" relationship. This type of relationship is used to make a complex object out of a set of simpler component objects. This is often referred to as *composition* (when a complex object is constructed from multiple simpler objects) or *decomposition* (when a complex object is disassembled into its constituent components).

An aggregate object is treated as an atomic unit, even though an aggregate object is comprised of multiple objects. This relationship is often called *is-a-part-of* (as opposed to *is-a*) when referring to composition, and *has-as-a-part* (as opposed to *has-a*) when referring to decomposition.

Aggregation is transitive, but not commutative. *Transitivity* means that if Object A *is-a-part-of* Object B, and if Object B *is-a-part-of* Object C, then Object A *is-a-part-of* Object C. An aggregation relationship is also antisymmetric, because if Object A *is-a-part-of* Object B, then Object B cannot also be *a-part-of* Object A.

Aggregation permits the physical grouping of logically related objects. This is one of the reasons CIM and DEN are so powerful: They both use an information model that makes extensive use of inheritance and aggregation. Aggregation defines groupings of objects, while inheritance enables these groupings to be reused.

Aggregations come in three basic forms: fixed, variable, and recursive. *Fixed aggregations* define a static structure that describes the composition of the aggregate. The number and type of component parts are statically defined. *Variable aggregates* define a fixed structure where the number of parts in each level may vary. That is, the overall structure is fixed, but the number of parts that comprise each level of the aggregate may vary. A *recursive aggregate* contains, either directly or indirectly, an instance of the same type of aggregate.

For example, CIM defines the PhysicalPackage class as a type of PhysicalElement that can contain or host other PhysicalElements. A PhysicalPackage has two subclasses, PhysicalFrame and Card. A PhysicalFrame refines the notion of "physical containment" expressed in PhysicalPackage by adding properties that characterize framed enclosures. The Card class is a type of physical container that serves two major functions:

- First, it can be plugged into another Card or motherboard, or can itself be used as a motherboard in a Chassis.

- Second, it refines the concept of "physical containment" expressed in PhysicalPackage by adding the ability to carry signals and provide a mounting point for PhysicalComponents (for example, a Chip) or other PhysicalPackages.

Finally, the PhysicalFrame class has two subclasses: Chassis and Rack. A Chassis adds additional attributes and relationships to the concept of a PhysicalPackage, mainly in its capability to represent objects such as a desktop or processing node. A Rack is a special type of PhysicalFrame into which Chassis can be placed. It, too, adds attributes and relationships. Except for Racks, any of these physical enclosures can contain other physical enclosures, and thus we can have a set of recursive containment relationships. This is illustrated in Figure 2.7.

Figure 2.7   Excerpt from the CIM physical model showing recursive physical containment.

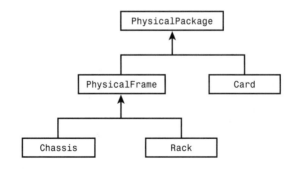

Benefits of Using Classes to Implement Relationships

Since associations and aggregations are implemented in classes in CIM and DEN, all the previous power and functionality inherent in classes can be applied to relationships. Here are the CIM definitions of an association and an aggregation in terms of classes (from the CIM 2.0 specification):

> An association is a class that expresses the relationship between two other classes. The relationship is established by the presence of two or more references in the association class pointing to the related classes.

An aggregation is a strong form of association. For example, the containment relationship between a system and the components that make up the system can be called an *aggregation*. An aggregation is expressed in CIM as a qualifier on the Association class (see the "User-Defined Data Types" and "Qualifiers" sections in Chapter 6). *Aggregation* often implies, but does not require, that the aggregated *objects* have mutual dependencies.

Association and Aggregation Hierarchies

Association and aggregation hierarchies are used to define the structure and functionality of relationships in both CIM and DEN. Association and aggregation hierarchies are both similar to inheritance hierarchies with the following major difference:

> Associations and aggregations define relationships between classes. Each involves a set of classes. However, since each aggregate class is itself comprised of a set of classes, each aggregate class serves as the root of its own class hierarchy. Furthermore, each aggregate class has a different composition. Therefore, multiple association and aggregation hierarchies must be used to completely describe a system. Also, association and aggregation hierarchies are particularly useful for identifying *potential* relationships among *instances* of classes.

Difference Between Inheritance and Relationship Hierarchies

Inheritance hierarchies are used to specify the refinement of behavior and functionality of individual objects. The hierarchy is used to categorize these objects according to the functionality they provide.

In contrast, association and aggregation hierarchies are used to specify how to assemble complex objects from simple objects. Associations and aggregations define the *rules* used to assemble objects that are categorized in the inheritance hierarchy, or to represent dependencies and functionality that affect multiple objects.

Both inheritance and aggregation hierarchies are represented as rooted tree structures. Both component and aggregate classes will appear in inheritance and relationship hierarchies. However, there is a marked difference in the semantics used to construct these trees. Inheritance hierarchies mandate that a class appears exactly once in the tree. Association and aggregation hierarchies do not require this at all. In fact, a class frequently must appear in multiple places in an association or aggregation hierarchy, because it could be contained in many different association and/or aggregation hierarchies.

For example, Figure 2.8 illustrates two inheritance sub-hierarchies (meaning that they are two sub-trees that are rooted off the same superclass). Figure 2.9 shows a single aggregation hierarchy that captures the notion that there is an aggregation between a NetworkElement class and a Protocol class.

Figure 2.8   Multiple inheritance sub-hierarchies.

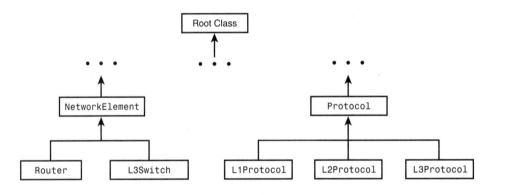

Figure 2.9   Single aggregation hierarchy between NetworkElement and Protocol.

Figures 2.10, 2.11, and 2.12 all show some of the different aggregation hierarchies that are implied by the single aggregation hierarchy of Figure 2.9. Each of these new aggregation hierarchies shown in Figures 2.10 through 2.12 represent a different view of using specialization or generalization applied to one or both of the NetworkElement and Protocol classes.

Figure 2.10   Implied aggregation hierarchies using specialization.

Figure 2.11   Implied aggregation hierarchies using generalization.

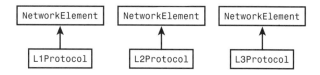

Figure 2.12   Implied aggregation hierarchies using component and aggregate specialization.

Advanced Concepts

This section briefly describes some advanced features of relationships that will be used in DEN applications and probably in the next release of DEN and CIM.

Roles

A *role* is the name of one end of an association. A role has a name that uniquely identifies the association. Roles are important because they provide the ability to associate objects without having to explicitly define the association.

Qualified Relationships

A *qualified relationship* is a relationship in which an additional attribute, called the *qualifier*, is used to distinguish between the set of objects on the many end of a one-to-many or many-to-many relationship. Qualification is used to restrict the multiplicity according to some criterion without losing the generality of the relationship.

For example, consider the *is-employed-by* relationship. This is illustrated in Figure 2.13. Here, we are identifying employees of the company, with no additional semantics. The 1 represents a cardinality of one on the company side of the relationship, while the asterisk represents a cardinality of "zero-or-more" on the employee side of the relationship. Thus, the overall multiplicity of this relationship is "one-to-many."

Figure 2.13   An unqualified relationship.

Now, if we add a qualifier that specifies the title of the employee, we effectively select only those employees whose title corresponds to the value of the title qualifier attached to the relationship. This is shown in Figure 2.14.

Don't be confused by the fact that the title qualifier is adjacent to the Company class. This is the standard way of representing qualified relationships and simply means that the company plus the qualifier will define zero or more employees. Also, note that the overall multiplicity is still specified as "one-to-many," but the qualifier may now restrict the "many" portion of the relationship to zero or more instances.

Figure 2.14   A qualified relationship.

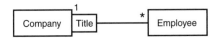

Constraints

A *constraint* is a means to specify a restriction of the values that an object can take. The difference between a constraint and a qualification is that a constraint expresses a functional relationship between different entities in an information model (for example, classes, class attributes, associations, and so on). For example, 30 percent of the bandwidth must be allocated to SNA traffic. On the other hand, a qualification identifies one object out of many that are specified in the relationship (for example, the interface identified as Ethernet 2, port adapter 1, port number 3, of the router named EngineeringRouter, and not any other interface of any other device). Put another way, a qualification relates two classes with a qualifier that is used to reduce the multiplicity of the association between the two classes. A constraint restricts the values that an instance can have.

Constraints can be placed on attribute values, parameters of a function, or relationships.

Constrained Multiplicity

Constrained multiplicity is useful to describe additional semantics between two objects. This is most often used in aggregations.

The most common form of constrained aggregations is to specify the multiplicity in terms of either a range of (not necessarily continuous) values or as the result of a function. The former enables a discrete set of values to be included in addition to a range, such as {1, 2, 5..8, 15}. This reads as the values 1, 2, 5, 6, 7, 8, and 15.

Sometimes the lower and/or the upper bound of the range is not a static integer but rather is determined by a function. The result of the function is the lower and/or upper bound of the multiplicity.

Finally, constrained multiplicity is also useful in identifying subclasses. That is, it can be used as a basis for specialization.

Ordered Relationships

Ordering is important, especially when considering how to map an information model to a directory. This is because directories that use LDAP as their access protocol do not guarantee the order of the result set to a query, unless custom controls are used.

Usually, ordering is unspecified in an information model. However, it can be specified when order is an important part of the semantics of the relationship.

CIM and DEN Relationships

CIM is based on a simple yet extensible class structure that represents a component to be managed using the ManagedSystemElement class. This has two subclasses: PhysicalElement and LogicalElement, which are used to model the physical and logical aspects, respectively, of a system, function, or component. Relationships are used to link these aspects together to form a complete model of the component or system.

CIM and DEN use classes to represent associations and aggregations. This enables all the power of classes, like inheritance, to be applied to relationships. CIM defines several types of relationships; here are arguably two of the most important types:

- *Dependency*—An abstract association, implemented as a class, that defines relationships where one object is dependent on another object type.

- *Component*—An abstract aggregation, implemented as a class, that defines "whole-part" relationships between ManagedSystemElements.

Both the dependency and the component relationships are base classes, and both have several important subclasses.

The CIM Dependency Relationship

Dependency relationships between ManagedSystemElements are represented by the CIM_Dependency relationship. It is frequently subclassed to describe how objects of one type depend on objects of another type. Two main types of dependencies are existence and functional dependencies.

Examples of existence dependencies are the Realizes association (between a LogicalDevice and its realization in PhysicalElements) and the HostedService association (between a Service and a System on which it resides). An example of a functional dependency is the ServiceSAPDependency association. This associates a Service with a ServiceAccessPoint and defines the referenced ServiceAccessPoint that is utilized by the Service to provide its underlying functionality.

The CIM Component Relationship

The Component aggregation is an abstract relationship that serves as the root of all composition relationships. CIM and DEN define numerous specializations of this relationship in order to determine concrete aggregations between descendent classes of ManagedSystemElement.

Element composition is represented by the Component association. All ManagedSystemElements can potentially participate in this relationship (or one of its specializations). This means that a System can be described by a set of simpler components, each of which can be individually managed (remember that a System itself is a subclass of ManagedSystemElement). This is a very powerful concept.

Examples of specializing the Component aggregation include the CIM_SystemComponent and the CIM_SystemDevice aggregations. The CIM_SystemComponent is a specialization of the CIM_Component aggregation that establishes "whole-part" relationships between a System and the ManagedSystemElements of which it is comprised. This enables an arbitrarily complex System to be built from a set of ManagedSystemElements. The CIM_SystemDevice aggregation is used to explicitly define the different LogicalDevices that are aggregated by a System.

Modeling the Physical and Logical Aspects of a System

CIM in general uses two cooperating class hierarchies (physical and logical) to model the aspects of a system. (DEN refines this notion to physical containment and connectivity, and logical containment and connectivity. However, the same root classes for the physical and logical aspects of the system are still used.) This is represented in Figure 2.15, where the following definitions apply:

- ManagedSystemElement—An abstract base class that represents all objects that are to be managed.

- PhysicalElement—An abstract base class that represents all physical objects that are to be managed (this is the root of the Physical class hierarchy).

- LogicalElement—An abstract base class that represents all logical (for example, non-physical) objects that are to be managed (this is the root of the Logical class hierarchy).

A LogicalElement represents a component, function, or service. A PhysicalElement is any object that has a distinct physical existence (for example, an identity). The distinction between a PhysicalElement and a LogicalElement is sometimes a bit harder to determine than it seems. A good test to determine if a component is a PhysicalElement is to ask if a label can be attached to it. For example, a modem is *not* a PhysicalElement. This is because it is impossible to attach a label to a modem. However, it is possible to attach a label to the *card* that implements the modem function. Put another way, once it is realized that a modem is a type of LogicalElement, we can then model the function of the modem in several ways (for example, as a set of SoftwareFeatures and SoftwareElements, along with other classes, that reside in a Digital Signal Processor). Note the inherent flexibility of this model; we can represent a single modem, a different type of modem(s), or even multiple modems by changing the software that is associated with the modem function. Thus, CIM enables us to differentiate between the physical packaging housing the modem function and the modem function itself.

A more technical explanation of this is that a PhysicalElement corresponds to just the physical packaging of a function. So when we attempt to model a dedicated router (for example, a device whose sole purpose is routing, as opposed to a general purpose computer that has routing capability), we see that the router itself is a very complex component that has both physical and logical aspects to it. Physical aspects include its chassis, various boards that fit into slots of the chassis, and connectors. These are all types of PhysicalElements. Logical aspects include the forwarding and routing functions that the router performs, as well as which personnel are authorized to log onto the router and change its configuration. Except for the person, these are all types of LogicalElements.

Figure 2.15 Modeling the physical and logical aspects of a system.

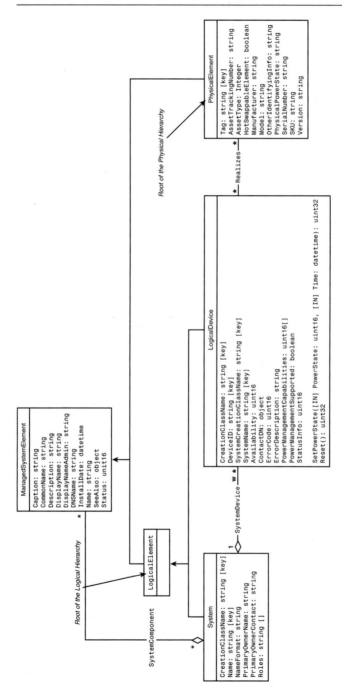

Refer to Figure 2.15. The `Realizes` association defines the mapping between a `LogicalDevice` and the physical component that implements the device. Thus, the model of the router consists of a set of classes with various relationships associating the classes to each other.

Associating Physical Classes with Logical Classes

If we are to model a router, we will need to associate classes that represent its physical aspects with classes that represent its logical aspects. This is where relationships are used.

Referring to Figure 2.15, we see that the `Realizes` relationship associates a `PhysicalElement` to a `LogicalDevice` (which is a subclass of a `LogicalElement`). This enables us to separate the modeling of the physical packaging of the functionality from the modeling of the logical functions and services that it performs. Inherent in this is a great amount of flexibility the packaging can change independent of the functions performed by the device, and the functionality offered can change independent of the packaging. For example, a 56 K modem can be modeled as an upgrade of a 28 K modem by adding a chip and/or software to the modem. This does not change the original modem package.

Sometimes, several associations need to be traversed. This is because a well-designed class hierarchy compartmentalizes knowledge into distinct classes. For example, a `System` is associated with a `LogicalDevice` using the `SystemDevice` association. If the system component being modeled has a physical representation, this can be found by first tracing the `SystemDevice` association, and then tracing the `Realizes` association.

Summary

This chapter has defined key aspect of object-oriented thinking and has related these to Object-Oriented Modeling. Key terminology, such as object, class, attribute, method, and relationship, have been defined.

Six important axioms of Object-Oriented Modeling are identity, abstraction, classification, encapsulation, inheritance, and polymorphism. These were related to CIM and DEN through various examples. The main reason that Object-Oriented Modeling is so important to the modeling of network elements and services is that network elements and services are inherently complex objects that require the modeling of not just their structural properties and functions, but also of their behavior and interaction with the rest of the system. CIM and DEN have been designed such that object, behavioral, and functional models can be integrated to describe all aspects of a component or a system.

CIM was defined as a layered information model. DEN was defined as an extension to CIM that provided additional network-specific knowledge, as well as specifying a methodology to map the model into a directory implementation.

Class, attribute, method, and relationship design were described. Although there is no one general approach to use in all situations, the techniques described in this chapter can be used to guide the developer in the development of the model.

Recommended Further Study and References

The following are general references for object-oriented analysis, design, and modeling. Each of the titles listed below is an excellent book in its own right and also has a rich set of references:

Booch, G. *Object-Oriented Analysis and Design with Applications.* Reading, MA: Addison Wesley, 1993.

Cox, B. J. and A. Novobilski. *Object-Oriented Programming*, Second Edition. Reading, MA: Addison Wesley Longman, 1991.

Hay, D. C. *Data Model Patterns: Conventions of Thought.* New York, NY: Dorset House, 1995.

Larman, C. *Applying UML and Patterns: An Introduction to Object-Oriented Analysis and Design.* Upper Saddle River, NJ: Prentice Hall, 1997.

Mullar, P. *Instant UML.* Chicago, IL: Wrox Press, 1997.

Myers, B. *Object-Oriented Software Construction.* Upper Saddle River, NJ: Prentice-Hall, 1998.

Myers, G. *Composite/Structured Design.* New York, NY: Van Nostrand Reinhold, 1978.

Quatrani, T. *Visual Modeling with Rational Rose and UML.* Reading, MA: Addison Wesley Longman, 1997.

Rumbaugh, J., M. Blaha, W. Premerlani, F. Eddy, and W. Lorensen. *Object-Oriented Modeling and Design.* Upper Saddle River, NJ: Prentice-Hall, 1991.

Schlaer, S. and S. J. Mellor. *Object-Oriented Systems Analysis: Modeling the World in Data.* Upper Saddle River, NJ: Prentice-Hall, 1988.

Yourdon, E. and L. L. Constantine. *Structured Design.* Upper Saddle River, NJ: Prentice-Hall, 1979.

Extending the Information Model

The purpose of this chapter is to describe how to extend an Information Model. The DEN Information Model is best viewed as a framework. This means that it provides a set of tools (classes, attributes, methods, and so on) that are meant to be used to establish a foundation for representing a system in the general sense, but are also designed to be extended to incorporate application-specific knowledge. The methods presented in this chapter can be used to extend the DEN Information Model.

Extending an Information Model: Class Design

This section describes different methods that can be used to extend an Information Model through extending the design of its classes. The next section describes how to extend an Information Model through extending the design of its relationships.

Abstract Versus Concrete Classes

Object-oriented design defines two basic types of object classes, called *abstract* and *concrete* object classes. They are differentiated based on whether they can be instantiated or not. That is, one is unable to create instances of an abstract class, whereas instances can be created of concrete classes. Abstract classes are often used as classification mechanisms (see Chapter 2, "What Is Object-Oriented Modeling?"), where the intent is to capture knowledge and not to create instances of objects.

An *object instance* is a data structure that represents an object in the application domain. From a modeling perspective, instances describe real-world entities that exist and can be manipulated in a system. A *concrete object class* is any object class that can be instantiated.

Sometimes, it is necessary to use a class to represent an important modeling concept without instantiating it. Such classes are called *abstract classes*. Their purpose is to group similar information and behavior into a single entity so that other classes may use and refine this information. For example, Figure 3.1 shows a portion of the DEN physical hierarchy.

Figure 3.1   A portion of the DEN physical model.

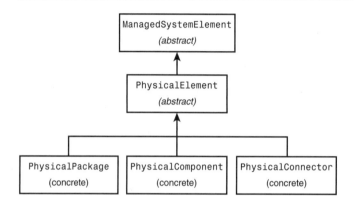

PhysicalElement is an abstract class. It inherits from ManagedSystemElement, so from a modeling perspective, it is used to refine the concept of a managed entity. It is not designed to be instantiated. Instead, it was designed to serve as the superclass for all classes that represent components of a system that have distinct physical identities. We therefore call the PhysicalElement class the *base class* (for example, the logical root) for all managed objects that have a distinct physical presence. In CIM, the most important of these subclasses of PhysicalElement are the PhysicalPackage, PhysicalComponent, and PhysicalConnector classes. PhysicalPackage adds the ability to contain or host other physical components. PhysicalComponent adds the ability to represent any low-level component that can be contained in a PhysicalPackage. Finally, PhysicalConnector represents any PhysicalElement that can be used to connect two or more devices.

The partitioning of the physical and logical aspects of an object is a fundamental concept in CIM and DEN, as it distinguishes purely physical objects (for example, a chassis) from entities that only have a logical presence, such as programs, processes, and services. It is especially useful to characterize complex objects, such as a router, that have many different physical and logical aspects. This was explained in Chapter 2 in the section "Modeling the Physical and Logical Aspects of a System." However, this is a fundamental notion, so the physical and logical base classes (PhysicalElement and LogicalElement, respectively) are repeated for convenience in Figure 3.2.

Figure 3.2 Modeling the physical and logical aspects of a system.

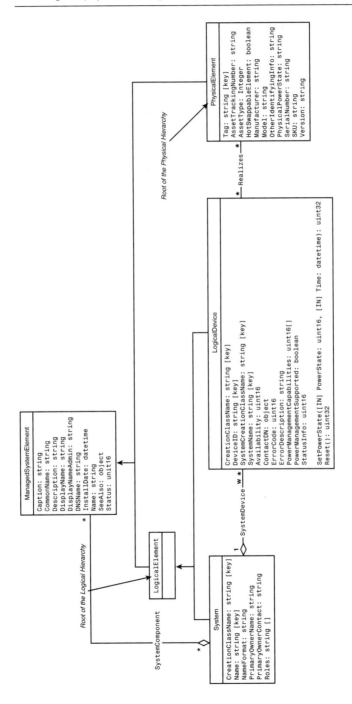

We never intend to instantiate the ManagedSystemElement, PhysicalElement, or LogicalElement classes, so they are all abstract classes. They exist solely to define fundamental concepts of our Information Model (describing an object that can be managed, and describing managed objects that have either a distinct physical presence or not, respectively). As mentioned in Chapter 2, they serve to anchor the rest of the Information Model by enabling the categorization and classification of more specialized concepts into these fundamental concepts (the ability to manage an object, and whether they are physical or not).

> ## Note
>
> The preceding discussion is accurate but simplified. Specifically, complex objects, such as a router, *cannot* be categorized as "just" a physical or logical entity; they are both. CIM and DEN use the principle of abstraction (as defined in Chapter 2) to represent different aspects of a complex object as different object classes. These different classes are then integrated into a single whole using relationships. Chapters 6 through 10 explore this in more detail.

For example, consider a modem. CIM and DEN distinguish between the *logical* functionality that represents how the modem communicates and the *physical* packaging of the modem (for example, the card that houses the hardware and software that performs the communication). A good test to determine whether an object is physical or logical is to see if you can pick up the entity and attach a label to it. If you can, it is a subclass of PhysicalElement. If you can't, it is most likely a subclass of LogicalElement.

Figure 3.1 shows a portion of the CIM/DEN physical model. There are three subclasses of the abstract class PhysicalElement, called PhysicalPackage, PhysicalComponent, and PhysicalConnector. Each of these inherits all the attributes defined by PhysicalElement but further refines the notion of a managed entity that has a physical presence. Specifically:

- PhysicalPackage adds the semantics of a physical entity that serves as a host for other physical entities.

- PhysicalComponent adds further semantics to PhysicalElement to represent any low-level component that is part of a PhysicalPackage.

- PhysicalConnector adds semantics to describe any PhysicalElement that is used to connect other PhysicalElements to each other. It also has the semantics of being able to transmit power and/or electrical signals between the PhysicalElements it is connecting.

Each of these three classes *refines* the concept of a managed physical entity. This is done by adding a set of attributes and relationships (and, in the case of `PhysicalPackage`, a method) to express new semantics of the particular type of object being represented. However, each of these three classes is still a type of physical entity. Thus, the `PhysicalElement` class served the purpose of defining a common point in the model where multiple types of objects that shared similar properties could be defined.

Generalization Versus Specialization

The previous example showed the result of how generalization and specialization can be mutually used to design a class hierarchy. Recall from Chapter 2 that generalization is used to construct a class hierarchy in a bottom-up fashion. Specifically, common attributes, methods, and relationships from different classes are combined into new parent classes.

On the other hand, specialization is used to refine existing functionality by creating new subclasses of existing classes that represent more specific concepts, and therefore add new attributes, methods, and relationships.

General Principles

Generalization is usually used to create a "placeholder" class that serves as the base class for common functions and knowledge. This base class will be refined (or specialized) through a set of new subclasses that each represents new aspects of added and/or enhanced functionality. In this case, the superclass is almost always an abstract class. A good example of this is the CIM `LogicalElement` class. It contains no attributes, methods, or relationships. Rather, it serves as the base class, from an organizational point-of-view, for all managed objects that are logical in nature.

Specialization almost always creates a subclass that has more functionality, but also a narrower focus, than its superclass. This takes three distinct forms:

- *Addition of functionality* in the subclass through adding new attributes, methods, and/or relationships

- *Extending the functionality* in the subclass through adding new parameters to an existing method

- *Restricting the focus of the subclass*, in the form of restricting the range of value and number of attributes, and/or restricting the return value of its methods

Note that these principles can also apply to generalization, except the focus is inverted. Instead of creating a subclass, a superclass is created, and instead of creating new attributes, methods, and relationships, existing ones are gathered into the superclass. The purpose of collecting attributes, methods, and relationships in the newly created superclass is to group functionality that is common to a set of subclasses into a single superclass. This is preferable to defining new functionality in a particular subclass because that loses the opportunity for reuse. Of course, a superclass could be created that has completely new attributes, methods, or relationships, but this is less common.

Thus, for generalization, we would have the following general principles for creating superclasses:

- Providing more generalized functionality in the superclass through defining new attributes, methods, and/or relationships that are common to its subclasses. Here, the idea is to look at the function of each of the subclasses and define new attributes, methods, and/or relationships that can be used to extend the general concept. For example, if we have a router class and a switch class, we might create a new superclass with appropriate attributes, methods, and relationships that can also represent a Layer 3 switch, which is actually a cross between a router and a switch. However, if all three of these devices inherit from a common superclass, we can provide a more streamlined design and avoid multiple inheritance problems (see "Single Versus Multiple Inheritance" later in this chapter).

- Identifying common functionality in the attributes, methods, and relationships of the superclass. This can be done in two different ways. The most common is to examine existing subclasses and move common attributes, methods, and relationships into a new superclass. The second way is to further examine the functionality and purpose of either the subclasses and/or their superclass, and to add attributes, methods, and relationships that not only capture their common function, but also enable new functions to be refined. This is the true power of classification: The resulting system aids the designer in analyzing and developing extensions to it.

- Generalizing the focus of each subclass into a common superclass. Here, we work backward, and where a subclass restricts the range of values and number of attributes (or restricts the return value of a method), the superclass defines a generalized form that has no restrictions. For example, if one type of router can have 13 slots, with two slots for system processor cards and up to 11 for networking cards, one might be tempted to represent that router with constraints on the number of cards it can have. We could still capture this knowledge but use it to generalize the concept of a network element that has different types of slots (system versus networking) and varying numbers of each. We could then verify this by looking at similar types of devices and designing a common superclass for them.

Note

We will discuss the concepts of addition, extension, and refinement of functionality as they relate to extending an object as well as an Information Model in the sections "Providing Additional Functionality," "Extending Existing Functionality," and "Restricting Existing Functionality" later in this chapter.

However, to gain a better understanding of these concepts, we will first discuss a simple example that introduces the concepts of how to use generalization and specialization. Next, we'll formalize the concepts of generalization and specialization by relating them to specialization theory. Then, we will discuss the concepts of addition, extension, and refinement of functionality. These sections will define more detailed concepts necessary for understanding how to extend both a general object model as well as an Information Model. They will all use specialization as a common example. However, each can be applied to generalization equally well. The only difference is one of perspective: Generalization combines attributes from different subclasses into a common superclass, whereas specialization refines the semantics of existing attributes or creates new attributes in a subclass.

Using Generalization and Specialization

It is instructive to see how a typical design can proceed. There are no specific rules that determine when to use generalization and when to use specialization. However, let's imagine that as a starting point, we have an existing class hierarchy and a set of new entities, as shown in Figure 3.3.

Figure 3.3   New classes identified for extending the model.

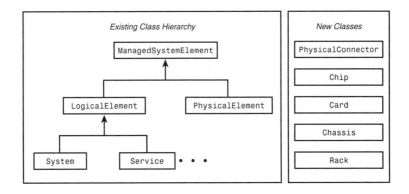

A typical design sequence covering the extension of the class inheritance hierarchy might occur as follows:

1. First, identify all the new entities comprising the system to be modeled. In this case, we can use abstraction to identify physical connectors, chips, cards, chassis, and racks (ignoring for the moment that there are other components to be added). These represent new entities that are not present in our existing model. Therefore, they are targeted to become new classes that will be integrated into the existing class hierarchy. This is called *extending our existing model*.

2. The task now is to link the new objects of the system being modeled to our existing class inheritance hierarchy. One way to do this is to use the concepts of generalization and specialization. We'll use the following approach:

   - Use generalization to find the highest points of commonality within the new objects to be modeled. This enables the new classes to be attached at the highest point in the existing class structure, enabling them to provide the most benefit by distributing their knowledge over as many classes as possible.

Note

Recall that in a directory implementation, there are two types of attributes (see the note in the section "Defining Basic Object-Oriented Terminology" in Chapter 2). These are called *"must have"* and *"may have"* attributes. The difference is that "must have" attributes must be instantiated, whereas "may have" attributes are not required to be instantiated. Therefore, extending a class should only be done using optional (for example, "may have") attributes, or existing implementations will be impacted.

   - Use generalization to re-examine the existing class hierarchy in light of the new concepts introduced by the new classes. Existing classes may be altered (for example, attributes and methods may be added or deleted), and new classes may be created and integrated with the hierarchy to best express these concepts.

   - Use specialization to refine concepts in both the new classes as well as in the existing classes of the class inheritance hierarchy.

3. Accordingly, generalization is first used to find common ancestors of the new objects. For example, a new PhysicalFrame class was created to represent the common properties and functionality of the Chassis and Rack classes before they were added to the tree (this actually was the case in CIM and DEN). This enables any future objects that represent a framed enclosure to be defined in extension schemas to CIM and DEN (see Chapter 6, "A Brief Introduction to CIM," for a definition of an extension schema). This is shown in Figure 3.4. It should be noted that not all classes are generalized at this point. This is okay because this entire process is an iterative one.

Figure 3.4   Generalizing the `PhysicalFrame` class.

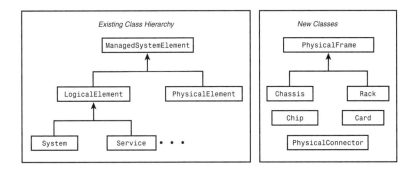

4. Generalization is used again to link these new classes to the existing class hierarchy (for example, `PhysicalPackage` was created to group together `Cards` and `PhysicalFrames`, and then `PhysicalPackage` was linked to `PhysicalElement`). (See Figure 3.5.)

Figure 3.5   Linking the extended classes to the class hierarchy.

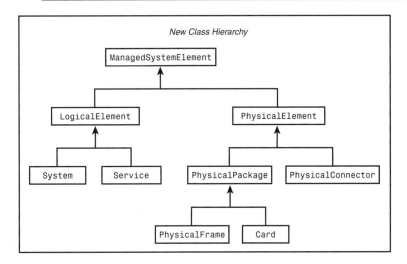

5. At this point, we've integrated everything but the `Chip` class with the existing class hierarchy. Here, we again generalize a `Chip` into a `PhysicalComponent` and make `PhysicalComponent` a subclass of `PhysicalElement`.

6. We can now specialize to add new functionality. For example, networking, memory, and other types of cards plug into one or more *slots* in a chassis-based device. We can specialize this functionality by creating a new subclass of PhysicalConnector, called Slot, which is a type of PhysicalConnector into which other PhysicalComponents can be inserted.

The completed excerpt from the CIM physical model is shown in Figure 3.6. Now, we can proceed in two ways. One way is to make the model more detailed by adding new attributes and methods to the inheritance class hierarchy. Another way is to identify relationships that exist between the classes in the class hierarchy. Either is correct; the choice depends on the type of information you want to model and the needs of the applications that will be using the model.

Figure 3.6   Completed excerpt of the physical model.

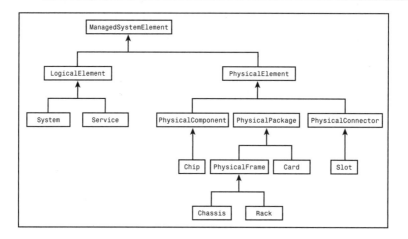

Differences in Class Creation

Both generalization and specialization can result in creating new classes. However, their respective effects are quite different. Generalization moves common attributes, methods, and relationships from existing classes into a new class that becomes the parent class of the affected existing classes. On the other hand, specialization creates new subclasses (for example, child classes) by refining the functionality and/or concepts of an existing class; nothing is "taken away" from the class.

This difference arises because generalization is used to find superclasses, while specialization is used to create subclasses. Which technique to use depends on how you are constructing your class hierarchy and what your frame of reference is at a particular time.

Defining a Basis for Specialization

When a new class is specialized from an existing class, the reason for the specialization is called the *basis for specialization*. The following sections describe how to refine the functionality of an existing class by refining its attributes, methods, and/or relationships.

The simplest basis of specialization for creating a new subclass is to define a new attribute that differentiates the subclass from its superclass. This basis can also be a new method or even a new relationship.

The basis for specialization, whether it is an attribute, method, relationship, or some combination of these, defines new functionality that the subclass has compared to its superclass. However, the new subclass operates in a more specific knowledge domain than its superclass. Thus, we say that a subclass provides greater functionality in a more restricted area than its superclass.

Compound Specialization and Generalization

When more than one basis attribute is used to either specialize or generalize a class, this is called *compound specialization or generalization*. This is sometimes necessary to properly characterize the nature of the specialization. It also helps avoid subclasses having overlapping domains as the basis for their specialization or generalization. It is usually good practice to avoid this, as it creates a less clear inheritance class hierarchy. It also complicates implementation, because it is harder to assign an object to a single class.

For example, consider modeling a network comprised of devices from different vendors that use different routed protocols (for example, protocols such as IP, DECnet, and AppleTalk that can be routed, as opposed to routing protocols—like BGP—that accomplish routing). Using compound specialization, we define our basis as two attributes: the VendorName and the RoutedProtocol attributes. The combination of these two attributes will then be used to create subclasses that characterize the different devices in the network. This is shown in Figure 3.7.

Note that compound specialization or generalization can always be transformed into simple specialization or generalization at multiple levels. It is impossible to provide a general rule as to which technique to use. Indeed, one single technique is not optimal for all situations. Compound specialization or generalization tends to produce inheritance hierarchies that are broad and shallow, while simple specialization or generalization tends to produce inheritance hierarchies that are narrow and deep.

Figure 3.7   Compound specialization.

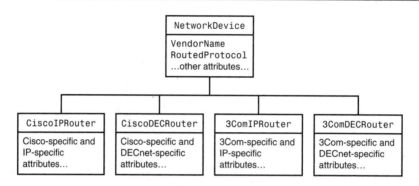

Continuing the example shown in Figure 3.7, we can simplify the compound specialization of VendorName-RoutedProtocol by expanding the single level of compound specialization to two levels, with one level being realized by the VendorName attribute and the next level being RoutedProtocol attribute. This is shown in Figure 3.8. Note that we could have also chosen to specialize first by RoutedProtocol attribute and second by VendorName attribute.

Figure 3.8   Transforming compound specialization into multiple simpler levels.

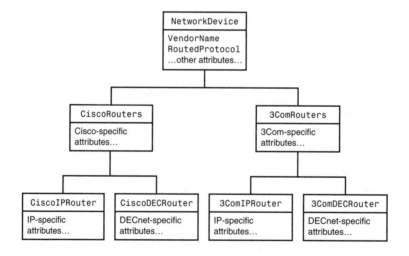

Providing Additional Functionality

Specialization most often is used to represent new or additional functionality. For example, referring to Figure 3.6, we see that a PhysicalElement has three subclasses: PhysicalComponent, PhysicalPackage, and PhysicalConnector. These are subclasses of PhysicalElement because they each realize different types of managed physical entities. This commonality means that they share (technically, inherit) the attributes and relationships of the PhysicalElement class (the PhysicalElement class currently has no methods, but if any were ever added, they would also be inherited by its subclasses). However, because these three subclasses each represent fundamentally new concepts, they each have their own additional set of attributes and relationships. See Chapter 6 for more information about the specific attributes and relationships of these subclasses.

Representing New Functionality

The simplest case is to create a subclass by adding attributes that represent the new functionality of that subclass compared to its superclass. This also applies to adding methods and relationships.

For example, the ManagedSystemElement class of CIM provides generalized concepts for managing an entity. It doesn't define the *type* of the entity, nor does it define the *semantics* that the entity has. PhysicalElement is one of the subclasses of ManagedSystemElement. PhysicalElement refines the notion of a managed entity into managing an object that has a physical presence. The PhysicalElement class represents this by adding attributes that are common to all objects that have a physical presence, such as Manufacturer, Model, and SerialNumber. These attributes are not part of the ManagedSystemElement class because that class is the superclass for physical as well as logical entities, and these three attributes are not part of a logical entity.

Note that PhysicalElement also adds new relationships. These relationships are used to further refine the notion of a managed object that has a physical presence. We'll talk more about the relationships of the PhysicalElement class in the Section "PhysicalElement" in Chapter 6.

So, in general, a new subclass can be created if its functionality requires new attributes, methods, or relationships to be defined.

Representing New Concepts

Sometimes, however, it is convenient to create a new subclass as a placeholder for representing a concept that is shared among its subclasses. A good example of this is the `LogicalElement` subclass (of `ManagedSystemElement`). It defines no new attributes, methods, or relationships. Rather, it is used to differentiate between the concepts of physical and logical managed entities. It is a convenient place to create different subclasses that correspond to different logical functions (for example, `System` and `Service`). Also, it helps classify the hierarchy into a physical and a logical side.

Extending Existing Functionality

Extending the existing functionality of a class most often takes the form of extending the definition of one or more methods of the class.

The idea behind method specialization is to refine the functionality and/or the semantics of the method as it appears in classes further down the hierarchy. This is because classes acquire increased capabilities (for example, through additional attributes or other semantics, such as relationships) as they become more and more specialized. Thus, a general method that was defined in a parent class may now have more specific definition in a subclass.

For example, the signature of the method may change. A *method signature* describes a method by defining the syntax and sequence of parameters to the method, along with the data type of the result of the method. Subclasses may be created by specializing the method signature of the superclass. In an Information Model, this means adding parameters to the method.

Extending the existing functionality of a class method is different when applied to an Information Model than it is when applied to an object model. This is because an object model allows the use of *overriding* an attribute or method value, whereas an Information Model does not. This is explained more fully in the section "Overriding Attributes and Methods" later in this chapter.

However, both an object as well as an Information Model can be extended through adding arguments to a method.

One way of specializing a method is to add new parameters to the method. Adding parameters is a natural consequence of refining the subclass: Because the subclass now has more attributes than its parent class, an existing method may need to change the number of parameters to access this functionality. Changing the data type of a parameter is not allowed, as this redefines encapsulated functionality. This is discussed in the section "Overriding Attributes and Methods" later in this chapter.

For example, consider a class Router that has a method that takes an IP address as a parameter. Now, let's say that we build a new type of router that can process IPX addresses in addition to IP addresses. We can use this fact as the basis of specialization and create a new subclass of the Router class, called MultiProtocolRouter. We can then subclass the existing method and add a new parameter, an IPX address, to it. The subclass has additional functionality (the ability to process IPX as well as IP addresses) compared to its superclass. This is reflected in the increased functionality of the method and the additional attributes that were added to the MultiProtocolRouter to represent this functionality.

Restricting Existing Functionality

There are three approaches to providing additional functionality through restriction:

- Restricting the values of attributes

- Restricting the enumeration of a given attribute

- Restricting the return value of a method

These are examined in the following three sections.

Attribute Value Restriction

The simplest way to create a new subclass is to restrict the values that an attribute can have. Suppose that we want to create different subclasses based on the numerical value of an attribute. For example, consider an interface processor card that may be configured to support a variety of signaling rates: T1, E1, T3, and E3. T1 and E1 transmit DS-1 formatted data at 1.544 Mbps and 2.048 Mbps, respectively. T3 and E3 transmit DS-3 formatted data at 44.736 Mbps and 34.368 Mbps, respectively. From a modeling point of view, we could define a single attribute, transmissionSpeed, that could be used to represent the maximum transmission speed of each of these four signaling rates.

The problem is that each of these different transmission methods requires different components (for example, a different physical connector). Now, imagine an inventory application that wants to instantiate the model. It needs to create an instance of the networking card class as well as an instance of the physical connector class. How does it know which type of connector to instantiate?

One way of solving this dilemma is to create four new subclasses, whose basis is determined by appropriately restricting the value of the transmissionSpeed attribute. Each of the subclasses could then contain the appropriate hardware and software to support the transmission-specific needs of the different configurations of the networking card. This is shown in Figure 3.9.

Figure 3.9   Specialization by restricting an attribute's values.

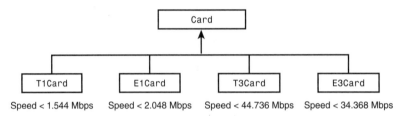

Note that this design is less than optimal. This is because the domain (for example, the range of values) of the basis attribute of each of the four subclasses overlaps. This is undesirable, because an object could be a member of more than one subclass. This runs contrary to the nature of specialization, whose purpose is to provide distinguishing functionality for a reduced scope of knowledge.

However, this situation is easily fixed by creating a compound basis for specialization that ensures that the domain of the compound attribute is unique over each of the four subclasses. This is done by adding additional attributes, methods, or relationships to the transmissionSpeed attribute so that the basis for subclassing becomes the *combination* of the transmissionSpeed attribute and one or more attributes, methods, or relationships.

CIM and DEN do not currently contain any examples of subclassing by restricting the value of an attribute. This is because this method is too specific to a particular application domain. The purpose of CIM and DEN is to provide a generic foundation that many applications can use. However, this is a good method to use when creating extensions of CIM or DEN. In fact, CIM and DEN contain many attributes in many different classes that could be used for this purpose. This enables extension schemata derived from CIM and/or DEN to use this technique to develop application-specific subclasses.

Attribute Enumeration Restriction

Another way to create a specialized subclass is to restrict the number of enumerated values that the basis attribute can have in the subclass. That is, if the basis attribute in the superclass can assume n values, that same basis attribute in the subclass will assume anywhere from 1 to $n-1$ values.

This most often occurs when the basis attribute in the superclass defines a typed value. For example, the purpose of the OperatingSystem class is to represent different types of operating systems, whether they are formally recognized as such or are simply a collection of software and/or firmware that make the hardware of the ComputerSystem (which they are associated with) usable. The OperatingSystem class has two attributes, OSType and OtherTypeDescription, that are used to define the specific operating system that the computer is using. The OSType attribute provides an enumerated set of common operating systems, while the OtherTypeDescription attribute provides the ability to define a new manufacturer and description of an operating system.

Note

Network devices are most often subclassed from UnitaryComputerSystem, which is a subclass of ComputerSystem. The UnitaryComputerSystem class represents a single node computer, such as a desktop computer. However, a network device could also be subclassed from a Cluster. This is a subclass of ComputerSystem that represents a computer comprised of two or more systems, each with compute capability, that function as an atomic unit. Both of these are described in much more detail in the section "System Common Model Classes" in Chapter 7, "CIM: The Foundation of DEN."

Applications can either define routers and switches directly from the UnitaryComputer System (or Cluster) class or create a new subclass to serve as the base class for defining routers and switches. In either case, an association is defined between the OperatingSystem and appropriate ComputerSystem classes. This association, called RunningOS, defines the type of operating system that is being used by the computer system. The OtherTypeDescription attribute can be used to define the specific network operating system, such as IOS from Cisco Systems, that is being used in the network device.

CIM and DEN do not currently contain any examples of subclassing by restricting the values that an enumerated basis attribute can have. This is because this method is again too specific to a particular application domain. However, CIM and DEN provide several CIM and DEN attributes (in addition to the operating system example given earlier) could be used this way, so that extension schemata can use this technique to develop application-specific subclasses.

Method Return Value Restriction

Another way of specializing a method is to restrict the return value of the method. Restricting the return value of the method is very similar in nature to restricting the values an attribute may have. The idea is that the subclass represents more detailed functionality, and therefore a method of that subclass cannot assume as general a set of values as the same method of its parent class.

CIM and DEN do not currently contain any examples of subclassing by restricting the return value that a method has. This is because this again is too specific to a particular application domain. However, CIM and DEN provide several instances of general methods in the core and many of the common models so that extension schemata can use this technique to develop application-specific subclasses. For example, the `StartService()` and `StopService()` methods of the `Service` class are defined as general-purpose methods; it is expected that extension models will subclass them and add parameters as well as possibly restrict the return type of the method to represent application-specific functionality.

Relationship Specialization and Generalization

Similarly, relationships may be specialized or generalized in the same ways as mentioned for class attributes and methods, and this may form the basis for specialization or generalization. Remember in CIM and DEN that a relationship is actually implemented as a class. Therefore, all the power and flexibility that is inherent in class design is available for the design of relationships. In fact, CIM and DEN have a rich relationship hierarchy. CIM implements a set of fundamental relationships, such as the notion of one entity depending on another entity, using relationships. These relationships are then subclassed to represent refinements of these ideas. This is discussed in more detail in Chapters 6 and 7.

Inheritance

This section delineates some advanced concepts concerning inheritance that were not mentioned in Chapter 2.

Strict Versus Selective Inheritance

Specialization theory defines a type of inheritance called *strict inheritance*. This means that every subclass *must* inherit each and every attribute and method from its ancestral classes and *must not* be deleted. This is quite different from conventional object-oriented programming, where classes can *selectively inherit* part of the attributes and methods of their superclasses. The advantage of such selective inheritance is that it facilitates code reuse. However, this fundamentally breaks an Information Model, in that an ancestor class is no longer treated as an atomic unit. CIM and DEN do not allow selective inheritance.

Single Versus Multiple Inheritance

There is a somewhat religious argument over the merits of multiple inheritance. Multiple inheritance permits a class to have more than one superclass, or parent class. The advantage of multiple inheritance is that it enables different information from multiple sources (for example, from each of the parent classes) to be combined into a single class. This also provides an increased opportunity for reuse. The disadvantages include a loss of simplicity and explicitness in being able to partition information. It may also cause implementation problems.

Multiple inheritance is most often used when two or more concepts have been specialized into different ancestral classes, and a subclass of one of the ancestral classes refers to its ancestor and a sibling of its ancestor. Note that this is different from compound specialization, where multiple attributes are used to form a single basis of specialization.

Currently, CIM and DEN do not use multiple inheritance. In fact, the Technical Development Committee of the DMTF has made a decision to try to avoid the use of multiple inheritance in order to keep CIM as simple and as general as possible. However, one of the methods that can map information in CIM to equivalent information in a directory that uses LDAP that may be of potential use in the future is a new method detailed in the *Families of Entries* specification. This document describes a model for grouping collections of attributes into families of directory entries. This enables the user to treat this information as either a set of related entries or as a single "compound" entry, and is accomplished using multiple inheritance in a very specialized way. Specifically, it is used as a means to associate multiple object classes with a single directory entry. This enables the directory server to determine parent-child relationships between the components of an entry. Note that this differs from the traditional use of multiple inheritance, which is for combining attributes and methods of different classes into a single class.

Overriding Attributes and Methods

Overriding attributes (or methods) is the process in which a subclass redefines the attributes (or methods) that it inherited from its superclasses. This is quite popular in conventional object-oriented programming, where virtual functions are often used to implement this.

In Object-Oriented Modeling, overriding is not permitted. This is because, when taken to its extreme, a subclass could completely redefine the meaning of an attribute or a method. One of the fundamental principles of object-oriented modeling is encapsulation. Encapsulation says that the underlying implementation is free to change as long as the external interface to the class does not change. Overriding changes the external interface of the class and, therefore, violates encapsulation.

Delegation

Delegation is the process of assigning one or more objects to perform certain operations on behalf of an object. The benefit of delegation is that it enables an object to present a consistent interface to the rest of the environment, even though other objects are actually performing operations on behalf of the object. Delegation is most often used in object-oriented software development, where functionality can be provided without having to be embodied in a class.

Unfortunately, delegation defeats the goal of building a rich classification scheme. It also runs contrary to the use of inheritance, generalization, and specialization, in that each of these techniques is built upon treating a class as an atomic entity. CIM and DEN are primarily concerned with building rich object taxonomies, whereas the purpose of delegation is to share behavior and *not* further develop the class hierarchy. Therefore, we will *not* use delegation in order to extend either CIM or DEN.

Extending an Information Model: Relationship Design

This section will concentrate on specific ways to extend an Information Model by extending the definition of its relationships. It will first cover the design of relationships, and then explore additional tools that help capture the semantics of the Information Model.

Understanding the more subtle differences between aggregations and associations is an important goal of this section. Throughout this discussion, remember that an aggregation is a special type of association. Therefore, everything that is said for associations also applies to aggregations. If a concept applies only to aggregations, then it is described in the sections on aggregations.

One fundamental principle is that attributes of one class should not be used to refer to other classes; associations should be used instead. The only time where this rule can be violated is when the Information Model is mapped to an implementation that does not have the capability to implement associations natively, such as a directory. However, this does not mean that if the implementation *is* a directory, the modeling of this reference does not have to be done by an association. In fact, it is critical that the Information Model first represent this relationship as an association, and then the association in the Information Model is mapped to an appropriate implementation. Otherwise, the design is inherently not extensible. For example, if the implementation is changed from a directory to a relational database, that part of the model would have to be redone.

Criteria for Creating Associations

Associations describe relationships between two or more objects that have some meaningful connection. How do you find associations, and what should or should not be an association?

Often, if you describe a concept or a service that is performed, you'll realize that what you're describing is in fact an association. The following are typical descriptions that indicate that an association is present:

- A depends on B.

- A is related to B.

- A references B.

- A communicates with B.

- A uses, manages, directs, or employs B.

- A is next to B (or some other type of physical relationship, other than containment).

- A is related to a transaction B.

Aggregations define a complex (aggregate) object in terms of its simpler constituent components. The following are typical descriptions of an aggregation:

- A is physically or logically a part of B.

- A is physically or logically contained in B.

- A is physically or logically composed of one or more objects, one of which is B.

Roles

Each end of an association is called a *role*. One test of an association is that its roles should be able to have meaningful descriptions.

Roles can have names, multiplicity, constraints, and qualifications. The name of a role is optional, but often aids in the description of the association or aggregation. Multiplicity, constraints, and qualifications are defined in the following sections.

Multiplicity

Multiplicity defines how many instances of A can be associated with B. Referring to Figure 3.10, we see that optionally, a Card may be inserted into zero or more slots. We know that this is an optional association because the cardinality of the card is 0 or 1. This means that the association isn't required, but if it is present, at most one instance of a card can participate. Similarly, if we examine the cardinality of the slot, we see that it is zero or more. Again, this means that slots aren't required to participate in this relationship, but if they do, there can be zero or more slots. The multiplicity of the role named CardInSlot is therefore zero-to-many.

Figure 3.10   Multiplicity of an association.

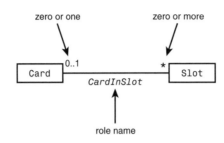

Multiplicity Intervals

Multiplicity is a very important concept for modeling aggregations, as it specifies exactly how many components are required to construct the aggregate. In general, there are many basic expressions of multiplicity, which can be expressed in terms of an *interval*. The following lists the most common types of multiplicity that are encountered.

Given a lower limit L and an upper limit U, the following represent the most common multiplicity expressions in terms of numeric intervals:

[0, 1]—The aggregate can *optionally* contain at most one component.

[0, *]—The aggregate can *optionally* contain zero or more components.

[1, 1]—The aggregate must contain one component.

[1, *]—The aggregate may contain one or more components.

[L, U]—The aggregate must contain at least L but at most U components.

[L, *]—The aggregate must contain at least L components.

[*, U]—The aggregate must contain at most U components.

Advanced Multiplicity Concepts

There are two additional ways of specifying multiplicity:

- Specifying a non-continuous interval

- Using an expression to specify the lower and/or the upper bound of the interval

Non-continuous intervals take the form of a set of discrete values. It is common for memory upgrades to be supplied in discrete values, such as 4, 8, 16, or 32 MB. Furthermore, it is also common for a constraint to be placed on the amount of memory. For example, to run a particular version of software, you must have a minimum amount of memory. Thus, to model the actual configuration of the card, it is not sufficient to supply a continuous range of values, because many of these values represent unrealistic or impossible configurations. Rather, the multiplicity consists of a set of discrete values. This is represented as a set of integers within braces, to avoid confusion with the representation of ranges (which are in brackets). Thus, we have:

[16, 32]—Represents the RANGE of values from 16 to 32

{16, 32}—Represents EITHER the value 16 OR the value 32

A generalization of this is to use attributes to define the lower and/or the upper bound of an interval. This arises in cases where one of these bounds is not known in advance but is instead dependent on the environment.

As a simple example, consider a particular type of router that has a number of slots n. Suppose that m of these are reserved for system controller boards. In theory, this leaves $n–m$ slots free for installing networking cards. Suppose that there are different models of this router, each having a different number of system slots m and networking slots n. Then we can define the multiplicity of the number of networking cards that can be installed as

$[0, n–m]$

Now, let's further suppose that not all cards have the same requirements. For example, the physical requirements (such as power consumption, cabling, and so on) and/or logical requirements (for example, a particular version of software is required, or a certain amount of system resources is consumed) could be different for different types of cards. Therefore, the number of cards of a particular type is not dependent on the number of free slots, but rather this and the type of cards that are occupying the used slots.

CIM and DEN do not currently contain any examples of either of these advanced forms of specifying multiplicity. This is because this is too specific to a particular application domain. However, CIM and DEN provide several instances of attributes in many of the common models so that extension schemata can use this technique to develop application-specific subclasses.

Multiple Associations Between Two Classes

Two objects may have multiple associations, aggregations, or a combination of each that relate to each other. This is perfectly reasonable, and simply means that the relationship between the two objects is complicated and consists of multiple different concepts.

There are several examples of this in CIM. For example, there are two associations, ServiceAccessBySAP and ServiceSAPDependency, that relate a Service object to a System object. In this case, the ServiceAccessBySAP association identifies the access points for a service, while the ServiceSAPDependency defines the use of a ServiceAccessPoint by a service. These are fundamentally different relationships that exist between two objects, and therefore should be modeled by separate associations.

Constraints

Constraints represent functional relationships between different entities in an object model. The purpose of a constraint is to restrict the values that an entity can assume with respect to its relationship with another entity. For example, the priority of one type of traffic may not be increased under any circumstances, given the current environment and other types of traffic flowing in the network. The following sections describe different types of constraints. Note that CIM and DEN do not currently have any examples of these types of constraints, because CIM and DEN are both general-purpose models. However, these types of constraints are often used in building an application-specific extension model of CIM or DEN.

Constraints on Class Attributes

Constraints can be placed directly on an attribute in a class, as in Figure 3.11. This figure shows that the priority of gold traffic is always greater than the priority of best-effort traffic. The constraint is drawn in braces near the class itself.

Figure 3.11   Placing a constraint on a class attribute.

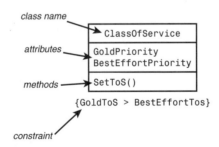

Constraints on Attributes Using Relationships

Constraints can also be placed directly on an attribute that is used to represent the dependency between two different classes. For example, the DEN policy class hierarchy specifies that a PolicyRule can consist of zero or more PolicyActions. However, an additional constraint is imposed, in that the policy actions may be ordered. This is again expressed through text in braces that is placed near the association, along with specifically identifying the attribute that is being constrained. This is illustrated in Figure 3.12.

Figure 3.12   Constraining an attribute of a class using a relationship.

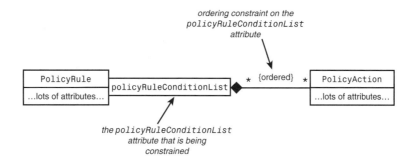

Constraining Attributes of Relationships

Another type of constraint is one that is placed directly on an attribute in an association or aggregation. Figure 3.13 shows a constraint between two attributes of two classes that are related to each other. The CIM CardInSlot association is used to describe the fact that cards plug into slots. CIM does not place a constraint on this association in order to ensure that it can be used for as many different applications as possible. However, many networking devices have a number of constraints that define which types of cards can plug into which slots in a chassis (for example, a controller card must go into slot #5, or a networking card can go in any even numbered slot). Thus, an *extension* model could subclass the CIM CardInSlot association in order to add these and other semantics by adding attributes that represent the constraints directly to the association.

Figure 3.13   Constraining an attribute of a relationship.

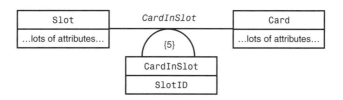

Constraining Relationships

Another type of constraint is one that depicts dependencies between two relationships. This is illustrated in Figure 3.14. This arises because there are two distinct relationships between instances of the same class, but one of the relationships is a subset of the other. Specifically, employees can be members of a project team, and a single employee can be designated as the technical leader of the project team. However, for an employee to be a technical leader of the project, that employee must also be a member of the project team. Thus, the *Technical-Leader* aggregation is a subset of the *Project-Member* aggregation.

Figure 3.14   Constraining two relationships.

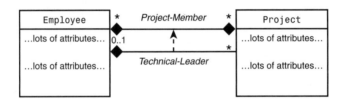

Qualifications

A *qualifier* is another way of restricting the multiplicity of an association. It is used with either one-to-many or many-to-many associations. The purpose of the qualifier is to distinguish among the set of objects that are identified by the other end of the association.

For example, refer to Figure 3.15. CIM defines two classes, called the `Directory` class and the `DataFile` class. We could extend CIM by adding a new association, `ContainsDataFile`, between these two classes. We could then *qualify* this association with a `FileName` attribute. That is, we would use the `FileName` attribute to identify a particular file from among the collection of files present.

Figure 3.15   Restricting multiplicity using a qualified association.

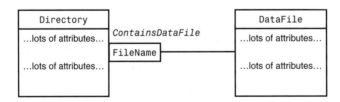

Relationship Hierarchy Implementation in CIM

Associations (and also aggregations, because they are a special type of association) are implemented in CIM and DEN as object classes. This means that class hierarchy diagrams can be drawn to represent the derivation and structure of associations and aggregations. It also means that associations and aggregations possess all of the rich features that classes offer, such as inheritance. Finally, it means that the guiding principles of class design identified in Chapter 2, such as encapsulation and object identity, should also be applied to associations and aggregations.

Aggregations Versus Associations

An *aggregation* is a special type of association. Aggregations always connote a whole-part relationship, where an aggregate object is comprised of a set of component parts. Semantically, this describes an object that has two distinct sets of interfaces. One interface enables the entire collection of objects (for example, the router and the networking cards that it contains) to be treated as a single atomic object. A second set of interfaces enables the set of objects that are "parts of the whole" to be treated as individual, yet related, objects. Aggregations are used in order to simplify the modeling of a complex object by creating an assembly of simpler objects that represent the complex object.

The following is a set of guidelines that can help determine whether to describe a relationship as an aggregation or as an association:

- An aggregation can always be described by the phrase *part of*. In an aggregation, one or more objects are always part of another larger object.

- An aggregation connotes a subordinate relationship between some of its constituent parts and the object that represents the whole (note that this may be a set of recursive relationships).

- Operations applied to the object that represents the whole are automatically propagated to all or some of its parts. For example, if an aggregate object is moved, all of its constituent parts are also moved. An even better indication is deletion: If an aggregate object is deleted, all of its component parts are also deleted. This is not true for associations.

- One or more attribute values assigned to the object that represents the whole are automatically propagated to all or some of its parts. For example, if a department has a cost center consisting of a special cost code, all of its employees, when working for that department, will use that cost code to account for their work.

Note

Note that in the case of an association or aggregation, CIM defines two *optional* qualifiers (see "Qualifiers" in Chapter 6), called DELETE and IFDELETED, that define the behavior if an association is deleted. Specifically, the DELETE qualifier indicates that the association must be deleted if any of the objects in the association are deleted as long as the respective object referenced in the association has the IFDELETED qualifier. It is the author's opinion that the particular deletion semantics used must be considered on an application-specific basis.

Aggregation Versus Inheritance Hierarchies

Both aggregation and inheritance hierarchies may be drawn in a hierarchical tree-structured form. However, there are a number of differences between these two types of hierarchies. These differences stem from the fundamental fact that they represent two different things. Inheritance is used to categorize objects and classify knowledge and concepts about those objects. Aggregation is used to define how complex objects are composed. Aggregation hierarchies are used to define how to assemble complex objects, and to capture operational semantics of that assembly. Put another way, an aggregation hierarchy is used to define potential relationships between *instances*, whereas a class inheritance hierarchy shows the subclass-superclass relationship between *classes*.

The distinction between inheritance and aggregation cannot be overemphasized. Inheritance represents a *specialized-from* relationship, whereas aggregation represents an *is-a-part-of* relationship. Furthermore, just because an object *is-a-part-of* another object does *not* mean that it must inherit anything from that object. Thus, an Information Model consists of multiple hierarchies: *one* inheritance hierarchy and *multiple* aggregation hierarchies.

Why multiple aggregation hierarchies? This is because more than one aggregation hierarchy may be needed to describe the composition of a complex object. Remember that in general a complex object can be comprised of multiple simpler objects, each of which can in turn be comprised of yet simpler objects. Therefore, multiple levels of aggregation could exist for a single complex object. Each of these different levels of aggregation is described by its own rooted hierarchy. The complete representation of the single complex object is therefore described by the collection of aggregation hierarchies.

For example, consider the inheritance hierarchy shown in Figure 3.16. This depicts a Layer3Switch class and a NetworkingCard class that can be installed in the Layer 3 switch as separate branches in the tree (much like the Chassis and Card classes of CIM).

Figure 3.16   Layer 3 switch and `NetworkingCard` inheritance hierarchy.

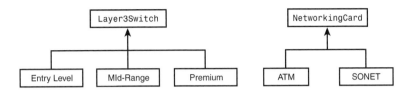

Now look at the aggregation hierarchy in Figure 3.17. This shows that the Layer 3 switch can optionally contain a set of networking cards.

Figure 3.17   Aggregation hierarchy for the Layer 3 switch.

The combination of the aggregation hierarchy of Figure 3.17 and the inheritance hierarchy of Figure 3.16 implies two different hierarchies:

- An aggregation hierarchy can be drawn for each subclass of the Layer 3 switch class, as shown in Figure 3.18.

- A separate aggregation hierarchy can be drawn for each subclass of the networking card class, as shown in Figure 3.19.

Figure 3.18   Aggregation hierarchies for the Layer 3 switch subclasses.

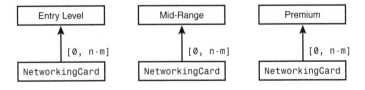

Figure 3.19   Aggregation hierarchies for the `NetworkingCard` subclasses.

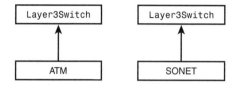

Drawing an Aggregation Hierarchy

As we have seen, aggregation hierarchies are slightly more complicated than association hierarchies. This is because an aggregation consists of multiple objects that are contained in other objects. Thus, an aggregation hierarchy is rooted at the aggregate (the whole part of the assembly) and proceeds downward through each of its components (the parts in the whole). Specifically, this means that an aggregation hierarchy shows different types of relationships between objects at multiple levels, whereas an inheritance hierarchy always shows a single type of relationship (inheritance) between objects at adjacent levels.

Because aggregation hierarchies describe how to assemble an aggregate object, the *same* component object may appear in multiple places in the aggregation hierarchy, as was shown in Figures 3.18 and 3.19. Compare this to inheritance hierarchies, where an object can *only* appear once, in a single place in the hierarchy.

An aggregation hierarchy is drawn by visiting each of the constituent components of the aggregate, enumerating the classes and relationships involved. This procedure is then repeated for each of the components of the aggregate (the transitive closure, if you will). This was shown in Figures 3.16 through 3.19.

Continuing the example illustrated in the previous figures, the Layer 3 switch can contain a number of different types of cards, such as networking cards, on-board memory cards, and other types of cards. Each of these cards can contain its own unique chips and connectors, and might also have on-board software that performs a service (for example, high-speed routing). These are all separate concepts that have their own aggregation hierarchies that describe them. Thus, there is a single aggregation hierarchy that describes the entire switch assembly and a set of aggregation hierarchies that describe each of the components of the Layer 3 switch (for example, one for each of the different cards contained in the Layer 3 switch).

As another example, consider describing the ports in a switch. In CIM and DEN, the `CIM_ProtocolEndpoint` class represents a port. A simplified conceptual inheritance hierarchy is shown in Figure 3.20. The purpose of the inheritance hierarchy is to describe the structural relationships of these three objects (switch, networking card, and port). This is why they each appear in separate branches of the inheritance hierarchy. In particular, note that the switch has both a physical part (represented by `PhysicalPackage`) as well as a logical part (modeled by a `UnitaryComputerSystem`), whereas the port is purely a logical element. The networking card also has a physical and a logical part of the model, but that was omitted from this figure for clarity. Recall also that the purpose of the inheritance hierarchy is to *classify* knowledge. The inheritance hierarchy cannot describe how these three objects are related to each other. (See Figure 3.20.)

Figure 3.20   Sample inheritance hierarchy.

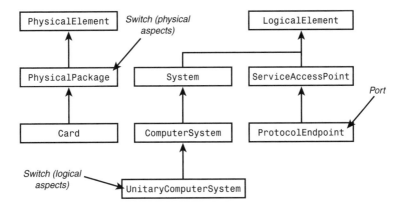

Compare this to (an equally simplified version of) the aggregation hierarchy, which is shown in Figure 3.21. Here, the class "switch" was used to focus on the concept, not to imply that there was an actual "switch" class in CIM or DEN. Conceptually, it describes the following relationships: A port *is-a-part-of* a networking card, which *is-a-part-of* a switch.

While the inheritance hierarchy shows these objects as separate objects in the tree, the aggregation hierarchy shows these objects as part of an assembly.

Figure 3.21   Sample aggregation hierarchy.

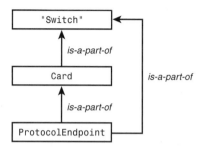

> **Note**
>
> The actual DEN inheritance and aggregation hierarchies are more complicated than these figures indicate. For example, the concept of a switch includes physical (for example, the chassis) as well as logical (for example, the bridging service) aspects. Each of these aspects has its own aggregation hierarchy, though they appear as one single inheritance hierarchy.

Using Aggregation and Inheritance Together

The inheritance and aggregation hierarchies are complementary concepts and should be used together to enable a complete understanding of the system being modeled. Inheritance hierarchies define the structure and behavior of classes, while aggregation hierarchies define how to assemble *instances* to create a more complex object. Although aggregation classes can have attributes and even methods, these attributes and methods are used to define concepts about the assembly. The attributes and methods of a class in an inheritance hierarchy are used to describe the function and behavior of that component.

Therefore, one needs to use both the inheritance and the set of applicable aggregation hierarchies in order to completely understand a complex object. For example, a router consists of a chassis that has slots into which cards plug in. Each card provides a type of networking function. Each of these objects (the router chassis, its slots, the cards, and the services that each card provides) is an individual object, each with its own attributes, methods, and relationships. The inheritance hierarchy describes the capabilities and functionality of each of these components. The aggregation hierarchy describes how they are assembled to form a particular type of router.

Higher-Order Associations

Associations may involve more than two objects. Such higher-order associations are in general more complicated to conceptualize and implement, but are sometimes necessary. For example, to distinguish between programmers that know a particular programming language that can work on a particular project, one could model this as a ternary association between the `Person`, `ProgrammingLanguage`, and `Project` classes.

CIM and DEN do not currently have a ternary or higher association. In fact, all of the various working groups try to avoid the use of associations between more than two object classes. This is in order to ensure as broad an applicability to multiple applications as possible.

Note

An extension to the CIM or DEN model may propose a higher-order association. Try to simplify this into a set of binary associations, perhaps using qualifications and/or constraints. The resulting model will be more general and easier to understand and reuse.

Metadata

Metadata is defined as data that describes other data. In CIM, metadata is used to define the *metaschema*, which is a formal definition of the model. The metaschema defines the terms used to express the model and its usage and semantics. See Chapter 6 for more information about the CIM metaschema.

A Checklist for Extending the Information Model

There is no one right way to proceed. Most of the design of the various CIM models (including DEN) has centered around first identifying a set of concepts, flushing this out (perhaps by specializing areas of the hierarchy that are best known) and then trying to normalize the result. This iterative approach of generalization followed by specialization has worked out well in the design of CIM and DEN.

This section will first present the concept of normalization, and then provide a general checklist for ways to extend the Information Model. It will conclude with a set of design principles to help guide the process of extending the Information Model.

Class Hierarchy Normalization

The process of normalizing a class inheritance or relationship hierarchy is similar to normalizing a database. Most of the CIM working groups use this technique as part of their methodology for designing common models, though it is not mandatory.

Class normalization, when applied to an object model, defines the "best" place to put a particular attribute or method. When this is applied to an Information Model, it also includes defining where the "best" place is to put a relationship.

Note

Class normalization is very important. If an attribute, method, or relationship is not put at the correct place in the class hierarchy, one or more of the following undesirable things may happen:

- Subclasses may not have access to one or more attributes, methods, and/or relationships that they need.

- Subclasses may be forced to inherit attributes, methods, and/or relationships they do not want.

- If an attribute is located in the wrong class, the semantics for that class may cause incorrect results (for example, if an attribute is mistakenly placed on the antecedent instead of the dependent end of an aggregation, it will mistakenly tell all dependents to be updated when it is updated).

- Two subclasses will define the same attribute, method, and/or relationship in different ways, which could lead to inconsistencies in the model and incorrect behavior.

Class hierarchy normalization does not have an equivalent to the "normal forms" of database normalization. Nevertheless, there are several important analogies between database normalization and class hierarchy normalization:

- The generalization of attributes, methods, and relationships (for example, their promotion from individual subclasses to a common superclass) is very similar to data normalization

- The prevention of deleting or redefining attributes, methods, and relationships is very similar to database schema normalization.

- The elimination of redundant information, which is done in database normalization through converting a schema to a desired normal form, corresponds to the insertion of abstract classes in the hierarchy to group common information.

Class hierarchy normalization should be done when the majority of the concepts in the model have been defined. It should also be done whenever the model is significantly altered, such as when new concepts are introduced.

Constructing and Extending an Information Model

There is no one "cookbook approach" that can be used for every situation. However, there are a set of general rules that can be followed that promise to help simplify the design process.

The following is a basic set of steps that can be followed to develop and extend an Information Model. Remember that this is an iterative approach, and some of these steps may need to be revisited during the course of the analysis.

1. Identify objects and classes, and group them into a rough inheritance hierarchy.

2. Identify the most important attributes and methods for these classes (to aid in better understanding their purpose).

3. Identify associations and aggregations between the objects in the class inheritance hierarchy.

4. Identify attributes and methods of the associations and aggregations.

5. Organize and simplify the inheritance hierarchy using generalization.

6. Expand the coverage of key concepts in the inheritance hierarchy using specialization.

7. Do the same for the relationship hierarchy.

8. Ensure that common queries can be easily and efficiently accommodated.

9. Iterate and refine the model as necessary.

A Checklist of Design Principles

The following is a checklist of design principles to use:

- Identify entities and concepts that are important to the system being modeled as early as possible. These are good targets for object and relationship classes.

- It is usually easier to create a lot of subclasses and then generalize them into a proper hierarchy than to first create a perfect hierarchy and then refine it.

- When specializing classes, ensure that only a single basis of specialization is used at each level in the class hierarchy. This will avoid problems with multiple inheritance. Remember that this also applies to superclasses that are created through generalization.

- Ensure that each subclass has its own unique domain, so that an object can always be assigned to a single subclass. Avoid creating subclasses that have overlapping domains. Obviously, overlapping domains are worse the higher in the hierarchy that they occur.

- In general, push concrete classes toward the bottom of the tree and place abstract classes at the top and middle of the tree. Don't be afraid to create an abstract class to model a concept (recall the use of `LogicalElement`).

- While doing the preceding, don't get obsessed with trying to perfectly model how a service interacts with physical and logical objects. This is, in general, very difficult to get right the first time. Furthermore, it usually requires understanding more of the environment than you think you need to so you get it right. Finally, modeling services requires the use of multiple classes and associations. Therefore, this is better done later in the model, after the particulars of the different object classes have been defined.

- Try to avoid class explosion. While it is sometimes tempting to create a subclass for each distinct aspect of a concept, try to keep the number of classes to a manageable level. Be especially careful of using a particular basis of specialization that causes a class explosion. If this happens, change the basis of specialization. For example, you might try creating more levels in the hierarchy that each have fewer subclasses.

- Try to normalize the hierarchy as soon as practical. This will provide insight into the overall design as well as ensure that the design is practical.

- Do not worry about the overall elegance of the hierarchy. Symmetricity is nice, but should not be a guiding principle. It is okay if the branches of the tree are not balanced, as long as the information that they represent is correct.

- Try to simplify all associations between more than two classes into binary associations.

- Examine your associations and aggregations and ensure that any attributes and methods specified in each association and aggregation are subclassed correctly. Remember that relationships are classes, too, and when new ones are defined, the designer should first ensure that the concept represented by the new relationship is unique. If not, then an existing relationship should be subclassed. Note that this has nothing to do with the types of objects in the relationship; it instead focuses on the nature of the relationship itself. This will be further discussed in Chapters 6 through 10, where the design of CIM and DEN are discussed.

- Don't worry if the exact details of constraints, qualifications, multiplicity expressions, and other forms of subclass creation aren't perfect. The most important thing is to get the overall concepts specified. You will find that this is an iterative process, and many of these items will change anyway.

- Try to avoid multiple inheritance if at all possible. But, if you must use multiple inheritance, ensure that the definitions of the attributes, methods, and relationships from one inheritance chain do not conflict with those from another inheritance chain.

Summary

This chapter has presented different ways to create and extend an Information Model. The CIM and DEN Information Models show the structure of the system being modeled, represented through a set of object classes and relationship classes.

A set of methods was described that can be used to create and/or extend an Information Model. The concepts of generalization and specialization were augmented to include a formal definition of the basis for creating superclasses and subclasses using generalization and specialization, respectively. Different types of bases and their uses were described, including the ability to provide new functionality as well as extend or restrict existing functionality.

Additional detail concerning class design was provided. Though popular in object-oriented programming, selective inheritance, overriding attributes and methods, and delegation were all discouraged as techniques to extend an Information Model. In addition, this chapter cautioned against using multiple inheritance.

Relationships were also examined. Multiplicity, constraints, and qualifications were designed and examined as ways of capturing the semantics of the Information Model. Care was taken to distinguish between inheritance and associations, and to help define the differences between associations and aggregations.

Finally, a list of guidelines to follow, as well as a checklist of design principles to use, was provided.

Recommended Further Study and References

The newly proposed LDAP Family of Entries draft can be found in the IETF LDAPEXT Working Group, which is located at

http://www.ietf.org/html.charters/ldapext-charter.html

It is authored by David Chadwick, and the latest version of the document can be found at

http://search.ietf.org/internet-drafts/draft-ietf-ldapext-families-00.txt

The following are general references for object-oriented analysis, design, and modeling. Each of the titles listed here is an excellent book in its own right and also has a rich set of references:

Booch, G. *Object-Oriented Analysis and Design with Applications.* Reading, MA: Addison-Wesley, 1994.

————. *Object Solutions: Managing the Object-Oriented Project.* Reading, MA: Addison-Wesley, 1995.

Gossain, S. and I. Graham. *Object Modeling and Design Strategies: Tips and Techniques (Advances in Object Technology, No. 15).* New York, NY: SIGS Books & Multimedia, 1998.

Jacobson, I. *Object-Oriented Software Engineering: A Use Case Driven Approach.* Reading, MA: Addison-Wesley, 1994.

Rumbaugh, J., M. Blaha, W. Premerlani, F. Eddy, B. Lorensen, and W. Lorenson. *Object-Oriented Modeling and Design.* Upper Saddle River, NJ: Prentice-Hall, 1991.

Rumbaugh, J., M. Blaha, W. Premerlani, F. Eddy, and S. Blaha. *Object-Oriented Modeling and Design: Solutions Manual.* Upper Saddle River, NJ: Prentice-Hall, 1991.

4

What Is a Directory?

The purpose of this chapter is to provide a brief background on directory technology and describe why directories are potentially so important for building Intelligent Networks. This chapter introduces the concept of a directory, and then compares it to other types of information repositories to further emphasize how a directory can be best utilized. Next, the advantages of directories, along with the role that they play in directory enabled networks, will be covered. Then, the salient characteristics of a directory, along with some insight into what are good and bad uses of a directory, will be provided.

The problem of proliferating application-specific directories (and other types of data stores) will then be covered. This is the motivation for using the directory as a unifying information repository.

Finally, this chapter will examine some of the problems in using a directory for networking as a foundation for future chapters.

What Is the Purpose of a Directory?

Two fundamental concepts of directories are the notion of a directory and the directory service. They are defined as follows:

- A *directory* is used to record information about a particular group of objects.

- A *directory service* stores and retrieves information from the directory on behalf of a set of authorized users.

The purpose of a directory is to store, identify, and retrieve a particular set of information about resources in an environment. This is done by structuring information in a way that is optimized for the applications using it. *Resources* represent objects, such as users, groups, file servers, and printers, that serve a defined purpose in the computing environment.

Directories enable information about resources in a (possibly distributed) computing environment to be published in a standard format. This enables authorized clients of the directory service to retrieve information about these resources. This standard format is arguably the most important benefit of a directory service, as it enables different types of directories, directory services, and systems that use the directory service to be built independently.

Note
A directory can be optimized for a set of applications by tailoring the way it organizes and stores information to best meet the needs of the application. This greatly benefits the target applications. However, this specialization of the directory schema has given rise to the proliferation of targeted directories that *isolate* information in their data stores. This isolation is a result of not representing information in a common way. This will be discussed in the section "Proliferation of Directories" later in this chapter.

Why Does Intelligent Networking Need a Directory?

As a developer of either Intelligent Networks or applications that use Intelligent Networks, you need a directory service for the following reasons:

- A directory is better suited to be used as a common information repository than other types of data stores.

- A directory is a natural publishing medium.

- Directories are the *de facto* medium for containing user and other types of information, and directory enabled network applications require user, network, and resource information to be integrated.

- Directories facilitate finding information.

- A directory enables different systems to be used to build different parts of the distributed system.

Directory as a Common Information Repository

A *common information repository* is one that can be used by all applications—regardless of their platform, language, and API dependencies—to store, search, retrieve and modify common (for example, *shared*) information. Directories were built to perform this function by offering standard ways to perform these operations in a distributed system.

Directories offer another fundamental advantage in implementing a common information repository over other types of data stores. This is the inherent ability of the directory to accommodate arbitrary information. It does this by organizing the information as a *hierarchy* which enables parent objects to serve as the naming authority for child objects. Thus, the hierarchical organization of the directory provides scoping as well as built-in navigation.

In addition, directory standards are becoming ubiquitous. This is driving vendors towards incorporating directory support for their applications. This in turn is influencing vendors to implement common repositories using directories instead of other types of data stores.

A Directory Is a Natural Publishing Medium

Directories are designed to be publishing mechanisms. This is primarily because of two reasons. First, they have been optimized to perform as many read operations as possible. Second, directories allow arbitrary information to be attached to and removed from the data store. This is done by treating information as an entry that has a number of attributes, each of which has a type and one or more values. One or more of these attribute values, called *distinguished values*, can be used to uniquely identify each directory object (see Figure 4.1). This is discussed in the section "Directory Entries" later in this chapter. The entries are organized by the directory hierarchy, as explained in the above section "Directory as a Common Information Repository." Thus, there are no restrictions on the information itself, which provides inherent extensibility for accommodating additional information.

Figure 4.1   The structure of a directory entry.

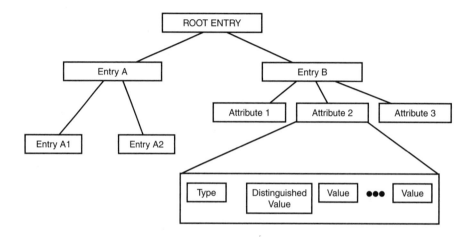

Directories Provide Integrated Information Support

Directories are the standard medium for storing user, application, printer, and other types of network resource information. DEN capitalized on this by defining a way to extend an existing directory schema to also represent network element and service information. The advantage of this is that information about network resources, elements and services are co-located. This enables the different applications that want to use and share this information to access a single repository. This greatly simplifies the design of the overall system.

Directories Facilitate Finding Information

A directory service is more than a naming service, such as DNS. A directory service enables both the searching and the retrieval of named information. The ability of directories to store a wide variety of information, as illustrated in Figure 4.1, makes them a natural choice for finding information.

In addition, directories present a standard interface for creating, modifying, and finding information. This interface is called the *Directory Access Protocol (DAP)* in X.500 systems. The IETF has defined a simplified, and very popular, version of DAP, called the *Lightweight Directory Access Protocol (LDAP)*. LDAP presents an interface consisting of a set of operations that an application can execute that tell the directory service what is desired of it. These operations consist of the following three categories of operations:

- *Query* (search and compare operations)

- *Update* (add, delete, and modify RDN operations)

- *Authentication* (bind, unbind, and abandon operations)

Note

Discussing how DAP and LDAP work, not to mention other lower-level protocols that the directory service uses, is beyond the scope of this book. See the section "Recommended Further Study and References" at the end of this chapter for more detailed information.

Directories Simplify Distributed Information System Design

A distributed system will in general require specialized data stores. Directory standards were built to enable different types of systems that comprise the directory to build independently from the systems that access the directory. This enables a distributed directory to be constructed using different nodes, each of which could be a specialized system that may have different performance and storage characteristics.

Most of the time, the directory is based on a client-server architecture. Depending on the needs of its clients, a set of many servers that are distributed across different physical locations may provide a single logical directory service. This can be done for many reasons, including the desire to increase local availability to its clients and to provide fail-over capabilities. In this case, it is important to remember that there is still one directory service that appears to a client, even though it is distributed among many servers.

What Is Different Between a Directory and Other Repositories?

The directory is not intended to be a general-purpose data store. Rather, it is a special type of information repository whose primary purpose is to efficiently store and retrieve information about objects relevant to an application or a set of applications. This is done via two important means:

- First, the information stored in a directory is done so in a *hierarchical* fashion. That is, the information infrastructure is based around parent-child relationships. This hierarchy is used for naming and scoping. Containment, not inheritance, is the driving factor of a good directory design.

- Second, the information in a directory is *attribute-based*. Refer again to Figure 4.1. This shows the directory as being comprised of a set of objects that are hierarchically related to each other. Each of the objects has a set of attributes that contain the information. Each attribute describes information pertaining to an aspect of the object, defined by the type of the attribute. The entry groups attributes together to completely describe the object. Thus, the information is spread through the attributes of the objects that form the infrastructure of the directory.

This structured way of representing information is particularly applicable to representing the physical and logical structural aspects of network elements and services. This is one of the major reasons why DEN was conceived as an extension of CIM, and why mapping DEN to an implementation based on using the directory is so attractive. This is one of the main points of Chapter 5.

Another difference between a directory and other types of repositories is how data is copied between different servers. Two methods, called *directory replication* and directory *synchronization*, can be used to do this, depending on the characteristics of the copy operation that you want to use. The implementation of replication and synchronization in a directory is very different than their implementation in other types of data stores. This is discussed in the section "Copying and Distributing Data Using Directory Replication and Synchronization" in this chapter.

Characteristics of a Directory

Directories have three salient functional characteristics. First, the storage of information in a directory is optimized so that it can be read much more frequently than it is written. This means that directories are very good at performing high-volume search operations, but not good at performing operations that require frequent writing. An example of the former is using a directory as the backing store for an address book. Here, the directory is being accessed as an intelligent search engine, and must be able to respond quickly to different user queries. However, the user (relatively) seldom changes anything in the address book. An example of the latter includes applications that require a value to change more frequently than the replication frequency of the directory (for example, statistics-based applications). Note also that the directory does not supply *transactional integrity* (for example, the directory cannot guarantee that writes to separate objects be treated atomically). This lack of transactional integrity is of concern to Directory Enabled Networks.

Second, directories provide a *unified namespace* for all resources for which they contain information. This means that common information can be located and shared by the different clients of the directory over a distributed network because each application can use the same method of referencing an object. A unified namespace enables network elements and services to be seamlessly integrated with other types of information, such as users, applications, and servers.

Finally, directories can efficiently distribute information among the various nodes that comprise a directory service through a process known as *directory replication*. This is a critical concept for network management and configuration.

How Directories Store Information

Directories store information about certain sets of objects, and organize the information describing these objects as a *tree*. This tree is sometimes called the *Directory Information Tree*, or *DIT*. To avoid confusion with the X.500 use of the term *DIT*, this will be called the *Directory Tree*, or *DT*. A simple DT is shown in Figure 4.2.

Figure 4.2   A sample Directory Tree.

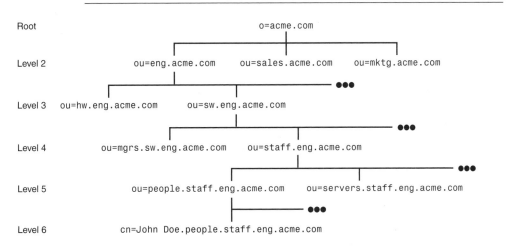

Note

DIT is, strictly speaking, an X.500 term that refers to a set of physically separate directories representing different information that are integrated to form a *global directory tree*. In the X.500 system, each directory server manages a portion of the global DIT. The confusion arises because many organizations refer to their directory tree as a *DIT*, even though it is a stand-alone directory and is *not* integrated into a global directory tree. Refer to the X.500 reference or to the accompanying Web site (www.macmillantech.com/strassner) for further information.

The Structure of Directory Information

Directory objects can theoretically contain any type of information, but most often describe physical or logical aspects of the business functions and/or information infrastructure of the organizations using the directory. This is another reason why application-specific directories have proliferated—there is no single authoritative schema that defines a set of classes and attributes that all directories must have. DEN specifically addressed this point by proposing a standard schema for managing network elements and network services.

Different directories structure the information contained in their DTs in different ways. Each DT organizes its information into a set of *directory objects*, where each directory object corresponds to an entry in the DT. Each entry is uniquely identified by a *Fully Qualified Distinguished Name (FQDN)*, which is usually abbreviated to *DN* for *Distinguished Name*. A DN uniquely identifies a directory entry in the DT. A DN can be viewed as a path from the root of the DT to the directory entry, and so in this respect is similar to how a file path uniquely identifies a file within a file system. However, the path specified by a DN is in reverse order to that of a file system.

The DN for an entry is built by taking the name of its parent entry and appending the Relative Distinguished Name (RDN) specified in the entry. Thus, the DN at any level is the set of RDNs that together specify a path from the root of the DT to the directory entry. This is shown in Figure 4.3.

Figure 4.3   The relationship between directory objects, entries, attributes, DNs, and RDNs.

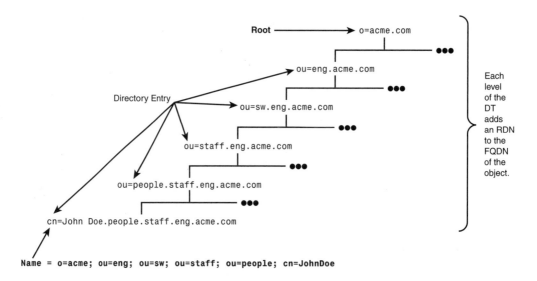

```
Name = o=acme; ou=eng; ou=sw; ou=staff; ou=people; cn=JohnDoe
```

Every object in the directory, called a *directory entry*, is uniquely identified by its DN. An object in the real world can be modeled as one or more directory entries. Each directory entry is an object that has a set of characteristics that describe the information carried by the object. These characteristics take the form of *attributes*. For example, a User object might have attributes that define the first name, last name, common name (full name), employee ID, phone number, and other data associated with that user. Each of these attributes is common to all instances of the User class. Two users, Joe Smith and Lori

Wright, will each have all of these attributes. Thus, any given directory object is comprised of the attributes of each directory entry that are used to form its FQDN. This is similar to class inheritance, but is not quite the same, as we will see in the section "Directories and Object-Oriented Modeling" later in this chapter.

The set of attributes that an entry has is determined by the *object class* of that entry. The object class defines which attributes *must* be included (for example, values must be specified for them) and which attributes *may* be included for a given entry. The complete set of object classes and attributes for a directory is defined as the *schema* of the directory.

Note

Optional attributes in a directory behave differently than NULL values in a relational database. Directories do not have to instantiate optional attributes when the object that an optional attribute belongs to is instantiated. This means that if that attribute is searched for, an error will be returned. In addition, since the attribute is optional, this means that two instances of the same object class may not have the same optional attributes instantiated.

Each attribute has a specific data type that may have restrictions qualifying the values of that data type (for example, a string with alphanumeric characters only). This is called the *syntax* of the attribute. In addition, a predefined set of matching rules are defined for each entry that specify whether this attribute is considered a match for a search or not (for example, given a string, ignore the case of each character in the string and see if this attribute's value equals the value that is being searched for). Attributes may in fact be multivalued, but do not have to be. Finally, all attributes have object identifiers that uniquely define them. These are *ASN.1 identifiers*.

For example, consider the following ASN.1 definition of a telephone number attribute (see Listing 4.1):

Listing 4.1   ASN.1 definition of a telephone number attribute.

```
telephoneNumber ATTRIBUTE::={
    WITH SYNTAX             PrintableString (SIZE( 1..ub-telephone-number))
    EQUALITY MATCHING RULE  telephoneNumberMatch
    SUBSTRINGS MATCHING RULE telephoneNumberSubstringsMatch
    SINGLE VALUE            FALSE
  ID                        id-at-telephoneNumber }
```

ASN.1 lets you define specialized rules based on previously defined rules. For example, the `telephoneNumberMatch` and `telephoneNumberSubstringsMatch` are special cases of the `caseIgnoreMatch` and `caseExactSubstringsMatch` rules, respectively. The difference is that `telephoneNumberMatch` and `telephoneNumberSubstringsMatch` both ignore all space and the "-" characters in the comparison.

ASN.1 and BER

ASN.1, or *Abstract Syntax Notation One*, is a means to define objects abstractly at different implementation layers. For example, a service at a higher layer may require transfer of abstract object definitions, while a lower layer service may transfer information as encoded strings of ones and zeroes. The directory uses ASN.1 (defined in X.208) as a means for defining objects and attributes. (Note that SNMP also uses ASN.1 and BER). ASN.1 is a flexible notation that allows the definition of a variety of data types, from simple types such as integers and strings to complex types such as sets, sequences, and combinations of other types.

A set of encoding rules, called *BER* (*Basic Encoding Rules*, defined in X.209), are used to represent objects as strings of ones and zeroes. BER describes how to represent or encode values of each ASN.1 type as a string of 8-bit octets. There is generally more than one way to BER-encode a given value.

Internet directories communicate using the Lightweight Directory Access Protocol (LDAP). LDAP requires that attribute values be transmitted as octet strings. Attributes are encoded in specific syntaxes as specified in RFC2252. *Syntaxes* define which character sets can be used for a given attribute. Similarly, *matching rules* are used to specify when an attribute value satisfies the result of a search operation. Matching rules can be specified for an entire value or for a substring.

Directories and Object-Oriented Modeling

Chapter 2, "Object-Oriented Modeling," defined six fundamental object-oriented principles: identity, abstraction, classification, encapsulation, inheritance, and polymorphism. It is important to understand how directories make use of these object-oriented principles, since both CIM and DEN are Information Models that use all of them, but directories are non-object-oriented repositories that cannot use all of them. Indeed, this mapping of object-oriented information to a directory is one of the main contributions of DEN.

Directories use the concept of identity and a modified form of abstraction, classification and inheritance. They do not have a concept of encapsulation or polymorphism, since they only contain attributes, not behaviors and relationships.

Identity means that each object can be uniquely distinguished within the system, and that two instances of the same class can be identified even if they have the exact same attribute values. Abstraction and classification play a part in the design of the DT, but are not used in the same pervasive and fundamental ways as they are in Object-Oriented Modeling. Directories do not encapsulate information, and because they do not have methods, they don't make use of polymorphism.

Perhaps the most misunderstood of these is the modified form of inheritance used by directories. Directory classes consist *only* of attributes, and therefore only the attributes of a superclass are inherited. Since directories do not really have a concept of encapsulation, it is more correct to say that the required and optional attributes defined by any directory object class are *grouped* together in the directory object class. However, directories do have an object class inheritance hierarchy that defines which attributes are required and optional for each entry in the DT.

Directories and Object-Oriented Technology

Strictly speaking, there is more difference than similarity between the use of object-oriented principles in theory and how they are implemented in the directory. However, most directory vendors like to describe their products using object-oriented terminology. So, here are the main differences between how object-oriented terms are defined and how they are used in a directory:

- **Classes**. A directory class is a collection of attributes. This is a much looser definition than the object-oriented definition of a class, which is an encapsulation of behavior and related data that are grouped together for some distinguishable common purpose.

- **Inheritance**. Directories use inheritance to include the attributes from parent classes in a child class. Object-oriented theory uses inheritance to refine the functionality of a parent class through its child classes. This means more than simply including attributes from the superclasses of a class—it refers explicitly to treating attributes and behavior as an encapsulated whole. This leads to concepts that don't exist in directories, such as overriding functions in a parent class, along with other more advanced concepts, such as defining new or refining existing relationships between objects.

- **Data Types**. The data type of an attribute in a directory is invariant and limited to one of a set of predetermined types. The data type of a property of an object-oriented class can exhibit a much richer structure, including defining completely new data types.

continues

Furthermore, many of these concepts are used differently. For example, directory operations execute on a directory entry, not on a directory object. This is because a directory object does *not* define what type of operations can be performed on or by the class. The directory object class does *not* encapsulate behavior and functionality; the directory entry is a collection of attributes that represents solely the attributes of a directory object. Finally, note that some directory concepts have no analog in object-oriented theory; a good example is how names are formed to make FQDNs.

Schema Checking

Schema checking is a feature that enforces all required attributes for an object class to be contained in a directory entry. It also ensures that *only* attributes defined by the object class corresponding to a directory entry are actually contained in the entry. This feature is available in most current directories. Its advantage is that it ensures that *only* classes and attributes that have been defined are allowed to be instantiated into a directory entry. This helps ensure the overall consistency of the schema.

Some directories can also check on additional properties and characteristics, but this behavior is vendor-specific. In general, there is no provision in a directory to prevent the user from entering inconsistent data. For example, there is nothing to stop a user from entering a telephone number as 1234567, 408-123-4567, or +1.408.123.4567. This is a problem because, in general, a client may not know how to form a string to search for the phone number. In fact, in this example, if the client used the value (408)123-4567 as the search criterion, the search would most likely fail because the default matching rules would not ignore the parentheses.

Problems with Directory Interoperability

All directories store information hierarchically, but each may use different methods to construct the hierarchy. All directories distribute information using various forms of replication and/or synchronization (these are defined later in this chapter) but, since there is currently no standard for either directory replication or synchronization, interoperability is not automatically guaranteed. All directories use access controls to protect the confidentiality of the data, but there is no common method used to implement access controls. This in turn makes interoperability quite difficult because, in order to share data, different access control mechanisms must be translated or somehow accommodated. Finally, there are no standard naming rules that are applied to a given type of object.

Referrals

Suppose that the directory service of an organization is comprised of many directory nodes. There are two choices for distributing the information:

- Copy all the information to all the nodes

- Ensure that each node contains all its important local data, along with a way to find data that it doesn't contain

If the second way is implemented, how is a client ensured that it can retrieve any data from any directory node?

Referrals are a generalized redirection mechanism. They enable one directory node to respond to a query for information that it does not contain with a URL (actually, a sequence of URLs) that should contain the information. This enables a directory entry, subtree, or an entire tree to be mapped to a URL, effectively enabling information to be linked, or referred, from node to node. Referrals provide the means to scale the directory to include multiple servers without having each server physically contain all entries. It is also a convenient way of partitioning information by enabling disparate information to be stored in separate servers. These servers may have their own administrative and access control mechanisms. Distribution of data among multiple servers also enables performance to be dramatically improved. This is represented in Figure 4.4.

Figure 4.4   Using referrals.

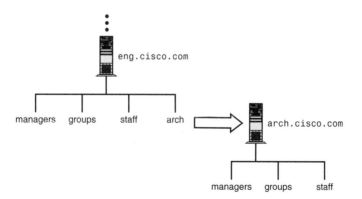

Referring to Figure 4.4, we see that the eng.cisco.com server is programmed to refer any queries it receives that reference arch.eng.cisco.com to the arch.cisco.com server.

Namespaces

Objects are differentiated by their *names*. Each object and its corresponding entry can have one or more names. Note, however, that each name that an object has is itself unique. *Namespaces* represent an essential way of organizing information that is fundamental to CIM and DEN.

Note

Sometimes, entities that need to be modeled in a directory require multiple directory objects to adequately represent them (the converse, however, is *not* a good idea). For example, using X.500 classes, the same person might need to be modeled as both an OrganizationalPerson (to represent his or her working for a specific organization) as well as a ResidentialPerson (to represent that person as a human being that is not affiliated with any specific business entity).

Modeling an entity with multiple directory objects should be used with caution. For example, consider a person that has multiple roles in an organization (for example, Marketing, Business Development, and Engineering). It might be tempting to create three different instances of OrganizationalPerson, one for each role that the person has. However, this is a bad practice because now every time a base attribute for that person is updated, each of these three classes must also be updated. If the organization has a lot of people for whom this applies, this rapidly becomes unmanageable.

Directory names are integrally related to the DT, which represents the overall hierarchy of the directory. Each node in the DT is an entry. Each entry is either a container node or a leaf node. The difference is that container nodes can contain other objects, whereas leaf nodes don't. Each object (whether it is a container or a leaf node) holds information about the object having the corresponding name.

Directories are rooted hierarchies. In other words, the DT has a single object that serves as its root. Though directory structures differ, the first level of objects below the root (for example, the "children" of the root object) are assumed to be used to organize the rest of the DT according to whatever unit best represents how the information is organized in the entity that is using the directory. This can include geographical, physical, political, business, or other ways of classifying and segregating the information.

Sometimes, representing this structure is complicated, especially if many different classification methods are required (for example, physical and business and geographical). In such cases, it might take several higher-level layers to represent this structure. For example, a large business might have the first level below the root correspond to the country that contains the information, the second level correspond to the overall business or organization, and the next levels correspond to divisions within that organization. At this point, one will either find unique objects that belong to that unit, or containers that group together similar types of objects.

Notice that as we move down the naming hierarchy, we build the FQDN of the object (one exception to this principle is that the root does not contribute a naming component). The name at any individual level of the DT is called the Relative Distinguished Name, or RDN. The DN of an entry is the DN of its parent appended with the RDN of that entry.

The RDNs of objects in a given container must be different. However, objects with the same RDN can be present in different containers. For example, you cannot have two Bob objects in the same container, but you could have one Bob object in a Users container and another Bob object in a Devices container that both have the same common parent. This is shown in Figure 4.5.

Figure 4.5   Uniqueness of RDNs.

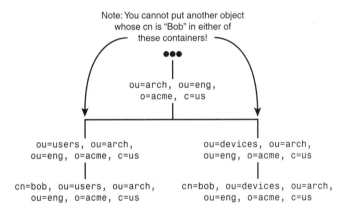

Advantages Provided by Directory Naming

Directory names provide a number of benefits:

- Uniqueness of names is automatically provided because each node must be uniquely named relative to its superior. RDN uniqueness relative to a superior name implies uniqueness for the resulting FQDN.

- Extensibility is provided through the ability to add new subordinate nodes at any level of the tree.

- Distribution and scalability are inherent benefits of the namespace. That is, a single namespace can effectively be divided into subtrees of contiguous entries. This allows multiple servers to share the workload while the overall logical model is retained.

- Management is enhanced by partitioning the namespace into subtrees that can be governed using separate policies for access control and administration.

Aliases

Sometimes, users and applications need more flexible ways to store and retrieve information. Most directories support the concept of an *alias*, which are structured in a similar way but provide an alternative name for the user or application to access the object.

Copying and Distributing Data Using Directory Replication and Synchronization

There are two ways to copy directory data between multiple nodes of a distributed directory. They are called *directory replication* and *directory synchronization*. However, there is a fundamental difference between them.

Note

This is actually a very complicated and technical discussion, so only a brief overview will be provided here. The reader is encouraged to look at two IETF working groups—the LDAPEXT (LDAP EXTensions) Working Group and the LDUP (LDAP Duplication and Update Protocol) Working Group—for more information. LDAPEXT is concerned with many issues designed to enhance LDAP in general, while LDUP is specifically concerned with directory replication. See http://www.ietf.org/html.charters/ldapext-charter.html and http://www.ietf.org/html.charters/ldup-charter.html, respectively.

Replication is used to distribute data, potentially over a number of separate replication cycles, to other servers in the organization. *Synchronization* is used to make the target server's data the same as the host server's data, in one operation. We will concentrate on replication, as that is most germane to the discussion of Directory Enabled Networks. The objective of using the directory in DEN is to distribute data as it is changed to every node that needs to know about the changed data; synchronization is more useful for startup and failover.

Replication is used to place data at different locations that are distributed throughout an organization. This is usually done to provide one or more of the following benefits:

- "Fast" local access for clients at a particular location by eliminating long-distance connections between the client and the directory server

- Shared data to other directory nodes (for example, a division can use its directory node to publish data that it wants to share with other divisions that are connected via other nodes; this way, the original division still maintains access control over its data)

- Corporate-wide high-availability access for critical applications

- Fault tolerance through replicating critical data (even whole DTs) to multiple servers (that way, if a hardware, software or network problem is encountered, there are still alternate sources for the data)

- Higher performance through either local access or by load balancing the data across multiple servers (this serves to reduce the access load on any single server)

A *replication topology* is defined as the collection of directory servers that constitute the "logical" directory service. This topology includes *replication agreements* between different nodes that determine which data are to be replicated (and updated) when, where, and between which servers. Replication policies define how the replication process is executed as well as how update conflicts (in the case of multi-master systems) are resolved.

A *single-master* (also known as *master-slave*) replication model defines a single server (the master) as the *only* server that can add, delete, and update replicated entries. Changes made by the master are carried to the rest of the directory nodes, which are read-only nodes. Conversely, a *multi-master* replication model enables different servers to write the same entry. This can cause a conflict if two servers write different values to the same entry during the same replication cycle (note that this is not necessarily the same *time*; rather, it is a *time period*). Special mechanisms must be put into place to detect and resolve conflicts. This is the subject of the LDUP working group (see `http://www.ietf.org/html.charters/ldup-charter.html`) and is beyond the scope of this book.

The Use of LDAP for Directory Enabled Networks

LDAP is the *de facto* standard way to access directory information in the Internet. LDAP defines a simplified object model for defining information that can be stored in the directory, and provides a corresponding namespace that determines how information is organized, stored and retrieved. Both the protocol and the object model are extensible—new functionality can be added to the protocol through defining extended operations and controls, and new classes and attributes can be added to the base schema of the directory.

Note

Many people describe LDAP as having an "Information Model." In the author's humble opinion, this is incorrect (see the definition of an Information Model in Chapter 2) and actually causes a disservice, in that it promulgates misunderstanding of a key modeling principle.

LDAP is a *protocol* used to access a schema, whereas an Information Model is used to build the information contained in a directory that is accessed by LDAP. Most directories do not use an Information Model; they instead have a collection of rules for defining a schema. This means that directories are incapable of directly representing modeling constructs (like *associations* and *aggregations*) and interrelationships between schema objects, both of which are crucial to an Information Model.

Advantages and Disadvantages of Using LDAP

LDAP is an open standard protocol, which encourages its adoption by multiple vendors. Since it is an open standard, vendors have been encouraged to write gateways that translate data between it and other proprietary protocols OS systems, such as X.500 and WHOIS++. This has led to LDAP becoming the ubiquitous way for accessing information from Internet directories.

Therefore, it is natural for DEN to want to use LDAP to access network element and service information. However, LDAP has a number of disadvantages, including:

- LDAP does not provide the rich semantics of a general-purpose query language. Specifically with respect to network management:

  - LDAP has limited search semantics. It lacks more powerful search methods, such as fuzzy search and SOUNDEX methods, that general-purpose query languages have. LDAP is really intended to search just for simple text.

  - LDAP has no relational support – no triggers or stored procedures, no concept of a "join," no dereferencing (for example, retrieve the objected referenced by the DN at this DN), no ability to index on arbitrary keys, and no conditional operators. This means that forcing an application to use LDAP to process relational queries is inefficient at best.

- LDAP has no transaction support, which means that multiple objects cannot be treated atomically. This is especially troublesome when the configurations of multiple devices must be changed at the same time.

- LDAP has limited data structure support for network management. Two examples are full support for ASN.1 data, and the use of tables (for example, to share SNMP data). Both of these features are lacking in LDAP.

- LDAP has limited operator support. For example, it has no bit-wise operators. This becomes a problem in networking, when it is common to use such operators (for example, in finding subnets or aggregates of a network).

- LDAP cannot evaluate arbitrary expressions. This limits the richness of the query that can be formed.

- LDAP has no "sanity checking" of its queries. This includes the inability to validate incoming and outgoing data as well as to prevent inappropriate queries and updates from being issued.

Additional Considerations for Using LDAP

In addition, it is important to realize that LDAP is "just" an access protocol, and other protocols must be used to perform certain key tasks. For example,

- LDAP is not an authentication protocol, it is a directory access protocol. While LDAP requires secure authentication in order to do secure updates of data, the base protocol (RFC2251) does not support this feature. Furthermore, requiring secure authentication is not the same as being an authentication protocol. Secure authentication is the subject of current work in the LDAPEXT working group. Furthermore, the authentication mechanisms that will likely be approved in LDAPEXT are aimed at simpler, lightweight implementations, not large-scale distributed implementations. Work on large-scale distributed security will likely start in the second half of 1999.

- LDAP is not a boot protocol. This is an important point. First, LDAP is much more complicated than, for example, BOOTP, and therefore inappropriate for devices that need a simple mechanism for booting. Secondly, using LDAP as a boot protocol for network devices would mean that the device must always access the directory in order to boot. Some devices don't even have an IP address when they are powered on, so this is obviously unsatisfactory. Also, this means that a device must be able to connect to the directory. There is no reason to introduce LDAP as a dependency (especially to network devices that are already deployed). Forcing a device to boot by using LDAP uses the directory incorrectly, because there are often dynamic parameters that must be customized during this process (also, what happens if the directory is unreachable?). However, accessing a common configuration and using this to change or add to current configuration settings is a much more appropriate use of the directory by a network device.

Conclusions Regarding the Use of LDAP

So, the key message is: Plan your directory deployment carefully. Don't try to make the directory accomplish everything by itself, and remember that the directory is "just" a data store (for example, realize its limitations). The directory is *not* a substitute for either middleware or even an intelligent repository.

Avoiding Bad Uses of a Directory

As directory usage becomes more frequent, it becomes very important to analyze the application to ensure that the directory is the appropriate type of data store to use. Good and bad uses can be found by analyzing the type of data that is best suited to be stored in (and that should not belong in) a directory. In addition, the characteristics of applications should be examined to ensure that a directory is best suited to store, find and retrieve their information.

Types of Data That Should Be Stored in the Directory

Although you can store almost any type of data in the directory, some types of data are better suited to being stored in a directory than others are. These types of data usually have some subset of the following characteristics:

- The data can be viewed as a collection of attributes that belong to a set of objects. For example, employee data can take the form of a set of User objects, where each User object has a set of attributes that distinguish it from other User objects.

- The data should be read much more often than it is written. For example, an employee ID (an attribute of a User object) is generally assigned once when the employee begins working for the organization, and doesn't change throughout the tenure of the user's employment. A MAC address of a device is generally defined once when the device is built and doesn't change. Conversely, router statistics are probably not well suited for directory storage, due to their high volatility and large size.

Note

Media Access Control, or *MAC*, address is the physical address of a device (technically, it is a standardized data link layer address). This enables the device to communicate with other devices on a network. Note that this is not the same as the network address of a device, which refers to a logical device.

- Directories are very well-suited to managing information about users and other objects whose attributes do not change frequently. This helps avoid having multiple data stores, and takes advantage of LDAP's natural strengths in search and retrieval.

- Directories can be adapted to manage the static portions of applications as well as devices. However, the nature of the data must be carefully examined before one decides that it should be put in the directory. Just because information is about the same object does *not* mean that all of that information should go in the same repository! This is exemplified by the difference between a MAC address, which doesn't change, and certain statistical information (such as flow rate), which change very frequently.

- Along these lines, directories are well suited to serve as a "global" configuration data store for applications and devices. The configuration data to be stored are static, and the replication capabilities of the directory enable the data to be distributed throughout the network so that users and applications can use it independent of their physical location.

- The data can be used by many applications, which might want to access the data from different physical locations. For example, knowing who the supervisor of an employee is can be used by purchasing applications, HR applications, and workflow applications.

Types of Data that Should Not be Stored in the Directory

In general, any data that exhibit one or more of the following characteristics is probably not a good candidate for storing in the directory:

- The data are frequently updated.

- Attribute-value queries are not likely to be sufficient. Instead, other types of queries, such as relational queries, will be required to retrieve information.

- The data are really for one (or, at most, a few) application and are not general in nature. In this case, a special-purpose data store that is dedicated to that application is probably better able to meet the search and retrieval needs of the application than a directory is.

Characteristics of Applications that Use the Directory

Two of the most common applications that directory services used today are White Pages and Yellow Pages searches. They are so named because of their close analogy to how searching through a telephone directory works.

White Pages directory searching uses search criteria that are based on the attributes of a directory object, such as a user name. For example, think of how you use the telephone book to find the telephone number of a person. If you know the name of a person, you can find that person's phone number by searching through the (alphabetized) listing of names in the White Pages until you find the person that you are looking for. If there are several people with the same name, then you can still retrieve the phone number of the correct person if you know additional information that can be used to distinguish between these people, such as the street address or city of the person whose phone number you are looking for. White Pages directory searches work exactly the same way. Given a set of attributes that can uniquely identify an object, you can retrieve additional information (for example, one or more attributes) about that object.

Yellow Pages directory searching instead retrieves information based on search criteria that define a category of information, such as "color printers." Again, think of a telephone book. Assume that you are looking for a transportation service. You pick up the Yellow Pages and search for the category "Transportation" (you don't use the white pages because you want to retrieve multiple listings for transportation services, and you don't know the name of a particular transportation service). Once you find that category, the Yellow Pages presents an alphabetized listing of transportation services, each with the same additional information (address and phone number). Yellow Pages directory searches works the same way. You're not looking for a specific entry; rather, you're looking for any entry that matches your search criteria.

Directories are well-suited to the management of user attributes. White and Yellow Pages searching work very well against the type of data that comprise user entries, as well as other objects that have a large collection of static string attributes. Furthermore, this helps prevent the proliferation of multiple data stores.

DEN had two objectives with respect to searching. The first was to extend traditional White and Yellow Pages searching to (the static portions of) network elements and services. The second was to extend White and Yellow Pages searching to searching over an *integrated* database of network and user information.

For example, consider a *virtual LAN (VLAN)*. A VLAN is a group of devices on a LAN that are configured so that they can communicate as if they were part of the same LAN, when in fact they are located on a number of different LAN segments. The DEN model of a VLAN enables an administrator to look for all devices that were part of a particular VLAN providing a specific network service for a given user. Representing this and other aspects of a VLAN as objects and object attributes can significantly simplify device configuration and network administration.

Directories can be used to manage devices and applications as long as care is taken to manage just the static aspects of devices and applications. Unlike users, devices and applications generally have more dynamic characteristics that also need to be managed. Therefore, caution must be exercised to ensure that directories manage just the static aspects of devices and applications, and not all aspects. An example of using the directory in such a way would be as a global store for configuration data for devices (for example, routers), with dynamic aspects of the device (for example, router flow rate statistics) contained in other data stores that are referenced using the directory. This has the advantage of using the directory as the single authoritative repository to obtain, directly or indirectly, all of the required information about an object that it manages. In other words, all applications can now issue a query to the directory to find where information resides, as opposed to having each application keep that knowledge. This simplifies administration, because when information sources change, only a single update to the directory (as opposed to updating each application) is needed.

Tip

Remember that directories can contain *pointers* to information stores that are better suited to manage the dynamic aspects of devices and applications. (Here, *dynamic* refers to information that can change faster than the replication frequency of the directory. An example of such information is a set of IP address leases.) This leverages the natural capabilities of the directory (such as replication) and makes use of the directory as a unifying information repository.

Finally, directories are intended to facilitate the sharing of information. This means that they are best used when the data that they store can be used by many applications, which might want to access the data from different physical locations. For example, knowing who the supervisor of an employee is can be used by purchasing applications, HR applications, and workflow applications.

Characteristics of Applications that Should Not Use the Directory

The following are examples of how not to use a directory:

- A directory is not a substitute for local storage (for example, a file system or a file server) of generalized data. Rather, it is a specialized database that is used to store, locate and retrieve specific types of information.

- A directory is not an ftp server or a web server. In addition, it is a bad idea to use a directory to store large, unstructured objects that require frequent update. A directory can be used to store pointers to where those types of servers can be found. Note, however, that though the directory supports URLs to do this, LDAP does not provide link tracking. Therefore, if the address of the Web or FTP server moves and receives a new URL, the administrator will have to manually update the corresponding directory entries.

- A directory is not a relational database; however, a directory can be implemented using a relational database. Some of the major differences between a directory and a relational database include:

  - LDAP does not provide transaction semantics (for example, two-phase commit and cascading deletes).

  - A directory is loosely consistent, whereas a relational database is tightly consistent. Loosely consistent means that there are times when the server that is sourcing the data changes has data that the replica servers do not from the client's point of view. This is much more of a problem for multi-master directories, but applies even to single-master directories. The obvious danger is that if the client reads data from an arbitrary server, it might not have the most up-to-date changes (for example, they might not have been replicated yet). This is because, in general, directories take many replication cycles before the data are consistent and resident in all nodes. Compare this to relational databases, where the act of committing a write ensures that the data are immediately consistent.

> **Note**
>
> Note that a directory *could* implement transactional replication. This would require that the directory nodes involved ensure that all changes between the "master" node and the other nodes are written successfully *before* the client is notified. This is somewhat contrary to the design of replication and is usually not implemented.

- A directory does not have relational semantics. For example, there is no concept of a "join," so relational queries will execute much more slowly using LDAP than if a relational database is used.

- A directory does not have triggers and stored procedures. This means that there is no way for the directory to specify, let alone take, one or more actions when data change. This is one of the more important features of a relational database.

- A directory contains information that is designed to be used by multiple applications and hosts. If the data in question are just for one application or host, then it is probably a better idea to store them locally.

Proliferation of Directories

Directories are very good information repositories. This has led to a proliferation of directories within an organization. The temptation is to develop multiple directories, and use different directories to each support a small targeted set of applications. Unfortunately, this creates several problems:

- First, application-specific data stores limit interoperability, because they foster the development of application-specific data formats, representations, and processing rules that can't be shared among different applications.

- Second, application-specific data stores become an obstacle to network growth because they make it harder to extend and share common types of data. Third, integration of these application-specific stores (for the first two reasons and more) requires a costly development effort.

- Finally, limitations in the access method (for example, the lack of a standard access control model) require application-specific APIs to be developed to access and manipulate the data. Note, however, that both the LDAPEXT and the LDUP working groups of the IETF are actively working to address these issues.

Finally, a large portion of the same information is stored repeatedly in these multiple directories. Several problems arise from storing multiple copies of information in multiple formats and places:

- Since the same information is entered into multiple directories, extra work must be expended to ensure that when common information is updated, that information is changed in each of the directories that contains that information. This is a manually intensive process.

- Most information describing an object can be conceptually divided into different sets of data: *common data* that all applications use, and *application-specific data* that pertains to a single application. For example, employee data, like salary and social security number, are really only useful to an HR application and not to an email application. Conversely, the HR application doesn't care about which POP or IMAP server the user is assigned to, but this information is critical to the email application. The large majority of information that comprises many objects (for example, a User object) can be used by multiple applications. Consider what happens if this information is spread across multiple directories, with each directory storing some, but not all, of the common information. There is now no guarantee that when a client connects to a directory, that specific directory will contain all of the common information that the client requires. This *partitioning* of common information is bad, because there is no easy way to combine that information (remember, unlike RDBMSes, there is no concept of a "join" in a directory).

- There is no naming control over the common information. This means that a user Joe Smith could be entered as `jsmith` in one directory and `Joe_Smith` in another. Now, when information associated with Joe Smith changes, it becomes very difficult to ensure that the appropriate attributes are updated in both objects, because they have different names. This problem is exacerbated by the fact that objects such as User and Network Element objects contain many attributes, each of which could be named differently.

The Problem with Directory Proliferation

This problem is often described as one of "*stovepipe*" *applications*—applications that use a data store for their own specific purposes, even though much of the information that is contained in their data store could be used by other applications. Stovepipe applications *isolate* common information from other applications that could use it in their private data stores to suit their own needs. This in turn forces organizations to use multiple directory services. This is exemplified by email systems, which often use proprietary directory services to store the same types of information, such as user names, passwords, and email addresses. These different directories are not usually able to share data between themselves, due to different data formats, naming conventions, protocols, and other factors. This results in the same information having to be managed in multiple directories, which causes an increased cost of ownership due to additional administrative, hardware and software costs.

For example, imagine that a company has two applications—a HR application and an email application—for which it wants to use a directory. It first develops a directory for the HR application. As it builds the directory, it will organize the information according to its application-specific needs. The organization of directory information is not just limited to the hierarchical relationships between the objects comprising the directory; it also effects how objects in the directory are named. For example, it might decide to store the name of the user object as multiple attributes—a first name, an optional middle name, and a last name—as well as have a single attribute that stores the entire name. Suppose that for a given user, John Doe, the name of the object corresponding to John Doe is John_Doe.

Now, imagine that this same company wants to leverage this directory for the email application. The email application might have its own rules defining how objects should be named that are different from the HR application. For example, it might form a name by taking some letters from the first and last names of the user and concatenating them. For the John Doe user, the email application might want to name it jdoe. This name conflicts with the naming structure previously defined by the HR application.

Therefore, the solution is that many companies have *multiple* directories, each fine-tuned to serve the needs of different applications. The problem is that both the John_Doe and the jdoe objects represent substantially the same information, and both must be updated every time changes need to be made to the object representing John Doe.

Global Directories

The problem of trying to support multiple directories that weren't completely interoperable gave rise to the desire for a *global directory service*. The idea behind the global directory is to provide a single, logically centralized repository that any application can access.

The X.500 ISO standard was intended to be a global directory service. While it has several features that make it very suited for this task, it also has a number of disadvantages, including its dependency on a communications layer that is not the Internet standard TCP/IP protocol and its difficulty in implementation and administration. LDAP was invented to simplify the implementation of a directory service as described by the Directory Access Protocol of X.500. The goal in the design of LDAP was to preserve the best qualities of X.500 while reducing its administrative costs and overall implementation complexity (hence the "L" for Lightweight).

Most current directory developments (LDAP or otherwise) are advertised as global direc-tory services. This means that a directory provides a single logical service that implements a consistent view of the namespace no matter how or where it is accessed. Note that the directory itself could be physically distributed (for geographic locality of the information, or to enhance reliability and availability, or for a number of other reasons). Even if there are multiple servers, the directory as a whole provides a single logical directory service.

Given the rigidity of naming, it is theoretically possible to combine independent directories under a single global namespace. While this is a laudable goal, there are some very big hur-dles than stand in the way of realizing a global directory. For example, this includes requir-ing each of the merged directories to have a compatible implementation. This in turn means that each directory would have a common information structure to represent the data, a common protocol with common operations to access the data, and a common set of access mechanisms to ensure that data confidentiality and integrity is not violated.

Note

This is, in the author's opinion, a very large task, and one that will require quite a bit of work. However, it is a very important task, and the benefits of realizing such a global namespace are many. This is where the value of standards comes in. Without standard pro-tocols and schemata, this goal is, frankly, unattainable.

Issues in Using a Directory for Networking

Networking involves a widely diverse set of applications and data. The most important point is to realize that a directory will *not* be able to serve all of the needs of different data stores that network applications currently use. However, the directory will be able to sig-nificantly improve and, in some cases, either simplify or provide added functionality, to many networking applications.

The problems in using a directory for a networking application lie in the basic limitations of a directory and in trying to directly substitute a directory for the existing data store(s) of a networking application. The former is independent of the specific type of application, and has been covered already in the sections describing examples of data not to store in the directory and example characteristics of applications that are not well-suited to use (only) a directory. We'll now discuss limitations of the directory that specifically effect networking.

Limitations of a Directory for Networking Applications

There are five main limitations of directories that adversely effect its use in networking applications. These five limitations can be overcome by augmenting the directory with additional information, as opposed to trying to embed this functionality in the directory service itself. These five limitations are listed below and discussed in the five following sections:

- There is *no standard Information Model* in use for existing directory objects, much less network objects.

- Information stored in a directory is bound to a single name representation and organization; there is *no common schema* for naming and describing network elements and services.

- Directory services are unable to differentiate between different network resources (for example, *lack of standard metadata*).

- Directory services are *not usually* used to *model* objects, they are used to *represent* them.

- Directories *cannot represent behavior* associated with objects that it contains.

The following sections will address each of these problems and offer a workaround.

Lack of an Information Model

Existing objects that are represented in directories are simple and have attribute values that stay relatively constant. Specifically, *simple* means that the object is rarely subject to change over its lifetime (for example, its attributes stay the same for the most part) and that it always serves the same purpose.

Unfortunately, this is not true of network elements. Values are subject to change in response to the dynamics of the network, and sometimes the roles of network elements are changed (for example, when the network topology is changed, or when new networking boards are added to an existing network element). Network elements require a rich modeling infrastructure, and hence a robust Information Model, for use by network applications. In addition, the Information Model must contain classes that enable the application to transition between different knowledge domains in the Information Model. That is, an application using the directory must be able to easily map between the physical containment domain (for example, what card is in what slot of what router) and logical containment (for example, which administrator is able to log on to the device and change its access control lists).

DEN has defined four such domains (physical and logical containment and connectivity), along with classes that can be used to map between them. For example, the wiring closet that a device is located in and the administrator that has the ability to login to the device and change its settings are examples of physical and logical containment, respectively. The key, then, is to be able to map these (purely) object-oriented constructs into a representation that the directory can accommodate.

Lack of a Consistent, Standard Schema

Subtle differences between the same information stored in different directory implementations will make it difficult for directory services to communicate with each other. Unless there is a single, definitive schema for representing the names of different objects in the directory (which requires a consistent naming methodology for each object class), objects which carry the same information may not be easily recognizable. Furthermore, there was (before DEN) no attempt to build a common schema (much less an Information Model!) to represent and model network elements and services.

This is why the DEN specification is so important; its purpose is to provide a single Information Model and schema in which network information can be shared. The DEN schema and Information Model are being standardized in the DMTF and also in the IETF. The DMTF is concerned mainly about how DEN will improve manageability, whereas the IETF is concerned with refining the (necessarily general) concepts of DEN and applying them to specific areas, such as policy and QoS.

Lack of Metadata Needed to Describe Objects and Their Roles

Traditional directory services are unable to differentiate between network resources such as a network printer, fax, or user. Existing schemes rely on esoteric, cumbersome naming methodologies to distinguish between these resources, and are not well suited to the needs of network elements and services. Furthermore, attributes for a given network resource differ between each application, so there is no guarantee that the desired information can be obtained, even if the network resource is located. Finally, some objects can play many roles. While this can be easily represented in an Information Model using appropriate relationships, it is much harder to represent in a directory.

Specifically, what are needed are methods to map the relationships in the Information Model to constructs that the directory supports. The DEN specification addressed this by including important metadata (for example, data about the information contained in an object) in the object classes that model and manage network elements and services. DEN (as well as CIM) also used a consistent naming methodology so that attributes of different objects that served a similar purpose were named similarly. Finally, DEN introduced the notion of *roles*, and this was carried on in the work of the Policy Framework Working Group (PFWG) of the IETF.

Lack of the Ability to Model Objects in the Directory

The fourth point focuses on the need to model network elements and services. Current directories lack the rich structure needed to model network resources, particularly network elements and services, along with other objects whose attributes and/or behavior change with time. The problem is that traditionally, most objects that are represented in the directory (such as users, computers, and printers) do not change their *ontological* purpose. For example, a User object may be moved between different branches of the DT because that person was transferred to a different division. However, the purpose and function that is represented by the user object stays the same. In fact, most of the attributes of the user object remain the same, with only a few essential ones changing.

This is not necessarily true of networking devices. For example, the networking boards inside a router can be changed, causing the router to run different protocols over different network media. Furthermore, this may change the *purpose* that the router has in the network from, for example, a core router (whose main function is to forward packets as fast as possible) to an access router (whose main role is to classify and filter packets).

To model this new purpose, entirely new classes and attributes need to be dynamically associated with the device. This is what is meant by the difference between *representing* the characteristics of an object and *modeling* the object. Existing directories are unable to cope with such changes.

In addition, very few directories are capable of representing objects that are inherently complex or hierarchical. This problem is further compounded because existing access protocols, such as LDAP, are not capable of processing such information. Networking devices require different knowledge domains, represented by different classes, to be combined and linked together to model the overall function of the device. DEN defines four fundamental knowledge domains (physical and logical containment and connectivity) to represent this information. DEN further describes ways in the model to link information from one domain to information in another domain under a single primary class.

Lack of the Ability to Model the Interaction Between Objects

Finally, traditional directories are used as "dumb" or "static" warehouses to store information. However, as network traffic grows, current and future applications will require more intelligent interaction between directory information and the network environment. This interaction could be a result of a specific business process that is being executed or caused by the specific state of the environment.

For example, the specific types of network resources that are available for a particular user for a given length of time might change, given the current network load and the other types of users who are currently logged on. On the other hand, it might be time to ensure that mission-critical traffic, such as quarter-ending financial data, gets high priority use of the network. Such situations must be actively planned for and anticipated, or else their needs will not be able to be met.

The Solution: Augment the Directory Service, Don't Change It

The solution is not to change the fundamental nature of the directory, but rather to address these limitations by using additional tools, mechanisms and software to work in concert with the directory. For example, many of these limitations can be addressed through the use of an appropriate Information Model to direct the design the schema that is stored in the directory. This doesn't mean that the directory has to solve all these problems itself; rather, it means that the directory should contain the tools (for example, classes and attributes) which other software can use to solve these problems. As an example, relationships (for example, associations and aggregations) are not expressible directly in directory schemata. However, relationships can be mapped into constructs that directories do support (such as properties and containment). The point is that the directory *itself* doesn't change, the *use* of the directory and its features changes.

The Directory as a Unifying Information Repository

The previous sections have described problems caused by the proliferation of application-specific directories as well as functionality that is lacking in the directory. Both of these have caused directories to become what is termed "islands of information," as described in the section "Modeling Network Elements and Services" in Chapter 1.

One of the driving ideas behind the idea of a unifying information repository is to address this problem. The idea behind building a global directory was to force all directories to interoperate. The idea between using a directory as a unifying information repository is to consolidate the disparate information repositories that currently exist into a single authoritative one. The directory is the ideal mechanism to do this, since it can either contain the data directly or point to other specialized data sources that do contain the data.

This is especially true of networking applications, since by their very nature such applications need diverse data from different data stores. Again, middleware and other services that can pre- and/or post-process information gathered from the directory can help integrate these diverse data stores.

Why Does Networking Want to Use a Directory?

LDAP is well suited to manage certain aspects of applications and network devices. Directories are a perfect mechanism for providing a logically centralized and physically distributed data store for configuration data and other types of static management information. This takes advantage of the partitioning and security features of the directory inherent in its namespaces as well as replication to provide scalability and reliability. This can be used to advertise and locate various network services, such as DHCP and IPSEC, as well as define how services are used (for example, IP Telephony) and who can use them (for example, RSVP and QoS).

DEN is the first step towards using the directory in this way. DEN extends the use of a directory from primarily a means to manage users, computers and printers to a general information repository that can also manage network elements and services. As such, it represents a completely new paradigm for leveraging the network. Current network management applications are built using applications and protocols that are designed to manage *individual* devices. DEN is a way to manage the network, as opposed to individual systems *in* the network.

Summary

This chapter has defined a directory service, shown why it is of use for networking, and what its inherent limitations are.

The fundamental purpose of a directory is to store, identify and retrieve various types of resources and information about them in a computing environment. It has been emphasized that the directory is *not* a general-purpose data store, but rather a special-purpose information repository. Characteristics of a directory service were examined, and a comparison with object-oriented theory was provided. This comparison is important to keep in mind, because one of the fundamental features of DEN is that it is a new way of designing directories and modeling network devices. Consequently, care must be taken to blend directory and (pure) Object-Oriented Modeling together.

Low-level functionality, such as naming, referrals, and replication, were introduced. The final section of this chapter contains references to more detailed information on these and other subjects related to directories.

Networking is a very rich collection of applications, with diverse functionality. Sometimes, examples are the best way of explaining new concepts. This chapter included sections that are intended to serve as general guidelines to define types of data that are amenable and not amenable to being stored in a directory, as well as good and bad examples of applications that use the directory.

Along these lines, this chapter introduced a problem: proliferation of application-specific directories. A solution of using directories as unified information repositories was recommended over the more drastic global directory solution that has been proposed. It should be noted that DEN is compatible with either solution.

Finally, networking devices have many interrelated facets, which are classified as knowledge domains, that are not present in the existing objects that are represented in directories. DEN specifically develops the concepts of four knowledge domains—physical and logical containment and connectivity—which play a crucial role in modeling a network device. The difference can be summed up as follows: unlike other objects, network elements require *modeling* in order to capture the richness of their functionality. Modeling is more than just producing a consistent schema; modeling involves understanding what data need to be modeled when and why, and how environment changes are reflected in the underlying model. It also places demands on the environment that is using the directory.

Recommended Further Study and References

Probably the best source of information on directories is in the two IETF working groups called LDAPEXT and LDUP. They can be found at the following URLs, which provide a detailed charter as well as a list of RFCs and Internet drafts:

This is the LDAPEXT home page:

`http://www.ietf.org/html.charters/ldapext-charter.html`

This is the LDUP home page:

`http://www.ietf.org/html.charters/ldup-charter.html`

This is the X-recommendations home page for the ITU:

`http://ecs.itu.ch/itudoc/itu-t/rec/x/bookshop.html`

Other pertinent references include the following, an excellent overview of LDAPv2 and how to use the LDAP APIs:

Howes, T. and M. Smith. *LDAP: Programming Directory-Enabled Applications with Lightweight Directory Access Protocol.* Indianapolis, IN: Macmillan Technical Publishing, 1997.

The following book is a thorough reference to directories in general and X.500 in particular:

Chadwick, D. *Understanding X.500: The Directory.* 1997.

5

Motivation for DEN

The purpose of this chapter is to describe the motivation for DEN. DEN represents a fundamentally different way of designing applications, one based on leveraging the power of a common model for representing information in a common repository. This is the basis of a new paradigm for designing Intelligent Networks and applications that take advantage of intelligence in those networks.

We Found the Schema, but Where Is the Network?

Object-Oriented Modeling has not been used much in network design. Instead, pre-DEN systems designed schemas to represent application-specific functions and used other means to represent the network. The fundamental problem with this approach is that there is no common means for representing clients of the network and the network itself, and so the binding of network clients to services that the network provides is prevented.

This was because network elements and services were not represented as objects in pre-DEN data stores. In fact, network elements and services were typically represented as specialized objects in proprietary stores, using proprietary formats, which prevented the sharing of such information. Examples range from using private (for example, vendor-specific) MIBs to represent data and capabilities of vendor devices, to different network management programs that stored data in proprietary formats using, for example, relational databases.

Note

One interesting example of the latter is CiscoWorks. It started out by storing device models and capabilities in a relational database using a proprietary format. CiscoWorks has evolved to using a directory and DEN and XML to exchange MOF data with other management applications.

DEN was designed partly because the market demanded a way to tie network services to users and applications in a standard way, and partly because application developers needed a way to share and exchange information about network elements and services from different vendors in a standard way.

Schemas Versus Information Models

CIM is perhaps the only well-known approach for describing a managed system using an object-oriented Information Model. Most pre-DEN systems simply defined schemata that were hard-wired to represent specific objects in a certain way. CIM and DEN advocate a fundamentally different approach, one in which an Information Model is used to describe the characteristics (data, methods, and events) of the objects in a system as well as the relationships between those objects.

The reason that this approach is so important is because schemata are generated from an Information Model. This enables multiple systems that employ different repositories (for example, a directory accessed using LDAP and a relational database accessed using SQL) to be derived from the same Information Model. Both repositories can be optimized for their specific needs while retaining the ability to exchange information with each other.

Why CIM Was Not Sufficient

CIM is a great Information Model. But it had two weaknesses that DEN, as a CIM Extension Model, corrected.

- First, CIM had not really considered directories at all. Consequently, CIM had no concept of the particular needs and limitations of directories. The DEN effort provided a new focus for CIM on how to map CIM information to a directory.

- Second, CIM did not represent network elements and services. An early version of a network model made good progress in representing basic connectivity issues but never tied these to network elements. Furthermore, network services and protocols were not represented. DEN addressed both of these.

Why It Made Sense to Move DEN into the DMTF

DEN can be viewed as the merging of protocol and network element and service information, along with a mapping to directories, with CIM. DEN, being an information model, evolved naturally into an extension model of CIM. This merging of information from CIM with information from DEN (and vice versa), helped make the DEN and CIM models more robust.

The real value of DEN is in its implementation as a standard. The DMTF already had working groups that consisted of modeling experts and a network's working group that was just getting started. This is why it was so important to move DEN to an official standards organization, without creating a new standards body to compete with the DMTF network modeling effort. Refer to Chapter 1, "The DEN Value Proposition," for more information on the DMTF.

The Dawn of Intelligent Networking

The network is maturing from a passive transport to an active infrastructure that can provide intelligent services. Previously, network vendors concentrated on building boxes whose main features were to switch or route as fast as possible and provide a lot of mechanisms to adjust various features such as queuing. But there has been a general shift from perceiving the network as a dumb pipe to a smart set of services. In fact, many people now define a network by the services that it provides, rather than any single metric such as bandwidth. This in turn means that network devices will be characterized not by the protocols that they support or how fast decisions can be made, but rather by the services that they offer and how easily they can be configured and managed.

This doesn't mean that existing network elements are not intelligent. Rather, the focus of building networks is changing from building boxes that transport data faster than before to building *systems* that intelligently handle data and adapt to the changing environment. Part of this new approach is an increased emphasis on manageability of the device. This represents a fundamental shift in the design of network elements as well as in their supporting components (for example, a policy server). This combination in turn enables applications to be designed that can leverage the power that the network provides.

It is important to realize that DEN is only one of several technology pieces; others include QoS and policy management standards that must be finished and integrated before Intelligent Networks are possible. However, DEN is a critical piece in this design, as it defines how to use a common repository to represent network devices and services in a common way. This enables the configuration of all applications and devices to be synchronized.

The Role of Directory Services

The rise of the Intelligent Network has caused a fundamental shift in the role of the directory, transforming it from a static repository for storing a limited set of application-specific information to a unifying information repository (see "The Directory as a Unifying Information Repository" in Chapter 4, "What Is a Directory?"). In this new role, the directory is used to store common information that all applications and network resources need. This enables components such as policy servers to understand what services users and applications are entitled to, what the current capabilities of the network are, and what must be done in order to grant network services to clients of the network.

Directories form the core component of a policy architecture, helping to control the interaction between clients of the network and the services that the network provides. A simplified architecture of a policy-controlled network is shown in Figure 5.1. This figure illustrates that the directory is involved in some degree in all aspects of policy-based networking.

- The *Management Tool* will retrieve policies for the system according to the privileges of the user accessing the system from the directories. It can also retrieve canonical definitions of policies (for example, what are the allowable conditions and actions of a policy) from the directory, since these are time-invariant.

- The *Policy Decision Point (PDP)* uses the directory to retrieve policies and policy definitional information (for example, the values to use to properly configure a queuing policy, such as Random Early Detection). It can also read other information about users, applications, service contracts, and even network capabilities from the directory and use this information to make decisions as well as to optionally write those decisions back to the directory.

- The *Policy Enforcement Point (PEP)*, which could be any number of different devices (for example, a network device such as a router or switch, a firewall, a server, or a host system), can use the directory in two different ways. First, it can pull common configuration information from the directory, so that common devices all have the same configuration to handle the same type of traffic, operate in the same role, provide the same service, and so on. Second, it can also read information about network devices and clients of the network and optionally write information back to the directory. Here, the decisions that are made are of a more granular level than the decisions made at the PDP. For example, the PEP might need to download specific information for traffic classification, whereas the PDP is more concerned with conformance of traffic to different classes of service that are provided by the network.

DEN defined the initial version of the policy information model that is now being standardized in the DMTF and the IETF.

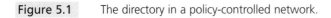

Figure 5.1   The directory in a policy-controlled network.

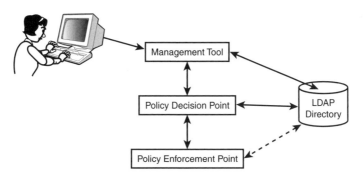

Migrating to an Intelligent Network

Networks have operated on a best-effort model. Recently, network element vendors have started including additional functions, in the form of advanced traffic conditioning mechanisms, to enable smarter networks to be built. Here, "smarter" means the ability to take advantage of advanced network traffic conditioning functions to provide different classes of service for network traffic. Examples of these include smart queuing (for example, priority, custom, and weighted fair queuing), congestion avoidance (for example, various forms of random early detection), and other mechanisms.

Up to now, smarter networks have provided additional services by focusing on using network devices that have more features. Unfortunately, when features are added to an already complex product, the configuration and management of that product increases significantly.

More importantly, adding features to individual devices misses the point. This strategy concentrates on building more powerful individual devices. The ability to interconnect simple devices so the network as a whole can provide an integrated set of services has been missing from network design. DEN is the first step in creating such an Intelligent Network, whose purpose is not just to forward traffic but to offer a set of dynamic, interoperable services that can be delivered on a per-user, per-application basis. DEN complements other efforts in the IETF, such as those in the RSVP Admission Policy (RAP), Differentiated Services, Integrated Services, and Policy Framework working groups.

These services are seamlessly layered together, as shown in Figure 5.2.

Note

Figure 5.2 is not meant to convey a specific architecture, nor is it meant to list every service that an Intelligent Network provides. Rather, it is aimed at conveying the conceptual layering of services by the Intelligent Network.

Figure 5.2   The layered services of the Intelligent Network.

Policy-Based Management				
Network Application Services				
File & Print Services	Messaging Services	Web Services	Object Services	Billing Services
Directory Services		Security Services		Management Services
Logical Network Infrastructure				
Multicast Services		Address Management and Resolution Services		
CoS/QoS Service Mechanisms		Routing Services		Switching Services
Physical Network Infrastructure				

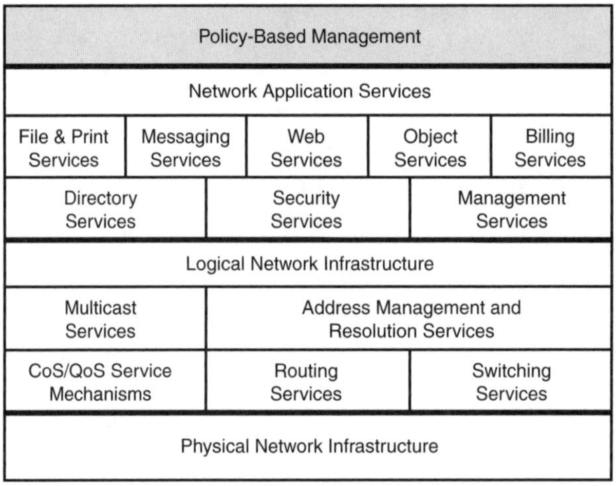

This figure makes two major points. First, the client's view of the capabilities of the network is now very different. In the past, each client viewed the network as containing the same elements. The Intelligent Network instead offers access to different services through a set of layered APIs. This serves to provide services targeted to different clients with different needs. Second, the functions of the Intelligent Network integrate mechanisms that previously were not associated with the network at all. This enables network vendors to better integrate these functions with the network and developers to leverage the result.

In addition, there are several subtle changes in how a network is defined and interacted with, compared to current networks, that this figure illustrates:

- The client can now configure and communicate with the network, using policy as an abstraction (for example, once "Gold Service" is defined, a device can be configured to support it and a user can be assigned to use it).

- Policy-based management of services involves more than just providing a specific QoS. It is the coordination of different services to meet a specified goal.

- There is a tight integration between each layer. Common services, such as security and naming, are applied to lower-level functions and capabilities (for example, QoS mechanisms) to furnish a complete solution.

Driving Factors of the Intelligent Network

There are several factors that are demanding the need for Intelligent Networks. This section will list five of the most compelling factors.

Internet and Related Technologies

The first, and most obvious motivating factor for the Intelligent Network, is the continuing commercialization, and hence reliance, on the Internet and related technologies. The Internet is emerging as the *de facto* communications infrastructure for organizations of all types. It takes many forms—Internet, intranet, and extranet—but the base technologies and motivation are all very closely related.

The increased usage of the Internet, along with its simplified and compelling interaction model and services, has profoundly changed corporate computing. IS and IT professionals want to use the established benefits of client-server and n-tier computing to implement their businesses. However, users want to take advantage of the simpler interaction and user interface of browsers. This has put pressure on corporate intranets to evolve to a more friendly system in which the simplicity and intuitiveness of the Internet is applied to the power and functionality of corporate applications. This has produced *extranets*, which are specialized networks of companies that have business partnerships with each other and are able to access each other's data and applications using browsers and other Internet tools and technologies.

However, there are two underlying problems inherent in the use of the Internet that the Intelligent Network can help solve.

- The Internet was built using a "best effort" model. That is, there was no planned differentiation of traffic based on who the user was or what application was running.

- The Internet was built as a fundamentally public entity. Intranets and extranets are fundamentally private entities, requiring robust security features in order to ensure that private data remains private.

The Intelligent Network can help solve these problems. The integration of naming and security services with other, lower-level mechanisms (for example, queuing), provides a single secure service that can be accessed by clients of the network.

Flat Rate Charging of Differentiated Services

A second important factor that will drive increased usage of the Internet is through enabling a business model wherein service providers can charge for differentiated services. Simply put, constraining the service provider to charging a flat rate of $19.95 for all desired services is economically unfeasible. This doesn't even pay for the building of additional infrastructure, so that the network may grow to accommodate the additional users who will want to take advantage of this service. However, in order to be able to charge for services on some basis (whether by user, by location, by quality, or whatever), the service provider needs to be able to identify, measure, and account for those services. The framework for doing this is provided by the Intelligent Network.

Accounting and Auditing

A third factor is accounting, both in the security sense (for example, know what user and application has access what service when, where, and how) as well as in the billing sense (provide billing records for user activities). Closely related to both of these is the concept of auditing (that is, actively or passively examining what a user is doing and comparing this to a set of permitted actions that the user can do). This is driven mostly by enterprise needs. Certain applications need to know who is accessing what resource at any given time, as well as who tried to access a resource that they did not have the permission for. The Intelligent Network integrates these capabilities into a common infrastructure.

Corporate Communication

A fourth factor is the customer (enterprise and the service provider) need to use new applications and tools for intra- and inter-company communication. Many people concentrate on the growing attention paid to multimedia applications, but this is simply one example of many different types of collaborative applications coming into widespread use. Other examples include video-conferencing and shared white boards. These applications require an infrastructure that can provide different granularities of services for different types of traffic, even if the different traffic is from the same application. For example, Microsoft's conferencing product, NetMeeting, generates network traffic that is composed of data, audio and video traffic that require different levels of QoS.

Location Independence

A final factor is location independence. Users want a consistent set of services to be available, independent of their physical location, or how they are connected at a given moment. This is evidenced by the growing number of remote and mobile users who interact with each other and with their colleagues who are connected to a local LAN (as well as the growing popularity of extranets).

This dissolution of the LAN-WAN barrier is best implemented through the use of an Intelligent Network, because of its ability to recognize the client of the network as well as to implement the unavoidable exceptions to this rule. For example, while a company may try to provide the same access privileges to the same set of information to a remote employee, certain data (for example, source code) may not be allowed to flow across public networks. Again, the Intelligent Network can prevent this through appropriate policy-based restrictions.

Embedding Intelligence in the Network

Historically, the network treated each user and application the same. In fact, the Internet was built on the premise that "best effort" was good enough. However, as discussed in the previous section, this is no longer sufficient. The Intelligent Network is instead defined by the set of services that constitute it. In this model, network clients request services of the network.

This is exacerbated by the recent movements towards converged networks (data, voice, and video running in the same network). Converged networks are a good reason why intelligence needs to also reside in the network. For example, it is not enough to embed extra intelligence in hosts that are using the network and have the hosts tell the network what to do. This relegates the network to serve as a "dumb transport" that simply ships bits between different systems.

To see why this is not sufficient, consider two service providers exchanging data on behalf of a host. This is shown in Figure 5.3. First, let's assume that the host is not malicious, and that the network administrator has configured this host to always send high priority traffic. Therefore, as far as the host is concerned, the traffic that it is sending is the most important thing in the universe (or at least the subnet), and so it marks the traffic with a DSCP (Differentiated Services Code Point) of 111000 to signal this. Let's assume that this is the highest classification of traffic. Now, if the network did nothing and simply transported the traffic, this traffic now has the highest classification, and other traffic will slow down (for example, through random dropping in TCP) to ensure that this traffic gets the highest priority. But what if the router in the figure connects other subnets, and one of them is the year-end financial traffic? The company's business needs will probably want that traffic to have priority over the traffic being sent in the host, but the host's traffic to have priority over other traffic in the host's subnet.

The problem is further exacerbated because the two service providers in the picture may have their own set of DSCP markings to indicate traffic priority. That is, Service Provider 1 (SP1) may think that inbound packets that are highest in priority should be mapped to a DSCP of 001010 (AF11, see RFC2475) is highest priority while Service Provider 2 (SP2) may use a DSCP of 010010(AF12). In this case, if the DSCP is not remarked at each of these points, then the wrong behavior will be applied to the traffic, even though the host marked it correctly.

So the problem is that in order to meet these business needs, we need distributed intelligence. It is insufficient for the host alone or the network alone to provide the intelligence. Rather, both need to cooperate.

Figure 5.3   Why intelligence is needed in the network.

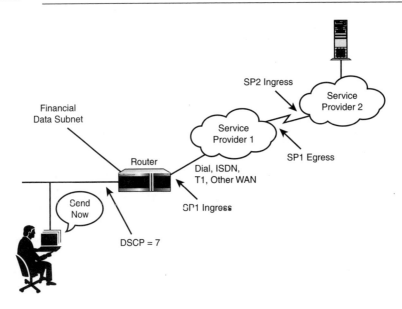

The Intelligent Network does more than hide the lower-level infrastructural services (as depicted conceptually in Figure 5.2) from its client; it encourages their integration. In this way, the Intelligent Network model is fundamentally different than a network operating system model. The latter assumes that all infrastructural services are provided in a single product or product suite. The Intelligent Network instead assumes that the products and technologies of different vendors can interoperate to provide a set of services that are independent of platform, operating system, and application.

Network Application Services

Referring again to Figure 5.2, the five top services (File and Print, Messaging, Web, Object, and Billing) are today implemented in necessarily constrained ways. For example, most file and print services are not distributed—they are bound to specific machines. This means that access to a file is location-dependent and hard to browse. Furthermore, if the file moves, there is no easy way to tell clients who are interested in the file that it has moved. Copying files to multiple locations simply exacerbates the problem of managing and maintaining coordinated access to and update of each of the several copies of the same file so that each copy is the same.

There is also little intelligence in such services. For example, if I take my computer into a new company, I can't print without knowing the name of a printer, what type of print driver it has, and other factors. Compounding this problem is the lack of knowledge of where the printer physically resides. Printers are rarely named "High-Speed HP Color Laser Printer next to Cube G5-07 on the Second Floor of Bldg 2," but are instead given shorter, less descriptive names. This is, of course, assuming that you successfully found the print server that manages the high-speed color laser printer, because the print server is probably named according to a completely different naming scheme, and it probably manages printers in multiple buildings. Finally, even if I do know that a certain printer is a color printer, what happens if it goes out of service? I now have to browse the network, looking for another color printer, and the whole vicious process starts over again.

Great strides are being made in the development of the three lower services (Directory, Security, and Management). However, they are still not as tightly integrated as they should be, and this is one of the major problems that is holding back the implementation of the Intelligent Network.

As stated in Chapter 4, directories provide a common and extensible way of naming entities. This allows such entities to be described, discovered, accessed, managed, and protected. But without robust security services to authenticate and authorize clients of the directory, directory services become compromised. Without a common means to store security keys and certificates, distributed security cannot be achieved. Finally, without a simple and compelling infrastructure to manage such services, they cannot be easily configured (which leads to synchronization problems) and will simply not be used to their fullest extent.

CIM and DEN represent the first step in solving this problem. They enable network devices, along with printers and other objects, to be described in a much more detailed and *standardized* fashion. By placing this information in a common repository, all applications can access it.

Logical Network Infrastructural Services

Currently, it is very hard to configure advanced services, such as QoS. This is because such services are implemented in a vendor-specific way and are tied to the particular physical infrastructure that is being managed. This set of services includes Layers 2 and 3 and covers, in addition to routing and switching, address management and resolution, multicast addressing, and other services. One of the primary goals of DEN was to simplify this by providing a standard way to model network elements and services. This then enables a standardized policy system, such as the one being developed in the Policy Framework working group of the IETF, to be built to control the management of users, network resources and services, and the interaction between these objects.

For example, the Dynamic Host Configuration Protocol (DHCP) is commonly used to assign important network information, such as the IP address, of host machines. The Domain Name System (DNS) provides name resolution for a TCP/IP network by mapping host names to IP addresses. Both DNS and DHCP can be used as part of the solution to help identify users and network resources. However, when one of these two components (for example, DNS and DHCP) are updated, the other component doesn't necessarily know about the update. For example, a user may get a new IP address lease, but the system may not know it. Some vendors are starting to use the directory as a unifying address management repository for both DNS and DHCP. This enables the association between the name of a user, the name of the machine that the user is logged into, and the IP address of the machine to be automatically maintained. Thus, if anything is changed, the other parts of the system will know. This tight integration between different layers of the Intelligent Network will help diminish the need for specialized address management and resolution protocols and ensure that networks can be more easily managed.

A New Management Paradigm

CIM and DEN enable managed objects, such as users, routers, and printers, to be administered based on their logical roles, defining characteristics, and relationships with other entities in the managed system. This is much more expressive and powerful than having to use, for example, a MAC address. Services are inherently logical abstractions, and tying them to a fixed attribute such as a MAC address or an IP address is no longer desirable or even feasible in certain circumstances. MAC addresses represent a part of an object, not a user or application, and don't contain the relevant relationships to such information. IP addresses are dynamic and can change. So tying an IP address back to a user is sometimes impossible.

Instead, the Intelligent Network binds services directly to clients of those services and to the entities that manage and produce those services. This assumes that when the user logs onto the network, there is a means to intercept the logon request and authenticate the user. At that point, IP addresses and other information may be bound to the user for the duration of the session. The intelligence lies in the ability to do this unobtrusively and securely. This abstraction removes the dependence on location and enables clients of the network to receive services based on a profile and/or a policy.

The Need for Policy-Based Management

The increased intelligence of the network comes with a price. More intelligence means more options in the network element to adjust. This complicates the configuration of the device and makes it harder to synchronize the configuration of different devices. This is especially true if there are different types of devices, each of which have slightly different mechanisms to provide the same service. For example, one device may use weighted fair queuing with eight queues and three threshold values, while another uses simple priority queuing with four queues. How do we ensure that "Gold Service" is mapped the same way in these two devices?

The answer lies in using policy-based management to control device configuration, ensuring that the relative capabilities of the device are mapped to the appropriate Service Levels. The key point here is that service providers and enterprise administrators will be able to manage users and applications via a directory-enabled policy management system. Policy-based management enables services to be centrally managed, and applied on an individual, group, role, time of day, or other aggregate basis. This is one of the most important values of DEN and will be discussed more thoroughly later in the book.

How DEN Facilitates Implementing Intelligent Networks

DEN defines how to use a common repository to represent network devices and services in a common way. The first common repository that will be used is the directory. The use of the directory is significantly expanded from the traditional use of directory services. As previously defined in Chapter 4, the directory will now be used as a unified information repository. This serves two purposes:

- Users and other computing and network resources (such as devices, operating systems, management tools, and applications) and services are all represented in a common model.

- Clients use the directory service to publish information about themselves, to discover other resources, and to obtain information about them.

> **Note**
>
> Care should be taken not to confuse the use of directory services with a general message passing service. The second bullet above refers to the use of the directory service as a searchable data store for relatively static data (for example, data whose content changes much less frequently than the fundamental replication frequency of the directory). The directory is certainly *not* a general purpose message passing system because:
>
> - It lacks notification and other features of message passing systems.
> - It lacks transactional and referential integrity.
> - It doesn't handle transient policy data.
> - It doesn't scale to handle large amounts of dynamic policy data.
> - The directory is loosely consistent, but policy needs tight consistency.
>
> A message passing service is used to provide dynamic information exchange between components of the policy system using a publish-subscribe interface. The directory still has a very important role, but one of a static nature, in which the components of the policy system use it to find definitional information.

What Makes the Network Intelligent?

We've defined the Intelligent Network as one which is characterized by the services that it provides, as opposed to other more conventional measures such as bandwidth. The intelligence in the network is distributed among the following components:

- Mechanisms in the device for classifying and handling different traffic types according to different conditions (for example, time of day, source IP address, protocol type, and others)

- Mechanisms in host machines that signal their needs to the network

- Mechanisms in policy servers that apply policies according to service level agreements (SLAs), or other types of contracts, to ensure that network resources are used appropriately

For the network to operate intelligently, all these mechanisms, plus some others, must operate in concert. For this to happen, there needs to be a standard way of representing information, a common repository, and a common notion of policy.

Common Information Representation

CIM and DEN are designed to represent information about systems that are being managed. Being information models, they are more concerned with modeling the system and its components and less concerned about implementation constraints. Though this handles the majority of the information required by the Intelligent Network, there are two important categories of data that are not included.

The first is information that does not really belong to or describe a managed object in the system, but rather exists as part of the system. For example, consider congestion in a router. It would be improper to model congestion as an attribute of the router, yet routers can, of course, become congested. Such information is critical in designing policies to provide QoS for different classes of traffic and in making real-time decisions for conditioning such traffic.

The second is information that can be modeled in CIM and DEN but presents implementation problems for certain types of repositories. For example, consider the following types of attributes: a MAC address of a device, a dynamically assigned IP address leased to a subscriber, a password of a user, and flow rate data for a router interface. All these could easily be assigned attributes in an information model. However, if the data store is a directory, then there are significant implementation problems with two of them.

To see why, let's first define the following types of data:

- *Static data*, which changes much slower than the replication frequency of the directory

- *Low-latency data*, which changes somewhat faster than the replication frequency of the directory and/or which requires on-demand replication, within some latency period, instead of scheduled replication

- *Transient data*, which changes much faster than the replication frequency of the directory and/or which is so voluminous that it doesn't make sense to store it

A MAC address is an example of static data, and there are no problems in storing it in the directory.

Leased IP addresses and passwords are different examples of low-latency data. Leased IP addesses, especially for a large Internet service provider, will change faster than the replication frequency of the directory in general. This means that we can't use directory replication to copy the data to the different replicas comprising the directory service. Passwords are an example of on-demand replication (it would be annoying, to say the least, to have to wait till the next morning to be able to log in again once your password was changed!). Although many directories can do on-demand replication, it is a fairly expensive operation. The problem with policy data is that many types of information have latency semantics, for which scheduled replication is not an option. (Note also that if you increase the replication frequency of the directory too much, queries and updates will get swamped by replication information.)

Note

Note that the service provider example of leased IP addresses is not in general the same as enterprise examples. Some enterprises assign lease times to their devices that are much longer than the replication frequency of the directory, so they would be classified as "static" data. This can be resolved by using policies that in effect assign a role to a device, and then configure the device accordingly. Storing this information in the directory enables common policies to be implemented across the enterprise.

Finally, flow-rate data, which is an example of transient data, is both too voluminous and too volatile to store persistently. However, it may make sense for a snapshot of the flow-rate data, over a suitable time interval, to be stored in the directory.

While CIM and DEN can model all three types of data, most data stores will have limitations that make them appropriate for some, but not all, of these types of data. The intelligence required in the network is dependent on the type of applications that are using the network, but in general will require some combination of static, low-latency, and transient data. CIM and DEN enable a Common Information Model to be used to integrate all three types of data. CIM does not address implementation specifics at all, and DEN concentrates only on directory implementations. Thus, care should be taken to ensure that an implementation can efficiently use the information model.

Common Repository

CIM does not specify a repository implementation, and DEN defines how to map information into a directory that uses LDAP as its access protocol. This combination of an information model to represent data and a mapping to a directory implementation is a good first step but is not complete. We still await industry standardization in areas such as access control and replication. Until then, the framework remains, but in general, interoperability will be limited to a coalition of vendors and their partners that use the same proprietary protocols and APIs.

Common Representation of Policy

DEN defined a policy Information Model that is being carried forward simultaneously in cooperation with the DMTF and the IETF. The DEN model has further evolved into a set of Internet drafts. One set describes a set of core classes for describing the structural composition of policy rules. A second set defines refinements necessary to represent both signaled and provisioned quality of service. These drafts are being used as the basis for defining policy schemata in both organizations.

The DMTF SLA working group is chartered with taking the DEN policy Information Model and ensuring that it is applicable to all types of environments, not just networking. This is why it owns the development of generic policy models, while the DMTF Networks working group owns the development of QoS policy models.

The IETF Policy Framework working group is chartered with defining an interoperable policy framework architecture, Information Model, and schemata.

Coordination between the DMTF and the IETF is ensured because the working group chairs of the DMTF Networks and SLA working groups (John Strassner and Ed Ellesson, respectively) are also the co-chairs of the IETF Policy Framework working group. John and Ed also act as liaisons between the two organizations.

Common Store Plus Policy Equals Intelligent Networks

Currently, network managers must try to integrate a multitude of separate application-specific directories (for example, email, human resources records, and so on) as well as multiple security schemes employed by each directory. This is problematic due to different representations (for example, naming as well as granularity of features) of information in each directory.

Directories were already being used to describe users and common network resources, such as file servers and printers. Therefore, if information describing network elements and services could be stored in the same directory as information describing users and other network resources, applications could go to a single repository to get their information. Thus, DEN had two important purposes:

- To define a Common Model for network elements and services, such that they could be implemented in any repository (hence, the merging of DEN with CIM)

- To define a specific mapping from that Common Information Model to a format suitable for implementation in a directory

This would also simplify the management of the network and its resources. For example, centralizing network configuration information would make network management and modeling easier, as well as ease deployment of QoS capabilities.

However, more is needed than simply accessing a common repository. Key enabling services, such as security, naming, and accounting, must be seamlessly integrated. In order for this to work, network and application vendors must support the same standards. The acceptance of DEN, and its move from an ad hoc committee to a formal standards organization, shows the willingness of network and application vendors, as well as customers, to use a common standard. Work on security and accounting standardization is continuing in the IETF.

Extensibility of the Information Model

Developers can accommodate their application-specific needs by deriving more detailed subclasses that meet those needs from the appropriate classes in the DEN framework. In this way, common representation of information (for example, objects, object attributes, and relationships between objects) is maintained. More importantly, a common namespace is maintained, which is crucial to interoperability.

Note that the relationships in DEN and CIM can be expressed in different ways (this is the subject of Chapter 9). Therefore, many vendors will extend their software development kits to provide APIs that shield the developer from these internal variances and instead provide a higher-level function to exercise these relationships.

DEN Is Not the Complete Solution

It is important to realize that while DEN provides a good foundation for how the Intelligent Network operates, it may not by itself contain all the information needed by applications that want to use Intelligent Networks. However, in most cases, DEN provides essential information that is required by those applications.

Consider, for example, an application that needs to keep track of the network state on a transaction basis. Such an application may want to access a particular network resource with a given set of criteria (for example, bandwidth, latency, and other requirements). To deliver consistent levels of service, the network must be capable of maintaining detailed information on the state of the connection and the devices that make up that connection.

In this example, DEN provides definitional information, such as which users and/or applications are allowed to ask for special services, what level of service each can request, possibly as a basis of some metric such as cost, when such services can be granted, and other operational factors. What DEN cannot provide is a detailed behavioral and/or functional (for example, data flow) model that tracks the state of each such transaction in the network.

DEN Compliance

The DEN vision is that, through the Common Information Model, applications that have completely different GUIs, APIs, and even purposes can exchange information and knowledge about common objects in a DEN repository. For example, an inventory application from one vendor could populate a DEN repository with information describing the salient characteristics of the network. An application from a second vendor could then use this information to probe the network and develop a representation of its logical topology. This could be used by a third vendor's application to provision various network services, while a fourth vendor's application could be used to provision additional network services and to manage various devices in the network. Each of these applications could run on different platforms, under different operating systems, using different APIs and GUIs. However, since they all use a common repository and a common way of representing information, they can all share and exchange information to the benefit of the owners and users of the network.

Note also that such a scheme still leaves room for vendor differentiation through added features and functions. All that is required is for the vendor to implement such features within the DEN framework (for example, as subclasses).

Compliance with the DEN information model is relatively straightforward. DEN is an extension of CIM, so the following elements are required:

- Compliance with the relevant portions of the CIM core schema

- Compliance with the relevant portions of the CIM Physical Model, which contains the physical portion of DEN

- Compliance with the relevant portions of the CIM Networks model, which contains the logical portions of DEN

- Compliance with any other common models that are appropriate to that application domain

In addition, to build a DEN-compliant LDAP schema, a vendor must follow the CIM-to-LDAP mapping guidelines provided by the Networks working group of the DMTF.

The DEN schema may be extended as long as the developer complies with the rules for defining schema extensions, as delineated by the CIM specification. (See the sections, "Recommended Extensions to the Information Model" and "Recommended Versus Supported Extensions to CIM," in Chapter 6.)

Compliance also includes publishing the complete information model and schema definitions, including all class, attribute, and relationship definitions and values, for a given version of the schema.

Summary

This chapter has discussed the major motivating factors for DEN:

- The desire to bind services available in the network to clients of the network

- The use of the combination of a common schema and a Common Information Model to share and exchange information about network elements and services among different applications

It reviewed why CIM by itself was not sufficient and why the DEN Ad-Hoc Working Group submitted its work to the DMTF.

A brief overview of Intelligent Networking was provided. Fundamentally, viewing the network as an active infrastructure that can provide services to its clients, rather than a passive transport, is a major change in the way of thinking about networks. The most important feature of this change is in emphasizing the building of devices that can fit together as systems, as opposed to being "the fastest packet forwarder." This new emphasis concentrates on manageability and providing services, not just mechanisms such as fancy queuing.

The Intelligent Network model was also described. It consists of a set of layered services. These services are integrated to form higher-level services used by a client. Factors driving this model include the increased usage of the Internet, and the need to transform it from a best-effort to a Differentiated Services model, the enabling of a business model where service providers can charge for Differentiated Services, increased security, the use of new applications and tools, and location independence.

The factors that make a network intelligent and how DEN helps make networks intelligent were explained. The focus is on using a common representation of information that is stored and retrieved from a common repository. It was also shown that Intelligent Networks and policy-enabled applications are well matched.

This chapter also cautioned against viewing DEN as a panacea. However, it was pointed out that DEN does serve a very important role in the development of the Intelligent Network.

Finally, DEN compliance was defined. Owners and users of the network benefit greatly from using a common repository and representing information in a standard format, which DEN defines. Vendors will embrace DEN because they can be compliant while being allowed to extend a DEN-Compliant Information Model and schema to represent their own differentiating features.

Recommended Further Study and References

The Burton Group has followed the development of DEN since its inception. Two important reports are

> Gauthier, L. "Directory-Enabled Computing: Directory Services Architecture," May, 1998.

> Petrosky, M. "Directory-Enabled Networks Initiative," December, 1997.

The following sites contain excellent references to various forms of queuing mechanisms:

http://www.aciri.org/floyd/red.html

http://www.aciri.org/floyd/cbq.html

http://www.ctr.columbia.edu/~campbell/andrew/publications/publications.html

The Differentiated Services, Integrated Services, Policy Framework, and RSVP Admission Policy working groups descriptions, documents, and other information can be found at these locations:

```
http://www.ietf.org/html.charters/diffserv-charter.html
```

```
http://www.ietf.org/html.charters/intserv-charter.html
```

```
http://www.ietf.org/html.charters/policy-charter.html
```

```
http://www.ietf.org/html.charters/rap-charter.html
```

The DEN specification as released by the DEN Ad-Hoc Working Group is located at

```
http://www.murchiso.com/
```

This specification has been divided mainly into the Physical and Networks models of CIM, though DEN did also influence some changes and additions to other CIM models. The CIM Core, Physical, Networks, and System models are the most important.

Please note that a new version of the DEN specification will be published in late 1999 by the Networks working group of the DMTF.

PART II

Inside DEN

CHAPTER

6

A Brief Introduction to CIM

The purpose of this chapter is to briefly introduce the *Common Information Model (CIM)*, define its goals, and describe its specification and the core, common, and extension models that it comprises. The CIM specification provides a complete meta-model for defining how management information should be represented and structured. It also defines additional constructs for closely integrating the needs of management applications with CIM. Finally, it provides an extensible mechanism for defining metadata that determine additional semantics for CIM objects.

Mapping between CIM and other management formats is very important. The *Managed Object Format (MOF) language* can be used for this mapping, and will be described briefly. MOF is a human-readable, textual format for describing richly structured management information, such as object definitions and relationships. MOF is constructed such that automated tools can process it (for example, compilers). In addition, the DMTF is currently investigating the use of eXtensible Markup Language (XML) as a standard way of mapping between different management formats using MOF, as well as serving as a transport for CIM data.

Finally, this chapter will provide an overview of CIM. This will include giving recommendations as to how to extend it and what features of CIM should and should not be used.

What Is CIM and What Are Its Goals?

CIM is an object-oriented information model that describes how a system may be managed. It supports enterprise-wide (instead of device-centric) management and provides a common definition of all types of management data. Its information model is independent of implementation. This facilitates the integration of diverse management information from different sources.

CIM reduces the complexity of the system being modeled by using most of the object-oriented techniques discussed in Chapter 2 and Chapter 3. In particular, it is an extensible classification system based on the principles of object identity, abstraction, encapsulation, and inheritance. It has been built using generalization and specialization to alternately add new high-level concepts to the model, as well as to refine existing concepts.

Above all, it is important to remember that CIM is an information model. It is *not* an implementation, nor does it specify a particular platform or technology to use for its implementation. However, CIM enables extension models to be constructed that address the specific needs of applications, platforms, and/or technologies.

CIM has both technical and deployment goals. The technical goal of CIM is to provide a common conceptual framework within which any component or system may be modeled and managed. Specifically, this framework should support the cooperative development of object-oriented information models and schemata across multiple organizations that use heterogeneous development tools and environments.

The deployment goal of CIM is to become a ubiquitous standard that all management vendors implement. This would enable information to be exchanged between applications regardless of GUI, APIs, differing platforms, or other variations between the applications.

CIM consists of a specification and an information model. These will be described in the following sections.

The CIM Specification

The CIM specification defines an object-oriented meta-model (for example, a model about the model) based on the *Unified Modeling Language (UML)*. UML is a language for describing managed entities and management information. The CIM specification also defines a namespace (including naming conventions) that enables its data to be integrated with existing data. Finally, the CIM specification describes how to map between information represented in CIM and other management formats, such as SNMP MIBs or LDAP-based directories. Refer to the CIM specification for more detailed information.

The CIM Meta-Model

The meta-model is a formal definition of CIM using object-oriented concepts. The meta-model defines the components of the model, the semantics of these components, and how they are used to describe concepts being modeled.

UML is used to define the structure of the meta-model. By adopting UML, CIM ensures that the meta-model can be easily understood by a variety of applications. The components of the CIM meta-model include *object* and *relationship* (both associations and aggregations are supported) classes. Each of these can have *attributes* (also called *properties*) and *methods.* In addition, CIM provides support for other constructs that enable event-based systems to better utilize CIM data. These are described in the section, "Additional Meta Constructs Supported by CIM" later in this chapter.

Data Type Support

CIM attributes are limited to its intrinsic data types, or arrays of those data types. Structured data types are constructed by creating new classes.

The following intrinsic data types are supported:

- UCS-2 strings (UCS stands for the Universal Multiple-Octet Coded Character Set)

- Signed and unsigned 8-, 16-, 32-, and 64-bit integers

- Boolean

- IEEE 4- and 8-byte floating-point

- Datetime

- Class reference

- User-defined data type

All these data types are well known except the datetime and user-defined data types, which are discussed in the following two sections.

Datetime Data Types

Two time- and date-related data types, namely dates (including time of day) and time intervals (representing elapsed time), share the same following data format:

`yyyymmddhhmmss.mmmmmmsutc`

Where

`yyyy` is a 4-digit year.

`mm` is the month.

`dd` is the day.

`hh` is the hour (24-hour clock).

mm is the minute.

ss is the second.

mmmmmm is the number of microseconds.

s is a "+" or "-" indicating the sign of UTC (Universal Coordinated Time; for all intents and purposes the same as Greenwich Mean Time) correction field, or a ":". In this case, the value is interpreted as a time interval, and yyyymm are interpreted as days.

utc is the offset from UTC in minutes (using the sign indicated by s). Note that there are some time zones that are not an integral multiple of 60 minutes away from UTC, which is why this value is in minutes. It is ignored for a time interval.

For example, Monday, December 28, 1998, at 1:14:15 PM PST would be represented as

19981228131415.0000000-600

Daylight Savings Time is accommodated by adjusting the UTC offset.

Similarly, time intervals use the same format, except that the interpretation of the fields is based on elapsed time. For example, an elapsed time of 1 day, 13 hours, 14 minutes, and 15 seconds would be:

00000001131415.000000:000

A UTC offset of zero is always used for interval time range specifications.

Refer to the CIM specification for more information concerning datetime attributes.

User-Defined Data Types

User-defined data types are defined by indicating additional data type semantics with appropriate qualifiers. For example, SNMP defines the notion of a *counter*. This is an integer that has special semantics associated with it: Increase to a maximum value, and then wrap back to zero and start over.

CIM does not define a new intrinsic data type of counter. Rather, CIM defines a new *qualifier* to indicate that an attribute whose data type is integer has the additional semantics of an SNMP counter.

Additional Meta Constructs Supported by CIM

The meta-model also supports the following important concepts, as described in the following sections:

- Events
- Triggers
- Indications
- Qualifiers

Events

An *event* is an external occurrence that represents some information being injected into the system or information that describes the system. The CIM model is currently being extended to include support for modeling events as objects. This would enable a common format for events to be defined, enabling applications to publish and subscribe to events in a standardized format. This standardized format is critical to enabling information about events to be exchanged.

> **Note**
>
> This is a very important step, as it enables information in CIM to be directly related to important occurrences in the environment being modeled. In addition, a mapping between generalized CIM events and specific events provided by other management applications (such as SNMP agents) is being defined by the CIM TDC (the architectural board of CIM).

Triggers

A *trigger* is a recognition of a change of state in one or more objects that are being managed. Such changes of state could include the creation, update, deletion, or access of information of an object instance and/or its attribute. Triggers are critical in building behavioral and functional models.

Triggers are beyond the scope of this book, though they represent a convenient and efficient means of tying object, behavioral, and functional models to the actual implementation of directory-enabled applications and network-enabled applications.

Indications

An *indication* is an object created as a result of a trigger. An indication is a class and has an association with zero or more triggers that can create instances of the indication. Again, indications form a critical part of behavioral and functional models.

Indications are beyond the scope of this book. They are an efficient means of tying event-based systems to the actual implementation of directory enabled applications and network-enabled applications.

Qualifiers

A qualifier is a directive that is used to define additional semantics for a class, attribute, or method in the model. For example, if a class has the qualifier ASSOCIATION, then that class is used to implement an association.

Qualifiers can be thought of as metadata about an attribute, method, method parameter, class, or instance. As such, qualifiers are *not* part of the definition itself. For example, a qualifier can be used to indicate whether a property value is modifiable (using the WRITE qualifier) or not. In this case, the qualifier does not alter the data or the attribute; rather, the qualifier is used to add semantics to the attribute that determine whether or not its content can be modified. Qualifiers always precede the declaration to which they apply.

Qualifiers also provide a way to extend the schema by enabling new types of qualifiers to be defined. This enables application-specific semantics to be defined and incorporated into the model.

For example, consider the concept of SNMP counters and gauges. These are integers that have additional semantics associated with them. Qualifiers enable these semantics to be defined without having to define new data types for the model.

There are four types of qualifiers. *Meta qualifiers* are used to refine the definition of an object class or attribute. For example, the ASSOCIATION and INDICATION qualifiers are used to indicate that an object class is being used to define an association or indication, respectively.

Standard qualifiers are a set of semantic refinements that all CIM implementations must support. These represent additions to the definition of a class, attribute, or method. For example, a qualifier can be used to indicate whether or not an attribute is read-only or can be modified.

The WEAK Qualifier

The WEAK qualifier is a very important standard qualifier. It is used when applications need to name instances within the context of other object instances. For example, if a management application wanted to differentiate between two identical routers in separate administrative domains, it must be able to explicitly identify and refer to each router in each administrative domain. In order to do this, the name of the router must include the name of the administrative domain in which it resides. This is done using an association that relates the router to the administrative domain in which it resides. This type of association is called a *weak association*, since the identity of the router depends on the name of the router and the name of the administrative domain. CIM supports the notion of weak associations, and the ability to propagate the key attributes between the objects of the weak association. It uses the WEAK qualifier to designate such relationships.

If any reference to the class has the WEAK qualifier, the attributes that are qualified as key in the other classes in the association are propagated to the referenced class. This is indicated using the PROPAGATED qualifier.

Optional qualifiers are standard qualifiers that do not have to be supported by a CIM-compliant implementation. They are defined because they represent semantics that frequently occur in applications. This way, non-interoperable user-defined definitions of these concepts may be avoided.

User-defined qualifiers represent the ability for specific applications to extend the information model. The only restriction of user-defined qualifiers is that they cannot redefine any of the other qualifiers that CIM provides.

MOF—A Language for Defining Management Models

A CIM-compliant model is described in a language called *Managed Object Format (MOF)*. This language is based on the standard Interface Definition Language (IDL). The purpose of MOF is to define the capabilities of a distributed service along with a common set of data types for interacting with those distributed services.

MOF defines a syntax for representing object class, attribute, method, and other model definitions. MOF enables a model and its components to be described in a human-readable textual form.

Basic MOF Concepts

All MOF keywords are case insensitive to enhance portability. The following sections provide an overview of the power and functionality of MOF. Refer to the CIM specification for detailed information regarding the grammar of MOF.

Comments

MOF supports the use of *comments*. Comments can appear anywhere, and are indicated with either a leading double slash (//) or a pair of matching slash-asterisk sequences (/*…*/). The first form is used for comments that fit on a single line, whereas the latter form is used to denote the beginning and end of text that should be treated as a comment.

Qualifiers

Qualifiers define metadata that specify additional semantics for a class, attribute, method, method parameter, or instance. As such, they add to the definition of the construct, and are not part of the definition itself. For example, the WRITE qualifier is used to indicate whether an attribute value is modifiable, or if it can only be read. This doesn't effect the definition of the attribute, but does effect how that attribute is used. Qualifiers always precede the declaration to which they apply.

Qualifiers have five modifiers that affect their use. The EnableOverride and DisableOverride keywords define whether this qualifier can be overridden or not. The ToSubclass keyword specifies that this qualifier is inherited by all subclasses, whereas the Restricted keyword mandates that this qualifier only applies to this class. Finally, the Translatable keyword specifies that the value of this qualifier can be specified in multiple locales. In this case, the language and country codes will be appended to the qualifier, separated by underscores.

Note

It is recommended that the EnableOverride and DisableOverride key words not be used. This is because Object-Oriented Modeling does *not* permit this type of overriding (often called canceling), as it violates encapsulation (see "Overriding Attributes and Methods" in Chapter 3). Overriding attributes and methods, though allowed by CIM, is strongly discouraged.

It is also recommended that the ToSubclass and Restricted keywords not be used, since selective inheritance is not supported in Object-Oriented Modeling (see "Strict Versus Selective Inheritance" in Chapter 3). If a qualifier is defined in a class, then all subclasses should inherit that qualifier.

Classes

Classes are declared as a set of definitions. These definitions define

- Any qualifiers that apply to the class as a whole

- The name of the class

- The name of the superclass from which the class is derived

- The attributes of the class

- The methods of the class

Subclasses are defined by first listing the name of the subclass, then appending a colon, and then appending the name of the superclass from which the subclass is derived. There are two restrictions for subclasses. First, they must be unique within a CIM namespace. Second, their superclass must have either been previously declared in the MOF specification, or already be registered with the CIM namespace that the MOF specification applies to.

Note

CIM is not a rooted hierarchy (for example, it has no single class, usually called Top, that is the root of the hierarchy). Therefore, it allows a class to be defined that has no super-classes; this is simply another top-level class that has no superclass.

The CIM TDC is currently thinking about rooting the CIM hierarchy. This will not take place before the CIM 3.0 time frame.

Attributes

Attributes are also composed of a set of definitions. These definitions consist of an optional list of qualifiers, a mandatory data type, and an optional initialization value.

Key Attributes and Uniqueness

Applications require a means to identify different instances of an object within a single namespace. CIM does this by designating one or more attributes of a class with the KEY qualifier. This designates the attribute as a key attribute. Key attributes function in a way analogous to RDNs of directory entries (see "The Structure of Directory Information" in Chapter 4). An object can be uniquely identified in a CIM namespace through the use of its key attributes.

If a new subclass is defined from a superclass, and the superclass or any of its parent classes have key properties, the new subclass cannot define any additional key properties. New key properties in a subclass can be introduced only if all of the superclasses of a given class do not already have keys.

> **Note**
>
> This means that many of the top-level classes in CIM do not have key properties. This enables their subclasses to define keys that are more suited to the purpose of the subclass.
>
> For example, the ManagedSystemElement class, which is the superclass of the PhysicalElement and LogicalElement subclasses, has no key properties defined. This is to allow physical and logical classes to define their own keys. The PhysicalElement class has two key attributes, CreationClassName and Tag. This means two things:
>
> • Every subclass in the physical hierarchy inherits these two keys.
>
> • No other subclass in the physical hierarchy can define a key attribute; if a new one is needed, it must go in the PhysicalElement class.

Methods

Methods also have a set of definitions. Here, the definition of each method consists of the name of the method, an optional qualifier list plus a mandatory signature. The signature is comprised of the return type of the method, along with the data types of any parameters that are used by the method. The only restriction on method return types and parameters is that they must be an intrinsically supported data type.

Constants

Character, string, integer, floating-point, and even object reference constants are supported. In addition, all data types can be initialized to the value NULL, which indicates that no value was supplied.

Expressing a CIM Object Class in MOF

Figure 6.1 shows an excerpt from the CIM Core Model MOF file. We will use this excerpt in order to visualize the salient characteristics of defining a CIM class in MOF. Note that this is only an example and does not exhaustively cover all of the different constructs that can be used to specify a CIM class. Refer to the CIM specification for more examples and a complete listing of the MOF grammar.

Figure 6.1   Expressing a CIM class in MOF.

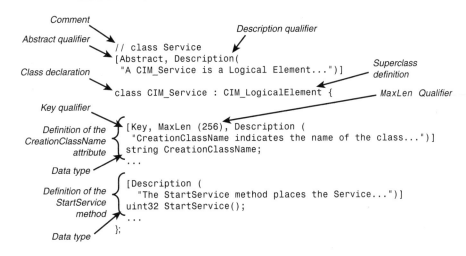

The class definition itself is defined using the keyword class and enclosing the class definition in braces. Qualifiers are enclosed in brackets and appear immediately before the component that they affect. For example, the first two qualifiers in Figure 6.1 (the abstract and the description qualifiers)

[Abstract, Description ()]

appear immediately before the class declaration. This means that they apply to the class itself. In this case, the Abstract qualifier defines the CIM_Service class to be abstract, while the Description qualifier provides explanatory text describing the purpose of the CIM_Service class.

The CIM_Service class is defined to be a subclass of the CIM_LogicalElement class. This is done by first listing the name of the class being defined (CIM_Service), then appending a colon, and then appending the name of the superclass (CIM_LogicalElement). There is no need to specify the complete genealogy of a class; all that is required is to specify its immediate superclass. The system will put all the pieces together.

Each component of a CIM object class, whether it is an attribute or a method, can optionally be qualified in some way. Referring again to Figure 6.1, we see that the definition of the CreationClassName attribute includes three qualifiers (Key, MaxLen, and Description) followed by the definition of the attribute itself. The Key qualifier is used to indicate that the CreationClassName attribute is a *key attribute*. This means that it is used to form the namespace path of the attribute (see the "CIM Namespace" section for more information about namespace paths). This function is analogous to an RDN of a directory entry or an index value in a database. CIM allows multiple key attributes to be declared for a class, meaning that such a class has a *composite* key consisting of all of the attributes.

The MaxLen qualifier is used to define the maximum number of characters that a string attribute can have. Here, we see that the CreationClassName attribute is limited to 256 characters.

The final part of the attribute definition is declaring the data type of the attribute. For the CreationClassName attribute, we see that it is declared as a string. Note that the MaxLen qualifier further qualifies this as a string of no more than 256 characters.

The last interesting thing about this excerpt is the method definition. Here, we see that the method StartService() also has qualifiers and a definition. The method definition will define the signature of the method (the order and data type of each of its parameters, along with the return value of the method). Here, we see that the StartService() method has no parameters and returns an unsigned 32-bit integer value.

Expressing a CIM Association Class in MOF

Figure 6.2 shows an excerpt from the CIM Core Model MOF file in order to visualize the salient characteristics of defining a CIM association in MOF. The procedure for defining an association is identical to that for defining a CIM class in MOF, except that there are a new set of qualifiers that can be used to define the characteristics of the association.

Figure 6.2   Expressing a CIM association in MOF.

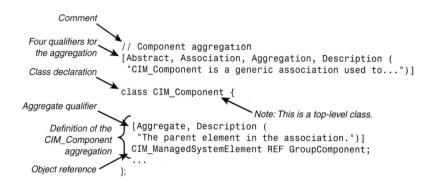

Again, we use qualifiers preceding the actual class declaration to define this class as not only an abstract class, but also an aggregation. Note that both the Association and the Aggregation qualifiers are required to do this. In addition, (though not shown in this example) multiplicity is specified through the use of appropriate qualifiers. For example, in the following MOF excerpt:

```
class CIM_HostedService:CIM_Dependency
{
    [Override ("Antecedent"), Max(1), Min(1),
     Description ("The hosting system") ]
 CIM_System REF Antecedent;
    [Override ("Dependent", Weak,
     Description ("The Service hosted on the System.") ]
  CIM_Service REF Dependent
}
```

We see that the cardinality of the antecedent is specified using the Max and Min qualifiers as Max(1), Min(1). This makes the cardinality 1. Similarly, since there is no qualification of the cardinality of the dependent, it is taken to be many (that is, zero-or-more).

The CIM_Component association is a top-level class, meaning that it has no superclass. Since it is also an aggregation, it has an aggregate part (for example, the "whole") and one or more component parts. The aggregate part is identified with the Aggregate qualifier.

Association and aggregation classes refer to the object classes that they define a relationship between. Hence, we see that an object of type ManagedSystemElement is defined to be the group component (that is, the aggregate) of the CIM_Component aggregation.

As previously mentioned, associations and aggregations are full-fledged classes. This enables rich relationships to be defined. As full-fledged classes, associations can benefit from all of the features inherent in classes. These include inheritance, as well as the ability to have attributes and methods defined as part of the relationship. The CIM_Component aggregation happens to be a very general relationship, and the part components are also of object type ManagedSystemElement. The purpose of this aggregation is to serve as a base class for other specialized aggregations. For example, the CIM_SystemComponent aggregation is a specialization of the CIM_Component aggregation that is used to define whole-part relationships between a System and the ManagedSystemElements that comprise it.

> **Note**
>
> Note the use of generalization and specialization in the design of relationships. The real benefit of the CIM_Component aggregation is to serve as a base class for further specialized relationships. This is an essential feature of CIM and DEN.

Another example of a general aggregation is the CIM_Container aggregation, which is a subclass of the CIM_Component aggregation. The CIM_Container aggregation represents the relationship between a contained and a containing PhysicalElement. It specifies that the aggregate, or the container, is an object of type PhysicalPackage, while the part components are objects of type PhysicalElement. Note that this is possible because both PhysicalPackage and PhysicalElement are subclasses of ManagedSystemElement, and that the CIM_Component aggregation defined both the whole and the part of the relationship as classes of type ManagedSystemElement.

The CIM_Container aggregation also defines an attribute, LocationWithinContainer, that is a free-form string used to represent the physical positioning of the PhysicalElement within the PhysicalPackage. This is an example of a subclass of an aggregation that refines the object classes of both the aggregate and the component objects that it associates. It also defines a new attribute that its superclass did not have. Subclasses of the CIM_Container class will inherit these refinements (including the new attribute).

Required Versus Optional Attributes

A directory implementation distinguishes between "*must have*" and "*may have*" attributes (see "Defining Basic Object-Oriented Terminology" in Chapter 2). "Must have" attributes are those that are required to be present in an object class. "May have" attributes are those that can optionally be present. However, CIM really has no notion of the difference between required and optional attributes. If your application needs this distinction, then you should define a CIM extension schema with new qualifiers to represent this.

A related concept is that of NULL. CIM supports the concept of NULL, meaning that no value has been provided. However, this is not the same as not providing the attribute. For example, in a directory implementation, an optional attribute does not have to be instantiated. In that case, when a search is performed on that attribute, the directory will return an ERROR. This is quite different than searching for something and not getting a result.

The CIM Namespace

CIM defines its own namespace. This is mandatory because CIM is independent of any specific repository. The CIM namespace enables different applications to identify and share management information by enforcing a naming mechanism that uniquely identifies each object, and its attributes and methods, in the model.

The CIM namespace consists of two components. In general, it isn't sufficient to think of the name of an object as the concatenation of its key attributes. This is because CIM allows multiple implementations, each with their own namespace, to coexist. Therefore, the name of an object consists of two components. The *namespace path* is used to select a specific namespace out of multiple namespaces, and thus provides access to the particular CIM implementation that is hosting the CIM object. The *model path* provides navigation among the objects in the CIM namespace. This is similar to naming in directories: The concatenation of CIM attributes that are designated *keys* forms a unique name just as the concatenation of RDNs forms a unique directory entry name. The combination of a namespace path plus a model path provides the ability to differentiate between two similarly named objects that are in separate namespaces.

The CIM namespace provides the following benefits:

- *Object identity*—The CIM namespace enables any object in the namespace to be uniquely identified and located. This enables the system to determine when multiple object names reference the same CIM object.

- *Application-independence*—Two applications can interoperate by exchanging CIM data. The power of this lies in the ability to maintain local relationships of the data being exchanged while incorporating the exchanged data into a new repository. This also enables different scoping hierarchies (for example, namespaces within namespaces) to be created.

- *Referencing and integrating data from multiple sources*—Each CIM namespace is self-contained. Therefore, if data about a system is contained in multiple data stores that each have their own CIM namespace, they can be related to each other through references between objects in each of the CIM namespaces.

- *Data synchronization*—Two applications, using CIM, can synchronize their data by using the namespace to detect and implement changes.

Fully qualified class names take the following form:

```
<schema name>_<class name>
```

An underscore is used as a delimiter between the <schema name> and the <class name>. The delimiter is not allowed to appear in the <schema name>, although it is permitted in the <class name>. This format enables the scope of class names to be limited to a particular schema and easily identified. Schema names are used to partition objects into their own namespaces, allowing the same CIM class to participate in multiple namespaces. These CIM classes can then be differentiated through the combination of the schema name and the class name. For example,

`CIM_ManagedSystemElement`

is the fully qualified name of the ManagedSystemElement class of the CIM hierarchy. In this example, CIM is the name of the schema and ManagedSystemElement is the name of the class. This uniquely identifies this class within the CIM namespace.

Mappings Between CIM and Other Formats

Other management applications have their own models. There are three possible ways to map these other models into CIM (and vice versa):

- *Content mapping*—A mapping is defined that maps non-CIM data directly into CIM data. Meta-model constructs are used as guidelines, but do not directly effect the mapping.

- *Meta-model construct-based mapping*—The CIM meta-model constructs are used to describe the meta-model constructs of the non-CIM model. This enables the non-CIM data to be expressed indirectly as CIM data. This technique relies on being able to express data and object structures and relationships as CIM constructs.

- *Meta-model equivalence mapping*—The meta-model constructs of the non-CIM model are translated to CIM meta-model constructs. This enables the non-CIM data to be translated into CIM data.

CIM

The second part of CIM is the information model itself. CIM supplies a set of classes that are used to implement an inheritance hierarchy and a set of relationship hierarchies. The combination of these hierarchies provide an extensible object-oriented framework by enabling a set of models of common objects and systems to be implemented. These are the Core and Common models of CIM, which are defined in "The Core Model" and "The Common Models" sections later in this chapter.

CIM itself is extensible. Specific extensions of these models, called *Extension models*, can be assembled according to the specific needs of an application.

The Core and Common models will discussed in detail in Chapter 7. DEN, which is itself an Extension model, is discussed in Chapters 8, 9, and 10.

The Three Layers of CIM

One of CIM's primary goals was to serve as an extensible object-oriented framework. This meant that it had to represent not only the set of applications that the designers of CIM had in mind during the design process, but also accommodate applications not specifically considered, as well as future applications not yet conceived.

This was accomplished by dividing up the task of building a single information model into a set of *layered* models. By defining a core layer that all models had to support and implement in order to be CIM-compliant, interoperability was assured. By defining a set of generic common models that addressed frequently occurring concepts (for example, computers, software, and so on), a common approach of modeling these concepts was created. This was a very important step because, without these common concepts, individual applications would redefine these concepts in different ways and data would not be sharable.

The Core Model

The *Core Model* describes concepts in the information model that are applicable to all areas of management. It is comprised of a set of classes, attributes, methods, and associations that define a set of fundamental concepts and relationships for describing managed systems and components. It forms the foundation for the class inheritance and relationship hierarchies. As such, the Core Model is the basis for all common and extension models.

The core schema establishes the top-level classification hierarchy of CIM by categorizing the components of a managed environment into ManagedSystemElements and other related classes, such as Products and SupportAccess. ManagedSystemElements define the fundamental attributes and relationships that enable systems and system components to be managed. Other classes defined in the core schema, such as Products, are designed to relate the use of managed objects to application-specific environments.

The Core Model does *not* have any specific implementation restrictions. That is, it is independent of platform and technology.

The Common Models

The *Common Models* are sets of classes, attributes, methods, and associations that define abstractions that occur frequently in particular management domains, but are independent of a specific technology or implementation. Each of these eight Common Models are specific enough to provide a basis for the development of management applications in that area, but are general enough to be widely applicable to a variety of management applications.

It is intended that each of these eight Common Models provide a foundation that can be extended to accommodate specific needs and requirements of that knowledge domain. That is, the classes, attributes, methods, and associations in each Common Model are intended to represent enough key concepts of that management domain to enable the design and implementation of a management application to be started. Furthermore, the overall structure exhibited by the Core and Common models is intended to serve as a guide for developing extension models that address specific implementation needs.

The eight Common Models are:

- *System*—Defines the key components of a system and how to assemble them. These include system, computer system, operating system, file, and processes.

- *Device*—Defines how to realize physical devices in hardware, along with how to model the connections between devices. These include mass storage devices, media, sensors, printers, power supplies, and other components.

- *Application*—Defines how to manage the installation of software in a system. This includes the concepts of software features and elements as well as the ability to check if conditions are met for installing software and actions to be taken as part of executing the software.

- *Network*—Defines specializations to the physical and logical element class hierarchies to model network elements and services. This also includes modeling network protocols and network systems.

- *Physical*—Defines the physical organization, containment structure and composition of devices and device interconnections.

- *User*—Models users, groups and organizations, and how these objects interact with the other components of a managed system.

- *Policy*—Builds on the original policy model proposed by DEN and generalizes this beyond network policy to a policy that can control any type of managed entity.

- *Database*—Models the operation of relational databases (this is still work in progress).

Each of the Common Models is also implementation-neutral. The Core Model plus the set of Common Models is defined as CIM.

Extension Models

Extension models represent specific extensions to the Common Model to address platform, technology, or other considerations. These models are specific to environments and/or implementations. For example, extensions may be developed to address the specific capabilities of different operating systems (for example, UNIX, and Microsoft Windows). Such extensions would still share the common infrastructure of the Core and Common models, and, therefore, still be interoperable.

Another example is extension models that assume a specific implementation, such as a directory. DEN is technically an extension schema. This is because it combines the Core Model and elements from many of the Common Models into a single information model that can then be mapped into a set of constructs that can be implemented in a directory.

Recommended Extensions to the Information Model

CIM presents an extensible classification mechanism through the combination of its Core and Common models. Therefore, the schema designer should first try to extend the model by designing subclasses of either the Core or an appropriate Common Model class. This applies equally to object classes that are part of the inheritance hierarchy, as well as to association classes that are part of the various relationship hierarchies.

The following is a list of supported extensions that can be made to CIM that are recommended in the spirit of DEN and Object-Oriented Modeling. When extending an Information Model, care should be taken to maintain its security permissions and restrictions, as well as to ensure that the interfaces (for example, the externally accessible attributes and behavior of CIM classes) presented to applications are preserved. Otherwise, the extension could make the model unusable by applications.

- An object or association class can be added to (but not deleted from) the Information Model. Specifically:

  - Adding new top-level object classes (for example, classes that do not have a superclass) is discouraged unless absolutely necessary. This is because it adds to and complicates the model without necessarily making the model more extensible. That is, if a new top-level class is added that has no relationship to the existing classes, the resulting model has more functionality, but has been "stretched" in a new direction, rather than extended in an existing direction.

- Adding new object subclasses is encouraged, though it is preferable to work in the Common Models as opposed to adding subclasses in the Core Model. Changing the Core Model has wide-ranging effects, and should be done with care.

- Adding new association classes or subclasses (whether they are top-level objects or not) is encouraged, as this enriches the overall model.

- An attribute can be added to (but not deleted from) either an object class or an association class.

- A method can be added to (but not deleted from) either an object or an association class.

- A qualifier can be added to (but not deleted from) any class, attribute, method, or relationship.

- A trigger may be added to (but not deleted from) a class.

Note

Changes such as the preceding can be added in a vendor's private application and still maintain CIM compliance. Alternatively, the vendor may propose such changes as formal additions, deletions, or modifications to the CIM specification. This is done through participation in a CIM working group, and writing a Change Request against the CIM specification and/or appropriate CIM model.

Recommended Versus Supported Extensions to CIM

The CIM specification is meant to appeal to as wide a variety of programmers and applications as possible. As such, it provides very general guidelines that are applicable to all types of development.

The philosophy of DEN is stricter, as described in Chapters 2 and 3 of this book. DEN is based on Object-Oriented Modeling, while CIM is meant to also accommodate object-oriented design. The following are supported features and extensions of CIM that are not recommended to be used when building directory and network enabled information models. The reasons for recommending against these features are described in Chapter 3.

- CIM specifies that a method or attribute of a subclass can override its inherited method or attribute of its superclass. As stated in Chapter 3, this is not recommended for either object or association classes.

- CIM allows the canceling of classes, attributes and methods. This is not recommended, as it alters the interface of the affected objects.

- Adding parameters to a method, or restricting the returned values of a method, are fine. However, CIM allows more general modifications, such as removing a method parameter or changing the data type of the return value of a method. In general, any alteration of the method signature that is not an addition of a method parameter, a restriction of the values that a method parameter can accept, or a restriction of the values returned by a method, is not recommended.

- CIM enables a class to become an association (or aggregation) as a result of the addition of an `Association` (or `Aggregation`) qualifier, plus references to each of the object classes to which it relates. This is not recommended, as changing an object class to a relationship in effect deletes the object class and adds a new relationship class. Deleting classes of any type is not recommended.

- CIM allows triggers to be deleted. This is not recommended.

- The following CIM qualifiers are not recommended for use:

  - `OVERRIDE` (standard qualifier)

  - `DELETE` (optional qualifier)

  - `IFDELETED` (optional qualifier)

Benefits of CIM

CIM provides the following important benefits:

- Provides a standard set of models that can be used as "building blocks" to model arbitrarily complex systems. This, in turn, provides

  - Standard ways of representing information about common objects, such as network devices, that enables vendors of different components and management applications to share information about them.

  - Standard ways to model common complex components, such as computer systems, by abstracting them into a set of simpler components that already have standard models.

- Models structural objects and relationships between objects as class hierarchies that are inherently extensible.

- Permits common understanding and sharing of different management data across multiple management systems.

- Allows integration of different management information from different sources that use different syntaxes and expressions.

CIM will enable different applications from multiple developers to describe and share diverse types of management data. CIM removes platform dependencies by providing a common information model in which to represent management information. This enables different applications to interoperate and share data with each other. For example, one application can be used to populate the model, while a completely different application can be used to derive information from that model, and a third application can be used to manage devices that are modeled. Without a common repository and a common way to represent, store and access data, this was impossible, because the applications had no way to share information with each other except by creating specific APIs to each other. Building APIs is a hard, complex task; it is language and platform dependent, and is subject to change as the application changes.

CIM solves this problem by defining a common format to represent and exchange information. It is independent of GUI, API, and language. In addition, since CIM is platform and implementation neutral, multiple types of repositories can be used to suit the needs of the applications being built.

The combination of a common repository and a common information format enables management information to be shared between different management systems and applications. The management data can collected, stored and analyzed using a common format (CIM), with application-specific data being stored in extensions to CIM. Then, each application can access common data from CIM and combine this with its own application-specific data stored as CIM extensions to perform its job.

Implementation Conformance

CIM specifies a minimum conformance level because, otherwise, it would not be possible to guarantee that information could be exchanged between heterogeneous management applications.

Currently, the mechanism for exchanging management information is to represent the information in MOF. A CIM-compliant system must be able to import and export MOF. This means that any meta instructions, as defined by the various qualifiers of CIM, must be adhered to. For example, if a qualifier requires an attribute to be read-only, then that metadata must be preserved during the mapping.

XML and CIM

The DMTF is currently evaluating the applicability of XML for representing structured management information of all types. XML is a rich language that is particularly well-suited to representing structured information. In addition, one of the benefits of endorsing XML would be to adopt it as a standard means for representing and transporting CIM information. This would require a mapping between the CIM meta-model and XML.

The following subsections provide a brief definition of XML and describe such a mapping.

What Is XML?

XML is a subset of the Standardized Generalized Markup Language (SGML). Markup languages are designed to be able to add structure and convey information about documents and data. This is done by adding markup constructs. Typically, these take the form of a start tag (indicating the start of the definition of markup data), optionally some content, and an end tag (indicating the end of the definition of markup data).

As a simple example, suppose that you wanted to identify a WAN interface for a router. An XML extract that does this (for this fictional example) is

```
<CLASS Name="Router">
<PROPERTY Name="WAN Interface">
198.210.1.1
</PROPERTY>
</CLASS>
```

XML has been standardized as a universal way for representing structured information by the World Wide Web Consortium (W3C).

XML is designed to represent structured data and semantic information about structured data in a textual format. XML is similar to the *HyperText Markup Language (HTML)*, the default language used in browsers. The main difference is that while HTML is used to convey *textual and graphical* information *about* a document, XML is used to represent *structured* data *in* a document.

One of the features of an XML document is that it can optionally have a description of its grammar attached to the document. This is called a *Document Type Definition (DTD)*. DTD describes the different constructs that can be used in the XML document, along with how they are structured.

Sometimes, management applications need to know how the data contained within an XML document should be rendered. XML documents can also specify one or more *eXtensible Style Language (XSL) style sheets*. XSL style sheets provide a generalized means to transform XML documents into other formats. This includes the ability to represent data contained in an XML document graphically. Any number of XSL style sheets can be associated with an XML document. This enables a management application, which needs to display the data in different ways, to change the display format by applying the appropriate XSL style sheet to the XML document.

Why XML?

XML is particularly well-suited for representing structured information. However, in order to represent CIM data, an XML vocabulary must be defined and agreed upon. The XML management vocabulary would be in effect a mapping of the CIM meta-model to an XML DTD. This enables any management information that can be modeled using CIM to be conveyed using XML, and vice versa. This would likely involve a set of XSL style sheets that translate between the CIM meta-model and XML.

Although a schema could be mapped from CIM to XML, the preferred approach would be to describe the CIM meta-model using an XML encoding.

Summary

This chapter briefly introduced CIM, defined its goals, and described the two components of CIM. These are the CIM specification and the common information model. The CIM specification provides a complete meta-model for defining how management information should be represented and structured. The CIM specification also defines additional constructs for closely integrating the needs of management applications with CIM. These include events, triggers, indications (for relating event-based applications to CIM), and qualifiers. Qualifiers are an extensible mechanism for defining metadata that define additional semantics for CIM objects.

The MOF language was briefly described. Its advantage is that it defines a simple, human-readable, textual format for describing richly structured management information.

The CIM namespace was briefly described. This is an important concept, as it enables different sets of objects to be integrated into a larger whole, while maintaining any local relationships between those objects.

Mapping between CIM and other management formats was discussed. The DMTF is currently investigating the use of XML as a standard way of performing these mappings, as well as serving as a transport for CIM data.

CIM itself was briefly described. It is a layered model, with Core, Common, and Extension models, was introduced. The Core Model defines a foundation for describing managed objects. The Common Models describe frequently occurring concepts and components in several common application areas, such as networks, systems and devices. Finally, Extension Models can be built to extend the concepts in the Core and Common models to meet application-specific needs.

Finally, recommendations were given that describe how to extend the common information model, and what features of CIM should and should not be used.

Recommended Further Study and References

For more information about the CIM specification, refer to the CIM home page:

`http://www.dmtf.org/spec/cims.html`

The CIM Specification and various versions of the CIM Schema are available for download from the above Web site. The MOF editor and parser, which are available to DMTF members only, are also available from the above Web site.

The main home page for DMTF members for the various DMTF working groups is

`http://www.dmtf.org/restricted/workgroup.html`

For more information about UML, refer to the following Web site:

`http://www.rational.com/uml`

And the following books:

Booch, G., Jacobson, I., and J. Rumbaugh. *The Unified Modeling Language User Guide.* Reading, MA: Addison-Wesley, 1998.

Eriksson, H. and M. Penker. *UML Toolkit.* New York, NY: John Wiley & Sons, 1997.

Fowler, M., Scott, K., and G. Booch. *UML Distilled: Applying the Standard Object Modeling Language.* Reading, MA: Addison-Wesley, 1997.

Larman, C. *Applying UML and Patterns: An Introduction to Object-Oriented Analysis and Design.* Upper-Saddle River, NJ: Prentice-Hall, 1997.

Quatrani, T. *Visual Modeling With Rational Rose and UML.* Reading, MA: Addison-Wesley, 1998.

Warmer, J. and A. Kleppe. *The Object Constraint Language: Precise Modeling with UML.* Reading, MA: Addison-Wesley, 1998.

The Interface Definition Language is defined by The Open Group as part of CORBA 1.1 in 1991. You can find more information on IDL and CORBA at this Web site:

```
http://www.omg.org/corba/
```

For more information about XML, go to the following Web site:

```
http://www.w3.org/XML/
```

For more information about XML vocabularies, go to the following Web site:

```
http://www.oasis-open.org/cover/xml.html#applications
```

CHAPTER

7

CIM: The Foundation of DEN

The purpose of this chapter is to provide a detailed technical background on CIM. This serves two goals:

- To familiarize the reader with the base CIM classes that are used by and serve as base classes for DEN

- To gain a better understanding of the information model, so that extensions to it for modeling network elements and services can be better designed

Overview of CIM

The *Common Information Model (CIM)* is an object-oriented information model that is designed to manage many common aspects of complex computer systems and their components. This includes the management of systems, software, users, and networks.

CIM defines a management model that consists of a common conceptual framework for describing a managed environment. This is done using an information model, which provides not only a fundamental classification of knowledge in the form of a class inheritance hierarchy, but also a set of aggregation hierarchies that define how managed objects in the system are related to each other. In addition, CIM defines a common set of classes (including relationships) that can be used to establish a common framework upon which to model and represent managed systems and their components.

CIM unifies the existing instrumentation and management standards (SNMP, DMI, CMIP, and so on) using object-oriented constructs and design. In particular, note that CIM does not try to replace any of these standards. Rather, CIM provides an information model that is independent of any particular storage format that defines how to use information from different sources, in different formats, to represent a managed system and its components.

CIM accomplishes this unification using an object-oriented information model. This approach enables abstraction, inheritance, and classification to be used to reduce the overall complexity of the system and its components. Abstraction enables the developer to focus on specific aspects of the system in exclusion of the rest of the system, in order to better understand those components. These entities can then be grouped into types (for example, classes) by identifying common characteristics (for example, attributes), relationships (for example, associations and aggregations) and behavior (for example, methods). Inheritance can then be used to help refine higher-level concepts. Subclasses are used to place the right level of detail at the right level in the model.

Of these concepts, the ability to depict relationships, such as dependencies and whole-part aggregations, are extremely powerful concepts. This differentiates CIM from previous efforts that have tried to capture such relationships using multi-dimensional arrays or data tables. CIM's object paradigm offers a more elegant approach in that relationships are modeled directly. Further semantics and information can be provided in properties (specifying common characteristics and features) and methods (which specify specific behavior) of the relationships.

Another important goal of CIM is to model all of the various aspects of the system being managed, not just a single area. To this end, a "Core" Model is created to provide a common set of base classes and relationships that are common to all managed systems. This is supplemented with a set of "Common Models" that address specific System, Device, Network, Database, User and Application domains. "Extension Models," such as DEN, are then built by taking the Core Model and parts of applicable Common Models. This serves as the foundation for building application-specific models.

CIM was originally focused on enabling enterprise management of devices and applications. While this is still somewhat true, the Networks model in particular addresses service provider needs as well. This reflects the blurring of enterprise and service provider needs, as evidenced by the outsourcing of enterprise intranets, virtual private networks, and other services provided to enterprise organizations by service providers.

A primary goal of CIM is to present a consistent view of the managed environment that is independent of the various protocols and data formats used by those devices and applications. DEN builds on this goal, modeling network elements and services, and their relationships to other entities in the managed system, as an extension of CIM. The DEN extended schema is primarily concerned with the expression and management of network element and network service information in both enterprise and service provider networks. DEN's representation of network element and service information complements and enhances the network model of CIM by defining a binding of how to represent this information in a directory.

Modeling Methodology

CIM uses a unique approach to modeling. This section defines this approach.

The CIM management model is divided into three layers:

- *Core Model*—A set of classes that provide a common inheritance and (set of) aggregation hierarchies that are applicable to all management domains.

- *Common Models*—Models that elaborate on specific management domains but are still independent of a particular technology or implementation. They include the System, Device, Physical, Network, Database, User, and Service Level Agreement models.

- *Extension Models*—Models that represent either a technology-, platform-, and/or implementation-specific extension of the Core Model and one or more of the Common models. DEN is one such extension. Extension models are built to address application- and/or platform-specific needs.

Physical Hierarchy Versus Logical Hierarchy

A fundamental design goal of CIM (and therefore DEN) is to separate the classification of objects into a Physical Hierarchy and a Logical Hierarchy (here, "hierarchy" means both the structural object classes that define inheritance relationships as well as the set of aggregation and association hierarchies, which define relationships between objects). This is a fundamental partitioning of knowledge that spans the core, common and extension models.

Difference Between Physical and Logical Entities

Physical entities represent any component of a system that has a physical identity. This can be simplified into a basic rule: If you can touch the entity, or attach a label to it, then it belongs in the Physical hierarchy.

On the other hand, logical entities represent any component of a system that is "realized" by installing and (re-)configuring physical elements, either directly or indirectly. Logical elements typically represent systems, system components and capabilities, and software. Also, when you talk about *managing* a component, you are talking about an abstract capability, and that means that you are using entities from the logical hierarchy. So, as a general rule: Logical elements are used to represent the functions and capabilities of systems and system components, as well as to manage those components.

Partitioning Physical and Logical Entities

CIM defines a ManagedSystemElement class as the root of all components that will be managed in the system, regardless of whether they are physical or logical entities. Two subclasses, appropriately called PhysicalElement and LogicalElement, represent the base classes of physical and logical managed entities. Conceptually, ManagedSystemElement provides the abstraction of a managed component of a system, and the physical and logical aspects of that managed component are represented in one or more subclasses of the PhysicalElement and LogicalElement classes, respectively. This is shown in Figure 7.1. (These classes will be defined shortly in the sections "The ManagedSystemElement Class and Its Relationships," "The PhysicalElement Class and Its Relationships," and "The LogicalElement Class and Its Relationships.")

Figure 7.1   Representing physical and logical entities in CIM.

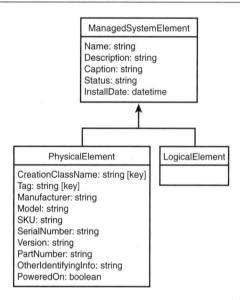

Note that the PhysicalElement class has attributes, while the LogicalElement class does not. While both are abstract base classes, the PhysicalElement class can define some common attributes and relationships that all managed physical entities must have. This is much harder to do for managed logical entities. In addition, the CIM Technical Development Committee (TDC) of the DMTF worried that new functions and services would need to be modeled in the future that we could not anticipate. Therefore, there was no real value in assigning attributes and relationships to the LogicalElement class; it was used solely for classification purposes.

Note

The CIM TDC is chartered with guiding the development of CIM. It is an architecture committee that defines and enhances the meta schema (the schema defining the schema), MOF, and the core schema and common schemata.

The CIM TDC consists of board members, alliance partner representatives and the chairs of the working groups (of course, each company only gets one vote).

This partitioning is so fundamental to CIM that it deserves more elaboration. The CIM designers like to refer to Webster's definition of "realization," which is "to make real; ... to bring into concrete existence; to accomplish."

Note that aggregation can apply both to physical as well as logical elements. A physical or a logical entity can be composed of multiple parts. For example, consider a chassis. It is composed of a physical enclosure, slots that accommodate cards, connectors that connect the cards to the enclosure, and many other things. All of these are physical entities; you can attach a label to any of them.

Similarly, an operating system can be described in terms of its components. For example, most operating systems have the concept of *processes* (also called *tasks*) that represent all or part of a program that is running. Processes are part of an operating system, so instances of the Process class are weak to instances of the OperatingSystem class that hosts the processes. This is represented by the OSProcess aggregation. Similarly, a Process may consist of a set of Threads. This represents the ability to execute portions of a Process in parallel. A second aggregation, called the ProcessThread aggregation, defines which Threads are associated with which Processes (see the section "Processes and Threads" later in this chapter).

These are all fundamentally logical concepts. The power of CIM is that it enables you to go from a logical concept (a process running in an operating system) to the physical realization of that logical concept (for example, the specific computer system that is hosting the operating system).

Note

This is a recurring theme that will be illustrated and referred to throughout the rest of this book. *Associations* and *aggregations* are used to link the physical and logical aspects of an object together, and to go from the physical domain to the logical domain (or vice versa). For example, the Realizes relationship is used to associate the particular card that is hosting the modem functionality (a physical entity) with the actual communication being done using the modem (a logical entity).

If an aggregation is present, then multiple relationships would be instantiated to relate each of the component parts to its logical (or physical) realization. For example, a System can host several types of LogicalDevices (for example, a Processor, a NetworkAdapter, and a Modem). For each of these relationships, an aggregation would be instantiated between the instance of the System class and each instance of the LogicalDevice subclass.

Sometimes this applies at several levels. For example, consider a multi-function card that contains both a modem as well as an Ethernet adapter. As we will see later in this chapter, the modem and the ethernet adapter are both instances of a LogicalDevice, and are both related to the instance of the Card class (which is ultimately a subclass of PhysicalElement) through the inherited Realizes association (also defined later in this chapter). You cannot attach a label to either the ethernet adapter or the modem. This is because both perform logical functions. The fact that they are hosted on a (physical) card means that one can attach a label to the Card that contains those two functions. Furthermore, the modem is actually composed of several things, including physical cabling and the actual software that realizes the communication functions provided by the modem.

The power of CIM is that it enables you to model these recursive relationships, and use the principle of abstraction to separate the physical aspects of a complex entity from its logical components. This in turn enhances the manageability of the entire entity (for example, you can differentiate between a software bug and a faulty cable).

Managing Components and Services

Furthermore, when you instrument the modem to manage it, you will be using logical entities (specifically, instances of the ServiceAccessPoint class, defined in the "Services and ServiceAccessPoints" section later in this chapter). Thus, CIM differentiates between the physical manifestation of the function and both the logical realization as well as the management of the function.

Other Design Themes

This section is a collection of the major additional design themes that are present in CIM.

CIM attempts to generalize as much knowledge as possible. Therefore, many of the classes and the relationships are defined to be abstract. Care should be taken that your application derives an appropriate subclass that is concrete. The most common error found in extension schemata is that an abstract association or aggregation is placed between two concrete classes.

Sometimes, and possibly not often enough, attribute types are used to prevent unnecessary class explosion. This builds on the discussion from the section "Generalization Versus Specialization" in Chapter 3, "Extending the Information Model." While different attribute values can certainly be used as a basis for specialization, it is equally correct to use a single enumerated attribute for the basis of generalization. In other words, a single enumerated attribute can be used to identify the "type" of object, as opposed to making as many subclasses as there are enumerated values. This obviously only works if the only difference between these subclasses is the value of the attribute that serves as the basis for generalization.

Complex objects are best represented by abstracting them into multiple simpler objects. Relationships can then be used to join these different "aspects" of an object back together.

Finally, multiple inheritance is sometimes desired. CIM doesn't support multiple inheritance. However, with clever class design, this problem can be solved. One common way to do this is to define two class hierarchies and then use an association to link them together. For simpler cases, an alternate method is to use a type attribute that can be used to provide the additional classification mechanism.

CIM Classes That Are Used in DEN

This section describes the various CIM classes in the Core and Common models that are either used in DEN, or are likely to be used in a network-enabled application.

> **Note**
>
> In the following descriptions, any relationship whose cardinality is not explicitly discussed is a zero-or-more to zero-or-more relationship (see the "Qualified Relationships" section in Chapter 2, "What Is Object-Oriented Modeling?"). This information is as defined in a late interim version of the 2.2 CIM schema.

Core Model Classes

The Core Model defines the fundamental classification of knowledge that represents entities, as well as relationships between entities, that are part of a managed system. It therefore represents a starting point for building any desired application model. Furthermore, the philosophy of CIM is such that the developer or analyst will not add classes to the Core Model, but rather to the Common Models. The purpose of the Core schema is to ensure that a uniform approach to modeling a managed environment is taken by all applications.

This section first describes the purpose of the Core Model. It then analyzes the classes and relationships that comprise it, concentrating on those classes and relationships that are of interest to DEN.

Modeling Principles of the Core Model

The Core Model recognizes that entities can be complex in nature. Therefore, CIM, when viewed as a knowledge hierarchy, is partitioned into three areas:

- Physical aspects of a managed entity

- Logical aspects of a managed entity

- Other aspects that are part of a managed environment

Physical aspects of an entity are those that occupy space. They represent objects that you can feel and touch. *Logical aspects* are abstractions (for example, software) that manage and coordinate aspects of the physical portion of the managed environment. Types of logical elements include systems, networks, components of a system or a network, services, and abstractions of hardware entities that perform functions (for example, a "printer").

CIM provides for an object to be either a member of one of the preceding three sub-hierarchies, or to incorporate aspects of two or all of them. For example, a chassis is a purely physical object, software is a purely logical object, and a router can be viewed as a product and a system that has both physical as well as logical properties and functions.

The real power of the Core Model is in the various associations that it defines. These associations provide a foundation for relating different aspects of a component, as well as different entities, to each other.

The remaining sections will describe each of the main elements of the Core Model in detail. It is very important that the Core Model be understood before progressing to the other Common Models.

The ManagedSystemElement *Class and Its Relationships*

The ManagedSystemElement class is the base class that represents any entity, whether it is a complex system or a component of a system, that is to be managed. Examples include software components, devices and other physical components, networks, and systems. In addition, the Component and Dependency relationships, along with several others, are defined for ManagedSystemElements.

An excerpt of the Core Model that shows the ManagedSystemElement class is shown in Figure 7.2. Note that this is not the entire Core Model, just the portion in which ManagedSystemElement is defined.

Figure 7.2 Core Model excerpt: ManagedSystemElement and its relationships.

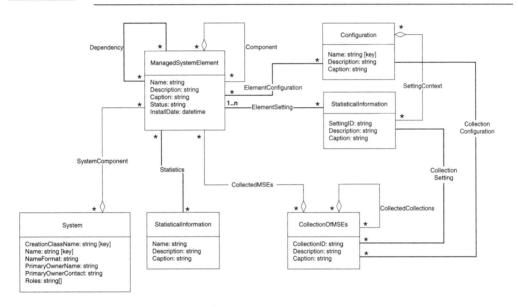

The ManagedSystemElement class has five properties. None of these properties are key properties, in order to enable the subclasses of the ManagedSystemElement class to define their own keys. Remember, the purpose of the ManagedSystemElement class is to define the abstraction of an entity that is being managed, and key properties are not necessary to do this. Key properties are instead used to refine different types of managed entities.

> **Note**
>
> In addition, remember that CIM restricts the definition of keys. Specifically, if a class defines one or more keys, then all subclasses of that class cannot define any keys. Thus, if keys were defined in ManagedSystemElement, then no other class in the managed object hierarchy would be able to define a key.

The five properties of the ManagedSystemElement class are

- The Caption attribute is a short one-line textual description of the entity. This is used mostly for GUI purposes when navigating CIM repositories. It is defined as a string of up to 64 characters.

- The Description attribute provides a free-form textual description of the entity.

- The InstallDate attribute defines when the entity was installed. However, the absence of a value does not indicate that the entity was not installed; it simply means that the date and time of installation was not known. This is a datetime data type.

- The Name attribute defines the label by which the object is known. It is defined as a string of up to 256 characters.

- The Status attribute is an enumerated string that indicates the current status of the object. The current values of the enumeration are "OK", "Error", "Degraded", "Unknown", "Pred Fail", "Starting", "Stopping", "Service", "Stressed", and "NonRecover". It is defined as a string of up to 10 characters.

The ManagedSystemElement class defines no methods. However, it does define seven important relationships, which are detailed in the following sections.

The Dependency Association

The first is a generic association that defines a dependency relationship between two objects. It is called Dependency. This is an abstract association, and is intended to be used as the superclass of specific associations that represent more detailed dependencies between two objects. Accordingly, the antecedent and the dependent of this relationship are both defined as ManagedSystemElements. The dependencies that can be related are loosely classified into functional dependencies (for example, the dependent object cannot function without the antecedent object), or dependencies that relate to some other aspect of the managed environment (for example, the dependent object cannot exist without the antecedent object).

The Component Aggregation

The next important association is the Component aggregation. This is a generic aggregation that is used to establish "whole-part" relationships between ManagedSystemElements. Accordingly, it is an abstract aggregation, and both the aggregate as well as the part components are defined to be ManagedSystemElements to enable more specific whole-part relationships to be defined as subclasses of this relationship.

The Statistics Association

The Statistics association is defined as a structural association that relates a ManagedSystemElement to a StatisticalInformation object. This relationship is used to define statistics that are captured for a given ManagedSystemElement. This enables a common representation and format of statistical information to be provided for any type of ManagedSystemElement as a subclass of the StatisticalInformation class. The reason for this separation is that statistics are usually specific to a particular view of the entity by a specific type of application. In other words, this represents special information that is not of general interest. Thus, by separating this information into a separate class hierarchy, but providing a relationship that links classes of that hierarchy to ManagedSystemElements, the two domains are effectively linked without having to involve the classes of one domain with the classes of the other domain.

The SystemComponent Aggregation

The next relationship, the SystemComponent aggregation, is actually a specialization of the more generic Component aggregation, and is used to establish "whole-part" relationships between a System and the ManagedSystemElements that compose the System.

Listing 7.1 consists of excerpts from the definition for the SystemComponent aggregation class:

Listing 7.1   The definition of the SystemComponent aggregation.

```
[Association, Aggregation, Description ...]
class CIM_SystemComponent:CIM_Component{ [Override ("GroupComponent"), Aggregate,
Description ("The parent System in the Association.") ]
    CIM_System REF GroupComponent;
...
};
```

There are three parts to this example:

- First, in order to declare the SystemComponent relationship as an aggregation, both the Association and the Aggregation keywords must be used.

- Second, SystemComponent is defined to be a subclass of the Component aggregation in the class definition by first listing the SystemComponent class, then appending a colon, and then appending its superclass (Component). Note that the entire genealogy does not have to be listed in the definition.

- Finally, the SystemComponent aggregation defines a relationship between the System and the ManagedSystemElements that are contained in the System. However, the parent class (Component) defines this as a relationship between ManagedSystemElements and ManagedSystemElements. Thus, we need the Override keyword to denote the fact that the aggregate has been specialized from a ManagedSystemElement to a System object.

Note

It is important to remember that the use of the keyword Override is for MOF definitional purposes only. From an object-oriented modeling point-of-view, we are restricting the type of class that can participate in this relationship. In particular, we are *not* changing the class itself. Furthermore, the fundamental purpose of the relationship—to define a whole-part relationship—is still the same.

The ElementConfiguration and ElementSetting Associations

The next two relationships, ElementConfiguration and ElementSetting, are very generic in nature. The ElementConfiguration relationship is a structural association whose purpose is to relate a Configuration object to one or more ManagedSystemElements. The multiplicity of this relationship is zero-or-more to zero-or-more. Similarly, the ElementSetting relationship is a structural association whose purpose is to relate a Setting object to one or more ManagedSystemElements. The cardinality of this relationship is one-or-more on the ManagedSystemElement side and zero-or-more on the Setting side. This means that if a Setting object is defined, then it must be associated with at least one ManagedSystemElement.

Configurations and Settings are currently being used to help define the *state* of the managed environment and its components. That is, they represent a set of commands and/or operational parameters that can be used to either transition a component or a system to a new state, or maintain its existing state. They therefore represent a link to accompanying behavioral models that can be used in conjunction with CIM.

> **Note**
>
> These relationships are really intended to serve as base relationships that can be subclassed to provide the appropriate scoping to the subclass of ManagedSystemElement that they refer to. This is why they, along with the Configuration and Setting classes, are very generically defined. This will be discussed further in the section "The Setting and Configuration Classes" later in this chapter when the Configuration and Setting objects themselves are discussed.

The PhysicalElement *Class and Its Relationships*

The PhysicalElement class is the root class of the physical portion of the CIM hierarchy. It is an abstract class, and is not meant to be instantiated. An excerpt of the Core Model that focuses on the PhysicalElement class is shown in Figure 7.3.

Figure 7.3   Core Model excerpt: PhysicalElement and its relationships.

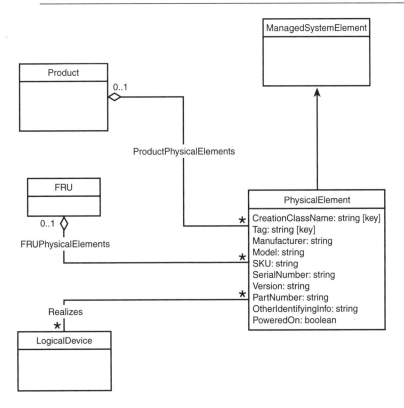

Remember, a physical entity is an object that can have a label physically attached to it. Therefore, entities like software programs and processes, services, and systems are not physical elements.

The PhysicalElement class has a composite key, consisting of the CreationClassName and Tag attributes. This composite key enables any instance of any subclass of the PhysicalElement class to be identified, regardless of whether the entity is an individual or aggregate component and where it is physically located. This is especially important, as objects of the PhysicalPackage class (which is a subclass of the PhysicalElement class) and the subclasses of the PhysicalPackage class may be defined as being removable and/or hot-swappable. Here, a removable component is defined as a component that is designed to be taken in and out of its enclosing physical container without impairing the functionality of the overall packaging of the entity. A component is defined to be hot-swappable if it is possible to replace that component with a physically different but equivalent component while its containing PhysicalPackage has power applied to it.

The reason that this is important is that a component that is removable and/or hot-swappable may be taken from its containing PhysicalPackage. This means that the component is temporarily outside of its scoping hierarchy. This may be done to move it to a different container, to move it into a parts inventory, or for other reasons. In any case, the component still physically exists, and must be able to be found regardless of whether it is inside its container or not. Therefore, the (composite) key for instances of the PhysicalElement class are defined independently of any container or location information.

The PhysicalElement class defines the following 10 attributes, which all physical entities inherit:

- CreationClassName defines the name of the class used to create an instance of this class. It is part of the composite key of the PhysicalElement class (and therefore all of the subclasses of the PhysicalElement class). Its purpose is to enable all of the different instances of this class and its subclasses to be uniquely identified. It is defined to be a string of up to 256 characters.

- Tag is the other part of the composite key of the PhysicalElement class. It is also defined to be a string of up to 256 characters. The Tag attribute is used to store data that can be used to help uniquely identify a particular instance of a PhysicalElement class (for example, the serial number of the physical component).

- Manufacturer is defined as a string of up to 256 characters, and is the name of the organization responsible for producing the PhysicalElement.

- Model is defined as a string of up to 64 characters, and is the name by which the PhysicalElement is generally known or cataloged by its manufacturer.

- SKU, or Stock Keeping Unit, is defined as a string of up to 64 characters, and is the SKU number assigned to the instance of this PhysicalElement class.

- SerialNumber is defined as a string of up to 64 characters, and is the serial number that is allocated by the manufacturer. This number can sometimes be used to identify the instance of the PhysicalElement class. However, there are cases where it is not unique, and so the Tag attribute is used as the key for the class.

- Version is defined as a string of up to 64 characters. It is the version number of the instance of this PhysicalElement class, as defined by the manufacturer.

- PartNumber is defined as a string of up to 256 characters, and is the part number assigned by the manufacturer to this instance of this PhysicalElement class.

- OtherIdentifyingInfo is a free-form string that is used to store additional data that could be used to differentiate between different instances of the same type of PhysicalElement class. Examples include bar code data, asset tags, and product numbers. However, if the only unique identifying information is already contained in one of the attributes of the class (for example, the Tag and the SerialNumber attributes), then this attribute would be NULL.

- PoweredOn is a boolean attribute that indicates if the instance of the PhysicalElement class is powered on (value is TRUE) or not (value is FALSE).

The PhysicalElement class defines three relationships: the ProductPhysicalElements aggregation, the FRUPhysicalElements aggregation, and the Realizes association.

The ProductPhysicalElements Aggregation

The ProductPhysicalElements aggregation is a structural relationship that defines the various PhysicalElement instances that compose a Product. The cardinality of this relationship is restricted to zero-or-one on the Product side. This means that the relationship does not have to exist, but if it does, at most one Product takes part in the relationship. The cardinality of the other side of the relationship is zero-or-more, which means that any number of PhysicalElements can be associated with a single Product.

The FRUPhysicalElements Aggregation

The FRUPhysicalElements aggregation is a structural relationship that defines the various PhysicalElement instances that compose a Field Replaceable Unit (which is represented by the FRU class in CIM). Again, the cardinality of this relationship is restricted to zero-or-one on the FRU side, while the cardinality of the other side of the relationship is zero-or-more. This means that any number of PhysicalElements can be associated with a single FRU.

The `Realizes` *Association*

The final relationship is the `Realizes` association. This very important association defines the `LogicalDevices` that are associated with this `PhysicalElement`. As we will see in the section "Members of the `LogicalElement` Hierarchy," a `LogicalDevice` is an abstraction or emulation of a physical entity for management purposes, has a distinct function that it provides (for example, a keyboard or monitor) and provides `Services` and access to `Services`. The `Realizes` association is a subclass of the more general `Dependency` association. The `Realizes` association refines the `Dependency` association by restricting the antecedent from a `ManagedSystemElement` to a `PhysicalElement` and restricting the dependent from a `ManagedSystemElement` to a `LogicalDevice`.

The `LogicalElement` *Class*

The `LogicalElement` class is one of the few examples of a class whose purpose is for classification and organization of knowledge only. It is an abstract class, and has no attributes or methods. It is the base class for all of the logical components of a `System` that represent non-physical functions. This includes abstract components, such as software programs and processes, as well as services, systems, and logical devices. It also includes the manageability aspects of these entities.

Members of the `LogicalElement` *Hierarchy*

The Core Model defines four important subclasses of the `LogicalElement` class. These are the `LogicalDevice`, `System`, `Service`, and `ServiceAccessPoint` classes. These four classes are described in the following subsections.

The `LogicalDevice` *Class and Its Relationships*

The `LogicalDevice` class and its relationships are illustrated in Figure 7.4.

The `LogicalDevice` class is an abstract class, and forms the base class of all objects that are abstractions or emulations of a physical component. The association with the physical component that the `LogicalDevice` class is representing is provided through the `Realizes` association.

A `LogicalDevice` is used to represent a particular function of a physical entity, and provides a way to capture services that are realized by the abstraction of that hardware as well as provide a means to manage it. For example, the current status of a printer is defined as an attribute of the `Printer` class, which is a subclass of the `LogicalDevice` class. Here, a subclass of the `LogicalDevice` class (`Printer`) is used to capture operational characteristics of the printer. Such characteristics are related to the particular printer instance through the `Realizes` association.

Figure 7.4   Core Model excerpt: `LogicalElement` and its relationships.

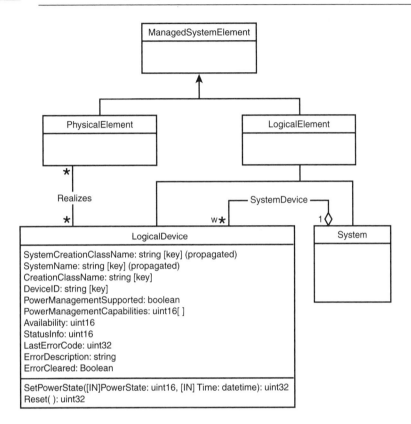

The `LogicalDevice` class receives two propagated attributes, and defines nine attributes, two relationships, and two methods. The `LogicalDevice` class has a composite key consisting of four key attributes. They are the `SystemCreationClassName`, `SystemName`, `CreationClassName`, and `DeviceID` attribute. The first two are propagated from the `System` class, which serves as the scoping container for all `LogicalDevices`. This provides the ability to uniquely identify the names of different instances of the same `LogicalDevice` that belong to different systems. The last two are defined to help distinguish between different instances of `LogicalDevices` within the same container.

Put another way, all `LogicalDevices` can be distinguished from each other by the combination of the following four attributes (which are concatenated to form the composite key of all `LogicalDevices`):

- The name of the `System` class that was used to create the instance of the system that hosts the instance of the `LogicalDevice`

- The name of the `System` itself

- The name of the `LogicalDevice` class that was used to create the instance of the `LogicalDevice`

- A unique feature that helps differentiate between different instances of the same type of `LogicalDevice`

The two propagated attributes are

- `SystemCreationClassName` is a *propagated key* from the `System` class. It is a string, whose maximum length is 256 characters. Referring to Figure 7.4, we see that a *weak* aggregation, `SystemDevice`, exists between an instance of a `LogicalDevice` and an instance of a `System`. Recall from "The Weak Qualifier" in Chapter 6, "A Brief Introduction to CIM," that a *weak* relationship is one in which an instance is named within the context of another object instance. In order to do this, a weak association is used to relate the instance of the `LogicalDevice` class to the instance of the `System` class in which it resides. The identity of the instance of the `LogicalDevice` class depends on the name of the `LogicalDevice` class as well as the name of the `System` class in which it resides. This latter is supplied by propagating the `SystemCreationClassName` from the `System` class to the `LogicalDevice` class. The former is supplied by the `CreationClassName` of the `LogicalDevice`.

- `SystemName` is also a propagated key from the `System` class. It is defined as a string, whose maximum length is also 256 characters. This is the name of the `System` in which the instance of the `LogicalDevice` class is defined.

The nine attributes that it defines are

- `CreationClassName` is a key attribute, and defines the name of the class that was used to create this instance (for example, the `LogicalDevice` class or the appropriate subclass of the `LogicalDevice` class). This is a string, whose maximum length is 256 characters.

- DeviceID is the final key attribute for the LogicalDevice class. It is also a string, whose maximum length is 64 characters, that contains additional information that can help uniquely identify different instances of this class. For example, DeviceID could contain the address of the printer in the earlier example, which would enable two printers of the same manufacturer to have the same name (for example, "Admin Printer") but still be uniquely identifiable in the network.

- PowerManagementSupported is a boolean attribute that indicates whether the instance of the LogicalDevice class has any power management capabilities or not. Note that this attribute does *not* indicate whether or not such features are currently active. This is instead defined by the PowerManagementCapabilities attribute.

- PowerManagementCapabilities is a 16-bit unsigned integer array. An array is used to enable multiple features to be listed for a device. Its purpose is to indicate the specific power management capabilities of this instance of the LogicalDevice class. Note that if the value of the PowerManagementSupported boolean attribute is FALSE, then the corresponding value for this attribute should be 1 (not supported). Furthermore, this should be the *only* value in the PowerManagementCapabilities array. Listing 7.2 is an excerpt from the Core MOF file shows the values that are currently supported (and also how to define an unsigned integer array):

Listing 7.2 MOF definition for the PowerManagementCapabilities attribute.

```
[Description(
    "Indicates the specific power-related capabilities of a LogicalDevice. The
    array values, 0=\"Unknown\", 1=\"Not Supported\" and 2=\"Disabled\" are self-
    explanatory. The value, 3=\"Enabled\" indicates that the power management
    features are currently enabled but the exact feature set is unknown or the
    information is unavailable. \"Power Saving Modes Entered Automatically\" (4)
    describes that a Device can change its power state based on usage or other
    criteria. \"Power State Settable\" (5) indicates that the SetPowerState method
    is supported. \"Power Cycling Supported\" (6) indicates that the SetPowerState
    method can be invoked with the PowerState input variable set to 5 (\"Power
    Cycle\"). \"Timed Power On Supported\" (7) indicates that the SetPowerState
    method can be invoked with the Power State input variable set to 5 (\"Power
    Cycle\") and the Time parameter set to a specific date and time, or interval,
    for power-on."),

Values {"Unknown", "Not Supported", "Disabled", "Enabled", "Power Saving Modes
Entered Automatically", "Power State Settable", "Power Cycling Supported","Timed
Power On Supported"} ]

    uint16 PowerManagementCapabilities[];
```

- Availability is a 16-bit unsigned integer whose value signifies the current availability and status of the instance of the LogicalDevice class. Listing 7.3 is an excerpt from the Core MOF file that shows the values that are currently supported. The ValueMap and Values qualifiers are used to associate specific array (indexed) values with text (e.g. "7" corresponds to "PowerOff").

Listing 7.3	MOF definition for the Availability attribute.

```
[Description (
   "The availability and status of the Device.  For example, the Availability
   property indicates that the Device is running and has full power (value=3), or
   is in a warning (4), test (5), degraded (10) or power save state (values 13-15
   and 17). Regarding the Power Save states, these are defined as follows: Value
   13 (\"Power Save - Unknown\") indicates that the Device is known to be in a
   power save mode, but its exact status in this mode is unknown; 14 (\"Power
   Save - Low Power Mode\") indicates that the Device is in a power save state
   but still functioning, and may exhibit degraded performance; 15 (\"Power Save
   - Standby\") describes that the Device is not functioning but could be brought
   to full power 'quickly'; and value 17 (\"Power Save - Warning\") indicates
   that the Device is in a warning state, though also in a power save mode."),

ValueMap {"1", "2", "3", "4", "5", "6", "7", "8", "9", "10", "11", "12", "13",
➡"14", "15", "16", "17", "18", "19"},

Values {"Other", "Unknown", "Running/Full Power", "Warning", "In Test", "Not
   Applicable", "Power Off", "Off Line", "Off Duty", "Degraded", "Not Installed",
   "Install Error", "Power Save - Unknown", "Power Save - Low Power Mode", "Power
   Save - Standby", "Power Cycle", "Power Save - Warning", "Paused", "Not Ready"},

MappingStrings {"MIF.DMTF¦Operational State¦003.5",
   "MIB.IETF¦HOST-RESOURCES-MIB.hrDeviceStatus"} ]

uint16 Availability;
```

- StatusInfo is a 16-bit enumerated unsigned integer, whose various values correspond to standard strings. These values are used to describe the current state of the LogicalDevice. Listing 7.4 is an excerpt from the Core MOF file defines the various values for this attribute.

Listing 7.4   MOF definition for the StatusInfo attribute.

```
[Description(
    "StatusInfo is a string indicating whether the LogicalDevice is in an enabled
    (value = 3), disabled (value = 4) or some other (1) or unknown (2) state. If
    this property does not apply to the LogicalDevice, the value, 5 (\"Not
    Applicable\"), should be used."),

ValueMap {"1", "2", "3", "4", "5"},

Values {"Other", "Unknown", "Enabled", "Disabled", "Not Applicable"},

MappingStrings {"MIF.DMTF¦Operational State¦003.3"} ]

uint16 StatusInfo;
```

- LastErrorCode is a 32-bit unsigned integer that is used to store the last error code reported by the LogicalDevice.

- ErrorDescription is a free-form string that can be used to store additional information pertaining to the error stored in the LastErrorCode attribute. It may also be used to store information on any corrective actions that may be taken.

- ErrorCleared is a boolean attribute. If it is TRUE, then it indicates that the error reported in the LastErrorCode attribute is now corrected.

The LogicalDevice class also defines two methods. The first, SetPowerState, is used to put a LogicalDevice into a specific power state. Its signature is

```
SetPowerState( [IN] PowerState: uint16, [IN] Time: datetime ) : uint32
```

This means that the SetPowerState method takes two input parameters (PowerState, a 16-bit unsigned integer, and Time, a datetime) and returns a 32-bit integer result. The PowerState variable enables the user to specify the desired power management setting, and the Time variable enables the user to specify when the power management setting specified in the PowerState attribute should be set. This can be either a discrete time value or a time interval. Finally, the SetPowerState method is defined to return 0 if successful and 1 if not successful.

Listing 7.5 is an excerpt from the Core MOF file that shows the definition of the SetPowerState method.

Listing 7.5   MOF definition for the SetPowerState method.

```
[Description(
    "SetPowerState defines the desired power state for a LogicalDevice and when a
    Device should be put into that state. The desired power state is specified by
    setting the PowerState parameter to one of the following integer values:
    1=\"Full Power\", 2=\"Power Save - Low Power Mode\", 3=\"Power Save -
    Standby\", 4=\"Power Save - Other\", 5=\"Power Cycle\" or 6=\"Power Off\". The
    Time parameter (for all state changes but 5, "\"Power Cycle\") indicates when
    the power state should be set, either as a regular date-time value or as an
    interval value (where the interval begins when the method invocation is
    received). When the PowerState parameter is equal to 5, \"Power Cycle\", the
    Time parameter indicates when the Device should power on again. Power off is
    immediate. SetPowerState should return 0 if successful, 1 if the specified
    PowerState and Time request is not supported, and some other value if any
    other error occurred.") ]

uint32 SetPowerState([IN] uint16 PowerState, [IN] datetime Time);
```

The other method defined for a LogicalDevice is the Reset method. As its name implies, this method instructs the LogicalDevice to be reset or rebooted. The return value is 0 if the method was successfully executed and 1 if the method was not successfully executed (including the case of the method not being supported for this LogicalDevice instance). The signature of the Reset method is

```
uint32  Reset ( );
```

The LogicalDevice class participates in two relationships. The Realizes association was already defined in the section "The ManagedSystemElement Class and Its Relationships," and serves to bridge between the physical and logical domains. It also participates in the SystemDevice aggregation, which defines the different LogicalDevices that are contained in a System. This relationship is more fully described in the next section.

The System Class and Its Relationships

The purpose of the System class is to aggregate a set of ManagedSystemElements. This aggregation is modeled as a single object in its own right, since the collection of instances of ManagedSystemElements serve one or more discrete purposes. That is, the collection of ManagedSystemElements, when assembled as parts of a greater whole, create a System.

The individual functions of each ManagedSystemElement that are contained in the System are still retained, but a new set of functions is produced by aggregating the ManagedSystemElements into a System. The System object defines how the ManagedSystemElements are to be put together. It also provides a way to *manage* the System itself as well as the individual ManagedSystemElements that comprise it.

The System class serves as the superclass for ComputerSystems, which are systems that possess some form of computing capability. This includes not just servers and PCs, but also things like routers and switches. An excerpt of the Core Model that focuses on the System class is shown in Figure 7.5.

Figure 7.5 Core Model excerpt: System and its relationships.

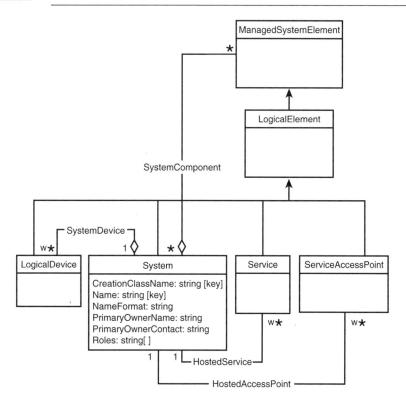

The System class has a composite key consisting of two key attributes. It also defines four other attributes:

- CreationClassName is one of the two key attributes of the System class. It defines the name of the class used in the creation of an instance. It is a string of up to 256 characters.

- Name is the other key attribute of the System class. It is inherited from ManagedSystemElement, and is overridden to be made a key for this attribute. It is a string of up to 256 characters.

Note

It is important to note that the use of the qualifier Override is for MOF definitional purposes only. From an object-oriented modeling point-of-view, the attribute itself is *not* being overridden. The attribute still serves to define the name of the instance, and its data type has not changed. The only thing that has changed is the *usage* of the attribute (from a general-purpose attribute in the ManagedSystemElement class to a special-purpose key attribute in the System class). This is similar to the earlier example of overriding the type of class that can participate in a relationship.

- NameFormat defines how the name of the System was generated. This is important to know, because Systems are used to provide scoping for many managed components. Knowing how the format of the name of the System was generated enables subclasses of the System class to generate the same System name key attribute. NameFormat is a string attribute, whose maximum length is 64 characters.

- PrimaryOwnerContact is a string attribute that can be used to contain information on how the primary owner of the System can be contacted. For example, it may contain the business phone number, email address, pager number, or other contact information. Its maximum length is 256 characters.

- PrimaryOwnerName is the name of the primary owner of the System. It is a string of up to 64 characters.

Note

These two attributes (PrimaryOwnerContact and PrimaryOwnerName) were defined *before* the CIM User Model was created. The CIM User Model will define detailed classes for describing users, organizations, and their relationships. These attributes still have use (for example, both of them could be populated from the relationship between a System and a User in order to simplify searching by certain implementations, such as a directory using the LDAP access protocol). However, care should be taken to ensure that they represent the current values as defined by the appropriate attributes of the User class.

- Roles is an array that specify the different types of roles that this System has in a managed environment. For example, a router (which, as we will see in Chapter 9, "The CIM/DEN Logical (Network) Model," is derived from System) may have several different roles. These may include "Access Device" and "Classification Device." The former enables users to access the network, whereas the latter is more concerned with classifying the type of traffic that is entering the device.

The System class participates in four relationships. The SystemComponent aggregation has already been defined in the section "The ManagedSystemElement Class and Its Relationships." The other three relationships are the SystemDevice aggregation, the HostedService association, and the HostedAccessPoint association.

The SystemDevice aggregation defines the different LogicalDevices that are contained in a System. It is a subclass of the SystemComponent aggregation. It is a *weak* relationship, since the System provides scoping for the LogicalDevices that it contains. The aggregate of this relationship is, of course, the System. The cardinality restricts this to exactly one instance by using both the Max and the Min qualifiers, as shown in Listing 7.6. The component parts are defined to be instances of the LogicalDevice class. Again, note the use of the Override qualifier, which is necessary on the definitions of both the aggregate as well as the part component of the relationship. This is because both sides of the relationship restrict the type of class that can participate in the relationship, among other reasons.

Listing 7.6   MOF definition of the SystemDevice aggregation.

```
[Association, Aggregation, Description (
   LogicalDevices may be aggregated by a System.  This relationship is made
   explicit by the SystemDevice association. ") ]

class CIM_SystemDevice:CIM_SystemComponent
{
[Override ("GroupComponent"), Aggregate, Max (1), Min (1),
   Description ("The parent system in the Association.") ]
CIM_System REF GroupComponent;

[Override ("PartComponent"), Weak,
   Description ("The LogicalDevice that is a component of a System.") ]
CIM_LogicalDevice REF PartComponent; }
```

The `HostedService` association is a subclass of the `Dependency` association. It refines the types of classes that can participate in a dependent relationship, and their interaction. Note that this is now a *weak* relationship, whereas its superclass (the `Dependency` association) is *not* weak). Furthermore, the cardinality of the antecedent (`System`) is defined to be exactly one, instead of zero-or-more, in the `HostedService` relationship.

The `HostedService` association defines the ability for a `System` to host (for example, contain, or provide) a set of `Services`. `Services` are usually associated with `LogicalDevices` and `SoftwareFeatures` that are hosted on the `System`. The cardinality of this relationship is one on the `System` side and zero-or-more on the `Service` side. This is because a `Service` cannot exist without a `System` in which it can reside. Thus, `Services` are weak with respect to the `System` that serves as their host. The Core Model does *not* represent `Services` that are hosted across multiple systems. This is instead modeled as an `ApplicationSystem`, and will be talked about later in this chapter in the section "The `ApplicationSystem` Class and Its Relationships."

Finally, the `HostedAccessPoint` association represents a dependency between a `System` and a `ServiceAccessPoint`. Therefore, it is a subclass of the more generic Dependency association. A `ServiceAccessPoint` represents a means to use, invoke, or manage a `Service`. Thus, we have a `System` which hosts one or more `Services`, and at least one `ServiceAccessPoint` for each hosted `Service`. This relationship is very similar to the `HostedService` association, in that both are weak relationships whose antecedent is an instance of the `System` class (or one of its subclasses). Furthermore, the cardinality is restricted to exactly one on the `System` side of both relationships. The difference is that for the `HostedAccessPoint` association, the dependent is an instance of the `ServiceAccessPoint` class (or one of its subclasses).

The `Service` Class and Its Relationships

The CIM `Service` class is used to represent the manageability of the functions provided by a `LogicalDevice` or a `SoftwareFeature`. The `Service` class does *not* model the function itself; rather, it enables the abstraction of the management of the functions provided by a `LogicalDevice` or a `SoftwareFeature`. Thus, the purpose of the `Service` object is to help configure and manage the implementation of the functions provided by a `LogicalDevice` or a `SoftwareFeature`.

There is a necessarily close relationship between the `System`, `Service`, and `ServiceAccessPoint` classes. `Services` are logical entities, and are always hosted in a `System`. `Services` represent the management aspects of the functions that a `System` provides, while `ServiceAccessPoints` furnish a way to manage the access to the functions that a `System` provides. Thus, `ServiceAccessPoints` are also hosted in a `System`.

An excerpt of the Core Model that focuses on the `Service` and the `ServiceAccessPoint` classes is shown in Figure 7.6.

Figure 7.6   Core Model excerpt: `Service`, `ServiceAccessPoint`, and their relationships.

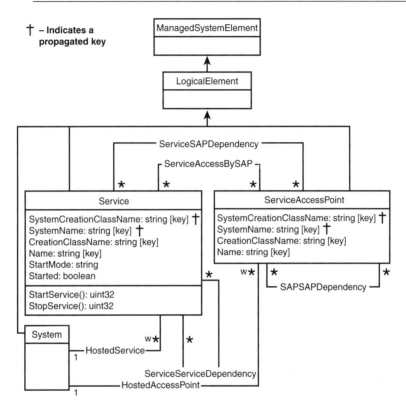

Together, instances of the `Service` and the `ServiceAccessPoint` classes (and their subclasses) separate the configuration and management of the function provided by instances of the `LogicalDevice` and `SoftwareFeature` classes (or their subclasses) from the implementation of these features. For example, the configuration of a printer that can only be accessed by a computer that is directly connected to it is very different than the configuration of that same printer if it is to be accessed by multiple systems through a network.

The following describe the attributes, methods, and most of the relationships of the
Service class. Some remaining relationships between the Service class and other classes will
be deferred until the appropriate Common Model is discussed (otherwise, it will become
very hard for you to refer to the appropriate MOF and Visio file). Of these, the following
four relationships are critical:

- DeviceServiceImplementation—defined in the Device Common Model. This association
  is used to define how a Service is implemented in a LogicalDevice (or one of its subclasses).

- DeviceSAPImplementation—defined in the Device Common Model. This association is
  used to define how a ServiceAccessPoint is implemented in a LogicalDevice (or one of
  its subclasses).

- SoftwareFeatureServiceImplementation—defined in the Application Common Model.
  This association is used to define how a Service is implemented in software using the
  SoftwareFeature class (or one of its subclasses).

- SoftwareFeatureSAPImplementation—defined in the Application Common Model. This
  association is used to define how a ServiceAccessPoint is implemented in software using
  the SoftwareFeature class (or one of its subclasses).

Additional network-specific relationships that involve the Service and the
ServiceAccessPoint classes will be covered in Chapter 9, when ProtocolEndpoints are
discussed.

The attributes of the Service class are as follows:

- SystemCreationClassName is a *propagated key* from the System class. It is a string, whose
  maximum length is 256 characters. This was described earlier in the description of the
  attributes of the LogicalDevice class.

- SystemName is also a propagated key from the System class. It is defined as a string, whose
  maximum length is also 256 characters. This was described earlier in the description of
  the attributes of the LogicalDevice class.

- CreationClassName defines the name of the class used to create an instance of this class.
  It is part of the composite key of the Service class. Its purpose is to enable all of the different instances of this class and its subclasses to be uniquely identified. It is defined to
  be a string of up to 256 characters.

- Name is the other key attribute of the Service class. It is inherited from ManagedSystemElement, and is overridden to be made a key for this attribute. The Name attribute is used to provide a unique name for the service that is being managed. It is a string of up to 256 characters.

- StartMode is a string that indicates whether the service is automatically started by some other entity, or whether it is only started upon specific request. It is a string of at most 10 characters. Two values are defined for this attribute: Automatic and Manual.

- Started is a boolean attribute that indicates whether the service has been started (value is TRUE) or stopped (value is FALSE).

The Service class defines two methods. The StartService method is used to place the service in the started state. As usual, an integer value of 0 is returned if the service was successfully started, and an integer value of 1 is returned if, for any reason, the service was not able to be successfully started. The signature of the StartService method is

```
uint32  StartService ( )
```

The other method that the Service class defines is the StopService method. This method is used to place the service into the stopped state. As usual, an integer value of 0 is returned if the service was successfully stopped, and an integer value of 1 is returned if, for any reason, the service was not able to be successfully stopped. The signature of the StopService method is

```
uint32  StopService ( )
```

The Service class participates in a number of associations, most of which will be described in the following sections. However, there is one important relationship that involves just instances of the Service class. This recursive association, ServiceServiceDependency, is a subclass of the Dependency association, and represents the dependency between multiple Services. That is, if one Service cannot be instantiated unless another Service is present, then the ServiceServiceDependency association is used to represent this. Naturally, both the antecedent and the dependent of this relationship are instances of the Service class. However, this association also defines an attribute, called TypeOfDependency, which is used to describe the nature of the dependency between the services. It is defined in Listing 7.7.

Listing 7.7   MOF definition of the ServiceServiceDependency association.

```
class CIM_ServiceServiceDependency:CIM_Dependency
{
[Override ("Antecedent"),
  Description ("The required Service.") ]

CIM_Service REF Antecedent;

[Override ("Dependent"),
  Description ("The Service that is dependent on an underlying Service.") ]

CIM_Service REF Dependent;

[Description ("The nature of the Service to Service dependency. This
  property describes that the associated Service must have completed (value=2),
  must be started (3) or must not be started (4) in order for the Service to
  function."),

Values {"Unknown", "Other", "Service Must Have Completed", "Service Must Be
  Started", "Service Must Not Be Started"} ]

uint16 TypeOfDependency; }
```

The ServiceAccessPoint Class and Its Relationships

The purpose of the ServiceAccessPoint class is to provide a means to manage and configure access to the function(s) represented by a service.

ServiceAccessPoints cannot be defined until a Service that they provide access to are defined, along with the System that contains the Services.

There are four attributes of a ServiceAccessPoint:

- SystemCreationClassName is a *propagated key* from the System class. It is a string, whose maximum length is 256 characters. This was described earlier in the description of the attributes of the LogicalDevice class.

- SystemName is also a propagated key from the System class. It is defined as a string, whose maximum length is also 256 characters. This was described earlier in the description of the attributes of the LogicalDevice class.

- `CreationClassName` defines the name of the class used to create an instance of this class. It is part of the composite key of the `Service` class. Its purpose is to enable all of the different instances of this class and its subclasses to be uniquely identified. It is defined to be a string of up to 256 characters.

- `Name` is the other key attribute of the `ServiceAccessPoint` class. It is inherited from `ManagedSystemElement`, and is overridden to be made a key for this attribute. The `Name` attribute is used to provide a unique name for the management access of the service that is being managed. It is a string of up to 256 characters.

The `ServiceAccessPoint` class participates in four basic relationships (others will be defined in the context of other Common Models). These are the `HostedAccessPoint`, `SAPSAPDependency`, `ServiceAccessBySAP`, and the `ServiceSAPDependency` associations.

One of them, `HostedAccessPoint`, has already been defined in the section "The `System` Class and Its Relationships." The other three are also subclasses of the `Dependency` relationship.

The `SAPSAPDependency` is a subclass of the `Dependency` association because it restricts the class of both the antecedent and the dependent of this relationship to instances of the `ServiceAccessPoint` class. It represents a dependency between multiple `ServiceAccessPoints`, indicating that the presence of other `ServiceAccessPoint` classes are required in order for a particular `ServiceAccessPoint` class to be able to provide access to its service. For example, a network printer must connect with network `ServiceAccessPoints` in order to send the print request over the network. (These are called `ProtocolEndpoints` and will be defined in Chapter 9).

The `ServiceAccessBySAP` is another subclass of the `Dependency` association, because it restricts the class of the antecedent to instances of the `Service` class, and the class of the dependent to instances of the `ServiceAccessPoint` class. This association represents the actual access points of a service. For example, there could be several ways to access a printer, such as using Netware, Windows, and UNIX. In this case, there would be (at least) three different instances of the `ServiceAccessPoint` class, corresponding to the three different systems that were using it. The antecedent in this association is a `Service`, and the dependent is a `ServiceAccessPoint`.

The final association is the ServiceSAPDependency. This represents the dependency between a ServiceAccessPoint and a Service. This relationship quantifies the dependency of the Service instance on the ServiceAccessPoint instance. For example, many Services depend on the ServiceAccessPoint of *another* Service. A good example is the relationship between a boot service and the BIOS disk service—the boot service may need to invoke one or more BIOS services, which are done by invoking the access points of the BIOS service. Hence, the antecedent is an instance of the ServiceAccessPoint class, while the dependent is an instance of the Service class.

The ComputerSystem Class

The ComputerSystem class is a subclass of the System class. A ComputerSystem represents a special collection of ManagedSystemElements that, as a collection, provide the capability to perform computations. Since a ComputerSystem is a subclass of System, instances of the ComputerSystem class often provide scope for the components, software and services that they contain.

The ComputerSystem class aggregates hardware, software and firmware. Examples of these include the hardware that forms the ComputerSystem, the operating system that the computer system is running, and the various services (for example, the ability to store information in a file system) that it provides.

The ComputerSystem class is defined as an abstract class, and serves mainly as a means to collect different relationships that are common to its subclasses. To this end, it defines no new attributes or methods (though it does override the NameFormat attribute).

The NameFormat attribute is overridden in the ComputerSystem class in order to change the way in which the name of the computer system is formed. Listing 7.8 provides an excerpt of the MOF definition of a ComputerSystem.

Listing 7.8   MOF defintion of the ComputerSystem class.

```
[Abstract, ... ]
class CIM_ComputerSystem : CIM_System
{
[Override ("NameFormat"), Description ("The ComputerSystem object and its
   derivatives are Top Level Objects of CIM. They provide the scope for numerous
   components. Having unique System keys is required. A heuristic is defined to
   create the ComputerSystem Name to attempt to always generate the same Name,
   independent of discovery protocol. This prevents inventory and management
   problems where the same asset or entity is discovered multiple times, but
   cannot be resolved to a single object. Use of the heuristic is optional, but
   recommended.
```

```
The NameFormat property identifies how the ComputerSystem Name is generated,
using a heuristic. The heuristic is outlined, in detail, in the CIM V2 System
Model spec. It assumes that the documented rules are traversed in order, to
determine and assign a Name. The NameFormat Values list defines the precedence
order for assigning the ComputerSystem Name. Several rules do map to the same
Value.

Note that the ComputerSystem Name calculated using the heuristic is the
System's key value. Other names can be assigned and used for the
ComputerSystem, that better suit a business, using Aliases."),

ValueMap {"Other", "IP", "Dial", "HID", "NWA", "HWA", "X25", "ISDN", "IPX",
"DCC", "ICD","E.164", "SNA", "OID/OSI"} ]

string NameFormat; };
```

The ComputerSystem class defines no methods. It does, however, define and participate in many different relationships. However, most of these are with classes that have not yet been defined. Therefore, these will be covered in the section "More About ComputerSystems" later in this section.

Building Products

It is important to relate the management aspects of components in a system to products. CIM provides three classes for this purpose: the Product, FRU, and SupportAccess classes.

The Product Class and Its Relationships

A Product is a concrete class that represents a set of PhysicalElements, software, and other Products, that are purchased from a supplier by a consumer. The Product class is really aimed at covering a form of acquisition, which includes licensing, warranty, and support implications.

The Product class also relates Products to Field Replaceable Units (FRUs), and defines a class and association for describing how support is obtained for a Product. Associations between the Product class and the PhysicalElement and SoftwareFeature classes define a Product in terms of PhysicalElements and software. In addition, a recursive association enables Products to contain other Products.

An excerpt of the Core Model that focuses on the Product class is shown in Figure 7.7.

Figure 7.7   Core Model excerpt: Product and its relationships.

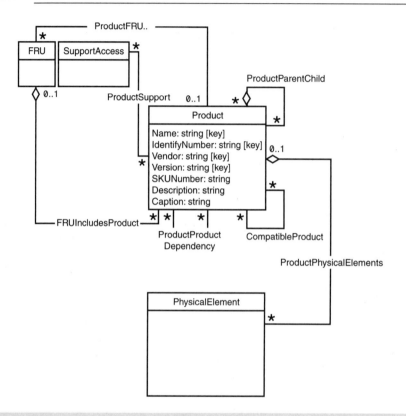

Note

It cannot be stressed enough that a Product represents only a unit of acquisition. As such, the only LogicalElement that is contained in a Product is software. Installing a Product typically results in the creation, removal, or upgrade of several other objects (typically, System, Application, and LogicalDevice objects). However, a Product does not contain these LogicalElements per se; rather, the LogicalElements are the result of installing the Product.

Product has a composite key, consisting of the Name, IdentifyingNumber, Vendor, and Version attributes.

The attributes of a `Product` are as follows:

- `Name` is part of the composite key of a `Product`, and is the name of the `Product` as defined by the supplier of the `Product`. It is a string of up to 256 characters.

- `IdentifyingNumber` is part of the composite key of a `Product`, and is a unique piece of information that helps differentiate an instance of a `Product` from other `Product` instances. Typically, this attribute contains the serial number of a device or software, the die number of a chip, and other unique information. It is a string of up to 64 characters.

- `Vendor` is part of the composite key of a `Product`, and is the name of the supplier of the `Product`. It is a string of up to 256 characters.

- `Version` is part of the composite key of a `Product`, and defines the version of the `Product` that was purchased. It is a string of up to 64 characters.

- `SKUNumber` is the Stock Keeping Unit information for the `Product`. It is a string of up to 64 characters.

- `Description` is a free-form string that contains a textual description of the `Product` (for example, its purpose and/or usage guidelines).

- `Caption` is a short, one-line description of the `Product`. It is intended for GUI applications, where space is at a premium and a short description of the object is required. It is a string of up to 64 characters.

The `Product` class does not define any methods. It does, however, define a number of important relationships that define various associations between `Products` and their components. The following three relationships (the `ProductParentChild` aggregation, the `CompatibleProduct` association, and the `ProductProductDependency` association) are all between `Product` instances. They are all optional relationships, having a cardinality of zero-or-more to zero-or-more. In addition, the `ProductPhysicalElements` aggregation is used to relate instances of the `PhysicalElement` class to an instance of a `Product` class.

The `ProductParentChild` aggregation represents a recursive relationship between products. For example, one `Product` may actually be composed of multiple `Products`, or it may accept other `Products` to augment its functionality.

The CompatibleProduct association is used to represent a generalized dependency between Products. Common dependencies include the ability to work together, to be installed together, or to run only if another quantity of another Product is already running. Note that the converse of these (for example, a Product can only run if another Product is not running), as well as any limitations and/or restrictions, can also be described in this relationship. The relationship contains a free-form string property, CompatibilityDescription, that can be used to contain the description of how they are compatible, or any limitations to their compatibility.

The ProductProductDependency association is a much stricter relationship than the CompatibleProduct association. The ProductProductDependency association indicates that one Product depends on either the installation or absence of another Product in order to function. This relationship is conceptually equivalent to the ServiceServiceDependency association. This relationship has a 16-bit unsigned integer property, TypeOfDependency, that describes the nature of the dependency. The values in this enumeration are "Unknown", "Other", "Product Must Be Installed", and "Product Must Not Be Installed".

The ProductPhysicalElements aggregation is an optional aggregation. It has a cardinality of zero-or-more on the PhysicalElement side, but has a restricted cardinality of zero-or-one on the Product side. The multiplicity of this relationship therefore means that it is not required, but if it is present, then at most one Product can aggregate any number of PhysicalElements. It defines the PhysicalElements that are contained in a Product.

The remaining relationships of a Product are between it and the FRU class, and between it and the SupportAccess class. These three relationships will be discussed in the next two sections, which discuss the FRU and the SupportAccess classes.

The FRU Class and Its Relationships

The FRU class represents a FRU. FRUs are defined by a vendor. Their purpose is to aggregate a set of Products, PhysicalElements, and/or software that represent either a replacement or an upgrade to the Product. Thus, an FRU represents a possible way to maintain or upgrade a Product without having to purchase a completely new Product.

An excerpt of the Core Model that focuses on the FRU class is shown in Figure 7.8.

Figure 7.8   Core Model excerpt: FRU and its relationships.

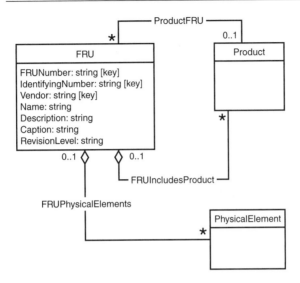

The FRU class has a composite key consisting of ordering information, a unique identifying number, and the name of the vendor that manufactures the FRU. This combination of information is the minimum required that can be used to uniquely identify a particular instance of a FRU from all other FRU instances in a system.

The FRU class defines the following seven attributes:

- FRUNumber is part of the composite key for the FRU, and is a string that describes the ordering information for the FRU. It is a string of up to 64 characters.

- IdentifyingNumber is part of the composite key for the FRU, and is a unique piece of information that is used to identify a FRU. For example, it can be the serial number of a PhysicalElement or software that is realized when a PhysicalElement is installed.

- Vendor is part of the composite key for the FRU, and is the name of the manufacturer of the FRU. It is a string of up to 256 characters.

- Name is a free-form string, and represents the vendor-assigned designation of the FRU.

- The Caption attribute is a short one-line textual description of the entity. This is used mostly for GUI purposes when navigating CIM repositories. It is defined as a string of up to 64 characters.

- The `Description` attribute provides a free-form textual description of the entity.

- `RevisionLevel` is a string that denotes the current revision level of the `FRU`. It consists of up to 64 characters.

The `FRU` class does not define any methods, but does define three important relationships (the `ProductFRU` association, the `FRUPhysicalElements` aggregation, and the `FRUIncludesProduct` aggregation).

The `ProductFRU` association defines a dependency relationship between a `Product` and a `FRU`. The purpose of this relationship is to define which components of the `Product` are being replaced or augmented by the `FRU`. The multiplicity of this relationship is zero-or-one on the `Product` side and zero-or-more on the `FRU` side. This means that a `Product` does not have to have this relationship, but if it is present, then at most one `Product` will have an association with one or more `FRU`s.

The `FRUPhysicalElements` aggregation is analogous to the `ProductPhysicalElements` aggregation. The `FRUPhysicalElements` aggregation defines the various `PhysicalElements` that are contained in a `FRU`. Again, the multiplicity of this relationship is zero-or-one on the `FRU` side to zero-or-more on the `PhysicalElements` side.

The `FRUIncludesProduct` aggregation is used to indicate that a `FRU` may be composed of multiple `Products`. However, the purpose of the `FRU` (for example, to replace and/or augment one or more functions of the `Product`) is still the same.

The `SupportAccess` Class and Its Relationships

The purpose of the `SupportAccess` class is to characterize how a given `Product` is supported.

An excerpt of the Core Model that focuses on the `SupportAccess` class is shown in Figure 7.9.

Figure 7.9 Core Model excerpt: `SupportAccess` and its relationships.

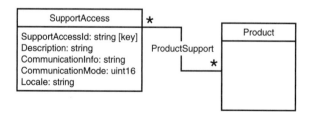

The attributes of the `SupportAccess` class are as follows:

- The `SupportAccess` class has a single attribute key, called `SupportAccessID`, which is a string that is defined by either the vendor supplying the `Product` or the organization that is responsible for deploying and maintaining the `Product`. This attribute is used to uniquely identify the way that support is provided for a given `Product`. It is a string of up to 256 characters.

- `CommunicationMode` defines the type of communications necessary in order to obtain support. It is an enumerated 16-bit unsigned integer. Listing 7.9 provides an excerpt from the Core MOF file that defines the various values that this attribute may have:

Listing 7.9 MOF definition of the `CommunicationMode` attribute.

```
[Description ( "CommunicationMode defines the form of communication in order to
    obtain support. For example, phone communication (value=2), fax (3) or email
    (8) can be specified."),

ValueMap {"1", "2", "3", "4", "5", "6", "7", "8"},
Values {"Other", "Phone", "Fax", "BBS", "Online Service", "Web Page",
"FTP", "E-mail"},
MappingStrings {"MIF.DMTF | Support| 001.5"} ]

uint16 CommunicationMode;
```

- `CommunicationInfo` is meant to supplement the information provided by the `Communication Mode` attribute. In general, the `CommunicationMode` attribute defines the type of support provided and the `CommunicationInfo` attribute provides additional information for that support. For example, if the value of the `CommunicationMode` attribute is equal to 2 (`"Phone"`), then the value of the `CommunicationInfo` attribute will be the corresponding phone number to be called.

- `Description` is a free-form string that contains a textual description of how support is provided (for example, by contract, through a support agency, and/or usage guidelines for obtaining support).

- `Locale` defines the geographic region and/or language dialect that is spoken in a particular geographic region to which support will be provided.

The `SupportAccess` class does not define any methods, but does define one association, `ProductSupport`.

The SupportAccess class defines one relationship, the ProductSupport association. This association defines how support is provided for a given Product. The multiplicity of this relationship is many-to-many, which means that the same SupportAccess class can represent support provided for multiple different Products, and also that various types of support (as indicated by separate SupportAccess instances) may be provided for a single Product.

The *Setting* and *Configuration* Classes

The Setting and Configuration classes are top-level objects that are used to define how ManagedSystemElements are configured. The Setting object is the workhorse, containing a set of parameters that define how a particular ManagedSystemElement will operate. Since there can be many types of Settings, the Configuration object is introduced to aggregate a group of Settings that all apply to a single object or to a group of objects.

There are two types of Settings that can be grouped together by the Configuration object. The first type are Settings that affect different aspects of the same object. For example, a router configuration file could control how different traffic is configured through the use of access control lists (ACLs). One set of ACLs could be used to control the configuration of edge interfaces, while another could be used to control the configuration of core interfaces. Thus, we would have two different instances of a Setting class, one for edge configuration and one for core configuration. It is possible, however, that both of these settings could apply to the same router. Hence, by grouping them into a Configuration object, we can logically associate them with a certain type of router. Configurations can contain Configurations, which enables the network manager to construct more complicated configurations that can apply to a larger set of devices. Abstracting common commands and parameters into reusable objects through the use of the Configuration and Setting classes greatly enhances the scalability and manageability of configuring and managing network elements and services.

The second type of grouping is to associate Settings that configure a device differently, in response to different conditions, to different Configurations. For example, a firewall might have morning, afternoon and evening settings. A network service might have Gold, Silver, and Bronze types of services, each of which can be associated with different users and applications for a number of different purposes. The Settings in both of these examples are related, since they all apply to the same object. However, the Settings in both examples are different, in that they configure the device to provide a different service.

In each of these two cases, CIM will make three different Configuration objects because each of the Settings contained in a particular Configuration must be applied at one time. Thus, you could not group the Gold, Silver, and Bronze settings into a single Configuration because each of these three Settings are different, and cause different actions to be executed. However, what you could do is to group other Settings with each network service (for example, group one set of DHCP and QoS Settings with the Gold network service, and possibly a different set of DHCP and QoS Settings with the Silver network service). This grouping of Configurations promotes reuse and enhances manageability, as it facilitates common management and administration of a set of related Settings.

The Setting Class and Its Relationships

The purpose of the Setting object is to define a set of related commands and operational parameters that can be used to configure one or more ManagedSystemElements. The Setting object is defined as an abstract object because it is used solely to define the concept of a group of settings and relationships between Setting objects, ManagedSystemElements, and Configuration objects. While it defines three attributes that are common to all types of settings, its real value is twofold:

- To serve as a means to classify setting objects

- To serve as an anchor point for defining relationships between Setting objects and both Configuration as well as ManagedSystemElement objects

A ManagedSystemElement may have multiple Setting objects associated with it, each of which control a different aspect of the configuration of the ManagedSystemElement. Furthermore, the current operational values of a ManagedSystemElement do not necessarily correspond exactly to the values of the attributes in the Setting objects that are associated with a ManagedSystemElement. This is because a Setting may not have been applied, or its application may be used to alter the values of one or more attributes of the ManagedSystemElement. One should always refer directly to the ManagedSystemElement in order to obtain the current operational values of the object.

Note

It is important to remember that Settings and Configurations represent the *desired* state of a managed entity, whereas the *current* state is represented by the set of values that the attributes of a managed entity has. The reader is cautioned that Settings and Configurations are not intended to model device configuration settings. This will be part of the CIM 2.3 effort.

An excerpt of the Core Model that focuses on the Setting and Configuration classes is shown in Figure 7.10.

Figure 7.10 Core Model excerpt: Setting, Configuration, and their relationships.

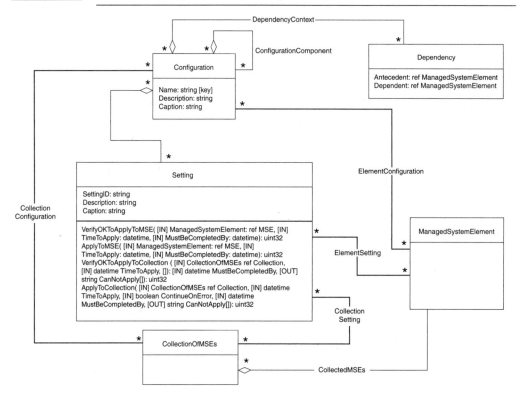

The Setting class does not define a key attribute. This is because the concept of a setting is too generic to define a key. Remember, defining a key in the Setting class means that its subclasses cannot define their own keys. It was thought that, due to the genericity of the Setting class, different subclasses might need the flexibility to define their own keys. This would allow the keys of each subclass to be better used to refine the nature and usage of the subclass.

The attributes of the Setting class are as follows:

- SettingID represents unique information that enables a particular Setting object to be identified. It is a string of up to 256 characters.

- Description is a free-form string that contains a textual description of the Product (for example, its purpose and/or usage guidelines).

- Caption is a short, one-line description of the Product. It is intended for GUI applications, where space is at a premium and a short description of the object is required. It is a string of up to 64 characters.

The Setting class defines four important methods. The first, VerifyOKToApplyToMSE, is used to ensure that it is safe to apply a specific Setting to a particular instance of a ManagedSystemElement at a given time or time interval. Its signature is

```
VerifyOKToApplyToMSE( [IN] CIM_ManagedSystemElement ref MSE,
     [IN] datetime TimeToApply, [IN] datetime MustBeCompletedBy ) : uint32
```

Here, the first input parameter, MSE, is a reference to a ManagedSystemElement object. This parameter represents the object to which the Setting will be applied. The second input parameter, Time, specifies a time or interval that will be used in performing the check. The third input parameter, MustBeCompletedBy, indicates a required completion time for the method. A return value of 0 indicates successful application of the Setting; a return value of 1 indicates that the method is not supported; a return value of 2 means that the Setting could not be applied within the time interval specified by the MustBeCompletedBy input parameter; any other return value indicates that some other type of error occurred in applying the method.

The second method is the ApplyToMSE method, whose signature is

```
ApplyToMSE( [IN] CIM_ManagedSystemElement ref MSE, [IN] datetime TimeToApply,
     [IN] datetime MustBeCompletedBy ) : uint32
```

This method performs the actual application of the Setting to the referenced instance of the ManagedSystemElement object. All three input parameters, as well as the return value, are the same as in the VerifyOKToApplyToMSE method.

The third and fourth methods are similar to the first two methods, but apply to a Collection of ManagedSystemElements as opposed to a single ManagedSystemElement. The effect of this method is to verify that it is okay to apply the method to each ManagedSystemElement in the collection. The signature of the verify collection method is

```
VerifyOKToApplyToCollection ( [IN] CIM_CollectionOfMSEs ref Collection, [IN]
datetime TimeToApply,
  [IN] datetime MustBeCompletedBy, [OUT] string CanNotApply [ ]): uint32
```

This is similar in operation to the VerifyOKToApplyToMSE method, except that it references a collection of ManagedSystemElements (instead of a single ManagedSystemElement), and provides one additional output parameter, CanNotApply. This is an array of strings that lists the keys of the ManagedSystemElements to which the Setting can NOT be applied. This enables those ManagedSystemElements to be revisited and either fixed, or other corrective action taken. (This is necessary because it is illegal to return an array of references).

The signature of the apply collection method is

```
ApplyToCollection ( [IN] CIM_CollectionOfMSEs ref Collection, [IN] datetime
TimeToApply,
   [IN] boolean ContinueOnError, [IN] datetime MustBeCompletedBy, [OUT] string
CanNotApply [ ]): uint32
```

This is similar in operation to the ApplyToCollection method, with the following differences. This method references a collection of ManagedSystemElements (instead of a single ManagedSystemElement). It provides one additional input parameter (ContinueOnError) and one additional output parameter (CanNotApply). ContinueOnError is a boolean that, if TRUE, applies the method to each ManagedSystemElement in the collection. If an error is encountered, it places the key(s) of each failed object in the CanNotApply array. If ContinueOnError is FALSE, then the method is applied to each object in the collection until an error is encountered, at which point it STOPS processing, places the key(s) of the failed object in the CanNotApply array, and returns with an error code of 2. The CanNotApply array is used as described above.

The Setting class defines one relationship, ElementSetting, and participates in a second relationship with the Configuration object (SettingContext), which is defined in the next section.

The ElementSetting association defines a dependency between a ManagedSystemElement and the Setting class(es) that are used to help define its configuration. Accordingly, the multiplicity is one or more on the ManagedSystemElement side and zero-or-more on the Setting side.

The Configuration Class and Its Relationships

The purpose of the Configuration class is to aggregate a set of Setting objects. This enables a group of Settings (or a subset of them) to be applied to the same object. More importantly, it increases the manageability of the system. Administrators no longer have to try and find separate settings to apply to a device; they can instead manage the configuration of the system through the use of higher-level objects. Furthermore, the Configuration class enables sets of related Setting objects to be grouped together and reused. For example, the configuration of a display adapter could contain various display settings (for example, VGA, SVGA, and XGA) that are dynamically applied depending on what the user chooses at startup.

An excerpt of the Core Model that focuses on the `Setting` and `Configuration` classes was shown in Figure 7.10. Unlike the `Setting` class, the `Configuration` class does define a key attribute. The reason for this lies in the difference between these two classes. The `Configuration` class groups `Setting` instances, and therefore can define a key (its `Name` attribute) to uniquely name the instance of the `Configuration` class, because this is common to all types of configurations. Typically, subclasses of the `Configuration` class are not required, because all the `Configuration` class is used for is *grouping*. However, the purpose of the `Setting` class is very different. It is used to group commands and parameters that affect the operation of a particular type of `ManagedSystemElement`. This requires the `Setting` class to be subclassed to represent the different characteristics of the `ManagedSystemElement` that is being controlled. Therefore, instances of different subclasses of the `Setting` class will necessarily be different, because they control the configuration of different objects. This is why the `Setting` class did not define a key. Note, however, that a single instance of a `Configuration` class can aggregate different instances of different `Setting` subclasses.

Referring to Figure 7.10, notice that the attributes of both the `Configuration` as well as the `Setting` classes are largely the same as that of `ManagedSystemElement`. However, there is a fundamental difference between the common attributes of these classes. This lies in the fact that `Configurations` and `Settings` can exist regardless of whether the object(s) that they apply to are present or not.

Note

Policies are closely related to configurations and settings. As we will see in Chapters 10 and 11, one important aspect of policies is managing and changing the configuration of objects in response to either dynamic conditions, or to provide functions that are either contracted for or assigned (for example, at login, because a user has a certain business role or belongs to a particular group). This is captured by using groups of related `Configurations` and `Settings`.

The `Configuration` class contains the following three generic attributes:

- `Name` is the key attribute of the `Configuration` class. Its purpose is to provide a unique name for instances of a particular `Configuration` class. It is a string of up to 256 characters.

- `Description` is a free-form string that contains a textual description of the `Configuration` (for example, its purpose and/or use).

- `Caption` is a short, one-line description of the `Configuration`. It is intended for GUI applications, where space is at a premium and a short description of the object is required. It is a string of up to 64 characters.

The Configuration class defines no methods. However, it does define two associations and two aggregations, which are described next.

The Configuration class defines four important relationships. The SettingContext aggregation associates one or more Setting objects with one or more Configuration objects. For example, a display adapter could have several associated settings, each of which controls one aspect of the display. Controlling the resolution of the display may require three separate Configurations, one each corresponding to VGA, SVGA, and XGA.

However, this is not the only user-adjustable parameter. For example, another Setting defining the number of colors to use would also need to be associated with a particular display resolution. Thus, we need to group these similar Settings together into separate Configurations. The specific Configuration that would be activated would depend on how the user chose to log into the system. The multiplicity is many-to-many, indicating that many Setting instances can be aggregated by a Configuration instance, and that a Setting instance can be grouped by multiple Configuration instances.

The ElementConfiguration class is an association that relates a Configuration object to one or more ManagedSystemElements. This association is used to assign certain behavior, such as operational settings to apply, to a particular ManagedSystemElement. Again, the multiplicity of this association is many-to-many, indicating that many Configuration instances can be associated with a given ManagedSystemElement instance, and that a Configuration class can apply to multiple ManagedSystemElement classes. This association has a boolean attribute, called ActiveConfiguration, that designates which Configuration instance is currently being applied to the ManagedSystemElement instance.

The ConfigurationComponents is a recursive aggregation, enabling Configuration objects to be nested. The purpose of this aggregation is to be able to group multiple Configurations in another Configuration. For example, a user might have one set of privileges given when logging into the corporate intranet directly over Ethernet, and a more restricted set of privileges when logging into the (same) corporate intranet remotely using PPP. In each case, the login contains a group of Settings that are used to configure the user's computer, so that the user can access resources on the corporate intranet. These two Configurations could be grouped into a higher-level Configuration, whose purpose is to manage the configuration of the user's computer as a function of how the user logs into the system. Similarly, this Configuration could be grouped into a higher-level group that applies to a department containing multiple groups.

The DependencyContext aggregation represents a set of dependencies between multiple Configuration objects. For example, consider a user's computer. That computer, which is represented by a ComputerSystem object in CIM, has one or more Configurations, corresponding to the privileges assigned to the user, the user's group, or the computer itself.

For example, one can only access secure information from a set of computers at a particular location. Now, what happens when the user is reassigned to a different department, and needs to move his or her computer? Another example is if the user is permitted mobile access, which may have more restricted access than when an employee uses the same computer in his or her departmental location. Presumably, a different set of Configurations will need to be applied. There could be a new set of dependencies between the new location that the ComputerSystem is attached to and the configuration of the ComputerSystem. This is represented by the DependencyContext aggregation.

The StatisticalInformation Class

The StatisticalInformation class is an abstract class. It is the base class for any class that collects statistical and/or measurement data for a ManagedSystemElement. The purpose of the StatisticalInformation class is to group related attributes together, so that metric data can be collected for a given ManagedSystemElement. In addition, this object and its subclasses provide the ability to store historical data for a ManagedSystemElement.

Note

The separation of statistical information from other information is representative of the power, flexibility, and organization of CIM. Statistical information is separated from the attributes that define a managed entity because statistics describe *how* an entity is performing. The attributes of an object describe the characteristics that define an object. This also enables applications that are concerned primarily with gathering and analyzing statistics to primarily use these classes and perhaps a few relationships (to reference the managed objects that the statistics relate to), instead of having to use and reference the entire model.

Statistics often come in groups that do not apply to one specific object. This is accommodated through separating the StatisticalInformation class from the object itself, and using relationships to associate the statistics to the entity or entities that they apply to.

One important thing to remember is that the current (CIM 2.2) version does *not* have the notion of history. In CIM 2.2, statistics are *not* tracked across time. Therefore, every time that a statistic is measured or retrieved, a new instance is created. If it is important to be able to distinguish one instance from another, then a subclass of the StatisticalInformation class must define a key (presumably defining a time stamp and/or sequence number as part of the key). In addition, if the user needs to track the historical significance of the statistical information being collected, then the user should subclass the StatisticalInformation class and add one or more attributes for keeping track of time-related information (for example, a timestamp attribute).

An excerpt of the Core Model that focuses on the StatisticalInformation class is shown in Figure 7.11.

Figure 7.11 Core Model excerpt: StatisticalInformation and its relationships.

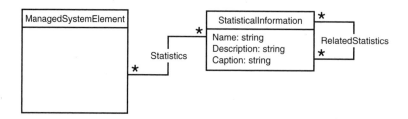

The StatisticalInformation class does not define a key attribute, for the same reason that the Setting class didn't. It contains the following three attributes:

- Name is a free-form string of up to 256 characters. When the StatisticalInformation class is subclassed, then this attribute may be overridden to serve as a Key attribute.

- Description is a free-form string that contains a textual description of the Product (for example, its purpose and/or usage guidelines).

- Caption is a short, one-line description of the Product. It is intended for GUI applications, where space is at a premium and a short description of the object is required. It is a string of up to 64 characters.

The StatisticalInformation class defines no methods, but does define two relationships. One of these is the Statistics association, which describes the dependency between a ManagedSystemElement and the Statistics that are defined for it. This was defined in the section "The ManagedSystemElement Class and Its Relationships."

The second relationship is RelatedStatistics, which is a recursive association (that is, both the antecedent and the dependent are instances of the StatisticalInformation class). It is used to define groups and/or hierarchies of related statistical information.

Device Common Model Classes

The Device Common Model is very robust. It is meant to show how different functions and services are realized in hardware (usually, the hardware is itself a subclass of PhysicalElement).

The Device Common Model represents functions and capabilities of the managed system that are realized using either discrete hardware entities (for example, a printer) or other functions that may not have a one-to-one correspondence with a physical entity (for example, a multi-function router card), or for that matter have a single physical representation (for example, processing and communication capabilities).

The power of the Device Common Model lies in its relationships. These relationships enable you to associate physical hardware and components with software as well as operational requirements, such as cooling, memory, and so on. The Device Common Model, in conjunction with the Network Common Model, enables you (for example) to model a router as a `PhysicalPackage` with a set of associated power, cooling, memory, and other requirements. Thus, by combining appropriate elements of the various CIM Common Models, you can create a customized, extensible, object-oriented model of your system and its components to whatever degree of detail necessary.

There are a wide variety of devices modeled. The Device Common Model includes Cooling Devices, Sensors, Printers, Scanners, Network Adapters, Batteries, Controllers (for example, serial, parallel, and video controllers), Power Supplies, Modems, Media Access and Mass Storage Devices, Alarm Devices, Processors, and User Devices (for example, keyboards, pointing devices, and so on). In addition, the Device Common Model describes important concepts, such as redundancy, device errors, and memory. In addition, through the appropriate relationships of `LogicalDevice`, ties into software can be realized. Describing each of these is beyond the scope of this book. However, there are certain essential classes that DEN depends on. These are briefly described in the following sections.

Members of the `RedundancyGroup` Hierarchy

A `RedundancyGroup` is a subclass of `LogicalElement`.

An excerpt of the Device Model that focuses on the `RedundancyGroup` class and its subclasses is shown in Figure 7.12.

Figure 7.12 Device Model excerpt: `RedundancyGroup`, its subclasses, and their relationships.

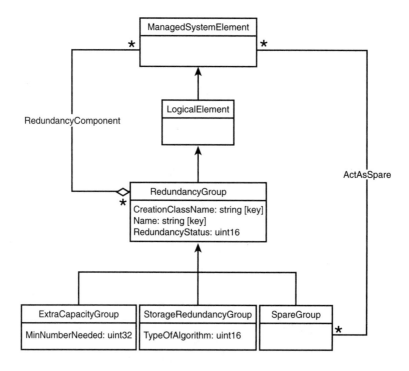

The `RedundancyGroup` class has a composite key, consisting of two attributes (`CreationClassName` and `Name`). The purpose of the `RedundancyGroup` class is to aggregate a set of `LogicalElements` that together provide redundancy for a given `ManagedSystemElement`. It is assumed that all objects of the `LogicalElements` that are aggregated in the `RedundancyGroup` class are instantiations of the same subclass of `LogicalElement`.

The following subsections describe the `RedundancyGroup` class and its subclasses.

The `RedundancyGroup` Class

The `RedundancyGroup` class has a (composite) key consisting of two attributes. Note that this is also the key for its subclasses. The `RedundancyGroup` class defines the following three attributes:

- `CreationClassName` defines the name of the class used to create an instance of this class. It is part of the composite key of the `RedundancyGroup` class (and therefore all of the subclasses of the `PhysicalElement` class). Its purpose is to enable all of the different instances of this class and its subclasses to be uniquely identified. It is defined to be a string of up to 256 characters.

- `Name` is the other key attribute of the `System` class. It is inherited from `ManagedSystemElement`, and is overridden to be made a key for this attribute. It is a string of up to 256 characters.

- `RedundancyStatus` holds the current state of the `RedundancyGroup`. It is an enumerated 16-bit unsigned integer with the following five settings:

Value	Name	Description
0	other	Ensures that all situations can be
1	unknown	described.
2	fully redundant	All of the configured redundancy is available.
3	degraded redundancy	One or more failures have been experienced that adversely affect the functions provided by the `RedundancyGroup`. However, the `RedundancyGroup` is still able to provide some measure of redundancy.
4	redundancy lost	Enough failures have happened such that no redundancy at all is available, and that the next failure that is experienced will cause complete failure of the `LogicalElement`.

The `RedundancyGroup` defines no methods. However, it does define one relationship.

The `RedundancyComponent` aggregation defines a set of `ManagedSystemElements` as being part of a `RedundancyGroup`. There are two semantic implications for this aggregation. First, all objects contained in this aggregation should be instantiations of the same subclass of `ManagedSystemElement`. Second, the set of `ManagedSystemElements` that are contained in a `RedundancyGroup` should be treated atomically. That is, in order for the `RedundancyGroup` to provide redundancy, the entire set of `ManagedSystemElements` that it aggregates must be present and working.

The `ExtraCapacityGroup` Subclass

`ExtraCapacityGroup` is a subclass of `RedundancyGroup`, and is shown in Figure 7.12. The purpose of the `ExtraCapacityGroup` class is to indicate that the set of aggregated `ManagedSystemElements` represented by the `ExtraCapacityGroup` have more capacity, or offer more capability, than is strictly needed to serve as a redundant system or component. For example, one might install an extra cooling device or power supply in addition to the primary and backup units. Such devices would be a member of this group.

The ExtraCapacityGroup has a single attribute, called MinNumberNeeded. This is a 32-bit unsigned integer, and defines the smallest number of ManagedSystemElements that are required to be operational in order to serve as a redundant component or system. This class defines no attributes or methods.

The StorageRedundancyGroup Subclass

StorageRedundancyGroup is a subclass of RedundancyGroup, and is shown in Figure 7.12. The purpose of the StorageRedundancyGroup class is to identify and group together various components that offer redundancy for mass storage. StorageRedundancyGroups are used primarily to protect user and system data, and they may overlap in protecting the same data.

The StorageRedundancyGroup class contains a single attribute, called TypeOfAlgorithm. This attribute defines the type of algorithm that is used for data redundancy. This is a 16-bit enumerated unsigned integer, whose values include "undefined", "other", "unknown", "copy", "XOR", "P+Q", "S", and "P+S".

The StorageRedundancyGroup class defines no methods. It does define two relationships, the PExtentRedundancyComponent and the AggregateRedundancyComponent aggregations. These are both low-level relationships whose use is specific to modeling memory. The former models the PhysicalExtents of a StorageRedundancyGroup, and the latter models the summary information about the addressable logical blocks which are in the same StorageRedundancyGroup and reside on the same physical media.

The SpareGroup Subclass

SpareGroup is a subclass of RedundancyGroup and is shown in Figure 7.12. The purpose of the SpareGroup class is to indicate that one or more of the elements aggregated by the SpareGroup class act as spares for other RedundancyGroups as well as components of the managed system. For example, a ComputerSystem may have several spare NICs. These NICs may not be able to be installed as redundant units, but are associated with one or more ComputerSystems and act as spares in case a ComputerSystem's NIC fails. This is realized through the ActsAsSpare association.

The SpareGroup defines a single association, called ActsAsSpare. This association defines which ManagedSystemElements in which SpareGroup can act as spares for a given component or system. This association also defines a boolean attribute, HotStandby, which indicates that the spare can operate in hot standby mode (for example, the spare can be replaced without turning power off to the system).

Members of the **NetworkAdapter** *Hierarchy*

NetworkAdapter is a subclass of **LogicalDevice**. Its purpose is to serve as a base class for the various types of network adapters that are used.

An excerpt of the Device Model that focuses on the **NetworkAdapter** class and its subclasses is shown in Figure 7.13.

Figure 7.13   Device Model excerpt: **NetworkAdapter**, its subclasses, and their relationships.

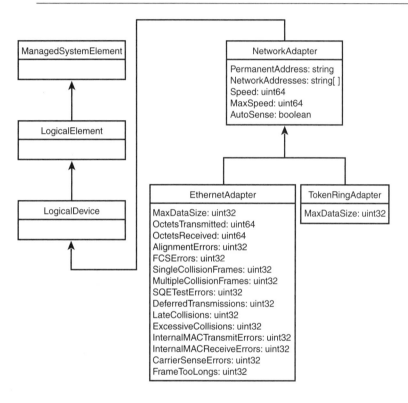

The **NetworkAdapter** *Class and Its Relationships*

The **NetworkAdapter** class is an abstract class; it serves solely as a classification mechanism in the CIM hierarchy. It inherits the composite key (as well as the other attributes, of course) of its superclass, **LogicalDevice**. The **NetworkAdapter** class does not define any methods or relationships, but does add the following attributes to those inherited from the **LogicalDevice** class:

- **PermanentAddress** indicates that a static network address has been hardcoded into the **NetworkAdapter** instance. Note, however, that it is possible for this address to be changed via either a software configuration change or a firmware upgrade. If either of these are done, then this attribute should be updated with the new address. If there is no hardcoded address, then this attribute should be left blank. This is a string of up to 64 characters.

- NetworkAddresses is an array of network addresses that the NetworkAdapter can use. This attribute specifies that each address in the array is indexed. Each network address is a string of up to 64 characters.

- Speed is an estimate of the current operational bandwidth in bits per second for this NetworkAdapter. For cases in which the bandwidth varies frequently, a nominal value may be used instead. This is a 64-bit unsigned integer.

- MaxSpeed is the maximum possible speed, again in bits per second, that can be used for this NetworkAdapter. This is also a 64-bit unsigned integer.

- AutoSense is a boolean attribute indicating whether the NetworkAdapter is capable of automatically (for example, without external operator intervention) determining the speed of the attached media that it should operate at. A value of TRUE indicates that it can automatically determine the speed of the attached media, and FALSE indicates that it cannot.

The EthernetAdapter Subclass and Its Relationships

The EthernetAdapter class is a subclass of the NetworkAdapter class. It is a structural class that represents the capabilities of an Ethernet adapter card. It is also shown in Figure 7.13. Note that the overriding of the NetworkAddresses attribute is not shown in this diagram.

This class adds many attributes from the Bridge MIB and the EtherLike MIB. However, it does not add any methods or relationships.

Note
RFC 1156 defines MIB-I, the core set of managed objects for the Internet suite of protocols. STD17/RFC 1213, defines MIB-II, an evolution of MIB-I based on implementation experience and new operational requirements. RFC 1493 defines a portion of the Management Information Base (MIB) for use with network management protocols in TCP/IP based internets. In particular it defines objects for managing MAC bridges based on the IEEE 802.1D-1990 standard between local area network (LAN) segments.

This class is currently being worked on by the Systems and Devices Working Group for the CIM 2.2 release. For example, attributes from the IETF Internet draft *Definitions of Managed Objects for the Ethernet-like Interface Types*, dated August 1998, are being added. The attributes shown in Figure 7.13 reflect the status of this class for CIM 2.1. Therefore, these attributes will not be discussed further, since they all correspond to attributes specified in a MIB. The one exception to this is the NetworkAddresses attribute. The EthernetAdapater class overrides the inherited definition of the NetworkAddresses attribute in order to specify an Ethernet 802.3 MAC address. As with its superclass, all attributes are indexed.

The TokenRingAdapter Subclass and Its Relationships

The TokenRingAdapter class is a subclass of the NetworkAdapter class. It is a structural class that represents the capabilities of a Token Ring adapter card. It is also shown in Figure 7.13. Note that the overriding of the NetworkAddresses attribute is not shown in this diagram.

This class is currently being worked on by the Systems and Devices Working Group for the CIM 2.2 release. The CIM 2.1 version of this class had two attributes: overriding the NetworkAdapter attribute and defining a new attribute (MaxDataSize) from the Bridge MIB. However, many more attributes are being added in CIM 2.2. Therefore, these attributes will not be discussed further, since they all correspond to attributes specified in a MIB. The one exception to this is the NetworkAddresses attribute. The TokenRingAdapater class overrides the inherited definition of the NetworkAddresses attribute in order to specify a Token-Ring 802.5 MAC address. As with its superclass, all attributes are indexed. In addition, it does not define any methods or relationships.

The DeviceErrorCounts Class and Its Relationships

The DeviceErrorCounts is a subclass of the StatisticalInformation class. The purpose of the DeviceErrorCounts class is to serve as a container for error-related statistical information for subclasses of LogicalDevice. The types of errors are as defined by CCITT (X.733) and ISO (IEC 10164-4).

An excerpt of the Device Model that focuses on the NetworkAdapter class and its subclasses is shown in Figure 7.14.

The DeviceErrorCounts class has a composite key, consisting of four propagated keys from LogicalDevice (which were actually propagated, as you will remember, from the System class) as well as an overriding of the Name attribute (which is inherited from the StatisticalInformation class). This set of keys is used to uniquely identify the LogicalDevice that serves as the scoping system for the StatisticalInformation class.

Figure 7.14   Device Model excerpt: `DeviceErrorCounts` and its relationships.

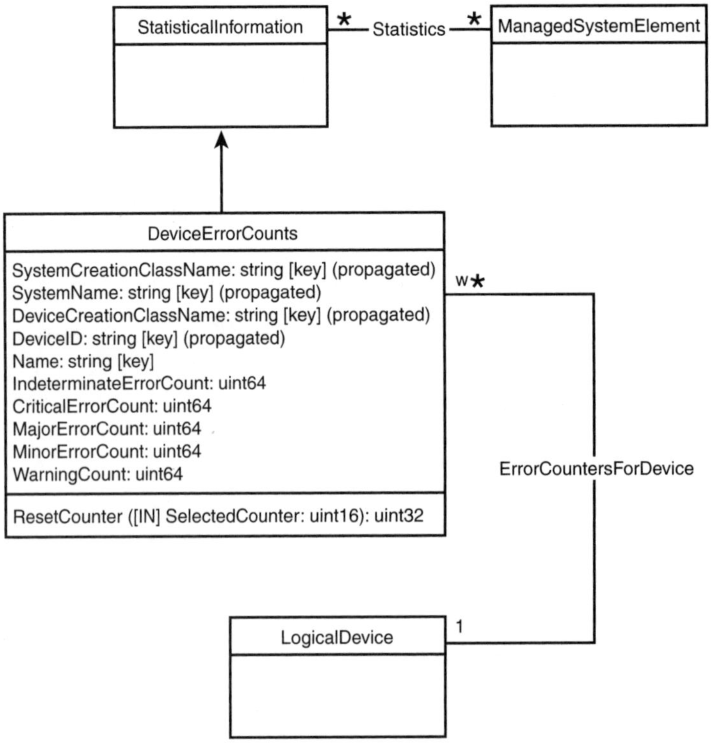

The `DeviceErrorCounts` defines the following important attributes:

- `SystemCreationClassName` is a *propagated key* originating from the `System` class, but propagated from the `LogicalDevice` class. It is a string, whose maximum length is 256 characters. Referring to Figure 7.14, we see that a *weak* aggregation, `ErrorCounters ForDevice`, exists between an instance of a `DeviceErrorCounts` class and an instance of a `LogicalDevice` class. This weak association is used to relate the instance of the `DeviceErrorCounts` class to the instance of the `LogicalDevice` class in which it resides. Remember that a `LogicalDevice` class is hosted in a `System`. The identity of the instance of the `DeviceErrorCounts` class depends on the name of the `DeviceErrorCounts` class as well as the name of the `LogicalDevice` class in which it resides, which in turn is derived from the `System` that hosts that `LogicalDevice` instance.

- SystemName is also a propagated key, originating from the System class and propagated from the LogicalDevice class. It is defined as a string, whose maximum length is also 256 characters. This is the name of the System in which the instance of the LogicalDevice class is defined. This identifies the instance of the LogicalDevice class that this particular instance of the DeviceErrorCounts class refers to.

- DeviceCreationClassName is a key attribute that is propagated from LogicalDevice. It defines the name of the class that was used to create this instance (for example, the DeviceErrorCounts class or an appropriate subclass of the DeviceErrorCounts class). This is a string, whose maximum length is 256 characters.

- DeviceID is a key attribute that is propagated from LogicalDevice. It is also a string, whose maximum length is 64 characters, that contains additional information that can help uniquely identify different instances of this class.

- Name is an key attribute that is inherited from LogicalDevice. This attribute is overridden in order to provide appropriate heuristics for naming instances of the DeviceErrorCounts class and its subclasses (as opposed to subclasses of LogicalDevice, which may have different naming heuristics). This is a string of up to 256 characters.

- IndeterminateErrorCount is a 64-bit unsigned integer that can be used to maintain a count of the number of all types of errors for the LogicalDevice.

- CriticalErrorCount is a 64-bit unsigned integer that is used to maintain a count of the number of critical errors for the LogicalDevice that this DeviceErrorCounts instance is associated with.

- MajorErrorCount is a 64-bit unsigned integer that is used to maintain a count of the number of major errors for the LogicalDevice that this DeviceErrorCounts instance is associated with.

- MinorErrorCount is a 64-bit unsigned integer that is used to maintain a count of the number of minor errors for the LogicalDevice that this DeviceErrorCounts instance is associated with.

- WarningCount is a 64-bit unsigned integer that is used to maintain a count of the number of warnings for the LogicalDevice that this DeviceErrorCounts instance is associated with.

The DeviceErrorCounts class defines a method called ResetCounter. The purpose of this method is to reset the various error and warning counters defined in the DeviceErrorCounts class. This may be necessary for the error processing instrumentation associated with the LogicalDevice instance that this instance of the DeviceErrorCounts class is associated with.

Its signature is

```
ResetCounter( [IN] SelectedCounter: uint16 ) : uint32
```

This method takes a single input parameter (`SelectedCounter`), which defines which counter is to be reset. This parameter is an enumerated integer with the following values:

Value	Description
0	all counters
1	the indeterminate error counter only
2	the critical error counter only
3	the major error counter only
4	the minor error counter only
5	the warning error counter only

Finally, the `DeviceErrorCounts` class defines a single association, called `ErrorCountersForDevice`.

This association is a subclass of the `Statistics` association (defined in the `Statistics` class), and defines the specific `LogicalDevice` instance that this `DeviceErrorCounts` instance applies to. This is a subclass, because:

- This is a *weak* association, whereas its superclass (the `Statistics` association) is not.

- The type of class on each end of the relationship has been changed.

- The cardinality of the `ErrorCountersForDevice` association, on the `LogicalDevice` side, is restricted to exactly one. This is because the purpose of this association is to identify the *one* device to which these error counters apply.

The StorageExtent *Class Hierarchy*

`StorageExtent` is an abstract subclass of `LogicalDevice`, and is shown in Figure 7.15. The purpose of the `StorageExtent` class is to describe the capabilities of various media that exist to store and retrieve data, as well as define how the devices that contain these media are managed. This class, and its subclasses, are being enhanced in CIM 2.2.

An excerpt of the Device Model that focuses on the `StorageExtent` class is shown in Figure 7.15. The following sections will also describe some of the subclasses of the `StorageExtent` class.

Figure 7.15   Device Model Excerpt: `StorageExtent` and its relationships.

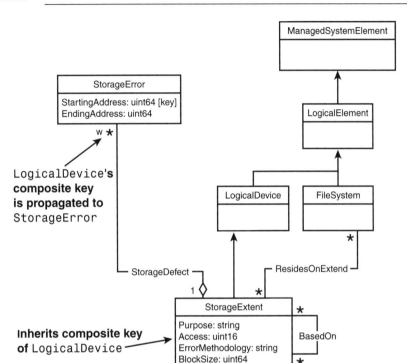

The `StorageExtent` class inherits the composite key of `LogicalDevice`. It defines the following attributes:

- `Purpose` is a free-form string that describes the media providing storage and/or the use of the media.

- `Access` is a 16-bit unsigned integer that defines whether the media is unknown (value = 0), readable (value = 1), writeable (value = 2), or both readable and writeable (value = 3).

- `ErrorMethodology` is a free-form string that describes the type of error detection and correction that is supported by this instance of the `StorageExtent` class.

- `BlockSize` is a 64-bit unsigned integer that defines the size in bytes of the blocks that constitute this `StorageExtent` instance. The value of 1 is reserved for instances in which either the block size is unknown or not a valid concept.

- `NumberOfBlocks` is the total number of consecutive blocks, each of size `BlockSize`, that constitute this `StorageExtent`. The total size of the `StorageExtent` can therefore be calculated by multiplying the value of the `BlockSize` attribute by the value of the `NumberOfBlocks` attribute.

The `StorageExtent` class defines no methods. It participates in one association (with `MediaAccessDevice`, called `MediaPresent`) and defines three relationships (the `ResidesOnExtent` and `BasedOn` associations and the `StorageDefect` aggregation).

The `MediaPresent` association is a subclass of the more general `Dependency` association. It is used to define the need for a `MediaAccessDevice` to be used to access a `StorageExtent`. It is a zero-or-more to zero-or-more dependency between a `MediaAccessDevice` and a `StorageExtent`.

The `ResidesOnExtent` association defines the usage of `StorageExtent` instances by a particular `FileSystem` (this class will be discussed in the section "The `FileSystem` Class and Its Relationships"). It is a subclass of the `Dependency` association. The subclass is required because this association restricts the types of classes that can be instantiated on each endpoint of the relationship.

The `BasedOn` association is another subclass of the `Dependency` association. The `BasedOn` association is a recursive relationship, meaning that both the antecedent and the dependent are instances of the `StorageExtent` class. The purpose of this relationship is to define composite `StorageExtents` from other `StorageExtents`. For example, it might be important for a particular application to use specific types of extents to construct storage with particular characteristics. This would be accomplished by subclassing the `StorageExtent` class to create specific subclasses that represent these characteristics. The composite (new) storage class can then be represented using the `BasedOn` association. This association has two 64-bit unsigned integer attributes. `StartingAddress` indicates where in the lower-level storage the higher-level storage extent begins. Similarly, `EndingAddress` indicates where in lower-level storage the higher-level storage extent ends.

Finally, the `StorageDefect` aggregation contains the set of `StorageErrors` for a particular `StorageExtent`. The purpose of the `StorageDefect` aggregation is to collect `StorageErrors` for a particular `StorageExtent`. This aggregation defines the cardinality at the aggregate end (for example, the instance of the `StorageExtent` class) as exactly 1. This ensures that errors are associated with one, and only one, particular instance of the `StorageExtent` class.

The cardinality at the part end (for example, the StorageError) is defined to be zero-or-more. This means that a given StorageExtent may not have an error (the 'zero' part), but if it does, then it could just as well have many errors. Note that this relationship is a weak relationship, since StorageError does not have any keys and can only exist within the scope of the StorageExtent that it is associated with.

The StorageError Class and Its Relationships

The StorageError class is not a subclass of StorageExtent, but is very closely related to it. The purpose of the StorageError class is to represent blocks of memory or media that should not be used because they contain some type of error. The composite key of StorageExtent (for example, the SystemCreationClassName, SystemName, DeviceCreationClassName, and DeviceID attributes) is propagated to StorageError. This is necessary because storage errors cannot exist outside of an object that they apply to. A single additional key, StartingAddress, is added to this propagated composite key. Together, these five attributes define which StorageError applies to which StorageExtent. The four propagated attributes identify the StorageExtent instance, and the additional StartingAddress attribute identifies which storage error instance (of possibly many storage errors) is being described.

The following attributes are defined for the StorageError class:

- StartingAddress is part of the composite key of the StorageError class. It identifies the starting address of the set of bytes that contain an error. It is a 64-bit unsigned integer.

- EndingAddress is not a key attribute. It is simply used to identify the ending address of the bytes that contain an error. It is a 64-bit unsigned integer.

The StorageError class defines no methods, and participates in a single relationship, the StorageDefect aggregation. This relationship was previously defined in the section "The StorageExtent Class Hierarchy."

The Memory Class and Its Relationships

The Memory class is a subclass of StorageExtent, and is the base class for different classes representing different types of memory.

An excerpt of the Device Model that focuses on the Memory class and its subclasses is shown in Figure 7.16. The following sections will also describe some of the subclasses of the Memory class.

Figure 7.16 Device Model excerpt: `Memory` and its subclasses and relationships.

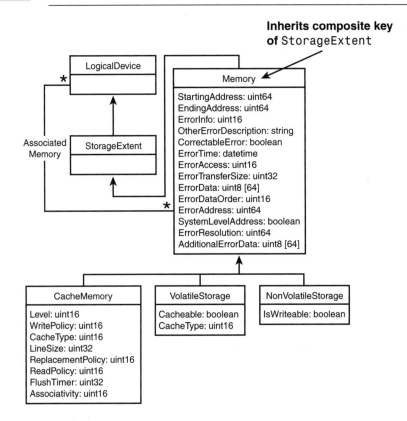

The `Memory` class inherits the composite key of its superclass, `StorageExtent` (for example, the `SystemCreationClassName`, `SystemName`, `CreationClassName`, and `DeviceID` attributes). The following are brief definitions of the attributes defined by the `Memory` class:

- `ErrorMethodology`, defined in the `StorageExtent` superclass, is overridden in the `Memory` class. This is to refine the more general notion of specifying any type of error detection and correction to a more specific type of error detection and correction. Possible values include parity or cyclical redundancy check algorithms, along with other mechanisms. This is a free-form string.

- `StartingAddress` is the address which indicates the beginning of this memory object. The starting address is specified in kilobytes, and uses a 64-bit unsigned integer as its data type.

- EndingAddress is the address which indicates the end of this memory object. The ending address is specified in kilobytes, and uses a 64-bit unsigned integer as its data type.

- ErrorInfo is an enumerated 16-bit unsigned integer that is used to describe the type of error that most recently occurred. This is meant to be used with the OtherErrorDescription attribute, which is described next. Listing 7.10 contains an excerpt from the Device Model MOF that defines this attribute.

Listing 7.10   Device Model MOF excerpt for the ErrorInfo attribute.

```
[Description ("An integer enumeration describing the type of error that occurred
most recently. For example, single (value=6) or double bit errors (7) can be
specified using this property. The values, 12-14, are undefined in the CIM Schema
since in DMI, they mix the semantics of the type of error and whether it was
correctable or not.  The latter is indicated in the property,
CorrectableError."),

ValueMap {"1", "2", "3", "4", "5", "6", "7", "8", "9", "10", "11", "12", "13",
          "14"},

Values {"Other", "Unknown", "OK", "Bad Read", "Parity Error", "Single-Bit Error",
   "Double-Bit Error", "Multi-Bit Error", "Nibble Error", "Checksum Error", "CRC
   Error", "Undefined", "Undefined", "Undefined"},

MappingStrings {"MIF.DMTF |Memory Device |002.12", "MIF.DMTF |
Physical Memory Array |001.8"},

ModelCorrespondence {"CIM_Memory.OtherErrorDescription"} ]

   uint16 ErrorInfo;
```

This listing indicates that the data type of ErrorInfo is a 16-bit unsigned integer. Fourteen enumerated values are defined for this attribute (this is the purpose of the ValueMap qualifier). These 14 values are defined in DMI. Notice that three of them (values 12, 13, and 14) cannot be used. The reason that they were defined anyway is because CIM always imports the full specification of an enumeration from another management system, even if some of the values cannot be used in the CIM context. The actual values to be associated with each of the 14 values are the strings defined in the Values array. Finally, note the use of the ModelCorrespondence qualifier. This qualifier relates this attribute to the OtherMemory Description attribute in the Memory class, which is described next. In effect, the value for the ErrorInfo attribute is one of the enumerated values specified earlier (except for values 12-14). However, if the value is 1 (for example, Other), then the value is defined by the OtherErrorDescription attribute. This provides an extensibility mechanism, so that implementations may define specific error types. The ModelCorrespondence qualifier is used to link these two attributes together, and provides the semantics of defining the particular type of error in the attribute and supplementing its description with additional information from the OtherErrorDescription attribute.

- OtherErrorDescription is a free-form string that is meant to be used with the ErrorInfo attribute. The purpose of this attribute is to provide more detailed information for the particular error identified by the ErrorInfo attribute when the value of the ErrorInfo attribute is set to 1 (for example, "Other"). If the value of the ErrorInfo attribute is not set to 1, then this attribute is not used. Note that the ModelCorrespondence qualifier must also be used in this attribute, and points back to the ErrorInfo attribute, as follows:

  ```
  ...ModelCorrespondence {"CIM_Memory.ErrorInfo"} ...
  ```

- CorrectableError is a boolean attribute that indicates that the most recent error for this memory device was correctable. Note that this attribute only has meaning as long as the value of the ErrorInfo attribute is *not* equal to 3 ("OK").

- ErrorTime is a datetime attribute that stores the date and time when the last memory error occurred. Again, this attribute only has meaning as long as the value of the ErrorInfo attribute is *not* equal to 3 ("OK").

- ErrorAccess is a 16-bit unsigned integer that has five enumerated values. It is used to store the type of memory access operation that caused the last error. The values are

Value	Meaning
1	"other"
2	"unknown"
3	"read"
4	"write"
5	"partial write"

Again, this attribute only has meaning as long as the value of the ErrorInfo attribute is *not* equal to 3 ("OK").

- ErrorTransferSize is a 32-bit unsigned integer attribute that indicates the size of the data transfer in bits that cause the last error. A value of 0 for this attribute indicates that no error is present. Again, this attribute only has meaning as long as the value of the ErrorInfo attribute is *not* equal to 3 ("OK").

- ErrorData is the actual data that was sent during the last memory access error. This is an array of 64 8-bit unsigned integers. The data occupies as many octets as needed (up to a maximum of 64), as determined by the ErrorTransferSize attribute. If the value of the ErrorTransferSize attribute is 0, then this attribute has no meaning.

- ErrorDataOrder is a 16-bit unsigned integer that has three enumerated values. The purpose of this attribute is to specify the ordering of data that is stored in the ErrorData attribute. The values can be 0 ("unknown"), 1 ("most significant byte first"), and 2 ("least significant byte first"). If the value of the ErrorTransferSize attribute is 0, then this attribute has no meaning.

- ErrorAddress is a 64-bit integer that specifies the address of the last memory error. The specific type of error is described by the ErrorInfo attribute. This attribute only has meaning as long as the value of the ErrorInfo attribute is *not* equal to 3 ("OK").

- SystemLevelAddress is a boolean attribute that indicates whether the address information in the ErrorAddress attribute is a system level address (TRUE) or a physical address (FALSE). This attribute only has meaning as long as the value of the ErrorInfo attribute is *not* equal to 3 ("OK").

- ErrorResolution is a 64-bit unsigned integer that defines the range, in bytes, for which the last error can be resolved. For example, if error addresses can be resolved to bit 12, then this means that errors can be resolved to 4K boundaries, and the value of this attribute is set to 12. This attribute only has meaning as long as the value of the ErrorInfo attribute is *not* equal to 3 ("OK").

- AdditionalErrorData is an array of 64 8-bit unsigned integers that can be used to hold additional error information. For example, if CRC is used for error detection and correction, then this attribute can be used to store the check bits. This attribute only has meaning as long as the value of the ErrorInfo attribute is *not* equal to 3 ("OK").

The Memory class does not define any methods. However, it does define one relationship (the AssociatedMemory association) and participate in two others. These other relationships, which are the ComputerSystemMemory aggregation and the AssociatedProcessorMemory association, will be covered when the ComputerSystem and Processor classes are discussed, respectively.

The AssociatedMemory association is a subclass of the Dependency association. The purpose of this association is to represent the dependency between certain types of LogicalDevices and their need for some type of memory. This could be used so that the LogicalDevice can store and retrieve data. It could also be used as a "scratchpad" for performing internal computations.

The NonVolatileStorage Class and Its Relationships

The NonVolatileStorage class is a subclass of the Memory class. It is used to represent any type of storage array that persists its data when power is turned off. This class has a single attribute, called IsWriteable, which is a boolean. This attribute is used to indicate whether this storage is writeable or not. If the storage is writeable, then the value of this attribute is TRUE. Note that this class is currently being revised as part of CIM 2.2.

This class defines no methods, but does define one association (BIOSLoadedInNV) to indicate if a BIOS is stored in this type of memory. This is not shown in Figure 7.16 for simplicity.

The VolatileStorage Class and Its Relationships

The VolatileStorage class is a subclass of the Memory class. It is used to represent storage arrays that do not persist their data when power is turned off.

This class has two attributes, both of which are used to indicate if this memory serves as a cache:

- Cacheable attribute is a boolean that indicates whether this memory serves as a cache (its value is TRUE if it is).

- CacheType attribute is used to indicate the particular type of cache. This attribute is a 16-bit unsigned integer that has five enumerated values:

Value	Meaning
1	"other"
2	"unknown"
3	"write-back"
4	"write-through"
5	"not applicable"

The last value (5) should be used if the Cacheable attribute is set to FALSE.

This class defines no methods or relationships.

The CacheMemory *Class and Its Relationships*

The CacheMemory class is a subclass of the Memory class. It is used to represent storage arrays that represent cache memories. The CacheMemory class defines the following attributes:

- Level defines the use (for example, level) of the cache. It is an enumerated 16-bit unsigned integer attribute with five values

Value	Meaning
1	"other"
2	"unknown"
3	"primary"
4	"secondary"
5	"Tertiary"

- WritePolicy defines how writes are performed in this cache. It is an enumerated 16-bit unsigned integer attribute with five values:

Value	Meaning
1	"other"
2	"unknown"
3	"write back"
4	"write through"
5	"varies with address"

- CacheType is an enumerated 16-bit unsigned integer attribute that is used to define whether this cache is used for instruction caching, data caching, or both. This attribute has the following five values:

Value	Meaning
1	"other"
2	"unknown"
3	"instruction"
4	"data"
5	"unified"

- `LineSize` defines the size in bytes of a single cache bucket or line. This is a 32-bit unsigned integer.

- `ReplacementPolicy` is an enumerated 16-bit unsigned integer that defines the algorithm used to determine which cache lines or buckets should be re-used. This attribute defines the following seven values:

Value	Meaning
1	`"other"`
2	`"unknown"`
3	`"least recently used (LRU)"`
4	`"first in first out (FIFO)"`
5	`"last in first out (LIFO)"`
6	`"least frequently used (LFU)"`
7	`"most frequently used (MFU)"`

- `ReadPolicy` defines the algorithm used by the cache for handling read requests. This is an enumerated 16-bit unsigned integer attribute with five values:

Value	Meaning
1	`"other"`
2	`"unknown"`
3	`"read"`
4	`"read-ahead"`
5	`"read and read-ahead"`

- `FlushTimer` defines the maximum amount of time, in seconds, that modified data may remain in the cache before they are flushed. A value of zero indicated that a cache flush is not controlled by a flushing timer. This is a 32-bit unsigned integer.

- `Associativity` is an enumerated 16-bit unsigned integer that defines the associativity of the system cache. The values are

Value	Meaning
1	`"other"`
2	`"unknown"`
3	`"direct mapped"`
4	`"2-way set-associative"`
5	`"4-way set associative"`
6	`"fully associative"`

This class defines no methods or relationships.

The `Processor` Class and Its Relationships

The purpose of the `Processor` class is to represent various types of processors that can be used as the computing element in various types of devices. For example, this class can be used not just to represent the processor in a computer system, but also the processor in a router or switch card, or the processor in an intelligent storage device.

An excerpt of the Device Model that focuses on the `Processor` class is shown in Figure 7.17. Note that this class is currently being revised as part of CIM 2.2.

The `Processor` class inherits the composite key of its superclass, `LogicalDevice`. The following are attributes that the `Processor` class defines:

- `Role` is a free-form string that is used to describe the role of the `Processor`. For example, a central processing unit is different from a math co-processor.

- `Family` is an enumerated 16-bit unsigned integer. This attribute is used to define the processor's family type. For example, the "Pentium Family" and the "IBM390 Family" are examples of processor family types. Listing 7.11 is an excerpt from the Device Model MOF that defines the full set of enumerations for this attribute.

Figure 7.17   Device Model excerpt: `Processor` and its relationships.

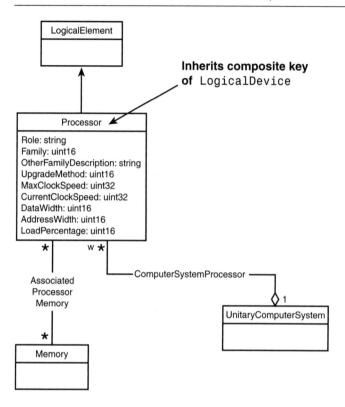

**Inherits composite key
of `LogicalDevice`**

Listing 7.11   Device Model MOF excerpt for the `Family` attribute.

```
[ Description( "The Processor family type. For example, values include "\"Pentium
    MMX\" (14) and \"C0040\" (96)."),

ValueMap {"1", "2", "3", "4", "5", "6", "7", "8", "9", "10", "11", "12", "13",
    "14", "15", "16", "18", "19", "25", "26", "27", "28", "32", "33", "34", "35",
    "36", "48", "64", "80", "96", "97", "98", "99", "100", "101", "112", "128",
    "144", "160", "180", "200", "250", "251", "260", "261", "280", "281", "300",
    "301", "302", "320"},

Values {"Other", "Unknown", "8086", "80286", "80386", "80486", "8087", "80287",
    "80387", "80487", "Pentium Family", "Pentium Pro", "Pentium II", "Pentium
    MMX", "Celeron", "Pentium II Xeon", "M1 Family", "M2 Family", "K5 Family", "K6
    Family", "K6-2", "K6-3", "Power PC Family", "Power PC 601", "Power PC 603",
    "Power PC 603+", "Power PC 604", "Alpha Family", "MIPS Family", "SPARC
    Family", "68040", "68xxx Family", "68000", "68010", "68020", "68030", "Hobbit
```

```
Family", "Weitek", "PA-RISC Family", "V30 Family", "AS400 Family", "IBM390
Family", "i860", "i960", "SH-3", "SH-4", "ARM", "StrongARM", "6x86",
"MediaGX", "MII", "WinChip"},

MappingStrings {"MIF.DMTF | Processor | 006.3"},

ModelCorrespondence {"CIM_Processor.OtherFamilyDescription"} ]

uint16 Family;
```

Note that the mapping strings are correlated against the master MIF file, and also that the OtherFamilyDescription attribute of the Processor class will be used to provide supplementary information.

> **Note**
>
> The *MIF*, or *Management Information Format*, is a language used by DMI (Desktop Management Interface) to described managed objects.

- OtherFamilyDescription is a string that is used to describe the processor family type when the Family attribute is set to 1 ("other"). If the value of the Family attribute is anything but 1, then this attribute has no meaning and should be set to NULL. Note that the MOF definition for this attribute also uses the ModelCorrespondence qualifier, with the value set to Processor.Family. This attribute is limited to 64 characters maximum.

- UpgradeMethod is an enumerated 16-bit unsigned integer that defines the means by which this processor can be upgraded. The MOF definition is provided in Listing 7.12.

Listing 7.12   Device Model MOF excerpt for the UpgradeMethod attribute.

```
[Description( "Method by which this processor can be upgraded, if upgrades are
supported. This property is an integer enumeration."),

ValueMap {"1", "2", "3", "4", "5", "6", "7", "8", "9"},

Values {"Other", "Unknown", "Daughter Board", "ZIF Socket", "Replacement/Piggy
Back", "None", "LIF Socket", "Slot 1", "Slot 2"},

MappingStrings {"MIF.DMTF | Processor | 006.7"}   ]

uint16 UpgradeMethod;
```

- MaxClockSpeed defines the maximum speed (in MHz) of this Processor. It is a 32-bit unsigned integer.

- CurrentClockSpeed defines the current operating speed (in MHz) of this Processor. It is a 32-bit unsigned integer.

- DataWidth defines the width of the data bus of the processor. It is a 16-bit unsigned integer.

- AddressWidth defines the width of the address bus of the processor. It is a 16-bit unsigned integer.

- LoadPercentage is a snapshot of the usage (for example, activity) of this processor, averaged over the last minute. It is a 16-bit unsigned integer.

The Processor class defines no methods. However, it defines the AssociatedProcessorMemory relationship and participates in the ComputerSystemProcessor relationship.

The AssociatedProcessorMemory Association

The AssociatedProcessorMemory relationship is a subclass of the AssociatedMemory association, which was defined by the Memory class. The purpose of this association is to define the dependency between a Processor and the Memory that is required. Since there are many different types of memory that a processor can require (for example, system memory or cache memory), the multiplicity of this association is zero-or-more to zero-or-more. In addition, an attribute, BusSpeed, is defined for this association. This attribute defines the speed of the bus, (in MHz) between the processor and the memory. Note that by placing this attribute on the association, we can represent different bus speeds between different memories that the processor uses.

Note

This is a good example of attaching data to an association. In this example, BusSpeed is *not* an attribute of either the Processor or the Memory, since there can be many different types of memory that the processor uses. Therefore, we place the attribute on the association that defines the particular processor-memory dependency that is being described.

Application Common Model Classes

The Application Common Model is oriented in this release of CIM to modeling the various stages of the life cycle of an application. An "application" is defined as a related set of software that end-users think of as an "application." The life cycle model that CIM currently has consists of four states, as shown in Figure 7.18.

Figure 7.18   Application Model excerpt: application life cycle.

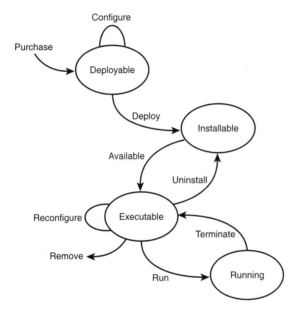

These states are described as follows:

- Deployable—The Deployable state is the beginning of the life cycle of a SoftwareElement. This state is achieved after the application has been purchased, including possibly performing some initial configuration of it. Additional procedures, such as licensing and arranging for support contracts, are also performed at this stage. At this point, the application is ready for installation.

- Installable—This step represents the knowledge necessary to successfully install the instance of the SoftwareElement, and what is required to transition to the Executable state. It consists of making the application available to its end-users. Note that additional configuration and support steps may take place in this state; they are not shown in Figure 7.18 for the sake of simplicity. This state also includes advertising to the set of targeted end-users the availability of the application, how to download and install it, how support will be performed, and other related information.

- Executable—This state represents the ability of the end-user to run the application. It is noted that some additional reconfiguration may take place at this stage (for example, define the preferences of the individual user to the application). From this state, the user could choose to run or uninstall the application. These actions correspond to transitioning to the executing or installable state, respectively. The user could also choose to remove the application. Executable doesn't transition to a definable state because it represents the desire of the user to not use the application, and this simple model assumes that the user is interested in using the application.

- Running—This state represents the application running. The Running state represents the ability to monitor and operate on a SoftwareElement that is executing. From this state, the user could terminate the application, in which case it returns to the executable state.

The Application Common Model is general enough to be used to describe a single software product as well as a complex, distributed application. It does this by defining the following five principal classes:

- ApplicationSystem—A general-purpose class that is used to represent an application. It provides the notion of "contained" software.

- SoftwareFeature—Represents the most important characteristics of a software program from an end-user point-of-view.

- SoftwareElement—Represents the individual files that comprise a SoftwareFeature.

- Check—Class represents one or more conditions that must be true in order to keep the SoftwareElement in its current state or approve its transition to a new state.

- Action—Represents the actual operations that are used to either keep the SoftwareElement in its current state or approve its transition to a new state.

Software is inherently a complex entity, and so the Application Model provides two classes to model software, SoftwareFeature and SoftwareElement. For example, a word processor needs the ability to spell-check, and a spreadsheet needs the example to do various types of recalculation. Each of these is a type of SoftwareFeature.

In reality, a SoftwareFeature is composed of a collection of SoftwareElements. A SoftwareElement partitions a SoftwareFeature into a set of components that can be individually managed. For example, the spell checker can be represented by a set of Files (for example, one that contains the spell checking function, another that contains the main dictionary used, and so on).

The combination of SoftwareFeature and SoftwareElement enable software products to be represented in terms that users and buyers understand, while still enabling the software to be managed.

The Application Common Model also introduces the concept of a state. Four primary states are defined: Deployable, Installable, Executable, and Running. A state, being a complex concept, is represented by two main classes. The Check class represents one or more conditions that must be true in order to keep the SoftwareElement in its current state or approve its transition to a new state. The Action class represents the actual operation(s) that is used to either keep the SoftwareElement in its current state or approve its transition to a new state.

The following sections describe the five principal classes of the Application Model that are applicable to DEN. A future release of the Application Common Model will represent "running" software in more detail.

The ApplicationSystem Class and Its Relationships

The ApplicationSystem class is a subclass of the System class. Its purpose is to represent an application that supports one or more specific business functions and which can be managed as an independent unit. The software aspects of the ApplicationSystem can be represented by instances of the SoftwareFeature class. These are defined by the ApplicationSystemSoftwareFeature aggregation.

An excerpt of the Application Model that focuses on the ApplicationSystem class is shown in Figure 7.19.

The ApplicationSystem class does not define any attributes or methods. This is done because there is very little in common between any two applications, and therefore avoiding imposing undue requirements on subclasses of ApplicationSystem that will be created to model specific applications. However, it does define one relationship, which is described next.

Figure 7.19 Application Model excerpt: `ApplicationSystem` and its relationships.

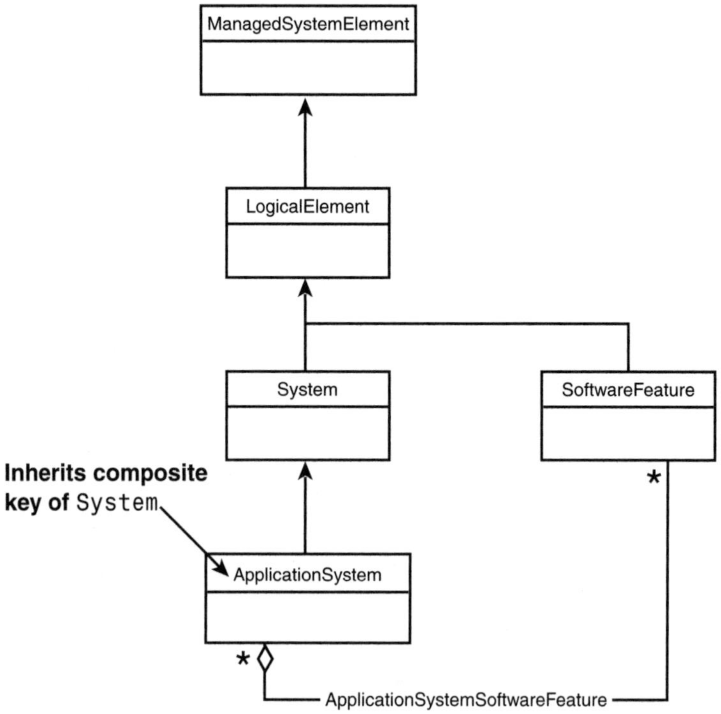

The `ApplicationSystemSoftwareFeature` *Aggregation*

The `ApplicationSystem` class defines one general-purpose aggregation. This is the `ApplicationSystemSoftwareFeature` aggregation. It is a subclass of the `SystemComponent` aggregation, and is used to identify the set of software features that are contained in a particular application. Note that this aggregation has nothing to do with software that is part of a product—that is defined by the `ProductSoftwareFeature` association that is described in the section "The `SoftwareFeature` Class and Its Relationships."

The `ApplicationSystemSoftwareFeature` aggregation has a multiplicity of zero-or-more to zero-or-more. This is to allow multiple software features to be aggregated by a single application, and multiple applications to use the same software feature.

The SoftwareFeature *Class and Its Relationships*

The SoftwareFeature class is a subclass of the LogicalElement class. Its purpose is to represent a specific function or capability of a software product or application. This class is intended to identify features that are meaningful to the end-user, as opposed to features that define how the product or application is built or packaged. The latter is captured by the SoftwareElement class, and related to the SoftwareFeature class through the SoftwareFeatureSoftwareElements aggregation.

The concept of a set of SoftwareElements that represent different aspects of a SoftwareFeature can be naturally extended to represent different components of a software feature that have platform-specific limitations. That is, the client portion of an application might run on several different platforms (for example, Windows 95, Windows NT, Solaris, and Macintosh). This situation requires multiple instances of SoftwareElement, one for each platform. However, from a management point-of-view, each of these can be aggregated into a SoftwareFeature. This simplifies management, as these same components can now be treated the same way, regardless of what platform they execute on.

SoftwareFeatures cannot exist by themselves; they must be defined in the context of a Product or an ApplicationSystem. This is explicitly rendered using the ProductSoftwareFeatures aggregation (discussed later) or the ApplicationSystemSoftwareFeature aggregation.

An excerpt of the Application Model that focuses on the SoftwareFeature class is shown in Figure 7.20.

The SoftwareFeature class has a composite key consisting of the propagated key of the Product class (that is, the IdentifyingNumber, Name, Vendor, and Version attributes) and the inherited Name attribute (from ManagedSystemElement) which it overrides. This enables a SoftwareFeature to be associated with a particular Product (alternatively, one can say that the Product class provides a *scope* for the SoftwareFeature class). The SoftwareFeature class overrides the propagated Name attribute in order to provide naming that is appropriate to software, as opposed to products. The definition of the Name attribute is the same as previous definitions of the Name attribute.

The SoftwareFeature class does not define any methods. However, it does define five relationships that are described next.

Figure 7.20   Application Model excerpt: `SoftwareFeature` and its relationships.

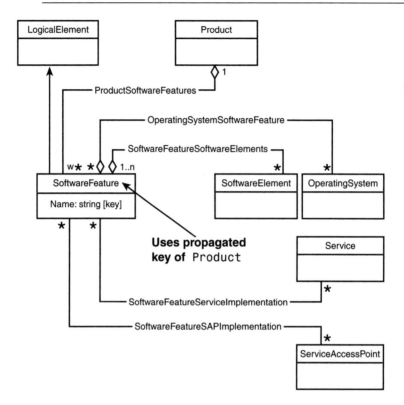

The `SoftwareFeatureSoftwareElements` *Aggregation*

The `SoftwareFeatureSoftwareElements` aggregation defines the specific `SoftwareElements` that are part of this `SoftwareFeature`. This is a subclass of the `Component` aggregation. It restricts the aggregate to an instance of the `SoftwareFeature` class, and also refines the cardinality of the aggregate end to one-or-more (from zero-or-more). The part component is also refined to be an instance of the `SoftwareElement` class, though its cardinality remains the same (zero-or-more).

The `ProductSoftwareFeatures` *Aggregation*

The `ProductSoftwareFeatures` aggregation defines the specific `SoftwareFeatures` that are part of this `Product`. This models how products are well-represented in the real world very well, since it emphasizes the essential functions of the product. The cardinality of the `Product` side of the aggregation is restricted to exactly one, and the cardinality of the `SoftwareFeature` side is zero-or-more. Note that this is a *weak* relationship, as the `SoftwareFeature` is defined to exist only in the context of a `Product`.

The OperatingSystemSoftwareFeature *Aggregation*

The OperatingSystemSoftwareFeature aggregation is defined later in the section "The OperatingSystem class and Its Relationships." It represents the set of SoftwareFeatures that together make up the functions of the operating system.

The SoftwareFeatureServiceImplementation *Association*

The SoftwareFeatureServiceImplementation association is a subclass of the Dependency association. This dependency relationship represents how a particular service is implemented in software. The multiplicity of this association remains zero-or-more to zero-or-more, since a SoftwareFeature may be used to implement many Services, and a Service may require multiple SoftwareFeatures. The subclass is used to restrict the antecedent to instances of type SoftwareFeature, and to restrict the dependent to instances of type Service.

The SoftwareFeatureSAPImplementation *Association*

The SoftwareFeatureSAPImplementation association is also a subclass of the Dependency association. This dependency relationship represents how a particular ServiceAccessPoint is implemented in software. The multiplicity of this association remains zero-or-more to zero-or-more, since a SoftwareFeature may be used to implement many ServiceAccessPoints, and a ServiceAccessPoint may require multiple SoftwareFeatures. The subclass is used to restrict the antecedent to instances of type SoftwareFeature, and to restrict the dependent to instances of type ServiceAccessPoint.

The SoftwareElement *Class and Its Relationships*

The SoftwareElement class is another subclass of the LogicalElement class. Its purpose is to represent all components of a SoftwareFeature object that can be individually managed and/or deployed, for a particular platform. The platform that a SoftwareElement applies to is identified by the underlying hardware architecture and operating system that the SoftwareElement runs on. Therefore, SoftwareElements are partly organized (for example, classified) by the operating system which they run on.

This class abstracts the complexity of a SoftwareFeature into its component parts so that each SoftwareElement that is contained in a particular SoftwareFeature can be managed independently. For example, a SoftwareFeature may be implemented by a set of files (for example, DLLs, or Dynamic Link Libraries). An update to the SoftwareFeature may be provided by replacing one or more of its files with a newer version.

An excerpt of the Application Model that focuses on the SoftwareElement class is shown in Figure 7.21.

Figure 7.21   Application Model excerpt: `SoftwareElement` and its relationships.

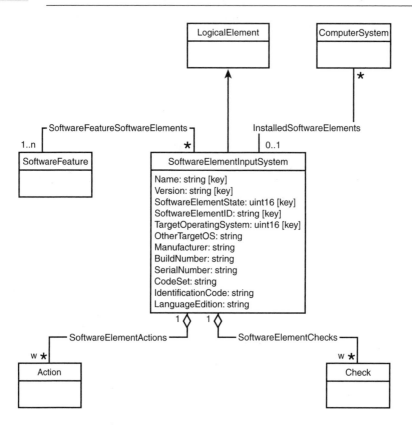

The `SoftwareElement` class has a composite key consisting of the `Name`, `Version`, `SoftwareElementState`, `SoftwareElementID`, and `TargetOperatingSystem` attributes. This enables a `SoftwareElement` to be uniquely identified by its name and version, what state it is currently in, some additional information that helps to differentiate between instances of the same class, and which operating system it is running on.

The following attributes are defined by the `SoftwareElement` class:

- `Name` is part of the composite key of the `SoftwareElement` class. It is a string, of a maximum of 256 characters, that represents the name of this `SoftwareElement` provided by its manufacturer.

- `Version` is part of the composite key of the `SoftwareElement` class. It is of the form:

```
<Major number>.<Minor number>.<Revision>
```
    or
```
<Major number>.<Minor number>.<letter>.<Revision>
```

It is a string of up to 64 characters.

- SoftwareElementState is part of the composite key of the SoftwareElement class. This attribute defines four possible states that all SoftwareElements must be in. Therefore, this attribute is an enumerated 16-bit unsigned integer, whose values corresponding to the strings "Deployable", "Installable", "Executable", and "Running".

- SoftwareElementID is part of the composite key of the SoftwareElement class. This attribute represents some unique information about this particular SoftwareElement instance, and is designed to be used in conjunction with the other composite keys of the SoftwareElement class in order to facilitate uniquely identifying different instances of the same SoftwareElement. It is a string of up to 256 characters.

- TargetOperatingSystem is part of the composite key of the SoftwareElement class, and is a string of up to 256 characters. This attribute contains the specific operating system that this particular SoftwareElement runs on. The value of this attribute may be verified by performing two checks, one by using an instance of the OSVersionCheck class and one by using an instance of the ArchitectureCheck class. The OSVersionCheck is used to verify that the correct version of the operating system is installed on the platform in which the SoftwareElement is being installed. The ArchitectureCheck is used to ensure that a specific SoftwareElement is compatible with the target platform. These are specific subclasses of the Check class, which will be described in the next section ("The Check Class and Its Relationships"). Listing 7.13 shows the current values of this attribute, taken from its MOF definition.

Listing 7.13   The MOF Values definition of the TargetOperatingSystem attribute.

```
... Values {"Unknown", "Other", "MACOS", "ATTUNIX", "DGUX", "DECNT", "Digital
Unix", "OpenVMS", "HPUX", "AIX", "MVS", "OS400", "OS/2", "JavaVM", "MSDOS",
"WIN3x", "WIN95", "WIN98", "WINNT", "WINCE", "NCR3000", "NetWare", "OSF",
"DC/OS", "Reliant UNIX", "SCO UnixWare","SCO OpenServer", "Sequent", "IRIX",
"Solaris", "SunOS", "U6000", "ASERIES", "TandemNSK", "TandemNT", "BS2000",
"LINUX", "Lynx", "XENIX", "VM/ESA", "Interactive UNIX", "BSDUNIX", "FreeBSD",
"NetBSD", "GNU Hurd", "OS9", "MACH Kernel", "Inferno", "QNX", "EPOC",
"IxWorks", "VxWorks", "MiNT", "BeOS", "HP MPE", "NextStep",  "PalmPilot",
"Rhapsody"},

ModelCorrespondence{"CIM_OperatingSystem.OSType"} ]

uint16 TargetOperatingSystem;
```

Note that this attribute uses the ModelCorrespondence qualifier to equate these values to the value of the OSType attribute of the OperatingSystem instance which this SoftwareElement instance depends on.

- OtherTargetOS contains the manufacturer and operating system type for a SoftwareElement when the value of the TargetOperatingSystem is 1 ("other"). If the value of the TargetOperatingSystem attribute is anything other than 1, then the value of this attribute should be NULL. It is a string of up to 64 characters. The MOF description of this attribute uses the ModelCorrespondence qualifier to ensure that the value of this attribute matches the value of the OtherTypeDescription attribute of the instance of the OperatingSystem class that this SoftwareElement instance is associated with.

- Manufacturer is used to store the manufacturer of this SoftwareElement. It is a string of up to 256 characters.

- BuildNumber is an internal identifier, used by the manufacturer of this SoftwareElement, to identify the specific compilation of this SoftwareElement. This is a string of up to 64 characters.

- SerialNumber is the manufacturer-assigned serial number of this SoftwareElement. This is a string of up to 64 characters.

- CodeSet is a description of the code used by this SoftwareElement. This is a string of up to 64 characters.

- IdentificationCode is a unique number, provided by the manufacturer of this SoftwareElement, that is used to uniquely identify different instances of this SoftwareElement. For example, this could be the part number or the SKU number of this SoftwareElement. This is a string of up to 64 characters.

- LanguageEdition identifies the specific language used, as detailed in ISO 639.

The SoftwareElement class does not define any methods. As previously mentioned, the SoftwareFeatureSoftwareElements aggregation identifies the set of SoftwareElements that are part of a specific SoftwareFeature. In addition, three new relationships are defined.

The SoftwareElementChecks Aggregation

The SoftwareElementChecks aggregation defines the different type of checks that can be applied to this SoftwareElement. The cardinality of this aggregation is defined to be exactly one on the SoftwareElement side, and zero-or-more on the Check side. Note that this is a *weak* relationship. This aggregation defines a single attribute, Phase, which is an enumerated 16-bit integer. It can have two values, "In-State" or "Next-State", that are used to define the type of check that is being performed.

The SoftwareElementActions *Aggregation*

The SoftwareElementActions aggregation defines the different type of actions that can be applied to this SoftwareElement. The cardinality of this aggregation is defined to be exactly one on the SoftwareElement side, and zero-or-more on the Action side. Note that this is a *weak* relationship.

The InstalledSoftwareElement *Association*

The InstalledSoftwareElement association is used to identify the specific ComputerSystem that a given SoftwareElement is installed on. To this end, the cardinality of this relationship is zero-or-one on the ComputerSystem side (meaning that this relationship is optional but, if instantiated, can involved at most a single ComputerSystem). The cardinality of this relationship on the SoftwareElement end is zero-or-more, meaning that zero or more SoftwareElements may be installed on a given ComputerSystem.

Note

You may wonder why the cardinality is zero-or-more instead of one-or-more. Doesn't a ComputerSystem *have* to have at least one SoftwareElement in order to function? The answer is threefold. First, although a ComputerSystem does indeed need at least one SoftwareElement in order to function, remember that CIM is a general management model. Thus, the system being managed could have a ComputerSystem that is not yet operational (for example, it is part of the system inventory) and thus, CIM could be used to track the SoftwareElements that belong to that ComputerSystem. Second, as a general rule, it is better to be as general as possible when designing classes. Thus, by having a cardinality of zero-or-more, we allow for the case of a ComputerSystem with embedded software. Finally, there may be some software that you are interested in modeling, and other software that you aren't. Hence, the cardinality allows you to talk about such software without modeling it.

The Check *Class and Its Relationships*

The Check class is a top-level abstract class. Its purpose is to represent different types of conditions that can be checked to determine if the SoftwareElement should either stay in its existing state, or transition into a new state.

The checks associated with a particular SoftwareElement are organized into two groups, using the Phase attribute of the SoftwareElementChecks aggregation. In-state checks are those conditions that can be satisfied when a SoftwareElement is in a specific environment. These conditions correspond to keeping the SoftwareElement in its current state. In contrast, conditions that must be met in order for a SoftwareElement to transition to a different state are called next-state checks.

The Check class has a composite key consisting in part of the propagated key of the SoftwareElement class. This is because Checks are associated directly with one or more SoftwareElements that they apply to. Thus, they use the composite key of SoftwareElement, consisting of the Name, Version, SoftwareElementState, SoftwareElementID, and TargetOperatingSystem attributes. To this is added the CheckID attribute of the Check class, which when combined with the propagated key of SoftwareElement, enables the specific instance of the Check class being applied to a given instance of the SoftwareElement class to be uniquely identified.

An excerpt of the Application Model that focuses on the Check class is shown in Figure 7.22.

Figure 7.22   Application Model excerpt: Check, Action, and their relationships.

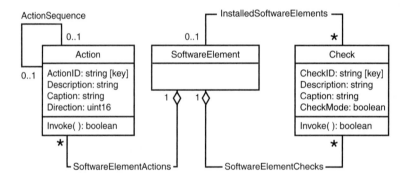

The following attributes are defined by the Check class:

- CheckID contains some unique information that can be used as a key attribute. It, in conjunction with the propagated composite key of the SoftwareElement class, is used to uniquely identify the Check instance that is being applied to a SoftwareElement instance. This attribute is a string of up to 256 characters.

- Description is a free-form string that contains a textual description of the Check (for example, its purpose and/or usage guidelines).

- Caption is a short, one-line description of the Check. It is intended for GUI applications, where space is at a premium and a short description of the object is required. It is a string of up to 64 characters.

- CheckMode is a boolean attribute that is used to indicate whether the condition is expected to exist or not in the environment (for example, a file is expected to be present, or an attribute is expected to have a certain value). When the value of this attribute is TRUE, then the condition is expected to exist in the system.

The Check class defines a method, Invoke, whose signature is

```
uint32  Invoke( )
```

This method is used to evaluate an instance of the Check class. The specific implementation of the Invoke method is left to the concrete subclasses of the Check class. The return values of this method are slightly different than in the rest of CIM. A zero is returned if the condition being checked is satisfied. A one is returned if the method is not supported. Finally, any other return value indicates that the condition is not satisfied.

The Check class defines one association, SoftwareElementChecks, which was previously described.

There are several subclasses of the Check class defined in CIM. The most important of these (with respect to DEN) are listed here:

- ArchitectureCheck is used to ensure that the SoftwareElement can run on a given platform.

- MemoryCheck defines the minimum amount of memory that must be available on a system.

- OSVersionCheck ensures that the version of the operating system can support this SoftwareElement.

- SoftwareElementVersionCheck specifies the particular version or range of versions of the SoftwareElement that is required for the current environment.

- VersionCompatibilityCheck is used to verify if the next state of a SoftwareElement can be created or not.

The Action Class and Its Relationships

The Action class is another top-level abstract class. Its purpose is to either transition a SoftwareElement to a new state, keep the SoftwareElement in its existing state, or remove the SoftwareElement completely.

Similar to the Check class, the Action class has a composite key consisting in part of the propagated key of the SoftwareElement class. This is because Actions are associated directly with one or more SoftwareElements that they apply to. Thus, they use the composite key of SoftwareElement, consisting of the Name, Version, SoftwareElementState, SoftwareElementID, and TargetOperatingSystem attributes. To this is added the ActionID attribute of the Action class, which when combined with the propagated key of SoftwareElement, enables the specific instance of the Action class being applied to a given instance of the SoftwareElement class to be uniquely identified.

An excerpt of the Application Model that focuses on the Action class is shown in Figure 7.22.

The following attributes are defined by the Action class:

- ActionID contains some unique information that can be used as a key attribute. It, in conjunction with the propagated composite key of the SoftwareElement class, is used to uniquely identify the Action instance that is being applied to a SoftwareElement instance. This attribute is a string of up to 256 characters.

- Description is a free-form string that contains a textual description of the Check (for example, its purpose and/or usage guidelines).

- Caption is a short, one-line description of the Check. It is intended for GUI applications, where space is at a premium and a short description of the object is required. It is a string of up to 64 characters.

- Direction is used to specify whether a particular Action object is part of a sequence of actions to install or uninstall a SoftwareElement. This is an enumerated 16-bit unsigned integer, whose values are "install" and "uninstall".

The Action class defines one method, Invoke, which is used to execute a specific sequence of operations that will either maintain the current state of the SoftwareElement, transition the SoftwareElement to a new state, or remove the SoftwareElement. Its signature is

```
uint32  Invoke( )
```

This method is used to evaluate an instance of the Action class. The specific implementation of the Invoke method is left to the concrete subclasses of the Action class. The return values of this method are slightly different than in the rest of CIM. A 0 is returned if the set of actions specified were executed successfully. A 1 is returned if the method is not supported. Finally, any other return value indicates that the set of actions specified were not executed successfully.

The Action class defines two relationships. One of them, SoftwareElementActions, has been previously described. The other, ActionSequence, is described below.

The ActionSequence Association

The ActionSequence association defines a series of operations that will be applied to the SoftwareElement to either transition it to a new state, maintain the SoftwareElement in its existing state, or remove the SoftwareElement completely.

There are several subclasses of the Action class defined in CIM. The most important of these (with respect to DEN) are

- RebootAction is used to reboot the system where the associated SoftwareElement is installed.

- ExecuteProgram causes one or more program elements to be executed on the system where the SoftwareElement is installed.

- FileAction is used to find, move, copy, or delete files that exist on the system in which the associated SoftwareElement resides.

- ModifySettingAction is used to modify a particular Setting for a specific entry with a specific value.

System Common Model Classes

The *System Common Model* focuses on providing classes, attributes, and relationships that enable general-purpose computer systems to be modeled. (Remember that *computer systems* is taken in the most general sense—the computing done by routers and switches makes them "computer systems.") These classes also serve to provide a framework for modeling other types of systems, such as an application or a network. The System Common Model does this by expanding the definition and usage of the System, Service, and ServiceAccessPoint classes defined in the Core Model. It also integrates the SoftwareFeature and SoftwareElement classes defined in the Application Common Model.

The portions of the System Common Model that are applicable to DEN center around the definition of and support for a computer system. Recall that a System is a LogicalElement that aggregates a well-defined set of ManagedSystemElements. The aggregate (that is, the System) operates as a functional whole, and can be identified as a single object in the managed environment. However, since it is an aggregation, it can be partitioned into a set of components, each of which can be individually managed. Furthermore, from a management point-of-view, every System consists of a set of defined ManagedSystemElements whose instances form the System. For example, a router is a single device that may have a number of networking cards installed in it that provide enhanced or additional functions. A router is modeled in DEN as a type of ComputerSystem (since routers *compute* routes) that contains a set of components. These components can be physical (for example, a chassis, power supply, cards, and so on) as well as logical (for example, the services provided by the router). It may also have a set of auxiliary components, such as an optional monitor, keyboard, and cabling that are used by a network administrator to configure the router. Thus, one can view a System either as a single object or a set of managed objects.

A System also has an important connotation. Some of the ManagedSystemElements that it contains provide critical functions to the System. For example, a router can still function if its top cover is removed. However, if the processor of one of its cards fails, then the functions provided by that card are lost. Depending on which card was crippled, the identity of the router may also be lost.

Systems can be identified by looking for complex objects that consist of multiple entities with the following characteristic: each entity in the complex object has one or more functions that it offers as well as one or more functions that it provides to the complex object as part of a cooperating aggregate. Note that objects that can be managed only in the context of another System are not themselves Systems. Rather, such an object would be a component of a System.

The System object is used to enumerate the ManagedSystemElement instances that are contained in it. The System object also provides semantics on how to assemble and configure its component parts. System objects represent different aspects of a system, and therefore are driven by the underlying applications that use the System as well as the needs of the other Common Models. For example, the Networks Common Model, along with DEN, added new aspects to the existing capabilities of the System object and its subclasses. These will be further explained in Chapters 9 and 10.

Note

The System Common Model is very detailed. Not all of its classes are directly applicable to a DEN model, and therefore will not be described in this book. The reader is encouraged to explore the System Common Model in more detail.

More About the ComputerSystem Class

A ComputerSystem is a special type of System that provides computing capabilities. A ComputerSystem aggregates hardware, software, and firmware. In addition, a ComputerSystem serves as an aggregation point for key components such as operating systems, file systems, processors, and other components. Finally, a ComputerSystem hosts Services and ServiceAccessPoints. ComputerSystems are a special subclass of System.

The System Common Model defines five additional relationships for a ComputerSystem. These are shown in Figure 7.23.

Figure 7.23   System Model excerpt: additional `ComputerSystem` relationships.

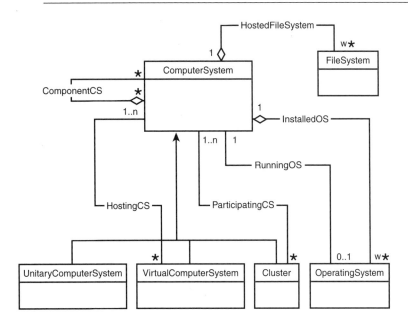

The `ComponentCS` Aggregation

`ComponentCS` is an aggregation that enables the instance of one `ComputerSystem` to aggregate instances of other `ComputerSystems`. This aggregation can be used for many different purposes, ranging from modeling a multi-processor machine to Intelligent Input-Output systems to the collection of networking cards that a single router (or switch) contains. The `ComponentCS` aggregation is a subclass of the `SystemComponent` aggregation, indicating that it refines the more general features present in the `SystemComponent` aggregation. This refinement consists of restricting both classes of the aggregation to be of type `ComputerSystem` (or one of its subclasses).

It is important to distinguish when to use the `ComponentCS` aggregation, and when to use a `Cluster`. The difference is that this aggregation models instances of atomic `ComputerSystems` that are in turn aggregated by a higher-level `ComputerSystem` instance. The important characteristic of this aggregation is that each of the component `ComputerSystems` are still distinguishable entities in their own right and must be treated and managed as such. On the other hand, a `Cluster` is a `System` whose aggregated `ComputerSystems` no longer have any individual identity. That is, you can *only* refer to them as a 'cluster' (implying that the group itself is atomic), and can no longer manage the component `ComputerSystems` individually.

The InstalledOS *Aggregation*

InstalledOS is another aggregation that is also derived from SystemComponent. It defines the OperatingSystem(s) that are installed on a given ComputerSystem. The usual meaning is for the OperatingSystem to be stored on either memory of the ComputerSystem or storage that is associated with the ComputerSystem (for example, a hard drive). Note that for network computers and similar devices (for example, the NetPC), this aggregation would represent an OperatingSystem that was downloaded via the network. This subclass restricts the classes participating in this relationship to ComputerSystem (as the group component) and OperatingSystem (as the part component). The cardinality of the group component is defined to be exactly one, since we are finding the operating systems that are installed on a particular computer system. The cardinality of the part component may be zero-or-more, where zero indicates that nothing is installed yet. Note that this is a weak association, since OperatingSystems are hosted in ComputerSystems. Finally, a boolean attribute, PrimaryOS, is defined that indicates which OperatingSystem, of possibly several that are installed, is the default OperatingSystem for the ComputerSystem.

The RunningOS *Association*

RunningOS is a subclass of the Dependency association. It is possible for a ComputerSystem to install multiple OperatingSystems and enable the user to choose which operating system the user wants to boot with. This association identifies the currently running operating system. Since at most a single operating system can run on any given computer, the cardinality of the antecedent (that is, the OperatingSystem) is set to zero-or-one (zero is allowed because the computer may not be booted yet, and hence no operating system is installed; this is a common case for network computers). The cardinality of the dependent (that is, the ComputerSystem) is set to exactly one, because we are concerned with a single computer system.

The HostedFileSystem *Aggregation*

HostedFileSystem is another subclass of the SystemComponent class. This aggregation is used to identify the FileSystems that are hosted by a given ComputerSystem. Accordingly, the aggregate (that is, the ComputerSystem) is set to exactly one, and the part components (that is, the FileSystem(s)) are set to zero-or-more. Zero is a valid value, because a network computer may not have a file system present. Finally, note that this is a *weak* aggregation, because the FileSystem is *hosted* by the ComputerSystem.

The `ParticipatingCS` Association

Finally, `ParticipatingCS` is a subclass of the `Dependency` association. It is used to identify the set of `ComputerSystems` that are contained in a `Cluster`. A `Cluster` is a special type of computer that contains multiple `ComputerSystems`. Each contained `ComputerSystem` is assigned to work on a set of tasks. This relationship identifies which `ComputerSystems` are participating in which `Cluster`. Since only a single `ComputerSystem` can be operational when the `Cluster` is first booted or established, the cardinality of this relationship on the `ComputerSystem` side is one-or-more.

The `ParticipatingCS` association defines two attributes. The `StateOfNode` attribute is an enumerated 16-bit unsigned integer, and is used to describe the condition of the participating `ComputerSystem` in the `Cluster`. The values defined include `"Unknown"`, `"Other"`, `"Joining"`, `"Paused"`, `"Available"`, `"Unavailable"`, and `"Degraded"`. The `RoleOfNode` attribute is also an enumerated 16-bit unsigned integer. It defines the specific type of relationship between a given `ComputerSystem` and its containing `Cluster`. Values include `"Unknown"`, `"Other"`, `"Peer"`, `"Primary"`, `"Secondary"`, and `"Standby"`.

The `UnitaryComputerSystem` Class

The `UnitaryComputerSystem` class is a subclass of the `ComputerSystem` class. This class is used to represent a variety of devices whose common characteristic is that they have a single `Processor` that performs their computations. Thus, the devices that the `UnitaryComputerSystem` class can be used to represent range from a desktop PC to a network computer to a router or switch.

The `UnitaryComputerSystem` has a number of required semantics. The most important of these is that a `ComputerSystem` has a single `Processor`, or node, that has at least one `OperatingSystem` and some `Memory`. Therefore, a `UnitaryComputerSystem` provides scoping for the `LogicalDevices` that it contains. Two examples of this are provided by the `ComputerSystemProcessor` and the `ComputerSystemMemory` aggregations. An excerpt from the System and Device Common Models is shown in Figure 7.24 that represents the `UnitaryComputerSystem` and its important relationships.

Similarly, `ComputerSystems` require software in order to provide computational capabilities, and therefore a `ComputerSystem` also provides scoping for one or more `OperatingSystems`. Note that an `OperatingSystem` can either be a `Product` (for example, Windows) or special firmware that is loaded into non-volatile storage, such as is found in some network devices. A `ComputerSystem` may contain multiple `OperatingSystems`, which are indicated using the `InstalledOS` aggregation. When more than one `OperatingSystem` is available on a `ComputerSystem`, the one that is "booted" at any point in time is indicated by the `RunningOS` association. All these also apply for `UnitaryComputerSystems`.

Figure 7.24 System Model excerpt: `UnitaryComputerSystem` and its relationships.

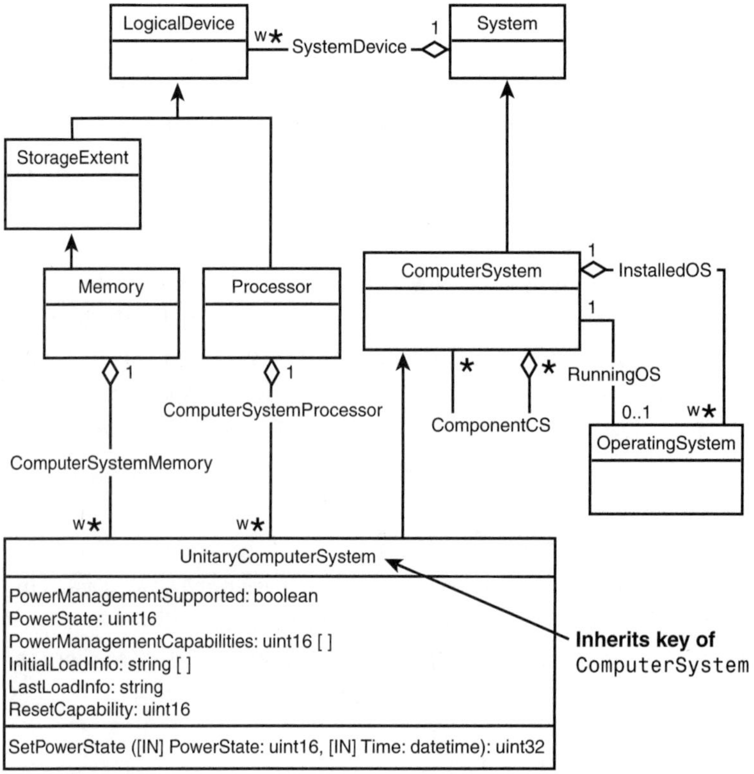

The `UnitaryComputerSystem` class defines the following attributes:

- `PowerManagementSupported` is a boolean attribute that indicates that the referenced `UnitaryComputerSystem` supports power management. It is meant to be used with the `PowerManagementCapabilities` attribute, which defines whether the power management capabilities of the `UnitaryComputerSystem` is currently enabled or not, and what those capabilities are. If the value of this attribute is `FALSE`, then the `PowerManagementCapabilities` attribute has no meaning.

- PowerState indicates the current power state of the UnitaryComputerSystem. This is an enumerated 16-bit unsigned integer. Values are as follows:

Value	Name	Description
0	"Unknown"	The state of power is not known.
1	"Full Power"	Full power is applied.
2	"Power Save—Low Power Mode"	The UnitaryComputerSystem is in a power save state that greatly reduces the power to the system, and therefore may exhibit degraded performance.
3	"Power Save—Standby"	The UnitaryComputerSystem is currently not functioning, but may be brought to full power "quickly."
4	"Power Save—Unknown"	The UnitaryComputerSystem is known to be in a power save mode, but that the exact mode and status of the UnitaryComputerSystem is not known.
5	"Power Cycle"	Power is currently being cycled to the UnitaryComputerSystem.
6	"Power Off"	Power to the UnitaryComputerSystem has been turned off.
7	"Power Save—Warning"	The UnitaryComputerSystem is both in a power save mode as well as in a warning state.

- PowerManagementCapabilities is an array of enumerated 16-bit integers. Each integer value has a specific meaning. Thus, the status (for example, "enabled") and capabilities (for example, "power saving modes entered automatically") are recorded in the array. The array enables multiple capabilities to be assigned. The values are as follows:

Value	Name	Description
0	"Unknown"	The state of power is not known.
1	"Not Supported"	Power is not supported.
2	"Disabled"	Power is disabled.
3	"Enabled"	Power management features are currently enabled, but the exact feature set is unknown or the information is unavailable.
4	"Power Saving Modes Entered Automatically"	The system can change its power state automatically, based on usage or other criteria.
5	"Power State Settable"	The SetPowerState method is supported.
6	"Power Cycling Supported"	The SetPowerState method can be invoked with the PowerState input variable set to 5.
7	"Timed Power On Supported"	The SetPowerState method can be invoked with the PowerState input variable set to 5 and the Time parameter set to a specific date and time, or interval, for power-on

- InitialLoadInfo is an array of free-form strings. This array contains all data required to find the initial way of booting the UnitaryComputerSystem (either through a device or a boot service). Load parameters may also be specified in this attribute.

- LastLoadInfo is a free-form string that identifies how the UnitaryComputerSystem was last booted (for example, through which device or service).

- ResetCapability is an enumerated 16-bit unsigned integer that describes what method is used to reset the hardware of the UnitaryComputerSystem. Values include 1 ("Other"), 2 ("Unknown"), 3 ("Disabled"), 4 ("Enabled"), and 5 ("Not Implemented").

The `UnitaryComputerSystem` class defines a single method, called `SetPowerState`. This method is used to place the `UnitaryComputerSystem` into a desired power state. Its signature is

```
SetPowerState( [IN] PowerState: uint16, [IN] Time: datetime ) : uint32
```

As can be seen, this method takes two input parameters. The first, `PowerState`, is the attribute that is described earlier. The second, `Time`, indicates the date and time or time interval that when the power state should be set. When the value of the `PowerState` input parameter is 5 (`"Power Cycle"`), then the `Time` parameter indicates when the `UnitaryComputerSystem` should be powered on again. A return value of 0 indicates that the `SetPowerState` method was successful in changing the power state of the `UnitaryComputerSystem` to the value indicated by its `PowerState` parameter. A return value of 1 indicates that the requested combination of power state and time to be applied is not supported. Any other return value indicates that an error occurred in the application of the `SetPowerState` method.

The `UnitaryComputerSystem` class defines two relationships, `ComputerSystemMemory` and `ComputerSystemProcessor`.

The `ComputerSystemMemory` Aggregation

`ComputerSystemMemory` is an aggregation that is a subclass of the `SystemDevice` aggregation. It indicates that memory is required for the `UnitaryComputerSystem` to operate. This is a *weak* relationship, since the `UnitaryComputerSystem` "owns" the memory, enabling multiple memory devices to be aggregated by the `UnitaryComputerSystem`.

The `ComputerSystemProcessor` Aggregation

`ComputerSystemProcessor` is another subclass of the `SystemDevice` aggregation, and is similar in nature to the `ComputerSystemMemory` aggregation. `ComputerSystemProcessor` is used to indicate that a processor is required of a `UnitaryComputerSystem`. Again, the processor is "owned" by the `UnitaryComputerSystem`, and therefore this is a *weak* relationship.

The `VirtualComputerSystem` Class

The `VirtualComputerSystem` is used to model the ability to emulate another hardware architecture or virtual machine. The `VirtualComputerSystem` class defines a single attribute, `VirtualSystem`, that is used to describe that type of system that is being virtualized. Note that since `VirtualComputerSystem` is a subclass of `ComputerSystem`, it inherits all of the attributes and relationships that `ComputerSystem` has. For example, the `RunningOS` association can be used to determine which operating system is currently running in the virtualized computer system.

The VirtualSystem class defines no methods, but it does define one relationship, HostingCS. The HostingCS association is a subclass of the more generic Dependency association, and is used to define the UnitaryComputerSystem that hosts the VirtualComputerSystem. Accordingly, the cardinality of this association is limited to one-or-more on the ComputerSystem, and zero-or-more on the VirtualComputerSystem side.

The Cluster *Class*

A Cluster represents a computer system that consists of other computer systems. The set of computer systems functions as an atomic whole. Each of the individual computer systems that are contained in the Cluster provides a dedicated function. Usually, individual components of the Cluster can be added or removed without adversely affecting the Cluster, as long as a minimum number of nodes that is particular to each Cluster is maintained. The ParticipatingCS association defines the ComputerSystems that participate in a given Cluster, and a ComputerSystem can in theory participate in more than one Cluster.

The Cluster class defines the following attributes:

- Interconnect is a free-form string that describes how each of the nodes that are contained in the Cluster are interconnected.

- InterconnectAddress indicates the address of the Cluster, which is dependent on how the nodes of the Cluster are interconnected.

- Types is an array of enumerated 16-bit unsigned integers. This array specifies how the Cluster is used. It is an array since a given Cluster may be used for more than one of these purposes. Values include:

Value	Meaning
"Unknown", "Other", "Failover"	The purpose of the Cluster is to provide improved failover capabilities.
"Performance"	The purpose of the Cluster is to provide improved performance capabilities.
"Distributed OS"	The purpose of the Cluster is to realize a distributed operating system.
"Node Grouping"	The purpose of the Cluster is to group a set of ComputerSystems in some way.

- `MaxNumberOfNodes` defines the maximum number of `ComputerSystems` that may participate at any given time in the `Cluster`.

- `ClusterState` defines the current state of the `Cluster`. Values include "`Unknown`", "`Other`", "`On-line`", "`Off-line`", "`Degraded`", and "`Unavailable`".

The `Cluster` class defines no methods, but does participate in two relationships. The `ParticipatingCS` association was previously defined when the `System` class was discussed. The `HostedClusterService` will be discussed when the `ClusteringService` class is discussed later in this chapter.

An additional set of classes and relationships can be used to further define the capabilities of `Clusters`. You are encouraged to study the System Common Model and look at the following important classes and relationships:

- `ClusteringService` (models the functions provided by a `Cluster`)

- `ClusterServiceAccessBySAP` (defines the relationship between a `ClusteringService` and its `ServiceAccessPoints`)

- `HostedClusterSAP` (this is a subclass of the `HostedAccessPoint` association, and is used to define the hosting `ComputerSystem` for a `ClusteringSAP`).

The `OperatingSystem` *Class and Its Relationships*

An `OperatingSystem` in CIM is defined as a set of software and firmware that makes a given `ComputerSystem` usable by providing a set of services that manage the resources of a `ComputerSystem`. Such resources include processes, jobs, threads, file systems, and other concepts that are defined in CIM. It is a subclass of `LogicalElement`.

An `OperatingSystem` cannot exist by itself; it must be hosted by another object. The hosting object for an `OperatingSystem` is, of course, a `ComputerSystem`. Therefore, the composite key of the `ComputerSystem` class is propagated to the `OperatingSystem` class. This propagated key consists of the `CreationClassName` (renamed as `CSCreationClassName`) and the `Name` (renamed as `CSName`) attributes. `OperatingSystem` then adds its own `CreationClassName` and `Name` attributes as part of the composite key (this is why the propagated `CreationClassName` and `Name` attributes were renamed `CSCreationClassName` and `CSName`, respectively). This collection of four attributes provides the ability to uniquely identify the instance of the `ComputerSystem` that is hosting the `OperatingSystem` (through the `CSCreationClassName` and `CSName` attributes) as well as the instance of the `OperatingSystem` that the `ComputerSystem` instance is using (through the use of the `CreationClassName` and `Name` attributes).

An excerpt from the System Common Model is shown in Figure 7.25 that represents the OperatingSystem and its important relationships.

Figure 7.25 System Model excerpt: OperatingSystem and its relationships.

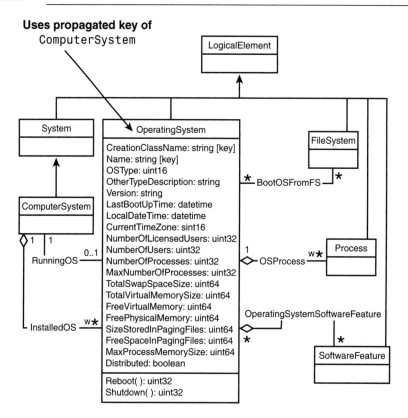

The following are attributes that the ComputerSystems class defines:

- CreationClassName is one of the four key attributes of the OperatingSystem class. It defines the name of the class used in the creation of an instance. It is a string of up to 256 characters.

- Name is another key attribute of the OperatingSystem class. It is inherited from LogicalElement, and is overridden to be made a key for this attribute. It is a string of up to 256 characters.

- OSType is an enumerated 16-bit unsigned integer that is used to indicate the specific type of operating system this instance is. Custom operating systems are handled by setting the value of this attribute to 1 ("Other") and then using the OtherTypeDescription attribute to provide the specific details of this attribute. For all other values of the OSType attribute, the OtherTypeDescription attribute has no meaning. The currently defined values of this attribute are shown in Listing 7.14.

Listing 7.14   The MOF Values definition of the TargetOperatingSystem attribute.

```
[ Description ( "A integer indicating the type of OperatingSystem."),

Values {"Unknown", "Other", "MACOS", "ATTUNIX", "DGUX", "DECNT", "Digital Unix",
    "OpenVMS", "HPUX", "AIX", "MVS", "OS400", "OS/2", "JavaVM", "MSDOS", "WIN3x",
    "WIN95", "WIN98", "WINNT", "WINCE", "NCR3000", "NetWare", "OSF", "DC/OS",
    "Reliant UNIX", "SCO UnixWare", "SCO OpenServer", "Sequent", "IRIX",
    "Solaris", "SunOS", "U6000", "ASERIES", "TandemNSK", "TandemNT", "BS2000",
    "LINUX", "Lynx", "XENIX", "VM/ESA", "Interactive UNIX", "BSDUNIX", "FreeBSD",
    "NetBSD", "GNU Hurd", "OS9", "MACH Kernel", "Inferno", "QNX", "EPOC",
    "IxWorks", "VxWorks", "MiNT", "BeOS", "HP MPE", "NextStep", "PalmPilot",
    "Rhapsody"},

ModelCorrespondence { "CIM_OperatingSystem.OtherTypeDescription" } ]

uint16 OSType;
```

- OtherTypeDescription is a string of up to 64 characters that is used to describe the manufacturer and type of operating system when the value of the OSType attribute of the OperatingSystem class is set to 1 ("Other"). When the value of the OSType attribute is any value other than 1, then the value of the OtherTypeDescription attribute should be set to NULL.

- Version is a free-form string that defines the current version of the OperatingSystem. The format of this information is either:

```
        <Major Number>.<Minor Number>.<Revision>
```
    or
```
        <Major Number>.<Minor Number>.<Revision Letter>
```

- LastBootUpTime is the date and/or time when the OperatingSystem was last booted.

- LocalDateTime defines the local date and time from the perspective of the OperatingSystem.

- CurrentTimeZone defines the number of minutes the OperatingSystem is offset from Greenwich Mean Time. This number can be positive, negative, or zero, and is therefore a signed 16-bit integer.

- NumberOfLicensedUsers defines the number of user licenses for the OperatingSystem. If this number is unlimited, then a value of 0 is entered. This is a 16-bit unsigned integer.

- NumberOfUsers defines the current number of user sessions that the OperatingSystem is storing state information for. This is a 32-bit unsigned integer.

- NumberOfProcesses defines the number of distinct process contexts that are currently loaded or running on the OperatingSystem. This is a 32-bit unsigned integer.

- MaxNumberOfProcesses is the maximum number of process contexts that the OperatingSystem can support. If there is no fixed maximum, then the value of this attribute should be set to 0. This is a 32-bit unsigned integer.

- TotalSwapSpaceSize defines the total swap space in kilobytes. This value may be NULL if swap space is not distinguished from page files. This is a 64-bit unsigned integer.

- TotalVirtualMemorySize defines the amount of virtual memory in kilobytes. This is a 64-bit unsigned integer.

- FreeVirtualMemory defines the amount of virtual memory in kilobytes that is currently unused and available. This is a 64-bit unsigned integer.

- FreePhysicalMemory defines the amount of physical memory in kilobytes that is currently unused and available. This is a 64-bit unsigned integer.

- SizeStoredInPagingFiles is the total number of kilobytes that can be stored in the paging files of the OperatingSystem. A value of 0 indicates that there are no paging files. This is a 64-bit unsigned integer.

- FreeSpaceInPagingFiles is the total number of kilobytes that can be mapped into the paging files of the OperatingSystem without causing any other pages to be swapped out. A value of 0 indicates that there are no paging files. This is a 64-bit unsigned integer.

- MaxProcessMemorySize is the maximum number of kilobytes that can be allocated to any single process. For OperatingSystems that do not have any virtual memory, MaxProcessMemorySize is typically the total amount of physical memory minus the memory used by the BIOS and operating system. For other OperatingSystems, this value may be infinity, in which case 0 should be entered. In other cases, this value could be a constant. This is a 64-bit unsigned integer.

- `Distributed` is a boolean that indicates whether the `OperatingSystem` is distributed across multiple `ComputerSystem` nodes. If it is, then these nodes should be grouped as a `Cluster`.

The `OperatingSystem` class defines two methods. The `Reboot` method is used to request a reboot of the `OperatingSystem`. The return value should be `0` if the request was successfully executed, `1` if the request is not supported, and some other value if an error occurred. The signature of this method is

```
Reboot( ) : uint32
```

The `Shutdown` method is used to request a complete shutdown of the `OperatingSystem`. The return value should be `0` if the request was successfully executed, `1` if the request is not supported, and some other value if an error occurred. The signature of this method is

```
Shutdown( ) : uint32
```

The `OperatingSystem` class defines five relationships. The `InstalledOS` and `RunningOS` relationships have previously been discussed in this chapter. The next sections will describe the `OperatingSystemSoftwareFeature` and `OSProcess` aggregations along with the `BootOSFromFS` association.

The `OperatingSystemSoftwareFeature` Aggregation

`OperatingSystemSoftwareFeature` is an aggregation that defines the specific `SoftwareFeatures` that are contained in an `OperatingSystem`. This aggregation is a subclass of the `Component` aggregation. Note that the `SoftwareFeatures` can be part of different `Products`.

The `OSProcess` Aggregation

`OSProcess` is an aggregation that associates a set of `Processes` that are running in this `OperatingSystem`. It is a subclass of the `Component` aggregation.

The `BootOSFromFS` Association

Finally, the `BootOSFromFS` association is used to define the `FileSystem`(s) that are used to load this `OperatingSystem`. This is a zero-or-more to zero-or-more association to account for the case of distributed operating systems, which could depend on several different file systems.

The File System Hierarchy

CIM represents the ability to store data locally as well as remotely through the use of logical files and file systems. An excerpt of the System Model that shows the FileSystem class and its relationships is shown in Figure 7.26.

Figure 7.26   System Model excerpt: FileSystem and its relationships.

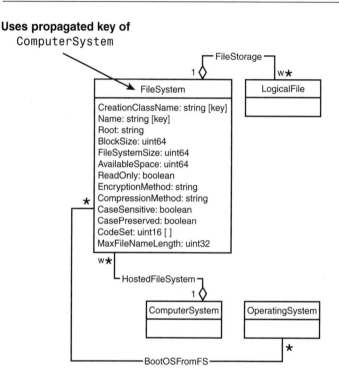

The FileSystem Class and Its Hierarchy

A FileSystem represents the ability to store a set of related files locally on or remotely associated with a ComputerSystem. Since FileSystems are contained by ComputerSystems, they are weak with respect to ComputerSystems. This means that the composite key of the ComputerSystem class (for example, the CreationClassName and Name attributes) must be propagated to the FileSystem class. Additional attributes from the FileSystem class (that is, its CreationClassName and Name attributes) must be added to the propagated attributes, to form a composite key. Therefore, the propagated attributes are renamed to

CSCreationClassName and CSName, respectively, to avoid clashing with the CreationClassName and Name attributes defined by the FileSystem class. The resulting composite key will then be able to distinguish between different instances of the FileSystem class that are used by different instances of the ComputerSystem class. The HostedFileSystem aggregation represents instances of the FileSystem class that are associated with instances of the ComputerSystem class.

A FileSystem consists of different types of logical files, which is modeled by the LogicalFile class. Three types of LogicalFiles are defined: Directories, Data and Executable Files. These correspond to the ability to serve as a container of other types of files (including additional directories), to contain data, and to execute processes and programs.

The FileSystem class defines the following attributes:

- CreationClassName is one of the four key attributes of the FileSystem class. It defines the name of the class used in the creation of an instance. It is a string of up to 256 characters.

- Name is another key attribute of the FileSystem class. It is inherited from LogicalElement, and is overridden to be made a key for this attribute. It is a string of up to 256 characters.

- Root is a free-form string that stores the path (or equivalent information) defining the root of the file system.

- Blocksize is a 64-bit unsigned integer that represents the number of bytes used in read and write operations of the FileSystem.

- FileSystemSize is a 64-bit unsigned integer that is used to store the total size of the FileSystem in bytes. If this value is not known, then a 0 should be entered.

- AvailableSpace is a 64-bit unsigned integer that indicates the total amount of free space in bytes for the FileSystem. If this value is not known, then a 0 should be entered.

- ReadOnly is a boolean attribute that indicates only read-only operations are allowed to be executed on this FileSystem.

- EncryptionMethod is a free-form string that indicates the specific type of algorithm or tool used to encrypt the FileSystem. If it is not possible or not desired to describe the encryption scheme (perhaps for security reasons), then enter either the value "Unknown" (if it is not known whether the FileSystem is actually encrypted or not), "Encrypted" (to represent that the FileSystem is encrypted, but the specific encryption scheme is not available), or "Not Encrypted" (to represent that the FileSystem is not encrypted).

- CompressionMethod is a free-form string that indicates the specific type of algorithm or tool used to compress the FileSystem. If it is not possible or not desired to describe the compression scheme, or if the compression scheme is not known, then it is recommended to use the string "Unknown" to represent this fact. The other recommended values are "Compressed" (to represent that the FileSystem is compressed but either its specific compression scheme is not known or not disclosed), and "Not Compressed" to represent that the FileSystem is not compressed.

- CaseSensitive is a boolean attribute that indicates that case sensitive file names are supported.

- CasePreserved is a boolean attribute that indicates that the case of file names are preserved.

- CodeSet is an enumerated 16-bit unsigned integer array that defines the various types of code sets that are supported by this FileSystem. Allowable values are "Unknown", "Other", "ASCII", "Unicode", "ISO2022", "ISO8859", and "Extended UNIX Code".

- MaxFileNameLength is a 32-bit unsigned integer that defines the maximum length of a file name within this FileSystem. If there is no limit on the file name length, then this attribute should be assigned the value 0.

The FileSystem class does not define any methods. It participates in two relationships that have been previously defined (HostedFileSystem and BootOSFromFS), as well as defines a new relationship, FileStorage.

The FileStorage aggregation is a subclass of the Component aggregation, and is used to define the set of LogicalFiles that are contained within a FileSystem. Accordingly, the cardinality on the FileSystem side of this relationship is exactly 1, since we are describing the relationship between a set of LogicalFiles and a single FileSystem. The LogicalFile is, of course, weak to the FileSystem that contains it.

The FileSystem class has two direct subclasses. None of these classes define any attributes or methods, because these would necessarily be implementation-dependent and application-specific. An excerpt of the System Model with these subclasses and their relationships is shown in Figure 7.27.

Figure 7.27   System Model excerpt: Subclasses of FileSystem and their relationships.

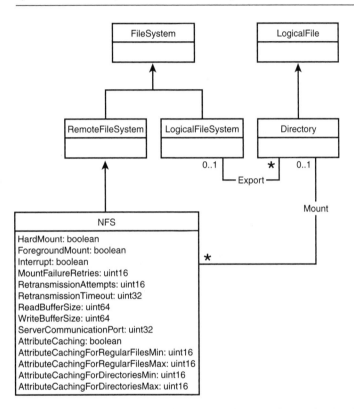

The LocalFileSystem subclass represents a file system that resides in the local media of its host ComputerSystem. This class defines no attributes or methods, but does define one additional relationship, called Export. This association indicates that the specified remote directories can be mounted on a local file system. This is an optional association, but if it exists, it is defined as associating many directories with a single LocalFileSystem. Hence, the cardinality on the LocalFileSystem side of the relationship is zero-or-one, while the cardinality on the Directory (this class is described in the next section, "The LogicalFile Class and Its Relationships") side of the relationship is zero-or-more.

The RemoteFileSystem subclass represents a file system whose contents are accessed using a network-related service. This implies that the file store is not on the local media of the ComputerSystem. This class defines no additional attributes or relationships. It does not define any relationships, but serves as the parent of the NFS class.

The NFS (NetworkFileSystem) subclass represents a FileSystem of another ComputerSystem that is mounted on this ComputerSystem (that is, the file system of the other ComputerSystem is being shared between the two ComputerSystems). The Directory class uses two associations, Mount and Export, to represent the ability of the remote ComputerSystem to enable one or more selected directories to be shared and accessed, respectively, by the other ComputerSystem. Directories that are mounted are accessed as though they were local to the ComputerSystem that is mounting them, and are added to the directories that are contained in the FileSystem of the local ComputerSystem.

The NetworkFileSystem class defines the following attributes:

- HardMount is a boolean attribute. If it is set to TRUE, then once the FileSystem is mounted, its ComputerSystem will continue to retry mounting the remote FileSystem. If set to FALSE, then its ComputerSystem will return an error if the remote FileSystem's ComputerSystem does not respond.

- ForegroundMount is a boolean attribute. If set to TRUE, then mounting retries are performed in a foreground process. If set to FALSE, then mounting retries are performed in the background.

- Interrupt is a boolean attribute. If set to TRUE, then interrupts are permitted for hard mounts. If set to FALSE, then interrupts are ignored for hard mounts.

- MountFailureRetries is a 16-bit unsigned integer that defines the maximum number of mount failure retries that are allowed.

- RetransmissionAttempts is a 16-bit unsigned integer, and defines the maximum number of retransmissions that are allowed.

- RetransmissionTimeout is a 32-bit unsigned integer. It defines the timeout interval (for example, how long to wait for a response before aborting the operation) in tenths of a second.

- ReadBufferSize is a 64-bit unsigned integer that defines the size of the read buffer in bytes.

- WriteBufferSize is a 64-bit unsigned integer that defines the size of the read buffer in bytes.

- `ServerCommunicationPort` is a 32-bit unsigned integer that defines the UDP port number of the remote `ComputerSystem` over which communication will be performed.

- `AttributeCaching` is a boolean attribute. If set to `TRUE`, then control attribute caching is enabled. If set to `FALSE`, then control attribute caching is disabled.

- `AttributeCachingForRegularFilesMin` is a 16-bit unsigned integer that defines the minimum number of seconds that cached attributes are held after file modification.

- `AttributeCachingForRegularFilesMax` is a 16-bit unsigned integer that defines the maximum number of seconds that cached attributes are held after file modification.

- `AttributeCachingForDirectoriesMin` is a 16-bit unsigned integer that defines the minimum number of seconds that cached attributes are held after an update of the directory.

- `AttributeCachingForDirectoriesMax` is a 16-bit unsigned integer that defines the maximum number of seconds that cached attributes are held after an update of the directory.

The `NFS` class does not define any methods, and uses the `Mount` association (defined later in the `Directory` class description) to share file systems of other `ComputerSystems`.

The `LogicalFile` Class and Its Hierarchy

A `LogicalFile` is a subclass of `LogicalElement`, and represents a named collection of data and/or executable programs. `LogicalFiles` exist only within the context of a `FileSystem`, and are therefore weak to `FileSystems`. Instances of the `LogicalFile` class are associated to instances of the `FileSystem` class through the `FileStorage` aggregation.

Notice that there are two sets of weak relationships. `LogicalFiles` are weak to `FileSystems`, which are in turn weak to `ComputerSystems`. Therefore, the composite key of the `LogicalFile` class consists of the propagated keys of the `ComputerSystem` (that is, its `CreationClassName` and `Name` attributes, renamed here to `CSCreationClassName` and `CSName`) and `FileSystem` (that is, its `CreationClassName` and `Name` attributes, renamed here to `FSCreationClassName` and `FSName`) classes plus its own attributes (that is, its `CreationClassName` and `Name` attributes). The `FileStorage` aggregation represents instances of the `LogicalFile` class that are associated with instances of the `FileSystem` class.

An excerpt of the System Model with the `LogicalFile` class and its relationships is shown in Figure 7.28.

Figure 7.28 System Model excerpt: `LogicalFile` and its relationships.

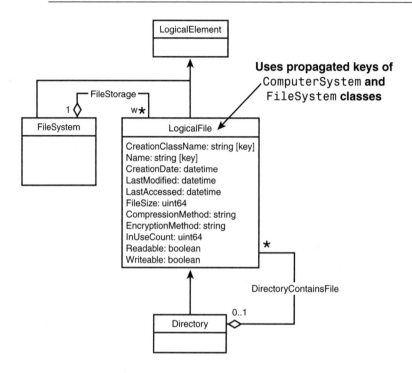

The `LogicalFile` class defines the following attributes:

- `CreationClassName` is one of the composite key attributes of the `FileSystem` class. It defines the name of the class used in the creation of an instance. It is a string of up to 256 characters.

- `Name` is another composite key attribute of the `FileSystem` class. It is inherited from `LogicalElement`, and is overridden to be made a key for this attribute. It is a string of up to 1024 characters.

- `CreationDate` is a datetime attribute that contains the date and time of the creation of the file.

- `LastModified` is a datetime attribute that contains the date and time that the file was last modified.

- `LastAccessed` is a datetime attribute that contains the date and time that the file was last accessed.

- FileSize is a 64-bit unsigned integer that defines the size of the file in bytes.

- CompressionMethod is a free-form string that describes the algorithm or tool used to compress the file. The following special values are recommended for the following uses. If it is not desired to describe the compression scheme, or if the compression scheme is not known, then "Unknown" should be used. If it is known that the LogicalFile is compressed, but the specific compression scheme is not known, then "Compressed" should be used. Similarly, the value "Not Compressed" should be used if the LogicalFile is known not to be compressed.

- EncryptionMethod is a free-form string that describes the algorithm or tool used to encrypt the file. The following special values are recommended for the following uses. If it is not desired to describe the encryption scheme, or if the encryption scheme is not known, then "Unknown" should be used. If it is known that the LogicalFile is encrypted, but the specific encryption scheme is not known, then "Encrypted" should be used. Similarly, the value "Not Encrypted" should be used if the LogicalFile is not encrypted.

- InUseCount is a 64-bit unsigned integer that indicates the number of file open commands that are currently active against the file.

- Readable is a boolean attribute that indicates that read operations can be performed on the file.

- Writeable is a boolean attribute that indicates that write operations can be performed on the file.

The LogicalFile class defines no methods. It participates in the FileStorage aggregation that was previously defined. It also defines another aggregation, DirectoryContainsFile.

The DirectoryContainsFile aggregation is used to define the hierarchical arrangement of LogicalFiles in a given Directory. This is a subclass of the Component aggregation, whose cardinality on the group end (for example, Directory) is set to zero-or-one. The group component is restricted to instances of the Directory class, and the part component is restricted to instances of the LogicalFile class.

The LogicalFile class has three subclasses. None of these classes define any attributes, because such attributes would necessarily be implementation-dependent and application-specific. An excerpt of the System Model with these subclasses and their relationships is shown in Figure 7.29.

Figure 7.29   System Model excerpt: subclasses of LogicalFile and their relationships.

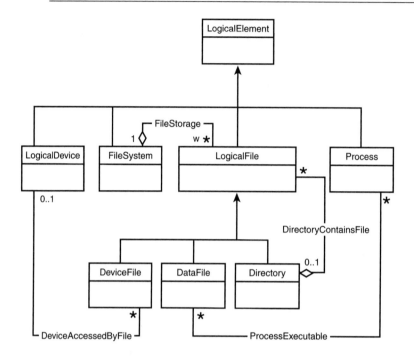

The Directory class represents a container that can group and organize other types of LogicalFiles, and provides a path to access the grouped files. It has no methods, but defines the aggregation DirectoryContainsFiles. This aggregation is a subclass of the Component aggregation, and makes the relationship between contained files and their container explicit.

The DataFile class represents end-user content. It may also represent system files needed by programs that contain data and constants needed by the program, or to carry out computations. It has no methods. The ProcessExecutable association, which is a subclass of the Dependency association, is defined by the DataFile class. This relationship represents a link between a Process and a DataFile, indicating that this DataFile is needed in the execution of the Process.

Finally, the DeviceFile class is used to represent a LogicalDevice. This is used mainly by operating systems that manage and control devices using a byte stream I/O model. This class defines no methods. It does define a new relationship, called DeviceAccessedByFile. This association is a subclass of the Dependency association, and is used to relate the DeviceFile to the LogicalDevice that it is associated with. The cardinality on the LogicalDevice side of this relationship is zero-or-one, and zero-or-more on the DataFile side. This means that not all LogicalDevices use this relationship, but if one does, then it may use zero-or-more DeviceFiles.

Additional Refinements to Services *and* ServiceAccessPoints

The System Model further refines the concepts of Service and ServiceAccessPoint. An excerpt of the System Model with these subclasses and their relationships is shown in Figure 7.30.

Figure 7.30 System Model excerpt: Service and ServiceAccessPoint subclasses and their relationships.

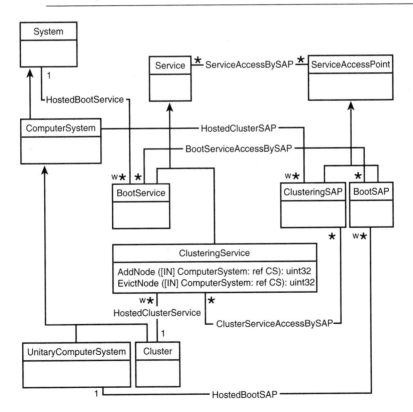

Two `Service` subclasses are currently defined for `ComputerSystem`. They are the `BootService` class and the `ClusteringService` class.

Similarly, two `ServiceAccessPoint` subclasses are currently defined for `ComputerSystem`. They are the `BootSAP` class and the `ClusteringSAP` class.

Neither of these four classes defines any attributes, because they would necessarily be implementation-dependent and application-specific. However, the `ClusteringService` class defines a method, and all four participate in relationships.

These classes are defined in the following sections.

The `BootService` Class

The `BootService` represents the functionality provided by an entity to load an `OperatingSystem` on a `System`. The entity that performs the booting service may be a `LogicalDevice` (such as a floppy drive or CD ROM drive with a bootable partition on which an `OperatingSystem` is loaded), software (for example, for a network computer), or for a device in a network (for example, BOOTP or DHCP services). The `HostedBootService` association represents this relationship. Note that it is associating a `System` (as opposed to a `ComputerSystem`) with a `BootService`. This is because the network may provide a booting service.

The `BootService` class does not define any methods. It defines two relationships. `HostedBootService` and `BootServiceAccessBySAP`.

`HostedBootService` is an association, derived from `HostedService`, that defines the hosting `System` for a particular `BootService`. The subclass is necessary because it is desirable to first restrict the dependent to be an instance of the `BootService` class, and second because such relationships will need to be subclassed to account for application and implementation needs. This class serves as an anchor point to define common associations (`HostedBootService` and `BootServiceAccessBySAP`). As such, it inherits the naming scheme defined for `Services`, inherits the proper contexts (for example, it is weak to a `System`), and enables these subclasses to be found easily by searching on the `CreationClassName` attribute of all `BootServices`.

`BootServiceAccessBySAP` is a subclass of `ServiceAccessBySAP`. This association defines the relationship between a `BootService` and the access points that are used to manage it. It is a subclass for the same reasons that `HostedBootService` is, as listed earlier.

The ClusteringService Class

The ClusteringService class is used to represent generic clustering functions. Two examples are the ability to add or remove a node from the Cluster. As with the other classes in this section, this is an anchor class and is meant to be subclassed in order to add the properties and methods required for particular types of clustering.

The ClusteringService defines two prototypical methods that all Clusters require. AddNode is used to bring a new node (which is an instance of a ComputerSystem class) into a Cluster. The signature of the AddNode method is

```
AddNode( [IN] CIM_ComputerSystem ref CS ) : uint32
```

The node to be added is specified in the CS input parameter. The return value is a 32-bit unsigned integer, and is 0 if the node was successfully added, 1 if the method is not supported, and any other number if an error occurred.

The signature of the EvictNode method is

```
EvictNode( [IN] CIM_ComputerSystem ref CS ) : uint32
```

The node to be removed is specified in the CS input parameter. The return value is a 32-bit unsigned integer, and is 0 if the node was successfully removed, 1 if the method is not supported, and any other number if an error occurred.

The ClusteringService class defines two important relationships, ClusterServiceAccessBySAP and HostedClusterService.

The ClusterServiceAccessBySAP association is a subclass of the ServiceAccessBySAP association. It represents the relationship between a ClusteringService and its access points. The subclass is defined to provide a relationship that already has the proper scoping relationships defined, so that subclasses of ClusteringService may use this common association.

The HostedClusterService association is a subclass of the HostedService association, and is used to define the hosting Cluster for the ClusteringService. The value of this relationship is that it provides the correct scoping and naming schemes to ensure that a ClusteringService is weak to its hosting Cluster.

The BootSAP Class

The BootSAP class represents the ability to access the boot service itself. Therefore, this class is hosted directly on the device that needs booting. This is defined to be an instance of the UnitaryComputerSystem class.

No methods are defined for the BootSAP class. It participates in the BootServiceAccessBySAP association that was just discussed, and defines one new relationship, HostedBootSAP.

The HostedBootSAP association is a subclass of the HostedAccessPoint association. It is used to define the hosting UnitaryComputerSystem for a given BootSAP. Again, the value of this relationship is to provide an anchor point to enable different subclasses of it (which are needed to meet application-specific needs) to all inherit a common set of features. This includes proper scoping between the ServiceAccessPoint, the Service, and the type of System that the Service and its ServiceAccessPoints are hosted on, as well as the ability to reuse the two pre-defined relationships of the BootSAP class.

The ClusteringSAP Class

The ClusteringSAP class is used to define the access points of a ClusteringService. This class is necessary because the ClusteringService is hosted on the Cluster, whereas the ClusteringSAPs are hosted on the individual nodes of the Cluster.

This class does not define any methods. It participates in the ClusterServiceAccessBySAP association which has been previously described. It also defines a new association, HostedClusterSAP.

The ClusterServiceAccessBySAP association is used to define the hosting ComputerSystem for a ClusteringSAP. This association is a subclass of the HostedAccessPoint association, so the proper scoping and naming contexts will have already been set up.

Other System Model Classes

A variety of other classes are defined in the System Model that may or may not be of use, depending on the granularity of your model. The following sections describe these classes and their relationships.

Processes and Threads

CIM provides the ability to model processes and threads, if desired. An excerpt of the System Model with these subclasses and their relationships is shown in Figure 7.31.

Processes, or tasks, represent a program (or part of a program) that is currently executing. Processes exist as part of an OperatingSystem; therefore, they are weak to OperatingSystems.

Figure 7.31   System Model excerpt: The `Process` and `Thread` classes and their relationship.

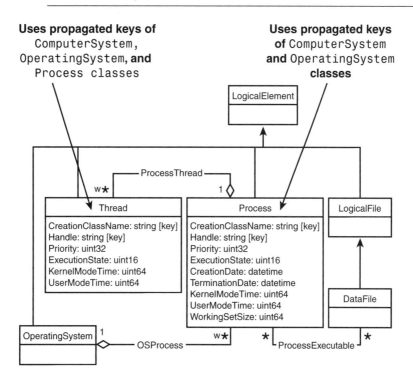

Since a `Process` is weak to an `OperatingSystem`, it must also be weak to a `ComputerSystem`, since it is the `ComputerSystem` that contains the `OperatingSystem`, and the `OperatingSystem` in turn contains the `Process`. Therefore, both the composite key of the `ComputerSystem` as well as the composite key of the `OperatingSystem` must be propagated to the `Process` class, where it will add its own unique attributes to complete the new composite key. Thus, we start with the `CreationClassName` and `Name` attributes of the `ComputerSystem` class (renamed to `CSCreationClassName` and `CSName`, respectively, to avoid name clashes). We then add the `CreationClassName` and `Name` attributes of the `OperatingSystem` class (renamed to `OSCreationClassName` and `OSName`, respectively, to avoid name clashes). Finally, we add the `CreationClassName` and `Handle` (this is a string of up to 256 characters that is used to uniquely identify the `Process`, such as a process ID) attributes of the `Process` class, and we can now identify a specific instance of a `Process` that is running in a given `OperatingSystem` that is hosted in a particular `ComputerSystem`.

Note

The attributes of the Process class will not be covered, as they are probably not of general interest to DEN applications. The Process class defines no methods, but it does define three relationships that may be useful for certain applications.

The OSProcess aggregation, which is a subclass of the Component aggregation, defines the Processes that are running in a given OperatingSystem. This is weak on the Process side of the relationship. Also, the cardinality of the OperatingSystem side is set to exactly 1, so that we can trace different instances of the same Process running on different OperatingSystems.

The ProcessThread aggregation, which is also a subclass of the Component aggregation, defines which Threads are associated with which Processes. This aggregation models multi-threaded programs. The cardinality of the Process side of the relationship is set to exactly 1, so that multiple instances of the same Process can be identified.

The ProcessExecutable association defines the dependency between a Process and a DataFile, when the Process requires the DataFile as part of its execution.

Threads represent the ability to execute units of a Process or task in parallel. A Process can have many Threads, each of which is weak to the Process.

Since a Thread is weak to a Process, the key for a Thread is more complicated. What we have is a Thread that is running in the context of a specific Process, which is running in a particular OperatingSystem, which is hosted on a particular ComputerSystem. Therefore, we need to propagate:

- The keys of ComputerSystem, renamed to CSCreationClassName and CSName

- The keys of OperatingSystem, renamed to OSCreationClassName and OSName

- The keys of Process, renamed to ProcessCreationClassName and ProcessHandle

- The keys of the Thread class, which are CreationClassName and Handle

Note

The attributes of the Thread class will not be covered, as they are probably not of general interest to DEN applications.

Jobs

CIM also models *jobs*, which are defined as a unit of work for a System. An example of a job is a print job. A Job is different than a Process in several important ways:

- First, a Job can be moved from one System to another during the course of its execution, whereas a Process cannot.

- Second, a Job may be placed into a JobDestination object, such as a queue, while it is waiting to execute (a Process has no concept of a JobDestination).

- Third, Jobs are classified by and defined in terms of the task that is submitted to the system; Processes are pre-defined operations that are performed by the OperatingSystem. In other words, Jobs are requests *to* the System to execute a specific task, whereas, Processes are inherent capabilities *of* the System.

- Finally, Jobs have a strong connotation of being performed on behalf of an end-user, whereas Processes may, but usually are not, performed on behalf of an end-user.

JobDestinations are hosted on, and therefore weak to, Systems. This is similar to the way that Services are hosted on (and therefore weak to) Systems. This means that the composite key of the System class (that is, the SystemCreationClassName and SystemName attributes) is added to the CreationClassName and Name attributes of the JobDestination class. Note that JobDestinations can also represent aliases for other JobDestinations.

Note

The attributes of the Job and the JobDestination classes will not be covered, as they are probably not of general interest to DEN applications. No methods are defined for either class. The Job class participates in one relationship, JobDestinationJobs, which is defined by the JobDestinations class. The JobDestinations class defines two relationships, HostedJobDestination and JobDestinationJobs.

The HostedJobDestination association, which is a subclass of the Dependency association, defines the System which hosts the JobDestination. The cardinality is exactly one on the System side, because JobDestinations are weak to the Systems that host them. The cardinality on the JobDestination side is zero-or-more, since a single System may host many different JobDestinations.

The JobDestinationJobs association, which is a subclass of the Dependency association, defines the JobDestination that a particular Job is submitted to.

BIOSFeature and BIOSElement

CIM provides two classes to describe BIOS (Basic Input Output System) capabilities of a System. *BIOS* is a set of low-level software functions that are used to bring up and configure a ComputerSystem. They are the BIOSFeature and the BIOSElement subclasses.

BIOSFeature is a subclass of SoftwareFeature. It models the capabilities of low-level software that is used to help boot and configure a ComputerSystem.

BIOSElement is a subclass of SoftwareElement, and represents the individual components of a BIOSFeature.

The BIOSFeatureBIOSElements aggregation is a subclass of the SoftwareFeatureSoftwareElements aggregation. This aggregation relates the individual BIOSElements to the BIOSFeature that they implement.

Summary

This chapter has presented an introduction to the design of the CIM Core and Common Models. The underlying modeling methodology was described briefly, emphasizing two points. These were the fundamental classification of physical versus logical aspects of a managed entity, and the use of associations and aggregations to model how a managed entity interacts with the rest of its environment.

The purpose of the Core Model is to provide a framework for developing a managed environment information model and schema. It partitions the knowledge hierarchy into physical, logical, and other aspects of a component and system.

The main classes of the Core Model were described. ManagedSystemElement is the root of the physical and logical hierarchies. An important aspect of this class are the relationships that it defines. Key among these are the Dependency and Component relationships, which serve as the base classes for defining dependency and whole-part relationships. PhysicalElement is the root of the physical portion of the CIM hierarchy, and defines three relationships. Two enable a Product and a FRU to aggregate a set of PhysicalElements. The other, Realizes, is the basis for bridging between the physical and logical hierarchies.

LogicalElement forms the root of the logical portion of the class hierarchy. This includes all non-physical functions, such as software, systems, and services. There are four subclasses of LogicalElement. LogicalDevice is the base class of all objects that abstract or emulate functions that are performed by a physical device. For example, the act of printing is not a physical function, but is rather a logical one. Even though (physical) pages come out of the (physical) printer, the act of printing is a function, and therefore is classified in CIM as a *logical* entity. Thus, attributes that control the printing process are found in the LogicalDevice hierarchy, not in the physical hierarchy.

The System class represents an aggregation of a set of ManagedSystemElements. The distinguishing characteristic of a System is that although the functions of each of the aggregated ManagedSystemElements are still present, a new set of functions is produced by aggregating the set of ManagedSystemElements into a new entity. The System class is the superclass of the ComputerSystem class, which represents network elements like routers and switches. The System class defines several relationships. The most important are the SystemDevice aggregation (used to define the LogicalDevices that are aggregated by a system), HostedService association (used to define which Services a System can host), and the HostedAccessPoint (used to define the access points from which a Service can be managed) association. The Service class is used to represent the implementation of functions provided by a LogicalDevice or a SoftwareFeature. Services are hosted in Systems. ServiceAccessPoints represent the ability to manage access to Services, and are also hosted in a System. Services and ServiceAccessPoints enable the configuration and management of functions to be separated from their implementation. Many different relationships are defined for each of these classes. The most important are ServiceServiceDependency (models the dependency of one Service on another Service), SAPSAPDependency (the same, but for ServiceAccessPoints), ServiceAccessBySAP (which defines the access points of a Service), and ServiceSAPDependency (which defines the dependency between a Service and a ServiceAccessPoint, quantifying the dependency of the Service instance on the ServiceAccessPoint instance).

ComputerSystem is a subclass of System, and represents Systems that have the ability to perform computations. It aggregates hardware, software, and firmware, and is the superclass of routers, switches, and other network elements.

Product represents a collection of PhysicalElements, software, and possibly other Products, that are purchased as a unit from a vendor. FRUs represent components of a Product that can either be replaced or upgraded, and thus provide possible alternatives to buying a completely new Product. SupportAccess models how a given Product is supported. These three classes are all inter-related using appropriate associations and aggregations.

Settings and Configurations are used to model the state of a managed entity, and how to either maintain that state, or transition to a new state. As such, they provide an effective linkage to a behavioral model that complements CIM's data and object representations. Configurations group Settings, and Settings consist of a related set of commands and/or operational parameters that control the configuration of a managed entity. It is important to remember that Settings and Configurations represent the *desired* state of a managed entity, whereas the *current* state is represented by the set of values that the attributes of a managed entity has.

StatisticalInformation is an abstract base class that is used to collect statistical information. This enables such information, which is fundamentally different than other information that describes the entity, to be separated into a different hierarchy. Thus, applications that are concerned primarily with statistics need only use these classes and perhaps a few relationships (to reference the managed objects that the statistics relate to), instead of having to use and reference the entire model.

The Device Common Model was then discussed. It is important to think of devices as not being tied, in a one-to-one fashion, to physical components. Rather, the purpose of this model is to represent the features and capabilities of the managed system or component, and to relate physical hardware with logical components, such as software and services.

The major classes of the Device Common Model were discussed. RedundancyGroup and its subclasses provide the ability to model redundancy, spare, and extra capacity or capabilities present in a group of ManagedSystemElements. NetworkAdapter and its subclasses represent specific types of interface adapters that are commonly found on networking and computer cards. In particular, the Ethernet and Token Ring adapter cards use many of the attributes defined in the applicable IETF MIB specifications. StorageExtents are fundamental to modeling, at a device level, how memory works and is implemented (this level of granularity may or may not be needed by networking and DEN applications). The Memory class (which is a subclass of StorageExtent), along with its relationships, provides an excellent abstraction layer to model the memory needs and capabilities of network elements and services. For example, the AssociatedMemory association represents the need for memory of certain types of LogicalDevices. Other types of memory, such as volatile, non-volatile, and cache memory, are also defined. A general error class, DeviceErrorCounts, as well as an error class that represents specific memory errors, StorageError, were also described. Finally, the Processor class was defined, which can be used to represent the processor in not only a computer, but also a router or switch.

The Application Common Model was described. Its purpose is aimed at modeling the installation, management, and deployment of a related set of software that end-users think of as an "application." This is related to a simple life-cycle model of an application.

The Application model defines five principal classes. The ApplicationSystem class represents an application that can be individually managed, and which incorporates software. The SoftwareFeature class represents the most important characteristics of a software program that an end-user is interested in. These correspond to major features of the application, such as the ability for a word processor to perform a spell check of the document. The SoftwareElement class partitions the SoftwareFeature into a set of individual components (for example, files or DLLs) so that they can be individually managed. The Check and Action classes are defined to enable the tracking of the state of an application. As usual, these classes interact with each other through associations and aggregations.

The purpose of the System Common Model is to extend the basic idea of a System as defined in the Core Model. That is, a System is a collection of managed objects that can be viewed and interacted with as an independent, single object. Systems are extended by defining new relationships as well as by providing new subclasses. Some of the new relationships defined for the System class include associating a System with its OperatingSystem and FileSystem, as well as enabling individual ComputerSystems to be clustered into a more powerful ComputerSystem. An OperatingSystem is defined as a set of software and firmware that provides intelligence for a ComputerSystem (for example, ability to manage its resources, perform computations, and so on). Both local and remote file systems are represented, along with a set of "logical file" objects. These represent the heart of a file system: directories, data files, and executable programs. Using these classes, a detailed model of the internals of network elements can be constructed.

The System Common Model defines additional Services and ServiceAccessPoints. These model the booting and clustering of a ComputerSystem.

Finally, the System Model contains other classes and relationships that may be useful if your application requires the ability to model the low-level features of a ComputerSystem. These include Processes, Threads, Jobs, JobDestinations, and BIOS concepts. Processes model tasks that are performed by the ComputerSystem, which may or may not be multi-threaded. Jobs are different from Processes in that a Job represents a task that is submitted to the ComputerSystem on behalf of one of its clients. JobDestinations represent the ability to queue a Job until it can be executed. Finally, the BIOSFeature and BIOSElement subclasses can be used to model the low-level software components of a Basic Input Output System.

Recommended Further Study and References

Several Internet RFCs are referenced. They can be obtained as follows:

- RFC 1156, "Management Information Base for Network Management of TCP/IP-based Interfaces," http://www.rfc-editor.org/rfc/rfc1156.txt.

- RFC 1213, "Management Information Base for Network Management of TCP/IP-based Interfaces: MIB-II," http://www.rfc-editor.org/rfc/rfc1213.txt.

- RFC 1493, "Definitions of Managed Objects for Bridges," http://www.rfc-editor.org/rfc/rfc1493.txt.

- RFC 1643, "Definitions of Managed Objects for the Ethernet-like Interface Types," ftp://ftp.isi.edu/in-notes/rfc1643.txt.

The DMTF has a public CIM tutorial available. It is a good overall introduction to CIM that complements this chapter, and is available at this URL:

```
http://www.dmtf.org/spec/cim_tutorial/
```

The DMTF also has a public set of whitepapers (that will grow in time) that talk about uses of CIM. They are available at the following URL:

```
http://www.dmtf.org/educ/whit.html
```

The DMTF has a public presentations page. This material is of general interest and is also relevant to the contents of this chapter and Chapters 8 through 10. In addition, presentations from conferences that had a major DMTF focus are provided on this page. It is available from the following URL:

```
http://www.dmtf.org/educ/pres.html
```

Finally, the 2.2 version of the CIM schema is publicly available from the following URL:

```
http://www.dmtf.org/spec/cims.html
```

DEN's Physical Model

The purpose of this chapter is threefold. First, it is important to explain how the physical model of network elements that was published in DEN was transformed into the CIM Physical Common Model. Second, it is important to understand the changes that took place in that transformation. Finally, the future of the Physical Common Model and its role in the DEN specification will be discussed.

Overview

The DEN schema incorporates concepts from both X.500 and CIM. It was originally conceived without knowledge of CIM, and was targeted "just" at modeling network elements and services. When the DEN Ad-Hoc Working Group became cognizant of CIM, the decision was made to integrate the ideas of DEN into CIM as much as possible.

DEN therefore became a formal extension model of CIM. DEN consisted of a Physical, Logical, and Policy Model. The DEN Physical Model eventually became the *CIM Physical Common Model* in CIM 2.1. The DEN Logical Model was incorporated into the *CIM Networks Common Model* in CIM 2.2. Finally, the DEN Policy Model served as the foundation for building the *CIM Policy Common Model*, which will be formally introduced in CIM 2.3. The translations of these DEN "sub-models" into CIM will be explained and analyzed in Chapters 9 and 10, respectively.

DEN will be released in the winter 1999 timeframe as a formal specification that includes these models, as well as appropriate portions of the Core and other Common models. The DEN specification will also provide a formal mapping of CIM into a schema suitable for implementation in a directory that uses DAP or LDAP as its access protocol.

Purpose of the DEN Physical Model

The purpose of the DEN Physical Model, as it was originally designed, was to provide a framework to store and retrieve information describing the physical characteristics of network devices. The DEN information model was independent of any specific repository. However, DEN also specified a mapping from a repository-independent form to a form that was amenable to being stored in a directory.

The DEN Physical Information Model describes both the characteristics of physical objects and the relationships between physical objects. The DEN Physical Model is aimed primarily at supporting inventory applications, along with systems that want to describe the topology of the network. It is important to note that the DEN Physical Model can use different data sources and integrate them using its underlying information model.

The DEN Physical Model

This section provides a brief overview of the DEN Physical Model. Its purpose is to enable you to track the changes in this model from its initial draft release (DEN Specification version v3.0c5) to its current form. This form includes CIM 2.1, plus additional changes that are pending the official release of CIM 2.2.

The DEN Physical Model strove to maintain compatibility with X.500 while incorporating many concepts from Version 2.0 of the CIM of the DMTF. X.500 defines the class `Device` to be the superclass for all physical devices, but doesn't add any structure to that definition. CIM refines this into two subclasses, called `PhysicalElement` and `LogicalElement`. `PhysicalElement` represents all physical aspects of a device, while `LogicalElement` represents the functional capabilities of the device.

The DEN Physical Model expands the hierarchy under `PhysicalElement` in a significantly different way than the CIM Device Common Model does. Recall from the previous chapter that the purpose of the Device Common Model is to show how different functions and services are realized in hardware. As such, the majority of classes in the Device Common Model are subclassed from either `LogicalDevice` or `LogicalElement`.

Instead, the DEN Physical Model seeks to model physical objects, the composition of physical objects, and their physical interconnections. The DEN Physical Model was redesigned to subclass entirely off of the CIM `PhysicalElement` class. While an application may use information from the DEN Physical Model in conjunction with other CIM Common Models, all physical properties of the managed environment will come from or be derived from the Physical Model.

The Transformation into the CIM Physical Common Model

The DEN Physical Model was originally built to model just the physical aspects of network elements. By integrating it into CIM, the CIM Technical Development Committee (TDC) (see the section "Partitioning Physical and Logical Entities" in Chapter 7, "CIM: The Foundation of DEN," for more information) was able to enhance the DEN Physical Model into a more general model that turned into the CIM Physical Common Model. This model did not lose any of its capability to model network elements; rather, it was enhanced so that it could model many general entities in addition to network elements.

The following sections provide more detail regarding the theoretical motivation for incorporating the DEN Physical Model into CIM, the principal classes present in the original DEN Physical Model, and the changes that were made to that model to generalize it into the CIM Physical Common Model.

Why Physical Classes Were Integrated into CIM

Prior to DEN, CIM viewed the managed environment as represented mostly by logical entities. In other words, CIM concentrated on modeling the informational, rather than the physical, aspects of the environment. The DEN Physical Model helped broaden the utility of CIM, and made it useful for manipulating information that represents and controls the state of the system, as well as any impact that changing the state of the system has on the actual physical environment. This was a large stride, since unlike the logical side of the environment, the physical parts of the system are not instrumented. In fact, the current state of physical entities in the system can usually only be indirectly inferred from other logical information about the system.

In order to do this, the basic ideas in the DEN Physical Model were analyzed and applied to other common entities that CIM wanted to model. These ideas were then fed back into the DEN Physical Model and it evolved into a new CIM Common Model.

Main Classes of the Original DEN Physical Model

The original DEN Physical Model concentrated on two important areas. The first centered around the concept of *physical containment* (implemented by the CIM `PhysicalPackage` class and its hierarchies) and additions to the functionality of the CIM `Card` class (and its subclasses) that plugs into the `PhysicalPackage` class. Each of these has two design alternatives that center around whether to make the referenced CIM classes robust enough to handle networking needs along with other needs, or whether specific subclasses for each discipline (for example, networking, host devices, and so on) should be used.

Originally, DEN took the latter approach. This was because it was thought that it would be inherently more extensible. So DEN specified two subclasses, NetworkPackage and NetworkCard, to provide these capabilities. In addition, it was thought that the NetworkPackage class was fundamentally different than other subclasses of PhysicalPackage. This difference was thought to lie in the nature of the abstractions that bind the logical and physical domains together. The utility of the NetworkPackage was to reduce the number of relationships that would need to be navigated. This is of particular importance when implementing DEN in a directory that uses (L)DAP as its access protocol, because having to traverse a large number of relationships will have severe performance implications. It also provides a symmetry between the physical and logical domains (NetworkPackage corresponds to NetworkElement, another DEN class from the DEN Logical Model, which will be covered in Chapter 9, "DEN's Logical Model"). This symmetry, though not mandatory, facilitates possible additional optimizations.

The proposed changes to NetworkCard center around the additional flexibility required in configuring networking cards. Networking cards come in two broad types: configurable and non-configurable. For the configurable types, there are many options, such as the ability to increase functionality through upgrading Application-Specific Integrated Circuits (ASICs) and/or different types of RAM, the ability to have an on-card boot memory device, and other options, that must be modeled. In addition, some cards require special adapter boards to interface to the outside world, or to ensure that legacy networking cards can be used with new chassis (or vice versa). Some cards also require special auxiliary processing cards. These all need to be modeled.

One of the most important behaviors that needs to be modeled is the concept of compatibility. Installing a networking card is a function of two different requirements:

- First, you must ensure that the network card is physically and electrically compatible with the slot that the networking card is going to be plugged into.

- Second, the device itself must be able to accept this new networking card.

The second requirement combines many different system requirements. For example, some cards of some vendors have to go into a pre-assigned slot. Some cards might not be able to be accepted due to a system limitation (not enough power or memory, wrong version of the operating system, and so on) even though they are physically and electrically compatible with a currently unoccupied slot. Some cards might also have dependencies on other cards that are currently installed (for example, you can only have a specified number of this type of networking card regardless of how many available slots there are).

The resolution to this dilemma is to use a method, called `IsCompatible`, that can be called to determine the answer to these and other similar requirements. It is assumed that the result of calling the method will be to populate the appropriate objects with an attribute that signals that this compatibility check has been made—though that is, of course, implementation-dependent.

Figure 8.1 shows the original DEN Physical Model.

Figure 8.1   Original DEN Physical Model Class hierarchy.

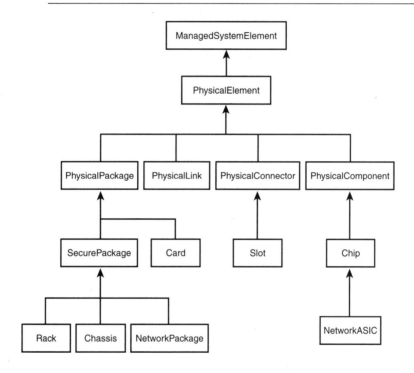

The following subsections will describe the original DEN model briefly so that you can better understand the changes that were made to it as it became the CIM Physical Common Model. Specific attention is given to correlating the changes between the original DEN specification and the current version of the CIM Physical Common Model.

Location

This class represents the location of a physical object. Locations may be nested in order to represent hierarchies of arbitrary depth. The most common such hierarchy is one in which network elements are contained in a WiringCloset, which is in a particular Floor of a specific Building of a Campus of a Site of an Organization. Therefore, it is assumed by DEN that appropriate subclasses of Location, such as WiringCloset and the others in this example, will be implemented as needed to model the appropriate physical containment, to the appropriate granularity, of physical entities in the managed environment.

The Location class had a composite key, consisting of two attributes, Name and LocationAddress. The Name attribute was called cn, or CommonName, when it was mapped into an LDAP representation.

The Location class was incorporated into the CIM Physical Common model. The following attributes were defined by DEN for this class:

- Name is the key attribute of the Location class. It defines the label by which the object is known. It is defined as a string of up to 256 characters.

- PhysicalPosition is the other key attribute of the Location class, and indicates the placement of a particular PhysicalElement. For example, it can specify the slot information on a hosting board, the mounting site in a Chassis, or even the latitude and longitude information from a GPS. It is a free-form string.

- LocationAddress is a free-form string that is used to physically identify where it is, such as a street address or a floor number. This was renamed to address in CIM.

- PhysicalLocationDN is used specifically for the LDAP mapping. It defines the Distinguished Name of a geographic location where physical devices can be installed. This is a pointer to an X.500 Locality entry. This corresponds to the PhysicalElementLocation association in the CIM model.

An association, PhysicalElementLocation, was defined to relate a physical object to a specific location. The cardinality of this relationship was zero-or-one on the PhysicalElement side and zero-or-more on the Location side. This means that this is a completely optional relationship but, if it is instantiated, then a specific physical object can be located in potentially many locations. Though this may seem odd at first, remember that a router, for example, may be located in a specific wiring closet located on a particular floor of a certain building. The wiring closet, floor and building are all subclasses of the Location object; hence the zero-or-more cardinality.

This class was incorporated into the CIM Physical Common Model. The `PhysicalLocationDN` attribute was not incoporated because it was LDAP-specific. It currently remains part of the DEN specification.

Device

This class represents the X.500 superclass for all devices. DEN proposed mapping it into the CIM `PhysicalElement` class. The attributes are mapped as follows:

Attribute Name	Containment	DEN Class Providing This
CommonName	MUST	ManagedSystemElement
description	may	ManagedSystemElement
localityName	may	an association
organizationName	may	an association
organizationalUnit	may	an association
owner	may	NetworkElement
seeAlso	may	ManagedSystemElement
serialNumber	may	PhysicalElement

PhysicalElement

This is an abstract class used to describe any physical system component having a distinct physical manifestation. As such, the component can be defined in terms of one or more labels that can be physically attached to it.

CIM 2.0 defined this class, and DEN extended it as follows:

- `HotSwappableElement` is a Boolean attribute that, if `TRUE`, means that it is possible to replace the `PhysicalPackage` that contains this `PhysicalElement` with a physically different but equivalent `PhysicalElement` while the containing `PhysicalPackage` still has power applied to it. All `HotSwappable` `PhysicalElements` are inherently removable and replaceable.

  This attribute, along with the related attributes `Removable` *and* `Replaceable`, *were moved into the* `PhysicalPackage` *class. The argument was that a* `PhysicalElement` *didn't know if it was hot-swappable or not, but its container did.*

- AssetType is a 16-bit unsigned integer, and defines the type of asset that this PhysicalElement is.

  This attribute was changed to PartNumber. *The reasoning was that part numbers were more general in usage than asset tracking numbers. This attribute remains in DEN, since networking devices often have both.*

- AssetTrackingNumber is a free-form string that contains a number assigned to an asset and recorded in a database. It provides the link between the asset tracking software and the physical object.

  *This attribute was deleted because its corresponding attribute (*AssetType*) was also deleted (in favor of using just the* PartNumber *attribute). However, this attribute remains in DEN, since networking devices often have both.*

- OtherIdentifyingInfo is a free-form string that contains supplementary information that is used to help identify different PhysicalElements.

  This attribute was added to the PhysicalElement *class.*

- PhysicalPowerState is an enumerated 16-bit unsigned integer that defines the current powered state of the device. Values include Unknown, Full Power, Power Save - Degraded, Power Save - Standby, Power Save - Unknown, Power Cycle, Power Save - Low Power Mode, Power Warning, and Power Off.

  This attribute was replaced with the more generic Boolean attribute PoweredOn, *and the concept of power state was moved to the logical hierarchy. DEN will conform to the CIM specification.*

The DEN Physical Model defined seven relationships that its version of the PhysicalElement class would participate in. These relationships were defined in the CIM Core and Physical Common models and reused by DEN. Therefore, they will not be further elaborated on.

PhysicalPackage

This class represents system components that physically contain other system components. The DEN version of the CIM PhysicalPackage class added the following attributes:

- BackplaneDescriptions is an array of free-form strings that defines whether the package has one or more backplanes that can be managed separately. For each backplane that can be separately managed, the characteristics of those backplanes are placed in the array. For example, many network devices use separate backplanes to interconnect network and system processor cards.

It was felt that this attribute was too specific to networking. It is currently not in any of the CIM Common Models, but remains in the DEN specification.

- CableManagementPackage is a free-form string that describes the cabling needs of this PhysicalPackage, independent of any other containers that this PhysicalPackage fits into. This is also useful for inventory and stocking purposes.

It was felt that this attribute was too specific to networking. However, a similar DEN attribute governing the overall cable management strategy for a PhysicalFrame *(the super-class of* Racks *and* Chassis*) was accepted. This attribute remains in the DEN specification.*

- CompatibilityList is an array of free-form strings that describes what may be contained by or in the PhysicalPackage. The purpose of this attribute is to help document specific requirements of this PhysicalPackage with respect to what types of components can be installed in it.

It was felt that this attribute was too specific to networking, and that existing attributes (for example, Description *and* OtherIdentifyingInfo*) could be used in its place. The DEN Ad-Hoc Working Group (AHWG) disagreed on the grounds that this information was specific and in addition to the information contained in the other attributes. This attribute remains part of the DEN specification.*

- ContainedComponentNumber is an unsigned 16-bit integer that specifies the number of contained components in this PhysicalPackage. The intent of this attribute was to facilitate enumeration for LDAP queries, and was not meant to be a CIM attribute.

It was felt that this was an optimization that was specific to LDAP, and so did not include it in the CIM Physical Common Model. Although the DEN AHWG agreed, this attribute represents the result of a common query that provides significant performance advantages over following associations in the model to get the same information. Therefore, it remains part of the DEN specification.

Note

This attribute could be placed on the Container aggregation to indicate the total number of contained objects. If CIM 2.2 does not do this, then you can certainly subclass the Container aggregation to provide this and other capabilities.

- ContainedPhysicalComponents is an array of object references to PhysicalElements that are contained in this PhysicalPackage. The intent of this attribute was to facilitate enumeration for LDAP queries, and was not meant to be a CIM attribute. This is equivalent to the CIM Container aggregation, except that this is intended specifically for an LDAP implementation.

This attribute points out the first of many DEN attributes and relationships that are equivalent to, but syntactically different than, the corresponding CIM attributes and relationships. Think of this as an LDAP equivalent of the Container *aggregation; you wouldn't have both.*

- CoolingRequirements is a free-form string that specifies the cooling requirements for this PhysicalPackage. Note that this is different than the AssociatedCooling relationship that associates the needs of a LogicalDevice with the capabilities of a CoolingDevice. The purpose of this attribute is to simply document the cooling needs of the PhysicalPackage.

It was felt that this attribute was unnecessary, as there were existing attributes (for example, Description*) that could be used for this purpose. The DEN AHWG disagreed, and so this attribute remains part of the DEN specification.*

- HotSwappablePackage is a Boolean attribute that, if TRUE, indicates that this PhysicalPackage has the capability to replace one or more PhysicalElements with physically different but equivalent PhysicalElements while power remains applied to the containing PhysicalPackage. All HotSwappable PhysicalPackages are inherently Removable and Replaceable.

This attribute was added to the CIM Physical Common Model.

- IndependentBackplanes is a Boolean attribute that, if TRUE, indicates that this PhysicalPackage has independent backplanes that can be managed separately.

This attribute was felt to be too specific to networking. It is not currently in any of the CIM Common Models, though it remains a part of the DEN specification.

- PowerRequirements is a free-form string that defines the overall power requirements for this PhysicalPackage as a function of the particular PhysicalElements that it contains.

This attribute was felt to be too specific to networking, as some PhysicalPackages *had self-contained power and others did not. Therefore, it was not added to any of the CIM Common Models, but remains an attribute of the DEN specification.*

DEN defined a key method that was incorporated into the CIM Physical Model. This method, IsCompatible, has the following signature:

```
IsCompatible([IN] PhysicalElement: ref ElementToCheck): uint32
```

This method was already described in the beginning of this section.

DEN also defined eight relationships that the PhysicalPackage class participated in. All these were moved into the CIM Physical Common Model except the PackageInNetworkPackage aggregation. This was because the NetworkPackage DEN class was not added into the CIM Physical Common Model, for reasons that will be explained when that class is covered.

SecurePackage

The DEN specification defined the concept of a SecurePackage. This subclass is a type of PhysicalPackage that serves as the parent for the Rack and Chassis classes. This class generalizes common properties that apply to Racks and Chassis, but not other subclasses of PhysicalPackage, such as Card, from the original CIM schema. This class later turned into the CIM PhysicalFrame class and was put into the CIM Physical Common Model.

The original SecurePackage class defined the following attributes:

- AudibleAlarm is a Boolean attribute that, if TRUE, indicates that this SecurePackage is equipped with an audible alarm.

   This attribute was kept, meaning that it was moved into the PhysicalFrame *class.*

- AudibleAlarmDescription is a free-form string that provides supplementary information for the AudibleAlarm property. It should only be filled in when the value of the AudibleAlarm attribute is TRUE.

   This attribute was not included, as it was felt that it could be incorporated in the Description *or another attribute. It remains part of the DEN specification.*

- CableManagementStrategy is a free-form string that contains information on how the various cables contained in the Chassis, Rack, or other type of PhysicalPackage are connected and bundled. This property contains information to aid in the assembly and service of the cables contained in a Chassis or Rack.

   This attribute was incorporated into the PhysicalFrame *class of the CIM Physical Common Model.*

- LockPresent is a Boolean attribute that, if TRUE, indicates that this PhysicalPackage is protected by some type of lock.

   This attribute was incorporated into the PhysicalFrame *class of the CIM Physical Common Model.*

- MountingOptions is an enumerated 16-bit unsigned integer that defines how the NetworkPackage is mounted. Values include: Stand-alone, Rack-mounted, free access, restricted access, and Enclosed in another chassis.

  This attribute was deleted because NetworkPackage *was deleted and because it was felt that other attributes could be used to store this information. Currently, this attribute still is part of the DEN specification.*

- SecurityBreach is an enumerated 16-bit unsigned integer attribute indicating whether a breach of the Rack was attempted. Values include Unknown, Other, No Breach, Unsuccessful (but attempted), and Successful (but attempted).

  This attribute was incorporated into the PhysicalFrame *class of the CIM Physical Common Model.*

- SecurityBreachDescription is a free-form string attribute that provides supplementary information for the SecurityBreach property. It should only be filled in when the value of SecurityBreach is Other.

  This attribute was incorporated into the PhysicalFrame *class of the CIM Physical Common Model, but renamed* BreachDescription.

- VisibleAlarm is a Boolean attribute that, if TRUE, indicates that the SecurePackage is equipped with one or more visible alarms (for example, LEDs or gauges).

  This attribute was incorporated into the PhysicalFrame *class of the CIM Physical Common Model, but renamed* BreachDescription.

- VisibleAlarmDescription is a free-form string attribute that provides supplementary information for the VisibleAlarm property. It should only be filled in when the value of VisibleAlarm is Other.

  This attribute was deleted because it was felt that it could be incorporated in the Description *attribute (or some other attribute). It remains part of the DEN specification.*

This class defined no attributes or methods.

Rack

This class was modified only by shifting some of its attributes into SecurePackage (which was later renamed PhysicalFrame). In addition, some attributes were renamed. The following table shows these changes (all CIM attributes are a part of the PhysicalFrame class unless otherwise noted):

DEN Attribute Name	CIM Attribute Name
RackHeight	Height, in PhysicalPackage
RackServiceDescriptions	ServiceDescriptions
RackServicePhilosophy	ServicePhilosophy
RackType	TypeOfRack, in Rack

The DEN class defined no new methods or relationships.

Chassis

A Chassis is a type of PhysicalPackage that encloses other PhysicalElements and provides a definable functionality in its own right, such as a desktop or a network device (for example, a router or a switch).

DEN extended the CIM Chassis class by adding the following attributes:

- ChassisServiceDescriptions is an array of free-form strings that provide more detailed explanations for any of the entries in the ChassisServicePhilosophy attribute. Each array entry is related to an entry in the ChassisServicePhilosophy attribute.

  This attribute was incorporated into the PhysicalFrame *class of the CIM Physical Common Model.*

- ChassisServiceOrdering is a free-form string that defines the order of installation of components into the Chassis.

  This attribute was deleted from both CIM and the DEN specification because its information could be put into other attributes (for example, ChassisTypeDescriptions*).*

- ChassisServicePhilosophy is an array of integers indicating how the Chassis is serviced. An array is used to enable multiple service instructions to be applied to the same Chassis. Values include Chassis Instructions, Card Instructions, Power Supply Instructions, Fan Instructions, Cable Instructions, Memory Instructions, and Other. If the value was Other, then application-specific information could be entered in the corresponding index value of the ChassisServiceDescriptions attribute.

  This attribute was incorporated into the PhysicalFrame *class of the CIM Physical Common Model.*

- ChassisSlotLayout is a free-form string that describes the slot positioning, typical usage, restrictions, individual slot spacings, or any other pertinent information for the slots in a Chassis.

  This attribute was deleted, but its semantics were expanded and captured in new relationships that were added to the CIM Physical Common Model.

- ChassisTypes is an enumerated, integer-valued array indicating the type of Chassis this object is.

  This attribute was incorporated into the Chassis class of the CIM Physical Common Model.

- ChassisTypeDescriptions is an array of free-form strings that provide more detailed explanations for any of the entries in the ChassisTypes attribute. Each array entry is related to an entry in the ChassisTypeDescriptions attribute. An array should only have a value if the corresponding array in the ChassisTypes attribute contains an entry.

  This attribute was incorporated into the Chassis class of the CIM Physical Common Model.

- CurrentRequiredOrProduced defines the amount of current required by this Chassis as a function of the components installed in the Chassis.

  This attribute was incorporated into the Chassis class of the CIM Physical Common Model.

- HeatGeneration defines the amount of heat generated by this Chassis as a function of the components installed in the Chassis.

  This attribute was incorporated into the Chassis class of the CIM Physical Common Model.

- IsParentEnclosure is a Boolean attribute that, if TRUE, means that this Chassis encloses another Chassis.

  This attribute was deleted in favor of defining just the Docked association.

- IsRootEnclosure is a Boolean attribute that, if TRUE, means that this Chassis is the outermost Chassis in the entire assembly.

  This attribute was deleted in favor of defining just the Docked association. However, it is still present in the DEN specification as a "may" attribute, since it greatly simplifies LDAP queries. The "may" attribute enables implementations that need this optimization to instantiate and use it, while other implementations do not have to instantiate it at all.

- MaxChassisSlotSpacing defines the maximum spacing between Slots in a Chassis, in inches.

  This attribute, along with MinChassisSlotSpacing, was simplified into a single attribute (DistanceBetweenSlots) and moved to the SlotInSlot association.

- `MinChassisSlotSpacing` defines the minimum spacing between `Slots` in a `Chassis`, in inches.

  This attribute, along with `MaxChassisSlotSpacing`, *was simplified into a single attribute (*`DistanceBetweenSlots`*) and moved to the* `SlotInSlot` *association.*

- `NumberOfCardSlots` defines the number of card slots that are built into a `Chassis`.

  This attribute gave rise to the `CardInSlot` *association. CIM therefore chose to delete it in favor of this association. However, in LDAP, this means that one would have to instantiate every* `CardInSlot` *association and keep track of the number, which is very expensive. Therefore, this attribute remains in the DEN specification as a query optimization.*

- `NumberOfPowerCords` is a 16-bit unsigned integer that defines the number of power cords that must be connected to the `Chassis` in order for all of the componentry inside the `Chassis` to operate correctly.

  This attribute was incorporated into the `Chassis` *class of the CIM Physical Common Model.*

The DEN specification defined four relationships. Three of them are part of the CIM Physical Common Model, and will be described in the next section. The fourth, `ChassisInNetworkPackage`, was deleted since the `NetworkPackage` class was deleted.

Card

This class represents a type of physical container that can be plugged into a `Slot` in a `Chassis`, or is itself a container that can accept other `Cards`. The semantics of this class includes any `PhysicalPackage` capable of carrying signals and providing a mounting point for `PhysicalComponents` (for example, `Chips`) or other `PhysicalPackages`. The `Card` class includes memory, as well as networking (such as a router interface processor) and other types of cards.

DEN extended the CIM `Card` class by adding the following attributes:

- `CardCompatible` is an attribute that is used to store the result of the negotiation process between a `Card` and a `NetworkPackage` to see if they are compatible. This is the result of the `isCompatible()` method, with the `Card` being the source and the `NetworkPackage` being the target.

  This attribute was deleted. It was felt that the `IsCompatible` *method was the most general concept that could be put into the Physical Common Model. This attribute is still in the DEN specification because it greatly aids the querying and searching when using a directory.*

- CardSlotLayout is a free-form string that describes the slot positioning, typical usage, restrictions, individual slot spacings or any other pertinent information for the slots on a Card.

  In CIM, this attribute was replaced by the more general association, AdjacentSlots. *This attribute is still in the DEN specification because it contains additional information not captured in the* AdjacentSlots *association. However, this information could (and probably should) move into the* AdjacentSlots *association in a future release of CIM.*

- CardUniqueness is a Boolean attribute that, if TRUE, defines this Card to be physically different from other Cards of the same type and therefore requires a special slot. The unique aspects of this Card are described in the CardUniqueRequirements attribute.

  This attribute was incorporated into the CIM Card *class, but was renamed to* SpecialRequirements.

Note

Note that the "uniqueness" described by the CardUniqueness and CardUniqueRequirements attributes only describe physical differences that necessitate installing this card in a special slot. This is because this is a physical class, and the CIM developers are very careful not to mix physical with logical requirements.

- CardUniqueRequirements is a free-form string that contains the physically unique requirements of this Card. For example, it must go in a certain slot number because it has special dimensions. This attribute should only be filled in if the value of the CardUniqueness attribute is TRUE.

  This attribute was incorporated into the CIM Card *class, but was renamed to* RequirementsDescription.

- Category is a free-form string that describes the overall function(s) of this card (for example, routing, switching, system management, and so on). This attribute is used to categorize the type of network card that this object is and facilitate queries.

  This attribute was removed from the CIM Card *class, as it was felt to be an optimization. It remains in the DEN specification to facilitate querying a repository that uses LDAP as its access protocol.*

- DaughterCardTypeList is an array of free-form strings that list the possible different types of companion boards that must accompany this Card in order for it to function properly.

  This attribute was removed from the CIM Card class, as it was felt to be too specific and it was impossible to supply a list of values for the array. It is currently in the DEN specification to standardize the modeling of this requirement, even though a standard set of values can not be supplied for the attribute.

- HostingBoard is a Boolean attribute that, if TRUE, indicates that this Card is a motherboard or, more generically, a baseboard in a Chassis.

  This attribute was incorporated into the CIM Card class.

- IsConfigurable is a Boolean attribute that, if TRUE, indicates that this Card has one or more options that can be configured before or after its purchase. Each of these options has a distinct physical manifestation (for example, additional memory, or faster CPU) that usually (but not always) results in occupying more room in the Card.

  This attribute was deleted from the CIM Card class. It was felt that a standard set of options should be able to be specified for this attribute, but unless the domain was narrowed to a specific field (for example, networking), it was impossible to do so. Thus, it was deleted from the Physical Common Model. It remains in the DEN specification.

- MaxMemoryCapacity is a 64-bit unsigned integer that indicates the maximum memory that this Card can use.

  This attribute was deleted from the CIM Card class, and the Memory class and its attributes were enhanced in the CIM Device Common Model. This attribute was also deleted from the DEN specification.

- MaxSlotSpacing is a 16-bit unsigned integer attribute that indicates the maximum spacing between slots in inches.

  This attribute was incorporated into the CIM AdjacentSlots association. This association is also used in the DEN specification.

- MinSlotSpacing is a 16-bit unsigned integer attribute that indicates the minimum spacing between slots in inches.

  This attribute was incorporated into the CIM AdjacentSlots association. This association is also used in the DEN specification.

- NumberOfPorts is a 16-bit unsigned integer attribute that indicates the number of ports supported by this Card.

  This attribute was deleted from both the CIM and the DEN Card classes because it isn't a physical attribute.

- NumberOfSlots is a 16-bit unsigned integer attribute that defines the number of slots in a Card, or the number of mounting points, sockets or 'slots' for daughtercards, memory chips/boards, and other types of Cards, that are supported by this Card.

  This attribute was deleted from the CIM Card class, as it is derived information (for example, the instantiated associations will also tell you indirectly how many slots are in a given Card). However, this attribute is still in the DEN specification, as this type of query is very expensive using LDAP.

- OnCardDRAMOptions is a free-form string that indicates the various DRAM configuration options that are available for this Card.

  This attribute was deleted from both the CIM and the DEN Card classes; instead, a new aggregation, MemoryOnCard, was defined.

- OnCardFlashOptions is a free-form string that indicates the various flash memory configuration options that are available for this Card.

  This attribute was deleted from both the CIM and the DEN Card classes; instead, a new aggregation, MemoryOnCard, was defined.

- OnCardSRAMOptions is a free-form string that indicates the various SRAM configuration options that are available for this Card.

  This attribute was deleted from both the CIM and the DEN Card classes; instead, a new aggregation, MemoryOnCard, was defined.

- RequiresDaughterBoard is a Boolean attribute that, if TRUE, indicates that this particular Card requires at least one auxiliary Card to function correctly.

  This attribute was incorporated into the Card class of the CIM Physical Common Model.

The DEN Card class defined no methods. However, it participated in seven relationships. The following relationships were deleted from both the CIM Physical Common Model and the DEN specification:

- The CardInNetworkPackage aggregation was deleted because the NetworkPackage class was deleted

- The DaughterCard aggregation was a specialized aggregation that defined the ability for a daughter card to plug into another Card. This relationship was already captured in the CardOnCard aggregation, and so it was removed.

- The LinkMediaOnCard aggregation was removed because the rest of the model was not able to support the detailed modeling required by this association.

The RunningCardOS association was deleted from the CIM Physical Common Model because it was felt to be too specific to networking. However, this association remains in the DEN specification because many network elements are chassis-based devices whose functionality is derived from the intelligence in the cards that are installed in it. This association enables the modeling of a network devices that has intelligent cards installed that are running different operating systems.

NetworkPackage

This class represented the physical characteristics that were particular to a networking device. It was used in DEN as the anchor class for transferring between the physical containment or connectivity domains and the logical containment or connectivity domains.

The Network working group, which now owns DEN, deleted this class as part of the CIM 2.2 effort. Here are the original definitions of the attributes for this class, and a brief discussion as to their status:

- DeviceGroupID was a 64-bit unsigned integer, and was used to uniquely identify this device as a member of a group of devices.

  This attribute was thought to be too "logical" in its use, and was deleted.

- Movable was a Boolean attribute that, if TRUE, indicates that this object is movable.

  It was replaced by the Removable *attribute in* PhysicalPackage.

- SlotCompatible is a 16-bit unsigned integer attribute that is used as part of the negotiation process between a Card and a NetworkPackage to see if they are compatible. This is the result of the isCompatible() method, with the NetworkPackage being the source and the Card being the target.

  This attribute was deleted because it was too specific in nature to be incorporated into the Physical Common Model. This attribute still could be useful in an extension model, but is also deleted in the DEN specification.

The NetworkPackage class participated in five relationships. These were all deleted in CIM. In the DEN specification, one of these still exists: UpgradeableByASIC. This is because ASICs (Application-Specific Integrated Circuit) play a fundamental role in providing network functions.

PhysicalLink

This class represents any physical object used to link other objects together. This usually represents the cabling of PhysicalElements together.

DEN extended this class by adding the following attribute:

- MediaType is an enumerated 16-bit unsigned integer attribute that indicates the specific type of media that is being used by this PhysicalLink.

  This attribute was incorporated into the PhysicalLink class of the CIM Physical Common Model, and then enhanced by the Systems and Devices Working Group.

The DEN version of this class participated in several relationships. All were either deleted or tabled pending more development of the Physical Common Model.

PhysicalConnector

This represents a PhysicalElement that is used to connect other PhysicalElements.

DEN extended the CIM PhysicalConnector class by adding the following attribute:

- InUse is a Boolean attribute that, if TRUE, indicates that this PhysicalConnector is in use by some other component of the system.

  This attribute was deleted from the Slot class of the CIM Physical Common Model. A new association defined in CIM 2.1, SlotInSlot, captures the semantics of this attribute.

Slot

This class represents a special type of `PhysicalConnector` into which circuit boards or adapter cards can be inserted. There are two common uses:

- One is to model the ability of a hosting board to accept a daughter card to add or complete the base functionality of the hosting board.

- The second is to represent the different expansion slots supported by a `Chassis`.

DEN extended the CIM `Slot` class by adding the following attributes:

- `SlotAdapter` is a Boolean attribute that, if `TRUE`, indicates whether this slot can accept an adapter that enables it to accept other types of cards (for example, fitting an adapter on two `Slot`s enable them to accept a `Card` that otherwise could not be accommodated).

  This attribute was deleted from both the CIM and DEN `Slot` *classes and replaced with a more generic association,* `SlotInSlot`.

- `SlotCategory` is a free-form string that enables `Slot`s to be classified (for example, PC-card slot versus networking slot). This is primarily to help querying using LDAP.

  This attribute was deleted from both the CIM and DEN `Slot` *classes, as* `PhysicalElement` *now contains more attributes that can be used to facilitate querying.*

- `SlotCompatibilityList` is an array of free-form that define the possible `PhysicalElement`s that may be contained in this `Slot`.

  This attribute was deleted from the CIM `Slot` *class because it was felt that it was too specific. This attribute is still in the DEN specification.*

- `SlotIndex` is a 16-bit unsigned integer attribute that represents an index into the system slot table. For example, this could be the hardware ID number (starting with 1) for each expansion slot, whether or not it is occupied.

  This attribute was incorporated into the CIM `Slot` *class, but renamed to* `Number`.

- `SlotUniqueness` is a Boolean attribute that, if TRUE, means that this `Slot` is physically different from other `Slot`s, and is intended to hold a special type of `Card` (for example, a doublewide card, or a longer card than normal).

  This attribute was incorporated into the CIM `Card` *class of the CIM Physical Common Model, but renamed to* `SpecialPurpose`.

- `SlotUniqueRequirements` is a free-form string that defines the physically unique characteristics of this `Slot`.

  This attribute was incorporated into the `Card` *class of the CIM Physical Common Model, but renamed to* `PurposeDescription`.

The DEN version of this class defined no methods. However, it participated in three relationships, all of which were incorporated into the CIM Physical Common Model. The `CardInSlot` association was incorporated without any modifications. The `CombinedSlots` association was renamed to `SlotInSlot` and then incorporated. Finally, `SharedSlots` was enhanced and became the `AdjacentSlots` association.

PhysicalComponent and Chip

These classes were CIM classes and were not modified by the DEN specification.

NetworkASIC

This class represents a special type of `Chip` that is used to upgrade the functionality of a networking device. Examples include upgrading the modem function of a device or implementing some type of networking functionality, such as fast switching.

This is a DEN class that was not added into the CIM Physical Common Model, as it was felt that it was too specific to networking. It has been removed from the current version of the DEN specification.

Changes Made in Migrating to the CIM Physical Model

Table 8.1 provides a mapping between the classes defined in the original DEN Physical Model and the resulting CIM Physical Common Model. All CIM 2.2 extensions that were approved before May 1, 1999, were also included in this mapping.

Table 8.1 Classes in the DEN Physical Model and CIM Physical Common Model.

DEN Class Name	CIM Class Name	Description and Status
Location	Location	CIM tightened up the data type definitions; the `PhysicalLocationDN` attribute is intended for LDAP use only.
Device	Device	Mapped into `PhysicalElement`.
PhysicalElement	PhysicalElement	Some attributes were incorporated in CIM; the rest remain as part of the DEN spec.

DEN Class Name	CIM Class Name	Description and Status
PhysicalPackage	PhysicalPackage	Some attributes were incorporated in CIM; the rest remain as part of the DEN spec.
SecurePackage	PhysicalFrame	Class renamed; some attributes were incorporated into CIM, and the rest remain as part of the DEN spec.
Rack	Rack	Some attributes were moved to PhysicalFrame, and some were renamed.
Chassis	Chassis	Some attributes moved to PhysicalFrame, and some were deleted.
Card	Card	Some attributes were moved to various relationships, some were renamed, and some were deleted.
NetworkPackage	deleted	
PhysicalLink	PhysicalLink	Now the same; DEN added an attribute to CIM 2.1.
PhysicalConnector	PhysicalConnector	The InUse attribute was not added to CIM.
Slot	Slot	Some attributes were deleted; relationships were renamed or enhanced.
PhysicalComponent	PhysicalComponent	Identical.
Chip	Chip	Identical.
NetworkASIC	deleted	Deleted from DEN spec.

As can be seen, the DEN Physical Model is largely a superset of the CIM Physical Common Model. The differences fall into two main categories:

- LDAP optimizations

- Classes and attributes that are specific to networking

The DEN specification is targeted for release in middle to late 1999.

The CIM Physical Common Model

The following section describes the CIM Physical Common Model, paying close attention to those classes needed for networking and skimming over the other classes.

Purpose of the Physical Common Model

The purpose of the CIM Physical Common Model is to model the physical characteristics, functions, and capabilities of managed objects. This model reinforces the distinction between physical and logical aspects of a managed object.

The Physical Common Model has three goals:

- Model the characteristics of physical entities, as well as the physical aspects of a managed entity

- Model the physical connectivity aspects of a managed environment

- Model the physical containment aspects of a managed environment

The first goal is achieved by creating a common superclass for physical objects, called PhysicalElement. This class serves as the parent for both purely physical objects (for example, a Chassis), as well as the physical aspects of a more complicated object. This latter is associated with its parent object through a set of associations, such as Realizes. In this way, the Physical Common Model leverages the basic concepts defined in the Core Model and extends them to the physical connectivity and containment domains.

Physical connectivity aspects are modeled through the use of dedicated relationships, such as ConnectedTo.

Physical containment aspects are modeled indirectly through separating the physical hierarchy into more granular classes that can capture containment as well as through dedicated relationships.

The following sections define the Physical Common Model. Its elements (except for the Location class) are all subclassed from the Core Model.

Location

The Location class specifies the position and address of a PhysicalElement. Locations can be nested to represent hierarchies of arbitrary depth (for example, a WiringCloset in a particular Floor of a specific Building of a Campus of a Site).

The Location class serves as a general superclass for you to customize how physical locations—such as the floor, building, campus, and site of the preceding example—are represented in your managed environment. It has a composite key consisting of two attributes: Name and PhysicalPosition. Together, they enable two similarly named objects to be differentiated from each other. Figure 8.2 illustrates the Location class.

Figure 8.2   Physical Model excerpt: Location and its relationships.

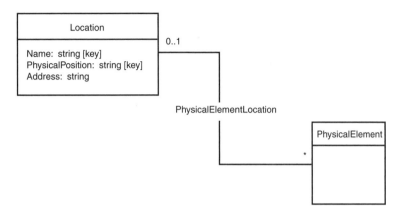

> ### Note
> Remember that the asterisk in Figure 8.2 represents a cardinality of zero-or-more.

The attributes of the Location class are defined as follows:

- Name is a free-form string, of up to 256 characters, that defines a label for the Location. It is a part of the key for the object.

- PhysicalPosition is a free-form string, of up to 256 characters, that indicates the placement of a PhysicalElement. This is a very general attribute, and can be used to specify a particular Slot in a PhysicalPackage, such as a Chassis, a mounting point on a Card, or even latitude and longitude information from a global positioning system. It is part of the key of the Location object.

- Address is a free-form string, of up to 1024 characters, that indicates a street, building, or other type of physical address for the Location of the PhysicalElement.

The Location class does not define any methods. However, it does participate in a single relationship, PhysicalElementLocation.

The PhysicalElementLocation *Association*

The PhysicalElementLocation relationship associates a PhysicalElement with a specific Location. This could be for general management purposes, or for specific functions like inventory maintenance or replacement. The cardinality of this association is zero-or-more on the PhysicalElement side, since not all PhysicalElements must have a location.

However, if they do have a location, then it could be shared among many objects that define this PhysicalElement. For example, the physical location of a Chassis could also be used for the location of the Cards and Slots that are contained in the Chassis.

The cardinality on the Location side of the association is defined to be zero-or-one. This is because a Location does not have to be attached to a physical object, but if it is, then at most one location can define the object (otherwise, we violate the laws of physics!).

PhysicalCapacity *and* MemoryCapacity

The PhysicalCapacity class is an abstract class that is used to describe the minimum and maximum requirements for a particular PhysicalElement. This can also be used to enumerate support for different types of hardware by this PhysicalElement. For example, the minimum and maximum memory requirements for a given PhysicalElement can be modeled as a subclass of PhysicalCapacity. Since this is so common, a subclass of PhysicalCapacity, MemoryCapacity, is also defined. Figure 8.3 illustrates the PhysicalCapacity class and its subclass and relationship.

Figure 8.3   Physical Model excerpt: PhysicalCapacity and its subclasses and relationships.

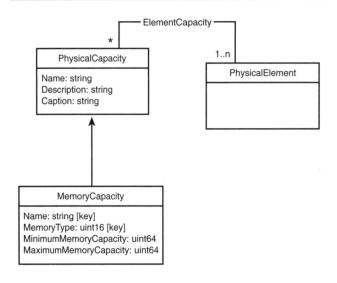

The PhysicalCapacity class defines no key attributes, because it is intended to be a superclass for application-specific classes that model capacities of physical entities. Since these are application-specific, it is impossible to define a specific key that is applicable to all applications. The attributes of the PhysicalCapacity class are defined as follows:

- Name is a free-form string of up to 256 characters that defines the label of the PhysicalCapacity object. Note that the Name attribute can be overridden to be a Key attribute when this class is subclassed.

- Caption is a short textual description (for example, one-line string) of up to 64 characters of the PhysicalCapacity object. It is intended primarily for GUI help-screen and information displays.

- Description is a free-form string that provides a textual description of the PhysicalCapacity object.

The PhysicalCapacity class does not define any methods. However, it does participate in a single relationship, ElementCapacity.

The ElementCapacity Association

The ElementCapacity association relates a PhysicalCapacity object with one or more PhysicalElements. The cardinality of this association is one-or-more on the PhysicalElement side and zero-or-more on the PhysicalCapacity side. This means that a PhysicalElement may have no known physical capacities, or it may be a complex object that has many different, unrelated physical capacities (for example, maximum number of cards that can be contained, minimum power, heating and cooling requirements, and so on). In this latter case, a single PhysicalElement would have relationships to multiple PhysicalCapacity objects. In addition, the same PhysicalCapacity object could be used to model the physical capacities of many different PhysicalElements.

The MemoryCapacity Subclass

The MemoryCapacity subclass is derived from the PhysicalCapacity class. The MemoryCapacity class describes the type of memory that can be installed on a PhysicalElement and its minimum and/or maximum configurations.

The attributes of the MemoryCapacity class are as follows:

- Name is a free-form string that defines the label of the PhysicalCapacity object. It is inherited from the PhysicalCapacity class, and is overridden in this class to serve as part of the composite key.

- MemoryType is an enumerated 16-bit unsigned integer that defines the type of memory that is represented by this object. This is a part of the composite key. The values are defined in Listing 8.1, and correspond to the values defined for the PhysicalMemory class (note the use of the ModelCorrespondence qualifier to do this).

Listing 8.1   MOF definition for the MemoryType attribute.

```
[...
Values {"Unknown", "Other", "DRAM", "Synchronous DRAM", "Cache DRAM", "EDO",
"EDRAM", "VRAM", "SRAM", "RAM", "ROM", "Flash", "EEPROM", "FEPROM", "EPROM",
"CDRAM", "3DRAM", "SDRAM", "SGRAM"},
ModelCorrespondence {"CIM_PhysicalMemory.MemoryType"} ]

uint16 MemoryType;
```

Note

All code listings, beginning with this one and continuing through Chapter 10, "DEN's Policy Model," are actually MOF fragments. As such, their format has been customized. The opening square bracket and ellipsis signify the start of the fragment. The end of the fragment is the last line in the example.

- MinimumMemoryCapacity is a 64-bit unsigned integer that defines the minimum amount of memory, in kilobytes, that is needed for the associated PhysicalElement to operate correctly.

- MaximumMemoryCapacity is a 64-bit unsigned integer that defines the maximum amount of memory, in kilobytes, that can be supported by the associated PhysicalElement.

ReplacementSet

The ReplacementSet class is used to define a set of PhysicalElements that must be replaced as a unit. This usually means that they must be treated as a single FRU. Figure 8.4 shows the ReplacementSet class.

Figure 8.4 Physical Model excerpt: `ReplacementSet` and its relationships.

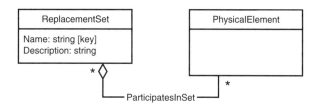

The `ReplacementSet` class defines the following attributes:

- `Name` is a free-form string, of up to 256 characters, that is used to define a label for the `ReplacementSet` object. It is the key for the object.

- `Description` is a free-form string that is used to describe and/or instruct how the components of this `ReplacementSet` are replaced.

The `ReplacementSet` does not define any methods. However, it defines a single relationship, `ParticipatesInSet`.

The `ParticipatesInSet` *Aggregation*

The `ParticipatesInSet` aggregation is used to define which `PhysicalElements` should be replaced together as a unit. The cardinality of this relationship is zero-or-more to zero-or-more.

`PhysicalPackage`

The `PhysicalPackage` class is used to represent `PhysicalElements` that can contain or host other `PhysicalElements`. Examples include a `Rack`, a `Chassis`, and a `Card`. Figure 8.5 illustrates the `PhysicalPackage` class.

The attributes of the `PhysicalPackage` class are defined as follows:

- `Removable` is a Boolean attribute that, if `TRUE`, means that a `PhysicalPackage` is designed to be taken in and out of the physical container in which it is normally found, without impairing the function of the overall packaging. Note that this has nothing to do with whether power is currently on or not. For example, an extra battery in a laptop is `Removable`, as are certain types of disk drives. However, the latter can also be removed while power is still applied to the laptop, making it `Removable` and `HotSwappable`. Compare this to the laptop's display, which is not `Removable`. In fact, trying to remove the display of a laptop would adversely impact the function of the overall packaging of the laptop.

- Replaceable is a Boolean attribute that, if TRUE, means that it is possible to replace the PhysicalElement with a different one. For example, some ComputerSystems allow the main Processor chip to be upgraded to one of a higher clock rating. In this case, the Processor is said to be Replaceable. As another example, some networking cards allow for various ASICs to be installed to replace or upgrade functionality that they provide. All Removable packages are inherently Replaceable.

- HotSwappable is a Boolean attribute that, if TRUE, means that it is possible to replace a PhysicalElement with a physically equivalent PhysicalElement while the containing PhysicalPackage has power applied to it. For example, a disk drive inserted using SCA connectors is both Removable and HotSwappable. All HotSwappable packages are inherently Removable and Replaceable.

- Height is a 32-bit real attribute that defines the height of the PhysicalPackage in inches.

- Depth is a 32-bit real attribute that defines the depth of the PhysicalPackage in inches.

- Width is a 32-bit real attribute that defines the width of the PhysicalPackage in inches.

- Weight is a 32-bit real attribute that defines the weight of the PhysicalPackage in pounds.

The PhysicalPackage class defines one method, called IsCompatible. This method is used to verify whether the referenced PhysicalElement may be contained by or inserted into the PhysicalPackage. Its signature is

```
uint32 IsCompatible([IN] CIM_PhysicalElement REF ElementToCheck);
```

The return value should be 0 if the request was successfully executed, 1 if the request is not supported, and some other value if an error occurred.

The PhysicalPackage class defines nine relationships. The PackageCooling, PackageTempSensor, and PackageAlarm relationships are probably not of interest to DEN applications, and so will not be discussed further (you can read their definitions in the Physical MOF file). The rest of these relationships, except the Container and the ComputerSystemPackage relationships, involve classes that have not yet been defined. Therefore, only the Container aggregation and the ComputerSystemPackage association will be described in the following sections.

Figure 8.5 Physical Model excerpt: `PhysicalPackage` and its relationships.

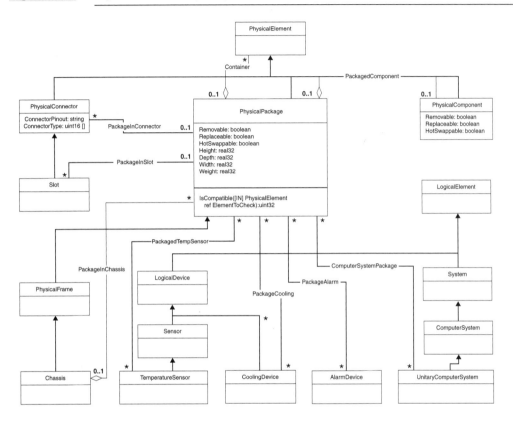

The `Container` *Aggregation*

The `Container` aggregation is a subclass of the more general `Component` aggregation and is used to represent the relationship between a `PhysicalPackage` (serving as the group component) and the set of `PhysicalElements` (that is, the part components) that it contains. The cardinality of this relationship is changed on the group component (that is, `PhysicalPackage`) from zero-or-more (as defined in the `Component` aggregation) to zero-or-one. This is because we are focusing on the various `PhysicalElements` that a specific `PhysicalPackage` can contain. The cardinality of the part component (that is, `PhysicalElement`) remains zero-or-more. In addition, this aggregation restricts the group and part components from `ManagedSystemElement` to `PhysicalPackage` and `PhysicalElement`, respectively. Finally, this aggregation defines a free-form string, `LocationWithinContainer`, to represent the specific physical positioning of the `PhysicalElement` within the `PhysicalPackage`.

The ComputerSystemPackage *Association*

The ComputerSystemPackage association is a subclass of the more general Dependency association. This relationship defines the PhysicalPackages that are used to make up a UnitaryComputerSystem. The antecedent and dependent are restricted to instances of the PhysicalPackage and UnitaryComputerSystem classes, respectively.

PhysicalFrame

The PhysicalFrame class is a subclass of PhysicalPackage. It serves as the superclass of Rack, Chassis, and other frame enclosures. Figure 8.6 illustrates the PhysicalFrame class.

Figure 8.6   Physical Model excerpt: PhysicalFrame and its relationships.

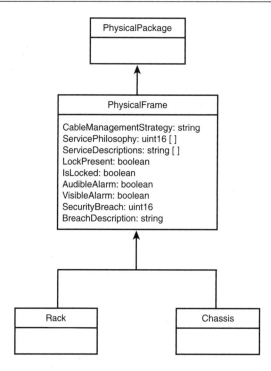

The attributes of the PhysicalFrame class are defined as follows:

- CableManagementStrategy is a free-form string that contains information on how the various cables are connected and bundled within the Frame. With many networking, storage-related and power cables, cable management can be a complex and challenging endeavor. Therefore, this attribute is used to contain information to aid in assembly and service of the cables contained in the PhysicalFrame.

- ServicePhilosophy is an enumerated array of 16-bit integers that indicates how the Frame is serviced. Extensibility is provided through the use of the Other value, which enables custom servicing to be described. Listing 8.2 shows the MOF definition for the values of this attribute.

Listing 8.2   MOF definition for the ServicePhilosophy attribute.

```
[...
ArrayType ("Indexed"),
Values {"Unknown", "Other", "Service From Top", "Service From Front", "Service
        From Back", "Service From Side", "Sliding Trays", "Removable Sides",
        "Moveable"},
ModelCorrespondence {"CIM_PhysicalFrame.ServiceDescriptions"} ]
uint16 ServicePhilosophy[];
```

- ServiceDescriptions is an array of free-form strings that provide more detailed explanations for any of the entries in the ServicePhilosophy array. The two arrays are related to each other through the use of the Indexed and ModelCorrespondence qualifiers.

- LockPresent is a Boolean attribute that, if TRUE indicates that the PhysicalFrame has a lock to protect it.

- IsLocked is a Boolean attribute that, if TRUE, indicates that the PhysicalFrame is currently locked.

- AudibleAlarm is a Boolean attribute that, if TRUE, indicates that the PhysicalFrame has an audible alarm of some type.

- VisibleAlarm is a Boolean attribute that, if TRUE, indicates that the PhysicalFrame includes some type of a visible alarm.

- SecurityBreach is an enumerated, 16-bit integer attribute that indicates whether a physical breach of the PhysicalFrame was attempted and, if so, what its status is. The value of 1 (Other) can be used to provide application-specific breach information. If the value is set to 1, then the specific breach description will be contained in the BreachDescription attribute. The possible values are

Value	Description
1	Other
2	Unknown
3	No Breach
4	Breach Attempted
5	Breach Successful

- `BreachDescription` is a free-form string that provides more information if the value of the `SecurityBreach` attribute is set to 1 (for example, `Other`). Otherwise, the value of this attribute should be set to `NULL`.

The `PhysicalFrame` class does not define any methods or relationships.

Rack

A `Rack` is subclassed from `PhysicalFrame`. It represents a type of `PhysicalFrame` that contains an enclosure in which `Chassis` and other types of `PhysicalPackages` are placed. Typically, a `Rack` is nothing more than the enclosure, with the important components contained in the `Chassis`, which is in turn contained in the `Rack`. Figure 8.7 illustrates the `Rack` class.

Figure 8.7   Physical Model excerpt: `Rack` and its relationships.

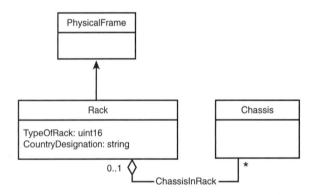

The attributes of the `Rack` class are defined as follows:

- `Height` is a 32-bit real attribute that defines the height of the `PhysicalPackage` in U's. A *U* is a standard unit of measure for the height of a `Rack` or rack-mountable component. It is equal to 1.75 inches or 4.445 cm.

> **Note**
>
> In order to change the definition of the measurement units from inches to U's, this attribute definition overrides the inherited attribute definition (from `Physical Package`). Note that this type of override is perfectly valid from an object-oriented point-of-view, because the semantics and syntax of the attribute are kept the same.

- TypeOfRack is an enumerated 16-bit integer that defines the type of Rack this object is. Five values are defined: Unknown, Standard 19 Inch, Telco, Equipment Shelf, and Non-Standard.

- CountryDesignation defines the country for which the Rack is designed. Country code strings are as defined in ISO/IEC 3166.

This class defines no methods. It participates in one relationship, ChassisInRack, which is defined in the following section, which describes the Chassis class.

Chassis

The Chassis class is another subclass of the PhysicalPackage class. It represents PhysicalFrames that are used to enclose other PhysicalElements. Figure 8.8 shows the Chassis class.

Figure 8.8   Physical Model excerpt: Chassis and its relationships.

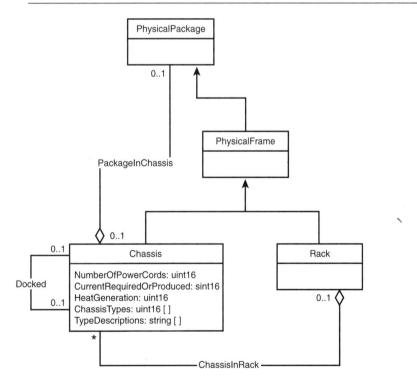

The attributes of the Chassis class are defined as follows:

- NumberOfPowerCords is a 16-bit integer that defines the number of power cords that must be connected to the Chassis in order for all the components contained in the Chassis to operate correctly.

- CurrentRequiredOrProduced is a 16-bit signed integer that defines the current required by the Chassis at 120V. If power is provided by the Chassis (as in the case of a uninterruptible power supply, or UPS), this attribute may indicate the amperage produced, as a negative number.

- HeatGeneration is an unsigned 16-bit integer that defines the amount of heat generated by the Chassis in BTUs/hour.

- ChassisTypes is an enumerated 16-bit array of integers that indicates the type of Chassis that this object is. Listing 8.3 defines the MOF for this attribute.

Listing 8.3	MOF definition for the ChassisTypes attribute.

```
[...
ArrayType ("Indexed"),
ValueMap {"1", "2", "3", "4", "5", "6", "7", "8", "9", "10", "11", "12", "13",
       "14", "15", "16", "17", "18", "19", "20", "21", "22", "23", "24"},
Values {"Other", "Unknown", "Desktop", "Low Profile Desktop", "Pizza Box",
       "Mini Tower", "Tower", "Portable", "LapTop", "Notebook", "Hand Held",
       "Docking Station", "All in One", "Sub Notebook", "Space-Saving", "Lunch
       Box", "Main System Chassis", "Expansion Chassis", "SubChassis", "Bus
       Expansion Chassis", "Peripheral Chassis", "Storage Chassis", "Rack Mount
       Chassis", "Sealed-Case PC"},
MappingStrings {"MIF.DMTF¦Physical Container Global Table|002.1"},
ModelCorrespondence {"CIM_Chassis.TypeDescriptions"} ]
uint16 ChassisTypes[]
```

Note

The qualifier ArrayType("Indexed") is used to define an array that maintains the order of its elements. Such an array is usually implemented based on an integer index for each of the array values.

- `TypeDescriptions` is an array of free-form strings that provides additional information for each of the `ChassisTypes` array entries. Note that each entry of this array is related to a corresponding entry in the `ChassisTypes` array through the use of the qualifier `ArrayType` (`"Indexed"`) (to index the array) and the `ModelCorrespondence` qualifier (to make them relate to each other). This means that each array is indexed, and the indices must line up.

The `Chassis` class does not define any methods. However, it does define three relationships: `Docked`, `ChassisInRack`, and `PackageInChassis`.

The Docked Association

The `Docked` association defines the "containing" relationship between a `Chassis` and the `Chassis` that it contains. This relationship is especially useful to represent the docking of a laptop. It is a subclass of the more general `Dependency` association, but alters both the multiplicity of the relationship and the types of classes that participate in it. The cardinality of both the antecedent and the dependent are changed from zero-or-more to zero-or-one. In addition, the class type of both the antecedent and the dependent are restricted to a `Chassis`.

The ChassisInRack Aggregation

The `ChassisInRack` aggregation defines the "containing" relationship between the `Rack` and the `Chassis` that it contains. It is a subclass of the more general `Container` aggregation, but alters both the multiplicity of the relationship and the types of classes that participate in it. The cardinality of the group component is changed from zero-or-more to zero-or-one, in order to identify the specific `Rack` that is being described (the zero enables this relationship to remain optional; this allows, for example, `Racks` to be inventoried without having to contain anything). The cardinality of the part component side of the relationship remains at zero-or-more, but its class type is restricted to a `Chassis`.

This aggregation also defines an attribute, `BottomU`, that indicates the lowest, or "bottom," U in which the `Chassis` is mounted.

The PackageInChassis Aggregation

The `PackageInChassis` aggregation defines the "containing" relationship between a `Chassis` and the `PhysicalPackages` that it contains. It is a subclass of the more general `Container` aggregation, but alters both the multiplicity of the relationship and the types of classes that participate in it (in a similar way to `RackInChassis`). The cardinality of the group component is changed from zero-or-more to zero-or-one, in order to identify the specific `Chassis` that is being described. The cardinality of the part component side of the relationship remains at zero-or-more, but its class type is restricted to a `PhysicalPackage`.

Card

The Card class is a subclass of PhysicalPackage. This might seem odd at first, but remember that this is the Physical Model. Therefore, a Card represents a type of physical container that can be plugged into a Slot in a Chassis or another Card, or is itself a motherboard in a physical container (such as a Chassis). In particular, a Card has no intelligence itself; rather, the intelligence is contained in components, such as special chips and software, that are contained on the Card. Figure 8.9 illustrates the Card class.

Figure 8.9   Physical Model excerpt: Card and its relationships.

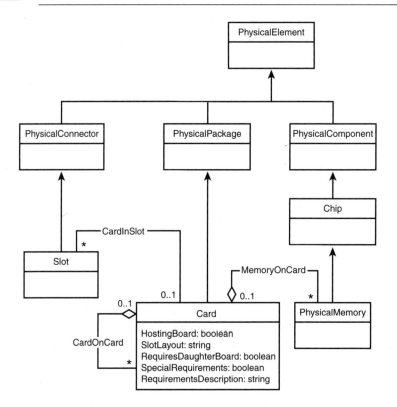

The attributes of the Card class are defined as follows:

- HostingBoard is a Boolean attribute that, if TRUE, indicates that this Card is a motherboard or, more generically, has the ability to host other Cards and physical components.

- SlotLayout is a free-form string that describes the slot positioning, individual slot spacings, typical usage and restrictions, or any other pertinent information for the slots on a Card.

- RequiresDaughterBoard is a Boolean attribute that, if TRUE, indicates that at least one daughterboard or some type of auxiliary Card is required in order for this Card to function properly.

- SpecialRequirements is a Boolean attribute that, if TRUE, indicates that this Card is physically different from other Cards that are to be installed in the Chassis or other type of physical enclosure. Therefore, this Card requires a special Slot. For example, a double-wide Card requires two Slots, and a Card that is different in some dimension (for example, longer) can be installed only in a Slot that can accommodate that type of Card. If this attribute is set to TRUE, then the corresponding attribute, RequirementsDescription, is used to specify the nature of the unique characteristics or purpose of this Card. As usual, this is indicated using the ModelCorrespondence qualifier.

- RequirementsDescription is a free-form string that is used to describe the unique characteristics of this Card, as compared to the other Cards contained in this enclosure. This attribute should only contain a non-NULL value when the corresponding Boolean attribute, SpecialRequirements, is set to TRUE.

This class defines no methods. However, it participates in three relationships: CardOnCard, MemoryOnCard, and CardInSlot. The CardOnCard aggregation will be defined in the following section. The other two relationships will be defined when the PhysicalMemory and Slot classes are defined later in this chapter.

The CardOnCard *Aggregation*

The CardOnCard aggregation is used to define the "containing" relationship between a Card and any daughter cards or auxiliary cards that it contains. It is a subclass of the more general Container aggregation, but alters both the multiplicity of the relationship and the types of classes that participate in it. The cardinality of the group component is changed from zero-or-more to zero-or-one in order to identify the specific Card that is being described. The cardinality of the part component side of the relationship remains at zero-or-more. Both the group and the part component are restricted to be of the class Card.

In addition, this relationship defines an attribute called MountOrSlotDescription. This attribute is a free-form string that describes how the daughter or auxiliary Card is mounted on or plugged into the main Card. This may be achieved through describing how the Card is mounted, or which Slot it should be connected to, or other information. This aggregation can be used instead of instantiating separate Connector and Slot objects if all that is required is to model the relationship of Cards to Chassis or other adapters. However, this does not preclude instantiating Connector and Slot objects in order to provide a richer model (for example, more detailed mounting or slot insertion data).

PhysicalConnector

The PhysicalConnector class represents any PhysicalElement that is used to connect other PhysicalElements together. The PhysicalConnector has the additional semantics of being able to transmit signals or power between the connected PhysicalElements. Figure 8.10 illustrates the PhysicalConnector class.

Figure 8.10 Physical Model excerpt: PhysicalConnector and its relationships.

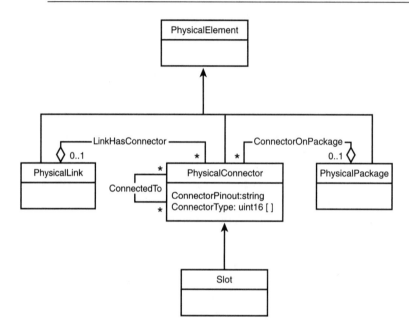

The attributes of the PhysicalConnector class are defined as follows:

- ConnectorPinout is a free-form string that contains the pin configuration (including signal usage) of a PhysicalConnector.

- ConnectorType is an array of 16-bit unsigned integers that defines the type of this PhysicalConnector. The use of the array enables the PhysicalConnector to be described by a set of predefined information, providing a better overall description of the PhysicalConnector. For example, a single PhysicalConnector could be described with the entries RS-232 (value=25), DB-25 (value=23), and Male (value=2). The MOF description of this attribute is provided in Listing 8.4.

Listing 8.4 MOF definition for the `ConnectorType` attribute.

```
[...
Values {"Unknown", "Other", "Male", "Female", "Shielded", "Unshielded",
        "SCSI (A) High-Density (50 pins)", "SCSI (A) Low-Density (50 pins)",
          "SCSI (P) High-Density (68 pins)", "SCSI SCA-I (80 pins)", "SCSI
          ➥SCA-II (80 pins)",
          "SCSI Fibre Channel (DB-9, Copper)", "SCSI Fibre Channel (Fibre)",
          "SCSI Fibre Channel SCA-II (40 pins)", "SCSI Fibre Channel SCA-II
          ➥(20 pins)",
          "SCSI Fibre Channel BNC", "ATA 3-1/2 Inch (40 pins)", "ATA 2-1/2
          ➥Inch (44 pins)",
          "ATA-2", "ATA-3", "ATA/66", "DB-9", "DB-15", "DB-25", "DB-36",
          "RS-232C", "RS-422", "RS-423", "RS-485", "RS-449", "V.35", "X.21",
          ➥"IEEE-488", "AUI",
        "UPT Category 3", "UPT Category 4", "UPT Category 5", "BNC", "RJ11",
        ➥"RJ45",
          "Fiber MIC", "Apple AUI", "Apple GeoPort", "PCI", "ISA", "EISA",
          ➥"VESA",
        "PCMCIA", "PCMCIA Type I", "PCMCIA Type II", "PCMCIA Type III", "ZV
        ➥Port", "CardBus",
          "USB", "IEEE 1394", "HIPPI", "HSSDC (6 pins)", "GBIC", "DIN",
          ➥"Mini-DIN", "Micro-DIN",
          "PS/2", "Infrared", "HP-HIL", "Access.bus", "NuBus", "Centronics",
          ➥"Mini-Centronics",
          "Mini-Centronics Type-14", "Mini-Centronics Type-20",
          ➥"Mini-Centronics Type-26",
          "Bus Mouse", "ADB", "AGP", "VME Bus", "VME64"} ]
    uint16 [];
```

This class does not define any methods. However, it participates in three relationships. Two of these, `ConnectedTo` and `ConnectorOnPackage`, are described next. The third, `LinkHasConnector`, is described later in this chapter when the `PhysicalLink` class is described.

The `ConnectedTo` Association

The `ConnectedTo` association is a subclass of the more general `Dependency` association. It is used to show that two or more `PhysicalConnectors` are connected together. The multiplicity of this relationship is the same as its parent (that is, zero-or-more to zero-or-more); however, the antecedent and dependent are both restricted to be of the `PhysicalConnector` class (or one of its subclasses).

The ConnectorOnPackage *Aggregation*

The ConnectorOnPackage aggregation is a subclass of the Container aggregation, and is used to represent the ability of a PhysicalPackage to contain PhysicalConnectors and other types of PhysicalElements. Making this aggregation specific enables more efficient navigation of the model, since connectors play a critical role in the realization of physical topology. The cardinality of the group component (PhysicalPackage) is restricted to zero-or-one, but the cardinality of the part component (PhysicalConnector) is left at zero-or-more. Finally, the group component is restricted to instances of the class PhysicalPackage, while the part component is restricted to instances of the class PhysicalConnector.

Slot

The Slot class is derived from the PhysicalConnector class, and represents PhysicalConnectors into which other components, such as Cards, can be inserted. Figure 8.11 illustrates the Slot class.

Figure 8.11 Physical Model excerpt: Slot and its relationships.

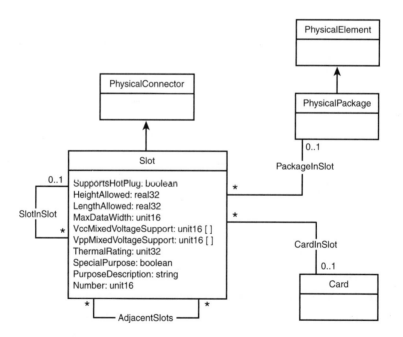

The attributes of the Slot class are defined as follows:

- ConnectorType is overridden in this class in order to conform to the master MIF file; semantically, it serves the same function as that provided by its inherited attribute.

> **Note**
>
> MIF, or Management Information Format, is used by the Desktop Management Interface to describe a mapping between management software and the components of a computer system that require management. This is a separate standard worked on in the DMTF.

- SupportsHotPlug is a Boolean attribute that, if TRUE, indicates that this Slot supports installing Cards with the power still on.

- HeightAllowed is a 32-bit real integer that defines the maximum height of a Card that can be inserted into this Slot, in inches.

- LengthAllowed is a 32-bit real integer that defines the maximum length of a Card that can be inserted into this Slot, in inches.

- MaxDataWidth defines the maximum bus width of Cards that can be inserted into this Slot, in bits. Acceptable values are 8, 16, 32, 64, and 128 bits.

- VccMixedVoltageSupport is an array of 16-bit enumerated integers that indicate all possible values of the Vcc voltage supported by this Slot. Currently, these values are defined as Unknown, Other, 3.3V, and 5V.

- VppMixedVoltageSupport is an array of 16-bit enumerated integers that indicate all possible values of the Vpp voltage supported by this Slot. Currently, these values are defined as Unknown, Other, 3.3V, 5V, and 12V.

- ThermalRating is a 32-bit unsigned integer that defines the maximum thermal dissipation of the Slot in milliwatts.

- SpecialPurpose is a Boolean attribute that, if TRUE, indicates that this Slot is physically unique and is intended to support special types of Cards, such as a system controller, networking, or graphics processor board. If the value of this attribute is set to TRUE, then the purpose of this Slot is defined in the attribute SpecialPurposeDescription.

- PurposeDescription is a free-form string that describes how this Slot is physically unique, and/or what type of special-purpose boards this Slot is designed to hold. This property only has meaning when the corresponding Boolean attribute, SpecialPurpose, is set to TRUE.

- Number is a 16-bit integer attribute that indicates the physical slot number of this Slot. This is, in reality, an index into the system slot table, which enables a Slot to be uniquely identified whether or not it is physically occupied.

The Slot class does not define any methods. However, it does define two relationships, SlotInSlot and AdjacentSlots. It also participates in two other relationships: PackageInSlot and CardInSlot.

The SlotInSlot Association

The SlotInSlot association is a subclass of the ConnectedTo association. The problem is that certain types of cards (especially networking cards) are very expensive. As new chassis are purchased, they may be incompatible with existing cards that have been purchased. Many vendors provide a special adapter card that serves as an interface between the new chassis and the old cards that are otherwise incompatible with the new chassis. This association represents the ability of a special adapter to extend the existing Slot structure to enable otherwise incompatible Cards to be plugged into a PhysicalPackage. The adapter effectively creates a new Slot and can be thought of (conceptually) as a Slot in a Slot.

The SlotInSlot association restricts the class of the antecedent and the dependent to instances of the Slot class (instead of PhysicalConnector). It also changes the multiplicity on the antecedent side from zero-or-more to zero-or-one.

The AdjacentSlots Association

The AdjacentSlots association is a top-level association that describes the layout of Slots on a PhysicalPackage. The association is between two instances of the Slot class, and the multiplicity of the association is zero-or-more to zero-or-more.

This relationship includes two attributes that are used to provide general layout information describing the Slots in the PhysicalPackage. The first, DistanceBetweenSlots, is a 32-bit real integer (which is an IEEE 4-byte floating-point number) that defines the distance in inches between two adjacent Slots in the PhysicalPackage. The second, SharedSlots, is a Boolean attribute that describes the dependency between two Slots that are located in close proximity to each other. Sometimes, the two Slots are so close that if one Slot is populated by an adapter Card, the other Slot must be left empty. If this attribute is set to TRUE, then the second Slot must be left unoccupied.

The `PackageInSlot` *Association*

The `PackageInSlot` association is a subclass of the more general `Dependency` association. High-end networking devices that are chassis-based often allow for enhancement and/or augmentation of their base functionality by enabling additional chassis-based devices to be installed in their enclosure. This is similar to installing a `Card` in a `Slot`.

The multiplicity of this relationship is changed. The cardinality of the antecedent, `Slot`, is zero-or-more, indicating that one or more of the `Slots` may be used to host the chassis-based device. The cardinality of the dependent, `PhysicalPackage`, is restricted to zero-or-one. This means that this relationship is not required but, if it is implemented, is defined for a single `Slot`.

The `CardInSlot` *Association*

The `CardInSlot` association is a subclass of the `PackageInSlot` association. It represents the dependency established when a `Card` is installed in a `Slot`.

The overall multiplicity of this association is the same as `PackageInSlot`. However, the dependent is changed from an instance of the `PhysicalPackage` class to an instance of the `Card` class.

PhysicalLink

The `PhysicalLink` class is used to represent the cabling together of `PhysicalElements`. This class is intended to serve as the subclass for specialized types of links (for example, ethernet and serial). Figure 8.12 shows the `PhysicalLink` class.

The attributes of the `PhysicalLink` class are defined as follows:

- `MaxLength` is a 64-bit real attribute that defines the maximum length of the `PhysicalLink` in feet.

- `Length` is a 64-bit real attribute that defines the current length of the `PhysicalLink` in feet. For some connections, this attribute may not be applicable and should be left uninitialized.

- `Wired` is a Boolean attribute, that, if `TRUE`, defines this `PhysicalLink` as an actual cable (instead of, for example, a wireless connection).

- `MediaType` is an enumerated 16-bit unsigned integer that defines the particular type of media through which communication is done. The current media values that are defined are `Unknown`, `Other`, `Cat1`, `Cat2`, `Cat3`, `Cat4`, `Cat5`, `50-ohm Coaxial`, `75-ohm Coaxial`, `100-ohm Coaxial`, `Fiber-optic`, `UTP`, `STP`, and `Ribbon Cable`.

Figure 8.12 Physical Model excerpt: `PhysicalLink` and its relationships.

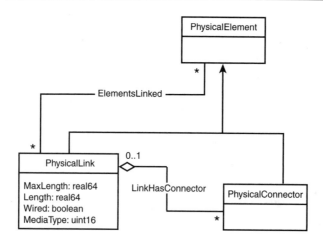

The `PhysicalLink` class defines no methods, but it does participate in two relationships, the `LinkHasConnector` aggregation and the `ElementsLinked` association. These are defined in the next sections.

The `LinkHasConnector` Aggregation

The `LinkHasConnector` aggregation is subclassed from the more general `Component` aggregation. It represents the use of a `PhysicalConnector` by a `Link` in order to actually connect `PhysicalElements`. The multiplicity of this relationship is zero-or-one on the aggregate (`PhysicalLink`) side and zero-or-more on the part (`PhysicalConnector`) side. The group component is restricted to instances of the `PhysicalLink` class, and the part component is restricted to instances of the `PhysicalConnector` class.

The `ElementsLinked` Association

The `ElementsLinked` association is subclassed from the `Dependency` association. This association is used to define which `PhysicalElements` are connected together by a `PhysicalLink`. The antecedent is restricted to instances of the `PhysicalLink` class, and the dependent is restricted to instances of the `PhysicalElement` class.

`PhysicalComponent`

The `PhysicalComponent` class is used to represent any low-level component that is physically housed within a `PhysicalPackage` that is itself not a `PhysicalLink`, `PhysicalConnector`, or `PhysicalPackage`.

A PhysicalComponent is therefore a generic base class for classifying physical objects that are contained in physical containers that do not belong to the PhysicalLink, PhysicalConnector, or PhysicalPackage classes. This also implies that if a PhysicalComponent is a complex object (for example, it is composed of several constituent objects), it does not need to be decomposed into those constituent objects (for example, it can be treated as an atomic object for manageability purposes). Figure 8.13 illustrates the PhysicalComponent class.

Figure 8.13 Physical Model excerpt: PhysicalComponent and its relationships.

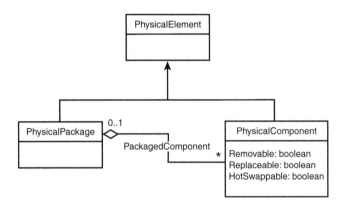

The attributes of the PhysicalComponent class are defined as follows:

- Removable is a Boolean attribute that, if TRUE, means that this PhysicalComponent is designed to be taken in and out of the PhysicalPackage in which it is normally found, without impairing the overall function of the device. Note that whether power is on or off has nothing to do with whether a PhysicalComponent is Removable or not.

- Replaceable is a Boolean attribute that, if TRUE, means that this PhysicalComponent is designed to be replaced or upgraded with a physically different PhysicalComponent. For example, some ComputerSystems, such as servers and routers, allow various chips (for example, the main processor or special-purpose ASICs) to be upgraded in functionality. This may be represented through an associated FRU class. All Removable PhysicalComponents are inherently Replaceable.

- HotSwappable is a Boolean attribute that, if TRUE, means that this PhysicalComponent was designed to be replaced with a physically different PhysicalComponent while the PhysicalPackage that contains the PhysicalComponent has power applied to it. All HotSwappable PhysicalComponents are inherently Removable and Replaceable.

The PhysicalComponent class does not define any methods. However, it participates in one relationship, the PackagedComponent aggregation.

The PackagedComponent Aggregation

The PackagedComponent aggregation is a subclass of the more general Container aggregation. The PackagedComponent aggregation defines the set of PhysicalComponents that are contained by a given PhysicalPackage.

The group component is restricted to instances of the PhysicalPackage class, and the part component is restricted to instances of the PhysicalComponent class. The cardinality of the aggregate (PhysicalPackage) is zero-or-one, meaning that this is an optional relationship but, if it is instantiated, it applies to a single PhysicalPackage. The cardinality of the part component (PhysicalComponent) side is zero-or-more, meaning that PhysicalComponents do not have to be installed in a PhysicalPackage but, if they are, any number can be installed.

Chip

The Chip class represents any type of integrated circuit, including ASICs, processors, memory chips, and so on. It is a subclass of PhysicalComponent. Figure 8.14 illustrates the Chip class.

Figure 8.14   Physical Model excerpt: Chip and its relationships.

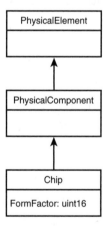

The Chip class defines a single attribute, as follows:

- FormFactor is an enumerated 16-bit integer attribute that describes the form factor for the Chip. Listing 8.5 shows the MOF for this attribute.

Listing 8.5   MOF definition for the FormFactor attribute.

```
[...
Values {"Unknown", "Other", "SIP", "DIP", "ZIP", "SOJ", "Proprietary", "SIMM",
        "DIMM", "TSOP", "PGA", "RIMM", "SODIMM"} ]
uint16 FormFactor;
```

The Chip class defines no methods or relationships.

PhysicalMemory

The PhysicalMemory class is a subclass of the Chip class, and is used to represent memory devices such as SIMMS, DIMMs, and other related devices. Figure 8.15 illustrates the PhysicalMemory class.

Figure 8.15   Physical Model excerpt: PhysicalMemory and its relationships.

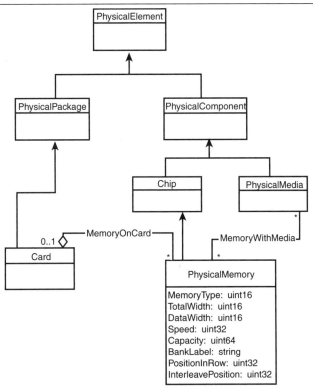

The PhysicalMemory class defines the following attributes:

- FormFactor is overridden in this class in order to conform to the master MIF memory device definition. Again, this type of override does not violate any of our object-oriented design principles, since it is not changing the semantics or the data type of the attribute.

- MemoryType is an enumerated 16-bit unsigned integer that defines the specific type of memory that this object is. This is also a useful attribute to query the repository on. Listing 8.6 defines the current values for this attribute.

Listing 8.6   MOF definition for the MemoryType attribute.

```
[...
Values {"Unknown", "Other", "DRAM", "Synchronous DRAM", "Cache DRAM", "EDO",
        "EDRAM", "VRAM", "SRAM", "RAM", "ROM", "Flash", "EEPROM", "FEPROM",
        "EPROM", "CDRAM", "3DRAM", "SDRAM", "SGRAM"},
MappingStrings {"MIF.DMTF |Memory Device |002.9"} ]
uint16 MemoryType;
```

- TotalWidth is a 16-bit unsigned integer that defines the total width, in bits, of the PhysicalMemory. This includes any check or error correction bits.

- DataWidth is a 16-bit unsigned integer that defines the data width of the PhysicalMemory, in bits.

- Speed is a 32-bit unsigned integer that defines the speed of the PhysicalMemory, in nanoseconds.

- Capacity is a 64-bit unsigned integer that defines the total capacity of this PhysicalMemory, in bytes.

- BankLabel is a string of up to 64 characters that is used to identify a block of memory, commonly called a *bank*.

- PositionInRow is a 32-bit unsigned integer that is used to specify the position of the PhysicalMemory in a *row* of memory, which corresponds to its data width. For example, if it takes two 8-bit memory devices to form a 16-bit row, then a value of 2 means that this PhysicalMemory chip is the second device in the row. Note that the value 0 is an invalid value for this attribute.

- InterleavePosition defines whether this PhysicalMemory objects is interleaved or not. The value of 0 is used to define it as non-interleaved. Otherwise, the value of this attribute corresponds to the position of this object (for example, 5 denotes the fifth position).

The `PhysicalMemory` class defines no methods. However, it participates in two relationships, the `MemoryOnCard` aggregation and the `MemoryWithMedia` association. The former is defined in the next section, and the latter is defined in the section describing `PhysicalMedia`.

The `MemoryOnCard` *Aggregation*

The `MemoryOnCard` aggregation is a subclass of the `PackagedComponent` aggregation. This aggregation is used to define the presence of physical memory on different types of `Cards`. Although the multiplicity of this relationship is the same, the group component is restricted to instances of the class `Card` and the part component is restricted to instances of the class `PhysicalMemory`.

PhysicalMedia

The `PhysicalMedia` class represents any type of documentation or storage medium, such as tapes and CD-ROMs. Figure 8.16 illustrates the `PhysicalMedia` class.

Figure 8.16   Physical Model excerpt: `PhysicalMemory` and its relationships.

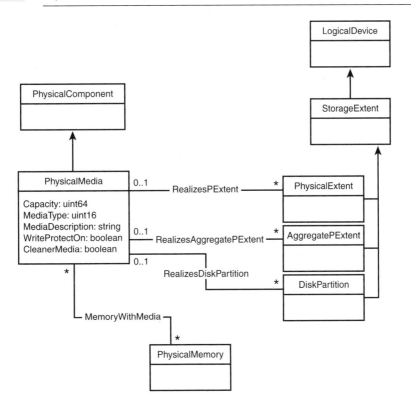

The PhysicalMedia class defines the following attributes:

- Capacity is a 64-bit unsigned integer that defines the size of the Media, in bytes.

- MediaType is an enumerated 16-bit unsigned integer that specifies the type of the PhysicalMedia. This attribute is related to the MediaDescription attribute through the use of the ModelCorrespondence qualifier. The MediaDescription attribute is used to provide more information for the media type defined in this attribute. Listing 8.7 defines the current values for this attribute.

Listing 8.7	MOF definition for the MediaType attribute.

```
[...
Values {"Unknown", "Other", "Tape Cartridge", "QIC Cartridge", "AIT Cartridge",
        "DTF Cartridge", "DAT Cartridge", "8mm Tape Cartridge", "19mm Tape
        Cartridge", "DLT Cartridge", "Half-Inch Magnetic Tape Cartridge",
        "Cartridge Disk", "JAZ Disk", "ZIP Disk", "SyQuest Disk", "Winchester
        Removable Disk", "CD-ROM", "CD-ROM/XA", "CD-I", "CD Recordable", "WORM",
        "Magneto-Optical", "DVD", "DVD+RW", "DVD-RAM", "DVD-ROM",
            "DVD-Video", "Divx", "Floppy/Diskette", "Hard Disk", "Memory Card",
            "Hard Copy"},
ModelCorrespondence {"CIM_PhysicalMedia.MediaDescription"} ]
uint16 MediaType;
```

- MediaDescription is a free-form string that provides additional information describing the type of media that is defined by the MediaType attribute.

- WriteProtectOn is a Boolean attribute that, if TRUE, specifies that this PhysicalMedia object is currently write-protected by some kind of physical mechanism, such as a protect tab on a floppy diskette.

- CleanerMedia is a Boolean attribute that, if TRUE, indicates that this PhysicalMedia object is used for cleaning purposes and not for data storage purposes.

The PhysicalMedia class defines no methods. It participates in four relationships. Three of these, the RealizesPExtent, the RealizesAggregatePExtent, and the RealizesDiskPartition associations, define the specific type of storage characteristics that this PhysicalMedia object has. These will most likely not be used in a DEN application, and so will not be covered here (you are encouraged to examine the Physical MOF for their definitions). The fourth relationship, the MemoryWithMedia association, is described next.

The `MemoryWithMedia` *Association*

The `MemoryWithMedia` association is a subclass of the more general `Dependency` association. It is used to define `PhysicalMemory` objects that are associated with a `PhysicalMedia` object.

The overall multiplicity of this association remains zero-or-more to zero-or-more, but the antecedent and dependent are restricted to instances of the `PhysicalMemory` and `PhysicalMedia` classes, respectively.

Modeling Examples

The following are some modeling examples to help increase your familiarity with the Physical Common Model, and to show its flexibility.

Discovering Physical Properties of a Logical Device

Discovering the physical properties of a logical device (for example, what physical router does this interface belong to?) is done in either a two- or a multi-step process. First, an association between the logical concept and the physical component is traversed. At this point, some of the physical characteristics of the device may be accessible, such as whether it is hot swappable, or who its manufacturer is, or what its serial number is. In general, however, another relationship must be traversed that provides access to the specific type of physical characteristic that you are looking for. For example, the location of a device would be found by traversing the `PhysicalElementLocation` association. The set of connectors on a given `PhysicalPackage`, such as a router, would be found by traversing the `ConnectorOnPackage` aggregation. The specific `Card` that is in a particular `Slot` of a given chassis-based device, such as a router, would be given as follows:

1. Find the router using the `Realizes` association (this yields a `Chassis`, a subclass of `PhysicalElement`).

2. Find the `Slot` by first traversing `PackageInChassis` to get to the containment aspects of a `Chassis`, and then traversing the `PackageInSlot` association (using the `Number` attribute of the `Slot`) to get to the specific `Slot` number.

3. Find the `Card` by traversing the `CardInSlot` association.

Modeling the Physical Characteristics of a Router

This section is an example of the physical model as applied to a Cisco 4700 router. The physical configuration of the Cisco 4700 router is fairly simple as far as network devices go. The 4700 has a chassis with three slots. Interface modules of various sorts can be plugged into the slots. In addition, the chassis itself has two physical connectors: a female DB-25 labeled CONSOLE and a male DB-25 labeled AUX.

In this example, a 4700 with two interface modules is modeled. The first slot has a module with six 10Base-T Ethernet interfaces. The second slot has a module with a single 100Base-TX Fast Ethernet interface. The third slot is empty.

The objects discussed in this example will belong to standard CIM classes; however, it is likely that, in real life, some of the objects would be instances of vendor-specific subclasses. For example, vendor-specific subclasses could be used to model additional attributes and relationships that are application- and/or vendor-specific, and hence not covered by the CIM Physical Common Model. Two likely possibilities are vendor-specific subclasses of the standard CIM Chassis and Card classes.

This example is significant in that standard CIM values can be applied to a commercial product without modification. This illustrates some of the power and flexibility of CIM.

Object Instances

There are five main objects that make up this model:

- Chassis

- Slots contained in a chassis

- CONSOLE and AUX connectors

- 10Base-T module

- 100Base-T module

The Chassis

The outer enclosure of the router is physically represented as an instance of the Chassis class. Values of interesting attributes of this class are:

- ServicePhilosophy: [2, 6] (Service From Back, Sliding Trays). Note that the ServicePhilosophy attribute is an array. Hence, as many values as are applicable for a specific object instance can be applied. In this case, there are two such values.

- NumberOfPowerCords: 1

- ChassisTypes: [23] (Rack Mount Chassis)

The Slots

As mentioned earlier, the router has three slots. These are represented by instances of the class Slot. The Number attribute of each of the three slots are 1, 2, and 3, respectively. Note that it is important to represent the empty Slot. This is because you may need to refer to this Slot in the future (for example, to answer a query asking if there are any available Slots that new networking Cards could potentially be installed into).

The CONSOLE and AUX Connectors

The CONSOLE and AUX connectors are represented by instances of the class PhysicalConnector. The value of the ConnectorType attribute for the CONSOLE object is [25, 23, 3] (RS-232, DB-25, Female). Remember that the ConnectorType attribute is an array; hence, it contains as many values as are needed to describe the type of connector that this instance is. The value of the OtherIdentifyingInfo attribute of the CONSOLE object is "CONSOLE". The value of the ConnectorType attribute for the AUX object is [25, 23, 2] (RS-232, DB-25, Male), and the value of the OtherIdentifyingInfo attribute is "AUX".

10Base-T Module

The 10Base-T module is an instance of the class Card. The six 10Base-T connectors are instances of the class PhysicalConnector. Their ConnectorType attribute values are each [35, 3] (RJ-45, Female).

Single 100Base-T Module

The 100Base-TX module is also an instance of the class Card. While the module only implements one 100Base-TX interface, the module actually has two connectors: an RJ-45 and a proprietary Media Independent Interface (MII). (Presumably, only one of the connectors can be in use at a time.) The ConnectorType attributes of these two connectors are [35, 3] (RJ-45, Female) and [1, 3] (Other, Female), respectively.

Association Instances

This section details the important associations that are present in this model.

Association Between Chassis and Slot

The association between the Chassis and a Slot is of type ConnectorOnPackage. There is one instance of this association for each slot. The GroupComponent attribute refers to the Chassis, while the PartComponent attribute refers to the Slot. ConnectorOnPackage is an aggregation of PhysicalConnector into PhysicalPackage; its use here is appropriate because Slot is a subclass of PhysicalConnector and Chassis is an indirect subclass of PhysicalPackage.

Association Between Chassis *and* Connector

The AUX and CONSOLE connectors are also associated with the Chassis through instances of the ConnectorOnPackage association class. Again, GroupComponent refers to the Chassis of the 4700 router, while PartComponent refers to the connector.

Association Between Slot *and* Card

There is one instance of the PackageInSlot association for each slot/card pair. The Antecedent attribute refers to the Slot, while the Dependent attribute refers to the Card. Thus, there are two instances of this association. There is no instance of this association connected to the empty slot.

Association Between Card *and* Connector

There is one instance of the ConnectorOnPackage association for each physical connector (RJ-45 or MII) attached to an (10Base-T or 100Base-TX) interface module. This is the same association that links the CONSOLE and AUX connectors to the chassis.

Modeling Physical Topology

As an example of how to model a physical connection between two devices, imagine two Cisco 4700 routers configured as described earlier. Imagine further that a patch cable connects the two RJ-45 connectors of the 100Base-TX modules. In order to model this connection, another class and two more associations will be introduced.

The wire is represented by an instance of the PhysicalLink class. The connectors on each end of the wire are represented by instances of the PhysicalConnector class. For the connectors terminating the wire, though, the values of the ConnectorType attribute are [35, 2] (RJ-45, Male), since these are male connector and not female connectors like those on the router modules. The connection between the wire and one of the terminating connectors is an instance of the class LinkHasConnector. Of course, there are two instances of this association, one for each end of the wire.

The connection between a connector terminating the wire and a connector attached to the 100Base-TX ethernet module is an instance of the class ConnectedTo. Again, there are two instances of this association. One connects one end of the wire to the first router, and the other connects the other end of the wire to the second router.

The Future of the Physical Common Model

The Physical Common Model is a very mature model. It is very stable and will not be redesigned or drastically changed. However, it is expected that it will be enhanced to cover the physical characteristics of more devices.

Some work likely to take place during the end of the CIM 2.2 session and during CIM 2.3 is support for intelligent I/O and storage area networks. In addition, printing, sensors, tape libraries, and fibre-channel devices will be modeled in CIM 2.2. All these will require additional support in the Physical Common Model.

Summary

This chapter has explained in detail the differences between the DEN and CIM physical models. The CIM Physical Common Model grew out of the DEN Physical Model. The difference between these models is that the DEN Physical Model was focused solely on the physical characteristics of network elements, whereas the CIM Physical Common Model strives to represent the physical characteristics of any managed system element.

It is important to remember that DEN is oriented towards modeling network elements and services. Therefore, DEN does not require all of the rich constructs that are available in the CIM Physical Common Model. However, DEN does not prohibit these constructs, and items such as modeling temperature sensors could certainly be included in a DEN-compliant model.

DEN specifies some additional informational elements that are not included in the CIM Physical Common Model. This is because DEN is an extension model of CIM. The information included in the DEN specification that is not included in the CIM Physical Common Model is either too specific to networking, or represent optimizations that are needed for a repository that uses LDAP as its access protocol. The former are not included in the CIM Physical Common Model because they represent physical information that does not generalize to other types of devices. The latter are not included in the CIM Common Model because CIM is independent of the specific technology used to build a repository.

Recommended Further Study and References

The DEN Specification, version 4, will be published in the second quarter of 1999. Please check the DMTF following home page for updated links to this specification:

```
http://www.dmtf.org/spec/denh.html
```

The CIM Physical Model is at

```
http://www.dmtf.org/spec/cims.html
```

CHAPTER 9

The CIM/DEN Logical (Network) Model

The purpose of this chapter is threefold. First, to explain how the logical model of network elements that was published in DEN was transformed into the CIM Network Common Model. Second, to consider the changes that took place in that transformation. Finally, to discuss the future of the Network Common Model and its role in the DEN specification.

Purpose of the DEN Logical Model

The purpose of the DEN Logical Model, as it was originally designed, was to provide a framework to store and retrieve information describing the logical characteristics of network elements and services. This built upon CIM's notion of separating the physical and logical aspects of managed objects. The DEN Logical Information Model describes both the containment and the connectivity characteristics of network elements and services, as well as the relationships between the objects representing network elements and services. The DEN Logical Model is aimed primarily at supporting the configuration of network devices, the management of services that these network devices supply, and modeling the logical topology (for example, connectivity map with respect to different protocols) of the network. It is important to note that the DEN Logical Model can use different data sources, such as SNMP data, and integrate them using its underlying information model. In fact, as we examine the DEN Logical Model, we will see a direct mapping of attributes in various classes of the logical model to external data, such as that provided by SNMP MIBs and the IEEE 802.1Q specification.

> **Note**
>
> Containment is fundamentally a *hierarchical* relationship. That is, the information is based around parent-child relationships.
>
> In DEN, containment is important to express physical and logical relationships (for example, a card is contained in a chassis, or this administrator can log into this device, but another administrator cannot). Containment can also be used to imply scoping in (for example) a directory implementation, to limit (and/or define) what operations are relevant to what objects.
>
> This structured way of representing information is particularly applicable to representing the physical and logical structural aspects of network elements and services. This is one of the major reasons why DEN was conceived as an extension of CIM, and why mapping DEN to an implementation based on using the directory is so attractive.

The DEN Logical Model

This section provides a brief overview of the DEN Logical Model. Its purpose is to enable you to track the changes in this model from its initial draft release (DEN Specification version v3.0c5) to its current form. This form includes the Network Model of CIM 2.2, plus some additional changes that are pending the official release of CIM 2.2. Note that many of the changes to the other CIM Common Models in the CIM 2.2 release are not covered, due to their volume and approval being so close to the publication of this book.

The DEN Logical Model expands the hierarchy under LogicalElement by focusing on three important areas:

- Logical aspects of network elements

- Protocols

- Network services

Logical aspects of network elements centered around a new subclass of UnitaryComputerSystem, called NetworkElement, that could serve as the base class for modeling switches, routers, access servers, and other types of networking devices. Other classes in the CIM 2.0 logical hierarchy, such as LogicalDevice, were also modified. The Protocol class was defined as a new subclass of LogicalElement, and serves as the base class for defining routed (for example, protocols such as IP that forward information) and routing (for example, protocols such as BGP that decide where to route information based on a particular routing algorithm) protocols. Finally, the Service class was subclassed to model three new types of services: "informational" services such as HTTP, "relay" services such as the forwarding of information by a router, and "network" services such as QoS, security, and other related services. ServiceAccessPoint was also subclassed to model accessing protocol information.

The Transformation into the CIM Network Common Model

The DEN Logical Model was transformed into the CIM Network Common Model by much the same process as the DEN Physical Model was transformed into the CIM Physical Common Model. The differences were due to the wider scope that the DEN Logical Model had. The DEN Physical Model focused completely on the physical aspects of network elements. However, the DEN Logical Model covered not just the logical aspects of network elements themselves (for example, a port) but also how other entities in the managed environment used those aspects. For example, DEN touched on the difference between users and administrators, as well as how users and administrators use services controlled by network elements. Users, profiles, and policies are part of the DEN Policy Model, and will be covered in the next chapter. It should be noted that these concepts were completely new to CIM, and gave rise to the formation of two new Common Models, the Policy and the User Common Models. Two new working groups, the SLA Working Group and the User Working Group, were formed to further develop these models.

The DEN Logical Model is illustrated in Figure 9.1.

As you can see, the DEN Logical Model touches four main points in the CIM Network Common Model. These are

- UnitaryComputerSystem

- ServiceAccessPoint

- Service

- A new subclass of LogicalElement

Figure 9.1   Mapping the DEN Logical Model into CIM.

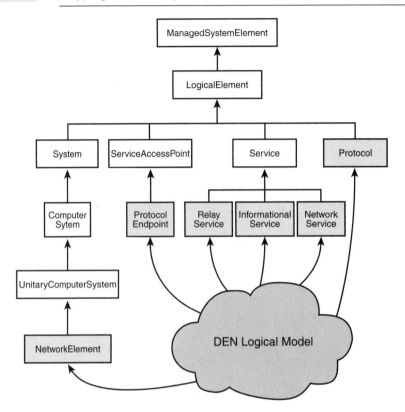

The integration of the DEN Logical Model into the CIM Network Common Model was more complex, which is why it did not show up until the 2.2 release of CIM. However, the benefits of this integration are even more pronounced than the benefits of integrating the DEN Physical Model with the CIM Physical Common Model. This is because the DEN Logical Model contains, and has the potential to affect, more objects and system functionality than the DEN Physical Model could. The Networks working group was able to enhance the DEN Logical Model into a more general model that could benefit many applications besides networking applications. The DEN Logical Model did not lose any of its capability to model network elements and services in this transformation; rather, it was enhanced so that it could model many general entities in addition to network elements. For example, a BGP (Border Gateway Protocol) model can describe the routers that are running BGP as well as the Autonomous System that the routers reside in, the routing policies that are used in that Autonomous System, and the network administrators that manage those routing policies.

The following sections provide more detail regarding the theoretical motivation for incorporating the DEN Logical Model into CIM, the principal classes present in the original DEN Logical Model, and the changes that were made to that model to generalize it into the CIM Network Common Model.

Main Classes of the Original DEN Logical Model

As mentioned previously, the original DEN Logical Model concentrated on three main areas. The first two centered around the modeling the logical aspects of network elements and services. The third modeled routed and routing protocols.

The following subsections will describe the original DEN model briefly so that you can better understand the changes that were made to it as it became the CIM Network Common Model. Specific attention is given to correlating the changes between the original DEN specification and the current version of the CIM Network Common Model.

NetworkElement

NetworkElement was intended to be a new base class for all networking devices. It is subclassed from an existing CIM class, UnitaryComputerSystem. This class was chosen because, in general, networking devices (for example, routers and switches) have many of the notions of a computer system as described by CIM. These notions include the ability to compute (for example, make routing decisions), the use of an operating system (for example, some networking cards contain their own operating system that is customized to make routing and forwarding decisions), and other distinguishing characteristics. For example, in CIM, services are hosted on systems. DEN uses this concept and applies it to routers. DEN models services like security, QoS, BGP routing decisions, and other functions of a network device as services that are hosted on a ComputerSystem (for example, a router). Note that, for simplicity, this version of the DEN specification only defined a network device that has a single computer (hence the choice of UnitaryComputerSystem). A similar network class could be derived from Cluster.

NetworkElement adds network-specific functionality to the basic concept of a UnitaryComputerSystem. This includes

- The ability to have special configuration files that control the functionality of the device, and enable administrators to modify the configuration (for example, as a function of observed traffic congestion)

- The ability to describe additional networking semantics (for example, there is a significant difference in the types of QoS mechanisms that are used in a border router and a router in the backbone of the network)

- The modeling of special interface requirements (for example, static routes and loopback interfaces)

- The concept of special networking software (for example, the association between features hosted on a networking card and the (network) operating system that provides those features)

NetworkElements interact with other entities in the managed environment in many ways. In CIM, these interactions are modeled using associations and aggregations. The NetworkElement class serves as an anchor point for these relationships.

The NetworkElement class, being a subclass of UnitaryComputerSystem, inherits the composite key of the System class. This composite key consists of two attributes, Name and CreationClassName.

The NetworkElement class was not incorporated into the CIM Network Common Model. This was because it was predicated on the idea that networking was done by dedicated devices that were somehow different than general-purpose computing devices. While that is true to some extent, it doesn't necessarily justify creating a new class from a modeling point of view. Instead, as will be seen, the CIM Network Common Model enhances the ComputerSystem class to incorporate many of the features of the NetworkElement class. This has the added advantage of being able to model computer systems that incorporate networking functionality, such as computers running the upcoming Windows 2000 operating system from Microsoft.

The remainder of this section will describe the attributes, methods, and relationships defined in the DEN NetworkElement class. Figure 9.2 illustrates this class.

The following attributes were defined by DEN for this class:

- Configuration is an OctetString attribute that is used to hold the current configuration of the device. This attribute is not currently included in the current CIM Network Common Model because it is too device-specific. Modeling the management of device configurations and states will be done in the CIM 2.3 timeframe, which is currently targeted for Q4 of 1999.

- ConnectionRequirementList is an array of DirectoryString attributes that represent a list of connections that this NetworkElement must have and maintain. This is an LDAP attribute, and represents a set of associations between the NetworkElement and the ProtocolEndpoints that represent the destinations that this network device is communicating with. This attribute is replaced with a set of associations if the target repository is not a directory that uses LDAP as its access protocol.

- `DeviceErrorCode` is an integer that contains a generalized error code that indicates the last type of error that this device had. This attribute is not currently modeled in the CIM Network Common Model because error handling needs a broader framework. This feature is slated for introduction in the CIM 2.3 timeframe.

- `DeviceErrorDescription` is a free-form string that contains a detailed description for the error identified in the `DeviceErrorCode` attribute. This attribute is also not currently modeled in the CIM Network Common Model, but its functionality will be included in the 2.3 version of the CIM Network Common Model.

- `DeviceType` is an enumerated 16-bit unsigned integer that defines the type of networking device this object is. Values include 1 (`physical (repeater, etc)`), 2 (`bridge`), 3 (`L2 switch`), 4 (`L3 switch`), and 5 (`router`). This attribute is moved into the `ComputerSystem` class, to enable applications to distinguish between dedicated devices like routers and computers that have routing capabilities.

- `DeviceUnavailable` is a Boolean attribute that, if `TRUE`, indicates that this device is currently unavailable. This attribute should be added to the CIM 2.3 release of the CIM Network Common Model.

- `InterfaceList` is an array of strings of up to 32 characters each that defines a list of interfaces supported by this device. Values include ATM, Ethernet, Fast Ethernet, channelized T1/T3, multi-channel (multi-protocol routing of multiple channels on 1 port) E1/T1, E3/T3, Token Ring, Fiber Distributed Data Interface (FDDI), Packet OC-3, ISDN, serial, and High-Speed Serial Interface (HSSI) interfaces. This attribute should be added to the CIM 2.3 release of the CIM Network Common Model.

- `MACAddressList` is an array of strings that contain the MAC addresses for this device. This attribute should be added to the CIM 2.3 release of the CIM Network Common Model.

- `NetworkAddressList` is an array of strings that represent the network addresses for this device. The format of the network address is defined by the value of the `NetworkAddressListType` attribute. This is currently implemented using associations in the current CIM Network Common Model. LDAP implementations may want to use a dedicated attribute, such as this, for query efficiency reasons.

- `NetworkAddressListType` defines the type of address used in the `NetworkAddressList` attribute. Values include 0 (`IPv4 address using CIDR format`), 1 (`IPv4 address using address-mask format"`), 2 (`IPX Address`), and 3 (`IPv6 address`). This attribute is enhanced and represented in separate areas in the CIM Network Common Model. For example, in the `IPProtocolEndpoint` class, the `AddressType` attribute serves a similar function.

- NetworkingSoftwareVersion defines the minimum version of the OperatingSystem that the NetworkElement uses that must be run in order for the network to function as desired. The version of the OperatingSystem that the NetworkElement is currently running (as defined by the RunningNetworkElementOS association) must be equal to or greater than this version. In the 2.2 version of the CIM Network Common Model, the RunningOS association is used to define the current operating system that is being run in the computer system. However, this association does not have the version information identified in this attribute. This information will probably be added in the 2.3 release of the CIM Network Common Model.

Figure 9.2 The DEN NetworkElement class.

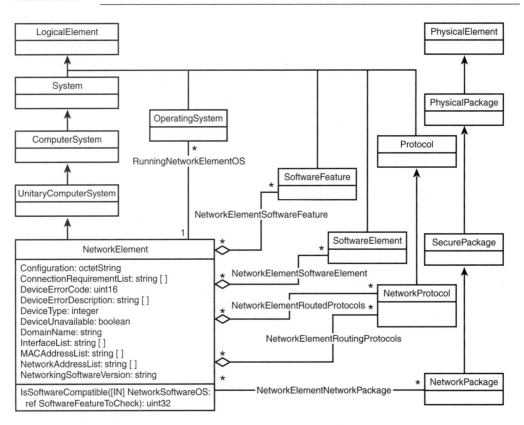

The NetworkElement class defines one method, IsSoftwareCompatible. The purpose of this method is to ensure that the software running on a component of the network (for example, a networking card) is compatible with the rest of the software running in the network element. Its signature is:

```
IsSoftwareCompatible:  ([IN] NetworkSoftwareOS ref SoftwareFeatureToCheck): uint 32
```

The NetworkElement class participates in nine associations. These are detailed in the following sections.

The AdministeredBy Aggregation

This aggregation associates people that have administration capabilities with a specific NetworkElement. The problem is that there is no standard user schema that every directory uses to represent users, groups of users, and organizations. Therefore, DEN defined a new class, SupportContact, as a class that can reference different types of users (for example, Person, OrganizationalPerson, Organization, OU, or OrganizationalRole) in an independent manner.

The aggregate is defined to be instances of the class NetworkElement, and the component is defined to be instances of the class SupportContact. The cardinality on the NetworkElement side is zero-or-one. The "zero" is required because, for inventory purposes, a NetworkElement may simply be stored and not actively administered at all. However, if a NetworkElement is administered, then this relationship defines, for this single device, the set of people that can administer it. Note that an administrator may not have been assigned to this NetworkElement, which means that this must also be an optional relationship. Therefore, the cardinality on the SupportContact side is zero-or-more.

This relationship is currently not in the 2.2 version of the CIM Network Common Model, because a user model has not yet been defined. When this is complete (scheduled for the 2.3 timeframe), then this relationship (or one similar) will be defined in both the CIM Network Common Model as well as in DEN.

The BackupAdministrators Aggregation

This relationship is identical to the AdministratedBy aggregation described earlier, except its purpose is to identify people who have a backup administration responsibility.

The NetworkElementNetworkPackage Association

The NetworkElementNetworkPackage association defines the set of NetworkPackages that together constitute this NetworkElement.

This association is not part of the CIM Network Common Model, since both the NetworkElement and the NetworkPackage classes are themselves deleted.

The NetworkElementSoftwareElements *Association*

The NetworkElementSoftwareElements association defines the set of SoftwareElements that this NetworkElement requires. This enables the individual files that provide the functionality of the network device to be individually managed. For example, if the operating system changes, one or more new files may be required to update the SoftwareFeature(s) that use those SoftwareElements.

This is a zero-or-more to zero-or-more aggregation, with the aggregate limited to instances of the NetworkElement class and the component limited to instances of the SoftwareElement class. Note that specific SoftwareElements associated with specific components of a NetworkElement using the DeviceSoftware association.

This relationship is not part of the CIM Network Common Model because the NetworkElement class was deleted. Furthermore, it is likely that such a relationship will be delegated to an extension model, as opposed to the Network Common Model, because it is becoming increasingly difficult to cleanly separate "networking" functions from other functions, as well as separate computers with routing functionality from dedicated routers.

The NetworkElementSoftwareFeatures *Association*

The NetworkElementsSoftwareFeatures association defines the set of SoftwareFeatures that this NetworkElement provides. In this case, a SoftwareFeature is not necessarily intended directly for the end-user. Rather, it represents a service, such as the ability to control congestion, offered by the device. Thus, the SoftwareFeatures of network devices are usually aimed at the administrators that configure the network devices.

This is a zero-or-more to zero-or-more aggregation, with the aggregate limited to instances of the NetworkElement class and the component limited to instances of the SoftwareFeature class. The 2.2 release of the CIM Network Common Model does not include this aggregation, since the NetworkElement class was deleted. Furthermore, it is likely that such a relationship will be delegated to an extension model, as opposed to the Network Common Model, because it is becoming increasingly difficult to cleanly separate "networking" functions from other functions, as well as separate computers with routing functionality from dedicated routers.

The Owner *Aggregation*

The Owner aggregation defines the set of people that own this NetworkElement. People are defined by the SupportContact class, as previously mentioned.

The 2.2 release of the CIM Network Common Model does not include this aggregation, since the NetworkElement class was deleted. However, it is likely that once the User Common Model is finalized in the 2.3 timeframe, this relationship (or a similar one) will become a part of the CIM Network Common Model. DEN will also be updated.

The NetworkElementRoutedProtocols *Aggregation*

The NetworkElementRoutedProtocols aggregation defines the particular routed protocols (for example, IP) that can be run by this NetworkElement. Note that this relationship does *not* define the specific routed protocols that are being run at a given time—this could be done, however, by enumerating the ProtocolEndpoints that each interface of the NetworkElement has.

This is a zero-or-more to zero-or-more aggregation, with the aggregate being restricted to instances of the NetworkElement class and the component being restricted to instances of the NetworkProtocol class. This aggregation represents all of the different routed protocols that are supported by a given NetworkElement.

The 2.2 release of the CIM Network Common Model does not include this aggregation, since the NetworkElement class was deleted. Furthermore, it is unclear that the protocol hierarchy developed in DEN will be incorporated into the CIM Network Common Model. This is because the DEN protocol hierarchy was oriented towards the OSI model, and many DMTF members have objected to that. However, most members did like the classification of protocols into routed and routing protocols. Work on resolving this is slated to being as soon as the 2.2 version of the CIM specification is completed.

The NetworkElementRoutingProtocols *Aggregation*

This aggregation is identical to theNetworkElementRoutedProtocols aggregation, with the exception being that it describes a different type of component (routing, versus routed, protocols) that are being aggregated by the NetworkElement.

The 2.2 release of the CIM Network Common Model does not include this aggregation, since the NetworkElement class was deleted. However, equivalent functionality is provided through the HostedRoutingServices and HostedForwardingServices associations. It is unclear that DEN's protocol hierarchy will be incorporated as is into the CIM Network Common Model; this will be resolved in the 2.3 timeframe.

The `RunningNetworkElementOS` *Association*

The `RunningNetworkElementOS` association indicates the currently executing `OperatingSystem` on this `NetworkElement`. This is a refinement of the `RunningOS` association—the change is in the restriction of the antecedent from a `ComputerSystem` to a `NetworkElement`. The multiplicity of the relationship remains the same.

Other Affected CIM 2.0 Logical Entities

There are several other CIM 2.0 classes in the logical hierarchy that DEN enhanced. This section describes their recommended enhancements and current disposition.

LogicalDevice

The following attributes were recommended to be added to the 2.0 version of the `LogicalDevice` class by DEN:

- `ContactDN` is a set of object references to people that can be contacted about this `LogicalDevice`. This may point to an individual Person as well as a `Group` (of people), an `Organization`, or an `OrganizationalUnit`. This attribute is intended for LDAP implementations, and would be replaced by an association between the `LogicalDevice` class and either a set of classes that defined people, or a single class (for example, `SupportContact` or its equivalent) that would in turn reference those classes.

  The 2.2 release of the CIM Network Common Model does not include this attribute, since it is specifically designed for LDAP implementations. Once the User Common Model is finished, the functionality called out by this attribute will be added to the model.

- `ErrorCode` is a 16-bit unsigned integer that contains a generalized error code that indicates the last type of error that this `LogicalDevice` had. This attribute was added to the 2.1 release of the CIM Core Model. It was called `LastErrorCode`, and changed to a 32-bit unsigned integer.

- `ErrorDescription` is a free-form string that contains a detailed description for the error identified in the `ErrorCode` attribute. This attribute was also added to the 2.1 version of the CIM Core Model.

DEN did not specify any additional methods or relationships to be added to the `LogicalDevice` class.

System

DEN recommended that two additional attributes be added to the definition of the System class. These were:

- PowerManagementCapabilities is an array of 16-bit unsigned integers that define the specific power-related capabilities provided by this LogicalDevice. It is an array so that multiple separate power management functions can be assigned to a single LogicalDevice.

  This attribute was not added to the CIM Core Model for systems. This is because a System is a very generic concept in CIM—it could be an autonomous system, a computer, or many other types of entities that may or may not have the concept of power management. Furthermore, power management must be differentiated in a more granular fashion when applied to Systems. For example, is the *entire* system controlled by the power management, or is just a part of it?

- PowerManagementSupported is a Boolean attribute that, if TRUE, indicates that the power of this LogicalDevice can be managed. This usually means that it can be put into a power save state. The specific power management features are defined in the PowerManagementCapabilities attribute.

  This attribute was not added to the CIM Core Model for the same reasons as the PowerManagementCapabilities attribute was not added to the CIM Core Model.

DEN did not recommend any new methods or relationships to be added to the System class.

UnitaryComputerSystem

The DEN specification recommended that a single attribute, SoftwareResetCapability, be added to the CIM UnitaryComputerSystem class. The purpose of this was to complement the existing ResetCapability attribute, which defined a "hard" reset of the UnitaryComputerSystem using either a power or a reset button. The SoftwareResetCapability attribute was intended to represent the capability to perform a "soft" reset of the UnitaryComputerSystem via software.

This attribute was not added to the CIM System Common Model, though it will be considered for the 2.3 CIM release.

Additions to the Service *Class Hierarchy*

The basic DEN service class hierarchy is illustrated in Figure 9.3. It expands the CIM Service class hierarchy by characterizing service objects that enable application developers to represent specific services that are available on the network.

Figure 9.3   The DEN Service class hierarchy.

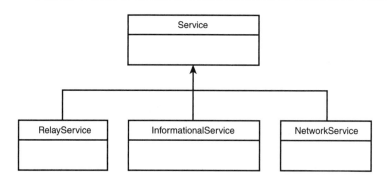

The next section describes some additions that DEN recommends to the CIM Service class. The following three sections discuss the new DEN subclasses of the CIM Service class.

Additions to the Service Class

The DEN specification recommended the following attribute be added to the CIM Service class:

- ServiceURL is a string of syntax LabeledURI. It is a URL that provides the protocol, network location, and other service-specific information required in order to access the service. This attribute was not added to the Service class because it is not appropriate for all services. Likewise, it was removed from the DEN specification. The ServiceURL attribute was added to the NetworkService class, described in the next section.

> **Note**
>
> This last example is an illustration of the dual nature of the DEN specification. DEN is both an *extension* of CIM and a *mapping* of data in CIM to a form suitable for storage and retrieval in a directory that uses LDAP as its access protocol.

The DEN specification defined no additional methods or relationships to be added to the CIM Service class.

RelayService

The RelayService class is an abstract class that represents any type of service that relays data between two or more points in a network. The relaying represents the receiving of data from one or more ProtocolEndpoints and sending that data via other Protocol Endpoints. Examples of this kind of service include routing, bridging, and repeating services. The RelayService class defines no methods, but it does define a single relationship, RelaysAmong. This is an abstract association, descended from ServiceSAPDependency, that relates a RelayService to the ProtocolEndpoints that are relaying the data. This class was not added to the CIM Network Common Model.

InformationalService

The InformationalService is a base class for representing generalized services, such as HTTP and SNMP, that are not instances of the RelayService or NetworkService (NetworkServices are defined in the next section) classes. It defines the following attributes:

- InfoServicePortRange is an array of free-form strings that defines the port or ports that this InformationalService will use.

- InfoServiceType is a free-form string that is used to categorize the different types of InformationalServices that exist in the system. This attribute is specifically targeted at simplifying the querying of a repository that uses LDAP as its access protocol.

- InfoServiceVersion is a free-form string that defines the specific version of the InformationalService.

The InformationalService did not define any methods. It did define four relationships, but these were subsequently removed.

The 2.2 release of the CIM Network Common Model does not include the InformationalService class or its subclasses. This work is targeted for the 2.3 release of this model. These classes remain part of the DEN specification.

NetworkService

The NetworkService class is an abstract base class for describing services that reside on the network. This enables application developers to match services to users, groups, and other objects. This is fundamentally different from the InformationalService class, which provides information as a requested service. Put another way, instances of the InformationalService class do not alter the data, they just supply it to a requester.

However, instances of the NetworkService class may add, delete, or otherwise modify the data that is being forwarded to the destination. They may also be used for configuring devices.

The 2.2 release of the CIM Network Common Model integrates the concept of a NetworkService class, though not all of its attributes.

The NetworkService class defines the following eight attributes:

- ServiceErrorCode is a 16-bit unsigned integer that contains a generalized error code indicating the last service failure experienced by this NetworkService object. This attribute is not integrated into the 2.2 release of the CIM Network Common Model because a more robust and extensible error handling mechanism is currently being worked on.

- ServiceErrorDescription is a free-form string that contains detailed information for the error code found in the ServiceErrorCode attribute. This attribute is not integrated into the 2.2 release of the CIM Network Common Model because the ServiceErrorCode attribute is not integrated into the model.

- ServiceKeywords is an array of strings, each up to 64 characters, that provide customized words to search for different types of services. This attribute is integrated into the 2.2 release of the CIM Network Common Model.

- ServiceName is a free-form string that provides a name for this NetworkService. This attribute is not integrated into the 2.2 release of the CIM Network Common Model, because the name attribute is already inherited from the Service class.

- ServicesContained is an array of object references (DN pointers for an LDAP repository) that identify a set of Service objects. This is an LDAP-specific attribute; the CIM equivalent is an aggregation. This attribute is not directly integrated into the 2.2 release of the CIM Network Common Model; rather, its semantics are implemented using a set of different relationships (for example, the NetworkServicesInAdminDomain aggregation). This attribute will remain part of the DEN specification.

- ServiceStartupConditions is an array of unsigned 8-bit integers that is used to specify any specific pre-conditions that must be met for this service to start correctly. This attribute is integrated into the 2.2 release of the CIM Network Common Model, but its name was changed to StartupConditions and its data type changed to an array of free-form strings.

- ServiceStartupParameters is an OctetString that specifies any startup parameters that must be entered for this service to start correctly. This attribute is integrated into the 2.2 release of the CIM Network Common Model, but its name was changed to StartupParameters and its data type changed to an array of free-form strings.

- ServiceType is a free-form string that specifies the type of NetworkService that this object represents. This attribute is intended primarily to aid directory searches (for example, it provides another differentiating attribute to categorize and search on). This attribute is not integrated into the 2.2 release of the CIM Network Common Model because it is for query optimization and not general purpose in nature. However, it will remain part of the DEN specification.

- ServiceURL is a string of syntax labeled URI that provides the protocol, network location, and other service-specific information required in order to access the service. This attribute is integrated into the 2.2 release of the CIM Network Common Model.

- ServiceUsage is a free-form string that specifies the guidelines for using this NetworkService. This attribute is not integrated into the 2.2 release of the CIM Network Common Model, as it is for query optimization tool. However, it will remain part of the DEN specification.

- ServicesContained is a set of object references (DN pointers for a directory) to a set of NetworkService objects. This attribute is an LDAP-specific attribute, and would be implemented as an aggregation in CIM. Therefore, it is not integrated into the 2.2 release of the CIM Network Common Model. It remains a part of the DEN specification.

The NetworkService class did not define any attributes or methods. It did define four subclasses to serve as the base class for defining different types of service objects. These four subclasses were for multimedia, AAAA (authentication, authorization, accounting, and auditing), security (for example, IPSec), and QoS. The QoSService class is being actively analyzed and refined, as described later. Work on the other classes will be postponed pending the outcome of refining the QoSService class, so that they may benefit from the experience gained in implementing the QoS hierarchy and emulate its structure.

QoSService is a base class for defining service objects that can be used to build quality of service guarantees. It is expected that each quality of service object will in general be composed of a set of service objects that each control one or more aspects of the overall service guarantee as described by the parent object.

The DMTF Networks and SLA working groups are working closely with the IETF Policy Framework working group to define a robust quality of service model that integrates the modeling and management of low-level device mechanisms with high-level policy control of those mechanisms. It is not enough to set parameters to control how weighted fair queuing works for a given traffic stream—such decisions must be made in light of other traffic that can flow through the interface, and must be made in a consistent manner throughout the enterprise.

DEN served to help bring greater awareness to this need. Once the work between the DMTF and IETF working groups is completed, the DEN specification will be revised to incorporate that work. This is likely to take several iterations, with the first iteration anticipated in 1999.

The DEN `Protocol` *Class Hierarchy*

The DEN specification stated that

> The protocol class hierarchy is subject to change as the DMTF Network working group refines the CIM Network schema. This specification proposes the following class hierarchy...

The CIM Network working group is studying how to model different types of protocols in a way that will satisfy the diverse users of CIM.

The DEN approach was to base the model on the OSI layers. This is illustrated in Figure 9.4.

`Protocol`

`Protocol` is a new subclass whose purpose is to separate networking protocols from other, more general, types of protocols. In this version of the DEN specification, it has three subclasses, one each for the first, second, and third layers of the OSI reference model (note that the `NetworkProtocol` class defines the notion of a protocol reference model, so other types of protocols besides the OSI model could be added in the future).

The `Protocol` class has not been implemented in the 2.2 release of the CIM Network Common Model. This is because there is still disagreement over how to devise a classification strategy that will be generic enough to cover all protocols in all reference models. As will be seen later in this chapter, some of these ideas are captured in the CIM Network Common Model through modeling the route calculation function of routing protocols. Additional work will be done in this area for the next (2.3) release of the CIM Network Common Model.

Figure 9.4   The DEN `Protocol` class hierarchy.

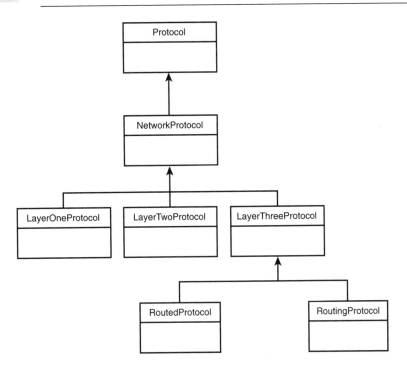

However, it is still important to understand the DEN approach to this classification. The following seven attributes were defined by DEN for this class:

- `HasProtocolStandardOptions` is a Boolean attribute that, if `TRUE`, indicates that this protocol instance implements all standard options of this protocol.

- `HasProtocolVendorID` is a Boolean attribute that, if `TRUE`, indicates that this protocol instance implements vendor-specific options of the protocol.

- `ProtocolName` is a free-form string that can be used to identify the name of the protocol.

- `ProtocolNumber` is a 32-bit unsigned integer that contains the assigned number of the protocol. This provides an alternate way to identify traffic from a protocol.

- `ProtocolStandardOptions` is an array of free-form strings that lists the standard protocol options implemented by this instance of the class.

- `ProtocolVendorID` is a free-form string that identifies the vendor that is implementing extensions to this instance of the protocol class.

- `ProtocolVendorOptions` is an array of free-form strings that lists the vendor protocol options implemented by this instance of the class. It is an array so that each option that is implemented may be identified.

The `Protocol` class defined no methods, but it did define one relationship, `ProvidesEndpoint`. This is a subclass of the `ServiceAccessBySAP` association, and is a one-or-more (on the `Protocol` side) to zero-or-more association between instances of a `Protocol` class and instances of a `ProtocolEndpoint` class. It was used to identify the protocol that was being carried over this connection. This was added to the CIM Network Common Model, except that the `Protocol` class was replaced with the `Network Server` class.

NetworkProtocol

The `NetworkProtocol` class is a subclass of the `Protocol` class. It is an abstract class, whose purpose is to represent the operational protocols that are run in the network. It contains three main subclasses (`LayerOneProtocol`, `LayerTwoProtocol`, and `LayerThreeProtocol`) that represent the operative layer of each protocol group.

The following two attributes were defined for the `NetworkProtocol` class:

- `LayeringReferenceModel` is an enumerated 16-bit unsigned integer that defines the particular organization that is used for representing the layering of different protocols. *Layering* means which protocol can use which other protocol of a protocol suite. For example, BGP is layered upon TCP. Its values currently include OSI, Internet, and B-ISDN.

- `OperativeLayer` is an enumerated array of 16-bit unsigned integers that defines the layer of the reference model in which this class is operating. The values of each array are specific to each `LayeringReferenceModel` attribute value. For example, for OSI, it includes the seven classic layers (Physical, Data Link, and so on) of the OSI protocol stack. There is a `ModelCorrespondence` between the `OperativeLayer` and the `LayeringReferenceModel` attributes, with one array in the former defined for each unique value in the latter.

This class defined no methods, but it did define two relationships, `NetworkElement RoutedProtocols` and `NetworkElementRoutingProtocols`.

The NetworkElementRoutedProtocols *Aggregation*

This aggregation defines the various routed protocols that this NetworkElement supports. This aggregation is not currently part of the 2.2 release of the CIM Network Common Model, but its functionality is being evaluated for possible incorporation into the 2.3 release of the CIM Network Common Model.

The NetworkElementRoutingProtocols *Aggregation*

This aggregation defines the various routing protocols that this NetworkElement supports. This aggregation is not currently part of the 2.2 release of the CIM Network Common Model, but its functionality is being evaluated for possible incorporation into the 2.3 release of the CIM Network Common Model.

The Subclasses of NetworkProtocol

The NetworkProtocol class defined three subclasses: Layer1Protocol, Layer2Protocol, and Layer3Protocol. These were the base classes for all protocols operating at Layer 1, 2, and 3, respectively, of the OSI reference model.

This defined a classification hierarchy that was predicated on using the OSI reference model. This decision is currently being rethought, so these classes and their subclasses will not be discussed further. As an example of this rethinking, DEN defined a BGP attribute class as a subclass of RoutingProtocol, which was a subclass of Layer3Protocol. The 2.2 version of the CIM Network Common Model provides a more powerful definition of the BGP protocol class, separating it into several different aspects that cover the attributes of the BGP protocol, the service that the BGP protocol provides, and its relationship to other entities (for example, routers that run BGP, and routing policies that affect routing decisions carried by BGP in an autonomous system). The result is a more extensive treatment of BGP while using all of the BGP material that the DEN specification provided.

The CIM Network Common Model

The purpose of the CIM Network Common Model is to model the logical characteristics, functions, and capabilities of managed objects that are contained in, and form, a network. This model reinforces the distinction between physical and logical aspects of a managed object.

The 2.2 release of the CIM Network Common Model is derived from the DEN Logical Model. Even though it is specific to networking, it covers many different concepts, and so is not limited to enhancing a single subclass of CIM like the Physical Common Model (which added classes to just the PhysicalElement class). In fact, the Network Common

Model drove the addition of several new concepts in CIM 2.2 which were added to the Core Model. That being said, the Network Common Model heavily leverages the Core and System models, and does not add any new top-level classes.

The Network Common Model has five main goals:

- Model the logical characteristics of network devices

- Model the logical characteristics of network systems

- Model various networking protocols

- Model the connectivity aspects of a managed environment

- Model the administration of networks and network elements

The first goal is achieved by enhancing the definition of a ComputerSystem, and defining appropriate additional classes and relationships that define essential networking concepts. These new subclasses are all based on existing classes defined in the Core Model, and include LogicalElement, ServiceAccessPoint, and ServiceStatisticalInformation. They include the classes necessary for route filtering (FilterList, FilterEntry, RoutingPolicy, and RouteMap), for representing network addresses (ProtocolEndpoint, AddressRange), and for gathering statistics (BGPStatistics, along with the various port and bridge statistics classes).

Modeling network systems builds on the first goal. This requires defining new subclasses of System (to reflect the emphasis on network, as opposed to general-purpose, systems) and CollectionOfMSEs. This produced the AdminDomain, AutonomousSystem, and LogicalNetwork classes, along with specialized classes (IPSubnet, IPRoute, and BGPCluster).

Networking protocols require the addition of a set of related new subclasses of Service, ServiceAccessPoint, and CollectionOfMSEs. BGP was modeled first for several reasons:

- First, it is the ubiquitous routing protocol in the Internet, and demand for modeling it was very high.

- Second, it is very complicated, and provides a good test of the protocol framework that is being developed.

The main BGP classes include RouteCalculationService, BGPService, BGPAttributes, BGPCluster, and BGPPeerGroup.

Connectivity aspects are modeled by defining SwitchPorts and ProtocolEndpoints. The 2.3 release will provide a much richer modeling of connectivity information, but will be based on this work.

Finally, networking cannot be covered without also covering administration and management. For example, the very definition of an AutonomousSystem centers around the common administration and management of a set of network devices and their routing policies. However, the User Common Model was not yet finished when the Network Common Model was submitted for member review. Therefore, the Network Common Model contains placeholder classes that will be associated with classes from the User Model (for example, defining who is the administrator for an autonomous system will be done by providing an association between the AutonomousSystem class and the appropriate user class).

A conceptual diagram defining the derivation of the Network Common Model is shown in Figure 9.5 through Figure 9.7. Figure 9.5 shows the Network Common Model classes derived from CollectionOfMSEs, System, and LogicalElement. Figure 9.6 shows the Network Common Model classes derived from Service and ServiceAccessPoint. Finally, Figure 9.7 shows the Network Common Model classes derived from the subclasses of StatisticalInformation.

Figure 9.5 Network Common Model classes derived from the CollectionOfMSEs, System, and LogicalElement classes.

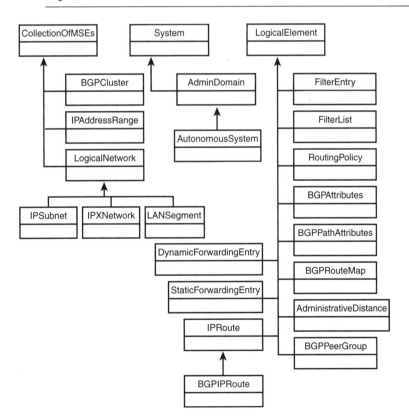

Figure 9.6 Network Common Model classes derived from the Service and ServiceAccessPoint classes.

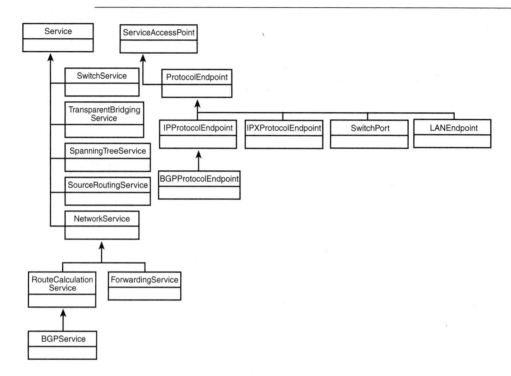

The following sections define the Network Common Model. All of its elements are subclassed from the Core Model.

Note

The Network Common Model did not add any new top-level classes. This is a very important point. It means that the Network Common Model can build directly off of and enhance the Core Model, as opposed to introduce new concepts that have no relation to the Core (or other) Common Models.

Figure 9.7 Network Common Model classes derived from the `StatisticalInformation` class.

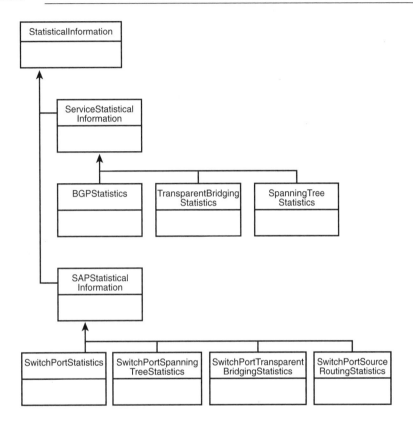

General-Purpose Networking Objects

The foundation of the Network Common Model is based on a set of objects that model basic networking concepts. These include logical connectivity and containment, along with defining network systems and administration.

The 2.2 release of the Network Common Model is focused around IP connectivity. Care has been taken to ensure that these foundational objects do not preclude the modeling of other technologies, such as ATM.

AdminDomain

The `AdminDomain` class is a subclass of the `System` class. Recall that a `System` is a `LogicalElement` that aggregates an enumerable set of `ManagedSystemElements` that operate as an atomic unit. This aggregation operates as a functional whole and requires a dedicated object to represent it. A `System` has the additional semantics of requiring that the entities that make it up must be put together in a specific way.

An `AdminDomain` is a special grouping of `ManagedSystemElements` that are all administered by the same user or group of users. From a networking point of view, it serves as an aggregation point to associate network elements and other resources that can be accessed by end systems. It therefore serves as a source of network services. The ability to group related devices that work together to provide one or more network services is fundamental to policy-enabled networking. Therefore, an `AdminDomain` is also used to group devices so that the same administrative policies are applied to all of the devices in the group.

An excerpt from the Network Common Model that illustrates the `AdminDomain` and its relationships is shown in Figure 9.8.

Figure 9.8   Network Common Model excerpt: `AdminDomain` and its relationships.

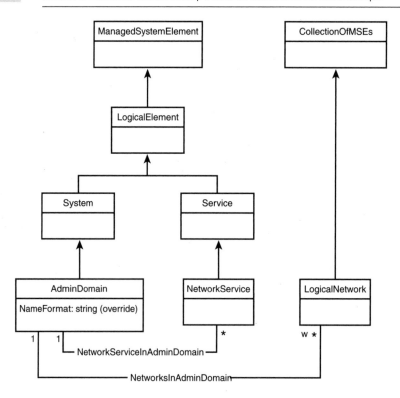

The `AdminDomain` class defines a single attribute, `NameFormat`. It inherits this attribute from the `System` class, but overrides it to control how the `Name` of the `AdminDomain` is generated. This naming heuristic can be different than that used for `Systems`, since `Systems` are by definition general-purpose in nature, whereas `AdminDomains` are used specifically to group various network resources together that must be administered in the same way, perhaps using the same policies.

The following MOF excerpt defines the current values for use in assigning the `Name` of the `AdminDomain`.

Listing 9.1 MOF definition for the `NameFormat` attribute.

```
[...
ValueMap {"Other", "AS", "NAP", "NOC", "POP", "RNP", "IP", "IPX", "SNA", "Dial",
"WAN", "LAN", "ISDN", "Frame Relay", "ATM", "E.164" },
Values {"Other", "Autonomous System", "Network Access Provide", "Network
Operations Center", "Point of Presence", "Regional Network Provider", "IP",
"IPX", "SNA", "Dial", "WAN", "LAN", "ISDN", "Frame Relay", "ATM", "E.164"} ]
string NameFormat;
```

The `AdminDomain` class defines no methods, but it does define two relationships, `NetworkServicesInAdminDomain` and `NetworksInAdminDomain`. Both of these relationships are described later in this chapter, the former in the `NetworkService` class, and the latter in the `LogicalNetwork` class.

AutonomousSystem

An `AutonomousSystem` (AS) is a fundamental concept in networking. Quoting from RFC 1771:

> The classic definition of an Autonomous System is a set of routers under a single technical administration, using an interior gateway protocol and common metrics to route packets within the AS, and using an exterior gateway protocol to route packets to other ASs.

It has become common for a single AS to use several interior gateway protocols and sometimes several sets of metrics within an AS. However, this is irrelevant to the definition of an AS. The defining factor of an AS is that the devices that make up the AS are all commonly administered, with consistent interior routing plans. Furthermore, the AS presents a consistent picture of what destinations are reachable through it. In this way, an AS enables the Internet to be partitioned into a set of separately administered domains that each have their own independent routing policies.

Figure 9.9 illustrates an AS and its relationships.

Figure 9.9   Network Common Model excerpt: `AutonomousSystem` and its relationships.

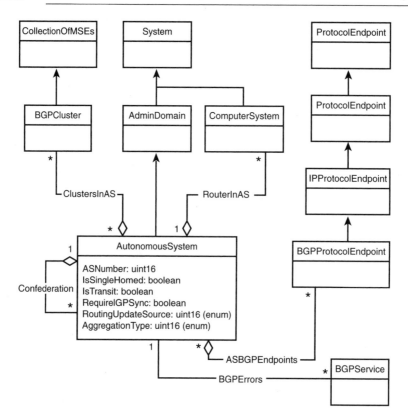

An `AutonomousSystem` class defines the following attributes:

- `ASNumber` is a 16-bit unsigned integer that has a range between 1 and 65,535, with the range 64,512 through 65,535 reserved for private use. Every AS must have a unique AS number, which is assigned to it by an Internet Registry or a Service Provider. IANA assigns and administers AS numbers.

- `IsSingleHomed` is a Boolean that, if `TRUE`, indicates that this AS reaches networks outside of its domain through a single exit point. This has important ramifications for BGP configuration.

- `IsTransit` is a Boolean that, if `TRUE`, indicates that this AS will advertise routes that it learns from other ASs. A non-transit AS will only advertise its own routes.

- RequireIGPSync is a Boolean that, if TRUE, indicates that this AS must not advertise destinations learned from internal BGP neighbors to external BGP destinations unless those destinations are also known via some internal gateway protocol. Otherwise, a BGP router may receive traffic that cannot yet be routed. However, this is a costly choice, so it is common practice to allow this rule to be broken under certain carefully controlled circumstances.

- RoutingUpdateSource is an enumerated 16-bit unsigned integer that defines how routing information is to be injected into BGP routes. Four choices are available. The first, Unknown, is self-explanatory. *Statically injected routes* are simple, but are independent of the status of the networks that they refer to. *Dynamic routes* cause all of the IGP routes to be distributed into BGP. Finally, *semi-dynamic routes* define a set of specific IGP routes that will be injected into BGP.

- AggregationType is an enumerated 16-bit unsigned integer that describes what type of route aggregation, if any, is being performed on this router.

Route aggregation summarizes ranges of routes into one or more aggregate routes in order to minimize the number of routes in the global routing table. A potential drawback of doing this is that specific path information (for example, AS_Path attribute value) is lost. This can lead to potential routing loops. However, BGP4 is well equipped to deal with this potential problem.

This enumeration consists of the following five values:

Value	CIM Attribute Value and Description
0	Unknown
1	None
2	Aggregate Only, where only the aggregate is advertised, and all of its more specific routes are suppressed
3	Aggregate Plus Specific Routes, where both the aggregate as well as its more specific routes are advertised (for example, send the aggregate to the NAP, but send the more specific routes to providers)
4	Aggregate Based on a Subset of Specific Routes, where the aggregate route is formed by looking at certain more specific routes and forming an aggregate on them, suppressing all others

This class defines no methods, but does participate in four relationships:

- The `ASBGPEndpoints` aggregation

- The `BPGClustersInAS` aggregation

- The `Confederation` aggregation

- The `RoutersInAS` aggregation

All of these except the `Confederation` and the `RoutersInAS` aggregations involved classes not yet defined. Therefore, these two aggregations will be defined here, and the remaining four will be defined when the class that they are associated with is defined.

The `Confederation` *Aggregation*

The `Confederation` aggregation is used to represent BGP confederations. This is an important concept in BGP, as BGP speakers in an AS are required to be fully meshed, which can lead to a huge number of TCP connections per router. Confederations reduce this peering requirement by partitioning one AS into a group of 'sub-ASs'. This enables all of the benefits of IBGP (the internal version of BGP) to be applied inside the confederation, while enabling EBGP (the external version of BGP) to be run between each confederation. For example, this enables certain BGP attribute values to be preserved between confederations. However, to the outside world, the AS with its confederations appear to be a single AS.

What is a Confederation?

A *confederation* is one way to reduce the meshing requirements for BGP speakers within an AS. It is described in detail in RFC 1965; a brief introduction to confederations is provided here so this class can be better understood.

The concept of a confederation is deceptively simple. The goal is to reduce the number intra-domain BGP connections while retaining the characteristics of an AS. Hence, confederations can be thought of as a set of sub-ASs that are contained in a parent AS.

For example, consider a single AS, called AS100. It may have many different connections to other ASs, as well as a set of internal routers that are interconnected. This is not only difficult to control from a routing policy point of view, but may require a large number of peering sessions, since each BGP speaker must be peered in a full mesh relationship. Now, assume that we can split this into some number of confederations. AS100 is still viewed as a single autonomous system from the outside world. The confederations are hidden from the outside world, and standard practice is to assign them AS numbers from the private AS list so that formal AS numbers are not used up (for example, AS65010, AS65020, and so forth).

Inside each confederation, all of the rules of IBGP apply. Furthermore, since each confederation behaves like an AS, then EBGP must be run between them. However, this enables important BGP attributes, like MED, Next_Hop, and LocalPreference, to be preserved when communicating between confederations.

The intention of confederations, besides minimizing the total number of peering sessions per router, is to aid in policy administration and reduce the management complexity of maintaining a large autonomous system. In addition, dividing an AS into confederations enables different IGPs to run in different confederations. This may be beneficial, or even required, depending on the characteristics of the router. It also helps in controlling potential route instabilities when running an IGP in a large system.

This aggregation is a subclass of the more generic SystemComponent aggregation. Both the aggregate as well as the part components are restricted to instances of AutonomousSystem. The multiplicity of this relationship is one to zero-or-more.

This aggregation also defines two 32-bit unsigned integers. ParentASNumber and ChildASNumber are the AS numbers of the parent and child AutonomousSystems that make up this aggregation.

The RoutersInAS Aggregation

The RoutersInAS aggregation is a subclass of the more generic SystemComponent relationship, and is used to define the set of routers (for example, ComputerSystems) that are contained in a given AutonomousSystem. This aggregation also has the additional semantics that all routers in a given AS share common configuration information, and are commonly administered.

The multiplicity of this relationship is one to zero-or-more, since a given router can only reside in a single AS, but an AS can aggregate any number of routers (including zero, if the AS is being defined but not populated yet). The aggregate is limited to instances of the AutonomousSystem class, and the part components are limited to instances of the ComputerSystem class.

This aggregation also defines the following attributes:

- BGPSupportedAttributes is an array of free-form strings that contain the BGP attributes supported by this router. This enables vendors that have extended the BGP protocol to add their own attributes in to be recognized by the system.

- AddCommunityValue is a Boolean attribute that, if TRUE, means that the community value of this router is added to the existing community value contained in the BGP message. FALSE means that the community value of this router replaces the existing community value. BGP Community values are used to affect routing decisions, and are explained briefly in the BGPAttributes class description later in this chapter.

- Role is an enumerated 16-bit integer that defines the function that this router plays in the AS. Its MOF definition is given in Listing 9.2.

Listing 9.2   MOF definition for the Role attribute.

```
[...
ValueMap { "0", "1", "2", "3", "4", "5", "6", "7" },
Values { "Unknown", "Other", "Conventional BGP Speaker", "Route Reflector",
         "Router Reflector Client", "Route Reflector Non-Client",
         "Peer Group Member", "Confederation Member" },
ModelCorrespondence {"CIM_BGPService.OtherRoleDescription"} ]
uint16 Role;
```

- OtherRoleDescription is a free-form string describing the type of function that this router has in its AS when the value of the Role attribute of this class is set to 1 (for example, Other). The format of the string inserted in this attribute should be similar in format to the values defined for the Role attribute. This attribute enables vendors to define application-specific roles and assign routers to them, so that the overall managed system reflects the terminology of the vendor. Accordingly, this attribute should be set to NULL when the Role attribute is any value other than 1.

NetworkService

The NetworkService class is an abstract base class that is derived from the Service class. This serves as the root of the network service hierarchy, which was defined in DEN.

Network services represent functions that are available from the network that can modify the traffic being sent through network devices. This is often done by reconfiguring the network devices that send and receive that traffic. For example, FTP is not a network service, as it simply passes data unchanged from source to destination. On the other hand, services that provide quality of service (for example, DiffServ) and security (for example, IPSec) do affect the traffic stream. QoS, IPSec, and other services are subclasses of this class. Figure 9.10 illustrates the NetworkService class and its relationships.

Figure 9.10   Network Common Model excerpt: `NetworkService` and its relationships.

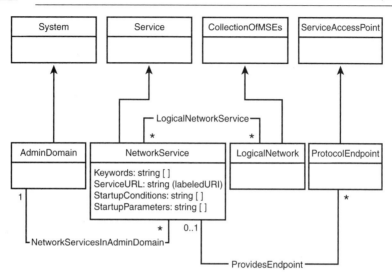

The `NetworkService` class defines the following attributes:

- `Keywords` is an array of free-form strings that can be used to store descriptive words and phrases for use in issuing queries for identifying and locating instances of this service.

- `ServiceURL` is a string, of syntax `labeledURI`, that provides the protocol, network location, and other service-specific information required in order to access the service.

- `StartupConditions` is an array of free-form strings that specify any application-specific pre-conditions that must be met in order for this service to start correctly. It is expected that subclasses will refine the inherited `StartService()` and `StopService()` methods, and then use this attribute to ensure that these refined methods will work correctly.

- `StartupParameters` is an array of free-form strings that specify any application-specific parameters that must be supplied to the `StartService()` and `StopService()` methods (or their subclasses) in order for this service to start correctly. It is expected that subclasses will refine the inherited `StartService()` and `StopService()` methods, and then use this attribute to ensure that these refined methods will work correctly.

The NetworkService class defines no methods, but does define three relationships. These are the NetworkServicesInAdminDomain (which is defined next), the LogicalNetworkService, and the ProvidesEndpoint associations. The last two associations are defined under the LogicalNetwork and ProtocolEndpoint, respectively.

The NetworkServicesInAdminDomain Association

The NetworkServicesInAdminDomain association is a specialization of the HostedService association. It is used to make explicit the dependency relationship that exists between an AdminDomain and the NetworkServices that are hosted in the AdminDomain. Put another way, this association defines the network services that are provided by this administrative domain. This association also provides the additional semantics that define these services as being commonly administered.

The antecedent is the AdminDomain that hosts the various network services and administers them, and the dependents are the NetworkServices that are hosted in the AdminDomain. The multiplicity of this relationship is one to zero-or-more. This is because this is a weak relationship, and therefore we must identify the single AdminDomain that is hosting the NetworkServices. However, multiple NetworkServices can be hosted in a given AdminDomain.

Note that this is a *weak* relationship, since the services are hosted in the AdminDomain. The Weak qualifier is not used in the Visio or the MOF because it is already inherited from the SystemComponent aggregation.

ForwardingService

The ForwardingService class is a subclass of the NetworkService class, and represents the generic ability of network devices to forward network traffic by receiving data from one or more ProtocolEndpoints and sending that data via other ProtocolEndpoints.

This class is different than the RouteCalculationService class (which is described later) in that it represents a way to forward traffic independent of having to calculate routing information. For example, traffic may be forwarded using static routing in a router, or by using a forwarding information database in a switch. Examples of this kind of service include routing, bridging, and repeating services.

Figure 9.11 illustrates the ForwardingService class.

Figure 9.11   Network Common Model excerpt: The ForwardingService class and its relationships.

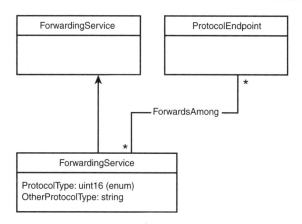

The ForwardingService class defines the following two attributes:

• ProtocolType is an enumerated 16-bit unsigned integer that defines the type of protocol that is being used to forward information. Listing 9.3 shows an excerpt of the MOF that defines the types of protocols currently recognized.

Listing 9.3   MOF definition for the ProtocolType attribute.

```
[...
ValueMap { "0", "1", "2", "3", "4", "5", "6", "7", "8", "9", "10", "11", "12" },
Values { "Unknown", "Other", "IPv4", "IPv6", "IPv4/IPv6", "IPX", "AppleTalk",
"DECnet", "SNA", "CONP", "CLNP", "VINES", "XNS" } ]
uint16 ProtocolType;
```

• OtherProtocolType is a free-form string of up to 32 characters that describes the type of protocol that is used to forward traffic when the value of the ProtocolType attribute of this class is set to 1 (for example, Other). Accordingly, this attribute should be set to NULL when the ProtocolType attribute is any value other than 1.

This class defines no methods, but does define one relationship, the ForwardsAmong association.

The ForwardsAmong *Association*

The ForwardsAmong association is a subclass of the more generic ServiceSAPDependency association, and represents the dependency that exists between the ProtocolEndpoints that are
used to forward data and the ForwardingService that is performing the forwarding of data.
This is a zero-or-more to zero-or-more association, with the antecedent and dependent
restricted to instances of the ProtocolEndpoint and ForwardingService classes, respectively.

RouteCalculationService

The RouteCalculationService is a subclass of the NetworkService class, and represents the
route calculation aspects performed by a router. This includes executing different routing
algorithms, such as BGP and OSPF as well as functions performed by the router when it
exchanges routing information.

Figure 9.12 illustrates the RouteCalculationService class.

Figure 9.12 Network Common Model excerpt: The RouteCalculationService class and its
relationships.

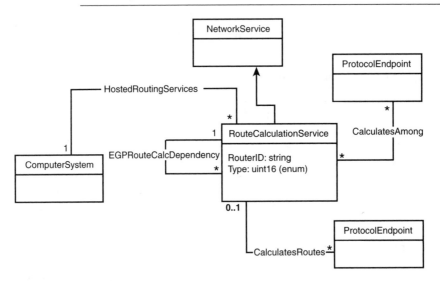

The RouteCalculation class defines the following two attributes:

- RouterID is a free-form string that uniquely identifies the router that is performing the
  route calculation. It is defined to be either the highest IP address or the highest loopback interface on the router.

- Type is an enumerated 16-bit unsigned integer that defines the routing algorithm used
  that this route calculation is being performed for. Its nine current values include
  Unknown, versions 1 and 2 of RIP and OSPF, and versions 1 through 4 of BGP.

This class defines no methods, but it does participate in four associations, `HostedRoutingServices`, `CalculatesAmong`, `EGPRouteCalcDependency`, and `CaluculatedRoutes`.

The `HostedRoutingServices` *Association*

The `HostedRoutingServices` association is derived from the more general `HostedService` association. The `HostedService` association defines a dependency between a `Service` and the `System` on which the `Service` resides. The `HostedRoutingServices` association defines the set of `RouteCalculationServices` (for example, routing protocols) that a given router (that is, a `ComputerSystem`) provides. These include different internal and external routing protocols. Each of these `RouteCalculationServices` are *weak* with respect to their hosting `ComputerSystem`. However, the `Weak` qualifier is not used in the MOF or the Visio because it is already inherited from the `HostedService` association.

The multiplicity of this association is defined as one to zero-or-more. This is because a single `ComputerSystem` must be identified to host the `RouteCalculationServices`, but that `ComputerSystem` can host many different types of routing services.

Recall that the `RouteCalculationService` class is used to represent different routing algorithms (such as BGP and OSPF) as well as functions performed by the router when it exchanges routing information. This association can be used to capture both of these aspects. This can be used to determine, for example, what different internal routing protocols are available for use with each external routing protocol.

The `CalculatesAmong` *Association*

The `CalculatesAmong` association is derived from the `ServiceSAPDependency` association. It represents the dependency that a `ProtocolEndpoint` has on the `RouteCalculationService` that provides its functionality.

The multiplicity of this relationship is zero-or-more to zero-or-more. The antecedent and dependent are restricted to instances of the `ProtocolEndpoint` and the `RouteCalculationService` classes, respectively. In addition, a single attribute, `IsStatic`, is defined. This is a Boolean attribute that, if `TRUE`, defines this `ProtocolEndpoint` to be a static route (`FALSE` means that this represents a dynamically learned route).

The `EGPRouteCalcDependency` *Association*

The `EGPRouteCalcDependency` association is a specialization of the `ServiceServiceDependency` association, and is used to capture the dependency that external gateway protocols (such as BGP) have on interior gateway protocols (such as OSPF).

The antecedent and dependent are each restricted to instances of the `RouteCalculationService` class. The multiplicity of this association is one to one, reflecting the dependency of a single instance of an EGP on the specific IGP that it is using.

This association also defines a single attribute, called `IGPInjection`, which is an enumerated 16-bit unsigned integer. This attribute reflects the fact that it is sometimes necessary to inject EGP information into an IGP. For example, injecting partial EGP information can be used to direct the corresponding outbound traffic towards specific exit points in the AS. The viability of this technique depends on many factors, but most importantly on the type of IGP that is being used. Furthermore, instabilities in the EGP will have disastrous effect on the IGP. This attribute defines three values, 1 – 3. These values mean that no, partial, or full EGP information is injected into the IGP, respectively. Again, injection of full information is not recommended, but is provided in an effort to model all possible cases.

The `CalculatedRoutes` assocation is used to identify all routes that are calculated by a specific `RouteCalculationService` used by a router. This enables every `RouteCalculationService` to have its own unique set of calculated routes. The antecedent and dependent are overridden to be instances of type `RouteCalculationService` and IPRoute, respectively. In addition, the cardinality of the `RouteCalculationService` is restricted to zero-or-one, in order to identify the specific `RouteCalculationService` that the `ProtocolEndpoint` instances apply to.

LogicalNetwork

A `LogicalNetwork` is an abstract class, derived from the `CollectionOfMSEs` class, that is used to group together a set of `ProtocolEndpoints` of a given type which are able to directly communicate with each other. This class does not represent a set of network elements; rather, it represents the set of interfaces that this group of devices provides to the outside world. As such, a `LogicalNetwork` represents the ability to send and/or receive data over a network.

Note that `LogicalNetworks` cannot exist outside of a `System` that hosts them. This is captured by the `NetworksInAdminDomain` association, which relates one or more `LogicalNetworks` to an `AdminDomain`. This is a weak association, and consequently the keys of the `System` class (`CreationClassName` and `Name`) are propagated to this class. These two attributes, along with the `CreationClassName` and `Name` attributes defines in this class, together make up the composite key of this class.

Figure 9.13 illustrates the `LogicalNetwork` class and its relationships.

Figure 9.13 Network Common Model excerpt: `LogicalNetwork` and its relationships.

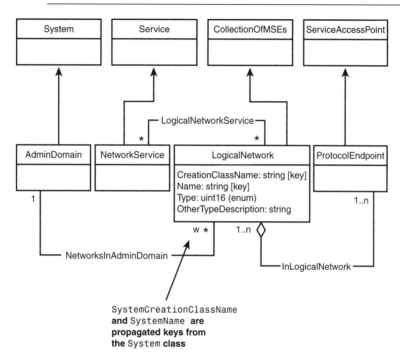

The `LogicalNetwork` class defines the following attributes:

- `Type` is an enumerated 16-bit unsigned integer that provides additional information that can be used to help categorize and classify different instances of this class. The current set of values are specified in Listing 9.4. Note the use of the `ModelCorrespondence` qualifier to link the `OtherTypeDescription` attribute to this attribute. This enables a vendor-definable extension mechanism by setting the value of `Type` to 1 (for example, `Other`) and then describing the application-specific value in the `OtherTypeDescription` attribute.

Listing 9.4 MOF definition for the `Type` attribute.

```
[...
ValueMap { "0", "1", "2", "3", "4", "5", "6", "7", "8", "9", "10", "11", "12",
"13", "14", "15", "16", "17", "18" },
Values { "Unknown", "Other", "IPv4", "IPv6", "IPv4/IPv6", "IPX", "AppleTalk",
"DECnet", "SNA", "CONP", "CLNP", "VINES", "XNS", "ATM", "Frame Relay",
"Ethernet", "TokenRing", "CDDI", "FDDI" } ]
ModelCorrespondence {"CIM_LogicalNetwork.OtherTypeDescription"} ]
string Type;
```

- OtherTypeDescription is a free-form string of up to 64 characters that describes the type of protocol that is being run by this LogicalNetwork when the value of the Type attribute of this class is set to 1 (for example, Other). Accordingly, this attribute should be set to NULL when the Type attribute is any value other than 1.

This class defined no methods. However, it participates in two associations (LogicalNetworkService and NetworksInAdminDomain) and one aggregation (InLogicalNetwork). The two associations are described next; the aggregation is described when the ProtocolEndpoint class is described later in this chapter.

The LogicalNetworkService Association

The LogicalNetworkService association represents network services that either originate and/or terminate in a particular LogicalNetwork. This enables management applications to associate specific network services, such as the origin of a VPN, with a specific LogicalNetwork.

The LogicalNetworkService association has a multiplicity of zero-or-more to zero-or-more, and is restricted to instances of the LogicalNetwork and NetworkService classes, respectively. It also defines a 16-bit unsigned integer, ContainmentType, that explicitly defines whether this network service originates, terminates, or originates and terminates in this LogicalNetwork. The values for this attribute are as follows:

Value	CIM Attribute Value and Description
0	Unknown
1	Originates In, meaning that this service originates in this LogicalNetwork but terminates in a different LogicalNetwork
2	Terminates In, meaning that this service terminates in this LogicalNetwork but originates in a different LogicalNetwork
3	Resides In, meaning that this service both originates and terminates in this LogicalNetwork

The NetworksInAdminDomain Association

The NetworksInAdminDomain association is used to define the set of LogicalNetworks that are contained in an AdminDomain. This association adds the semantics that this set of LogicalNetworks are all administered by the same network administrator that administrates the AdminDomain.

This association is not subclassed from the Dependency association because, as can be seen in Figure 9.13, a LogicalNetwork is not a subclass of ManagedSystemElement, and the Dependency association requires both the antecedent and the dependent to be subclasses of ManagedSystemElement.

This is a weak relationship. Therefore, the multiplicity of this relationship is defined to be one to zero-or-more. Since an AdminDomain hosts the LogicalNetworks, we can define only one AdminDomain which is hosting the LogicalNetworks. However, that AdminDomain can contain as many LogicalNetworks as needed. Note that the MOF and Visio do not use the Weak qualifier because it is already inherited from its superclass, HostedService.

IPSubnet

The IPSubnet class is derived from the LogicalNetwork class. An IPSubnet represents a group of related IPProtocolEndpoints that can communicate with each other directly using IP. Note that this class is aimed at describing the characteristics of the grouping of IPProtocolEndpoints and *not* the characteristics of the underlying devices that provide those interfaces.

Figure 9.14 illustrates the IPSubnet class.

Figure 9.14   Network Common Model excerpt: the IPSubnet class.

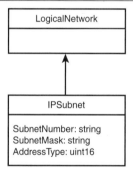

The IPSubnet class defines the following attributes:

- SubnetNumber is a free-form string that contains the IP address of the entire subnet, formatted according to the appropriate convention as defined in the AddressType attribute of this class. This is one of the two attributes that form the composite key for this class.

- SubnetMask is a free-form string that is the other attribute that forms the composite key of this class. It, too, is formatted to be consistent with the addressing scheme defined in the AddressType attribute.

- AddressType is a 16-bit unsigned integer that defines the format of the IPAddress and SubnetMask attributes. The current formats that are defined are Unknown, IPv4, and IPv6.

IPRoute

The IPRoute class is a subclass of LogicalElement, and represents a generic form of a routing table entry. It defines a route as a tuple, consisting of a source, a destination, some path metric information, and how the destination is to be reached. The source and destination addresses may be either individual IPProtocolEndpoints or IPSubnets.

Figure 9.15 illustrates the IPRoute class.

The IPRoute class has nine attributes that form its composite key. These correspond to the four propagated keys of the System (that is, SystemCreationClassName and SystemName) and Service (that is, ServiceCreationClassName and ServiceName) classes, along with three keys that are defined in this class. These are the CreationClassName, IPDestinationAddress, IPDestinationMask, AddressType, and NextHop attributes. This is in order to make an IPRoute instance *weak* to a ForwardingService instance.

Figure 9.15   Network Common Model excerpt: The IPRoute and BGPIPRoute classes and their relationships.

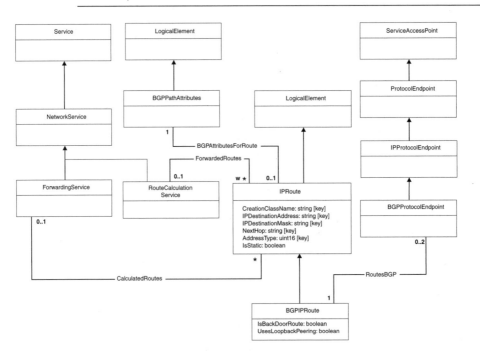

The IPRoute class defines the following attributes (the four propagated keys are not repeated here):

- CreationClassName is one of the nine attributes that form the composite key of this class. It is a free-form string that identifies the class that created this instance. This enables subclasses of the IPRoute class to be created that represent specific types of routing protocol ProtocolEndpoints.

- IPDestinationAddress is one of the nine attributes that form the composite key of this class. It is a string that contains the IP address which serves as the destination of the traffic, formatted according to the appropriate convention as defined in the AddressType attribute of this class.

- IPDestinationMask is one of the nine attributes that form the composite key of this class. It is a string that contains the IP address which serves as the destination of the traffic, formatted according to the appropriate convention as defined in the AddressType attribute of this class.

- NextHop is one of the nine attributes that form the composite key of this class. It a string that contains either the address of the directly connected interface of the next-hop router or the interface to which the destination is connected to (for example, Ethernet0).

- AddressType is one of the nine attributes that form the composite key of this class. It is an enumerated 16-bit unsigned integer that defines how to format the address and mask of the source and destination addresses that defines this IPSubnet). The allowable values are IPv4 and IPv6, though the escape value of Unknown is also defined.

* IsStatic is a boolean that, if TRUE, indicates that this ProtocolEndpoint represents a static route. FALSE means that it represents a dynamically-learned route.

This class defines no methods. However, it does define three associations, ForwardedRoutes, RoutesBGP, and BGPAttributesForRoute. The first is described next; the others will be explained when the BGPProtocolEndpoint and the BGPPathAttribute classes are explained later in this chapter.

The ForwardedRoutes *Association*

The ForwardedRoutes association is a subclass of the general Dependency association, and makes explicit the routes that are used by a specific ForwardingService. Thus, every ForwardingService can have its own unique set of routing destinations.

The antecedent and dependent are restricted to instances of the ForwardingService and IPRoute classes, respectively. Since this is a *weak* relationship, the cardinality of the ForwardingService end is set at exactly 1. The cardinality of the IPRoute end is zero-or-more to zero-or-more, since there can be as many different routing entries as needed for a specific ForwardingService.

This association also defines the following two attributes, which are used to describe the preference of this routing entry over other routing entries that also go to the same destination:

- AdminDistance is a 16-bit unsigned integer that contains the current administrative distance of this route. Note that the AdministrativeDistance class contains the default values, not the current values, of administrative distances that are to be used with routes.

- PathMetric is a 16-bit unsigned integer that contains a value corresponding to the overall preference of this route compared to other routes that reach the same destination.

IPAddressRange

The IPAddressRange class is a subclass of the CollectionOfMSEs class. It represents a grouping of specific addresses (*not* the network elements that provide these addresses!) that are intended to be used as a group (for example, for allocation of DHCP IP address leases).

Figure 9.16 illustrates the IPAddressRange class.

The IPAddressRange class defines the following attributes:

- StartAddress defines the starting IP address of the AddressRange, formatted according to the appropriate convention as defined in the AddressType attribute of this class.

- EndAddress defines the ending IP address of the AddressRange, formatted according to the appropriate convention as defined in the AddressType attribute of this class.

- TypeOfAddress is an enumerated 16-bit unsigned integer that defines how to format the address and mask attributes of this AddressRange. The three values that are currently defined are Unknown, IPv4, and IPv6.

- AllocationRegion is an enumerated 16-bit integer that defines the region that addresses can be allocated to. The MOF describing the definition of the different address ranges that are allocated is shown in Listing 9.5.

Figure 9.16   Network Common Model excerpt: the `IPAddressRange` class.

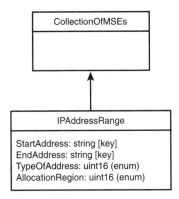

Listing 9.5   MOF definition for the `AllocationRegion` attribute.

```
[...
ValueMap {"1", "2", "3", "4", "5", "6", "7", "8", "9" },
Values {"Unknown",
        "Multiregional: 192.0.0.0 to 193.255.255.255",
        "Europe: 194.0.0.0 to 195.255.255.255",
        "Others: 196.0.0.0 to 197.255.255.255",
        "North America: 198.0.0.0 to 199.255.255.255",
        "Central & South America: 200.0.0.0 to 201.255.255.255",
        "Pacific Rim: 202.0.0.0 to 203.255.255.255",
        "Others: 204.0.0.0 to 205.255.255.255",
        "Others: 206.0.0.0 to 207.255.255.255" } ]
  uint16 AllocationRegion;
```

This class defines no methods or relationships at this time.

IPXNetwork

The IPXNetwork class is a subclass of LogicalNetwork, and represents a network that uses the IPX network protocol. Figure 9.17 illustrates the IPXNetwork class.

The IPXNetwork class defines a single attribute, NetworkNumber, which is an IPX network number formatted as eight hexadecimal digits.

This class defines no methods or relationships at this time.

Figure 9.17   Network Common Model excerpt: the `IPXNetwork` class.

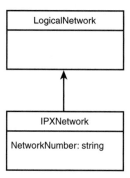

LANSegment

The `LANSegment` class is another subclass of the `LogicalNetwork` class. It represents a collection of `LANEndpoints` (which is a subclass of `ProtocolEndpoint`) that are able to directly communicate with each other without any intermediate routing or bridging services.

Figure 9.18 illustrates the `LANSegment` class.

Figure 9.18   Network Common Model excerpt: the `LANSegment` class.

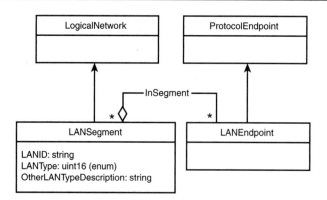

The `LANSegment` class defines the following three attributes:

- `LANID` is a free-form string, of up to 64 characters, that contains a unique identifier for this LAN Segment. It corresponds with the `LANID` attribute of the `LANEndpoint` class.

- `LANType` is an enumerated 16-bit unsigned integer An indication of the kind of technology used on the LAN. The current values are defined as follows:

Value	CIM Attribute Value
0	Unknown
1	Other
2	Ethernet
3	TokenRing
4	FDDI

- OtherLANType is a free-form string, of up to 64 characters, that describes the type of technology used on the LAN when the value of the LANType attribute of this class (or any of its subclasses) is set to 1 (that is, Other). This property should be set to NULL when the LANType attribute is any value other than 1.

This class does not define any methods, but does define one relationship, InSegment, which is defined in the section where the LANEndpoint class is described.

Networking Protocol Objects

The 2.2 version of the Network Common Model defines a set of classes and relationships that can model different networking protocols. This version of the Network Common Model concentrates on providing a framework for modeling protocols. In addition, a sub-model for BGP is provided, due to its heavy usage and its emergence as the *de facto* standard for Internet routing. The BGP sub-model is compatible with the following IETF RFCs: 1657, 1700, 1771, 1965, 1966, and 1997.

This portion of this chapter will first discuss core foundation classes, such as the ProtocolEndpoint and RouteCalculationService classes, that are common to all routing protocols. Then, it will describe the BGP classes that form the BGP sub-model.

ProtocolEndpoint

ProtocolEndpoint is an abstract class that represents a communication point of the network element (for example, a router interface or a switch port) from which data may be sent or received. ProtocolEndpoints represent the abstraction of router interfaces and switch ports so that they can be associated with LogicalNetworks. The ProtocolEndpoint class builds on the DEN work and adds additional associations to reflect different types of network communication.

Figure 9.19 illustrates the ProtocolEndpoint class.

Figure 9.19   Network Common Model excerpt: the `ProtocolEndpoint` class and its relationships.

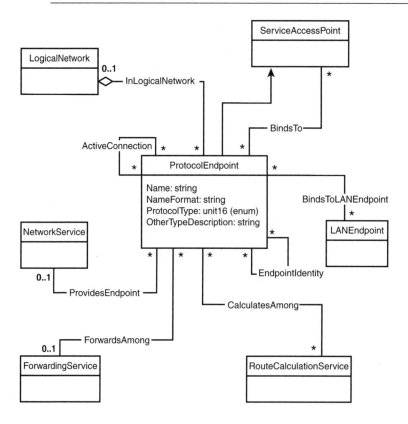

The `ProtocolEndpoint` class defines the following attributes:

- `Name` is a free-form string, of up to 256 characters, that is inherited from its parent (`ServiceAccessPoint`) but overridden in this class. The override consists of using the value of the `Address` attribute, optionally appended with an instance identifier consisting of an underscore followed by a string of characters, whose format is defined in the `NameFormat` property, that can be used to differentiate instances hosted on the same `System` or `LogicalNetwork` which have the same address.

- `ProtocolType` is an enumerated 16-bit unsigned integer that is used to categorize and classify different instances of this class.

Its current values are shown in Listing 9.6.

| Listing 9.6 | MOF definition for the Type attribute. |

```
[...
ValueMap { "0", "1", "2", "3", "4", "5", "6", "7", "8", "9", "10", "11", "12",
"13", "14", "15", "16", "17", "18" },
Values { "Unknown", "Other", "IPv4", "IPv6", "IPv4/IPv6", "IPX", "AppleTalk",
"DECnet", "SNA", "CONP", "CLNP", "VINES", "XNS", "ATM", "Frame Relay",
"Ethernet", "TokenRing", "CDDI", "FDDI" } ]
ModelCorrespondence {"CIM_ProtocolEndpoint.OtherTypeDescription"} ]
string Type;
```

- OtherTypeDescription is a free-form string that contains more detailed information describing the type of ProtocolEndpoint that this instance is when its Type attribute is set to 1 (for example, Other). This attribute should be set to NULL when the Type property is any value other than 1.

- NameFormat is a string attribute that contains the naming heuristic that is chosen to ensure that the value of the Name property is unique. For example, one might choose to prepend the name of the port or interface with the value of the ProtocolType attribute that this instance is (e.g., IPv4_).

This class defines no methods, but does participate in eight relationships. Six of these, the InLogicalNetwork, BindsTo, ActiveConnection, ProvidesEndpoint, ForwardsAmong, and EndpointIdentity relationships, are described next. The other two relationships, CalculatesAmong and BindsToLANEndpoint, are defined when the RouteCalculationService and the LANEndpoint classes are described later in this chapter.

The ProvidesEndpoint Association

The ProvidesEndpoint association is a subclass of the ServiceAccessBySAP association. It is used to define the ProtocolEndpoints (which are, of course, ServiceAccessPoints) that provide management access to the NetworkService.

The antecedent and dependent are restricted to instances of the ProtocolEndpoint and the ForwardingService classes, respectively. The multiplicity of this relationship is zero-or-one to zero-or-more. This is because a NetworkService does not have to define a ProtocolEndpoint to manage it (the "zero" part), but it should (the "one" part). Once defined, the NetworkService may in fact be a complicated service that requires many different access point (for example, a VPN, which consists of several services that are "tunneled" on top of each other). Hence, there may be many ProtocolEndpoints that are needed to manage this NetworkService.

The ForwardsAmong *Association*

The ForwardsAmong association is a subclass of the ServiceSAPDependency association. It represents the dependency that exists between the ProtocolEndpoints that are used to forward data and the ForwardingService that is performing the forwarding of data.

It is instructive to compare the use of ProtocolEndpoints in this association versus the ProvidesEndpoint association. Here, the ProtocolEndpoints are used to relay data from a source to a destination. Compare this to their use in the ProvidesEndpoint association, where they are used to provide access to manage a NetworkService.

The antecedent and dependent are restricted to instances of the ProtocolEndpoint and the ForwardingService classes, respectively. The multiplicity of this relationship is zero-or-more to zero-or-more. This is because many ProtocolEndpoints may be required to forward data between a source and a destination, and the ForwardingService may actually be made up of multiple layered services, each using the same ProtocolEndpoint. In addition, the type of forwarding service may change, with the new ForwardingService configured to use the same ProtocolEndpoint. Note that the ForwardingService is different than the NetworkService. The ForwardingService provides the additional semantics of relaying the data in the NetworkService from the source to the destination. The NetworkService represents generic functions that are available from the network that configure and/or modify the traffic being sent. They do not carry the additional semantics of forwarding traffic.

The InLogicalNetwork *Aggregation*

The InLogicalNetwork aggregation is a subclass of the CollectedMSEs aggregation. It explicitly defines the set of ProtocolEndpoints that make up a given LogicalNetwork. The aggregate is restricted to instances of the class LogicalNetwork, and the part component is restricted to instances of the class ProtocolEndpoint. The multiplicity of this relationship is zero-or-one to zero-or-more. The cardinality on the LogicalNetwork side is zero-or-one, since a LogicalNetwork does not have to be defined. If it is defined, then it may either not be configured (in which case there are zero ProtocolEndpoints) or, if it is configured, may contain many ProtocolEndpoints. Similarly, a ProtocolEndpoint can only be contained in a single LogicalNetwork (it can't exist in two places at the same time!).

The ActiveConnection *Association*

The ActiveConnection association is a subclass of the SAPSAPDependency association. It defines a connection that is currently carrying traffic between two ProtocolEndpoints. The multiplicity of this relationship is zero-or-more to zero-or-more, since connections don't have to be instantiated but, when they are, can be single- or multi-point connections. In addition, a connection can be multiplexed between two different services.

The particular type of traffic that is carried over these two ProtocolEndpoints is defined by the attributes that this class defines, which are defined here:

- TrafficType is an enumerated 16-bit integer that defines the type of traffic that is carried over this connection. There are currently six values defined:

Value	CIM Attribute Value
0	Unknown
1	Other
2	Unicast
3	Broadcast
4	Multicast
5	Anycast

Note that the standard mechanism of using the value of 1 (Other) to indicate a different type of traffic is used here to ensure extensibility.

- OtherTypeDescription is a free-form string, of up to 64 characters, that describes the type of traffic that is being exchanged between these two ProtocolEndpoints when the value of the Type attribute is 1 (Other). If the value of the Type attribute is not 1, then the value of this attribute should be NULL.

- IsUnidirectional is a Boolean attribute that, if TRUE, means that this connection supports only uni-directional traffic. A value of FALSE means that this connection supports bi-directional traffic.

The BindsTo Association

The BindsTo association is a subclass of the SAPSAPDependency association. It is used to define the dependency between two ProtocolEndpoints, with one ProtocolEndpoint requesting protocol services from another ProtocolEndpoint. This binding establishes a layering of two protocols, the upper layer represented by the antecedent and the lower layer represented by the dependent. The antecedent is restricted to instances of the class ServiceAccessPoint, and the dependent is restricted to instances of the class ProtocolEndpoint. The multiplicity of this relationship is zero-or-more to zero-or-more.

The EndpointIdentity Association is a subclass of the LogicalIdentity association. It is used to indicate that two ProtocolEndpoints represent different aspects of the same type of ServiceAccessPoint. For example, a BGPProtocolEndpoint and an IPProtocolEndpoint could be related to each other using this relationship.

The antecedent and dependent (called `SystemElement` and `SameElement`, respectively) are both overridden to be instances of the `ProtocolEndpoint` class. The multiplicity of this relationship is zero-or-more to zero-or-more.

IPProtocolEndpoint

The `IPProtocolEndpoint` class is a subclass of the `ProtocolEndpoint` class. This class is used to represent interfaces that are dedicated to running IP, and adds attributes that are specific to running IP.

Figure 9.20 illustrates the `IPProtocolEndpoint` class.

Figure 9.20   Network Common Model excerpt: the `IPProtocolEndpoint` class.

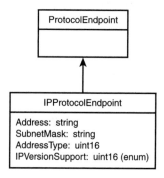

The `IPProtocolEndpoint` class defines the following attributes:

- `Address` contains the IP address of this `ProtocolEndpoint`, formatted according to the appropriate convention as defined in the `AddressType` attribute of this class.

- `SubnetMask` defines the mask for the IP address of this ProtocolEndpoint, formatted according to the appropriate convention as defined in the `AddressType` attribute of this class.

- `AddressType` is an enumerated 16-bit unsigned integer that defines how to format the address and mask attributes for this `IPProtocolEndpoint`. Values include `Unknown`, `IPv4`, and `IPv6`.

- `IPVersionSupport` is an enumerated 16-bit unsigned integer that defines whether this `IPProtocolEndpoint` can support IPv4 and/or IPv6. This dedicated attribute is necessary because it is not possible to tell from the address alone if a particular `IPProtocolEndpoint` can support IPv4 and/or IPv6. It has the following four values:

Value	CIM Attribute Value
0	Unknown
1	IPv4 Only
2	IPv6 Only
3	Both IPv4 and IPv6

This class defines no methods or relationships.

IPXProtocolEndpoint

The IPXProtocolEndpoint class is a subclass of the ProtocolEndpoint class, and is used to represent an IPX communication point from which data may be sent or received.

It defines a single attribute, Address, which contains an IPX address. This is formatted as eight hexadecimal digits representing the network number, followed by a colon, followed by twelve hexadecimal digits that represent the host address.

This class does not define any methods or relationships.

LANEndpoint

The LANEndpoint class is a subclass of the ProtocolEndpoint class. A LANEndpoint represents a special type of ProtocolEndpoint that may send and receive data frames directly to other LANEndpoints that are on the same LAN without requiring intermediate routing or bridging services.

Figure 9.21 illustrates the LANEndpoint class.

The LANEndpoint class defines the following attributes:

- LANID is a string that uniquely identifies this LANEndpoint. It is related to a LANSegment's LANID attribute through the use of the ModelCorrespondence qualifier.

- LANType is an enumerated 16-bit unsigned integer An indication of the kind of technology used on the LAN. The current values are defined as follows:

Value	CIM Attribute Value
0	Unknown
1	Other
2	Ethernet
3	TokenRing
4	FDDI

Figure 9.21   Network Common Model excerpt: the LANEndpoint class and its relationships.

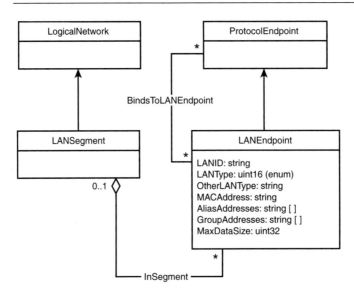

- OtherLANType is a free-form string, of up to 64 characters, that describes the type of technology used on the LAN when the value of the LANType attribute of this class (or any of its subclasses) is set to 1 (for example, Other). This property should be set to NULL when the LANType attribute is any value other than 1.

- MACAddress is a string of 12 characters that represents the unicast address used to communicate with this LANEndpoint. The MAC address is formatted as 12 hexadecimal digits (for example, \"010203040506\"), with each pair representing one of the six octets of the MAC address in canonical bit order according to RFC 2469.

- AliasAddresses is an array of strings that contain the other unicast addresses that may be used to communicate with this LANEndpoint.

- GroupAddresses is an array of strings that contain the set of multicast addresses that this LANEndpoint listens to.

- MaxIFieldRecv is a 16-bit unsigned integer that defines the length in bits of the largest information field that may be sent or received by this LANEndpoint.

This class defines no methods, but does define two relationships, BindsToLANEndpoint and InSegment. These two relationships are defined here.

The BindsToLANEndpoint *Association*

The BindsToLANEndpoint association is a subclass of the more generic BindsTo association, and is used to make the dependency between a LANEndpoint and a more generic ProtocolEndpoint that resides on a higher protocol layer on the same system explicit. Accordingly, the antecedent and dependent are restricted to instances of the LANEndpoint and ProtocolEndpoint classes, respectively. The multiplicity of this relationship remains at zero-or-more to zero-or-more.

The BindsToLANEndpoint association defines a single attribute, called FrameType. This is an enumerated 16-bit unsigned integer that defines the specific framing method for the upper layer ProtocolEndpoint that is bound to the LANEndpoint. The specific values are as follows:

Value	CIM Attribute Value and Description
0	Unknown
1	Ethernet
2	802.2
3	SNAP
4	Raw802.3 (This is only known to be used with the IPX protocol.)

The InSegment *Aggregation*

The InSegment aggregation is used to define a LANEndpoint as a member of a specific LANSegment. This is a subclass of the more generic InLogicalNetwork aggregation. In this aggregation, the aggregate is restricted to instances of the class LANSegment, and the part component is restricted to instances of the LANEndpoint. The multiplicity of this relationship, however, remains zero-or-one to zero-or-more.

FilterEntry

The FilterEntry class is a subclass of the LogicalElement class. It represents the basic ability of a network device to classify and filter traffic based on certain criteria, such as the source or destination IP address. Once traffic is identified, it can either be dropped or forwarded (with possibly further processing) to its destination. More importantly, a FilterEntry is the basic building block of FilterLists.

Note

An example of a FilterEntry is an *Access Control Entry*, or *ACE*, from Cisco's IOS. Note that there are different forms of this in Cisco's Internetwork Operating System, or IOS, depending on whether the ACE is meant to be part of a standard or extended Access Control List (ACL).

Figure 9.22 illustrates the `FilterEntry` class and its relationships.

Figure 9.22 Network Common Model excerpt: The `FilterEntry` and `FilterList` classes and their relationships.

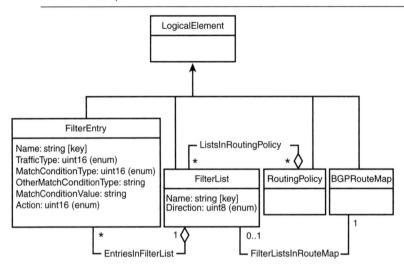

A `FilterEntry` is weak to the `ComputerSystem` (that is, the network device) that contains it. Therefore, the key attributes of the `ComputerSystem` must be propagated to the `FilterEntry` class. These are renamed as `SystemCreationClassName` and `SystemName`. These are combined with the `CreationClassName` and `Name` attributes to form the composite key of the `FilterEntry` class. In addition, the `FilterEntry` class defines the following attributes:

- `CreationClassName` is a free-form string that identifies the class that created this instance. This enables subclasses to be created that represent specific types of filter entries.

- `Name` is a free-form string, of up to 256 characters, that is inherited (from `ManagedSystemElement`) but overridden in this class to serve as its key.

- `TrafficType` is an enumerated 16-bit unsigned integer that defines the type of traffic that is being filtered. This is used to select among possible filtering rules that can be used in the `MatchCondition` attribute of this class. The current values defined are `Unknown`, `IP`, and `IPX`, having the values 0, 1, and 2, respectively.

- MatchConditionType is an enumerated 16-bit integer that defines one of a set of ways to filter traffic. Extensibility is built in through the standard mechanism of using the value 1 (that is, Other). If the value of this attribute is set to 1, then the specific type of filtering performed by this FilterEntry is defined in the OtherMatchConditionType attribute of this class.

The MOF description of this attribute is shown in Listing 9.7.

Listing 9.7   MOF definition for the MatchConditionType attribute.

```
[...
ValueMap { "1", "2", "3", "4", "5", "6", "7", "8", "9" },
Values {"Other", "Source Address and Mask", "Destination Address and Mask",
        "Source Port", "Source Port Range",
        "Destination Port", "Destination Port Range",
        "Protocol Type", "Protocol Type and Option" },
ModelCorrespondence { "FilterEntry.OtherMatchConditionType" } ]
uint16 MatchConditionType;
```

- OtherMatchConditionType is a free-form string that is used to supply the specific type of filtering for this FilterEntry if the value of the MatchConditionType attribute in this class is equal to 1 (for example, Other). This value should be NULL if the value of the MatchConditionType attribute is any value other than 1.

- MatchConditionValue is a free-form string that defines the value of the condition that filters the traffic. It corresponds to the condition specified in the MatchConditionType attribute. If, however, the value of the MatchConditionType attribute is 1, then it corresponds to the condition specified in the OtherMatchConditionType property.

- Action is an enumerated 16-bit integer that defines whether the action should be to forward or deny traffic meeting the match condition specified in this filter.

This class does not define any methods, but does define a single aggregation, EntriesInFilterList. This will be defined in the next section, where the FilterList class is described.

FilterList

The FilterList is a subclass of LogicalElement, and is an aggregation of a set of FilterEntries. This enables complex routing decisions to be defined by combining simpler FilterEntries that each perform specialized processing and filtering of traffic.

Figure 9.22 illustrates the FilterList class and its relationships.

A FilterList is also weak to the ComputerSystem (that is, the network device) that contains it. Therefore, the key attributes of the ComputerSystem must be propagated to the FilterList class. These are renamed as SystemCreationClassName and SystemName. These are combined with the CreationClassName and Name attributes to form the composite key of the FilterEntry class. These are the same attributes as those used in FilterList, and their descriptions are consequently the same. In addition, the FilterList class defines the following new attribute:

- Direction is an enumerated 16-bit unsigned integer that defines whether this FilterList is used for input, output, or both input and output filtering, having the values, 1, 2, and 3.

This class defined no methods. However, it does participate in three relationships. Two of these, the ListsInRoutingPolicy aggregation and the FilterListsInRouteMaps association, will be defined when the RoutingPolicy and BGPRouteMap classes are defined, respectively. The third, EntriesInFilterList, is defined here.

The EntriesInFilterList Aggregation

The EntriesInFilterList aggregation is derived from the more generic Component aggregation. It is used to define a set of FilterEntries that are aggregated by a particular FilterList.

Note

In Cisco IOS software, a FilterList corresponds to an Access Control List (ACL). FilterLists can represent both standard as well as extended forms of Cisco ACLs. They also provide the ability to represent protocol-specific ACLs, such as IP vs. IPX ACLs.

The multiplicity of this aggregation is one to zero-or-more. The cardinality of the aggregate, which is restricted to instances of the class FilterList, is defined to be exactly 1 so that FilterLists can be distinguished from each other. The cardinality of the part component, which is restricted to instances of the FilterEntry class, is zero-or-more. This reflects the fact that a FilterEntry can be defined without having any FilterEntries associated with it, or it can have as many FilterEntries associated with it as it needs. Note that the same FilterEntry can be used in multiple FilterLists.

FilterEntries are aggregated into a FilterList, and therefore the action that each FilterEntry has is often dependent on the order in which it is seen in the FilterList. Most ACLs, which are examples of FilterLists, filter the traffic by comparing it with each FilterEntry in succession. As soon as the traffic parameters being examined (for example, source IP address) match the traffic parameters contained in the FilterEntry, the processing stops. Therefore, the position of a given FilterEntry in the FilterList is critical.

Accordingly, this class also defines a single attribute, Sequence, that defines the position of this FilterEntry relative to all other FilterEntries that are contained in this FilterList.

RoutingPolicy

The RoutingPolicy class, which is a subclass of the LogicalElement class, is used to implement routing policies. A routing policy is defined as a set of FilterLists, along with other appropriate constructs, that function as an atomic unit.

One example is its use in BGP. Here, a RoutingPolicy can be used to change how traffic is filtered by changing values of various BGP attributes in a consistent manner.

Figure 9.23 illustrates the RoutingPolicy class and its relationships.

Figure 9.23   Network Common Model excerpt: the RoutingPolicy class and its relationships.

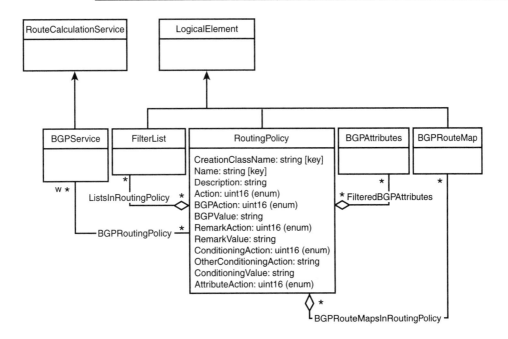

The RoutingPolicy class defines the following attributes:

- CreationClassName is part of the composite key of this class. It is a free-form string that identifies the class that created this instance. It is expected that the RoutingPolicy class will serve as the base class for subclasses that implement application-specific routing policies. The use of CreationClassName enables different instances of different subclasses of the RoutingPolicy class to be identified.

- Name is the other composite key of this class. Name is a free-form string, of up to 256 characters, that is inherited (from ManagedSystemElement) but overridden in this class to serve as its key.

- Description is a free-form string that provides a textual description of the routing policy.

- Action is an enumerated 16-bit unsigned integer that defines the type of action that will be performed if the traffic being filtered meets the match conditions of this filter policy. There are essentially four choices: forward the traffic unmodified, forward the traffic after either doing some alteration to its semantics (for example, modify one or more of the BGP attributes that it is carrying), forward the traffic for further processing that may result in subsequently modifying the traffic or its semantics, or prevent the traffic from being forwarded. These are listed in the MOF excerpt provided in Listing 9.8.

Listing 9.8 MOF definition for the Action attribute.

```
[...
ValueMap { "1", "2", "3", "4", "5", "6", "7", "8", "9" },
Values { "Accept As Is", "Accept With BGP Changes", "Accept and Remark Packet",
         "Accept With BGP and Remark Changes", "Accept With Other Actions",
         "Accept With BGP Changes and Other Actions",
         "Accept with Remark Changes and Other Actions",
         "Accept with BGP and Remark Changes and Other Actions",
         "Deny" } ]
uint16 Action;
```

- BGPAction is an enumerated 16-bit integer that defines one or more BGP attributes that should be used to modify this routing update. Listing 9.9 provides the applicable MOF excerpt to define the different BGP attributes that can be used for this purpose.

Listing 9.9   MOF definition for the `BGPAction` attribute.

```
[...
ValueMap { "1", "2", "3", "4", "5", "6", "7", "8", "9", "10" },
Values { "Origin", "AS_Path", "NEXT_HOP", "Multi_Exit_Disc", "Local_Pref",
"Atomic_Aggregate", "Aggregator", "Community", "Originator_ID", "Cluster_List" } ]
uint16 BGPAction;
```

- `BGPValue` is a free-form string that defines the value for the corresponding `BGPAction`.

- `RemarkAction` is an enumerated 16-bit integer that defines how to remark the traffic that has successfully matched the filter condition portion of this routing policy. Listing 9.10 provides the applicable MOF excerpt that describes the different types of remarking actions.

Listing 9.10   MOF definition for the `RemarkAction` attribute.

```
[...
ValueMap { "1", "2", "3", "4", "5", "6", "7" },
Values { "Change DSCP", "Change ToS", "Change 802.1Q Value", "Change CIR",
         "Change CBR", "Change ABR", "Change VBR" } ]
uint16 RemarkAction;
```

- `RemarkValue` is a free-form string that defines the value for the corresponding `RemarkAction`.

- `ConditioningAction` is an enumerated 16-bit unsigned integer that defines actions besides forwarding, remarking, or dropping, to be taken for this traffic. Listing 9.11 defines the different types of actions that can be assigned to this traffic.

Listing 9.11   MOF definition for the `ConditioningAction` attribute.

```
[...
ValueMap { "1", "2", "3", "4", "5", "6", "7" },
Values { "Other", "Input Flow Policing", "Output Flow Policing",
         "Input Aggregate Policing", "Output Aggregate Policing",
         "PoliceByMarkingDown", "PoliceByDroppingDown" } ]
uint16 ConditioningAction;
```

- `OtherConditioningAction` is a free-form string that may be used to define an application-specific type of conditioning for the traffic that is not described by one of the values of the `ConditioningAction` attribute. As usual, this is triggered if the value of the `ConditioningAction` attribute is 1. If the value of the `ConditioningAction` attribute is any other value, then the value of the `OtherConditioningAction` attribute should be set to NULL.

- `ConditioningValue` is a free-form string that defines the value for the corresponding `ConditioningAction`.

- `AttributeAction` is an enumerated 16-bit integer that controls whether BGP attribute values replace, get prepended, or get appended to the existing value of the corresponding attribute in the traffic being filtered. This can be used to affect routing decisions.

This class defines no methods, but does participate in four different relationships. These are the `ListsInRoutingPolicy`, `FilteredBGPAttributes`, and `BGPRouteMapsInRoutingPolicy` aggregations, along with the `BGPRoutingPolicy` association. The `ListsInRoutingPolicy` aggregation will be described here. The other three relationships will be described in the `BGPAttributes`, `BGPRouteMap`, and `BGPService` classes, respectively.

The `ListsInRoutingPolicy` Aggregation

The `ListsInRoutingPolicy` aggregation is a subclass of the `Component` aggregation. This aggregation is used to define a set of `FilterLists` that make up a particular `RoutingPolicy`.

The multiplicity of this relationship is zero-or-more to zero-or-more, since any `FilterList` can potentially be aggregated by any `RoutingPolicy`, and multiple `RoutingPolicies` can potentially use the same `FilterList`.

A 16-bit unsigned integer attribute, called `Sequence`, is also defined in this relationship. The purpose of this attribute is to define the position of this `FilterList` relative to all other `FilterLists` that are contained in this `RoutingPolicy`. It is a higher-level version of the `Sequence` attribute found in the `EntriesInFilterList` aggregation.

AdministrativeDistance

The `AdministrativeDistance` class is used to control path selection when the same route is learned by multiple means, each of which involves using a different protocol. The lower the distance, the higher the preference for that protocol. This table affects *all* routes. Therefore, it should not be used if what is desired is to fine-tune a particular routing decision, since if the administrative distance of a protocol is altered, it affects all routes that use that protocol.

Figure 9.24 illustrates the AdministrativeDistance class and its relationships.

Figure 9.24 Network Common Model excerpt: the AdministrativeDistance class and its relationships.

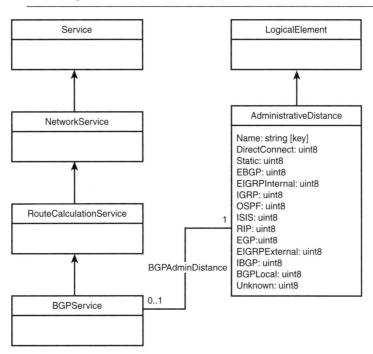

The AdministrativeDistance class defines the following attributes (note that all are unsigned 8-bit integers except for the first attribute, Name):

- Name is the key of this class. Name is a free-form string, of up to 256 characters, that is inherited (from ManagedSystemElement) but overridden in this class to serve as its key.

- DirectConnect defines the administrative distance for directly connected peers. It has a default value of 0.

- Static defines the administrative distance for statically connected peers. It has a default value of 1.

- EBGP defines the administrative distance for peers using EBGP. It has a default value of 20.

- EIGRPInternal defines the administrative distance for peers using internal EIGRP. It has a default value of 90.

- IGRP defines the administrative distance for peers using IGRP. It has a default value of 100.

- OSPF defines the administrative distance for peers using OSPF. It has a default value of 110."

- ISIS defines the administrative distance for peers using ISIS. It has a default value of 115.

- RIP defines the administrative distance for peers using RIP. It has a default value of 120.

- EGP defines the administrative distance for peers using EGP. It has a default value of 140.

- EIGRPExternal defines the administrative distance for peers using external EIGRP. It has a default value of 170.

- IBGP defines the administrative distance for peers using IBGP. It has a default value of 200.

- BGPLocal defines the administrative distance for peers using BGP locally. It has a default value of 200.

- Unknown defines the administrative distance for peers using an unknown protocol. It has a default value of 255.

This class does not define any methods. It participates in one relationship, the BGPAdminDistance association. This relationship will be defined in the description for the BGPService class.

The BGP Sub-Model

The BGP sub-model combines its own classes with those in the network infrastructural model (for example, those described in the sections "General-Purpose Networking Objects" and "Networking Protocol Objects") to model BGP. This model describes the operation of the BGP protocol, special configurations of routers running BGP (for example, peer groups, confederations, and clusters), and detailed manipulation of routing information through the use of BGP path attributes, filters, and route maps.

Note that confederations are described in the section "The Confederation Aggregation" in the "AutonomousSystem" section. The concept of autonomous systems are used by other entities than BGP, and it is more convenient to describe Confederations as part of autonomous systems.

The following sections describe the BGP sub-model in more detail.

BGPProtocolEndpoint

The BGPProtocolEndpoint class is a subclass of the ProtocolEndpoint class.

> ## Note
>
> Note that the BGPProtocolEndpoint class is *not* a subclass of the IPProtocolEndpoint class. This is because an IPProtocolEndpoint class may be instantiated *prior* to running BGP on that endpoint. If the BGPProtocolEndpoint class was a subclass of IPProtocolEndpoint, then we would have an unpleasant situation: if an IPProtocolEndpoint was instantiated first, and then it was decided that this endpoint should run BGP, then we would have to delete the instance representing the IPProtocolEndpoint and instantiate a new BGPProtocolEndpoint.
>
> This design instead allows the original IPProtocolEndpoint to remain, a new BGPProtocolEndpoint to be instantiated, and the two endpoints (the IPProtocolEndpoint and the BGPProtocolEndpoint) to be associated with each other through the EndpointIdentity association (described in the section "The EndpointIdentity Association" later).

This class is used to represent interfaces that are dedicated to running BGP, and adds attributes that are specific to running EBGP vs. IBGP. The difference between EBGP versus IBGP is twofold:

- How BGP attributes are carried and propagated,

- How each neighbor processes routing updates from its neighbor.

In particular, routers running EBGP must be physically connected. If there is an intermediate router between them, this is referred to as EBGP multihop, and the routers are said to be logically connected. These additional semantics require this subclass to be instantiated, in effect turning an IPProtocolEndpoint into a BGPProtocolEndpoint.

Figure 9.25 illustrates the BGPProtocolEndpoint class.

Figure 9.25 Network Common Model excerpt: the `BGPProtocolEndpoint` class and its relationships.

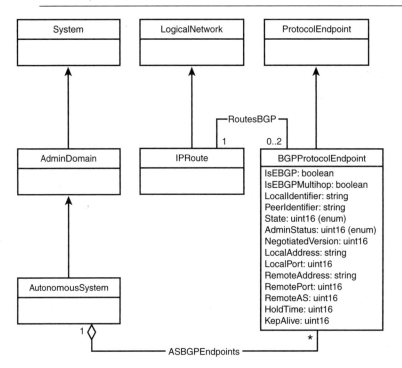

The `BGPProtocolEndpoint` class defines the following 14 attributes:

- `IsEBGP` is a Boolean attribute that, if `TRUE`, signifies that this `BGPProtocolEndpoint` is running the external version of BGP (`FALSE` means that this router is running the internal version of BGP).

- `IsEBGPMultihop` is a Boolean attribute that, if `TRUE`, means that this is a logical connection (for example, the router interfaces that are running BGP) are not directly connected. `FALSE` means that the router interfaces are directly connected.

- `LocalIdentifier` is a string attribute that contains the unique identifier of the local BGP router. This is often the router ID.

- `PeerIdentifier` is the unique identifier of the peer BGP router, which is also often its router ID.

- `State` is a 16-bit enumerated unsigned integer that defines the current connection state of the BGP Peer. It defines the following values: 1 ("Idle"), 2 ("Connect"), 3 ("Active"), 4 ("OpenSet"), 5 ("OpenConfirm"), and 6 ("Established").

- `AdminStatus` is a 16-bit enumerated unsigned integer that defines the desired state of the BGP connection. Values include 1 ("Start") and 2 ("Stop").

- `NegotiatedVersion` is a string attribute that defines the negotiated version of the BGP protocol that is running between the two peers.

- `LocalAddress` is a string atttribute that contains the local IP address of this router's BGP connection.

- `LocalPort` is a 16-bit unsigned integer that contains the local port number for the TCP connection of this router's BGP connection.

- `RemoteAddress` is a string attribute that contains the remote IP address of this router's BGP connection.

- `RemotePort` is a 16-bit unsigned integer that contains the remote port number for the TCP connection of this router's BGP connection.

- `RemoteAS` is a 16-bit unsigned integer that contains the remote AS number for this router's BGP connection.

- `HoldTime` is a 16-bit unsigned integer that defines the maximum amount of time in seconds that may elapse between the receipt of successive KEEPALIVE or UPDATE messages (please refer to the bgpPeerHoldTime variable of RFC1657).

- `KeepAlive` is a 16-bit unsigned integer that defines the time interval in seconds for the KEEPALIVE timer established with the peer (please refer to the bgpPeerKeepAlive variable of RFC1657).

This class defines no methods, but does define two relationships that are described here. These are the `RoutesBGP` association and the `ASBGPEndpoints` aggregation.

The `RoutesBGP` Association

The `RoutesBGP` association is a subclass of the `Dependency` association, and is used to define the two `BGPProtocolEndpoints` that serves as the source and destination addresses of a BGP route.

This association restricts its instances to the BGPIPRoute and BGPProtocolEndpoint classes. The cardinality of the BGPIPRoute instance is defined to be exactly one, and the cardinality of the BGPProtocolEndpoint instance is defined to be at most two. This enables a specific BGP route to be defined exactly in terms of its source and destination addresses.

The ASBGPEndpoints *Aggregation*

The ASBGPEndpoints aggregation is a subclass of the SystemComponent aggregation, and defines the different router interfaces that are running BGP in the AutonomousSystem. This is a collection of BGPProtocolEndpoints, not routers, that this AutonomousSystem can advertise as its entry and exit points. Accordingly, the aggregate is restricted to instances of the AutonomousSystem class, and the part components are restricted to instances of the BGPProtocolEndpoint class. The multiplicity of this class is defined as zero-or-one to zero-or-more, since it is an optional relationship, but a given BGPProtocolEndpoint cannot be a part of multiple AutonomousSystems.

The EndpointIdentity Association

The EndpointIdentity association, which is a subclass of the more general LogicalIdentity association, indicates that two ProtocolEndpoints represent different aspects of the same underlying object. In addition to the BGP example described earlier, consider the following example. In the DHCP sub-model that will be released in CIM 2.3, we need to define the concept of a DHCP allocated address. Now, DHCP addresses are IP addresses. It would, however, be incorrect to add DHCP-specific properties to an IP address, because many IP addresses are statically assigned (instead of dynamically assigned using DHCP). This association enables a particular endpoint to have both "IP" as well as "DHCP" attributes.

The EndpointIdentity association has a multiplicity of zero-or-more to zero-or-more. Both ends of this relationship are restricted to instances of the ProtocolEndpoint class.

BGPIPRoute

The BGPIPRoute class is a subclass of the IPRoute class, and is used to associate source and destination addresses to a route carrying BGP information. The source and destination addresses may be either individual endpoints or IP subnets.

Figure 9.26 illustrates the BGPIPRoute class.

Figure 9.26   Network Common Model excerpt: the `BGPIPRoute` class and its relationships.

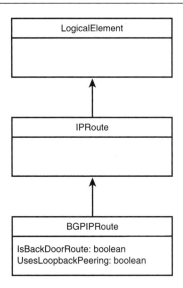

The `BGPIPRoute` defines two attributes that can be used to tune BGP. The `IsBackDoorRoute` attribute is a Boolean attribute that, if TRUE, defines this route to be a "back door" route. *Back door routes* are used to alter the priority that the route is given when installed into the routing table. This attribute, if TRUE, enables a route learned by an IGP to have a lower administrative distance than a similar route learned by EBGP and be installed instead.

The `UsesLoopbackPeering` attribute is another Boolean attribute that, if TRUE, defines this route to use a loopback interface. Loopback interfaces are used to eliminate dependencies on using specific physical interfaces. The loopback interface instead instructs the router to use any available interface.

BGPService

The `BGPService` class is a subclass of the `RouteCalculationService` class, and is used to represent the basic operation of BGP from a routing point of view. Note that most of these attributes are mapped directly to corresponding attributes from RFC 1657, or have been influenced from other BGP RFCs.

Figure 9.27 illustrates the `BGPService` class and its relationships.

Figure 9.27   Network Common Model excerpt: the `BGPService` class and its relationships.

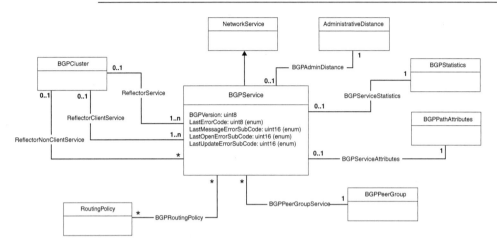

The `BGPService` class defines the following attributes:

- `BGPVersion` is an 8-bit unsigned integer that contains the version of the BGP protocol that this router is using. This is part of the BGP peer negotiation process.

- `LastErrorCode` is a 16-bit unsigned integer that defines the type of the notification message that is to be sent when BGP detects an error. This message contains an error code, an error subcode, and error data. The six types of errors defined in BGP4 are provided in Listing 9.12, which shows the MOF excerpt for the `LastErrorCode` attribute.

Listing 9.12   MOF definition for the `LastErrorCode` attribute.

```
[...
ValueMap { "1", "2", "3", "4", "5", "6" },
Values { "Message Header Error", "OPEN Message Error",
         "UPDATE Message Error", "Hold Timer Expired",
         "Finite State Machine Error", "Cease" } ]
uint16 LastErrorCode;
```

- LastMessageErrorSubCode is a 16-bit unsigned integer that defines the BGP error sub-code for HEADER message errors if the value of the LastErrorCode attribute of this instance is equal to 1 (Message Header Error). If the LastErrorCode attribute is equal to any other value, then this attribute should be set to NULL. The specific message value codes are defined in Listing 9.13.

Listing 9.13   MOF definition for the LastMessageErrorSubCode attribute.

```
[...
ValueMap { "1", "2", "3" },
Values { "Connection Not Synchronized", "Bad Message Length", "Bad Message Type" },
ModelCorrespondence {"BGPService.ErrorCode"} ]
uint16 LastMessageErrorSubCode;
```

- LastOpenErrorSubCode is a 16-bit unsigned integer that defines the BGP error subcode for OPEN message errors if the value of the LastErrorCode attribute of this instance is equal to 2 (OPEN Message Error). If the LastErrorCode attribute is equal to any other value, then this attribute should be set to NULL. The specific message value codes are defined in Listing 9.14.

Listing 9.14   MOF definition for the LastOpenErrorSubCode attribute.

```
[...
ValueMap { "1", "2", "3", "4", "5", "6" },
Values { "Unsupported Version Number", "Bad Peer AS", "Bad BGP Identifier",
         "Unsupported Optional Parameter", "Authentication Failure",
"Unacceptable Hold Time"}, ModelCorrespondence {"BGPService.ErrorCode"} ]
uint16 LastOpenErrorSubCode;
```

- LastUpdateErrorSubCode is a 16-bit unsigned integer that defines the BGP error subcode for UPDATE message errors if the value of the LastErrorCode attribute of this instance is equal to 3 (UPDATE Message Error). If the LastErrorCode attribute is equal to any other value, then this attribute should be set to NULL. The specific message value codes are defined in Listing 9.15.

Listing 9.15   MOF definition for the LastUpdateErrorSubCode attribute.

```
[...
ValueMap { "1", "2", "3", "4", "5", "6", "7", "8", "9", "10", "11" },
Values { "Malformed Attribute List", "Unrecognized Well-Known Attribute",
         "Missing Well-Known Attribute", "Attribute Flags Error",
         "Attribute Length Error", "Invalid Origin Attribute", "AS Routing
         Loop", "Invalid NEXT_HOP Attribute",
```

continues

Listing 9.15   Continued

```
        "Optional Attribute Error", "Invalid Network Field",
        "Malformed AS_path" },
ModelCorrespondence {"BGPService.ErrorCode"} ]
uint16 LastUpdateErrorSubCode;
```

The `BGPService` class defines no methods. However, it does participate in eight relationships. Two of these, `BGPAdminDistance` and `BGPRoutingPolicy`, will be discussed in this section. Of the remaining six relationships, three of them (`ReflectorService`, `ReflectorClientService`, and `ReflectorNonClientService`) will be discussed when the `BGPCluster` class is discussed. The `BGPServiceStatistics` and the `BGPServiceAttributes` associations will be described when the `BGPStatistics` and the `BGPPathAttributes` classes, respectively, are described. The final relationship, `BGPPeerGroupService`, will be discussed when `BGPPeerGroups` are described.

The `BGPAdminDistance` Association

The `BGPAdminDistance` association is a specialization of the `Dependency` association, and defines the dependency realized in calculating routing decisions using administrative distances. Specifically, it associates an instance of the `BGPService` class with the administrative distances (as defined in the `AdministrativeDistance` class instance) that are used to control the (BGP) routing decisions that it makes. This enables centralized control over the definition of administrative distances, which is critical because this changes the preference for routing *all* traffic using that protocol.

The antecedent is restricted to instances of the `BGPService` class, and the dependent is restricted to instances of the `AdministrativeDistance` class.

The multiplicity of this relationship is zero-or-more to one. A given `BGPService` class does not have to use values from the `AdministrativeDistance` class (they could be supplied from somewhere else) but, if it does, then it can use exactly one instance. However, the same `AdministrativeDistance` instance could be used by many different instances of the `BGPService` class.

The `BGPRoutingPolicy` Association

The `BGPRoutingPolicy` association is a specialization of the `Dependency` association, and defines the relationship between a `BGPService` and the `RoutingPolicy` that controls it.

The antecedent is restricted to instances of the RoutingPolicy class, while the dependent is restricted to instances of the BGPService class. The multiplicity of this relationship is zero-or-more to zero-or-more, since many routing policies can be used to control individual aspects of the overall BGP routing service, and many different instances of the BGPService class can use the same RoutingPolicy.

BGPAttributes

The BGPAttributes class is a subclass of the LogicalElement class, and is used to define the set of BGP attributes that are supported for a given BGP service. The purpose of this class is *not* to model per-path information, but rather to define the set of BGP attributes that can be used in an AutonomousSystem. This will enable any filtering that is done which manipulates these attributes to be done in a common way. Per-path BGP information is modeled using the BGPPathAttributes class.

Figure 9.28 illustrates the BGPAttributes class and its relationships.

Figure 9.28   Network Common Model excerpt: the BGPAttributes class and its relationships.

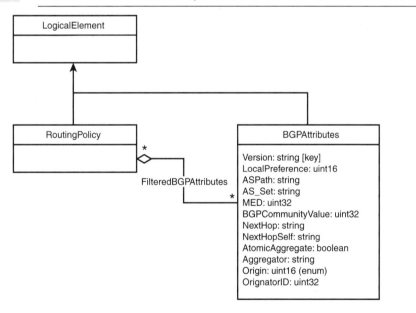

The BGPAttributes class defines the following attributes:

- Version is the key of this class. It is a free-form string, and defines the version of the BGP protocol that is being used.

- LocalPreference is a 16-bit unsigned integer that defines the priority, or preference, of a route. This can be used by an AS to define its preferred outbound route. When there are multiple routes for the same destination, this attribute instructs BGP to choose a preferred route by comparing the value for this attribute for each route and choosing the route with the highest LocalPreference value. In fact, this attribute is at the highest level of the decision process. If there are multiple routes to the same destination, then the route with the highest LocalPreference value will be chosen, even if other routes have shorter path lengths.

- AS_Path is a free-form string that defines the set of AS numbers through which routing information carried in this UPDATE message has passed, in the sequence that they were visited. Users can manipulate which routes are chosen by prepending one or more instances of the AS number of their AutonomousSystem to the AS_Path. This makes the overall path length longer, and if all other things being equal, BGP will choose the route with the shortest path length.

- AS_Set is a free-form string that contains an unordered set of all attributes carried in specific routes so that this information will not lost when it is aggregated.

- NextHop is a free-form string that defines the IP address of the border router that either announced the route, or from which the route was learned.

- NextHopSelf is a proprietary Cisco parameter that can be used to ensure that the next hop is reachable from within the AS. It is included because of the frequency of use of this parameter in the Internet.

- MED, or MultiExitDiscriminator, is a 32-bit unsigned integer that is used on external (for example, inter-AS) links. It is used when an AS has multiple entry points to tell other ASs which is the preferred entry point into this AS. Lower MED values have preference.

- BGPCommunityValue is a 32-bit unsigned integer that defines a group of destinations that all share a similar property. Communities are not restricted to a single network or even AS, and can span multiple ASs. This attribute is used to simplify routing policies by basing policies on a logical value, as opposed to an IP address or an AS number. Some community values are reserved for global Internet use, and others can be defined by Service Providers as they see fit.

Routers can have more than one community attribute, and can also add or modify community values before forwarding them to other peers. This enables a router to base its routing decisions on one or more logical parameters.

- `AtomicAggregate` is a Boolean attribute that, if `TRUE`, means that information loss occurred because of route aggregation. This is because the aggregate is formed from different sources that have different attributes. For example, a less-specific route could have been selected instead of a more specific one.

- `Aggregator` is a free-form string that identifies the AS number and IP address of the router that has generated an aggregate.

- `Origin` is a free-form string that is generated by the AS that originates the routing message. There are three types of origins - `IGP`, `EGP`, and `INCOMPLETE`. These correspond to whether the information was learned internally in the AS, externally via an `EGP`, or by some other means. BGP prefers the path with the lowest `ORIGIN` type, where `IGP` is preferred over `EGP`, and `EGP` is preferred over `INCOMPLETE`.

- `OriginatorID` is a free-form string that contains the router ID for the `ORIGIN` attribute.

This class defines no methods, but it does participate in one relationship, `FilteredBGPAttributes`. This aggregation is described here.

The `FilteredBGPAttributes` Aggregation

The `FilteredBGPAttributes` aggregation is a subclass of the `Component` aggregation, and is used to define the set of BGP Attributes that are used by a particular `RoutingPolicy`. This enables different routing policies of different ASs to agree on the attributes that they will use.

The multiplicity of this aggregation is zero-or-more to zero-or-more. The aggregate is restricted to instances of the `RoutingPolicy` class, and the part component is restricted to instances of the `BGPAttributes` class.

BGPPathAttributes

The `BGPPathAttributes` class is used to provide per-path BGP information. This class represents the current values of various BGP parameters that are used by the `BGPService` to communicate routing information. The attributes in this class map to the corresponding BGP4 MIB variables in RFC 1657, and the class itself behaves much like the `bgp4PathAttrTable` in that RFC.

The purpose of that table is to contain path attributes received from all BGP4 peers. The format of the table is one entry per path to a network.

Figure 9.29 illustrates the `BGPPathAttributes` class and its relationships.

Figure 9.29   Network Common Model excerpt: the `BGPPathAttributes` class and its relationships.

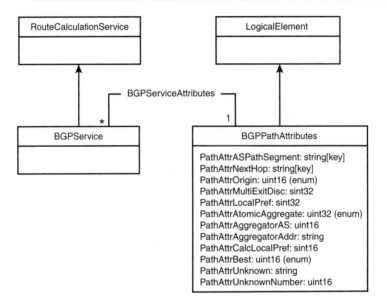

The `BGPPathAttributes` class defines the following attributes:

- `PathAttrASPathSegment` is a string attribute that contains one or more AS numbers, represented as either an `AS_SET` or an `AS_SEQUENCE`. An `AS_SET` is an unordered set of AS numbers that lists all ASs (for example, the entire path) that an `UPDATE` message has traversed. An `AS_SEQUENCE` is an ordered set of AS numbers that lists the path that an `UPDATE` message has traversed.

- `PathAttrOrigin` is an enumerated 16-bit unsigned integer that defines the ultimate origin of the path information. There are three possible values:

Value	CIM Attribute Value and Description
`IGP`, meaning that the origin of the route is interior to the AS that this router is in	
`EGP`, meaning that the origin of the route is external to the AS that this router is in	
`INCOMPLETE`, meaning that the origin of this route cannot be determined	

This attribute is mapped to the `bgp4PathAttrASPathSegment` MIB variable, which is actually an encoded `OctetString`. Its length is defined as a minimum of 2 and a maximum of 256 octets. One octet is reserved for the type of path information that is being stored (for example, is this data an `AS_SET` or an `AS_SEQUENCE`), and another octet is reserved to store the number of AS numbers in the path. This leaves up to 254 octets to represent AS numbers that are in the path. Note that the AS numbers are themselves encoded as 2 bytes according to the following algorithm:

```
first-byte-of-pair = ASNumber / 256
second-byte-of-pair = ASNumber & 255
```

- `PathAttrMultiExitDisc` is a 32-bit signed integer that is used to discriminate between multiple adjacent `AutonomousSystems`. A value of -1 indicates the absence of this attribute. The range of this attribute is defined to be -1 to 2,147,483,647.

- `PathAttrLocalPref` is a 32-bit signed integer that defines the originating BGP4 speaker's degree of preference for an advertised route. A value of -1 indicates the absence of this attribute. The range of this attribute is defined to be -1 to 2,147,483,647.

- `PathAttrAtomicAggregate` is an enumerated 32-bit unsigned integer that is set as an indication that information loss was experienced as a result of route aggregation. Put another way, it defines whether or not the local system has selected a less specific route without selecting a more specific route. There are two values, 1 and 2, indicating that a less specific route has not and has been selected, respectively. This is a 32-bit integer to correspond to the IETF MIB.

- `PathAttrAggregatorAS` is a 16-bit unsigned integer that corresponds to the `Aggregator` attribute. It is used to specify the AS number and the last BGP4 speaker that generated an aggregated route. A value of `0` indicates the absence of this attribute. The range of this attribute is defined to be 0 to 65,535.

- `PathAttrAggregatorAddr` is the IP address of the last BGP4 speaker that performed route aggregation. A value of `0.0.0.0` indicates the absence of this attribute.

- `PathAttrCalcLocalPref` is a 16-bit signed integer that defines the degree of preference calculated by the receiving BGP4 speaker for an advertised route. A value of -1 indicates the absence of this attribute. The range of this attribute is defined to be -1 to 2,147,483,647.

- `PathAttrBest` is an enumerated 16-bit unsigned integer that is an indication of whether or not this route was chosen as the best BGP4 route. There are two possible values, 1 (`FALSE`) and 2 (`TRUE`). This is a 16-bit unsigned integer instead of a Boolean in order to be compatible with the `bgp4PathAttrBest` MIB variable in RFC 1657.

- PathAttrUnknown is an array of strings that contains one or more path attributes not understood by this BGP4 speaker. The MIB variable is an OctetString, and contains a 1-octet length field and up to 255 additional octets of data. The length is placed in a separate attribute of this class, PathAttrUnknownNumber. The ModelCorrespondence qualifier is used to relate this attribute to the PathAttrUnknownNumber attribute.

- PathAttrUnknownNumber is a 16-bit unsigned integer that defines the number of unknown attributes that are present in the PathAttrUnknown attribute. The ModelCorrespondence qualifier is used to relate this attribute to the PathAttrUnknown attribute.

This class defines no methods, but does define a single relationship, the BGPServiceAttributes aggregation. This is described here.

The BGPServiceAttributes Aggregation

The BGPServiceAttributes aggregation is a specialization of the Component aggregation, and defines the set of BGP attributes that are transmitted in per-path UPDATE messages.

The aggregate and part component are restricted to instances of the BGPService and BGPPathAttributes classes, respectively. The multiplicity of this relationship is zero-or-one to one. A BGP service doesn't have to transmit BGP attributes but, if it does, it is related to exactly one instance of the BGPPathAttributes class. This is because the per-path information is specific to each BGPService instance, and each BGPService instance can transmit a different set of BGP attributes. This reflects the particular role that a given router plays in the AS.

BGPCluster

The BGPCluster class is subclassed from the CollectionOfMSEs class. The purpose of this class is to model BGP clusters, which are one way to reduce the full meshing requirement of BGP speakers in an autonomous system. The full meshing requirement is, of course, is a potentially serious problem, because it can lead to a huge number of TCP connections per router.

What Is a BGP Cluster?

A *BGP cluster* is a special configuration of routers that work together that reduces the full meshing requirement of BGP speakers. This is explained more fully in RFC 1966, but a brief introduction is provided here so that the BGPCluster class and its relationships can be more easily understood.

BGP clusters use the idea of a route reflector. This is a specially configured router that acts as a concentration point for other routers, called *clients*. The clients peer with the route reflector, and the route reflector passes (that is, reflects) new information to its clients. The set of clients and route reflectors form a (BGP) cluster. Non-clients are routers that peer with the route reflector.

To see how this works, first look at Figure 9.30. This illustrates a set of three routers, named Eeyore, Pooh, and Tigger. Pooh is physically connected to Eeyore and Tigger, but Eeyore and Tigger are not physically connected. Since they are all BGP speakers, they run a full IBGP mesh between them. If Eeyore receives a routing update, then it must pass the update to both Pooh and Tigger, who will then forward the information to their respective external peers.

Figure 9.30   Internal AS peering requirements without a route reflector.

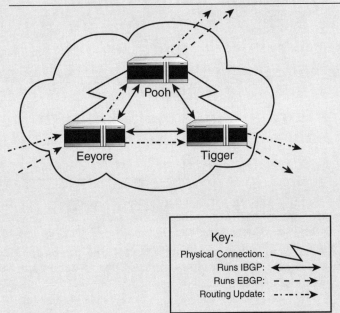

Now look at Figure 9.31. Here, we've configured router Pooh as a route reflector. Now, any updates received from Eeyore or Tigger will automatically be reflected (that is, passed on) to Tigger and Pooh, respectively. Eeyore and Tigger are called *clients of the route reflector*. Being clients, they no longer have to run a full IBGP mesh.

continues

Figure 9.31   Internal AS peering requirements using a route reflector.

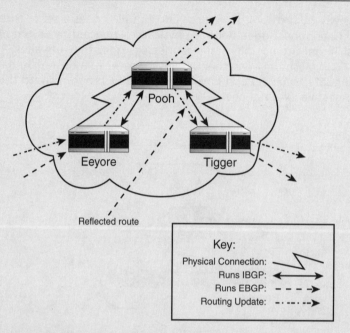

Figure 9.32 shows a BGP cluster, with a route reflector, two clients of the route reflector, and two non-clients of the route reflector. Note that the non-clients must be fully meshed with the router reflector and each other.

Finally, an AS can have more than one route reflector, and there can be more than one route reflector in a cluster. Of course, there can also be more than one cluster in an AS.

Figure 9.32 A route reflector, with its clients and non-clients.

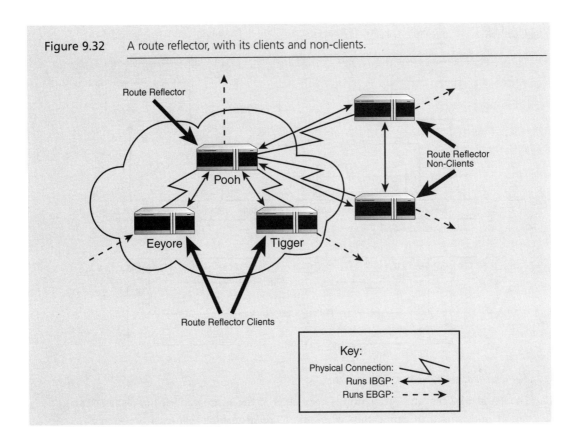

Figure 9.33 illustrates the `BGPCluster` class and its relationships.

The `BGPCluster` class defines a single attribute, `ClusterID`. This attribute is a 32-bit unsigned integer, and serves as the key for this class. It represents a 4-byte cluster ID that allows each route reflector in a cluster to be uniquely identified. In addition, this enables route reflectors to recognize updates from other route reflectors in the same cluster.

This class defines no methods, but participates in five relationships. Two of these, `RoutersInCluster` and `BGPClustersInAS`, are aggregations. The other three, `ReflectorService`, `ReflectorClientService`, and `ReflectorNonClientService`, are all associations. These five relationships are described here.

Figure 9.33 Network Common Model excerpt: the `BGPCluster` class and its relationships.

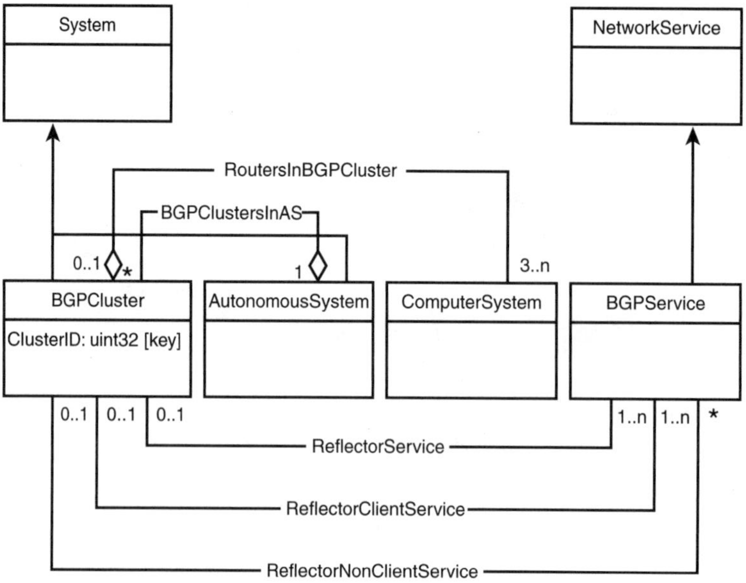

The `RoutersInBGPCluster` *Aggregation*

The `RoutersInCluster` aggregation is a subclass of the more generic `CollectedMSEs` aggregation, and is used to define the "whole-part" relationships that exist between a `BGPCluster` and the `ComputerSystems` (that is, the routers) that it contains. At least three routers are required to form a cluster - a reflector and two clients.

This aggregation also has the additional semantics of having the routers that form a cluster share common configuration information, along with being commonly administered.

The aggregate (that is, the "collection") is restricted to instances of the `BGPCluster` class. Its cardinality is defined as zero-or-one. The part component (that is, the "member") is restricted to instances of the `ComputerSystem` class. Its cardinality is three-or-more. Thus, the overall multiplicity of this aggregation is zero-or-one to three-or-more. This means that this is an optional relationship but, if it is instantiated, then at least three `ComputerSystems` must be associated with the `BGPCluster`.

The BGPClustersInAS *Aggregation*

The BGPClustersInAS aggregation establishes whole-part relationships between an AutonomousSystem and the BGPClusters that it contains. In addition, this aggregation provides the added semantics of applying the same configuration information and administration procedures to the clusters, since they are all part of the same AutonomousSystem.

Note that this aggregation is not derived from the CollectedMSEs aggregation, because the aggregate is an AutonomousSystem, not a CollectionOfMSEs. In addition, the part component is restricted to instances of the BGPCluster class. The multiplicity of this relationship is exactly one on the AutonomousSystem side and zero-or-more on the BGPCluster side. This is because the same BGPCluster cannot belong to more than one AutonomousSystem, but an AutonomousSystem can contain many BGPClusters.

The ReflectorService *Aggregation*

The ReflectorService association is a top-level association that will serve as the base class for defining BGP routing policies for the reflector of this Cluster. No attributes are provided because they are a function of the routing policies employed, as well as the way that the BGPCluster will be administered.

The multiplicity of this association is zero-or-one to one-or-more, with the antecedent and dependent restricted to instances of the BGPCluster and BGPService classes, respectively. This association is optional (hence the "zero" in the cardinality of the antecedent) but, if it is instantiated, then at least one BGPService must be associated. Multiple BGPServices can be used to represent different peering relationships with the reflector of this BGPCluster.

The ReflectorClientService *Aggregation*

The ReflectorClientService association is a top-level association that will serve as the base class for defining BGP routing policies for clients of the reflector of this Cluster. No attributes are provided because they are a function of the routing policies employed, as well as the way that the BGPCluster will be administered.

The multiplicity of this association is zero-or-one to one-or-more, with the antecedent and dependent restricted to instances of the BGPCluster and BGPService classes, respectively. This association is optional (hence the "zero" in the cardinality of the antecedent) but, if it is instantiated, then at least one BGPService must be associated. Multiple BGPServices can be used to represent different peering relationships with the clients of the reflector of this BGPCluster.

The `ReflectorNonClientService` *Aggregation*

The `ReflectorNonClientService` association is a top-level association that will serve as the base class for defining BGP routing policies for the reflector of this `Cluster`. No attributes are provided because they are a function of the routing policies employed, as well as the way that the `BGPCluster` will be administered.

The multiplicity of this association is zero-or-one to zero-or-more, with the antecedent and dependent restricted to instances of the `BGPCluster` and `BGPService` classes, respectively. This association is optional (hence the "zero" in the cardinality of the antecedent) but, if it is instantiated, then zero or more `BGPServices` may be associated, since `BGPClusters` do not have to have non-clients of the reflector. However, if they do, then multiple `BGPServices` can be used to represent different peering relationships with the non-clients of the reflector of this `BGPCluster`.

BGPPeerGroup

A `BGPPeerGroup` is a subclass of `LogicalElement`, and is used to represent a set of BGP neighbors that share the same update policies. This enables an administrator to assign policies to the peer group, instead of having to assign the same routing policy to each individual router. This in turn enables the routers in the peer group to optimize BGP UPDATE messages.

> ## Note
> Peer groups are used to simplify administration, not restrict it. Routers that have certain special routing requirements can still be a member of a peer group; these special requirements are simply added to the policies defined by the peer group.

Since BGP peer groups offer route optimization, certain restrictions apply to their configuration. For example, all EBGP peer group members should belong to the same IP subnet. However, this is beyond the scope of this book.

Figure 9.34 illustrates the BGPPeerGroup class and its relationships.

Figure 9.34   Network Common Model excerpt: the BGPPeerGroup class and its relationships.

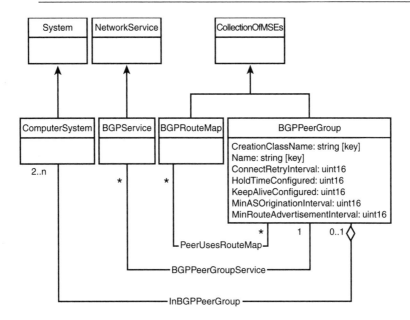

The BGPPeerGroup class defines the following attributes:

- CreationClassName is one of the two attributes that form the composite key of this class. It is a free-form string that identifies the class that created this instance.

- Name is the other attribute that forms the composite key of this class. Name is a string, of up to 256 characters, that is inherited from LogicalElement but overridden in this class to serve as its key attribute.

- ConnectRetryInterval is a 32-bit unsigned integer that defines the time interval, in seconds, for the connect-retry timer of the router (see RFC 1771 for a description of the use of this and other timers used in BGP).

- HoldTimeConfigured is a 16-bit unsigned integer that defines the time interval in seconds for the hold time configured for this BGP speaker with a peer. This attribute is used as part of the negotiation process to establish a peering relationship.

- KeepAliveConfigured is a 16-bit unsigned integer that defines the time interval in seconds for the keep-alive timer configured for this BGP speaker with a peer. This attribute is used as part of the negotiation process to establish a peering relationship.

- MinASOriginationInterval is a 16-bit unsigned integer that defines the time interval in seconds for the MinASOriginationInterval timer. This attribute is used as part of the negotiation process to establish a peering relationship.

- MinRouteAdvertisementInterval is a 16-bit unsigned integer that defines the time interval in seconds for the MinRouteAdvertisementInterval timer. This attribute is used as part of the negotiation process to establish a peering relationship.

This class does not define any methods, but does define three relationships. The InBGPPeerGroup aggregation and the BGPPeerGroupService association are defined here; the BGPPeerUsesRouteMap association will be defined when the BGPRouteMap class is defined later in this chapter.

The InBGPPeerGroup *Aggregation*

The InBGPPeerGroup aggregation is a subclass of the more generic Component aggregation, and defines the specific routers (that is, ComputerSystems) that participate in a PeerGroup.

The aggregate is restricted to instances of the BGPPeerGroup class, and has a cardinality of zero-or-one. This means that this relationship is not required, but if it is instantiated, then it identifies the specific BGPPeerGroup that the BGPRouteMaps are aggregated by.

The part component is restricted to instances of the ComputerSystem class (that is, a router). There must be at least two routers to form a BGP peer group, so the cardinality of this side of the relationship is two-or-more. Thus, the overall multiplicity of this relationship is zero-or-one to two-or-more.

In addition, this aggregation defines a number of attributes that are needed to define the policies in the peer group. These are mapped from RFC 1657, and are as follows:

- LocalIdentifier is a string that contains the unique identifier of the local BGP router.

- PeerIdentifier is a string that contains the unique identifier of the peer BGP router.

- State is an enumerated 16-bit unsigned integer that defines the current connection state of the BGP peer. The values of this attribute reflect the six states of the BGP Finite State Machine, and are:

Value	CIM Attribute Value
1	Idle
2	Connect
3	Active
4	OpenSet
5	OpenConfirm
6	Established

- AdminStatus is a 16-bit unsigned integer that defines the desired state of the BGP connection. The value of this attribute is either 1 (Stop) or 2 (Start).

- NegotiatedVersion is a string that defines the negotiated version of BGP (for example, BGP4) that will be used between the two peers.

- LocalAddress is a string that contains the local IP address of this router's BGP connection.

- LocalPort is a 16-bit unsigned integer that contains the local port number for the TCP connection of this router's BGP connection.

- RemoteAddress is a string that contains the IP address of this router's peer.

- RemotePort is a 16-bit unsigned integer that contains the remote port number for the TCP connection of this router's BGP connection.

- RemoteAS is a 16-bit unsigned integer that contains the remote AS number for this router's BGP connection.

- HoldTime is a 16-bit unsigned integer that defines the maximum amount of time in seconds that may elapse between the receipt of successive KEEPALIVE or UPDATE messages.

- KeepAlive is a 16-bit unsigned integer that defines the time interval in seconds for the keep-alive timer established with the peer.

The BGPPeerGroupService Association

The BGPPeerGroupService association is a subclass of the Dependency association, and defines the relationship between a BGPService and the BGPPeerGroup that hosts it.

The antecedent and dependent are restricted to instances of the BGPPeerGroup and BGPService classes, respectively. The multiplicity of this relationship is one to zero-or-more. This means that this relationship is optional. However, if it is instantiated, then a single BGPPeerGroup can provide zero or more BGP services within the routers that make up the peer group as well as to other routers that are outside of this peer group.

BGPStatistics

The BGPStatistics class is a subclass of the ServiceStatisticalInformation class, and contains statistical information for BGPPeerGroup sessions. It contains a number of attributes, all of which correspond to statistics-oriented MIB variables from RFC 1657. They are defined as follows:

- InUpdates is a 32-bit unsigned integer that contains the number of BGP UPDATE messages received on this router's BGP connection. This is a 32-bit counter.

- OutUpdates is a 32-bit unsigned integer that contains the number of BGP UPDATE messages transmitted on this router's BGP connection. This is a 32-bit counter.

- InTotalMessages is a 32-bit unsigned integer that contains the total number of BGP messages received on this router's BGP connection. This is a 32-bit counter.

- OutTotalMessages is a 32-bit unsigned integer that contains the total number of BGP messages transmitted on this router's BGP connection. This is a 32-bit counter.

- LastError is an array of 32-bit unsigned integers that contains the last error code and error subcode for this router's BGP connection. If no error has occurred, then each integer in the array is zero.

- FsmEstablishedTransitions is a 32-bit unsigned integer that contains the total number of times that the BGP Finite State Machine has transitioned into the established state for this router's BGP connection. This is a 32-bit counter.

- FsmEstablishedTime is a 32-bit unsigned integer that indicates how long, in seconds, this peer has been in the established state, or how long since this peer was last in the established state. It is set to zero when a new peer is configured or when the router is booted. This has the semantics of a 32-bit gauge.

- InUpdateElapsedTime is a 16-bit unsigned integer that defines the time in seconds since the last BGP UPDATE message was received from the peer. This has the semantics of a 32-bit gauge.

This class defines no methods, but does define a single association, BGPServiceStatistics, which is defined here.

The BGPServiceStatistics Association

The BGPServiceStatistics association is a subclass of the ServiceStatistics association, and is used to define statistics collected for a BGP specific session. The statistics collected can be for an individual router, a peer group, a cluster, or a confederation.

The antecedent and dependent are restricted to instances of the BGPService and BGPStatistics classes, respectively. The cardinality of the BGPService class is zero-or-one, meaning that statistics do not have to be collected for it but, if they are, then the corresponding statistics are for a particular BGPService object. The cardinality of the BGPStatistics object is zero-or-more, since a history of different statistical data gathered over a specific time interval may need to be gathered.

BGPRouteMap

The BGPRouteMap class is a subclass of the LogicalElement class, and is used to represent a route map. This is a common way to control and modify routing information, as well as to define when a route should be redistributed between routing domains. Route maps are placed in router configuration files, and several instances of the same route map may be used to implement different actions. Route maps may use FilterLists for more sophisticated processing if needed.

What is a Route Map?

A *route map* is very similar to an access list. The difference is that a route map can specify how a packet that is matched is changed in addition to permitting or denying the forwarding of packets.

A route map has a name, so that another process may invoke it. A route map has a match condition, a set action, a permit or deny action, and a sequence number. If the condition is matched, then any set actions are executed. After all set actions have been executed, the permit or deny action is executed. The sequence number enables multiple instances of the same route map to be used.

Figure 9.35 illustrates the BGPRouteMap class and its relationships.

The BGPRouteMap class defines the following attributes:

- CreationClassName is one of the two attributes that form the composite key of this class. It is a free-form string that identifies the class that created this instance.

- Name is the other attribute that forms the composite key of this class. Name is a free-form string, of up to 256 characters, that is inherited from its parent (LogicalElement) but overridden in this class to form its key.

- Direction is an enumerated 16-bit unsigned integer that defines whether this RouteMap is used for input (1), output (2), or both input and output processing (3).

- Action is an enumerated 16-bit unsigned integer that defines whether the traffic meeting the match condition specified in this RouteMap should be forwarded (1) or denied (2).

- `MatchConditionType` is an enumerated 16-bit integer that specifies the criteria that must be matched in order for the corresponding `MatchAction` to take effect. The matching of the criteria may be specified by using a `FilterList`. It uses the standard mechanism of defining the value of 1 (that is, `Other`) as another attribute that can contain application-specific match conditions.

Figure 9.35   Network Common Model excerpt: the `BGPRouteMap` class and its relationships.

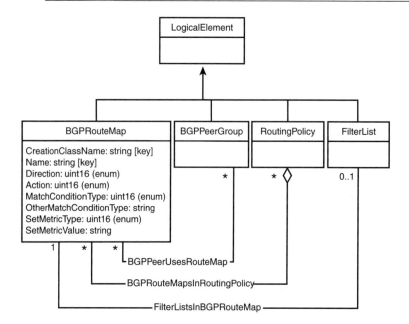

Listing 9.16 lists the different types of conditions that are predefined.

Listing 9.16   MOF definition for the `MatchConditionType` attribute.

```
[...
ValueMap { "1", "2", "3", "4", "5", "6", "7", "8", "9" },
Values {"Other", "Source Address and Mask", "Destination Address and Mask",
        "Source Port", "Source Port Range", "Destination Port", "Destination
        Port Range", "Protocol Type", "Protocol Type and Option" },
ModelCorrespondence { "RouteMap.OtherMatchConditionType" } ]
uint16 MatchConditionType;
```

- `OtherMatchConditionType` is a free-form string that contains an application-specific match condition that should be used when the value of the `MatchConditionType` attribute in this class is 1 (for example, `Other`). If the value of the `MatchConditionType` attribute is anything else, then the value of this attribute should be `NULL`.

- `SetMetricType` is an enumerated 16-bit unsigned integer that defines an additional action to take for BGP filtering if the `MatchCondition` is satisfied. The actual value of the metric is specified in the `SetMetricValue` property.

Listing 9.17 lists the different types of conditions that are pre-defined.

Listing 9.17   MOF definition for the `SetMetricType` attribute.

```
[...
ValueMap { "1", "2", "3", "4", "5", "6", "7", "8", "9" },
Values { "Origin", "AS_Path", "NEXT_HOP", "Multi_Exit_Disc", "Local_Pref",
          "Atomic_Aggregate", "Aggregator", "Community", "Originator_ID" } ]
uint16 SetMetricType;
```

- `SetMetricValue` is a string that contains the value of the BGP metric that is being set for the BGP attribute defined in the `SetMetricType` property.

The `BGPRouteMap` class defines no methods, but does define three relationships. These are the `BGPPeerUsesRouteMap` association, the `BGPRouteMapsInRoutingPolicy` aggregation, and the `FilterListsInBGPRouteMaps` association, and are described here.

The `BGPPeerUsesRouteMap` Association

The `BGPPeerUsesRouteMap` association is a subclass of the `Dependency` association. It is used to define the `BGPRouteMaps` that are used by a particular `BGPPeerGroup` object. Multiple instances of the same `BGPRouteMap` may be used in the same `BGPPeerGroup` instance, and are distinguished by using the Sequence attribute of this association.

The aggregate and dependent are restricted to instances of the `BGPPeerGroup` and `BGPRouteMap`, respectively. The multiplicity of this relationship is zero-or-more to zero-or-more. This is because many different `BGPRouteMaps` can be used in the same `BGPPeerGroup`, and the same `BGPRouteMap` can be used in many different `BGPPeerGroups`. However, in both cases, this dependency does not have to exist (hence, the "zero-or-more" in the cardinality of both the antecedent and the dependent).

This relationship also defines a 16-bit unsigned integer, called Sequence. This integer is used to distinguish between different instances of the same `BGPRouteMap` that are used by the same `BGPPeerGroup`.

The `RouteMapsInRoutingPolicy` Aggregation

The `RouteMapsInRoutingPolicy` aggregation is a subclass of the `Component` aggregation, and is used to define the `BGPRouteMaps` that are used by a particular `RoutingPolicy` object. Multiple instances of the same `BGPRouteMap` may be used in the same `RoutingPolicy` instance; they are distinguished by using the Sequence attribute of this aggregation.

The aggregate and part component are restricted to instances of the RoutingPolicy and BGPRouteMap classes, respectively. The multiplicity of this relationship is again zero-or-more to zero-or-more, since the same BGPRouteMap may be used by different RoutingPolicy objects, and multiple BGPRouteMaps may be used by the same RoutingPolicy object. Again, since this is an optional relationship, the cardinality on both sides must be zero-or-more.

This relationship also defines a 16-bit unsigned integer, called Sequence, that can be used to differentiate multiple instances of the same BGPRouteMap that are used by the same RoutingPolicy object.

The FilterListsInRouteMaps Association

The FilterListsInRouteMap association is a subclass of the Dependency association, and is used to associate a FilterList with a BGPRouteMap.

In general, FilterLists do not have to use route maps of any type. However, if a FilterList is being used to filter and redistribute BGP routing information, then a BGPRouteMap is an efficient way to do this. Consequently, the antecedent is restricted to instances of the class FilterList, and its cardinality is zero-or-one. Since there can be only one BGPRouteMap associated with a FilterList, the dependent is restricted to instances of the class BGPRouteMap, and its cardinality is exactly one. Therefore, the overall multiplicity of this relationship is zero-or-one to one.

Multi-Protocol Bridge Objects

The multi-protocol bridge is a sub-model of the network model, and is used to model bridges that can communicate using different protocols. It is based on RFCs 1493 and 1525.

SwitchPort

The SwitchPort class is a subclass of the ProtocolEndpoint class. This object represents the internal portion of a port on a bridge or switch, from which frames are transmitted and received. In this sub-model, it represents the internal interface to the bridge or switch, which is where important internal functions of the switch (for example, spanning tree services) are interfaced to the outside world. In the VLAN sub-model, it has the added semantics of representing the VLAN aspects of a switch port.

Figure 9.36 illustrates the SwitchPort class and its relationships.

Figure 9.36   Network Common Model excerpt: the `SwitchPort` class and its relationships.

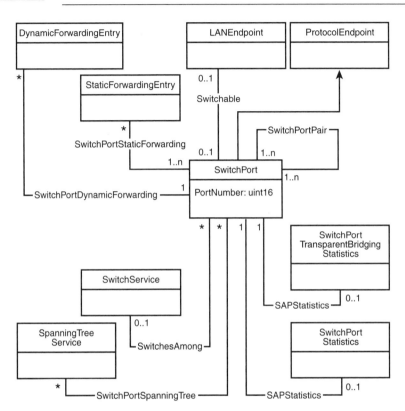

Note that the `SwitchPort` does not represent the packet-handling aspects of the switch port. This is done through a `ProtocolEndpoint` that connects to the `SwitchPort`, as shown in Figure 9.37. This will be discussed further through the remainder of this section.

The `SwitchPort` class defines a single attribute, called `PortNumber`. This is a 16-bit unsigned integer that serves as the numeric identifier for the port in the switch. This enables the ports in the switch to be uniquely identified.

The `SwitchPort` class defines no methods, but does participate in eight relationships. The `SwitchPortPair` and `Switchable` associations are defined here. The remaining associations will be discussed when the classes that they depend on are described later in this chapter.

Figure 9.37   Part of the packet handling interface in a switch.

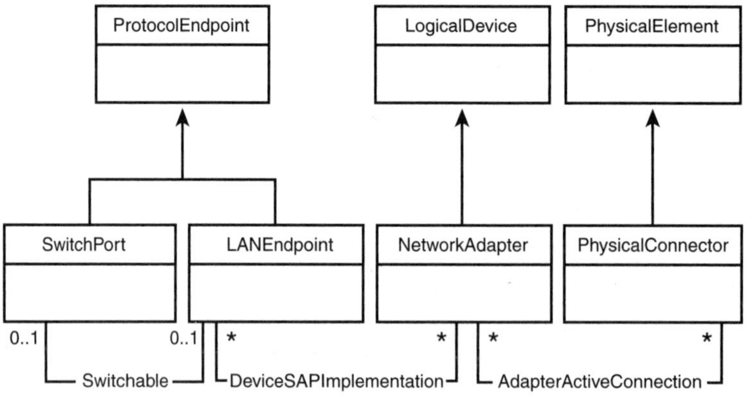

The SwitchPortPair *Association*

The SwitchPortPair association is a subclass of the SAPSAPDependency association, and represents information about the port pairings of a switch that is used by the SourceRoutingService of a switch.

The antecedent and dependent are restricted to instances of the classes SwitchPort, and represent the higher and lower numbered ports of the tuple, respectively. Since this is a dependency relationship between at least one port to at least one port, the multiplicity of this relationship is one-or-more to one-or-more.

This association defines the following two attributes that characterize the pairing of the switch ports:

- BridgeNum is a 16-bit unsigned integer that uniquely identifies the path between the two ports provided by this source routing bridge. The bridge number is used to differentiate between multiple paths connecting the same two LANs.

- BridgeState is an enumerated 16-bit unsigned integer that defines the state of the BridgeNum attribute. There are three possible values: 1 (Enabled), 2 (Disabled), and 3 (Invalid). Note that writing a value of 3 (Invalid) removes the instance of this association.

The Switchable *Association*

The Switchable association is a subclass of the BindsTo association, and describes the dependency that a SwitchPort has on a particular LANEndpoint. The antecedent and depen-dent are restricted to instances of the SwitchPort and ProtocolEndpoint classes, respectively. The multiplicity of this relationship is zero-or-one to zero-or-one, indicating that it is a completely optional relationship, but if instantiated, at most one SwitchPort is bound to at most one LANEndpoint.

SwitchService

The SwitchService class is a subclass of the Service class, and represents the generic ability of a bridge or switch to forward packets. The SwitchService object represents the switch-ing aspects of the switch or bridge (that is, an instance of the ComputerSystem class) in which SwitchService is hosted. Additional switching functions are incorporated as subordi-nate services related to this class via ServiceComponent associations.

Figure 9.38 illustrates the SwitchService class and its relationships.

Figure 9.38   Network Common Model excerpt: the SwitchService class and its relationships.

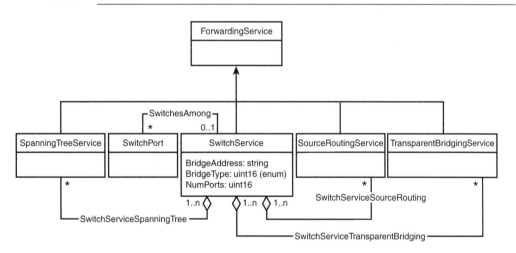

The SwitchService class defines the following attributes:

- BridgeAddress is a string of 12 characters that contains the MAC address that uniquely identifies this SwitchService. This forms a unique bridge identifier when it is concate-nated with a SpanningTreeService priority attribute. Twelve characters are necessary in order to properly format the MAC address according to RFC 2469.

- `NumPorts` is a 16-bit unsigned integer that contains the number of switch ports controlled by this `SwitchService`.

- `BridgeType` is an enumerated 16-bit unsigned integer that defines the specific type of switching service can be performed. The values are listed in the MOF excerpt in Listing 9.18 (note that srt stands for `sourceroute-transparent bridging`).

Listing 9.18   MOF definition for the `BridgeType` attribute.

```
[...
ValueMap {"1", "2", "3", "4"},
Values {"unknown", "transparent-only", "sourceroute-only", "srt"},
Mappingstrings {"MIB.IETF | RFC1493-MIB.dot1dBaseType"} ]
uint8 BridgeType ;
```

This class defines no methods, but does participate in four relationships. The `SwitchesAmong` association is described here. The other three aggregations (`SwitchServiceSpanningTree`, `SwitchServiceSourceRouting`, and `SwitchServiceTransparentBridging`) are described when the `SpanningTreeService`, `SourceRoutingService`, and `TransparentBridingService` classes are described, respectively.

The SwitchesAmong Association

The `SwitchesAmong` association is a subclass of the `ServiceSAPDependency` association, and is used to represent the ability of the `SwitchService` to switch frames between `SwitchPorts`.

The antecedent and dependent are restricted to values of the `SwitchPort` and `SwitchService` classes, respectively. This relationship is optional. However, if it is instantiated, then it defines the dependency between a specific `SwitchService` and a set of `SwitchPorts`. Therefore, the multiplicity of this association is zero-or-more to zero-or-one.

TransparentBridgingService

The `TransparentBridgingService` is a subclass of the `Service` class, and is used to represent the learning and transparent bridging aspect of `SwitchService`.

Transparent bridging refers to the ability of bridges and switches to pass frames along one hop at a time based on the use of internal tables that associate a port (that is, a `SwitchPort` in our model) with an end node (for example, a `LANEndpoint`). Since this process occurs transparently to the end nodes in the network, it is called transparent bridging.

Figure 9.39 illustrates the `TransparentBridgingService` class and its relationships.

Figure 9.39 Network Common Model excerpt: the `TransparentBridgingService` class and its relationships.

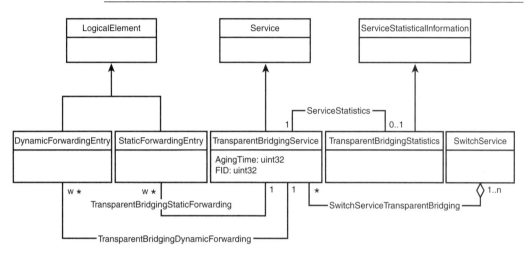

The `TransparentBridgingService` class defines the following two attributes:

- `AgingTime` is a 32-bit unsigned integer that defines the timeout period in seconds for removing dynamically learned forwarding information. The 802.1D specification recommends a default of 300 seconds for this attribute.

- `FID`, or Filtering Database Identifier, is a 32-bit unsigned integer that is used by VLAN-aware switches that have more than one filtering database.

This class defines no methods, but it does participate in four relationships. The `SwitchServiceTransparentBridging` aggregation is described here. The `TransparentBridgingStaticForwarding` and `TransparentBridgingDynamicForwarding` associations will be described when the `StaticForwardingEntry` and the `DynamicForwardingEntry` classes are described later in this chapter. Finally, the `ServiceStatistics` association will be described in the "Statistics for the Multi-Protocol Bridge Sub-Model" section later in this chapter.

The `SwitchServiceTransparentBridging` Aggregation

The `SwitchServiceTransparentBridging` aggregation is a subclass of the `ServiceComponent` aggregation, and is used to represent the whole-part relationship that associates an aggregate `SwitchService` to its component `TransparentBridgingServices`.

The antecedent and dependent are restricted to instances of the SwitchService and TransparentBridgingService classes, respectively. The SwitchService has a cardinality of one-or-more for all types of switches and bridges. The cardinality of the TransparentBridgingService is zero-or-more for VLAN-aware switches, but should be restricted in an implementation to zero-or-one for most VLAN-unaware switches.

SpanningTreeService

The SpanningTreeService is a subclass of the Service class, and represents the capability of a switch or bridge to help build a distributed spanning tree. A spanning tree is used to ensure that a particular portion of the network is loop-free. (For more information, refer to the IEEE 802.1 Spanning-Tree Protocol standard).

Figure 9.40 illustrates the SpanningTreeService class and its relationships.

Figure 9.40   Network Common Model excerpt: the SpanningTreeService class and its relationships.

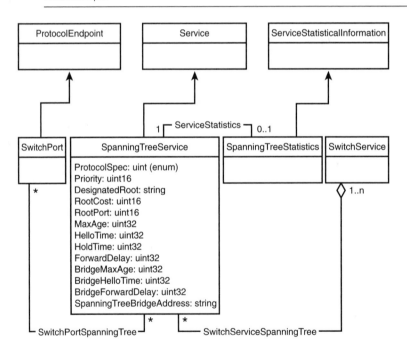

The `SpanningTreeService` class defines the following attributes:

- `ProtocolSpec` is an enumerated 16-bit unsigned integer that defines the version and type of the spanning tree protocol that is used by this switch. The values are listed in Listing 9.19 in the following MOF excerpt.

Listing 9.19   MOF definition for the `ProtocolSpec` attribute.

```
[...
ValueMap {"1", "2", "3"},
Values {"unknown", "decLb100", "ieee802d"},
Mappingstrings {"MIB.IETF¦RFC1493-MIB.dot1dStpProtocolSpecification"} ]
uint16 ProtocolSpec;
```

- `Priority` is a 16-bit unsigned integer that can be assigned to the switch for use in constructing the spanning tree. It is the value of the writeable portion of the Bridge ID, consisting of its first two octets. The unique identifier for a switch is constructed by concatenating the MAC address associated with the switch for spanning tree operations to the 2-byte priority. Choice of the priority value influences election of the root bridge.

- `DesignatedRoot` is a string of 16 characters (to represent 8 octets of information, with each pair of characters representing one octet of information) that contains the bridge identifier of the root of the spanning tree as determined by the Spanning Tree Protocol as executed by this node.

- `RootCost` is a 16-bit unsigned integer that defines the cost of the path from this switch to the root switch.

- `RootPort` is a 16-bit unsigned integer that contains the port number of the port having the lowest cost path to the root bridge.

- `MaxAge` is a 32-bit unsigned integer that contains the current value for the maximum age of all dynamic Spanning Tree information. Age is defined as current time minus the time that the information was first learned. All dynamically learned information will be periodically refreshed.

- `HelloTime` is a 32-bit unsigned integer that contains the current value of the interval between transmission of bridge configuration information by the switch on any port for which it is the spanning tree root or trying to become so, as learned from the network.

- `HoldTime` is a 32-bit unsigned integer that defines the minimum interval between transmission of bridge configuration information through a given port, as learned from the network.

- ForwardDelay is a 32-bit unsigned integer that defines the time spent by a port in the listening state before transitioning to the learning state and in the learning state before transitioning to the forwarding state, as learned from the network. This value is also used during the period of a topology change as the maximum age of Spanning Tree information before discard.

- BridgeMaxAge is a 32-bit unsigned integer. It represents the value of the MaxAge attribute that is to be used by all switches in the network if this switch becomes the root switch.

- BridgeHelloTime is a 32-bit unsigned integer. It represents the value of the BridgeHelloTime attribute that is to be used by all switches in the network if this switch becomes the root switch.

- BridgeForwardDelay is a 32-bit unsigned integer. It represents the value of the BridgeForwardDelay attribute that is to be used by all switches in the network if this switch becomes the root.

- SpanningTreeBridgeAddress is a string of 12 characters that contains the MAC address used by the spanning tree service when it must be uniquely identified. When concatenated with the Priority attribute of the SpanningTreeService, a unique bridge identifier is formed. This attribute is only useful for switches that support multiple spanning tree services. The twelve characters represent six octets of information, two characters per octet, according to RFC 2469.

This class does not define any methods. However, it does participate in three relationships. Two of these, the SwitchPortSpanningTree association and the SwitchServiceSpanningTree aggregation, are defined here. The third is another instance of the ServiceStatistics association, and will be defined in the section "Statistics for the Multi-Protocol Bridge Sub-Model" section later in this chapter.

The SwitchPortSpanningTree Association

The SwitchPortSpanningTree association is subclassed from the ServiceSAPDependency association, and represents the dependency that the ports of a switch have on the spanning tree that determines their forwarding behavior.

In switches that support more than one spanning tree, the same port may participate in multiple spanning trees. This is true for several popular switches, and is also true in the proposed multiple spanning tree proposal for 802.1Q. Consequently, the multiplicity of this relationship is zero-or-more to zero-or-more. In addition, the antecedent and dependent are restricted to instances of the SwitchPort and SpanningTreeService classes, respectively.

This association defines the following attributes:

- Priority is an 8-bit unsigned integer that contains the priority assigned to the port. This is the value contained in the first octet of the two-octet port ID; the other octet contains the port number.

- State is an enumerated 16-bit unsigned integer that contains the current state of the port as determined by the spanning tree protocol. There are six possible values, which are defined in Listing 9.20.

Listing 9.20   MOF definition for the State attribute.

```
[...
ValueMap {"1", "2", "3", "4", "5", "6"},
Values {"disabled", "blocking", "listening", "learning", "forwarding", "broken"},
Mappingstrings {"MIB.IETF¦RFC1493-MIB.dot1dStpPortState"} ]
uint16 State;
```

- Enable is an enumerated 16-bit unsigned integer that defines whether this port is enabled or disabled. A value of 1 means Enabled, and a value of 2 means Disabled.

- PathCost is a 16-bit unsigned integer that defines the contribution of this port to the path cost of paths towards the spanning tree root which include this port.

- DesignatedRoot is a string that contains the bridge identifier of the root bridge for the segment to which this port is attached, as transmitted by the designated bridge for the segment.

- DesignatedCost is a 16-bit unsigned integer that defines the cost of the path to the root offered by the designated bridge for this segment.

- DesignatedBridge is a string that contains the bridge identifier of the designated bridge for the segment to which this port is attached.

- DesignatedPort is a 16-bit unsigned integer that contains the port identifier of the port on the designated bridge serving the segment to which the port is attached.

The SwitchServiceSpanningTree Aggregation

The SwitchServiceSpanningTree aggregation is a subclass of the ServiceComponent aggregation. It represents the dependency between a SwitchService and the set of SpanningTreeServices that it contains.

The aggregate and part components are restricted to instances of the cardinality of the SwitchService and SpanningTreeService classes, respectively. The cardinality of the SwitchService is one-or-more. This is because this is an aggregate association, and at least one instance of the SwitchService is required to form a higher-level service. The cardinality of the SpanningTreeService is zero-or-more for VLAN-aware switches, but should be restricted to zero-or-one for a VLAN-unaware switch.

DynamicForwardingEntry

The DynamicForwardingEntry class is a subclass of LogicalElement, and represents an entry in the forwarding (filtering) database associated with the transparent bridging service. This represents an entry that is learned dynamically from the network.

Figure 9.41 illustrates the DynamicForwardingEntry class and its relationships.

Figure 9.41 Network Common Model excerpt: the DynamicForwardingEntry class and its relationships.

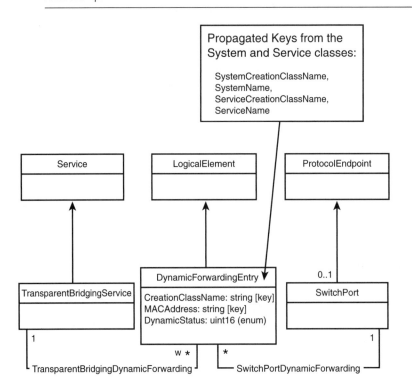

The DynamicForwardingEntry class has a composite key that is made up of the propagated keys from the System and Service classes (the CreationClassName and Name attributes, renamed to SystemCreationClassName, SystemName, ServiceCreationClassName, and ServiceName, respectively), along with two attributes that are defined in this class (CreationClassName and MacAddress). This is necessary because two relationships that associate instances of this class are *weak* relationships.

The DynamicForwardingEntry class defines the following attributes:

- SystemCreationClassName is a string of up to 256 characters that is part of the composite key of this class. It is propagated from the System class. This attribute defines the class of the System that contains this instance of the DynamicForwardingEntry class.

- SystemName is a string of up to 256 characters that is part of the composite key of this class. It is propagated from the System class. This attribute defines the name of the System that contains this instance of the DynamicForwardingEntry class.

- ServiceCreationClassName is a string of up to 256 characters that is part of the composite key of this class. It is propagated from the Service class. This attribute defines the class of the Service that contains this instance of the DynamicForwardingEntry class.

- ServiceName is a string of up to 256 characters that is part of the composite key of this class. It is propagated from the Service class. This attribute defines the name of the Service that contains this instance of the DynamicForwardingEntry class.

- CreationClassName is a string of up to 256 characters that is part of the composite key of this class. This attribute defines the class used in the creation of this instance of the DynamicForwardingEntry class.

- MacAddress is a string of 12 characters that is part of the composite key of this class. This attribute defines the unicast MAC address for which this TransparentBridgingService has forwarding and/or filtering information. The MAC address should be formatted as twelve hexadecimal digits, with each pair of digits representing one of the six octets in canonical bit order according to RFC 2469.

- DynamicStatus is an enumerated 16-bit unsigned integer that defines the status of the entry. There are five possible values, which are defined in Listing 9.21.

Listing 9.21   MOF definition for the DynamicStatus attribute.

```
[...
ValueMap {"1", "2", "3", "4", "5"},
Values {"other", "invalid", "learned", "self", "mgmt"},
Mappingstrings {"MIB.IETF¦RFC1493-MIB.dot1dTpFdbStatus"} ]
uint16 DynamicStatus;
```

This class does not define any methods, but does participate in two relationships, the `TransparentBridgingDynamicForwarding` and the `SwitchPortDynamicForwarding` associations. These two associations are defined here.

The `TransparentBridgingDynamicForwarding` Association

The `TransparentBridgingDynamicForwarding` association is a subclass of the `Dependency` association, and relates an instance of the `TransparentBridgingService` to the entries of its forwarding database. The forwarding database, represented by the `DynamicForwardingEntry`, is *contained* in the service, which is represented by the `TransparentBridgingService`. Therefore, the `DynamicForwardingEntry` is *weak* to the `TransparentBridgingService`.

The antecedent and dependent are restricted to instances of the `TransparentBridgingService` and the `DynamicForwardingEntry` classes, respectively. Since this is a weak relationship, the cardinality of the `TransparentBridgingService` is exactly 1. The cardinality of the `DynamicForwardingEntry` is zero-or-more.

The `SwitchPortDynamicForwarding` Association

The `SwitchPortDynamicForwarding` association is a subclass of the `Dependency` association, and is used to represent the dependency that exists between a `DynamicForwardingEntry` and the `SwitchPort` to which the entry applies.

The antecedent and dependent are restricted to instances of the `SwitchPort` and `DynamicForwardingEntry` classes, respectively. The cardinality of the `SwitchPort` is exactly 1, and the cardinality of the `DynamicForwardingEntry` is zero-or-more.

StaticForwardingEntry

The `StaticForwardingEntry` is a subclass of the `LogicalElement` class, and represents an entry in the static (destination-address filtering) database associated with the `SwitchService`.

Figure 9.42 shows the `StaticForwardingEntry` class.

Figure 9.42 Network Common Model excerpt: the StaticForwardingEntry class and its relationships.

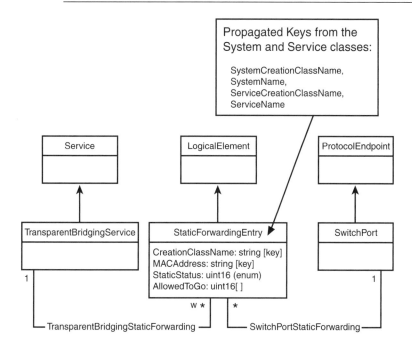

The StaticForwardingEntry class has a composite key that is made up of the propagated keys from the System and Service classes (the CreationClassName and Name attributes, renamed to SystemCreationClassName, SystemName, ServiceCreationClassName, and ServiceName, respectively), along with two attributes that are defined in this class (CreationClassName and MacAddress). This is necessary because two relationships that associate instances of this class are *weak* relationships.

The StaticForwardingEntry class defines the following attributes:

- SystemCreationClassName is a string of up to 256 characters that is part of the composite key of this class. It is propagated from the System class. This attribute defines the class of the System that contains this instance of the StaticForwardingEntry class.

- SystemName is a string of up to 256 characters that is part of the composite key of this class. It is propagated from the System class. This attribute defines the name of the System that contains this instance of the StaticForwardingEntry class.

- ServiceCreationClassName is a string of up to 256 characters that is part of the composite key of this class. It is propagated from the Service class. This attribute defines the class of the Service that contains this instance of the StaticForwardingEntry class.

- ServiceName is a string of up to 256 characters that is part of the composite key of this class. It is propagated from the Service class. This attribute defines the name of the Service that contains this instance of the StaticForwardingEntry class.

- CreationClassName is a string of up to 256 characters that is part of the composite key of this class. This attribute defines the class used in the creation of this instance of the StaticForwardingEntry class.

- MacAddress is a string of 12 characters that is part of the composite key of this class. This attribute defines the destination MAC address (which can be unicast, multicast, or broadcast) to which the filtering information applies. The MAC address should be formatted as twelve hexadecimal digits, with each pair of digits representing one of the six octets in canonical bit order according to RFC 2469.

- StaticStatus is an enumerated 16-bit unsigned integer that defines the status of the entry. There are five possible values, which are defined in Listing 9.22.

Listing 9.22 MOF definition for the StaticStatus attribute.

```
[...
ValueMap {"1", "2", "3", "4", "5"},
Values {"other", "invalid", "permanent", "deleteOnReset", "DeleteOnTimeout"},
Mappingstrings {"MIB.IETF¦RFC1493-MIB.dot1dTpFdbStatus"} ]
uint16 StaticStatus;
```

- AllowedToGo is an array of 16-bit unsigned integers that contain the port numbers to which frames with the destination MAC address arriving on the port represented by the SwitchPortStaticForwarding association are allowed to be forwarded.

This class does not define any methods, but does participate in two relationships, the TransparentBridgingStaticForwarding and the SwitchPortStaticForwarding associations. These two associations are defined here.

The TransparentBridgingStaticForwarding Association

The TransparentBridgingStaticForwarding association is a subclass of the Dependency association, and represents the dependency of a specific TransparentBridgingService to the entries of its static (for example, the destination-address filtering) database. The forwarding database, represented by the StaticForwardingEntry, is *contained* in the Service, which is represented by the TransparentBridgingService. Therefore, the StaticForwardingEntry is *weak* to the TransparentBridgingService.

The antecedent and dependent of this relationship are restricted to values of the TransparentBridgingService and the StaticForwardingEntry classes, respectively. Since this is a weak relationship, the cardinality of the TransparentBridgingService is exactly one. The cardinality of the StaticForwardingEntry is zero-or-more.

The SwitchPortStaticForwarding *Association*

The SwitchPortDynamicForwarding association is a subclass of the Dependency association, and is used to represent the dependency that exists between a StaticForwardingEntry and the SwitchPort to which the entry applies.

The antecedent and dependent are restricted to instances of the SwitchPort and StaticForwardingEntry classes, respectively. The cardinality of the SwitchPort is exactly 1, and the cardinality of the StaticForwardingEntry is zero-or-more.

SourceRoutingService

The SourceRoutingService class is a subclass of the Service class, and represents the capability of a switch to participate in the source routing of frames received at its ports.

Figure 9.43 shows the SourceRoutingService class.

Figure 9.43 Network Common Model excerpt: the SourceRoutingService class and its relationships.

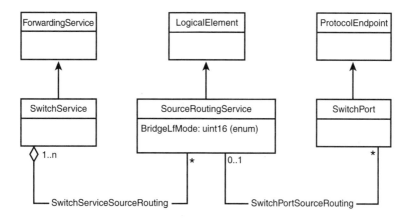

The SourceRoutingService class represents source-route bridging, which is fundamentally different than transparent bridging. In source-route bridging, the entire route to a destination is pre-determined in real-time prior to the sending of any data to the destination.

This class defines a single attribute, BridgeLfMode, which is an enumerated 16-bit integer that indicates whether this bridge operates using (the older) 3-bit length negotiation fields or (the newer) 6-bit length negotiation fields. The values 1 and 2 correspond to the 3-bit and 6-bit fields, respectively.

This class defines no methods, but does define two relationships. These are the
`SwitchServiceSourceRouting` aggregation and the `SwitchPortSourceRouting` association, and
are described here.

The `SwitchServiceSourceRouting` *Aggregation*

The `SwitchServiceSourceRouting` aggregation is a subclass of the `ServiceComponent` aggregation, and represents the set of `SourceRoutingServices` that make up a `SwitchService`.

The aggregate and part components are limited to instances of the `SwitchService` and
`SourceRoutingService` classes, respectively. The cardinality of the `SwitchService` is defined
to be one-or-more (it must be at least one since this aggregation represents a composite
`Service`). The cardinality of the `SourceRoutingService` is zero-or-more for VLAN-aware
switches, but should be set to zero-or-one for a VLAN-unaware switch.

The `SwitchPortSourceRouting` *Association*

The `SwitchPortSourceRouting` association is a subclass of the `ServiceSAPDependency` association, and represents the dependency that exists between the source-routing information in
the network and how that affects an individual `SwitchPort`.

The antecedent and dependent are restricted to instances of the `SwitchPort` and the
`SourceRoutingService` classes, respectively. The cardinality of the `SourceRoutingService` is
zero-or-one. This means that it is an optional relationship but, if it is instantiated, then it
refers to a particular `SourceRoutingService`. The cardinality of the `SwitchPort` is zero-or-
more.

This association defines the following attributes:

- `HopCount` is a 16-bit unsigned integer that contains the maximum number of routing
descriptors allowed in either an All Paths or Spanning Tree Explorer frames.

- `LocalSegment` is a 16-bit unsigned integer that contains the segment number that
uniquely identifies the segment to which this port is connected. Current source routing
protocols limit this value to the range 0 through 4095. A value of 65535 signifies that
no segment number is assigned to this port.

- `BridgeNum` is a 16-bit unsigned integer that contains the bridge number that uniquely
identifies a bridge when more than one bridge is used to span the same two segments.
Current source routing protocols limit this value to the range 0 through 15. A value of
65535 signifies that no bridge number is assigned to this bridge.

- TargetSegment is a 16-bit unsigned integer that contains the segment number that corresponds to the target segment this port is considered to be connected to by the switch. Current source routing protocols limit this value to the range 0 through 4095. A value of 65535 signifies that no target segment is assigned to this port.

- SteSpanMode is an enumerated 16-bit unsigned integer that determines how the port behaves when presented with a Spanning Tree Explorer (STE) frame. The value Disabled (2) indicates that the port will not accept or send STE packets; any STE packets received will be silently discarded. The value Forced (3) indicates the port will always accept and propagate STE frames. This allows a manually configured Spanning Tree for this class of packet to be configured. The value Auto-span (1) can only be returned by a bridge that both implements the Spanning Tree Protocol and has use of the protocol enabled on this port. The behavior of the port for STE frames is determined by the value of the State attribute of the SwitchPortSpanningTree association for the port.

  If the port is in the "forwarding" state, the frame will be accepted or propagated. Otherwise, it will be silently discarded.

Statistics in the Multi-Protocol Bridge Sub-Model

This sub-model makes use of two of the four common statistics classes from the Core Model. In particular, the ServiceStatisticalInformation and SAPStatisticalInformation classes are used as the parents of all statistics classes in this sub-model. The design, therefore, is to define specialized statistics objects that are derived from these two classes, and use instances of the ServiceStatistics and SAPStatistics associations, respectively, to relate the specialized statistics class in the sub-model to the object that the statistics are being gathered for. Figure 9.44 shows this design without any class attributes.

The following sections describe the function of the six statistics subclasses in the multi-protocol bridge sub-model.

Figure 9.44   Network Common Model excerpt: the multi-protocol bridge statistics class hierarchy.

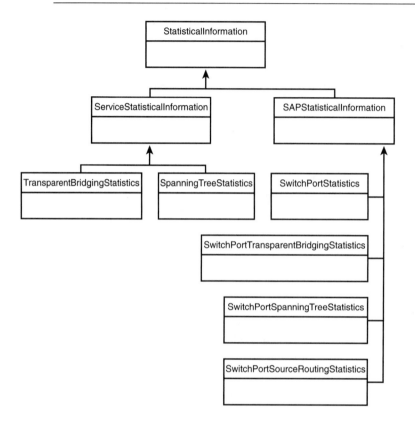

The TransparentBridgingStatistics *Subclass*

The TransparentBridgingStatistics class is a subclass of the
ServiceStatisticalInformation class, and is used to provide statistical information regarding the Transparent Bridging Service of a particular switch.

Figure 9.45 shows the TransparentBridgingStatistics class.

This class defines a single attribute, called LearnedEntryDiscards. This is a 32-bit unsigned integer that contains the total number of Forwarding Database entries, which have been or would have been learnt, but have been discarded due to a lack of space to store them in the Forwarding Database.

Figure 9.45   Network Common Model excerpt: the `TransparentBridgingStatistics` class and its relationships.

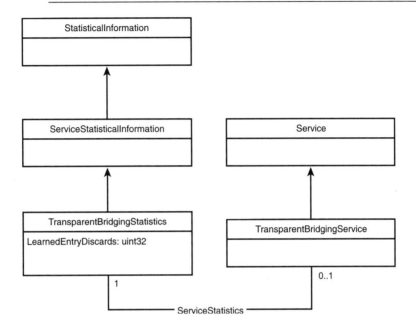

This class defines no methods, and is related to the `TransparentBridgingService` through an instance of the `ServiceStatistics` association. The cardinality of this association is exactly one on the `TransparentBridgingStatistics` side and zero-or-one on the `TransparentBridgingService` side.

The SpanningTreeStatistics Subclass

The `SpanningTreeStatistics` class is a subclass of the `ServiceStatisticalInformation` class, and is used to gather statistical information regarding the `SpanningTreeService`.

Figure 9.46 shows the `SpanningTreeStatistics` class.

Figure 9.46 Network Common Model excerpt: the `SpanningTreeStatistics` class and its relationships.

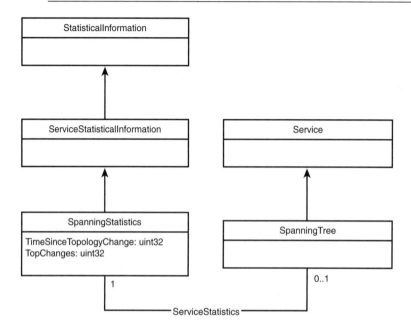

This class defines the following two attributes:

- `TimeSinceTopologyChange` is a 32-bit unsigned integer that contains the time since the last topology change was detected by the switch.

- `TopChanges` is a 32-bit unsigned integer that contains the total number of topology changes detected by the switch since the counter was last reset or initialized.

This class defines no methods, and is related to the `SpanningTreeService` through an instance of the `ServiceStatistics` association. The cardinality of this association is exactly one on the `SpanningTreeStatistics` side and zero-or-one on the `SpanningTreeService` side.

The `SwitchPortStatistics` Subclass

The `SwitchPortStatistics` class is a subclass of the `SAPStatisticalInformation` class, and contains statistics regarding a generic switch port, independent of the specific kind of switching done on frames arriving at the port.

Figure 9.47 shows the `SwitchPortStatistics` class.

Figure 9.47   Network Common Model excerpt: the SwitchPortStatistics class and its relationships.

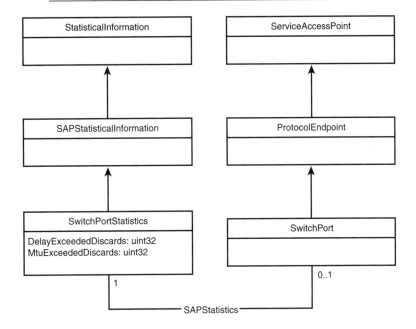

This class defines the following two attributes:

- DelayExceededDiscards is a 32-bit unsigned integer that contains the number of frames discarded by this port due to excessive transit delay through the bridge.

- MtuExceededDiscards is a 32-bit unsigned integer that contains the number of frames discarded by this port due to an excessive size.

This class defines no methods, and is related to the SwitchPort through an instance of the SAPStatistics association. The cardinality of this association is zero-or-one on the SwitchPort side and exactly one on the SwitchPortStatistics side.

The SwitchPortTransparentBridgingStatistics Subclass

The SwitchPortTransparentBridgingStatistics class is a subclass of the SAPStatisticalInformation class, and contains statistical information for a specific switch port that performs transparent bridging.

Figure 9.48 shows the SwitchPortStatistics class.

Figure 9.48   Network Common Model excerpt: the `SwitchPortStatistics` class and its relationships.

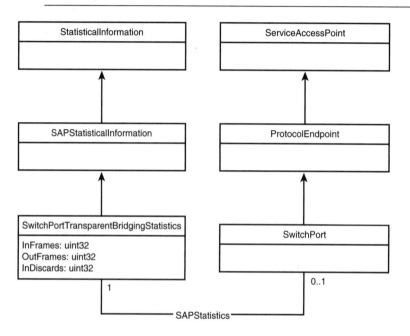

This class defines the following three attributes:

- `InFrames` is a 32-bit unsigned integer that contains the number of frames that have been received by the port from its segment.

- `OutFrames` is a 32-bit unsigned integer that contains the number of frames that have been transmitted by the port to its segment.

- `MtuExceededDiscards` is a 32-bit unsigned integer that contains a count of the valid frames received which were discarded (that is, filtered) by the forwarding process.

This class defines no methods, and is related to the `SwitchPort` through an instance of the `SAPStatistics` association. The cardinality of this association is zero-or-one on the `SwitchPort` side and exactly one on the `SwitchPortTransparentBridgingStatistics` side.

The `SwitchPortSpanningTreeStatistics` Subclass

The `SwitchPortSpanningTreeStatistics` class is derived from the `SAPStatisticalInformation` class, and contains statistical information for a switch port participating in the spanning tree computation.

Figure 9.49 shows the SwitchPortSpanningTreeStatistics class.

Figure 9.49   Network Common Model excerpt: the SwitchPortSpanningTreeStatistics class and its relationships.

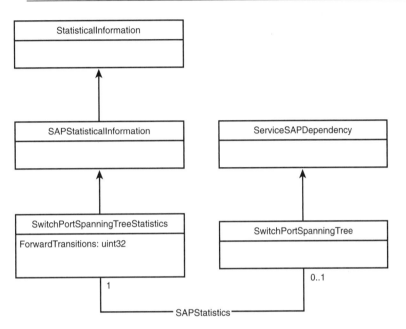

This class defines a single attribute, ForwardTransitions, which is a 32-bit unsigned integer that contains the number of times that the port has transitioned from the Learning state to the Forwarding state.

This class defines no methods, and is related to the SwitchPort through an instance of the SAPStatistics association. The cardinality of this association is zero-or-one on the SwitchPort side and exactly one on the SwitchPortSpanningTreeStatistics side.

The SwitchPortSourceRoutingStatistics *Subclass*

The SwitchPortSourceRoutingStatistics class is derived from the SAPStatisticalInformation class, and contains statistical information for a switch port that supports source routing.

Figure 9.50 shows the SwitchPortSourceRoutingStatistics class.

Figure 9.50   Network Common Model excerpt: the `SwitchPortSourceRoutingStatistics` class and its relationships.

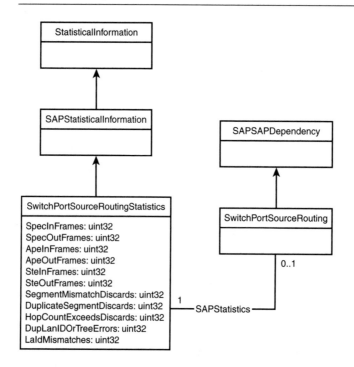

This class defines the following attributes:

- `SpecInFrames` is a 32-bit unsigned integer that contains the number of Specifically Routed frames (for example, Source Routed Frames), that have been received from the segment attached to the port.

- `SpecOutFrames` is a 32-bit unsigned integer that contains the number of Specifically Routed frames (for example, Source Routed Frames), that the port has transmitted on its segment.

- `ApeInFrames` is a 32-bit unsigned integer that contains the number of All Paths Explorer frames (for example, All Routes Explorer frames), that have been received by the port from its segment.

- `ApeOutFrames` is a 32-bit unsigned integer that contains the number of all Paths Explorer Frames (for example, All Routes Explorer frames), that have been transmitted by the port on its segment.

- SteInFrames is a 32-bit unsigned integer that contains the number of spanning tree explorer frames that have been received by the port from its segment.

- SteOutFrames is a 32-bit unsigned integer that contains the number of spanning tree explorer frames that have been transmitted by the port on its segment.

- SegmentMismatchDiscards is a 32-bit unsigned integer that contains the number of explorer frames that have been discarded by the port because the routing descriptor field contained an invalid adjacent segment value.

- DuplicateSegmentDiscards is a 32-bit unsigned integer that contains the number of frames that have been discarded by the port because the routing descriptor field contained a duplicate segment identifier.

- HopCountExceedsDiscards is a 32-bit unsigned integer that contains the number of explorer frames that have been discarded by the port because the Routing Information Field has exceeded the maximum route descriptor length.

- DupLanIdOrTreeErrors is a 32-bit unsigned integer that contains the number of duplicate LAN IDs or Tree errors. This helps in detection of problems in networks containing older IBM Source Routing Bridges.

- LanIdMismatches is a 32-bit unsigned integer that contains the number of ARE and STE frames that were discarded because the last LAN ID in the routing information field did not equal the LAN-in ID.

This class defines no methods, and is related to the SwitchPort through an instance of the SAPStatistics association. The cardinality of this association is zero-or-one on the SwitchPort side and exactly one on the SwitchPortSourceRoutingStatistics side.

VLAN Objects

The VLAN sub-model combines features commonly found in proprietary implementations with the IEEE 802.1Q specification. It builds on the general networking protocols objects and especially the multi-protocol bridge sub-model, and adds several VLAN-specific classes to model VLAN-aware switches. This section describes these classes.

What is a VLAN?

A *VLAN*, or *virtual local area network*, is a *logical* grouping of network devices that are connected to a set of LAN switch ports. The VLANs are configured using special management software. Non-VLAN-capable switches make multiple LAN segments appear to be part of a single LAN segment. VLAN-capable switches, however, make it possible to configure multiple VLAN segments. Depending on the VLAN technology used, the VLANs may be totally isolated from each other at Layer 2, or they may allow some sort of filtering of packets. The key point is that VLANs allow a physical infrastructure of switches to be configured to provide a desired logical Layer 2 infrastructure.

VLANs are used to group geographically dispersed users, servers, and other network devices into a single broadcast domain. Unlike traditional LANs, VLANs enable you to group users by function or interest, as opposed to being constrained by the physical locations of the devices that the users are connected to. The method of grouping varies according to vendor, but the most popular schemes are grouping based on port, MAC address, protocol used, or by intercepting the user login. Typically, a VLAN will contain a group of users with similar computing needs along with the servers and hosts they access most often. On the other hand, VLANs can be used to isolate one group of users from the other users on a network.

VLAN

The VLAN object is a subclass of the ServiceAccessPoint class, and represents the ability of a switch to offer a VLAN function. This means that in a given switch, there should be an instance of the VLAN object for every VLAN that is available in the switch. The type of the VLAN can be inferred from the VLANService(s) with which the VLAN is associated in the VLANFor association.

Figure 9.51 shows the VLAN class.

An instance of a VLAN class may be associated with more than one VLANService. This is necessary to correctly model switches that support both 802.1Q VLANs and proprietary VLANs from the switch vendor.

In typical VLAN-aware switches, packets can be assigned to a VLAN based on the port on which they are received (port-based VLANS), based on the source MAC address (MAC-based VLANs), or based on the value of a set of bits in the packet (protocol-based VLANs). This model provides a framework for the developer to subclass one or more of the VLAN objects to represent application-specific needs. For example, if the modeling of the specific VLAN assignment needs to be represented, then the VLAN class, along with the InboundVLAN and OutboundVLAN associations, must be subclassed to represent these application-specific assignments.

Figure 9.51   Network Common Model excerpt: the VLAN class and its relationships.

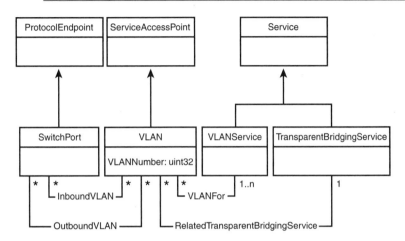

The VLAN class defines a single attribute, VLANNumber. This is a 32-bit unsigned integer that is the internal number of this VLAN.

This class defines no methods, but participates in four relationships. The RelatedTransparentBridgingService, along with the InboundVLAN and OutboundVLAN associations, are described here. The VLANFor association is described under the VLANService class.

The RelatedTransparentBridgingService Association

The RelatedTransparentBridgingService association is a subclass of the ServiceSAPDependency association, and relates the VLAN to the forwarding database (for example, filtering database) that it uses. Recall that a TransparentBridgingService represents a forwarding database. Thus, this association is used to determine which port a packet should be transmitted on, given that it is assigned to the VLAN and that it has a particular destination MAC address.

The antecedent and dependent are restricted to instances of the VLAN and TransparentBridgingService classes, respectively. Many VLANs may use the same forwarding database, but a switch does not have to be VLAN-aware. Therefore, the cardinality is zero-or-more on the VLAN side and exactly one on the TransparentBridgingService side.

The InboundVLAN Association

The InboundVLAN association is a subclass of the SAPSAPDependency association, and is used to model the dependency between a SwitchPort and a VLAN. This captures the ability of the switch to receive a packet on a given port and assign it to a particular VLAN.

The antecedent and dependent are restricted to instances of the `VLAN` and `SwitchPort` classes, respectively. The multiplicity of this relationship is zero-or-more to zero-or-more. This is because many ports can forward to a given VLAN, and many VLANs can use the same input port. In both cases, additional information (for example, a VLAN tag) can be used to determine the specific VLAN to forward the packet to. The zero is including in the cardinality of each side of the relationship because it is an optional relationship.

This class defines the following two attributes:

- `Tagged` is a Boolean attribute that, if `TRUE`, means that packets already tagged with the number in the `VLANNumber` attribute will be accepted when arriving at this port. If the `Tagged` attribute is false, it means that any untagged packets arriving at this port might be classified into the associated VLAN. If there is no such association, then the packet will be dropped.

- `Default` is a Boolean attribute that, if `TRUE`, means that untagged packets received by the `SwitchPort` are assigned to the Dependent VLAN by default. For 802.1Q-compliant ports, this attribute should be true on the association instance connecting a `SwitchPort` to the `VLAN` corresponding to the port's PVID. Note that the `Default` attribute should never be true if the `Tagged` attribute is true — it applies only to untagged packets.

The `OutboundVLAN` Association

The `OutboundVLAN` association is a subclass of the `SAPSAPDependency` association, and represents the dependency between the VLAN service and the outbound `SwitchPort`. If this association is not instantiated, then any packet that has been assigned to the VLAN and whose destination address is associated with that port will be dropped by the switch without being transmitted. If this association is present, then a packet that is assigned to this VLAN can be forwarded successfully to this outbound port.

The antecedent and dependent are restricted to instances of the `VLAN` and `SwitchPort` classes, respectively. The multiplicity of this relationship is zero-or-more to zero-or-more. This is because a given VLAN can forward packets to many ports, and many VLANs can use the same output port. The zero is including in the cardinality of each side of the relationship because it is an optional relationship.

This class defines a single attribute, `Tagged`. This is a Boolean attribute that, if `TRUE`, instructs the packet to be transmitted in encapsulated form, tagged with the associated VLAN tag. If this attribute is `FALSE`, then the packet will be transmitted without any VLAN tag.

VLANService

The VLANService class is a subclass of the Service class, and represents the VLAN aspects performed by a switch. Figure 9.52 shows the VLANService class.

Figure 9.52   Network Common Model excerpt: the VLANService class and its relationships.

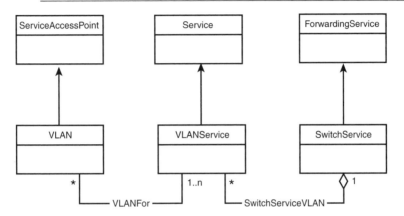

The VLANService class performs two main functions. First, it represents the VLAN function of the switch (classifying packets into VLANs, dropping broadcast packets based on VLAN, and so on). Second, it represents the service of deciding, in collaboration with other switches, what VLANs should be active on a trunk. This is usually done using specific protocols, such as the GVRP of the IEEE 802.1Q specification, or Cisco's proprietary VTP. The second aspect of the service is supported by a protocol (the GVRP protocol or the VTP protocol, for example). Note that these protocols, as well as others, are not modeled in the 2.2 release of the Network Model.

VLANService is an abstract class, so it must be subclassed so that instances can be distinguished by their class (for example, distinguishing GVRP from VTP). The Name attribute (inherited from its Service superclass) can be used to store a name assigned to a set of VLAN-aware switches (for example, the VTP domain name in Cisco Catalyst switches).

A VLANService should be instantiated in a VLAN-aware switch even if there is no GVRP-like protocol. However, some switches support both the 802.1Q VLAN standard and a proprietary VLAN protocol from the switch vendor. In such a case, two instances of VLANService should be instantiated, each having an associated VLAN object for each VLAN that it has.

This class defines no attributes or methods, since it is a base class for defining vendor- and protocol-specific subclasses. It does participate in two relationships, VLANFor and SwitchServiceVLAN, which are described here.

The VLANFor Association

The VLANFor association is a subclass of the ServiceSAPDependency association, and is used to represent the dependency that exists between a VLAN and a VLANService. The antecedent and dependent are restricted to instances of the VLAN and VLANService classes, respectively. Since there must be at least one VLANService present in order to instantiate this object, the multiplicity of this relationship is zero-or-more to one-or-more.

The SwitchServiceVLAN Aggregation

The SwitchServiceVLAN aggregation is a subclass of the ServiceComponent aggregation, and is used to define the set of VLANServices that are contained in a given SwitchService.

The aggregate and part component and restricted to instances of the SwitchService and VLANService classes, respectively. Since this relationship describes the VLANServices that make up a (higher-level) SwitchService, the multiplicity of this relationship is exactly one (on the SwitchService end) to zero-or-more (on the VLANService end).

802dot1QVLANService

The 802dot1QVLANService class is a subclass of the VLANService class. It is used to represent a switch that supports 802.1Q. Attributes will be added to this class in a future release of the Network Common Model, once the associated specifications are finalized in the IEEE.

The RelatedSpanningTree Association

The RelatedSpanningTree association is a subclass of the ServiceServiceDependency association, and identifies the spanning tree in which a forwarding database (for example, a TransparentBridgingService) is nested. This is needed for VLAN-aware switches.

The antecedent and dependent are restricted to instances of the TransparentBridging Service and SpanningTreeService classes, respectively. Since this defines the set of TransparentBridgingServices that are related to a single SpanningTreeService, the multiplicity of this relationship is zero-or-more to zero-or-one.

Modeling Examples

The following are some modeling examples to help increase your familiarity with the Network Common Model, and to show its flexibility.

Discovering Logical Properties of a Network Device

Discovering the logical properties of a network device (for example, what physical router does this interface belong to, and what type of protocols is it running?) is done in several ways, depending on what logical properties you are interested in.

Finding Out More Information About the Network Device

The Network Common Model does not have a dedicated router or switch class. Rather, it represents these as types of ComputerSystems (see "The ComputerSystem Class" in Chapter 7) that are distinguished using the Dedicated enumerated attribute. This attribute is used to indicate whether the ComputerSystem is a special-purpose System (that is, dedicated to a particular use) or a "general-purpose" System. This attribute contains several values that are used to identify dedicated networking devices (for example, Router, Switch, Layer 3 Switch, Central Office Switch, Hub, Access Server, and Firewall). So, you can find all of the networking devices that are dedicated routers by querying on this attribute. This provides a means to identify a dedicated networking device when not much other information is available describing it.

The ComputerSystem class also has a Roles enumeration, which is an array of free-form strings that can be used to identify the different roles that the device has. So, your administrator could set up a system that ensures that all network devices populate this attribute using a standard convention. For example, standard networking functions, such as access vs. distribution vs. core, could be defined to describe the role of this networking device in the overall network. Other information, such as "Internet gateway router", could be added on an as-needed basis. This attribute is designed to support focused queries that are looking for types of devices (not necessarily dedicated networking devices) that perform a particular function in the network.

Alternatively, one could subclass ComputerSystem and add a dedicated attribute, such a Keywords, to the subclass. The Keywords attribute could be defined as an array of strings that contain standard (at least for your applications) words and/or phrases that help identify a device. This would be especially useful if a directory using LDAP as its access protocol is used, due to LDAP's limited search semantics.

If you know some additional information about the device, then there are a set of dedicated associations that you can traverse to find more information. For example, suppose you are looking for all of the routers that are in AS100. Well, we know that the AutonomousSystem object has an attribute, ASNumber, that is its AS number – in this case, it would be set to 100. We can now follow the RoutersInAS aggregation to identify the set of routers that belong to this AS.

The preceding works in an even more abstract way. Suppose you have just discovered a new ProtocolEndpoint. What router (for example) does it belong to? There are actually two ways to find this out, depending on what information you know. If you know what protocol is being run, then you can follow the ProvidesEndpoint association to the ForwardingService class (this works because ForwardingService is a subclass of NetworkService). The ProtocolType enumerated attribute of the ForwardingService can then be used to identify the protocol, which is a type of network service. The NetworkServicesInAdminDomain association then relates this network service to a particular AdminDomain, such as an autonomous system. You can then follow the RoutersInAS aggregation to identify the particular router.

An alternate way makes use of the InLogicalNetwork aggregation, which associates the ProtocolEndpoint with a specific type of LogicalNetwork, such as an IPSubnet or a LANSegment. You can then use the NetworksInAdminDomain association to find the administrative domain that this device is a part of.

Finally, you can follow the BindsTo relationship that identifies a ServiceAccessPoint for this ProtocolEndpoint. You can then follow the HostedAccessPoint association to the ComputerSystem that hosts this ProtocolEndpoint (again, since ComputerSystem is a subclass of System, it inherits this association).

Modeling the Protocols That a Router Is Running

The Network Common Model defines two classes, ForwardingService and RouteCalculationService, that model the ability to forward packets and determine how to route packets to a destination, respectively. The protocols of interest that you will be modeling should all be derived from one of these superclasses. For example, BGP, being a routing protocol, is derived from the RouteCalculationService superclass.

There is an inherent symmetry in this model, shown by different classes working together towards a common goal. In the case of BGP, not only do you have a BGPService, you also have BGPEndpoints, BGPIPRoutes, BGPStatistics, BGPPathAttributes, and other specialized subclasses that together model how BGP functions. Not every protocol needs as many classes as BGP (and some may even need more, depending on what aspects of the protocol and how it works are to be modeled), but the BGP framework provides a good example of when to reuse existing classes and relationships, and when a refinement is needed. Note also that some of the parent classes, such as `ProtocolEndpoint` and `IPRoute`, are probably "good enough" to capture basic connectivity information.

Modeling Logical Topology

Logical connectivity can be modeled on several levels, depending on how much detail you need in your model.

At the highest level, everything is connected using some type of `ProtocolEndpoint`. So, for a simple case of a host connecting to a router, the simplest model would be similar to the one shown in Figure 9.53.

Figure 9.53   A simple network connectivity model.

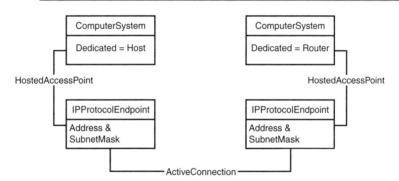

This model ignores many of the intricacies involved, such as cabling and network adapters, and concentrates on showing connectivity between the host and the router.

This example can get as robust as needed. For example, the different layers in the protocol stack could be modeled, as shown in Figure 9.54.

Or, some physical aspects could be included, such as those shown in Figure 9.55.

Figure 9.54 A more advanced network connectivity model.

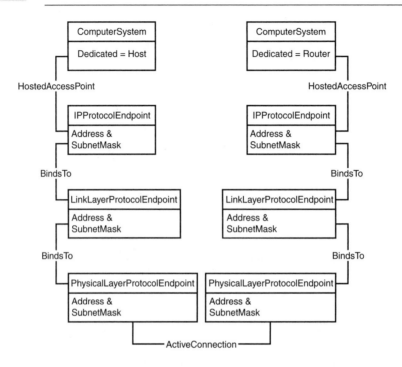

Figure 9.55 shows two associations between PhysicalConnector and NetworkAdapter. The Realizes association relates the NetworkAdapter to the PhysicalConnector. However, there could be a multi-function adapter that can output to one of several PhysicalConnectors. The Realizes association relates each PhysicalConnector to the NetworkAdapter, and the AdapterActiveConnection association defines which of the PhysicalConnectors identified by the multiple Realizes associations is actually carrying the data.

This later model still ignores many of additional physical and logical aspects of this connection. For example, physical aspects for the router not yet modeled would include the rack that it is in (if any), along with the chassis and its collection of networking (and other) cards and cables, and other objects. Logical aspects of the router would include what administrative domain it is part of (and possibly what autonomous system, if required), what protocols it was running, and other features.

Figure 9.55   A more advanced network connectivity model including physical aspects.

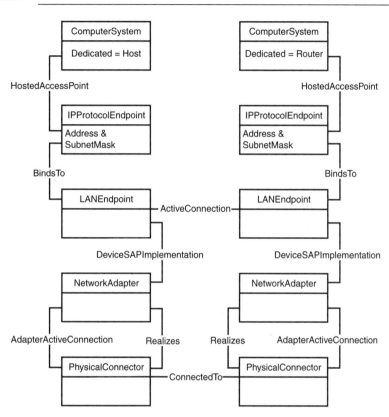

The Future of the Network Common Model

This is the first release of the Network Common Model. It has undergone extensive review from both the Networks working group as well as the DMTF member community. However, it was purposely limited in several areas in order to first gain implementation experience, and is expected to be enhanced to add requested functionality.

Some work likely to take place during the end of the CIM 2.2 session and during CIM 2.3 is support for additional protocols (OSPF and RIP are obvious candidates), additions to the general networking objects to bring CIM even closer in alignment with various important IETF MIBs, and work on ATM and possibly Frame Relay. It is likely that VPNs, as well as other tunnel services, will also be modeled in the 2.3 version of the Network Model. Finally, QoS mechanisms will be modeled in support of the IETF and DMTF policy efforts.

Summary

This chapter has explained in detail the differences between the DEN and CIM logical models. The CIM Network Common Model grew out of the DEN Logical Model. The difference between these models is that the DEN Logical Model was focused solely on the logical characteristics of network devices, whereas the CIM Network Common Model strives to represent the logical networking characteristics of any ManagedSystemElement.

DEN specifies some additional informational elements that are not included in the CIM Network Common Model. This is because DEN is an extension model of CIM. The information included in the DEN specification that is not included in the CIM Network Common Model are mostly optimizations that are needed for a repository that uses LDAP as its access protocol. These are not included in the CIM Network Common Model because CIM is independent of the specific technology used to build a repository.

Recommended Further Study and References

The DEN Specification, version 4, will be published in the fourth quarter of 1999. Please check the DMTF home page here for updated links to this specification:

`http://www.dmtf.org/spec/denh.html`

An overview of the Network Model was presented in the 1999 DMTF Annual Conference, sessions C304 and C305, by John Strassner. This presentation is available on the DMTF Networks Working Group Web site, and should also be publicly available on the DMTF Web site and is available at `http://www.dmtf.org/educ/conf199/press.html`

There are quite a few RFCs for autonomous systems and BGP. The most important of these are

S. Willis, J. Burruss, J. Chu, RFC 1657 Category: "Definitions of Managed Objects for the Fourth Version of the Border Gateway Protocol (BGP-4) using SMIv2", `http://www.rfc-editor.org/rfc/rfc1657.txt`

Y. Rekhter and T. Li, RFC 1771, "A Border Gateway Protocol 4 (BGP-4)", `http://www.rfc-editor.org/rfc/rfc1771.txt`

Y. Rekhter and P. Gross, RFC 1772, "Application of the Border Gateway Protocol in the Internet", `http://www.rfc-editor.org/rfc/rfc1772.txt`

P. Traina, RFC 1773, "Experience with the BGP-4 protocol", `http://www.rfc-editor.org/rfc/rfc1773.txt`

J Hawkinson and T. Bates, RFC 1930, "Guidelines for the Creation, Selection, and Registration of an Autonomous System", http://www.rfc-editor.org/rfc/rfc1930.txt

P. Traina, RFC 1965, "Autonomous System Confederations for BGP", http://www.rfc-editor.org/rfc/rfc1965.txt

T. Bates, R. Chandra, RFC 1966, "BGP Route Reflection: An alternative to full mesh IBGP", http://www.rfc-editor.org/rfc/rfc1966.txt

R. Chandra, P. Traina, T. Li, RFC 1997, "BGP Communities Attribute", http://www.rfc-editor.org/rfc/rfc1997.txt

E. Chen, T. Bates, RFC 1998, "An Application of the BGP Community Attribute in Multi-home Routing", http://www.rfc-editor.org/rfc/rfc1998.txt

J. Stewart, T. Bates, R. Chandra, E. Chen, RFC 2270, "Using a Dedicated AS for Sites Homed to a Single Provider", http://www.rfc-editor.org/rfc/rfc2270.txt

A. Heffernan, RFC 2385, "Protection of BGP Sessions via the TCP MD5 Signature Option", http://www.rfc-editor.org/rfc/rfc2385.txt

C. Villamizar, R. Chandra, R. Govindan, RFC 2439, "BGP Route Flap Dampening", http://www.rfc-editor.org/rfc/rfc2439.txt

E. Chen, J. Stewart, RFC 2519, "A Framework for Inter-Domain Route Aggregation", http://www.rfc-editor.org/rfc/rfc2519.txt

DEN's Policy Model

The purpose of this chapter is threefold. First, it is important to explain how the Policy Model of network elements that was published in DEN will be transformed into the CIM Policy Common Model. Second, it is important to understand the changes that are taking place in this transformation. Finally, because the Policy Model is the last portion of the DEN specification, the future of the DEN specification will be discussed.

Overview

The DEN specification is made up of three sub-models. These are the Physical, Logical, and Policy Models. Policy is a new concept to CIM; therefore, DEN provided a generic as well as a network-specific definition of Policy.

The DEN Policy Model proved to be very popular. An IETF working group, called the Policy Framework working group, was chartered after its initial meeting (which is somewhat unusual) to define an architecture, core schema (that is, one that can be used by all IETF working groups) and network QoS-specific schemata, all based on the DEN Policy Model. Similarly, the DMTF chartered a new working group (the service level agreement working group) to evolve the DEN Policy Model. This work will be fed back into the DEN specification, which will then be updated by the Networks working group of the DMTF.

Note

At the time of this writing, I am the chair of the Networks Working Group of the DMTF, and I co-chair the Policy Framework and the LDUP Working Groups of the IETF. You are encouraged to participate in these working groups.

Purpose of the DEN Policy Model

The purpose of the DEN Policy Model, as it was originally designed, was to provide an Information Model and extensible class hierarchy that enabled application developers to represent policies that controlled access to and allocation of network resources. The DEN Policy Model was designed to be independent of any specific repository. However, DEN also specified a mapping from a repository-independent form of its Policy Model to a form that was amenable to being stored in a directory that used LDAP as its access protocol.

The DEN Policy Model describes a simple, yet powerful, model that can represent both the characteristics of conditions that trigger policy and the actions that need to be taken when a particular set of conditions is identified. The DEN Policy Model is aimed primarily at supporting applications that need to control access to and allocation of network resources.

The DEN Policy Model

This section provides a brief overview of the DEN Policy Model. Its purpose is to enable you to track the changes in this model from its initial draft release (DEN Specification version v3.0c5) to its current form in the IETF Policy Framework working group (which is identical to its form in the DMTF service level agreement and Networks working groups). This form is based on the initial DEN Policy Model, plus additional changes that are pending the official acceptance of the applicable Internet drafts (in the IETF Policy Framework working group) to proposed standards.

Conceptual Model

The underlying Information Model was originally focused on controlling network elements and services. However, the general goal of CIM is to extend and generalize where possible. In order to produce a more general model that was applicable to any entity, we needed a simple and extensible model that captured the common structure of policies. The DEN Policy Model was a solid first step in achieving this goal.

Classifying Policy

First, it was decided that there would be two types of policies: simple and complex. Simple policies are those that can be expressed in a simple form. The most popular form of expressing a policy is using an IF statement. The archetypal representation of a policy is

IF a set of conditions is satisfied, THEN take the following set of actions.

Simple policies can be efficiently represented in schemas or MIBs. Examples of this are VLAN assignments, simple yes/no QoS requests, and IP address allocations.

Complex policies are policies that are built from simple policies, and consist of a complex set of conditions and actions. Complex policies model intricate interactions between objects that have complex interdependencies. Examples of this include a sophisticated user logon policy that sets up application access, security, and reconfigures network connections based on a combination of user identity, network location, logon method and time of day.

Policies can be further classified into two categories: *service policies* and *usage policies.* Service policies describe services available in the network. Usage policies describe which policies will use which services when the policies are satisfied. Usage policies describe particular mechanism(s) employed to either maintain the current state of the object, or to transition an object from one state to a new state, in order to utilize the specified services. Put another way, service policies describe what the network is capable of providing, and usage policies describe how to configure the network in order to take advantage of one or more services that the network provides.

Execution Model

The Execution Model of a DEN policy is simple yet powerful. It consists of two components, a decision-making process and an execution, or action, process. The decision-making process compares the current state of the network to a desired state described by the set of conditions that differentiate this policy from other policies. The execution process is enabled once the decision-making process defines that this policy is applicable and its conditions are all satisfied. The execution process implements either a change to a new policy state or the maintenance of the current policy state through a set of management commands. When such a set of management commands is applied to network elements, they change the current configuration of the network device.

Each policy is a declarative statement consisting of a Boolean expression that describes a situation to which the policy applies. When the expression is true, one or more actions are executed. This version of the DEN specification makes two important simplifications:

• When the expression is false, *no* actions are executed.

• All conditions of a policy must be satisfied in order to execute the set of actions contained in the policy.

Policies can be nested, which enables complex policies to be constructed from simple policies. This also enhances reusability.

General policies can be used to control how groups of entities use a service or a set of services, while specific policies, which inherit from more general ones, control the use of a specific service by a particular entity. Thus, policies make use of generalization and specialization just like other classes.

It is important to note that policy is separate from enforcement and auditing.

Structure of a Policy

Common to either type of policy are the IF and THEN clauses. The IF clause is modeled as a set of conditions that determine if this policy is applicable or not. The THEN clause is modeled as a set of actions that either maintain the current state of the object or transition the object to a new state. In order to keep the semantics of the policy simple, it was decided that the actions of a given policy would only be executed if all of the conditions in its corresponding IF clause were true.

These semantics are packaged into two objects, called PolicyCondition and PolicyAction. These objects are formed into a policy rule using the PolicyRule object. The PolicyRule object serves to aggregate a set of conditions and a set of actions, and adds structure to these two sets to represent the particular semantics of a policy rule. To provide further extensibility, a PolicyGroup object is introduced. Its purpose is to aggregate a set of PolicyRule objects so that they can be treated as an atomic, more complex, rule.

Note
The DEN model had the idea of nesting policies but did not formalize this into the PolicyGroup class. This was done by the service level agreement and Networks Working Groups of the DMTF after DEN was submitted to the DMTF.

This leads to the Conceptual Model shown in Figure 10.1.

One thing that is misunderstood about policies is that many people think of policies as being "static" and "dynamic." This is incorrect. The "policy" is always a static entity. It may be parameterized, but it is still static. It is the *state* that policy depends on that is dynamic. In other words, the definition of the policy is constant; the application of the policy may depend all or in part on the environment. This dependency is expresed through the (dynamic) values taken in the condition.

Figure 10.1 Conceptual Model of the DEN Policy class hierarchy.

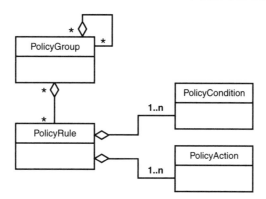

The DEN Policy Model describes information that constitutes a policy rule and information that can be used by the Policy Decision Point (PDP) in making decisions about attributes. There are additional data, in the form of dynamic attributes, which may be required to evaluate and/or execute the actions of a policy. However, these data are not part of the DEN repository. Data described by DEN include the characteristics, rights and privileges of objects, as well as relationships between objects. Dynamic data, which are not described by DEN, include volatile attributes that are of interest at the specific time of enforcement or policing of the policy. Policing is a particularly good example of the merging of the static and dynamic natures of policy data, in that static rules are applied to a dynamic environment to monitor and/or effect a change. DEN could specify where to obtain the dynamic data for a given policy (for example, from a designated collector node in the system). However, DEN is not responsible for storing or merging this data with static data. This is the responsibility of the PDP. In summary, DEN provides a robust framework to perform policy decision-making and enforcement, but is not by itself (or should it be) a complete solution.

This model will be explained in more detail in the section "The DEN Policy Class Hierarchy" later in this chapter.

Application of Policy

DEN Policies represent a binding of business goals and objectives to a set of commands that change the configuration of appropriate network resources to meet the business goals and objectives. However, a translation must be made between these business goals and objectives and their realization in the network. An example of this could be a service level agreement (SLA). For example, a business goal could be that one subscriber gets Gold service while another subscriber gets Silver service. Let's assume that the difference between Gold, Silver, and best effort is the combination of bandwidth, jitter, delay, and loss that traffic from one service gets with respect to traffic from other services. The problem is that the network devices are not able to equate (for example) "Gold service" with a configuration. Furthermore, the network administrator does not want to specify policies in the low-level terminology that makes sense to devices (for example, use this type of queuing algorithm with these parameters). Hence, a translation must occur between the policy as expressed in business terms and the policy as expressed in a form that can be applied to the device to change its configuration. The draft DEN specification realizes this need, but does not address how to implement it.

Note

This is precisely what is being addressed in the IETF Policy Framework Working Group. Because this work is being fed back into the appropriate DMTF Working Groups, the new DEN specification will reflect this.

Translating the requirements of the SLA into policies and mechanisms is necessarily vendor-specific. Therefore, the base DEN specification does not address this either.

What the base DEN specification DOES address is the definition of the structure of a policy rule, its constituent components, and how the static aspects of policies are stored in a DEN-compliant repository.

Reuse

Reuse is of prime importance to DEN, and is applied in several areas. The lowest level of reuse offered is in the conditions and actions of an individual policy. Three important benefits are gained by making the IF and THEN clauses objects in their own right:

- Common conditions and actions can be used as building blocks to develop more complex conditions and actions.

- Manageability is improved because common conditions and actions can be identified and handled in the same way.

- Refinement of common conditions and actions to meet application-specific needs is more easily achievable.

This last point deserves further explanation. Suppose that you have developed a set of actions that describe network configuration changes in response to a certain event. One of these actions involves changing the QoS setting of the traffic, for example, using a differentiated services code point, or DSCP. This is, for example, dependent on the source address and destination address of the traffic. We'll call this policy A, consisting of condition A and action A.

Now, suppose that a new common action needs to be defined, called policy B. It is also dependent on the source and destination address of the traffic, but does two things. First, it changes the QoS setting of the traffic as above, and second, it encrypts the traffic. Thus, policy B consists of condition A, action A, and action B.

If the two policies (A and B) were implemented as a single atomic class, then each time I wanted to change a condition or an action, I would have to change the entire class. Instead, by defining a policy to contain one or more condition and one or more action objects, I can change one or more of the constituent condition and action objects without having to change the entire policy. The policy, in effect, becomes a "shell" that contains some common information and pointers to a set of condition and action objects.

In addition, I can then develop two new policies, C and D. Policy C refines condition A to include a source port range and a destination port range. Policy D is based on the protocol type and the time of day. Both policy C and policy D can use actions A and B, or develop new actions. Having conditions and actions as separate objects that can be reused simplifies the development of new policies.

Reuse can also occur at two higher levels. The first is at the `PolicyRule` level, and the second is at the `PolicyGroup` level. DEN defines a `PolicyRule` object as a container of a set of `PolicyCondition` and `PolicyAction` objects. `PolicyRule` objects can be aggregated by `PolicyGroup` objects. For example, consider a company-wide Logon Policy. The company may be geographically distributed, and so may have several subordinate location-dependent policies. This is modeled by a `PolicyGroup` (representing the company) containing, for example, two instances of the `PolicyGroup` object, corresponding to an East Coast and a West Coast location. The security policy enforced in the East Coast and the West Coast locations could each use the same general security mechanisms to control access to the company's intranet. However, they might need different logon policies. For example, employees in the East Coast might use static IP addresses, whereas employees in the West Coast might use dynamically assigned IP addresses. Thus, the East Coast and West Coast `PolicyGroup` instances would share the same security `PolicyRule` but use different logon `PolicyRules`. This is shown in Figure 10.2.

Figure 10.2 DEN policy classes applied to the logon example.

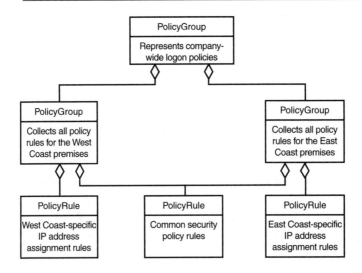

Finally, in real-life policy systems, which can contain thousands of policies, patterns develop that reuse a set of common conditions and actions, as well as rules, to develop more complex policies. This is where it is very important to have an extensible and efficient reuse mechanism, as in the DEN Policy Model.

The Policy Architecture Model Used by DEN

To understand the DEN Policy class hierarchy, we first need to understand the context in which the DEN policy classes are envisioned to be used. A simplified block diagram of a policy system that will use the DEN Policy class hierarchy is shown in Figure 10.3.

This block diagram was not developed in the DEN Ad-Hoc Working Group. Rather, this architecture emerged in the IETF, primarily from the RAP (RSVP Admission Policy) Working Group. It was adopted by DEN, and then enhanced by the IETF Policy Framework Working Group. What follows is a description of a snapshot of this architecture in the timeframe of the issuance of the DEN draft specification (July, 1998).

Figure 10.3 Simplified policy-enabled architecture.

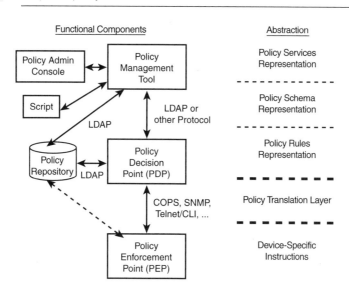

Architectural Components

In this architecture, policy is created, edited, and managed through a logically centralized administration point, called the Policy Management Tool. Figure 10.3 illustrates three different methods of interfacing to the Policy Management Tool. The first two represent two similar ways of entering data: a user using a GUI console and a generalized programmatic interface. The third is really a feedback mechanism, and enables the Policy Decision Point (PDP) to interact with the Policy Management Tools when there is a question about the definition or use of a policy.

The Policy Repository is used to store policies and definitional data that is used to make policy decisions (for example, threshold values). It can be, for example, a directory or a database. The important point is that its policy data is represented using the DEN Policy class hierarchy.

Usually, policy decisions are made in the PDP and implemented in the PEP (which could be a router, a host, or any other device capable of enforcing policy decisions). However, sometimes a PEP must also make decisions. For example, if the condition depends on the values of certain fields in the packet header, the PDP can not be used, since there is not enough time for the packet to be shipped from the PDP to the PEP, and the PDP does not have detailed knowledge of each PEP (so that it could instruct each PEP how to react). The architecture supports both a single device that contains a local PDP as well as a PEP, or one could separate the PDP and PEP into distinct physical entities.

There is at least one PDP per administrative domain. However, there are multiple PEPs per administrative domain. The PEPs are organized into groups. Each group of PEPs is controlled by a PDP.

Note that there are two ways for a PEP to obtain and act on its policies. The normal way is for this information to be passed using a dedicated policy protocol, such as COPS (the Common Open Policy Service protocol, defined in the IETF RAP Working Group). However, for some special situations, it may be more efficient to enable a device to pull information from the directory (using LDAP) without going through an intermediate layer. The former mechanism is used when highly structured information along with state is passed to the PEP. The latter is used when simple actions, such as downloading ACLs or even a simple configuration file, is needed.

Figure 10.4 illustrates how these various components could be combined in a single administrative domain. Other, more complex interconnections, could also be supported. The key to this extensibility is in the flexible structure inherent in the DEN Policy Model.

Figure 10.4   Simplified policy-enabled architecture.

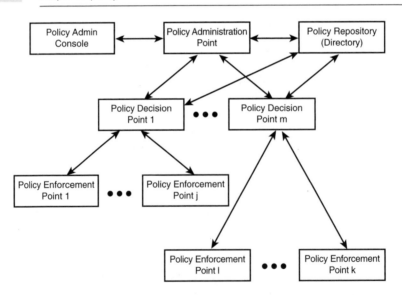

Application of the DEN Policy Classes

Policy is a means to control access to and allocation of network services and resources. DEN policies are generalized rule sets that perform these functions. An important portion of the DEN Policy Model is a set of shared classes that enable application-specific navigation between different knowledge domains (for example, physical and logical containment and connectivity). This enables a comprehensive policy strategy to be delivered to a variety of entities (or aspects of those entities) of different types. For example, the specification of a policy might require an administrator to change ACLs on a device. This requires the coordination of many different entities. For example:

- We must find the specific set of network administrators who have the authority to change ACLs on the devices; this is reflected in the logical containment model.

- We must also find the specific set of devices to change. This involves the coordination of several models:

  - The physical containment model can be used to determine the specific location of each device. This may take the form of which rack in which wiring closet in which floor of which building of which campus the device is located.

  - The physical connectivity model can be used to determine which devices are physically connected to each other.

  - The logical connectivity model can be used to determine which devices communicate with each other. This information can then be used to help determine if applying the policy to any one of the targeted devices will have any adverse effects on other devices or networks.

- We must also find the PDP that controls each device. This is so the PDP can examine the proposed policy and determine if it conflicts with any other policy that is already installed in the targeted device. The PDP not only will access the directory for policy information, it also will access it to obtain other related information (for example, topology information).

The DEN Policy Class Hierarchy

The DEN Policy class hierarchy is shown in Figure 10.5.

The following subsections will describe the original DEN Policy Model briefly so that you can better understand the changes that were made to it as it becomes standardized in the IETF and the DMTF. A formal CIM mapping is still in process. However, the classes and attributes will be analyzed to give you a feel for what classes, attributes, and relationships will be carried over into the CIM Policy Common Model. When the current snapshot of the CIM Policy Common Model is described later in this chapter, specific attention will be given to correlating the changes between the original DEN specification as described in this section and the current version of the IETF Core Policy Model (which will be part of the DEN Policy Common Model).

Figure 10.5 The DEN Policy class hierarchy.

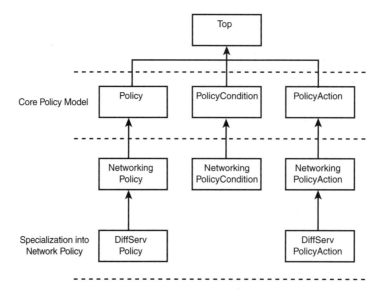

The Policy *Class*

The Policy class is a subclass of the Top class, and is used to encapsulate information governing the use of and interaction between network resources and services in a particular context. A Policy is a named object that represents an aggregation of one or more PolicyCondition and one or more PolicyAction objects. You can view a Policy object as a template of attributes and behaviors that describe a function or a set of functions that can be invoked that control how various entities interact with each other.

Note

One potential problem is matching policy classes to the layout of the directory tree. There is no standard for organizing the contents of the directory tree. Therefore, an administrator is free to define the tree as he or she sees fit. In practice, this means that the tree is already defined before DEN and its policy classes are considered. Therefore, DEN needs to fit into the existing structure of the tree, as opposed to redefine it.

The specific problem is that entities that require policy may be scattered throughout the tree. Fortunately, one of the strengths of the directory is in its containment model. Therefore, DEN recommends that instances of the Policy class be attached to the appropriate container (for example, OU) through the use of the PolicyContainmentAuxClass (an auxiliary class, which will be defined later in this section).

The `Policy` class defines the following attributes (note that all attributes were expected to be carried over into CIM except where noted):

- `cn`, or common name, is a string attribute that is derived from the X.500 specifications. It specifies a (possibly ambiguous) name by which the object is commonly known. This name conforms to the naming conventions of the country or culture with which it is associated. This would be a key attribute in a CIM implementation, and equated to the `Name` attribute. It may be used to form the RDN in an LDAP implementation.

- `PolicyActionSet` is a set of DN pointers that reference a set of `PolicyAction` objects. This set of pointers represents the set of actions that will be executed if the conditions of the Policy are satisfied. It is assumed that the actions will be executed in the order listed, although this is hard to enforce in an LDAP implementation.

  This is an LDAP-specific implementation attribute. In a CIM representation, this attribute would not be present, and would be replaced by an aggregation between a `Policy` object and the `PolicyAction` objects that it contains.

- `PolicyConditionSet` is a set of DN pointers that reference a set of `PolicyCondition` objects. This set of pointers represents the set of conditions that will be evaluated to determine if this Policy is applicable to the event being processed.

  This is an LDAP-specific implementation attribute. In a CIM representation, this attribute would not be present, and would be replaced by an aggregation between a `Policy` object and the `PolicyCondition` objects that it contains.

- `PolicyEnabled` is a Boolean attribute that, if TRUE, means that this particular policy is enabled. This attribute is retained in both the CIM and IETF models.

- `PolicyErrorCode` is a 16-bit unsigned integer that provides a generalized error code indicating a policy failure. This attribute was rejected in the CIM and IETF models in favor of developing a more robust, MIB-based error handling mechanism.

- `PolicyErrorDescription` is a free-form string that provides a detailed textual description of the error code identified in the `PolicyErrorCode` attribute. This attribute was rejected in the CIM and IETF models for the same reasons as described above.

- `PolicyKeywords` is an array of free-form strings provides a set of one or more keywords that a policy administrator may define to assist directory clients in locating the policy objects applicable to them. This attribute is retained in both the CIM and IETF models.

- `PolicyKind` is an enumerated 16-bit unsigned integer that defines whether this is a service or a usage policy. This attribute was deleted from the CIM and IETF representations in favor of a more robust classification mechanism.

- `PolicyModality` is an enumerated 16-bit unsigned integer that specifies whether the action(s) contained in this policy should be applied if the condition(s) is satisfied (value = 0) or not satisfied (value = 1). This attribute was deleted from the CIM and IETF models because it was decided that there were too many complications from allowing this freedom. Instead, policies were specifically limited to the semantics of actions that would be executed only if the overall condition of the policy evaluated to true.

- `PolicyName` is a free-form string that is a user-friendly name for this policy class. This attribute will be incorporated in the CIM and IETF models.

- `PolicyType` is a free-form string that contains the type of policy that this class is. This attribute is used to categorize different types of policies. This attribute was deleted from the CIM and LDAP models in favor of a more robust classification mechanism.

- `PolicyUsage` is a free-form string that contains descriptive text that describes how this policy is to be used. This attribute will be incorporated in the CIM and IETF models.

The `Policy` class defines no methods. However, it defines seven relationships, which are described below.

The `AdministratedBy` Aggregation

The `AdministratedBy` aggregation defines people that can administer a particular `NetworkElement`. People are represented by the CIM `SupportContact` class, which can be used to reference instances of the appropriate class that identifies one or more people that are administrators. Possible classes include the `Person`, `OrganizationalPerson`, `Organization`, `OU`, and `OrganizationalRole` classes.

The aggregate is restricted to instances of the `NetworkElement` class, and the part component is restricted to instances of the `SupportContact` class. The cardinality of this relationship is zero-or-one on the `NetworkElement` side and zero-or-more on the `SupportContact` side.

This relationship will be implemented (but not in this form) in the CIM model (it is irrelevant in the IETF model, as the IETF does not model such relationships). However, while its semantics will be implemented and the name kept, the aggregate will be `ComputerSystem` (because `NetworkElement` was deleted). Also, the part component will not be `SupportContact`, but rather a superclass in the to-be-finalized CIM User Common Model that serves the same purpose as that identified in DEN (`SupportContact` does not have these semantics).

The BackupAdministrators *Aggregation*

The BackupAdministrators aggregation is the same as the AdministratedBy aggregation, except that the administrators identified in this relationship are backup, or secondary, to the administrators identified in the AdministratedBy aggregation. Otherwise, everything else applies, including implementing this relationship in CIM and DEN.

The CanConfigure *Aggregation*

The CanConfigure aggregation defines one or more people that are allowed to configure this NetworkElement. Again, the SupportContact class is used to reference people from the appropriate classes that describe people.

The aggregate is restricted to instances of the NetworkElement class, and the part component is restricted to instances of the SupportContact class. The cardinality of this relationship is zero-or-one on the NetworkElement side and zero-or-more on the SupportContact side.

This relationship will be implemented (but not in this form) in the CIM model (it is irrelevant in the IETF model, as the IETF does not model such relationships). However, while its semantics will be implemented and the name kept, the aggregate will be ComputerSystem (because NetworkElement was deleted). Also, the part component will not be SupportContact, but rather a superclass in the to-be-finalized CIM User Common Model that serves the same purpose as that identified in DEN (SupportContact does not have these semantics).

The ContainedPolicies *Aggregation*

The ContainedPolicies aggregation defines the set of finer-level policies that comprise this more higher-level policy. For example, in the logon policy example previously mentioned, the company logon policy would have two instances of this aggregation, one for the West Coast logon policies and one for the East Coast logon policies.

The aggregate as well as the part component are restricted to instances of the Policy class. The cardinality of this relationship is zero-or-one on for the aggregate and one-to-more for the part component.

This relationship will be implemented (but not in this form) in the CIM and IETF models. Instead, a new class (PolicyGroup) with additional semantics and relationships will be introduced to perform this task.

The ContainedPolicyActions *Aggregation*

The ContainedPolicyActions aggregation defines the set of PolicyAction objects that make up a Policy. The aggregate is restricted to instances of the Policy class, and has a cardinality of zero-or-one. The part component is restricted to instances of the PolicyAction class, and has a cardinality of one-or-more. The cardinality of the part component is important: DEN mandated that a Policy have at least one action (as well as one condition). The CIM and IETF mappings change this to zero-or-more, as we will see later in this chapter.

This relationship will be implemented (but not precisely in this form) in the CIM and IETF models. The differences lie in the semantics of how it is used and the cardinality of the part component.

The ContainedPolicyConditions *Aggregation*

The ContainedPolicyConditions aggregation defines the set of PolicyCondition objects that make up a Policy. The aggregate is restricted to instances of the Policy class, and has a cardinality of zero-or-one. The part component is restricted to instances of the PolicyCondition class, and has a cardinality of one-or-more. The cardinality of the part component is important: DEN mandated that a Policy have at least one condition. The CIM and IETF mappings change this to zero-or-more, as we will see later in this chapter.

This relationship will be implemented (but not precisely in this form) in the CIM and IETF models. The differences lie in the semantics of how it is used and the cardinality of the part component.

The Owner *Aggregation*

The Owner aggregation defines the people that own this NetworkElement. People are defined by a SupportContact class, which contains references to one or more people that are contained in appropriate classes (such as OrganizationalPerson) that represent people.

The aggregate is restricted to instances of the Policy class, and has a cardinality of zero-or-one. The part component is restricted to instances of the NetworkElement class, and has a cardinality of zero-or-more.

This relationship will be implemented (but not precisely in this form) in the CIM model; it is not applicable to the IETF model. NetworkElement will be replaced by ComputerSystem, and SupportContact will be replaced by a yet-to-be-determined class in the CIM User Common Model that provides the semantics of this aggregation (SupportContact doesn't).

The *NetworkingPolicy* Class

The NetworkingPolicy class is a subclass of the Policy class, and is a base class for grouping together different networking policies (as opposed to other types of policies). The primary purpose of this class is to establish a base class in the hierarchy that more specific networking policies classes can refine. The one example of this in DEN is the DiffServPolicy class, which is described in the next section. This class is likely to be replaced in both the DEN and the IETF models in favor of a richer hierarchy for networking and other domains.

The NetworkingPolicy class defines a single attribute, called ConfigurationMethod. This is an enumerated 16-bit unsigned integer that defines how the configuration file of this network element was constructed. Values include:

Value	DEN Attribute Value and Description
0	Unknown
1	Other
2	Standard Configuration File
3	User-Overridden Configuration File
4	Manually

This class defines no methods, but does define one relationship, Traffic Conditioning Agreement (TCA), which is described below.

The *TCA Aggregation*

The TCA aggregation defines the Traffic Conditioning Agreements for a particular network device. A Traffic Conditioning Agreement is a special form of service level agreement.

The aggregate is restricted to instances of the NetworkElement class, and has a cardinality of exactly one. The part component is restricted to instances of the NetworkingPolicy class, and has a cardinality of zero-or-more.

This relationship will be implemented (but not precisely in this form) in the CIM and IETF models. The ComputerSystem class will replace the NetworkElement class as the aggregate, but it is still unclear what class the part component will be restricted to. This should be defined in the near future.

The DiffServPolicy *Class*

The DiffServPolicy class is a subclass of the NetworkingPolicy class, and is used to define policies that apply specifically to using differentiated services (as defined by the IETF) as a tool for realizing the result required by certain networking policies.

This class is subject to review and is likely to change. The IETF Policy Framework Working Group is going to be producing at least one QoS schema draft, which will contain an LDAP schema for RSVP and differentiated services. If it does not contain an information model for these services, then it will be defined in the DMTF. This class will be considered as input for this process, but will likely be changed; therefore, this class will not be discussed further.

The PolicyCondition *Class*

The PolicyCondition class is a subclass of Top, and describes a set of conditions to be met in order to determine whether the action(s) associated with a particular Policy should be executed. It can also be viewed as the means to determine whether a given set of network elements are in the correct policy state or not, or whether a given set of network elements should be transitioned to a new policy state. If a Policy requires multiple conditions to be met (for example, filter on subnet x and subnet y), then it will aggregate multiple PolicyCondition objects, one for each distinct condition.

The PolicyCondition class defines the following attributes:

- cn is the common name of the policy condition and is required for LDAP mapping. The same comments for the cn attribute of the Policy class apply here as well.

- PolicyConditionName is a free-form string that contains the user-friendly name of this PolicyCondition object. This attribute will be implemented in the CIM and IETF models.

- PolicyConstraint is the data that expresses the constraint of this PolicyCondition. This is an OctetString in the LDAP mapping, and is likely to be split into several coordinated attributes in the CIM mapping. Its purpose is to enable vendor-specific conditions to be encoded in binary form in this object. However, because CIM doesn't have OctetStrings as a native data type, multiple attributes (for example, at least one for the length and one for the values—remember that CIM does support different types of arrays) are used to decode the OctetString. This attribute will be implemented in the CIM and IETF models.

- PolicyConstraintEncoding is a string in the CIM mapping and an OID in the LDAP mapping. It is used to uniquely identify the encoding used to express the constraint. This allows vendors to publish their "language" for expressing policy constraints and identify it unambiguously. A policy engine can readily determine whether it supports the PolicyConstraintEncoding and gracefully report an error if it does not. This attribute will be implemented in the CIM and LDAP mappings.

- PolicyConstraintSequence is a 16-bit unsigned integer that assigns an order to each PolicyCondition that a Policy object refers to. The purpose of this attribute was to enable different policy condition instances contained in a Policy object to be prioritized. The IETF and DMTF have debated this very thoroughly, and it is very likely that this attribute will be deleted from both the IETF as well as the DMTF models. This is because it introduces too much complexity and moves the policy engine to a procedural, as opposed to declarative, model.

This class does not define any methods or relationships (other than the ContainedPolicyConditions aggregation that it participates in with the Policy class, which has already been described).

The NetworkingPolicyCondition *Class*

The NetworkingPolicyCondition class is a subclass of the PolicyCondition class. The purpose of this class is to provide a canonical representation of network policy. This enables policy conditions to be exchanged between multiple vendors' policy servers, providing interoperability of policy conditions. It also simplifies the parsing of policy rules by the policy server. In addition, it helps simplify the GUIs that must represent the structure of policy rules so that administrators can edit them. Finally, it helps in determining if any policy rules may potentially conflict with each other.

This class is subject to review and is likely to change depending on the QoS schema draft(s) produced by the IETF Policy Framework Working Group. This class has already been considered as input for this process. Therefore, a brief overview of its attributes will be presented.

The NetworkingPolicyCondition class defines the following attributes:

- ApplicationNameCondition is a free-form string that defines the name of the application that this condition applies to. One use of this attribute would be for certain applications that do not use a fixed port, but use specific ports or ranges of ports, to be grouped together and treated as an atomic unit.

- DestinationDeviceCondition is a free-form string in the CIM mapping and an OctetString in the LDAP mapping. It defines a particular value that can be used to uniquely identify the destination device that this condition applies to. The value is defined by the value of the DestinationDeviceConditionType attribute.

- DestinationDeviceConditionType is an enumerated 16-bit unsigned integer that defines the type of destination that this condition applies to. Values are:

Value	DEN Attribute Value and Description
0	Unknown
1	Other
2	DNS Name
3	Host Name
4	IP Address Using CIDR Format
5	IP Address Using IPv4 Format
6	IP Address Using IPv6 Format
7	IP Address Using IPX Format
8	MAC Address

- PortNumberRangeDestCondition is a string that defines the destination port or range of ports that this condition applies to.

- PortNumberRangeSourceCondition is a string that defines the source port or range of ports that this condition applies to.

- ProtocolCondition is a string that defines a condition on a protocol that must be satisfied as part of a condition of a Policy. For example, one might want to trap all DECnet and IPX traffic. The LDAP implementation used an OctetString to encode a simple matching expression directly in the attribute.

- ReceivedDSByteCheck is a string that specifies a condition to match incoming traffic based on the contents of the DS byte of the received packet's IP header. The format is a string of the form

  xxxxxxxx:xxxxxxxx

  where each x is either 0 or 1. The left substring is termed Mask and the right substring Match. The DS byte of the received packet's IP header is ANDed with Mask, and the result is compared against Match. The combination of Mask and Match allows definition of DS byte based profiles where certain bits in the DS byte may be ignored for the purpose of comparison.

- `SourceDeviceCondition` is a string that defines the source device that this condition applies to. The value used to uniquely identify the source device is defined by the value of the `SourceDeviceConditionType` attribute.

- `SourceDeviceConditionType` is an enumerated 16-bit unsigned integer that defines the type of source device that this condition applies to. Values are:

Value	DEN Attribute Value and Description
0	Unknown
1	Other
2	DNS Name
3	Host Name
4	IP Address Using CIDR Format
5	IP Address Using IPv4 Format
6	IP Address Using IPv6 Format
7	IP address Using IPX Format
8	MAC Address

- `TimeOfDayValidityRef` is an LDAP attribute (it would be implemented as an association in CIM). It is a DN that references a `TimeOfDayValidity` object for specifying time as a condition parameter for determining when this condition is valid. Time is specified relative to Greenwich Mean Time.

This class defines no methods or relationships.

The `PolicyAction` Class

The `PolicyAction` class is a subclass of `Top` that describes a set of actions to be invoked when the conditions for a `Policy` are satisfied. Network policy actions usually direct the changing of the configuration of one or more network elements in order to achieve a desired policy state. This state corresponds to providing one or more different behaviors for each network element. For networking policy actions, this could involve changing the code point or denying the forwarding of traffic.

If a `Policy` requires multiple actions to be executed (for example, remark the traffic and police it), then it will aggregate multiple `PolicyAction` objects, one for each distinct action.

This class is subject to review and is likely to change depending on the QoS schema draft(s) produced by the IETF Policy Framework Working Group. This class has already been considered as input for this process. Therefore, a brief overview of its attributes will be presented.

The `PolicyAction` class defines the following attributes:

- `cn` is the common name of the policy condition, and is required for LDAP mapping. The same comments for the `cn` attribute of the `Policy` class apply here as well.

- `PolicyActionData` is a set of attributes in the CIM model and an OctetString in the LDAP model. It provides a general escape mechanism for representing policy actions that have not been modeled with specific attributes (in the subclasses of `PolicyAction`). The specific encoding of data is determined by the OID value stored in the `PolicyActionEncoding` attribute. A PDP can readily determine whether it supports the values stored in an instance of `PolicyActionData` by checking the value from `PolicyActionEncoding` against the set of values that it recognizes.

- `PolicyActionEncoding` is a string in CIM and an OID in the LDAP mapping. It is used to identify the encoding and semantics of the values of `PolicyActionData` in this instance.

- `PolicyActionName` is a free-form string that contains the user-friendly name of this object.

- `PolicyActionSequence` is a 16-bit unsigned integer that assigns an order to each `PolicyAction` that a `Policy` object refers to. The purpose of this attribute was to enable different policy action instances contained in a `Policy` object to be prioritized. The IETF and DMTF have debated this very thoroughly, and it is very likely that this attribute will be deleted from both the IETF as well as the DMTF models. This is because it introduces too much complexity and moves the policy engine to a procedural, as opposed to declarative, model.

This class did not define any methods or relationships, other than the `ContainedPolicyActions` aggregation (with the `Policy` class) that was previously described.

The `NetworkingPolicyAction` Class

The `NetworkingPolicyAction` class is a subclass of the `PolicyAction` class. This class is analogous to `NetworkingPolicyCondition`, and provides a canonical representation of common networking policy actions. This enables policy conditions to be exchanged between multiple vendors' policy servers, providing interoperability of policy actions. It also simplifies the parsing of policy rules by the policy server. In addition, it helps simplify the GUIs that must represent the structure of policy rules so that administrators can edit them. Finally, it helps in determining if any policy rules may potentially conflict with each other.

This class is subject to review and is likely to change depending on the QoS schema draft(s) produced by the IETF Policy Framework Working Group. This class has already been considered as input for this process. Therefore, a brief overview of its attributes will be presented.

The NetworkingPolicyAction class defines the following attributes:

- ChangeAccessAction is a string that defines a change in access privilege for a particular type of traffic on a device. Note that this does *not* specify the mechanism (for example, ACL) by which this change is made.

- TrafficAction is an array of enumerated 16-bit unsigned integers that defines the type of action to be applied to this type of traffic. Values include:

Value	DEN Attribute Value and Description
0	Unknown
1	Other
2	Permit
3	Deny
4	Remark
5	Encrypt
6	Decrypt
7	Start Accounting
8	Stop Accounting
9	Start Auditing
10	Stop Auditing
11	Start Logging
12	Stop Logging

- TrafficPrioritySetting is a string that defines the value of the relative priority setting indicated in the TrafficPriorityType attribute.

- TrafficPriorityType is an enumerated 16-bit unsigned integer that defines the specific type of prioritization method that will be applied to the network device. Values include:

Value	DEN Attribute Value and Description
0	Unknown
1	Other
2	None
3	IP Precedence
4	DiffServ
5	TokenRing
6	802.1q
7	ATM
8	Frame Relay
9	MPLS
10	RSVP

- TrafficQueueAssignment is a 16-bit unsigned integer that defines the particular queue that this traffic should be assigned to. Note that this does not specify the *type* of queue. This way it is independent of implementation and can be used to assign traffic to different queue types (for example, class-based and priority-queues).

- TrafficQueueBehavior is a string that is used to assign a device-specific behavior to condition the traffic.

This class does not define any methods or relationships.

The DiffServAction Class

The DiffServAction class is a subclass of the NetworkingPolicyAction class, and is used to describe actions that are specific to the IETF Differentiated Services effort.

This class is subject to review and is likely to change. The IETF Policy Framework Working Group is going to be producing at least one QoS schema draft, which will contain an LDAP schema for RSVP and differentiated services. If it does not contain an information model for these services, then it will be defined in the DMTF. This class will be considered as input for this process, but will likely be changed. Therefore, this class will not be discussed further.

The `PolicyContainmentAuxClass` *Class*

The `PolicyContainmentAuxClass` class is an auxiliary class used to bind policies to an appropriate container object in the directory tree. This enables the DEN schema to integrate with an existing directory schema, as opposed to forcing the user to redo the schema. Note that auxiliary classes are directory constructs, and so this class does not appear in the CIM model.

This class defines a single attribute, called `PoliciesContainedList`. This is a set of object references to a set of `Policy` objects that are aggregated by the container object to which this auxiliary class has been attached.

The `TimeOfDayValidity` *Class*

The `TimeOfDayValidity` class is a subclass of `Top` (this changed in the current IETF draft to be a subclass of `PolicyCondition`), and provides a means of representing the time periods during which a policy rule is valid. For all times that fall outside these time periods, the `Policy` has no effect. A policy rule is treated as valid at all times if it does not specify a `TimeOfDayValidity` condition.

The `TimeOfDayValidity` class is defined as a subclass of the `PolicyCondition` class. This is to allow the inclusion of time-based criteria in the condition of a `Policy`.

This class is subject to review and is likely to change depending on the QoS schema draft(s) produced by the IETF Policy Framework Working Group. This class has already been considered as input for this process. Therefore, a brief overview of its attributes will be presented.

The `TimeOfDayValidity` class defines the following attributes:

- `cn` is the common name of the policy condition, and is required for LDAP mapping. The same comments for the `cn` attribute of the `Policy` class apply here as well.

- `PolicyValidityDayMask` is a string that defines the days in the month when the policy is valid. The format is a mask of 31 positions, with a "1" meaning that the policy is enabled for that day of the month and a "0" meaning that the policy is not enabled for that day of the month. The first bit represents Day 1 and continues to the 31st bit, representing Day 31; months having less than 31 days MUST define those corresponding bit values as 0.

- `PolicyValidityMonthMask` is a string that defines the months when the policy is valid. The format is a mask of 12 bits, with a "1" meaning that the policy is enabled for that month and a "0" meaning that the policy is not enabled for that month. The first bit represents January, the second February, and so on, up to bit 12 (December).

- `PolicyValidityPeriodName` is a string that contains the user-friendly name of this class.

- `PolicyValidityPeriodTime` is a string that defines when this policy is valid. The format of this string is:

  `yyyymmddhhmmssTZ:yyyymmddhhmmssTZ`

  where substrings on either side of the colon must be valid dates in the form `year-month-day-hour-minute-second-timezone`. In addition, the Julian equivalent of the right side is larger than that of the left side.

- `PolicyValidityTimeMask` is a string that defines the time when the policy is valid. The format is a mask as follows:

  `hhmmssTZ:hhmmssTZ`

  where substrings on either side of the colon must be valid times in the form `hour-minute-second` and the Julian equivalent of the right side is larger than that of the left side.

- `PolicyValidityWeekMask` is a string that defines the days when the policy is valid. The format is a mask of 7 bits, with a "1" meaning that the policy is enabled for that day and a "0" meaning that the policy is not enabled for that day. Bit 1 represents Monday, bit 2 represents Tuesday, and so on, up to bit 7 (Sunday).

This class does not define any methods or relationships.

Transformation into the IETF Policy Model

The DEN Policy Model was originally built to model just the logical aspects of controlling network elements and services. This meets the goals of the IETF. However, if this model is to be integrated into CIM, then it should be enhanced into a more general model that can in theory describe a policy to control the physical and/or logical aspects of any managed entity. Otherwise, it doesn't really follow the underlying CIM philosophy.

The remainder of this chapter will discuss the current IETF Policy Model. This information is accurate up to and including the second interim meeting of the IETF Policy Framework Working Group, held May 27–28, 1999.

Policy: CIM Goals Versus IETF Goals Versus DEN Goals

CIM and various working groups of the IETF will always have different goals. This is because the IETF focuses on protocols and network element and service applications. CIM, being a generalized Information Model, attempts to take concepts that apply to one domain and generalize them if possible.

The danger is, of course, conflicting object models. Therefore, a compromise was reached between these two conflicting goals. This was to let the IETF take the lead on developing an architecture, Information Model, and schema for network QoS applications. The DMTF would then take this model and generalize it to suit their goals. The result would be an Information Model that was compatible with the IETF model but addressed other knowledge domains besides network QoS. Thus, the CIM version of the Policy Model must by definition lag the IETF Version.

Note that an update to the DEN specification can still be released, as soon as the IETF version is stable. This is because DEN is focused solely on defining policy that can control access to and allocation of network resources.

The Current IETF Policy Architecture Model

There has been a lot of recent debate over how sophisticated an architecture the IETF needs to standardize. This actually took the form of separate Internet drafts that defined conflicting architectures. As of this writing, these differences have been resolved into a common converged architecture that contains a set of agreed-upon elements from both drafts.

This, of course, effects the Policy Information Model. For example, if a function is decided to be included in the architecture, then the information model and schema must support that function.

Figure 10.6 shows a simplified view of the current IETF converged architecture. It is similar to the DEN architecture of Figure 10.3, except that some important variations in terms of how policy services will be packaged have changed.

Figure 10.6   Current simplified IETF policy architecture.

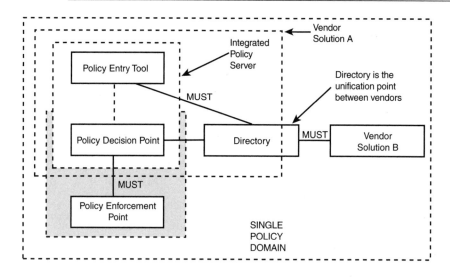

The first change is that several packaging options have emerged that alter the DEN picture. Figure 10.6 shows the following important possibilities that represent different vendor packaging options:

- Combining the means to enter policies with the PDP
- Combining the PDP with the PEP
- Combining both of the above options
- Combining a directory with a PDP and/or a policy entry console

These options have significant effects on the communication mechanisms needed to convey information between different functional elements.

Along these lines, there are some hard issues that are still being worked on in the architecture. One of these is conflict detection and resolution. Some people advocate a conflict detection and resolution function that is part of the PDP. Others advocate a separate function that is globally connected to all PDPs. A third alternative is to have two types of conflict detection—local within the PDP and global to coordinate the PDPs. This latter is necessary because one PDP might object to a new policy being installed while another PDP might not.

There are other issues as well. In order to move forward, the IETF Policy Framework Working Group has captured these and other requirements and has built an information model and schema that contain provisions to satisfy these requirements. The following section describes the current IETF policy information model.

The Current IETF/CIM Policy Information Model

Figure 10.7 shows a simplified view of the current IETF and CIM policy class hierarchy. The intent of this figure is not to show all of the detail (for example, associations and attributes) that make up the Policy Model. Rather, Figure 10.7 is used as an overview to help visualize the changes made from the DEN Policy Model.

Figure 10.7   Current CIM/IETF `Policy` class hierarchy.

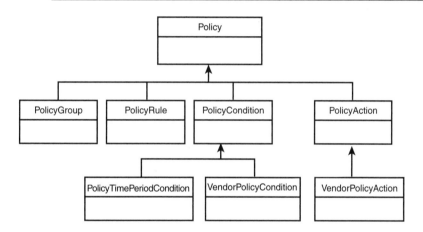

The following sections will describe this Information Model in more detail. The information presented herein is current as of the second interim meeting of the IETF Policy Framework Working Group. It is documented in version 3a of the core schema draft from the IETF Policy Framework Working Group, which is a private copy of the public draft (`draft-ietf-policy-core-schema-03.txt`). This draft will be revised at least once more, but the changes should be relatively minor. It is slated for release as part of the CIM 2.3 release, and will be implemented as part of the new Policy Common Model.

Note

You can find the latest version of this document by searching the IETF Web site (`http://www.ietf.org/internet-drafts/draft-ietf-policy-core-schema-03.txt`) or our Web site (`www.macmillantech.com/strassner`).

The *Policy* Class

The `Policy` class is an abstract class that is a subclass of the root of the tree (for example, the `Top` class). It is shown in Figure 10.8.

Figure 10.8   The `Policy` class.

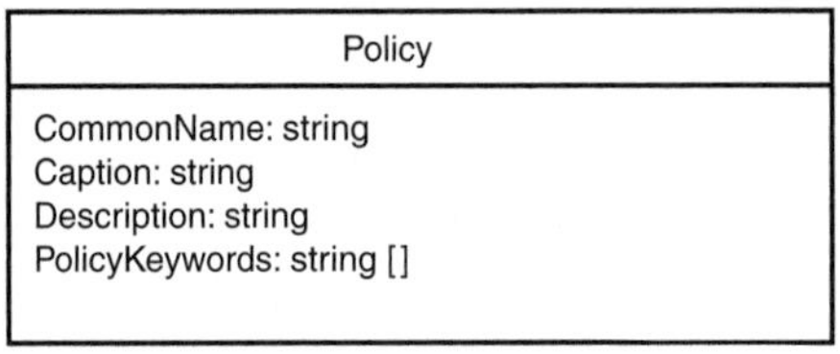

```
+---------------------------------------+
|                Policy                 |
+---------------------------------------+
| CommonName: string                    |
| Caption: string                       |
| Description: string                   |
| PolicyKeywords: string []             |
|                                       |
+---------------------------------------+
```

The `Policy` class serves as the root of the classification hierarchy. It is also used in the LDAP mapping as a mechanism for identifying policy-related instances in the Directory Information Tree (DIT). Recall that the DIT has most likely been populated, and this population most likely did not consider the needs of policy. Therefore, it is imperative that the policy hierarchy interface with any existing DIT, as opposed to mandating a redesign. To accomplish this, the LDAP mapping will attach an auxiliary class, `PolicyElement`, to this class. This "tagging" enables all subclasses of the `Policy` class to be found using a search for an auxiliary class of "`PolicyElement`" (or one of its attributes). This, in turn, aids searching as well as bulk loading and retrieval of policy information.

The `Policy` class defines the following attributes:

- `cn` is the common name of the policy condition, and is required for LDAP mapping. The same comments for the `cn` attribute of the `Policy` class apply here as well.

- `Caption` corresponds to the `Caption` attribute defined in CIM, and is a short textual description (for example, one-line string) of up to 64 characters of the object. It is intended primarily for GUI help-screen and information displays.

- `Description` corresponds to the `Description` attribute defined in CIM, and is a free-form string that provides a textual description of the object.

- `PolicyKeyword` is an array of free-form strings, each up to 64 characters long, that provides a set of one or more keywords that a policy administrator may define to assist directory clients in locating the policy objects applicable to them. Keywords are of one of two types. The first are keywords that are defined in the core schema document, or in documents that define subclasses of the classes defined in the core schema document. These keywords provide a vendor-independent, installation-independent way of identifying and locating policy objects. Examples include "Engineering," "Billing," and "Review in December 1999."

The core schema document defines the following keywords for identifying policy objects: UNKNOWN, POLICY, CONFIGURATION, USAGE, SECURITY, SERVICE, MOTIVATIONAL, INSTALLATION, and EVENT.

The other type of keywords are those that are specific to subclasses of the Core Schema classes. These are defined in additional Internet drafts, such as the QoS schema draft. By convention, keywords defined in conjunction with class definitions are in uppercase. Installation-defined keywords can be in any case.

This class does not define any methods or relationships.

The PolicyGroup *Class*

The PolicyGroup class is a subclass of the Policy class, and is used as a generalized aggregation container. It enables either instances of the PolicyRule or PolicyGroup classes, but not both, to be aggregated in a single container. This restriction enables the associated semantics to be greatly simplified. There is no limit to the degree of nesting. Loops, including the degenerate case of a PolicyGroup that contains itself, are not allowed when PolicyGroups contain other PolicyGroups.

The PolicyGroup class is shown in Figure 10.9.

Figure 10.9   The PolicyGroup class and its relationships.

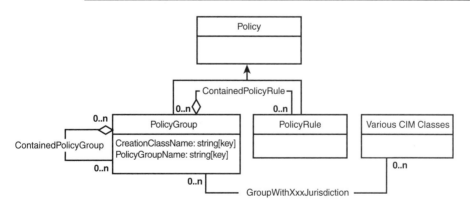

The PolicyGroup class defines the following two attributes:

- CreationClassName defines the name of the class used to create an instance of this class. It is part of the composite key for this class. Its purpose is to enable all the different instances of this class and its subclasses to be uniquely identified. It is defined to be a string of up to 256 characters.

- `PolicyGroupName` is a free-form string, of up to 256 characters, that provides a user-friendly name for a policy group. This is normally what will be displayed to the end user as the name of this class.

This class does not define any methods, but does participate in two aggregations and a set of associations. These are defined next.

The `ContainedPolicyGroups` Aggregation

The `ContainedPolicyGroups` aggregation enables `PolicyGroups` to be contained in other `PolicyGroups`. This nesting ability is critical for scalability and manageability, as it enables complex policies to be constructed from multiple simpler policies for administrative convenience. In the LDAP schema, the `ContainedPolicyGroups` relationship is mapped to the `PolicyGroupsAuxContainedSet` attribute in the auxiliary class `PolicyGroupContainmentAuxClass`.

The aggregate and part component are restricted to instances of the `PolicyGroup` class. The multiplicity of this relationship is zero-or-more to zero-or-more.

The `ContainedPolicyRules` Aggregation

The `ContainedPolicyRules` aggregation enables one or more `PolicyRules` to be contained in a `PolicyGroup`. This grouping is primarily for administrative convenience, as well as an aid to the understanding of the underlying semantics of the policies that are being used. Note that a `PolicyRule` may also be used by itself, without belonging to a `PolicyGroup`. In the LDAP schema, the `ContainedPolicyRule` relationship is mapped to the `policyRulesAuxContainedSet` attribute in the auxiliary class `policyRuleContainmentAuxClass`.

The aggregate is restricted to instances of the `PolicyGroup` class, and the part component is restricted to instances of the `PolicyRule` class. The multiplicity of this relationship is zero-or-more to zero-or-more.

The `GroupWithXXXJurisdiction` Associations

The `GroupWithXXXJurisdiction` set of associations is still being defined. The antecedent in all cases is the `PolicyGroup` class. Some of the dependents (that is, the names of classes that correspond to the "XXX" in the name of the association) that are being discussed include the `ManagedSystemElement`, `Setting`, and `Configuration` classes. In addition, a to-be-defined superclass in the CIM User Common Model will be needed to relate the jurisdictional authority that people have to policy groups.

The purpose of these associations is to make the dependency that exists between a `PolicyGroup` and various entities that use that `PolicyGroup` explicit.

The PolicyRule *Class*

The PolicyRule class is another subclass of the Policy class, and represents the "If <Condition is Met> then <Execute Action>" semantics associated with a Policy. It does this by aggregating a set of PolicyCondition and a set of PolicyAction objects.

The PolicyRule class is shown in Figure 10.10.

Figure 10.10 The PolicyRule class and its relationships.

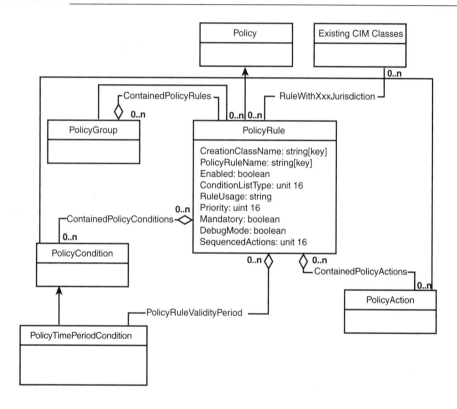

A PolicyRule condition, in the most general sense, is represented as either an ORed set of ANDed conditions (Disjunctive Normal Form, or DNF) or an ANDed set of ORed conditions (Conjunctive Normal Form, or CNF). Individual conditions may either be negated or not negated. The actions specified by a PolicyRule are to be performed if and only if the PolicyRule evaluates to TRUE.

The conditions and actions associated with a policy rule are modeled, respectively, with two subclasses of the `Policy` class, called the `PolicyCondition` and `PolicyAction` subclasses. In the LDAP implementation, these are made into auxiliary classes, so that they can either be attached to an instance of the `PolicyRule` class itself, or to an instance of the `PolicyInstance` class. This will be discussed more in the section "The IETF/CIM Policy Model: LDAP Implementation." Briefly, applications that require a minimum of LDAP access calls can retrieve these objects in one call if they are aux classes, while retaining the flexibility to reference other objects if more complex rules are required.

The `Policy` class defines the following attributes:

- `PolicyRuleEnabled` is an enumerated 16-bit unsigned integer that indicates that this `PolicyRule` is currently enabled. This lets a policy administrator enable or disable a `PolicyRule` without having to add it to, or remove it from, the directory. The defined values for this attribute are:

Value	CIM Attribute Value and Description
1	`Enabled`
2	`Disabled`
3	`Enabled for Debug` (a special mode where policies can be stimulated but not executed)

- `PolicyRuleConditionListType` is an enumerated 16-bit unsigned integer that is used to specify how the policy rule conditions are represented. Currently, there are two values for this attribute:
  1: disjunctive normal form (DNF)
  2: conjunctive normal form (CNF)

- `PolicyRuleConditionList` is a string that provides an unordered list of DN pointers that identify a set of policy conditions associated with this policy rule. Each DN pointer in this string has the following format:

`groupNumber : +¦- : DN ;`

where `groupNumber` is an integer that groups the conditions into first-level groups for the DNF or CNF representation of the overall `PolicyRule` condition; +¦- represents the characters plus ("+") and minus ("–")—the "+" indicates that the condition is not negated, and the "–" indicates that it is negated—and `DN` is a pointer to the `PolicyCondition` object.

This is an LDAP-specific attribute, and would be replaced by a set of aggregations between the `PolicyRule` object and one or more `PolicyCondition` objects. The `GroupNumber` and `IsNegative` attributes are placed in the aggregation, and have the same meaning as the `groupNumber` and + or – characters in the string.

- `PolicyRuleActionList` is an unordered array of strings of the form `n:DN` that identify a set of policy actions associated with this policy rule. When `n` is a positive integer, it indicates a place in the sequence of actions to be performed, with smaller integers indicating earlier positions in the sequence. The special value `0` indicates `Don't Care`. Negative integers are not allowed.

  If two or more actions have the same non-zero sequence number, they may be performed in any order, but they must all be performed at the appropriate place in the overall action sequence.

- The `policyRuleSequencedActions` attribute is used to indicate whether the order defined in this attribute is required, recommended, or not to be used at all.

  This is an LDAP-specific attribute, and is replaced in the CIM model by a set of aggregations between the `PolicyRule` object and one or more `PolicyAction` objects.

- `PolicyRuleValidityPeriodList` is an unordered set of DN pointers to one or more `PolicyTimePeriodCondition` objects, indicating when the policy rule is scheduled to be active and when it is scheduled to be inactive. The rule is scheduled to be active if it is active according to at least one of the `PolicyTimePeriodCondition` objects pointed to by this attribute.

  This is an LDAP-specific attribute, and is replaced by a set of associations between the `PolicyRule` object and one or more `PolicyTimePeriodCondition` objects.

- `PolicyRuleUsage` is a free-form string that contains descriptive text recommending how this policy should be used.

- `PolicyRulePriority` is an unsigned 16-bit integer that enables policy rules to be prioritized relative to each other. Policy rules that have this attribute are prioritized higher when the value of this attribute is larger. Prioritization among policy rules provides a simple and efficient mechanism for resolving policy conflicts.

- `PolicyRuleMandatory` is a Boolean that, if TRUE, indicates that evaluation of this `PolicyRule` is mandatory. Note that this attribute does *not* mean that the actions associated with this `PolicyRulePolicyRule` will automatically be executed. This attribute simply means that this `PolicyRule` *must* be evaluated.

- PolicyRuleSequencedActions is an enumerated 16-bit unsigned integer that provides the policy administrator with a means of specifying how the ordering of the policy actions associated with this PolicyRule is to be interpreted. Three values are supported:

Value	CIM Attribute Value and Description
1	Mandatory, which means perform the actions in the indicated order, or don't perform them at all
2	Recommended, which means perform the actions in the indicated order if possible, otherwise perform them in another order
3	Don't Care, which means perform them at all cost regardless of their order

This class does not define any methods. However, it participates in four aggregations and a set of associations. The ContainedPolicyRules aggregation was already discussed, but the other three aggregations and the set of associations are defined below.

The ContainedPolicyConditions Aggregation

The ContainedPolicyConditions aggregation is used to aggregate zero or more instances of the PolicyCondition class into an instance of the PolicyRule class.

The aggregate is restricted to instances of the PolicyRule class, and the part component is restricted to instances of the PolicyCondition class. The multiplicity of this relationship is zero-or-more to zero-or-more. This is because this relationship is not mandatory but, if it is instantiated, then a given PolicyRule object can aggregate multiple PolicyCondition objects and multiple PolicyRule objects can use the same PolicyCondition object.

This relationship contains two attributes:

- GroupNumber is a 16-bit unsigned integer that represents the GroupNumber portion of the PolicyRuleConditonList attribute. It is used to group together the different terms of the condition expression.

- ConditionNegated is a Boolean attribute that, if TRUE, means that this condition should be negated. It corresponds to the "+" or "–" characters embedded in the PolicyRuleConditonList attribute.

Note that there must be at least one PolicyCondition present in a PolicyRule. In the CIM model, this means that at least one ContainedPolicyConditions aggregation must be instantiated. The cardinality is zero-or-more to allow for policies that are in an incomplete state. In the LDAP model, this is more complicated, and is explained in the PolicyRule subsection under the section "The IETF/CIM Policy Model: LDAP Implementation" later in this chapter.

The ContainedPolicyActions *Aggregation*

The ContainedPolicyActions aggregation is used to aggregate zero or more instances of the Action class into an instance of the PolicyRule class.

The aggregate is restricted to instances of the PolicyRule class, and the part component is restricted to instances of the PolicyAction class. The multiplicity of this relationship is zero-or-more to zero-or-more. This is because this relationship is not mandatory but, if it is instantiated, then a given PolicyRule object can aggregate multiple PolicyAction objects and multiple PolicyRule objects can use the same PolicyAction object.

This relationship contains a single attribute, called ActionOrder. This is a 16-bit unsigned integer that corresponds to the n portion of the PolicyRuleActionList format. It is used to assign a particular execution order to a specific PolicyAction object relative to other PolicyAction objects that are contained in a given PolicyRule.

Note that there must be at least one PolicyAction present in a PolicyRule. In the CIM model, this means that at least one ContainedPolicyActions aggregation must be instantiated. The cardinality is zero-or-more to allow for policies that are in an incomplete state. In the LDAP model, this is more complicated, and is explained in the PolicyRule subsection under the section "The IETF/CIM Policy Model: LDAP Implementation" later in this chapter.

The PolicyRuleValidityPeriod *Aggregation*

The PolicyRuleValidityPeriod aggregation enables one or more PolicyTimePeriodCondition objects to be aggregated by a PolicyRule class. This enables a time period to be treated as another additional condition to be evaluated along with any other conditions specified for the policy rule.

The aggregate is restricted to instances of the PolicyRule class, and the part component is restricted to instances of the PolicyTimePeriodCondition class. The multiplicity of this relationship is zero-or-more to zero-or-more. This is because this relationship is not mandatory but, if it is instantiated, then a given PolicyRule object can aggregate multiple PolicyTimePeriodCondition objects and multiple PolicyRule objects can use the same PolicyTimePeriodCondition object.

The RuleWithXXXJurisdiction Associations

The RuleWithXXXJurisdiction set of associations is still being defined. The antecedent in all cases is the PolicyRule class. Some of the dependents (for example, the names of classes that correspond to the "XXX" in the name of the association) that are being discussed include the ManagedSystemElement, Setting, and Configuration classes. In addition, a to-be-defined superclass in the CIM User Common Model will be needed to relate the jurisdictional authority that people have to policy rules.

The purpose of these associations is to make the dependency that exists between a PolicyRule and various entities that use that PolicyRule explicit. These associations are semantically different that the GroupWithXXXJurisdiction associations. The latter are used to assign jurisdictional authority to PolicyGroups. The RuleWithXXXJurisdiction associations focus on whether the PolicyRule was executed successfully or not by a given entity. Accordingly, there will be a set of attributes associated with this relationship. Two likely candidates are a Boolean indicating whether execution was successful or not and a time stamp attribute.

The PolicyCondition Class

The PolicyCondition class is a subclass of the Policy class. An instance of a PolicyCondition represents one term of the overall condition of a PolicyRule, which may be expressed in DNF or CNF. If the overall condition of the PolicyRule is evaluated to TRUE, then the actions prescribed by the PolicyAction objects contained in this PolicyRule will be executed.

The PolicyCondition class is shown in Figure 10.11.

This class defines the following attributes:

- CreationClassName defines the name of the class used to create an instance of this class. It is part of the composite key for this class. Its purpose is to enable all of the different instances of this class and its subclasses to be uniquely identified. It is defined to be a string of up to 256 characters.

- PolicyConditionName is a free-form string, of up to 256 characters, that provides a user-friendly name for a policy condition. This is normally what will be displayed to the end user as the name of this class.

This class does not define any methods. It participates in a single relationship, ContainedPolicyConditions, which has already been defined.

Figure 10.11 The `PolicyCondition` class and its relationships.

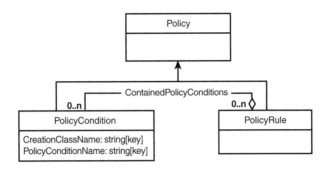

The `VendorPolicyCondition` Class

The `VendorPolicyCondition` class is a subclass of the `PolicyCondition` class. Its purpose is to provide a general escape mechanism for representing policy conditions that are specific to a particular vendor and cannot be modeled with a specific set of known attributes. Instead, the two attributes `ConstraintData` and `ConstraintEncoding` are used to define the content and format of the condition.

The `VendorPolicyCondition` class is shown in Figure 10.12.

Figure 10.12 The `VendorPolicyCondition` class and its relationships.

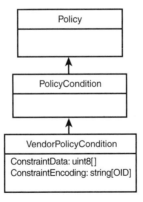

In the LDAP mapping, the data types of these two attributes are OctetString and OID, respectively. The CIM mapping is still being discussed; however, it is likely to be an array of either strings or unsigned 8-bit integers for the ConstraintData attribute, and a string for the ConstraintEncoding attribute.

This class defines the following two attributes:

- ConstraintData enables policy information describing a condition to be transported in a vendor-specific encoding. The format of the policy information is determined by the value stored in the ConstraintEncoding attribute.

- ConstraintEncoding serves as a unique identifier of vendor-specific policy information encodings. This attribute serves as a pointer into a registry of policy data formats.

This class does not define any methods or relationships.

The PolicyAction Class

The PolicyAction class is a subclass of the Policy class, and is used to execute one or more operations that will affect the target object(s) in order to achieve a desired policy state or maintain an existing policy state. The actions associated with a PolicyRule are executed if and only if the overall condition(s) of the PolicyRule evaluates to TRUE. A PolicyAction ordinarily changes the configuration of one or more of the objects that it affects.

The PolicyAction class is shown in Figure 10.13.

Figure 10.13 The PolicyAction class and its relationships.

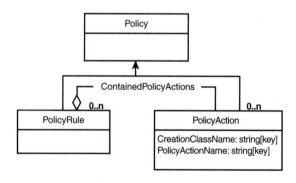

A `PolicyRule` contains one or more `PolicyActions`. However, there are two important differences between how a `PolicyAction` is aggregated by a `PolicyRule` compared to a `PolicyCondition` is aggregated by a `PolicyRule`:

- A `PolicyRule` can contain multiple lists of `PolicyCondition` instances, arranged in either DNF or CNF. However, for `PolicyActions`, the semantics are deliberately simplified to restrict a `PolicyRule` to contain only a single list of `PolicyActions`.

- A policy administrator can assign an order to the actions associated with a `PolicyRule`, but cannot assign an order to the conditions associated with a `PolicyRule`. In addition, an indication of whether or not the indicated order is mandatory, recommended, or of no significance can be attached to each `PolicyAction` object.

This class defines the following attributes:

- `CreationClassName` defines the name of the class used to create an instance of this class. It is part of the composite key of this. Its purpose is to enable all of the different instances of this class and its subclasses to be uniquely identified. It is defined to be a string of up to 256 characters.

- `PolicyActionName` is a free-form string, of up to 256 characters, that provides a user-friendly name for a policy condition. This is normally what will be displayed to the end user as the name of this class.

This class does not define any methods. It participates in a single relationship, `ContainedPolicyActions`, which has already been defined.

The `VendorPolicyAction` Class

The `VendorPolicyAction` class is a subclass of the `PolicyCondition` class. Its purpose is to provide a general escape mechanism for representing policy actions that are specific to a particular vendor and cannot be modeled with a specific set of known attributes. Instead, the two attributes `ActionData` and `ActionEncoding` are used to define the content and format of the condition.

The `VendorPolicyAction` class is shown in Figure 10.14.

Figure 10.14 The `VendorPolicyAction` class and its relationships.

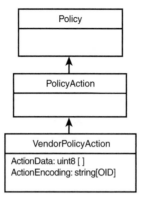

In the LDAP mapping, the data types of these two attributes are OctetString and OID, respectively. The CIM mapping is still being discussed; however, it is likely to be an array of either strings or unsigned 8-bit integers for the `ActionData` attribute, and a string for the `ActionEncoding` attribute.

This class defines the following two attributes:

- `ActionData` enables policy information describing a condition to be transported in a vendor-specific encoding. The format of the policy information is determined by the value stored in the `ActionEncoding` attribute.

- `ActionEncoding` serves as a unique identifier of vendor-specific policy information encodings. This attribute serves as a pointer into a registry of policy data formats.

This class does not define any methods or relationships.

The `PolicyTimePeriodCondition` Class

The `PolicyTimePeriodCondition` class is a subclass of the `PolicyCondition` class, and is used to represent the time periods during which a policy rule is active. At all times other times, the policy rule has no effect.

The `PolicyTimePeriodCondition` class is shown in Figure 10.15.

Figure 10.15 The `PolicyTimePeriodCondition` class and its relationships.

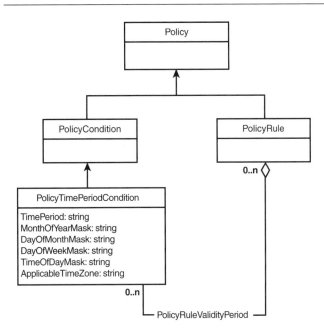

This subclass enables time periods, which are among the most common condition used across different types of policies, to be included as criteria as easily as other types of conditions that make up a `PolicyRule`. If a given `PolicyRule` does not include an instance of this class, then it is treated as active at all times.

Time sometimes requires a lot of detail to specify. Accordingly, this class defines additional attributes that supplement the main attribute (`TimePeriod`) which provide more granular specification of certain aspects of time. The values of all attributes present in an instance of the `PolicyTimePeriodCondition` class are ANDed together to determine the validity period(s) for the instance. For example, suppose that you wanted a certain policy rule to be active only on each Friday of the month, from 1 p.m. to 8 p.m., ending each quarter of the 1999 calendar year (for example, March, June, September, and December). This could be implemented as follows:

- Set the overall validity range to be January 1, 1999, through December 31, 1999.

- Set the month mask to be "001001001000" (this sets March, June, September, and December to enabled and disables all other months).

- Set the day-of-the-week mask to "0000100" (Fridays).

- Set the time-of-day range of 1300 through 2000.

Any attributes that are not present in an instance of the `PolicyTimePeriodCondition` class are implicitly treated as having their value `Always Enabled`.

The following attributes are defined for the `PolicyTimePeriodCondition` class:

- `TimePeriod` is a structured string attribute that identifies an overall range of calendar dates and times over which a policy rule is valid. It is formatted as a string consisting of a start date and time, then a colon (:), and followed by an end date and time. Dates are expressed as substrings of the form yyyymmddhhmmss. For example:

  `19990120073000:19990131173000`

  represents January 20, 1999, 7:30 a.m. through January 31, 1999, 5:30 p.m.

- `MonthOfYearMask` is a structured string attribute that refines the definition of the valid time period that is defined by the `TimePeriod` attribute. These attributes work together, with the `TimePeriod` attribute used to specify the overall time period that the policy is enabled for, and the `MonthOfYearMask` used to select which months of that time period the policy is active for.

  This attribute is formatted as a string containing 12 ASCII 0s and 1s, where the 1s identify the months (beginning with January) in which the policy rule is valid. For example, the value

  `"100100100100"`

  indicates that a policy rule is valid only in the first month of each calendar quarter (for example, January, April, July, and October).

  If this attribute is omitted, then the policy is valid for all 12 months.

- `DayOfMonthMask` is a structured string attribute that refines the definition of the valid time period that is defined by the `TimePeriod` attribute. These attributes work together, with the `TimePeriod` attribute used to specify the overall time period that the policy is enabled for, and the `DayOfMonthMask` used to select which days of that time period the policy is active for.

This attribute is formatted as a string containing 31 ASCII 0s and 1s, where the 1s identify the days of the month (beginning with Day 1 and going up through Day 31) on which the policy rule is valid. For example, the value

`"1000010000100001000010000100001"`

indicates that this `PolicyRule` is valid only on every fifth day of this month (assuming that it is a month that has 31 days). If a month has less than 31 days, the mask positions corresponding to days that the months do not have are ignored.

- `DayOfWeekMask` is a structured string attribute that refines the definition of the valid time period that is defined by the `TimePeriod` attribute. These attributes work together, with the `TimePeriod` attribute used to specify the overall time period that the policy is enabled for, and the `DaysOfWeekMask` used to select which days of the week of that time period the policy is active for.

  This attribute is formatted as a string containing 7 ASCII 0s and 1s, where the 1s identify the days of the week (beginning with Monday and going through Sunday) on which the policy rule is valid. For example, the value

  `"1111100"`

  indicates that a `PolicyRule` is valid only on weekdays (Monday through Friday).

- `TimeOfDayMask` is a structured string attribute that refines the definition of the valid time period that is defined by the `TimePeriod` attribute. These attributes work together, with the `TimePeriod` attribute used to specify the overall time period that the policy is enabled for, and the `TimeOfDayMask` used to select which time periods in a given day of the week of that time period the policy is active for.

  This attribute is formatted as a string containing two times separated by a colon (`:`). The first time indicates the beginning of the time period, while the second time indicates the end of the time period. Times are expressed as substrings of the form `hhmmss`, where `hh`, `mm`, and `ss` each represent two digits indicating the hour, minutes, and seconds of time, respectively.

  The second substring always identifies a later time than the first substring. However, if a time range spans midnight, the value of the second string may be smaller than the value of the first substring. For example, the range `080000:170000` identifies the range from 8 a.m. to 5 p.m. the same day, and the range `170000:08000` identifies the range from 5 p.m. on one day to 8 a.m. the following day.

When a range spans midnight, it by definition includes parts of two successive days. When one of these days is also selected by either the MonthOfYearMask, DayOfMonthMask, and/or the DayOfWeekMask, but the other day is not, then the policy is active only during the portion of the range that falls on the selected day. In the last example, the range extended from 5 p.m. on one day until 8 a.m. the following day. Now, if the DayOfWeekMask selects Monday and Tuesday, then this policy will be active during the following three intervals:

From midnight Sunday until 8 a.m. Monday

From 5 p.m. Monday until 8 a.m. Tuesday

From 5 p.m. Tuesday until 11:59:59 a.m. Tuesday

- ApplicableTimeZone is a structured string attribute that refines the definition of the valid time period that is defined by the TimePeriod attribute. These attributes work together, with the TimePeriod attribute used to specify the overall time period that the policy is enabled for, and the ApplicableTimeZone attribute used to define the time zone that is enforced for this time period.

This attribute is formatted as a string containing used to explicitly define a time zone for use by this time period. If this attribute is NULL, then local time (at the PEP where the PolicyRule is enforced) is assumed.

This attribute specifies time in UTC, using an offset indicator. The UTC offset indicator is either a 'Z', indicating UTC, or a substring of the following form:

"+" or "−"	direction from UTC: '+' = east, '−' = west
hh	hours from UTC (00..23)
mm	minutes from UTC (00..59)

This class does not define any methods or relationships.

The IETF/CIM Policy Model: LDAP Implementation

The LDAP implementation of the CIM Policy Model is being standardized in the IETF Policy Framework Working Group in cooperation with the Networks and service level agreement Working Groups of the DMTF. The output of this standard will then form the basis of the DEN Policy Model.

However, there are several significant differences between the IETF/CIM Policy Model and the corresponding LDAP implementation. These differences are due partly to the limitations of LDAP (which were discussed in Chapter 4, "What Is a Directory?"), and partly to take into account how information is organized in a directory. This organization is different from other types of repositories (for example, relational databases); therefore, a specialized mapping is needed.

Directory Navigation Issues

Navigation is performed very differently when using a directory compared to other types of policy repositories. CIM, of course, is an Information Model that deliberately does not take into account any special functions or limitations of the target repository. Directories excel at using containment to focus searches. However, the CIM model doesn't have a notion of containment that is used for navigation.

The danger of not having classes that help optimize navigation in the DIT is that without such classes, a directory-based implementation will not be scalable enough for use as a generalized policy repository. The CIM model doesn't have, and shouldn't have, such classes. However, an LDAP mapping can be derived that adds classes to the CIM model in order to represent navigation (much like DEN mapped physical and logical characteristics of CIM into a directory implementation).

Using Auxiliary Classes

Auxiliary classes provide a convenient means for accomplishing these goals. As mentioned in Chapter 4, auxiliary classes function much like a #include file does in C or C++ programming. Auxiliary classes "attach" to other classes, effectively adding their attributes to the attributes contained in the class that they are attaching to. The LDAP mapping, though still preliminary, uses three important mapping techniques. These are denormalizing, pointing to specific locations in the DIT, and getting around some search limitations of LDAP.

Denormalization

Denormalizing data is a common practice in optimizing relational databases, and can be effectively used in a directory implementation as well. This is not normally used in constructing a CIM Common Model because it is assumed that navigation has no penalties associated with it. In addition, one focus of the information model is to identify relationships between objects, and to model these with associations and/or aggregations, as appropriate. CIM builds the relationships, and then assumes that they can be "strung together" and traversed as required.

The problem is that each association corresponds to an LDAP object access. Following DNs and retrieving objects that are pointed to by the DN is a relatively expensive operation in LDAP. Strategic denormalization of data (for example, repeating data in several classes) enables the number of LDAP object accesses to be significantly reduced.

Identifying Key DIT Locations

Efficient searching requires knowing where to start the search in the DIT. This concept is not really present in the CIM Policy Model, because this is a technique that is specific to the type of implementation used for the repository. However, this is a key concept for directory implementations, because the alternative is to search the entire DIT.

This goal is complicated by the fact that the DIT may have already been organized by some means that did not take the needs of policy into account. This can be overcome by the use of auxiliary classes that can be "attached" to important locations in the DIT. This can be used to establish an arbitrary number of search locations in the DIT, independent of how the DIT is organized, by simply searching for either a specific auxiliary class or one (or more) of the attributes of an auxiliary class.

Bulk Load and Retrieval

Another factor that must be taken into account is how policy information can be efficiently loaded and retrieved. This is again the problem of a policy application not necessarily having control over the structure of the DIT. It can once again be solved by the judicious use of auxiliary classes.

Again, an auxiliary class can be used to "flag" a container (or other object) in the DIT as an object that has policy information. Depending on the directory, one can either search on the presence of the auxiliary class itself, or on one of its attributes.

Promoting Extensibility

Auxiliary classes can help represent complex structures. Suppose you had a single `PolicyCondition` subclass with a large number of attributes of several different types (for example, attributes that describe user, application, and host characteristics). This presents significant reusability problems, because every time one of the attributes in one of the types (user, application, and host) needed to change, the entire class would have to change. In addition, you would need another class to combine these new subclasses in order to avoid attribute collision.

A better design would be to use three auxiliary classes, one each for the three different types (user, application, and host in this example) of attributes. You have now isolated changes into three, not one, separate domains. This allows you to change one or more attributes in one domain without adversely affecting the other two domains.

Problems with Auxiliary Classes

Auxiliary classes are a very useful tool. However, there are problems with using auxiliary classes with respect to current directory implementations. There are two main problems, one small and one large.

The small problem is that you can't attach multiple instances of the same auxiliary class, because you would then have attribute collision (that is, the same attribute is trying to be used multiple times in different places). The solution for this problem is to plan your policies so that this doesn't happen.

The large problem is that support for auxiliary classes varies by directory vendor at the time of this writing. In practice, this means that certain features of auxiliary classes are not supported in the same way for all directories. The solution for this problem varies by vendor, but can usually be solved simply by either restricting the use of auxiliary classes in certain cases, or by ensuring that the auxiliary class has an attribute to search on (because some directories have trouble with searching on auxiliary object classes).

Another, more subtle, problem is that auxiliary classes are constructs specific to directory implementations. This means that although you can take the CIM Policy Model and map it to an LDAP implementation that uses auxiliary classes, mapping this information back to the CIM Policy Model will be much more difficult. This is especially true if you add information not present in the CIM Policy Model to the auxiliary classes. In addition, mapping this information to other types of repositories (such as relational databases) that do not support the notion of auxiliary classes is problematic.

It is therefore highly recommended that you develop a comprehensive strategy for mapping policy information to and from directories prior to developing detailed schemata if you are going to use directory-specific constructs, such as auxiliary classes.

Alternatives to Auxiliary Classes

Instead of using auxiliary classes, you can implement the CIM Policy Model directly and follow DN references. The obvious problem is that this could generate a lot of references that you would have to dereference serially.

One possible solution to this is to define a new extended control to unwind the references. The advantage of this approach is that you don't have to deal with differences in vendor support for auxiliary classes. The obvious disadvantage is that this is not standardized yet (though an Internet draft is being submitted).

Note

Experience has shown that using auxiliary classes as an exclusive solution is not wise. Though auxiliary classes present an efficient solution for the majority of cases, mapping information stored in auxiliary classes will be very hard to map back into a common form.

On the other hand, not using auxiliary classes at all is simply not practical. Therefore, judicious use of auxiliary classes, supplemented by additional mechanisms, should be employed.

LDAP Implementation

The LDAP mapping is conceptually divided into two parts. Figure 10.16 shows the preliminary LDAP mapping using auxiliary classes of the base concepts in the IETF/CIM Policy Model presented in Figure 10.7.

Note

Note that the IETF and DMTF have adopted a convention of specifying CIM attributes in InitCaps, whereas the LDAP mapping has the first letter in lower case and all subsequent word boundaries in InitCaps. Thus, the CIM attribute `PolicyRuleEnabled` would be changed to the LDAP attribute `policyRuleEnabled`.

Figure 10.16   The LDAP `Policy` class hierarchy without the subtree pointer and containment classes.

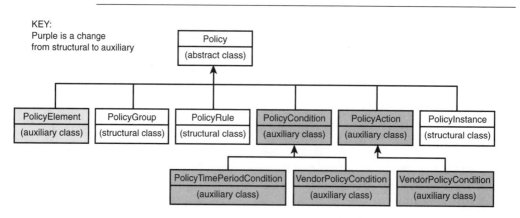

Figure 10.16 adds two new classes to the policy class hierarchy, and changes five of the existing classes from structural classes to auxiliary classes. The reasoning for this will be explained in the following sections. In addition, changes to the definitions of the attributes have been made to accommodate standard directory practices. For example, CIM specifies

a string as a data type. Directories have many different types of strings, such as IA5Strings, PrintableStrings, and DirectoryStrings.

Figure 10.17 shows three additional classes; one is used to identify subtrees in the DIT, and the other two are used to capture containment relationships.

Figure 10.17   The LDAP Policy class hierarchy, showing just the subtree pointer and containment classes.

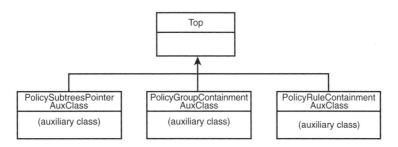

The following sections describe the differences between the LDAP mapping and the IETF/CIM model.

The Policy Class

The changes to this class are solely to identify the particular type of string that is used.

The PolicyRule Class

The differences between the CIM and LDAP Mappings in the PolicyRule class are shown in Figure 10.18.

Figure 10.18   Differences between the CIM and LDAP mapping of the PolicyRule class.

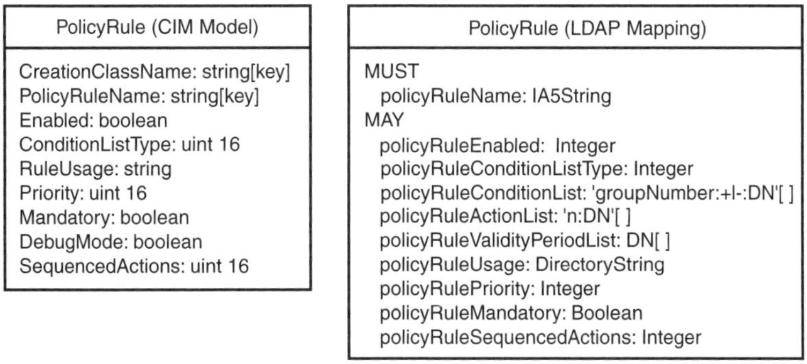

PolicyRule (CIM Model)	PolicyRule (LDAP Mapping)

CreationClassName: string[key]
PolicyRuleName: string[key]
Enabled: boolean
ConditionListType: uint 16
RuleUsage: string
Priority: uint 16
Mandatory: boolean
DebugMode: boolean
SequencedActions: uint 16
	MUST
	  policyRuleName: IA5String
	MAY
	  policyRuleEnabled: Integer
	  policyRuleConditionListType: Integer
	  policyRuleConditionList: 'groupNumber:+l-:DN'[ ]
	  policyRuleActionList: 'n:DN'[ ]
	  policyRuleValidityPeriodList: DN[ ]
	  policyRuleUsage: DirectoryString
	  policyRulePriority: Integer
	  policyRuleMandatory: Boolean
	  policyRuleSequencedActions: Integer

The following table maps the differences in naming and data type of the attributes from the CIM model to the LDAP mapping for this class.

CIM Mapping	LDAP Mapping
CreationClassName: string[key]	objectClass
PolicyRuleName: string[key]	policyRuleName: IA5String
Enabled: Boolean	policyRuleEnabled: Integer
ConditionListType: uint16	policyRuleConditionListType: Integer
None	policyRuleConditionList: "groupNumber:'+|-':DN" []
None	policyRuleActionList: "n:DN" []
RuleUsage: string	policyRuleUsage: DirectoryString
Priority: uint16	policyRulePriority: Integer
Mandatory: Boolean	policyRuleMandatory: Boolean
DebugMode: Boolean	policyRuleDebugMode: Boolean
SequencedActions: uint16	policyRuleSequencedActions: Integer
None	policyRuleValidityPeriodList: DN []

There are five differences (besides refining the specific type of string used) between the CIM and the LDAP mappings of this class:

- There is no CreationClassName in the LDAP mapping, because all LDAP object classes have an objectClass attribute that serves to define the type of class that this LDAP object is. Note, however, that objectClass is usually *not* used as a key.

- The data type for policyRuleEnabled in the LDAP mapping has been changed from a Boolean to an integer.

- The policyRuleConditionList attribute is an array of structured DN pointers. This attribute represents the ContainedPolicyConditions aggregation in the CIM model. Note that structured DN pointers require a fairly large amount of processing on the client end.

- The policyRuleActionList attribute is an array of structured DN pointers. This attribute represents the ContainedPolicyActions aggregation in the CIM model.

- The policyRuleValidityPeriodList attribute is an array of structured DN pointers. This attribute represents the PolicyRuleValidityPeriod aggregation in the CIM model.

The PolicyGroup Class

The changes to this class are as follows:

- There is no CreationClassName in the LDAP mapping.

- The policyRuleName attribute refines the type of string used to an IA5String.

- The ContainedPolicyGroups aggregation is replaced with a set of DN pointers as defined by the policyGroupAuxContainedSet attribute of the PolicyGroupContainmentAuxClass auxiliary class.

- The ContainedPolicyRules aggregation is replaced with a set of DN pointers as defined by the policyRuleAuxContainedSet attribute of the PolicyRuleContainmentAuxClass auxiliary class.

- The GroupWithXXXJurisdiction association is replaced with a set of DN pointers as defined by the policyGroupAuxJurisdictionSet attribute of the PolicyGroupJurisdictionAuxClass auxiliary class.

The PolicyInstance Class

This is a new structural class that is not present in the CIM model. The purpose of the PolicyInstance class is to serve as an "anchor point" for auxiliary classes to attach to. As you will soon see, the LDAP mapping changes the PolicyCondition, PolicyAction, and PolicyTimePeriodCondition classes from structural classes to auxiliary classes. This is in order to realize better reuse in an LDAP environment. Thus, a PolicyRule can contain instances of these three classes through three attributes that point to an instance of the PolicyInstance class that has the PolicyCondition, PolicyAction, and PolicyTimePeriodCondition classes attached to it. This is shown in Figure 10.19.

The DN pointer attributes (policyRuleConditionList, policyRuleActionList, and policyRuleValidityPeriodList) conceptually point to the attached PolicyCondition, PolicyAction, and PolicyTimePeriodCondition class instances, respectively. This provides much greater freedom in reuse and subclassing in a directory implementation.

Figure 10.19 Using the `PolicyInstance` class and appropriate auxiliary classes to represent CIM aggregations.

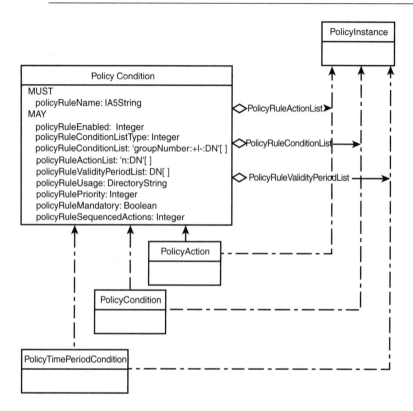

The `PolicyCondition` *Class*

The changes to this class are as follows:

- This class, which was a structural class in CIM, is changed to an auxiliary class in the LDAP mapping.

- There is no `CreationClassName` in the LDAP mapping.

- The `policyConditionName` attribute refines the type of string used to an IA5String.

- The `ContainedPolicyCondition` aggregation is replaced with a set of DN Pointers as defined by the `policyRuleConditionList` attribute in the `PolicyRule` class. However, because the `PolicyCondition` class is now an auxiliary class, it must be attached to a structural class for this to work. The `PolicyInstance` structural class is used to anchor (different) instances of the `PolicyCondition` class, so that this aggregation can be more efficiently realized in a directory implementation.

The `PolicyAction` *Class*

The changes to this class are as follows:

- This class, which was a structural class in CIM, is changed to an auxiliary class in the LDAP mapping.

- There is no `CreationClassName` in the LDAP mapping.

- The `policyActionName` attribute refines the type of string used to an IA5String.

- The `ContainedPolicyAction` aggregation is replaced with a set of DN Pointers as defined by the `policyRuleActionList` attribute in the `PolicyRule` class. However, because the `PolicyAction` class is now an auxiliary class, it must be attached to a structural class for this to work. The `PolicyInstance` structural class is used to anchor (different) instances of the `PolicyAction` class, so that this aggregation can be more efficiently realized in a directory implementation.

The `PolicyTimePeriodCondition` *Class*

The following table maps the differences in name and data type of the attributes from the CIM model to the LDAP mapping for this class.

CIM Mapping	LDAP Mapping
TimePeriod: string	ptpConditionTime: PrintableString
MonthOfDayMask: string	ptpConditionMonthOfYearMask: PrintableString
DayOfMonthMask: string	ptpConditionDayOfMonthMask: PrintableString
DayOfWeekMask: string	ptpConditionDayOfWeekMask: PrintableString
TimeOfDayMask: string	ptpConditionTimeOfDayMask: PrintableString
ApplicableTimeZone: string	ptpConditionTimeZone: PrintableString

Other than the above name and data type changes, the only other difference between the CIM and the LDAP mappings of this class are that the `PolicyTimePeriodCondition` class has been changed from a structural class to an auxiliary class.

The *VendorPolicyCondition* Class

The changes to this class are as follows:

- The type of class has been changed from a structural class to an auxiliary class
- The name of the Constraint attribute has been changed to vendorPolicyConstraintData; the data type has been changed from an array of unsigned 8-bit integers to an OctetString.
- The name of the ConstraintEncoding attribute has been changed to vendorPolicy ConstraintEncoding; the data type has been changed from a string to an OID.

The *VendorPolicyAction* Class

The changes to this class are as follows:

- The type of class has been changed from a structural class to an auxiliary class.
- The name of the ActionData attribute has been changed to vendorPolicyActionData; the data type has been changed from an array of unsigned 8-bit integers to an OctetString.
- The name of the ActionEncoding attribute has been changed to vendorPolicyActionEncoding; the data type has been changed from a string to an OID.

The *PolicyElement* Class

The PolicyElement class is an auxiliary class that is used to "tag" objects in the DIT as being "policy" objects. This enables us to use a DIT whose structure is not conducive to policy actions without modification. This class does not define any attributes.

This class can be used for a variety of purposes. Three examples are

- Tagging a class as a class that has policy information associated with it
- Tagging a class as a class that should be controlled using a policy
- Tagging a class that should be part of a bulk load and/or retrieval operation

In all cases, a simple search can be used to get a list of all classes that meet the criteria. This can be filtered by subclassing the PolicyElement class (but still keeping it as an auxiliary class) to contain attributes of interest, and then searching on those attributes.

The *PolicySubtreesPointerAuxClass* Class

This class is an auxiliary class, and is used to identify different locations in the DIT that contain policy information. It is intended to be attached directly to the Top class to facilitate locating policy information in the DIT.

This class defines a single MUST attribute, called `policySubtreesAuxContainedSet`. This is an array of DN pointers to objects in the DIT that represent subtrees that contain policy information.

The `PolicyGroupContainmentAuxClass` Class

This is an auxiliary class that contains a single attribute, called `policyGroupsAuxContainedSet`. This is an array of DN pointers that define which `PolicyGroups` are contained in a given `PolicyGroup`. This represents the `ContainedPolicyGroups` aggregation in the CIM model.

By making this an auxiliary class, it can be attached to any desired `PolicyGroup` class no matter where that `PolicyGroup` class is located. This is important, because the aggregation that this mechanism is representing is independent of the location of classes in the DIT. The attachment works as follows. Suppose that there is an object, which is an instance of the `PolicyGroup` class, which aggregates other `PolicyGroup` classes. Call this object the "parent" object. Further suppose that there are a set of objects that are in various locations in the DIT that are also instances of the `PolicyGroup` class. Call these objects "child" objects. This attachment enables all "child" objects to point back to the "parent" object and vice versa.

The `PolicyRuleContainmentAuxClass` Class

This class is identical in purpose and function to the `PolicyGroupContainmentAuxClass`, except that it is used to point instances of a `PolicyRule` object to a `PolicyGroup` object. It also contains a single attribute, called `policyRulesAuxContainedSet`. This is an array of DN pointers that define which `PolicyRules` are contained in a given `PolicyGroup`. This represents the `ContainedPolicyRules` aggregation in the CIM model.

Simple and Complex Policy Rules

This design is very flexible. Its use of auxiliary classes for modeling policy conditions and policy actions enables a policy rule to be modeled in two distinctly different ways. These are termed simple and complex policy rules, respectively.

Simple policy rules are built by subclassing the `policyRule` class and attaching the conditions and actions to the subclassed `policyRule` instance. This promotes simplicity and fast access. Alternatively, complex policy rules can be built by using the `policyInstance` class as an anchor to attach instances of the `policyCondition` and `policyAction` classes (or their subclasses). These instances are then pointed to by one of three different attributes in the `policyRule` object: `policyRuleConditionList`, `policyRuleActionList`, or `policyRuleValidityPeriodList`. this promotes reusability, as the conditions and actions can be reused among different policy rules.

In addtion, one can have combinations of these, where (for example) the conditions are attached to a subclass of a `policyRule` object and the actions are attached to instances of the `policyInstance` class and pointed to by the `policyRule` class.

Summary

This chapter has described the DEN Policy Model, and explained how it grew into its present form. The DEN Policy Model serves as the foundation of the IETF Policy Framework Working Group's work. This working group has, in cooperation with various DMTF working groups, enhanced the DEN Policy Model and focused it on representing policy to control access to network elements and allocation of network resources. This work will result in a Core Schema document issued by the IETF Policy Framework Working Group that will serve as a foundation to model policy for all IETF working groups. This work is making significant progress, and should be an RFC before the end of the year.

An LDAP mapping of the IETF Core Schema work is also being developed, again in conjunction with various DMTF Working Groups. In addition, the Policy Framework Working Group is developing a set of schemata, derived from the Core Schema, that model network QoS policies. These schemata will serve as a model for other IETF Working Groups, such as IPsec, DHC, and ISPS, for developing application-specific policy schemata in their respective areas.

This work will then be used by the DMTF service level agreement Working Group to develop a generalized Policy Model that can be used for managed objects (not just network elements and services). It will also be used by the DMTF Networks Working Group to develop an enhanced information model that represents the management of low-level network mechanisms that are used to provide network QoS services.

Recommended Further Study and References

The DEN Specification, version 4, will be published in the second quarter of 1999. Please check the DMTF home page below for updated links to this specification:

`http://www.dmtf.org/spec/denh.html`

The following are references for tracking the (still-developing) IETF Work:

Bhattacharya, P., and R. Adams, W. Dixon, R. Pereira, R. Rajan, "An LDAP Schema for Configuration and Administration of IPSec based Virtual Private Networks (VPNs)," `draft-ipsec-vpn-policy-schema-00.txt`, October 1998.

Gai, S., J. Strassner, D. Durham, S. Herzog, H. Mahon, F. Reichmeyer, "QoS Policy Framework Architecture," `draft-sgai-policy-framework-00.txt`, Feb 1999.

Pereira, R., P. Bhattacharya, "IPSec Policy Data Model," `draft-ietf-ipsec-policy-model-00.txt`.

Srisuresh, P., L.A. Sanchez, "Policy Framework for IP Security," `draft-ietf-ipsec-policy-framework-00.txt`, February 1999.

Strassner, J., "Policy Architecture BOF Presentation," 42nd IETF Meeting, Chicago, Illinois. October, 1998.

Strassner, J. and Ellesson, E. , "Terminology for Describing Network Policy and Services," `draft-ietf-policy-terms-00.txt`, Feb 1999.

Strassner, J., Ellesson, E., and Moore, B. "Policy Framework Core Information Model," `draft-ietf-policy-core-info-model-00.txt`, Feb 1999.

———. "Policy Framework LDAP Core Schema," `draft-ietf-policy-core-schema-04.txt`

Wahl, M., S. Kille, and T. Howes, "Lightweight Directory Access Protocol (v3): UTF-8 String Representation of Distinguished Names," December 1997, RFC 2253.

The following drafts in progress that are of general interest to policy and QoS:

Weiss, W., Strassner, J., and Westerinen, A., "Information Model for describing network policy and services", `draft-weiss-policy-device-qos-model-00.txt`

Snir, Y., Ramberg, Y., and Strassner, J., "QoS Policy Framework Information Model and Schema", `draft-snir-policy-qos-infomodel-00.txt`

PART III

Applications of DEN

CHAPTER 11

Policy-Based Networking

The purpose of this chapter is to provide insight into the emerging generation of policy-based networking. This chapter will concentrate on examining how policies are used to control access to and utilization of network resources in a coordinated way across a service provider or Enterprise domain.

Overview

This chapter will build on the previous three chapters, and show real-world examples of how DEN is being used to build next generation Intelligent Networks and applications. Specific examples will be given from Cisco products and solutions as representative examples of the emerging industry move to policy-based networking

Motivation

There are many factors that serve to motivate the creation and deployment of this new class of application. Arguably, the most important of these are to

- Enable intelligent, environment-based access to and control of network resources

- Improve network management, especially device configuration and provisioning

- Provide personalized network services

Intelligent Networking

Policy-based networking links the various users of the network with the computing systems and resources that these users wish to utilize. Policies are needed to ensure that business uses and requirements are met. This is getting increasingly difficult with the proliferation of applications, each having different needs. Supplying more bandwidth will not solve the problem. Rather, controlling the mix of different traffic types, as opposed to providing more bandwidth, is the fundamental advantage that an Intelligent Network offers.

Now, if the Intelligent Network can be controlled using policies that represent the needs of the business, then business will run better, and users will become more productive. For example, without a comprehensive set of policies that can be enforced at a granular level, non-critical applications could be consuming valuable network resources at the expense of mission-critical applications. While, in theory, you could control an Intelligent Network and its applications by configuring policies device-by-device, in practice that is impossible for even medium-sized networks. Not only does this lead to inconsistencies in the implementation of policies across devices, it does not provide a global view of the network and how network resources are being used to manage the different types of traffic flowing through the network. What is really needed is centralized policy control. This provides a way to link the power of the Intelligent Network to the needs of the business.

Chapter 5, "Motivation for DEN," described the move towards Intelligent Networking, and why DEN could play a crucial role in realizing Intelligent Networks and networked applications.

DEN provides a method of representing and sharing information between applications, network services, and network elements that provide Intelligent Network services. It is these services, accessed on an individual or group basis, that enable the realization of Intelligent Networking. This common representation and sharing of information is possible because of the following fundamental features provided by DEN:

- The entire end-to-end process of a user using a given application, connecting to a network resource through the network, and performing one or more operations can now be modeled. This has never been able to be done before in a generic manner, which is why it has been so hard to provide responsive, personalized network services. Being able to model this process enables the developer to leverage the power of the network for all applications (not just one or two) in a consistent fashion. This, in turn, enables network traffic to be controlled in a comprehensive fashion, while allowing specific traffic for individual and groups of users to be assigned a more granular quality of service.

- The DEN Information Model serves as a single repository for all data. On one end of the spectrum, the needs and characteristics of its users, and which applications and services they have rights to use, can be described. This is complemented by the ability to describe network elements and the services that are provided by a particular set of network elements. Thus, by joining these two heretofore-disparate pieces of information, the ability to model end-to-end services on a per-user or per-group basis is achieved.

- DEN can be used to help make applications network-aware. By providing a common means of representing and sharing information about network elements and services, applications can communicate their needs to each other and to the network. This enables differentiated value-added network services to be supplied on a per-application basis.

- Similarly, DEN can be used to make networks application-aware. Intelligent Networks are policy-driven, but are also aware of the different types of traffic that are flowing through them at any given time. If a particular device had to query its Policy Decision Point every time a new type of packet was received, nothing would ever get done. The network needs to realize the needs of individual applications that are using it, and vice versa. For example, interactive scientific visualization is an extremely computationally intensive operation that consists of a number of coordinated sub-tasks. Dedicated networks are, as of this moment, still too expensive to be employed for such applications. Therefore, visualization network traffic must peacefully coexist with other traffic that is on the network. However, if the visualization is to be interactive in nature, then its demands on the network will vary greatly and in a semi-random manner, depending on the interests of its users. This requires more than current protocols and differentiated services-enabled networks can provide. The answer lies in the ability of the network element itself to recognize and act proactively to such traffic, and is currently the subject of active research. However, without a comprehensive information model, such research cannot proceed.

Improved Network Management

One of the original driving factors of DEN was the desire to create a new type of network management, one that unified the needs of applications, users, host machines, network services, and network elements. This again required a common representation of data and a common means to store and retrieve that data in a secure way.

Once data could be represented and accessed in a common way, the next immediate goal was to reduce the number of isolated administrative islands, or "stovepipe" applications, that cannot communicate with each other. This would not only simplify the administration of network services, it would also enable a scalable distributed administration to be introduced. The directory could be used to provide a location- and access-independent identity, where authentication and authorization to network services could utilize the rich hierarchical access control mechanisms of the directory.

DEN enables the directory to be used as a centralized repository for shared configuration information for network services, as well as a means to control access to and allocation of network resources. For example, the network administrator can design common configurations for classes of similar devices. These devices can be identified through attributes, roles, or other means. The (common) configuration information can be placed in the directory, and all that is needed is for the devices to know the location of the directory to retrieve their configuration.

This also enables centralized policies to be designed to control access to and allocation of network resources. Policies and policy information can be stored in a centralized repository, enabling PDPs, as well as PEPs, and other network components to store and retrieve policy information. The power of the directory is not just to store policy information. Applying policies requires the coordination of many different tasks. The directory can simplify this coordination by providing storage for user authentication (for example, public keys and certificates) and authorization information (for example, user-based access control lists), as well as device and service authentication and authorization. For example, when a user logs on to a policy-enabled network, the user is authenticated and authorized using information in the repository. This same information can be used to coordinate a number of related tasks that provide a more powerful yet customized user experience. For example, once the user is identified and authenticated, information in the centralized repository can be used to assign the user to a particular VLAN that has been preconfigured to provide the network services that the user requires for this session. Given the groups that the user belongs to, certain network services can be started automatically. The user can be granted certain special capabilities, such as the ability to request bandwidth (for example, by using RSVP) or a given service. These are all examples of network services that use centralized related information to provide an integrated, compelling end-user experience.

Personalized Networking

Personalized networking is the ability to provide customized network services for a given individual or group of users that are different than what is given to other users of the network by default. For example, certain users may obtain network services that are better in some way (for example, more bandwidth, less jitter, and so on) than the default "best-effort" service.

This requires the coordination of many different facilities. Users, along with applications and services that are executed on behalf of a user, must be identified and given the appropriate type and level of service. Network devices must be identified and possibly reconfigured to provide differentiated levels of service. The network itself must be modeled to ensure that the set of resources allocated to a given set of network services is consistent with the business goals and policies that are being enforced.

For example, service providers need the ability to differentiate their service offerings based on providing added value. This added value is achieved through the delivery of end-to-end services that offer a wide variety of pricing options based on the type of service, quality of service, and usage. There are two distinct market segments that this can be applied to: consumer-based Internet services and services necessary to outsource a corporate intranet. In both cases, an open, standards-based solution must be used that can integrate with existing legacy system while providing a minimum of (and preferably no) disruption to their currently deployed services.

This builds on the transformation of the network infrastructure from being viewed as a fat "dumb" pipe to an intelligent framework that can provide network services. This, in turn, leads to what I call a "service-centric architecture." The goal of such an architecture is to enable the user to invoke services indirectly (instead of launching an application or working with individual objects, such as a document) as part of an overall business process. For example, when trying to establish a video conference with another person, the user no longer needs to perform a series of manually-intensive operations; rather, the service-centric architecture lets the user request the video conference service, who the user wants to connect to, and it does the rest. This enables the user to be more productive and alleviates the user from the manual management of the files or objects that the user is working with. It also makes optimum use of the resources of the network.

The New Role of Directories

Directories are emerging as the most popular type of repositories for these new applications. The use of directories and information models is driving the development of new types of network devices and applications that can take advantage of this information.

These tools represent a fundamentally new way of developing applications, and can be used to produce more intelligent applications. CIM and DEN play a crucial role in this new genre of application development.

For example, an increasing number of vendors are now announcing network elements, such as routers and switches, that have embedded LDAP clients, event services, and other advanced components that enable network devices to communicate more effectively and efficiently with each other as well as with directories, PDPs, and other components of the intelligent architecture.

DEN shows how to transform the directory into a logically centralized repository for hosting diverse information for different application domains. The inherent organizational structure of the directory is used to manage information of multiple types. This set of applications is characterized by using a directory as a means to manage and administer multiple types of information, of which networking information is included, but is not the central focus.

What Are Directory- and Network-Enabled Applications?

Directory- and network-enabled applications are two terms that are often misused or misunderstood. They are both used to describe a new genre of intelligent applications. These applications use Information Models to bind clients of the network to services that the network provides. Although people have a tendency to use these terms interchangeably, there is a difference.

A directory-enabled application is an application that uses the directory as its main repository. This doesn't necessarily mean that it is CIM- or DEN-compliant, though that is often the case. It also doesn't necessarily mean that the network is involved at all.

A network-enabled application is an application that takes advantage of the network. As with directory-enabled applications, a network-enabled application doesn't necessarily mean that it is CIM- or DEN-compliant, though that is often the case. And while a network-enabled application obviously uses the network, it doesn't necessarily use a directory as its main repository, nor does it use a CIM or DEN model of network elements and services to leverage network functions.

Why all the confusion over terminology? Market forces encourage people to claim compliance with new standards and terms, and this is a new, emerging area that everyone is paying attention to.

In this chapter, the use of these two terms will be avoided. Instead, we will use the term *policy-enabled network application* to mean an application that

- Is DEN-compliant (which also means that it is CIM-compliant)
- Controls network resources through using policies
- Binds clients of the network to services that the network provides without having the application to know low-level details about how to configure the network

How to Integrate DEN

One problem that faces policy-enabled network applications is how to integrate the DEN Information Model and schema that they need into an existing Directory Information Tree (DIT). The problem is that the DIT is usually already defined (that is, an existing schema is in place). This existing schema was probably developed to serve one or more specific applications which were most likely *not* policy-enabled network applications. If a policy-enabled network application required the DIT to be rebuilt, or even required its own special repository to work alongside the existing schema, then the market would simply not embrace policy-enabled networking. Furthermore, this would make it impossible for the directory to unify existing information with the new policy information.

A directory is recommended for storing policy information because it is a particularly good mechanism for implementing *containment*. This enables the construction of policies to integrate seamlessly with existing schemata through the use of auxiliary classes, as explained in Chapter 10, "DEN's Policy Model." In effect, auxiliary classes function as "policy tags" that allow policy classes and information to be attached to classes in the existing DIT structure without rebuilding or changing the DIT.

Containment also enables the policies to be focused in a specific context. That context can apply to a single user or a group of users, applications, devices, and services. Inheritance is used to fine-tune the application of policy in this context. For example, high-level default policies can be applied at an OrganizationalUnit (OU) level, and then refined at individual levels that are contained within the OU. These could be additional OUs, groups, or even users. The effect is one of structured refinement of policies: The most general policies are specified at the top of the tree, and the more specific policies are defined at lower levels of the tree.

The Need for Policy-Based Networking

The promise of Intelligent Networks is the delivery of higher levels of reliability, quality of service, and security. Policy-based networking is a comprehensive solution that enables the delivery of this promise. This is shown in Figure 11.1.

Figure 11.1 illustrates four major problems facing the deployment of the Intelligent Network (configuration complexity, inconsistent policies, lack of application control, and insufficient visibility) and four solutions brought by policy-based networking (automated policy configuration, centralized policy control, network application recognition, and active audit of policies, respectively).

Figure 11.1   The need for policy-based networking.

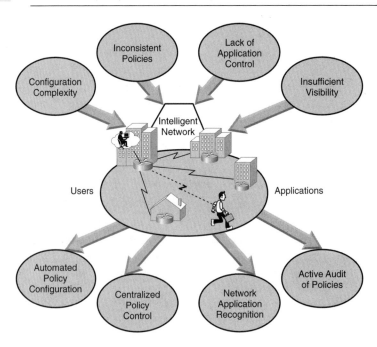

Solving Configuration Complexity

Today, the Intelligent Network provides a rich set of features—such as quality of service and security. Individual network devices are growing in features and functions, offering an increasingly wide variety of mechanisms for controlling network services such as QoS. However, this comes as a price: increased complexity of configuring the network device. In addition, this effect multiplies in the network, since as the configuration complexity of individual devices increases, the chance that the network as a whole will have conflicting configurations grows.

The performance of the network must be related to the business needs of the corporation(s) that are using the network. Network services must change in response to the changing environment (for example, new users logging on, old users logging off, new traffic patterns, and so on). The goal of the Intelligent Network is to adapt to these changing conditions by providing dynamic and automatic configuration of the appropriate low-level network mechanisms in the associated network devices in the Intelligent Network.

Performing this configuration, especially for a large number of devices, is a very complex task. Configuring policies on a device-by-device basis is difficult and can lead to inconsistent policies. Instead, centralized policy control is needed.

Automating Policy Configuration

Networks are too large and too complex to allow devices to be individually configured. Not only is this impractical from an administrative point-of-view, it increases the chance of having inconsistent policies exist in the network. This would be disastrous, since

- It means that some network devices are misconfigured and, therefore, providing the wrong service levels to one or more types of traffic.

- It also means that the overall order among the different types of traffic in the network as a whole may be wrong.

Policy-based networking solves this problem by using a highly distributed, logically centralized system to administratively control the various components of the network and of the policy system itself. This is discussed more throughout this chapter.

Network Recognition of Application Needs

Up until now, it has been difficult to associate business application policies with the network. By providing different levels of service, the network can provide different services for the various types of traffic that it carries. This is the first step in equating business rules to network performance.

However, the Intelligent Network needs more than this. The network needs to be able to recognize and activate policies for specific applications and user groups. This requires additional intelligence, distributed not just in the network, but in the controlling entities of the network and, where appropriate, the hosts and servers that are using the network.

This takes several forms and addresses the following problems:

- *How does the network know who the user is?* Many environments, such as those that use dynamically assigned IP addresses, render the identity of the user in question. Without knowledge of whom the user really is, the appropriate policies cannot be applied. Vendors have designed a variety of solutions to this problem, the most popular of which are application "shims" and proprietary protocols that can be used to identify the current user to the network.

- *How does the network ensure appropriate transport for different applications?* Applications must be treated, not as opaque traffic or instances of a protocol, but as part of the business that is being run. The network must know that month-end financials that is running over SAP/R3 is more important than ensuring that the humans crush the orcs in Warcraft 2 (though perhaps not as fun). The role of the policy server is to enable these mappings to be known to the network, so that each and every node in the network doesn't have to repeatedly query its policy server asking how each different type of traffic should be treated.

- *How does the administrator know that the network is delivering the services that it should?* The network must be able to be modeled as a system in its own right, so that it can be proactively monitored. What is important is not just the status of an individual device, but how that device is functioning in its subnet and/or delivering services to its clients.

In short, the network needs to be linked more closely to the applications that it transports. The Intelligent Network will use policy to deliver application data according to its business-critical nature.

Providing More Secure Policies

There is still one important piece of policy-based networking that has not been covered yet. That is its inherent ability to provide more granular information about how, when, why, and by whom a particular resource is used and accessed.

Just like other types of policies, security policies can be applied to users, applications and devices individually or by group. This is shown in Figure 11.2.

Figure 11.2   The role of security policies.

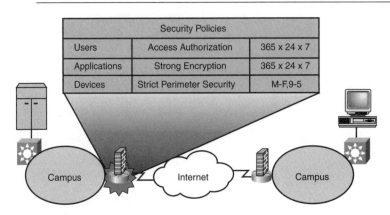

By establishing security policies and integrating them with other types of policies (for example, QoS and IP address assignment), we can protect the different types of applications that are critical to our businesses. These policies are especially important when information is transmitted over the Internet!

In the same manner that we set up our QoS policies, we can define and implement our Security policies. For instance, our ERP application is given top security, while NetShow receives only standard security protection. This is shown in Figure 11.3.

Figure 11.3   Aligning network resources with business priorities.

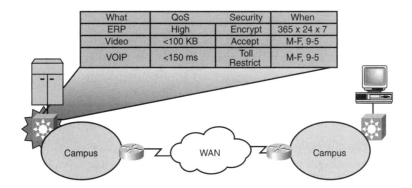

What	QoS	Security	When
ERP	High	Encrypt	365 x 24 x 7
Video	<100 KB	Accept	M-F, 9-5
VOIP	<150 ms	Toll Restrict	M-F, 9-5

As an example of a security policy integrated with a QoS policy, imagine that a corporation is running SAP ERP applications. The QoS policy should be the highest available in order to ensure that its traffic gets priority in all cases across the entire network, no matter what the traffic mix is. To further ensure this, we can create a policy that restricts the use of multimedia applications so that they can only consume a limited amount of available network bandwidth when they are running.

However, both of these applications have security requirements. Again, we see the difference between them: SAP traffic is required to be encrypted, whereas the multimedia traffic is not.

Note

The Policy classes discussed in Chapter 10 are very amenable to this approach. Specifically, we could have two different sets of PolicyRules, one for the SAP ERP traffic and one for the video traffic. Each set has two subclasses, one to implement the QoS PolicyRule and one to implement the Security PolicyRule. These can then be grouped into respective PolicyGroups, which can in turn be grouped into an overall PolicyGroup.

In addition, note that the time-of-day restrictions are eloquently handled through the attachment of the PolicyTimePeriodCondition class.

Theory of Policy-Based Networking

Historically, network management has focused on "individual device management" (that is, setting device parameters one at a time). A major drawback of this approach is the lack of a good mechanism to control and coordinate common configuration parameters and commands. That is, given a network-wide policy, how can it be applied in a consistent fashion across multiple network devices, and how can you be certain that the multiple devices that require common configuration changes as part of a coordinated change receive those changes at the same time?

While the mechanics of coordinating, managing and implementing network management are challenging, a more serious problem is the underlying philosophy used. This is perhaps best exemplified by the use SNMP. While SNMP is a pervasive and even very effective tool for network management, the problem is that SNMP was aimed at managing an individual device. This philosophical decision caused the following problems:

- Since SNMP is aimed at individual devices, the differences in these devices prohibit a standard MIB from being specified for all device types.

  » *This gave rise to a proliferation of MIBs, but didn't solve the problem. This was because the MIBs were either too generic (and therefore didn't manage device-specific features) or too specific (in which case the device could not be compliant with and support the MIB).*

- This was temporarily solved by the multiplication of proprietary MIBs.

  » *This worked well for an individual device. However, as soon as this was applied to a network of heterogeneous devices, this solution failed. The reason was the prohibitive expense, caused by extremely complicated design, required for a single device manager to accommodate this set of heterogeneous devices, each with their own private MIB(s).*

- Another drawback of designing a solution around the management of a single device was scalability. Here, the problem was the inherent *push* model used by SNMP.

  » *This works well for a small number of devices that are reporting similar information to a centralized manager. But this doesn't scale well when large numbers of devices of different characteristics, which have different information that they want to convey, send diverse information to a single manager. That manager is forced to accommodate a huge amount of information as well as varying types of data.*

Policy management is one way to control this explosion of volume and diversity of data. It enables information to be organized in more powerful ways (for example, objects, with relationships associating objects to each other) than simple tabular representations. The CIM and DEN models, in particular, are very conducive to this approach. Future versions of CIM and DEN will also add a powerful query language (that is quite similar to the standard SQL92 query language) and events, making the information model even more powerful.

Note

One challenge for the IETF and the DMTF is to harmonize the growing philosophical and implementation mismatches between the CIM/DEN Information Model and what can be built using LDAP. Work defining a standardized approach to representing associations and aggregations in a directory implementation is already underway. Adding events and a query language will either cause the definition of an intermediation layer to translate between these concepts and a directory implementation, or additions and enhancements to the LDAP protocol, or both.

Policy-enabled networking offers a more scalable alternative to individual device management. This framework provides policy definition, modification, distribution, verification, and administration for a heterogeneous set of network devices.

Intra-Domain Versus Inter-Domain Issues

The work currently underway in the IETF and the DMTF is concentrating on defining policy-based management in a single administrative domain. The Internet2 effort, in conjunction with the IETF, is leading the definition of interdomain policy administration and management.

Policy administration and management within a single policy domain can have heterogeneous devices and even policy servers that control those devices. However, the important point is that they are all within a single administrative boundary, and therefore all have knowledge of the policies and policy decisions that are being executed within the domain. This has three important corollaries:

- At the intra-domain level, a single administrative organization creates, stores and enforces a set of policies through a centralized Policy Service. The building blocks of the Policy Service must be constructed so as to share a common view of the policies.

- Heterogeneous PDPs and PEPs are envisioned. A given PDP (or its proxy) is responsible for translating between the shared definition of policy and the device-specific configuration that implements that policy for the PEPs that it controls.

- The focus of intra-domain policy administration and management is on the specification of low-level policies that can be used to configure and manage the network resources that supply network services that this administrative domain provides to its clients.

Inter-domain policy management is much different. Here, the focus is to interconnect separate administrative domains that control their own private network resources so that an end-to-end service can be specified, monitored, and obtained. This is done through *a priori* bilateral agreements between neighboring administrative domains. In this model, each domain is responsible for its own internal resource management. Domains external to a given domain only see abstract, opaque services (for example, Gold, Silver and Bronze). They do *not* see the specific policies that control the network elements that provide those services.

In general, at the inter-domain level, different Policy Domains do not share a common view of policies. Rather, they cooperate and exchange traffic on the basis of service level agreements (SLAs) using, for example, bandwidth brokers. SLAs are pre-negotiated contracts between adjoining administrative domains that together control the services provided in an end-to-end fashion. This is illustrated in Figure 11.4.

Figure 11.4   Using SLAs to construct an end-to-end service.

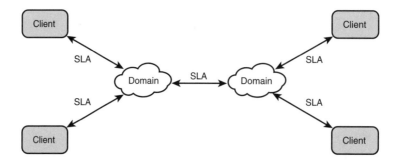

SLAs define a set of services that can be contracted for. A special type of Policy Server is responsible for taking these requirements and coordinating multiple administrative domains so that the same relative treatment of traffic within each of the administrative domains is provided. This effectively links the disparate administrative domains together, and specifies how they can work together to provide end-to-end services as specified by the SLA.

SLA links specific technologies employed within a given administrative domain to the business objectives as represented by the SLA. Individual administrative domains may manage internal resources in any way they see fit, to fulfill both internal and external obligations.

Generalized Intra-Domain Policy-Based Architecture

Figure 11.5 illustrates a generalized policy-based architecture for a single administrative domain. The following sections describe this generalized architecture in more detail.

Figure 11.5   General form of an intra-domain policy-based architecture.

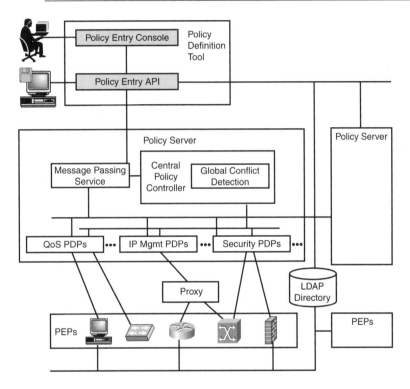

Policy Management Tool

Policies are defined, edited, and managed using a centralized policy management tool. This consists of a GUI interface (for example, the Policy Entry Console in Figure 11.2) and/or a generalized programmatic interface (that is, the Policy Entry API). The Policy Entry API (PEAPI) enables programs, as well as the output of the PEC, to participate directly in the creation, editing, installation, removal, and management of policy information. It serves as the interface through which programs and the PEC interact with the Policy Service. The PEAPI is also responsible for validating new and edited policy information, and then sending it on to the Policy Server for further processing.

The other main function of the Policy Entry Console (PEC) is to enable the network administrator to store, view, search, and delete policies and related policy support information. The PEC reads policy information from the Directory (and possibly other sources) and creates an overall view of the policies and policy information in the Policy Server.

The combination of the PEC and PEAPU provide a number of important services for administering policy information, including:

- Authentication and authorization of the user on whose behalf the program using the PEC is operating, and determine what operations this user is allowed to perform.

- Viewing and editing of the overall configuration of the Policy System.

- Management of the message passing interface, including registering with a message passing service either as a publisher, subscriber, or both, as well as sending and receiving messages, and other necessary but less important functions.

- Construction of the messages to be sent from a PEC or a program via the messaging system. The messages themselves are used to perform various operations, including the following:

  - Add new policies or policy information

  - Delete existing policies or policy information

  - Modify existing policies or policy information

  - Enable/disable individual and/or groups of policies

  - Communicate the success or failure, and optionally the reason, of attempted policy change messages

Policy Server

The Policy Server consists of three major functions. These include a Message Passing Service, a Central Policy Controller, and one or more PDPs.

The Message Passing Service

The Message Passing Service can take many forms. The most general of these is a publish-subscribe system that communicates using self-describing events. Other simpler forms include a bus-based architecture based around the directory, augmented with a simple form of notification.

In any case, the purpose of this component is to communicate incremental updates of policies. These could be changes to existing policies as well as the notification of a new policy that should be installed. This component coordinates the creation, modification, validation, administration, management, and installation of policies by providing a standard form of communication (events) between the various components that make up the Policy Server.

The use of a Message Passing Service in addition to the directory service is a fundamental architectural decision that, while under discussion in the IETF, is how many vendors are currently proceeding. This reflects using the Directory for what it's good at (for example, a searchable data store for relatively static data) and not misusing the directory for tasks that it is not well suited for. These tasks include

- Basic messaging functions, such as delivery of richly structured information and notification that new data is available.

- Enforcing transactional and referential integrity of operations (recall that directories operate on the principle of loose consistency, and some operations require tight consistency).

- Although policies are static, the data that they use to base decisions on are transient.

The Central Policy Controller

The Central Policy Controller (CPC) is the single logical point through which all policy changes are passed. It may be a single entity, or consist of several physically distinct entities. In either case, it represents the function to coordinate and synchronize policy changes in the Policy Server. In other words, it ensures that the effect of policy change in the Policy Server is both predictable and consistent.

The CPC coordinates the evaluation of policy changes to ensure that the results of the policy operation are valid. For example, the CPC can check to ensure that deleted policies do not create an inconsistent state, and that new and modified policies do not conflict with other installed policies.

The CPC enables complex policy conflict detection and verification to be performed. It contains a Global Conflict Detection component, which is responsible for performing detection of common conditions that are not specific to any particular PEP that have conflicting actions.

Global conflicts are those based on the properties of the policy and not the specific devices (or their interfaces) to which the policy applies. Two policies globally conflict with each other when all their conditions are satisfied, but one or more of the actions of one policy conflict with one or more of the actions of the other policy. The conditions of two policies are both satisfied when their criteria are both met simultaneously. The actions of two policies conflict when they cause different operations to be applied to the same resource. For example, if Policy A specifies that traffic should be forwarded for a particular source IP address, but Policy B specifies that traffic should be denied for that same source IP address, these policies will conflict with each other if each of their conditions are all satisfied.

As another example, imagine the specification of the following two policies:

- Policy A provides Gold Service for all engineering managers.

- Policy B provides Bronze Service for anyone that is running FTP

Now, what happens when an engineering manager runs FTP? Does that person get Gold or Bronze Service? The Global Conflict Detection component resolves this and similar conflicts once, rather than mandating that all PDPs perform the exact same calculations.

The CPC also enables the PDPs to democratically decide if a new policy change should be allowed or not. One way to do this is to pass the proposed policy on to each of the PDPs, and have each of the PDPs *vote* as to whether it can implement this policy. The CPC collects the votes and then decides whether the policy should be implemented now, sometime in the future, or not at all, for a set of the PDPs that it communicates with.

Often, policies that appear to conflict globally actually do not conflict with each other. This is because the administrator may intend to use these policies at different times, such as in response to different network conditions. For example, two policies might mark a certain type of traffic differently (for example, using different differentiated services code points) for the same set of source and destination IP addresses. Normally, this would be a global conflict. However, if the administrator defined one policy to be used under normal or congested conditions, and the other policy to be used only under certain emergency conditions, then that specification effectively resolves the conflict. This is important, because the two policies should be stored intact in the repository. They are differentiated according to other factors, some of which may also be stored in the repository. These factors may be as simple as populating the keyword attribute for the policies or as complicated as subclassing the policy and defining specific metadata that governs its operation and application.

The PDP

The Policy Decision Point (PDP) is the Policy Service component that communicates with policy-capable network elements. For network devices that are not policy-capable, a Policy Proxy is used to translate between their means of communication and control capabilities and those of the PDP.

The PDP is the component of the Policy Server that controls the application of device configuration changes. These device configuration changes are the result of one or more policy decisions that are made by the PDP on behalf of the PEP(s) that it controls.

Figure 11.5 shows a single administrative domain that consists of two Policy Servers. Each Policy Server consists of a set of heterogeneous PDPs and PEPs. The PDPs are organized according to the type of policy that they administer. Three examples shown in Figure 11.5 are QoS, IP Address Management, and Security.

This approach is more general than having a single PDP handle all of its PEPs, and is also more realistic. Here's why:

- PEPs may reside in different physical locations that make it physically impossible for the same PDP to communicate with them.

- The PDP will generally have some, but not all, of the knowledge of the capabilities of a PEP. It is much easier to construct a PDP that manages a certain set of devices, as opposed to trying to construct a PDP that manages all types of devices.

- Furthermore, even if the PDP did know exactly what the capabilities were of each of the devices that it was managing, it in general would not be cognizant of the (changing) network topology that connected them.

- It may be desirable to load balance multiple PDPs to reduce traffic between a PDP and its set of PEPs.

- A network element may need to connect to more than one PDP to acquire its policy (for example, a firewall or an access server).

- Finally, existing policy servers currently on the market, as well as those being planned for the near future, usually address one type of policy to the exclusion of other types.

There may be multiple PDPs of the same category within a given Policy Server. This is often necessary to accommodate the differences in the PEPs that are being controlled, or because different vendors are involved. Some vendors may want to build a specialized PDP for a specific type of device (for example, a switch versus a router versus a host). Other vendors have very rich mechanisms available that require additional specification beyond what is available in the standards. For example, proprietary mechanisms that are not yet standardized will require additions to the Information Model to control them.

Each PDP is responsible for managing one or more PEPs. The PDP is responsible for translating a policy into a form that the device can understand. An example of this translation is as follows:

1. Specify an SLA in business terms. Example:

   Engineering managers get Gold Service for coding

2. Specify one or more SLOs (Service Level Objectives) that are used to implement the SLA. Example:

   a. The following users are Engineering managers {...}
   b. Network resources for coding have the following IP addresses {...}

3. Translate the preceding to a more specific form amenable to device configuration. Example:

   ```
   IF User IN EngManagerGroup THEN Remark to Gold
   ```

4. Map all variables in generic form to a more specific form amenable to device configuration. Example:

   ```
   IF SourceIPAddress IN {...} AND DestIPAddress IN {...}
   THEN Remark Using DSCP of 5
   ```

5. Map all device-independent variables to a form that is device-specific for that class of device. Example:

   DSCP of 5 means to use Weighted Fair Queueing, Four Queues, Three Threshold Values, for this particular PEP

6. Finally, map this to a device-specific form using the appropriate mechanisms (for example, MIBs) that are specific to the PEP being configured

Local conflict detection is done within each PDP. This is a more fine-grained version of the global conflict detection done in the CPC. Local conflict detection is used to detect conflicting actions in policies that have device- and/or topology-specific conditions. For example, one policy might require three queues with a set of corresponding thresholds and drop behaviors, while another policy might require eight queues with a different number of thresholds and drop behaviors. What happens when both of these policies are assigned to the same device interface?

The PDP is responsible for understanding the policies currently installed in the devices that it controls, as well as mapping policies into specific configuration changes for those devices. Changes to policies may also change the configuration of some network elements. The PDP is responsible for determining which devices are affected by a particular modified policy, and ensuring that the modified policy can be installed without conflict.

The PEP

Each PEP tells the PDP what actions it is capable of performing and how it wants its policy to be specified to it (for example, the particular form of conditions and actions that are transmitted to it). This may be communicated by several means, including dedicated policy protocols like COPS. A proxy may be inserted between the PDP and the PEP in cases where the PEP does not speak the same protocol that the PDP speaks.

Network devices support different types of mechanisms. These mechanisms can be available either in software or in hardware. Therefore, policies must be abstract enough to allow for those differences, while remaining specific enough to provide useful direction to the PEP.

Policy-Based QoS

This section will describe one approach to abstracting some of the many QOS mechanisms that are available today so that they can be used in a policy system. While the process of abstracting such mechanisms is general, many of the following examples are specific to Cisco products.

Network managers are concerned with tailoring their network to support a mix of different applications. It's important to have a range of QoS mechanisms available in the network infrastructure, to help in deploying new applications quickly and successfully.

Cisco IOS has a very rich set of QoS queuing and priority mechanisms to support different network and application scenarios.

Intelligent QoS Mechanisms

Cisco offers many different types of low-level QoS controls. The following provides a brief description of four popular types of QoS mechanisms:

- *Admission control.* This ensures that traffic is admitted to a link at an agreed-upon rate.

- *Congestion management.* This is used to provide prioritization and queuing of outgoing traffic onto a slow link, so that high priority traffic is not delayed behind less time-sensitive traffic.

  Such mechanisms, which include priority queuing, custom queuing and weighted fair queuing, enable routers to provide varying levels of service to different traffic flows or types. This allows preferential treatment to applications that require different levels of service, when there is bandwidth contention due to congestion.

- *Congestion Avoidance.* This is used to prevent congestion from occurring in the first place. Weighted Random Early Detection (WRED) is perhaps the best known of these mechanisms, and operates by associating specific priorities to packets and discarding low priority packets, when buffers surpass a predetermined utilization.

- *Traffic Shaping.* This set of mechanisms include the feedback mechanisms provided by Frame Relay or ATM, to ensure that congestion doesn't occur within the network, by controlling flow into the network to only what can be supported. Cisco's Generic Traffic Shaping is an example of this type of mechanism.

Different QoS Mechanisms

Priority queuing is the simplest of the QoS mechanisms. It mirrors the defined behavior of IP Precedence by partitioning the traffic into different queues that have different priorities assigned to them. Priority queuing then uses an absolute scheduling algorithm that first empties all traffic in the highest priority queue. It then empties traffic from the next highest priority queue, and so forth. Priority queuing is used when the traffic mix corresponds to absolute levels of importance. It ensures that important traffic gets the fastest handling at each point where it is used. The problem with priority queuing is that lower-priority traffic can be locked out by higher-priority traffic. Priority queuing is illustrated in Figure 11.6.

Figure 11.6   Priority queuing.

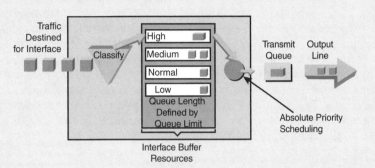

Class-based, or custom, queuing was designed to allow various traffic types to share the network with some applications that have specific minimum bandwidth or latency requirements. In these environments, bandwidth must be shared proportionally between applications and users. Custom queuing is used to provide guaranteed bandwidth at a potential congestion point, ensuring that the specified traffic receives a fixed portion of the available bandwidth. The remainder of the remaining bandwidth will shared to other traffic. For example, encapsulated SNA requires a guaranteed minimum level of service. You could reserve half of available bandwidth for SNA data, allowing the remaining half to be used by other protocols such as IP and IPX. The problem with custom queuing is that it is in reality FIFO by class, and so is still unpredictable within a class. Custom queuing is illustrated in Figure 11.7.

Figure 11.7   Custom queuing.

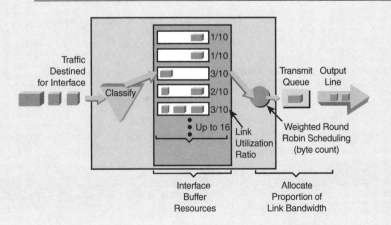

continues

Weighted Fair Queuing (WFQ) is the most sophisticated queueing mechanism. It attempts to provide predictable traffic latency, and guarantee that reserved flows achieve a certain bandwidth and latency. This is often used in situations where it is desirable to provide consistent response time to varied traffic (for example, some traffic types require light use of network resources, while other traffic types require much heavier use of network resources) without adding excessive bandwidth. WFQ does two things simultaneously: it schedules interactive traffic to the front of the queue to reduce response time, and it fairly shares the remaining bandwidth between high bandwidth flows. This ensures that a given traffic type is not starved for bandwidth. The problem with WFQ is that it requires more resources to run than the other alternatives. WFQ is illustrated in Figure 11.8.

Figure 11.8   Weighted fair queuing.

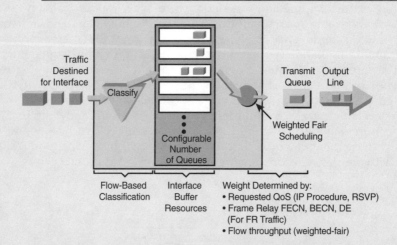

Congestion avoidance techniques monitor network traffic loads in an effort to anticipate and avoid congestion at a likely bottleneck in the network. This is different than the congestion management techniques described earlier, which attempt to manage and control congestion once it occurs. The most common example of congestion avoidance is Weighted Random Early Detection (WRED).

WRED works by monitoring traffic load and dropping packets if the congestion begins to increase above a pre-determined flight. The result of the drop is that the source detects the dropped traffic and slows its transmission. WRED can use IP Precedence or RSVP information to determine the rate to drop traffic at. WRED is illustrated in Figure 11.9.

Figure 11.9   Weighted random early detection.

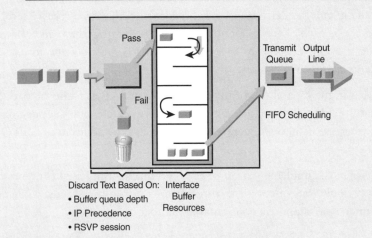

Generic Traffic Shaping is used to manage traffic and congestion on a particular inter-face. It reduces outbound traffic flow to avoid congestion by constraining specified traffic to a particular bit rate (also known as the token bucket approach), while queu-ing bursts of the specified traffic. Thus, traffic adhering to a particular profile can be shaped to meet downstream requirements, eliminating bottlenecks in topologies with data-rate mismatches. WRED is illustrated in Figure 11.10.

Figure 11.10   Generic traffic shaping.

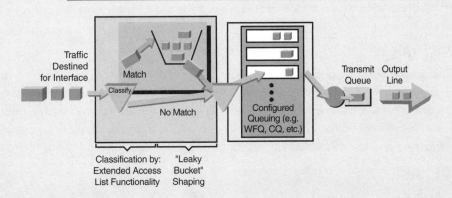

For more information on Quality of Service, refer to *Windows 2000 Quality of Service*, published by Macmillan Technical Publishing.

Delivering End-to-End QoS

QoS is meaningless unless it is applied end-to-end, from source to destination. This also increases the difficulty in delivering QoS, because now the same relative level of QoS must be supplied across each of the different components that together carry the traffic from source to destination. This means that end-to-end QoS must equate, for each of the network elements that form the path:

- Differences in the capabilities of the network elements that form the path between the source and the destination (for example, one network element supports WFQ by default, whereas the next network element only has the ability to do FIFO and priority queuing).

- Differences in the implementation of the QoS mechanisms used (one network element can support only four queues with three different drop thresholds, while another network element can support a configurable number of queues).

- Differences in the various technologies used (for example, Committed Information Rate in Frame Relay versus Constant Bit Rate in ATM versus IP Precedence in Layer 3 routing).

- How to map higher-level traffic treatments, such as RSVP and differentiated services, into the specific lower-level QoS mechanisms that are available in a given network element (for example, use IP Precedence to define the priority to assign to a given queue).

- How to map the preceding tools to higher-level specification of policy (for example, Gold, Silver, and Bronze Services are defined as High, Medium, and Normal Queues, respectively, for a network element that uses priority queuing).

Managing QoS

Defining and managing policies throughout the network requires a common repository. This repository represents information in a common way, so that all applications can both access as well as share this information. This means that applications can both publish as well as retrieve information about objects of interest. In addition, applications can use the repository to discover other network resources and obtain information about them.

The DEN Policy Model can be used for two purposes:

- To define policies that control which network resources a given consumer can use in the context of a particular application or service

- To define the structure of a policy, so that its conditions form a means of deciding whether the actions of this policy should be applied or not

This combination of *access to* and *allocation of network resources* enables higher-level policies to control who can log on to the network, what capabilities they will be granted, what their preferences are, and what types of operations they can perform.

For example, suppose that we want to add distance learning traffic to our current traffic mix. Distance learning has its own set of network requirements. Unfortunately, most distance learning applications require high bandwidth (for example, 250 – 1500 Kbps). A QoS policy can be used to restrict the distance learning application so as to protect business-critical network resources. This could be done by using RSVP to reserve resources from the network in combination with a policy to limit bandwidth at the remote office location that uses RSVP to ensure that other business critical applications are not adversely affected by the running of this training application.

Applications of Policy-Based Networking

Cisco's vision of policy-based networking combines Intelligent Network elements, policy servers and applications with multiple types of repositories. This is because policy requires access to data that is fundamentally different in terms of storage needs, rate of change, and volume. Trying to put these different types of data into a single repository simply will not work. Instead, Cisco advocates the use of different types of repositories, each suited to the specific storage and retrieval needs of the data that it contains.

Directories are simple, yet specialized, types of databases. They are not designed to collect information from multiple sources and then make a policy decision. Specifically, directories are not good candidates to store the state of a device, let alone the state of a network. Directory-enabled applications are designed to be able to pull static information from the central repository and then operate on that data autonomously. In a policy-based networking system, the directory still stores information, but a PDP or PEP interprets this information in the context of other data.

Example: Layer 3 Packet Filtering

The following is an example of a policy that is used to determine whether or not a user can invoke a specific service at a particular time.

Suppose that an interactive multimedia training program is made available to the managers of a company. However, employees that are not managers cannot use this program. Furthermore, due to its high bandwidth requirements, this program can only be run during non-business hours.

Assume that an employee tries to run the program at any time. Access to the program is granted through the directory. Therefore, the access control properties of the directory service itself can be used to ensure that the employee, if not a manager, is denied access.

But what if the user is a manager? Then, a more complicated set of steps must be executed in order to verify that this user can run this program at this time. Assume that it is 1:30 p.m. on Monday afternoon, and that a manager attempts to run the multimedia application. The following set of steps describe the series of transactions that take place to determine if the manager is allowed to run the program or not.

1. The intelligent device (for example, a router) determines that the inbound packet is from the interactive multimedia training program by examining the IPSourceAddress, protocol type, and application's port number.

2. The COPS client on the router transmits a request to its policy server, asking it to determine if the person represented by this IPSourceAddress is authorized to run the interactive multimedia training program corresponding to this application's port number and ProtocolType.

3. Upon receipt of the COPS request, the policy server utilizes LDAP to access the directory server to obtain the user profile of the object (user profiles is also a DEN concept). If the manager is authorized to use the interactive multimedia, then this will show up as one or more attributes in one or more classes in the directory. Otherwise, the attribute will not be set, and the manager will not be permitted to use the interactive multimedia training program.

4. The policy server queries its local time server to obtain the current time-of-day of this request.

5. The PDP makes a decision when its gathered enough information to know what it is lacking. In this case, the policy decision will be no, because the time-of-day condition is not met.

6. The PDP transmits the policy decision to the router via the COPS protocol. Note that if the decision had been positive, then COPS would also have to ship configuration information to the PEP.

7. The router, based on the policy decision, constructs a packet filter that either accepts or denies the video traffic of the manager until (for example) 5:00 p.m.

Example: Remote User Authentication

Assume that a user attempts to access his or her corporate intranet from the road, using a DHCP-based client. Corporate policy requires the user to be authenticated before being permitted to access the corporate network. A result of this will be for the remote access server to assign an appropriate IP address to the remote user. The following list describes one set of possible steps involved in authenticating the mobile user and assigning a IP address to that user. In this case, the Policy Server is being used to authenticate the user, provide an IP address to the user, determine what network resources the user has access to, and possibly even assign QoS settings for that user.

1. The user dials into his or her corporate intranet from the road, thereby connecting to the remote access server.

2. The remote access server initiates a dialog with the user, asking the user for his or her username and password.

3. The user supplies the username and password.

4. The remote access server queries the directory, attempting to match an entry that has the supplied username and password.

5. If this is not successful, then the remote access server displays a suitable error message on the user's client machine and the process stops. If this is successful, then the remote access server retrieves all applicable policies governing how the connection should proceed and what rights and permissions the user has.

6. Another authentication process could optionally be inserted, depending on the security requirements of the session.

7. At this point, the user is authenticated. The policy server now queries the directory server to retrieve the profile of the user. The profile specifies what privileges and access rights the user has, and what resources the user can access.

8. The user profile is retrieved by the policy server.

9. The user profile specifies the authorization data and other information needed to complete the connection. There are two paths to proceed, depending on whether the rest of the data is in a directory or another special-purpose database (for example, a RADIUS and/or a DHCP database):

   • If this information is contained in the directory, then LDAP will also be used to retrieve this information.

   • If this information is in a different database or databases, then this process may need to use different protocols, such as RADIUS or DHCP, to connect to those databases. This information may need to be subsequently translated into LDAP, because the Policy Server may not support these other protocols directly, and/or for ease of querying. The translation could be quite complicated (for example, translation from RADIUS vendor-specific attributes).

10. We'll assume in this case that the user profile specified that a RADIUS server should be used to construct the IP address. The policy server contacts the RADIUS server in order to obtain an IP address lease.

11. The RADIUS server responds back with either an accept or reject message, and associated information.

12. The policy server logs this information as appropriate for future use (for example, the policy server can now associate traffic from a specific IP address with a specific user for QoS purposes).

13. Depending on the RADIUS response, the remote access server either authenticates or blocks the dial-in user.

Cisco's Policy-Based Architecture

This section will use the CiscoAssure Policy Networking architecture as an example for illustrating the previous points in this chapter.

Overview

Network administrators will define policies and behavior, either programmatically and/or using a GUI. These definitions will be defined using business terms, so that they can be more efficiently related to business rules.

These definitions will then be translated into an intermediate form, either in the Policy Definition Tool (see Figure 11.5) or in the Policy Server. If there are multiple Policy Servers, then they must synchronize and replicate these business rules between them. If there is more than one administrative domain, then the business rules must be synchronized and replicated across multiple administrative domains. This will provide a consistent view of policies that control network elements and services across all affected administrative domains. This is critical for providing an end-to-end service.

A key part of the Cisco policy-enabled networking architecture is that the Policy Server abstracts port and interface parameters. This enables the Policy Server to control devices in an abstract sense, rather than having to have intimate knowledge of the capabilities and configuration methods of each of the devices that it controls.

CiscoAssure implements this architecture using four building blocks: policy administration, policy servers, registration and directory services, and Intelligent Network devices.

The policy administration portion consists of both an interactive GUI tool as well as APIs that offer programmatic and scripted interfaces. This is where business rules are transformed into network, security, and other types of policies. The policy administration component uses a directory so that rules and policies can be centrally configured and managed.

CiscoAssure can have more than one policy server. Each policy server distributes and activates policies for various network services that it controls, such as QoS and security. The architecture of CiscoAssure enables different policy servers, each governing different types of policies, to communicate with each other and deliver coordinated policy management.

One of the types of data that is used by a CiscoAssure policy server comes from specialized databases, including registration (for example, DNS and DHCP servers) and directory services. These services provide a dynamic binding between network addresses and user group identities.

Mapping Business Rules to QoS Policies

This section will discuss the flow of policy data from the PDP to the PEP, starting immediately after the network manager has specified a policy and it has been validated by the Policy Server (refer again to Figure 11.5). This first step is ignored because it is straightforward, and will vary widely as a function of the particular vendor implementing the policy console and associated APIs.

Policies are mappings between business rules and device enforcement mechanisms. Although the business rules can be simple to specify, the mappings themselves may be quite complex. This section will discuss this mapping for one particular domain: network quality of service.

The mapping takes as input a vendor- and device-independent specification of QoS and outputs a vendor- and device-specific form of that policy, utilizing the native QoS mechanisms available in each network device. This is done so that the policy does not depend on a particular technology, device type, or vendor. Application recognition mechanisms may be used at the input in cases where more information is needed than just IP addresses, port numbers, or protocol types, or when these data may be either ambiguous or unresolvable. This mapping then uses some protocol (for example, COPS) to transfer this information from the PDP to either a Policy Proxy or the PEP directly. The policy information may be translated to a device-specific form either before it is downloaded by the device or by the device itself, depending on the power of the individual device.

Application Recognition

As stated previously, the Intelligent Network requires more application recognition and awareness, since it transports the business information that is generated by the application.

Some policies can be implemented completely by the network. For example, well-known traffic flows (for example, http and ftp) can be identified by looking at well-known ports in the TCP and UDP headers. Users and network resources can sometimes be identified if, for example, the IP address is static or if it comes from a certain range of addresses (this is used for managing groups of users that do not need individual differentiation, such as the sales force). However, many policies cannot. The network needs some clue from the host generating the traffic to help identify what the traffic is being used for, who generated it, and other factors. Given this additional information, the PDP can decide what policies apply to that traffic.

Some examples of where the network needs help are

- Identifying end-users if their addresses are dynamically assigned using DHCP
- Identifying end-users if an intermediate network address translation device is used between the user generating the traffic and the network device receiving it
- Identifying application traffic for many applications that use dynamic ports
- Identifying users or applications if the traffic is encapsulated in a security tunnel (since the encapsulation may not allow either to be seen)

Various types of application recognition can be performed. Network devices can include the ability to filter many things, such as Layer 4 port numbers, Layer 3 IP addresses, and Layer 2 MAC addresses. In addition, some policy solutions include agents that are installed on a host or server, which communicate directly with the PDP. Other policy solutions include proprietary protocols that provide additional information to help distinguish the traffic.

The COPS Protocol

COPS is a dedicated protocol for transporting policy information. Although the initial goal for COPS was to support QoS policy, it was designed to be extensible and can be extended to support other network services, such as security and multicast.

COPS is a simple query and response protocol that can be used to exchange policy information between a policy server (that is, a PDP) and its clients (that is, PEPs). It enables dynamic policy information to be exchanged between policy servers and policy enforcement nodes. COPS is stateful and allows for policy requests and responses to be exchanged in both solicited and unsolicited fashions.

The main characteristics of the COPS protocol include

- *Client/Server Model.* COPS uses a client/server model, where the PEP sends requests, updates, and deletes to the remote PDP and the PDP returns decisions back to the PEP.

- *Extensibility.* COPS uses self-identifying objects to insulate it from any application-specific dependencies. This enables the protocol to be used for general administration, configuration, and enforcement of policies regardless of their type, data content or context.

- *TCP.* COPS uses TCP as its transport protocol. This ensures reliable message exchange between policy clients and their server.

- *Security.* The protocol relies on existing protocols, such as IPSEC, for security.

- *State.* The protocol is stateful in four main aspects:

  - Requests from the client PEP, and the corresponding decisions from the remote PDP, are installed or remembered by the remote PDP until they are explicitly deleted by the PEP.

  - Decisions from the remote PDP can be generated asynchronously at any time for a currently installed request state.

- A PDP can push configuration information to the client, and subsequently remove that information from the client when it is no longer applicable.

- State from various events may be inter-associated, enabling the PDP to respond to new queries differently because of previously installed Request/Decision state(s) that are related.

COPS is preferred over both SNMP and LDAP for installing policy configurations and communicating policy information. With respect to SNMP, COPS has richer semantics (for example, transaction capabilities, compared with SNMP "sets" of leaf elements) than SNMP. In addition, COPS uses TCP for large transactions, compared to SNMP/UDP. Finally, COPS scales better, since the device being configured initiates transactions in COPS, compared to external initiation for SNMP.

COPS is preferred over LDAP for many reasons. First, LDAP was not designed to carry and understand dynamic state information. Second, there is no support for unsolicited notifications, and notifications of changes are still the subject of much debate in the LDAP community. LDAP replies reflect neither the dynamic state of the network nor the semantics of the data. Finally, LDAP requires much more code to implement than COPS does, which is a serious concern for low-end devices and devices that have limited resources.

Deploying Qos Policies

CiscoAssure provides a framework that enables policies to be defined, managed, and used to control the configuration of QoS capabilities of both routers and switches. This section will describe in detail one of the important components of CiscoAssure, the QoS Policy Management (QPM) subsystem.

Architectural Overview

A simplified block diagram of the QPM architecture is shown in Figure 11.11.

The architecture consists of five major components. The first is an administration tool that is GUI-driven. This is used for the definition, management, and administration of QoS policies. It represents the network administrator's views of the deployed policies in the system.

The second is the Policy Server. This performs the major functions of the PDP described earlier in this chapter. It stores policies and policy information in a logically centralized, but possibly physically distributed, set of databases. For simplicity, this third component is shown as a single database in Figure 11.11.

Figure 11.11 Simplified QoS Policy Management architecture.

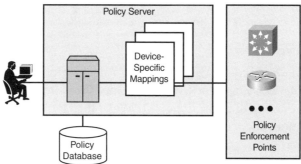

The fourth component is a special part of the Policy Server. This consists of a set of mappers that translate generic policy rules into device-specific configuration commands. The mappers perform a dual role. First, they provide the afore-mentioned translation. Second, they also enable the Policy Server to communicate with the PEP that it is controlling using a protocol that that particular PEP understands (for example, COPS, Telnet/CLI, SNMP, and so on).

The final component is, of course, the individual PEPs that make up the Intelligent Network. The wide variety of PEPs that Cisco makes mandate specialized combinations of Policy Servers and mapping tools. This is because there is a large diversity in the capabilities, protocols, and commands to adjust the configuration of these devices. In addition, the Policy Server must support legacy devices to protect the investment of the customer.

Policy Deployment Cycle

The typical cycle in deploying QoS policies is as follows:

- Specification of business policies into an intermediate form more suitable for device configuration using a GUI interface

- Define devices that you want to control using policies

- Translation of higher-level policy rules, defined using the GUI system, into network configuration commands

- Validation of configuration commands to ensure that the target PEP supports the QoS features chosen by the user

- Storage and distribution of validated policy rules for groups of devices and interfaces

- Ability to monitor the progress of distributing policies among multiple devices

- Ability to view QoS policies deployed on a network-wide basis graphically

Defining Policy-Controlled Devices

Devices must be identified to QPM. This is done manually (for now) by the user, who identifies a target device by name or IP address. Once the user supplies the appropriate password(s) needed to log onto the device, QPM can then log onto the target device and obtain pertinent information about that device. This includes information that identifies the particular characteristics of the device, such as its model number, software release, and interface information. This information is stored in the policy repository. The GUI is then populated by creating a folder containing the user-visible subset of this information for that device. A folder is used because the GUI uses an explorer metaphor, and the folder connotes that multiple policies and associated information can be defined for a particular object.

Initializing the Policy System

Once a new device is identified to QPM, its configuration is read and appropriate policy rules are created in the policy database representing the current configuration of the device. The Policy Server can then read this information to populate the GUI so that the user can see the current configuration of the device.

User Interaction

At this point, the user is ready to interact with the system. The GUI presents a customized (by device characteristics) view of the information that can be controlled by user-defined policies. The user can then use an intuitive drag-and-drop GUI interface to create policy rules. This GUI is in the form of a partitioned explorer view, showing the device's existing policy rules, and the conditions and actions that make up a policy rule that has been selected in the interface. This enables the user to visually examine existing policy rules, promoting reuse as well as assisting the user in creating new or modified policy rules.

The user can also create policy-controlled services. These take one of two general forms. The first is enabling and/or modifying a set of predefined application service treatments (for example, services denoting Oracle and PeopleSoft traffic). The second is a general interface that enables the user to define custom treatment of the traffic corresponding to a particular application service using common building blocks (for example, the protocol(s) and transport layer port and address information associated with the application).

The construction of a policy rule is also GUI-driven, once again using a drag-and-drop interface supplemented by pop-up dialogs that present predefined choices for more granular specification of QoS components. This aids the user in expressing QoS policy rules. At the same time, it also defines implicitly the translation process between high-level business policies and low-level device configuration commands. By presenting the user with a set of choices that represent possible conditions and actions, the user is relieved of the burden of trying to express syntactically and semantically correct policy rules for network devices. This also enables the policy rule to be algorithmically mapped to device configuration commands, reducing the complexity of translating policy rules that are in a form that make sense to network administrators to QoS configuration commands that are in a new form that make sense to network devices.

To apply the QoS policy rule to traffic on a router or switch, the user defines a policy statement for the specified interface of a particular network device. This is done by combining the appropriate building blocks to form policy conditions and policy actions.

Validation

Once a policy is defined and the appropriate QoS action is chosen, the user can validate the defined policy. This enables the user to view all proposed devices changes. The user can assess whether all or only some of the proposed device changes should be committed. In addition, any conflicts that have been detected by the system are displayed to the user. The user now has the ability to fix these conflicts manually or override them.

Note

Sometimes, policies aren't really conflicting with each other, even though from a syntactic analysis they appear to be. For example, a user could define two policy rules, one assigning Gold treatment to a particular flow and another assigning Silver treatment (that is, not as "good" in one or more metrics, such as bandwidth and jitter).

These two policies appear to be in conflict. However, there could be extenuating circumstances that are not expressible in the policy conditions of these two rules that restrict their application. For example, the first rule could be applied only under "normal" travel conditions, whereas the second rule could be intended for "exceptional" traffic conditions. An example of "exceptional" conditions might be the need to downgrade the service allotted to this traffic type because there is a financial crisis, and trading applications (which represent different traffic types) need as much available bandwidth as possible.

There is no way to predict application-specific requirements like this example. Thus, QPM allows the storage of what appears to be conflicting policy rules, allowing either additional software or human intervention to resolve the apparent conflict.

Once the user tells QPM to validate the policy rules, QPM will simulate making all requested changes and display a status report. Policy status is either Pass or Fail. Failure indicates that the policy rule, though valid, was unable to be loaded into the selected device. Detailed information indicating the reason for the failure, along with providing the user a recommended action. This provides the user with a final check before committing these changes to the selected target PEPs.

Application

After the validation step is complete, the user is asked to confirm the application of the proposed policy changes. Configurable distribution control mechanisms are available to enable the user to take corrective action in the event of distribution failures.

QPM allows the user to view all policy statements that were committed, along with the status of the policy distribution. New configuration changes are highlighted by the system for easy identification.

An audit log history of all policy configuration changes is stored for viewing by the user.

QoS Policy Rule Administration

QoS policy administration is done primarily through a GUI interface. It enables the user to define policy rules for individual and groups of devices and device interfaces. In addition, it also enables the definition of policies for different application services, and enables the user to bind these QoS policies to general devices (for example, by type of device or the role of the device in the network) or specific devices. A graphical interface allows QoS policies to be specified using an intuitive "drag-and-drop" style, supplemented with pop-up dialogs. Finally, the QoS Policy administration tool provides a network-wide view of deployed QoS policies.

QoS Policy Repository

The QoS Policy Repository is a combination of several different repositories. A directory is used to provide DEN-compliant storage and retrieval of policy rules and additional definitional policy information, such as device-specific parameters and configuration rules. Other repositories may be used in conjunction with the database to provide data-specific policy information.

QoS Policy Server

The QoS Policy Server interrogates supported devices for essential information, such as the specific capabilities that the device supports, what version of software it is running, and other important attributes. Using this information, it can then translate policy statements defined in the GUI component into device-specific ACL configuration commands. The QoS Policy Server is also responsible for validating, storing, and distributing policy rules to PEPs or PEP Proxies. In addition, the Policy Server is responsible for identifying conflicting policy rules and either resolving those conflicts or presenting those conflicts to the administrator so that they can be resolved by the policy administrator. Finally, the Policy Server is responsible for detecting and reporting any errors that occurred during the device configuration process, as well as maintaining a history of all configuration changes.

QoS Policy Rule Definition

Policy rules, or statements, can be defined for applications, devices, and other objects. Figure 11.12 shows a screen shot for a simple policy statement, ERP Application, that is used to select SQL traffic and assign the action "accept with traffic priority 4" to that traffic. This is a combination of forwarding the traffic and remarking it to have a priority of 4.

Figure 11.12 A simple policy rule.

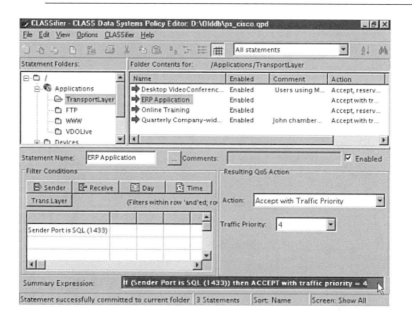

First, the user decides what type of policy rule he or she is going to define. In this case, the user has selected to write a policy rule that filters application transport layer traffic, and forwards it with a remarked priority of 4.

The user then defines the condition and action terms that make up this policy. The various traffic filtering condition terms are available in the lower left portion of the screen. The condition can contain any combination of the following:

- Source IP address or host name

- Destination IP address or host name

- Source port

- Destination port

- MAC address

- Session protocol

Complex filter conditions can be defined using Boolean operators to combine these basic building blocks into more complex combinations. A screen shot of a portion of the GUI interface that is used to define conditions is shown in Figure 11.13.

Figure 11.13   Defining a policy condition.

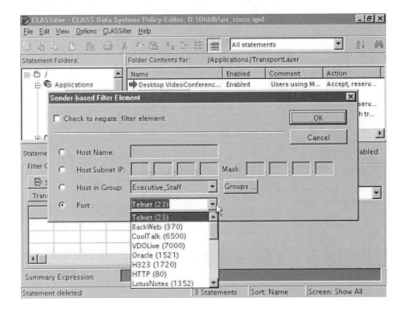

A number of QoS actions can be chosen, including shaping (for example, GTS or CAR, which stands for Committed Access Rate), Coloring (policy-based routing and CAR), or different types of queuing (for example, priority, custom, and weighted fair queuing). The particular type of QoS action is determined by the specific software version that is being run by the devices, along with the properties of the device interface. The Policy Server translates the policy into ACL statements and converts the ACL statement into the appropriate device-specific configuration commands.

A screen shot of a portion of the GUI interface that is used to define conditions is shown in Figure 11.14.

Figure 11.14 Defining a policy action.

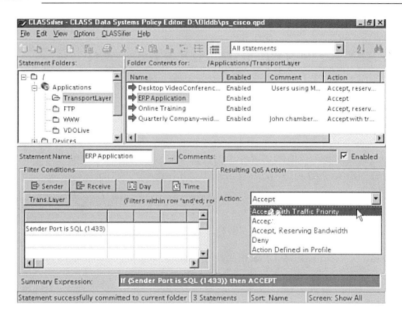

Summary

A policy-based solution distributes and integrates intelligence in the host, the network, and the surrounding infrastructure. Within this environment,

- Hosts can provide additional information to a policy server to help it make policy decisions.

- Policy servers distribute policy, in the form of policy rules and other definitional information that can be used in configuring network elements, hosts, and resources, to hosts and network devices.

- Network devices, controlled by policy, can be dynamically configured to classify, enforce and police traffic according to changing environment conditions.

Recommended Further Study and References

If you are interested in scientific visualization and active networks, see

Foster, I. and Kesselman, C. "The Grid—A Blueprint for a New Computing Infrastructure," Morgan Kaufman, 1999.

If you are interested in the Internet2 effort, please see the following URL for a comprehensive list of pointers to information about the Internet2 effort:

http://dir.yahoo.com/Computers_and_Internet/Internet/Internet_2___Abilene_Project/

www.merit.edu/working.groups/i2-qbone-bb

For readers interested in the COPS protocol, see

http://www.ietf.org/html.charters/rap-charter.html

and appropriate drafts and RFCs specified in the RAP working group, such as

http://www.ietf.org/internet-drafts/draft-ietf-rap-cops-06.txt

Current Use of DEN in the Industry

Standards-based networking is gaining increasing importance for two principal reasons:

- First, it enables a customer to avoid being locked into a single vendor. This results in competition, which produces lower prices, higher value, and better products.

- Second, it provides the means for customers to make their own decisions about best-of-breed products, and which solutions they should endorse.

The purpose of this chapter is to describe how CIM and DEN are currently used in the industry. First, the notion of CIM and DEN "compliance" is defined. Second, examples of two completely different products manufactured by Cisco—one focusing on the Enterprise and one on the service provider community—will be examined. This will provide a better appreciation for how CIM and DEN have affected the products and solutions for a large company.

The remainder of this chapter will describe DEN solutions from other vendors, both small and large, in order to describe in more detail how DEN has affected the industry as a whole.

When Is a Product "DEN-Compliant"?

The DMTF will be issuing formal compliance statements for CIM and DEN in the fall of 1999. The following provides a snapshot view of the current thinking regarding the compliance process. It also addresses what compliance statements the DMTF is likely to require of vendors who want their products labeled as either CIM- and/or DEN-compliant. It cannot be stressed enough that, in order for a product to be DEN-compliant, it must also be CIM-compliant.

Motivation for Formal Compliance Requirements

In today's information technology environment, management information about the configuration, performance, and state of the equipment and services is gathered, stored, and made available to the operations staff using a wide variety of proprietary and standard data. Information models can play a critical role in the standardization of these data formats. The goal of the Common Information Model (CIM) is to provide the basis for a normalized exchange of management data between devices and managing systems, between applications using managing systems, and between managing systems. To assure the desired level of interoperability between such devices and systems requires that there be clear and verifiable guidelines for compliance to the CIM model.

There are several benefits in using a common information model:

- First, it provides a single, common source from which platform- and technology-dependent schemata can be developed. Using a single common source for these different schemata enables CIM data to be mapped to various repositories, such as relational databases, directory servers, and SNMP stores.

- Second, it enables applications to be designed for particular platforms (for example, UNIX and Windows) that have differing requirements. These two points are very important. Complex system and network management applications require a large variety of different types of information, along with different access rates and mechanisms. No one single repository or application is capable of meeting all of these diverse needs. However, multiple repositories that represent data in the same way can *share* their application and/or domain-specific data with other repositories and applications in the system.

- Third, it enables the CIM repositories to be used as a single source for configuration information, enabling applications running on different platforms to exchange and share data seamlessly.

- Finally, it provides for consistent network management through the implementation of common policies.

Basic Rules for CIM and DEN Compliance

The goal of the DMTF's CIM compliance certification program is to standardize the application of "CIM-compliant" to products. The advantage of using CIM-compliant products is that users of such products will be guaranteed a definable level of interoperability with other CIM-compliant products through the exchange of relevant information, appropriate to the role and function of each management application or device.

In order to be labeled CIM-compliant, a product must implement the relevant portion of the Core schema, along with appropriate portions of the particular Common schema areas that the product is utilizing. Because many management applications manage only a single aspect of a managed entity, it is unreasonable to expect such applications to support additional schema that is beyond the functionality of the application. This is true even if such schema is in the same schema (Core or Common) that the application is using. For example, if an application was only interested in performing physical inventory, it is unreasonable to force it to contain schema for managing logical aspects of the entities that it is providing an inventory for, even though both physical and logical aspects of a device are captured in the Core schema.

Specific compliance requirements are likely to include the following:

- The current mechanism for describing management information is the *Managed Object Format (MOF)*. Therefore, applications that wish to be compliant with CIM must be able to import and export properly formed MOF constructs. This must include support for CIM class and instance definitions, as well as proper handling of namespaces and query support.

- All management applications must provide support for some or all of the Core Model, plus some or all the appropriate Common Models.

  - Since it is impossible to anticipate the specific needs of each product, the decision as to which classes must be included can only be made for the Core Model.

  - Management applications are concerned with managing three types of data: Physical, Logical, or Both. All categories must include the `ManagedSystemElement` class and its recursive relationships, `Dependency` and `Component`.

  - Applications that are concerned only with physical data must include the `Managed SystemElement` class, its two recursive relationships, and the `PhysicalElement` class.

  - Applications that are concerned only with logical data do not need to include the `PhysicalElement` class. Instead, they must include the `ManagedSystemElement` class, its recursive relationships, and the `LogicalElement`, `System`, `Service`, and `ServiceAccess Point` classes (though it is very likely that the `LogicalDevice` class will also need to be included). In addition, it must include the relationships that associate these classes with each other as well as with `ManagedSystemElement` (for example, `SystemComponent`, `SystemDevice`, `HostedService`, `HostedAccessPoint`, `ServiceServiceDependency`, `SAPSAPDependency`, `ServiceSAPDependency`, and `ServiceAccessBySAP`).

- Applications that manage both the physical and the logical aspects of entities will include all the preceding classes, as well as relationships that connect the physical and logical hierarchies together (for example, Realizes).

- An extension may *not* redefine CIM Object classes, nor may it use them for a purpose different than what the CIM Object class was defined for in the CIM model. Specific examples include not allowing the canceling of (that is, not using) attributes, methods and/or relationships that are defined in a class, as well as redefining the data type of an attribute or the signature of a method.

- Any compliance statement must call out the specific CIM Schema version (for example, CIM Specification v2.1).

- CIM Object classes instantiated in the CIM-compliant application must, at a minimum, include all key properties and all properties marked as required. *Key properties* enable instances to be uniquely identified within a given namespace. *Required properties* have the REQUIRED qualifier present and set to TRUE, and indicate properties that must be included in a class.

Note

Key properties define how naming and navigation are performed in CIM. Therefore, to be CIM-compliant, an application must use the key qualifier for these purposes. Simply including the key qualifier but not using it for naming and navigation is insufficient and would result in the application not being deemed CIM-compliant.

Recall that CIM has no explicit notion of requiring that a property be included, whereas LDAP does (for example, "must" versus "may" properties). The REQUIRED qualifier can serve as the link between LDAP "must" properties and CIM properties that must be included.

Notice that several of the top-level classes in the Core schema have been left off of the required list. Here is the reasoning for this:

- The Product, FRU, SupportAccess classes and their relationships are important for modeling an infrastructure that is based on units of acquisition. This may or may not be applicable to a given management application, and hence these classes and their associations are optional.

- The Configuration and Setting classes are useful for defining a means to change the state of an entity. Some management applications are concerned with tracking the state of its entities, and these classes may form the basis for modeling state changes. Such state changes are usually made on managed objects to either affect a transition to a new state, or to maintain the existing state of the managed object. However, these are only applicable to management applications that are concerned with managing the state of their objects. Hence, these classes and their associations are optional.

- Finally, the StatisticalInformation class, along with its immediate children (for example, SystemStatisticalInformation) and relationships (for example, Statistics) form a powerful, extensible framework for modeling statistics for a particular management application. However, not every application needs to model statistical information. Therefore, these classes and their relationships are also optional.

Verifying CIM Compliance

The idea of a compliance test suite is currently being discussed. This offers an independent means to verify whether a given extension is compliant with the basic foundational aspects of CIM.

The DMTF is considering creating a Compliance Review Board that determines whether a given submission should be formally given the title "CIM-compliant" or "DEN-compliant." The Compliance Review Board would review all submissions and accept only those that were sufficiently (and correctly) documented that would facilitate third-party support, and would also administer and run the test suite. The test suite has two purposes:

- Ensures that MOF descriptions, navigation and scoping, and queries all meet at least the minimum requirements set forth in the compliance specification.

- Examines the attendant documentation to verify that the extensions are properly described. Without good documentation, extensions will be impossible to standardize and reuse.

Compliance When the Information Model Is Extended

At any point in time, most CIM-compliant management applications will implement features and services beyond those described by the standard CIM schema. In order to allow sufficient flexibility for vendors to implement their own value-added features, while still ensuring interoperability of CIM-compliant applications or devices, it is necessary to provide for the orderly extension of CIM beyond the ratified schema. It is desirable that the process of gaining compliance for proposed extensions also be useful to the ongoing process of defining the ever expanding scope of ratified CIM schema. For example, if an extension for modeling management of Virtual Private Networks (VPNs) is proposed, and if this extension is not already part of the Networks model, then it would be desirable to include this extension into the Networks model. Therefore, the DMTF is considering forming a Compliance Review Board that will serve as a registration authority for well-formed extension schema from member companies. This would also enable a particular working group to contact the submitter of the proposed extension in order to jointly develop changes to the extension (in the event that changes were needed to incorporate it into the specific working group). Extensions will likely be submitted to a CIM Compliance Review Board of the DMTF.

Extensions should whenever possible be incorporated into the base information model. This prevents multiple extensions from being built that conflict with each other, as well as enhances the base information model. Therefore, at such time as the appropriate CIM working group undertakes to extend the relevant Common schema area, it will seek to incorporate such well-formed registered extensions into the ratified schema. When there is conflict between well-formed registered schemata and ideas in the working group, the working group will use technical diligence to choose an approach that will best allow for on-going development of schema in the area. Either the TDC and/or the DMTF Compliance Group will arbitrate in such decisions.

Note

The CIM Technical Development Committee (CIM TDC), is chartered with coordinating all technical activities of the DMTF. This includes the development of CIM, the Desktop Management Interface (DMI), DEN, and the associated technologies required to deliver Web Based Enterprise Management (WBEM) to the customer.

Members of the TDC include Cisco, Compaq, Dell, Hewlett-Packard, Intel, Microsoft, NEC, Novell, SCO, Sun, Symantec, and Tivoli (IBM), plus chairs of the working groups.

Compliance with DEN

One must be careful to distinguish between support for DEN and a vendor's specific implementation of directory-enabled services and applications. By defining a common schema across directories and network products, DEN opens the way for applications and services to be built that can operate independently of the underlying directory service and network equipment. The ultimate purpose of DEN is to provide an information model and schema that enables different vendors to interoperate regardless of platform and technology used to implement their DEN repositories.

Interoperability comes in two forms: the ability to share information and the ability to reuse information. The former means that applications made by different vendors can share information while they are running. The latter means that one application from one vendor can reuse information that another application from a different vendor has operated on. For example:

- Application X from Vendor A can populate the repository with information about various network elements and/or services that it wants to manage.

- Application Y from Vendor B could then use some or all of this information to provision part or all of the network (for example, according to policies that it has defined).

- Application Z from Vendor C could then perform various types of statistical analysis on the newly provisioned network elements and services.

In the preceding scenario, none of the three applications needed any prior knowledge about each of the other applications. The DEN specification defined a technology- and platform-independent information model, which was presumably mapped into application-specific schemata that were platform- and/or technology-dependent. However, since each was derived from the same information model, data (as well as access to that data, via navigation and scoping) was able to be defined in a common way. This enables these disparate applications, with possibly different user interfaces and APIs, to be able to share and reuse information.

As stated earlier, in order to be DEN-compliant, a product must first be CIM-compliant. This is because DEN is an extension of CIM itself. A schema provider is compliant with a given version of the DEN schema when the following occur:

- It is fully compliant with CIM.

- It publishes the complete information model and schema definitions for that version of the schema.

- Extensions to the schema published by the schema provider conform to the definition of extending the CIM schema provided earlier.

- Additional classes and attributes published by the schema provider that are not defined in the CIM or DEN information models are *not* presented as extensions to the schema.

- All relationships are fully documented and are limited to associations and aggregations.

A schema consumer is compliant with a given version of the DEN schema when the following occur:

- Usage of object instances defined in the schema is in accordance with the usage model prescribed in the formal specification of the version(s) of the schema for which support is claimed.

- Extensions to the schema published by the schema consumer conform to the definition of schema extensions given earlier.

- Additional classes, attributes, and relationships published by the schema consumer that are not defined in the schema are *not* presented as extensions to the schema.

- Additional relationships that are not associations or aggregations are not presented as extensions to the schema.

Overview of Directory-Enabled Products and Applications

The purpose of this section is to provide a brief overview of different products that are taking advantage of DEN. First, an in-depth overview of Cisco's use of directory-enabled applications, along with how DEN will be used to make increasingly intelligent network devices, is provided. The second section consists of a survey of other DEN initiatives and activities of a selected set of vendors. This is organized alphanumerically by company for convenience.

Cisco's Directory-Enabled Network Strategy

Cisco Systems has a concentrated focus on DEN and making networks "increasingly more intelligent."

Cisco's January, 1999 *Packet* magazine featured an article on DEN. Its subhead summarized the effect of DEN nicely: "Enterprises and service providers look to a new generation of solutions based on directory-enabled networks to provide greater functionality while simplifying management."

Cisco has many projects focused on these areas; two very different ones will be described to provide a sense of the impact that DEN has on a large company. First, however, common foundation technology that is incorporated in both the enterprise and the service provider products will be described.

Foundation Technology: CNS/AD

Cisco Networking Services for Active Directory (CNS/AD) is a foundation technology for various Cisco strategic initiatives, including DEN, rapid service provisioning with the Cisco Service Management, and policy-based management with CiscoAssure Policy Networking. CNS/AD enables networks to become more application-aware and applications to become more network-aware. One of the principle ways that this is done is by enabling developers to more easily leverage the advanced networking services found in Cisco IOS software and networking products.

As a foundation technology, CNS/AD will provide a set of platform-independent APIs to enable ISVs and internal IT staffs to more closely link their applications to the powerful services of Cisco IOS software. Specific extensions made to DEN are used to model specific Cisco IOS software features, such as QoS mechanisms. CNS/AD provides the directory and event services that both the enterprise as well as the service provider solutions will use to govern network behavior.

CNS/AD builds on Microsoft's Active Directory, which contains numerous important base services, such as multimaster replication and integrated security. CNS/AD contains enhancements developed jointly by Cisco and Microsoft to extend Active Directory to handle more dynamic data. Its services and APIs are illustrated in Figure 12.1.

Figure 12.1   Conceptual overview of CNS/AD.

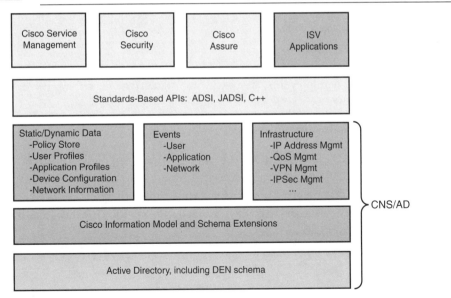

By coupling a DEN-based directory, such as Microsoft's Active Directory, with Cisco value-added features, CNS/AD offers customers a robust repository for a wide range of data. This enables policy and provisioning servers to dynamically configure the network to better link users to network services. Features of CNS/AD enable a user to

- Store and manage information securely from a variety of authenticated sources, such as applications and network devices that include the CNS/AD client

- Provide definitions for, registration of, and processing of a large variety of network and network-related events through a generic publish/subscribe interface

- Provide high-level, extensible APIs that enable applications to take advantage of directory-based networking services

- Maintain state information on network devices, users, and applications that enables administrators to provide coordinated, policy-based actions and management

Cisco builds upon the DEN industry initiative and defines various schema and information model extensions to DEN that represent Cisco-specific network devices and services. Uses for these data include the storage and replication of data such as DHCP leases, network state and configuration information, and optimization of network services. This information can be used in policy-based networking decisions and operations, such as provisioning network services.

CNS/AD also includes a directory-based event services engine. It uses the directory for defining and registering

- Events

- Data contained within events, along with metadata (data describing the data) about the events

- Publishers and subscribers of events

Using the CNS/AD client event APIs, event consumers can register for events. As event producers generate events, the event server filters these events and sends them to the appropriate event consumers. This enables a wide variety of applications to communicate via a standard mechanism and exchange detailed information. It also allows these applications to respond to events as they occur.

Security services must be integrated seamlessly within a directory. This is done in CNS/AD by using CIM, DEN, and extensions to both to model the security needs of users, network devices, and other resources on the network. This enables enterprise managers and service providers to have centralized control over the information and services that users, applications, and network devices can produce as well as consume. In CNS/AD, users, applications, and network devices all authenticate themselves using the directory. This enables the establishment of a trusted relationship between each participant, and ensures that each producer and consumer of information receives the appropriate credentials before any information is exchanged.

CNS/AD provides IP address management services, along with other infrastructural services such as IPSec and VPN management, by using the directory (with appropriate DEN-based extensions). The directory provides storage and replication of data for each of these services (for example, IP addresses and tunnels). In addition, through its event engine, CNS/AD ensures that information for these services dynamically reflect what is happening on the network.

CNS/AD is packaged as a set of tools, including server and client libraries and APIs, sample source code, and full documentation, to enable developers to take advantage of the services that Cisco network devices offers. These APIs empower the CNS/AD client to perform sophisticated pre- and post-processing operations to simplify access to directory-based information that applications require. For example, if an application needed to know all the devices participating in a particular virtual LAN (VLAN), the CNS/AD APIs would perform the necessary pre- and post-processing of this request so that this inherently complex query could be phrased as a single, simple query. Without these APIs, a developer using LDAP Version 3.0 alone would need to issue dozens of directory calls and perform the associated processing (for example, split the incoming request into multiple LDAP queries and then combine the many responses into a single result). In addition, the CNS/AD APIs also enable the result to be represented as an object in its own right. This scenario offers tremendous performance advantages when subsequent operations get and set information regarding this VLAN.

Enterprise Focus: CiscoAssure

The boom in the intranet is causing more business applications to be dependent on an Intelligent Network. As a result, enterprise network managers require the capability to control the use of the network and to allocate and prioritize network resources for different applications and user groups.

Network managers need policy control over bandwidth-hungry applications, which consume bandwidth at the expense of performance and drive up the cost of expensive wide-area resources. A misbehaved application can potentially shut down the business. The network manager needs to be able to map these business requirements into specific policies that link business needs with the desired network behavior.

The intelligent network provides a rich set of QoS and security mechanisms to enable business applications. However, utilizing these features can be a complex exercise for network managers. There is a real need to provide dynamic and automatic configuration of features in the intelligent network. Network devices must be dynamically tuned to support increased user mobility and new classes of applications such as Internet webcasting and multimedia applications that support data, voice, and video simultaneously.

Architecture

A conceptual architecture of CiscoAssure is shown in Figure 12.2. It is based on the following five building blocks:

- Policy Administration, which provides the ability to centrally configure rule-based policies that control the services that an intelligent network provides

- Policy Services, which provide the dynamic binding to associate network addresses and other identifying information with users, applications, and other consumers of network services

- The leveraging of existing Network Management Services, combined with the incorporation of new management protocols, into a single integrated Web-based management framework

- Intelligent Network Elements that enable, monitor and enforce policy-based services

- Common Repository Services, based on DEN, that are able to model and help control the configuration of network devices and hence the state of network services

Figure 12.2   Conceptual overview of CiscoAssure.

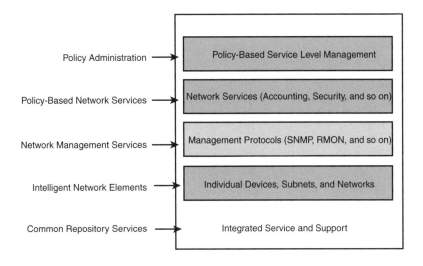

Vision

The CiscoAssure vision for network management centers around integrating knowledge into the management process and enabling policy-based service-level management using DEN. Key to this is the ability to incorporate existing intelligence and management tools (for example, current QoS mechanisms that are provided by various network devices and existing network management protocols, such as SNMP and RMON) with new tools and protocols (for example, RSVP, Differentiated Services, CIM, and DEN) in a new, Web-based framework. Even more important, CiscoAssure uses the rich DEN policy model to control the configuration of these devices to dynamically adjust the network to provide the services required of it in a changing environment. This represents a new management paradigm, as illustrated in Figure 12.3.

Figure 12.3 Traditional management paradigm is insufficient.

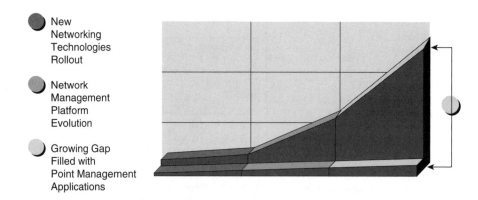

- New Networking Technologies Rollout
- Network Management Platform Evolution
- Growing Gap Filled with Point Management Applications

Network Management Framework

CiscoAssure represents one embodiment of thinking differently about network management. It will deliver a distributed system of network management modules, services, and other elements that are seamlessly integrated through the combination of an underlying information model (DEN, with appropriate Cisco extensions) and Web-based technologies.

Some of the services provided include the following:

- Physical and logical topology

- Network services that are bound to the user and/or application that is using the network

- Traffic monitoring and analysis

- User tracking and reporting

- Auto-discovery of new devices

Through the use of DEN and new management frameworks that DEN and CIM help realize, CiscoAssure seeks to usher in a new era of device configuration management. This new era takes advantage of the common representation of management data, thereby enabling different specialized applications to work together to provide a more powerful solution than existing network management applications. This is because existing network management applications are unable to leverage data provided by different solutions that address different facets of the management problem.

The underlying framework for these features is the integration of Intelligent Network policy with standards-based directory services. The directory provides a central repository and a common naming service for all network resources—including users, systems, printers, and network devices, and end-user applications. Through directory integration, the network manager only has to go to one place (the directory) to add new users or devices, or to change access rights to network resources.

Figure 12.4 illustrates this new architecture.

Figure 12.4   The new network management paradigm.

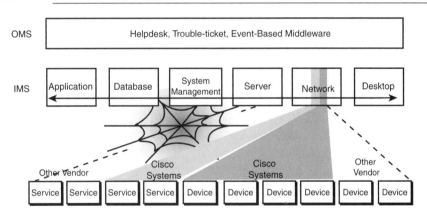

OMS: Overall Management Solution
IMS: Individual Management Solution

Figure 12.4 shows three types of components:

• The overall management solution

• A set of individual management products that are contained by the overall management solution

• A set of devices and services that are under control of the network management application

Cisco's view is that the end-to-end management solutions of the future extend beyond network management and must intimately embrace the manageability of applications, servers, databases, desktops. Thus, in this new environment, Cisco will supply Internet-powered tools for managing the Cisco infrastructure of the network, and try to ensure through the implementation of standards such as DEN that these tools integrate with the rest of the components that comprise the overall management solution. This goes beyond simple data exchange, and includes Web-based integration and interaction of tasks and processes. For example, to change the configuration of a device, one application might require the results of a different application in order to choose certain options. This represents exchange of data as well as interoperation of the two applications.

Below the individual management systems are four areas, representing services from Cisco and other vendors, and network devices from Cisco and other vendors. One of the unique features of this architecture is that Cisco is explicitly defining as a requirement that its devices and services must be able to fit into this environment and add value.

This is best expressed by an additional feature of this new architecture: the ability to accommodate plug-in modules. By relying on standards like DEN, new devices and services that are DEN-compliant can be integrated under the network management system.

Service Provider Focus: Cisco Service Management

Service providers want to offer different services that are tailored to accommodate the wide range of their customer and application requirements. This is due to several reasons, the main ones being trying to keep up with the advances in network technology, as well as in trying to accommodate new applications. This is, of course, contrary to their other main goal, which is trying to streamline their operations and decrease the administrative burden of provisioning and managing applications and services.

DEN, along with other approaches like Differentiated Services from the IETF, provides most of the necessary tools to fix this contradiction. One example of a product taking this approach is Cisco's *Cisco Service Management (CSM) system.* CSM is a set of management solutions oriented for the service provider that provide enhanced management of end-to-end services across a diverse set of network technologies. It also contains APIs that can be leveraged to integrate, customize and extend the value of these applications for a service provider.

CSM, like CiscoAssure, uses CNS/AD as foundation technology for integrating the different applications that comprise the CSM suite. CSM leverages many of the features of CNS/AD for providing, managing, and optimizing network services (for example, associate users and applications with network services and resources, provide event-based networking services, and provide a DEN-based directory). CSM will enable service providers to quickly define, deploy, operate, and bill for new services, including VPNs, Internet telephony, managed network services, and electronic commerce (e-commerce). This forms the basis for a scalable, cost-effective means for billing applications as a function of the customers who use them, along with tracking users' consumption of network services, regardless of their login location or address.

CSM addresses the complete life cycle for service offerings that service providers require. As described in the CSM Statement of Direction, this consists of four phases: Service Planning and Administration (the ability to effectively plan the network), Multiservice Provisioning (the ability to rapidly provision the network services and users), Service Operations and Assurance (the ability to provide proactive, guaranteed service levels), and Accounting and Billing (the ability to accurately charge for services).

Other Vendors' DEN Initiatives

The products from the following companies represent public information that each has announced in its support of DEN and CIM. The general theme of these products is to enable a unified modeling approach, along with a standard representation of data, of network elements and services. The following products realize this theme in several different variations:

- DEN is used as the cornerstone of a strategy to help plan the development and deployment of next-generation networks and networked applications.

- DEN is used to provide definitional data to mission-critical systems, such as policy-based networking systems.

- DEN is used to link business processes to networked applications and services.

- DEN is used as the basis for extending network management to a proactive, predictive model from today's passive, reactive model.

3Com

3Com's early desktop focus has helped to differentiate it from its networking competitors. 3Com is developing and delivering technologies and products that include the desktop as an active participant in the intelligent network. In addition, 3Com places a heavy emphasis on Layer 2 switching.

Several white papers are available from the 3Com Web site that shows its interest and support in DEN and directory-enabled networking. One of the more interesting ones is "Directory Enabled Networks and 3Com's Framework for Policy–Powered Networking."

Note

There are some inaccuracies in this white paper. First, Cisco and Microsoft jointly founded the DEN initiative (the white paper implies that only Microsoft did). Second, CIM is *not* a data definition language for describing schema, nor is it the property of Microsoft—it is an information model that is owned by the DMTF.

In this white paper, 3Com identifies two distinct uses for directories, device configuration and policy-powered networking. With respect to device configuration, 3Com says: "Directory support for device configuration management allows network devices to retrieve their configuration parameters directly from a directory server."

3Com's approach to device configuration management revolves around storing configuration parameters for each network device in a common directory. Once a network device is properly configured (for example, address of the directory server, along with specific parameters, such as QoS and Differentiated Services Code Point (DSCP) values for desired traffic and applications), the network device can contact the directory and acquire its configuration parameters. In principle, this is certainly more attractive than either manually initiating a TFTP download or making a Telnet connection to each device and performing a box-by-box configuration.

Note

Do not construe from this example that it is a good idea to put *all* information in the directory. Although some policy information is essentially static in nature, policy decision-making and policy enforcement are inherently dynamic operations. Thus, it is best to limit the use of the directory in policy-based networking to containing boot or startup information, along with definitional information that a policy server requires in order to make its decisions.

3Com's NETBuilder II router family is designated as the first 3Com product to support an LDAP client. This sets the stage for implementing a DEN-compliant directory as part of 3Com's strategy. 3Com has announced that their Layer 2 and Layer 3 switches, remote access server platforms, and desktops will also become LDAP-enabled.

3Com has also announced that it will use DEN as part of its policy-powered networking solutions. 3Com differentiates using the directory for policy-based control of the network (they call this *policy-powered networking*) from device configuration. As 3Com points out later in this paper:

> "Directories are simple databases; they are not designed to collect information from multiple sources and then make a policy decision. The key difference between a directory configuration system and a policy-powered networking system is statefulness."

In other words, when using policy to control network devices, some entity other than the directory (for example, a Policy Server) interprets information supplied by numerous sources (including the directory) in a specific context. While the information stored in the directory doesn't change, its application and use with respect to the environment does change.

3Com is focusing its initial policy-based products and technologies on supporting QoS and automating network device and address management. 3Com's Transcend Policy Server will use an LDAP-compatible directory to store network device configuration parameters. This directory will implement DEN and/or specific schema defined by 3Com that is DEN compliant.

Bay Networks/Nortel Networks

Bay Networks defined a strategy called *adaptive networking*. This was very similar to the goals of DEN, and was based around defining a new product line that could let the network "adapt" to changing user requirements by changing the configurations of some or all of its devices.

Nortel Networks' *Security and Policy Management solution* permits or denies access to Web-based applications and services based on policies and identification information stored in a standard directory, and establishes a certified and encrypted channel between the user and application or service. Role-based policy management allows administrators to profile access capability and authorization for various users and databases.

In Nortel's strategy note titled, "A Policy-Based Approach to Application-Optimized Networking," support for DEN is identified as part of their short- and long-term goals. The Bay/Nortel policy framework is "…designed to support a DEN-compliant schema within any LDAPv3-compliant directories."

In the first phase of the rollout (scheduled for the second quarter of 1999), targeted policy services (for example, Differentiated Services and RSVP) will be modeled in DEN. In Phase 3, which is scheduled for sometime in the year 2000, Bay/Nortel will increase the level of DEN support, along with providing a version of DEN that is optimized to meet the needs of large Carriers and service providers. Here, the emphasis is on integrating the needs of Enterprises with those of Carriers and service providers. Bay/Nortel envision two related subsets of DEN: one optimized for Enterprise needs and one optimized for the needs of Carriers and service providers.

Note
As of this writing, this work has not yet been submitted to the DMTF.

Cabletron Systems

Cabletron recently announced an aggressive new initiative for directory-enabled hardware and software. It also announced a set of professional services that complements their directory-enabled network products.

Cabletron's *SmartNetworking Services* is aimed at enabling "...the integrated management of application, computing and network infrastructures intelligently linked with the people and the organizations they support."

This embodies the spirit of DEN, which is to bind services available from the network to clients of the network that want to use those services. Cabletron is using DEN models and the directory as their repository to correlate network traffic to users and applications. This enables them to link business processes to network performance.

Cabletron's SmartNetworking Services are comprised of three components:

- The directory is used to store policies and other information that enables business processes to be linked to the capabilities of the network. This is done by capitalizing on the directory's ability to provide user-specific access to network resources. This may be based on static parameters (for example, who the person is) and/or dynamic policies (for example, time of day, role of the person in the organization, and other factors).

- Policy control is used to define business rules and enforce their behavior in the network.

- Finally, integrated accounting enables performance, usage, and billing to be associated with each business service. Access to information is important, but it is equally important to be able to account for what users are demanding of the network and what network resources are being utilized.

On March 22, 1999, Cabletron and Novell announced the signing of a software license agreement that will bundle and integrate Novell Directory Services® with Cabletron's SPECTRUM, SmartSwitch, and SmartSwitch Router platforms. This announcement described a "...partnership to deliver standards-compliant directory enabled networking (DEN) products that will reduce cost of network ownership and administration for enterprise customers, while significantly improving manageability and the quality of network service."

This announcement also stated that "...Cabletron and Novell will collaborate to develop solutions based on the DEN specifications in order to promote the adoption of these open standards industry-wide."

This work appears to be centered around simplifying and automating network configuration and administration processes, which in the past have been error-prone and time-consuming. These efforts center around Cabletron's SmartSwitch Router 2000/800/8600 Gigabit LAN/WAN routing platform, which is a Layer 3 switch. This product line offers standards-based multiprotocol routing along with the ability to control applications by switching packets at Layers 2, 3, and 4. It is an impressive endorsement of directory enabled networking in general and DEN in particular that Cabletron would dedicate its new premiere product line to directory enabled networking.

Check Point Software

Check Point Software is an interesting case of a company that makes specialized products (primarily in the areas of network security, traffic control and IP address management), but is still incorporating DEN into its products. For example, their Meta IP product was built to design, manage and maintain network services for enterprise networks that need IP address and name resolution services. They are migrating to a directory-based repository that uses DEN to model various functions, including the process of leasing an IP address, correlating users to IP addresses, and managing the overall allotment of IP addresses in the enterprise.

Check Point has also formed a partnership with Microsoft around directory-enabled policy management for Windows NT. This is detailed in the press release entitled, "Check Point Software Technologies and Microsoft Expand Strategic Partnership."

FORE Systems

FORE Systems was one of the early adopters and supporters of DEN. They have aggressively incorporated DEN into their product lines and continue to champion it (see, for example, their presentation at the 1999 Networld + Interop Conference in Singapore, among others).

In their press release, "FORE Systems Introduces Industry's Most Advanced Directory-Enabled Networking Solution," FORE announced the introduction of the *Extensible Directory Services Agent (EDSA)*. This product is the cornerstone of FORE's Policy-Based Network Management (PBNM) solution, and uses DEN and a centralized directory to define, manage and administer policies for FORE's ESX family of routing switches. Echoing the design of DEN, FORE says that its "…EDSA approach also is compatible with the DEN standards initiative now under development. The EDSA architecture was uniquely developed to be directory and schema neutral, supporting a broad range of directory services and ensuring the EDSA can handle new schema and directory services from different vendors and standards efforts."

The highlights of this solution that take advantage of FORE's DEN solution include the following:

- The containment feature of the directory is used to apply policies at different points in the directory. This causes all the objects beneath the applied point to inherit the specified policy. This not only dramatically reduces the amount of time required to apply policies, but it helps ensure that the policies are the same and are applied in a consistent manner.

- A corollary to the preceding feature is that generalized policies can be set and enforced for generic objects (for example, an OrganizationalUnit) and be subsequently refined by more specific policies (for example, for an OrganizationalPerson that is contained in the OrganizationalUnit).

From the article in *InternetWeek.com* by John Fontana, "FORE Adds Directory Agent For Enterprise-Wide Policy Networking," a customer (talking about FORE products) states that the "...next logical step is taking a directory and pushing it down to the network level and using LDAP and DEN. That is the only level where you can guarantee quality of service."

FORE is doing exactly this with its EDSA, which will support LDAP compliant directories. EDSA runs on the ESX lines of Layer 3 switches, and will be the first implementation of FORE's DEN architecture. EDSA was developed using technology from Fore's acquisition of Berkeley Networks.

FORE will add an agent that provides naming services, along with dedicated application agents (for example, for VoIP and e-commerce) later in 1999. These application-specific agents will provide priority service mappings for these and other applications to mechanisms directly on the switch.

In FORE's "Extensible Directory Services Agent" white paper, FORE touts DEN as a way to control and manage network services. Specifically, they say:

> "DEN represents an entirely new network control model that tames large collections of diverse network services, allowing them to be centrally configured and managed. These network services include prioritization, forwarding, security, addressing, inventory control and many others."

FORE has also announced that it will use DEN to manage additional network services besides those of its ESX routing switch. Along these lines, in the May 1999 Networld + Interop show, FORE demonstrated a DEN-based system that uses a Netscape directory server to manage its ESX routing switch. This demo shows how, using policy, a user can manage the different resources required for a policy-enabled network using DEN.

Lucent

Lucent is supporting DEN through its own products and with other partners. For example, in the press release "Lucent and Novell work jointly to accelerate development and adoption of directory-enabled networking standards," Lucent says:

> "Lucent Technologies...and Novell, Inc. today announced the two companies are working together to advance the development and adoption of directory-enabled networking standards and policy-based networking. These new standards will help integrate network equipment, such as switches and routers, with directory services and will allow customers to improve their network management and cost controls."

Furthermore, in the same article, they say:

> "Lucent and Novell will collaborate to develop solutions based on the Common
> Information Model (CIM) and Directory-Enabled Networks (DEN) specifications
> in order to expedite the acceptance and implementation of these open standards
> throughout the industry. "Directory-enabled networking brings applications and
> devices together in a way that simplifies network management, and allows customers
> to set priorities for their network applications based on business needs," said Karyn
> Mashima, vice president of enterprise networks at Lucent."

Lucent is planning on using the directory to ensure that network resources are used for
the most productive activity possible. The directory provides a natural scoping to apply
policies to control network resources, ranging from an individual user to groups of users to
an entire organization. Applications can enjoy similar treatment. This combination enables
network administrators to offer guaranteed access to critical network resources through
allocations based on corporate policy.

Lucent's support for these policies will be provided initially by their Cajun P550 Gigabit
Routing Switch. Support for the other members of its Cajun Campus product, along with
additional offerings in the company's data networking enterprise portfolio, will follow.

Another area that Lucent will use DEN in is for advanced IP address management through
its QIP product line. DEN will be used for managing DNS and DHCP, enabling better
management of these two services, as well as better configuration and performance.

Finally, Lucent will be using DEN for their Policy Management Systems. *CajunView* is a
suite of tightly integrated applications that enables the configuration, monitoring, administration, and troubleshooting of switched and shared networks. In addition to using generic
management frameworks, such as HP's OpenView or Tivoli's TME, Lucent also makes use
of DEN-enabled products and technologies. For example, the following is an excerpt from
their CajunView Suite product description:

> "Policy management could also be achieved through the direct manipulation of the
> attributes of objects in a DEN-based (Directory Enabled Networks) Directory Service."

This enables CajunView to use DEN at various levels of abstraction—the entire network
down to settings in an individual device's configuration file.

Newbridge Networks

Newbridge is also very committed to directory and policy-based management. Newbridge has an affiliate strategy program, wherein Newbridge works with its partners on various solutions. One of the solutions in this program is DEN.

Novell

Novell was one of the first supporters of DEN, and its support has increased as DEN has matured. For example, here is a quote from Christopher Stone, Sr. vice president of Strategy and Business Development, from Novell's Brainshare '99 Conference:

> "We are using LDAP for compatibility with other directories and their related applications, and we are supporting the DEN initiatives and other standards initiatives around this area. We will help to drive all of those initiatives and eventually you will get to this notion of community."

Even more significantly, the latest version of NDS (version 8) announces support for DEN (see the Reviewer's Guide Reference).

Novell has been actively supporting DEN through various industry partnerships. Foremost among these are many networking vendors, including Cabletron, Cisco, Lucent, and Nortel Networks. Novell Directory Services (NDS) will be integrated into Cabletron's SPECTRUM, SmartSwitch, and SmartSwitch Router platforms in the second quarter of 1999. Cisco plans to offer NDS integration with Cisco Assure, Cisco Network Registrar, and Cisco User Registration and Tracking in the second quarter of 1999. Lucent and Nortel Networks will bundle and integrate NDS with the Cajun P550 switch and Bay Network's Optivity Policy Services, respectively, by the second quarter of 1999.

Ukiah Software

Ukiah Software is an example of a startup company that has backed DEN and incorporated it into its product line. The following URL reference is part of a presentation on their NetRoad policy-based management software that uses DEN.

```
http://www.ukiahsoft.com/NetRoad%20APS%20presentation/sld016.htm
```

Ukiah Software defines an intelligent network as one that is policy-enabled. Its mission is to provide a policy management solution that will help enable the transition from a dumb physical network infrastructure to an intelligent one. Their focus is on enabling network administrators to make better mappings of business policies to the network policies that control network behavior.

Ukiah thinks that, as IP networks move towards providing converged data, voice, and video traffic, the need for policy management will be even more important. This includes both low- and high-level issues, such as ensuring that certain QoS parameters (for example, bandwidth, delay, jitter, loss), as well as mission-critical applications, receive the priority and service that they require.

Ukiah Software's *NetRoad Active Policy System* is fully directory-enabled. As stated in their presentation, the directory is used to "collect, correlate and store dynamic network data, as well as provide access to standard directory services." Its first release uses policy management to deliver network QoS. Features include definition, editing, and management of QoS policies, as well as the ability to enforce and monitor policy. Future releases will deliver policy management for services beyond QoS, such as security, accounting, and billing.

Ukiah Software also has a firewall, called *NetRoad FireWALL*, that provides multilevel IP firewall security and Network Address Translation (NAT). It is interesting to note that this firewall is also directory-enabled, utilizing policy to manage and control the preceding features.

Industry Presentations on DEN

There are many sources for presentations on DEN. Here is a representative sampling:

Lucent Technologies and Novell to present directory-enabled networking seminar program across Europe. March, 1999.
`http://www.lucent.com/press/0399/990326.nsa.html`

Networld Interop, Las Vegas, NV. Workshop W848: "Policy, QoS, and DEN," 1999.
`http://www.interop.com/LasVegas/Education/Descriptions/ws.html`

Networld Interop, Singapore, "Directory Enabled Network—The Cornerstone to Policy Based Network Management," Fore University Workshop, 1999.
`http://www.interop.com.sg`

John Strassner. "Directories and Policy-Based Networking." EMA, March, 1999.

———. "The Networks Model and DEN," presented at the DMTF Annual User's Conference, June, 1999.

———. "Policy-Based Network Management," ComNet, January, 1999.

———. "Policy-Based Network Management," Networld+Interop, Las Vegas, NV. May, 1999.

Summary

This chapter has provided a perspective on the importance of DEN, and its effect in the networking industry. A snapshot of some of the current thinking regarding defining a standard notion of compliance for both CIM and DEN was provided. Key to this was the notion of registering extensions and providing a test suite.

Examples of using DEN and CIM throughout the networking industry were provided. Highlights included using DEN

- In enterprise and service provider solutions

- As the cornerstone for developing and deploying next-generation networks and networked applications

- In advanced policy-based networking solutions

- To link business processes to networked applications and services

- As the basis for extending network management to a proactive, predictive model from today's passive, reactive model

A number of trends were also identified as follows:

- The evolution to standardized schema simplifies device configuration, especially when devices from multiple vendors are used. For example, when a generic schema is defined for a particular type of device that plays a specific role in the network, all devices having that role can use the information in the schema.

- Backup, replication, and synchronization of network configuration files are automatically performed by the directory service.

- Replication of common configuration parameters are automatically performed by the directory service.

- Since the desktop configuration, access rights, and other policies are stored in the directory service and not on the PC's hard drive, a user always receives the same network and application configuration regardless of attachment point to the network. This means that nomadic and traveling users have a consistent experience every time that they access network.

- Centralized end-to-end policy management ensures that business objectives are being met in a reliable and consistent manner via automatic enforcement mechanisms in the network.

Recommended Further Study and References

For information on Cisco's directory-enabled networking initiative, see

"Moving Forward With DEN," *Packet Magazine*, January, 1999.
`http://www.cisco.com/warp/public/784/packet/jan99/10.html`

"Cisco Networking Services for Active Directory,"
`http://www.cisco.com/warp/public/cc/cisco/mkt/servprod/sms/common/tech/cnsad_wp.htm`

"Cisco Networking Services for Active Directory,"
`http://www.cisco.com/warp/public/cc/cisco/mkt/enm/cns/tech/cns_sd.htm`

"Cisco Networking Services for Active Directory—Enabling the Power of the Network,"
`http://www.cisco.com/warp/public/cc/cisco/mkt/enm/cns/prodlit/cns_ds.htm`

"Network-Aware Business Solutions,"
`http://www.cisco.com/warp/public/cc/cisco/mkt/enm/cns/tech/kpmg_wp.htm`

"CiscoAssure Policy Networking—Statement of Direction,"
`http://www.cisco.com/warp/public/cc/cisco/mkt/enm/cap/tech/assur_sd.htm`

"CiscoAssure Policy Networking End-to-End Quality of Service,"
`http://www.cisco.com/warp/public/cc/cisco/mkt/enm/cap/tech/caqos_wp.htm`

"CiscoAssure Services,"
`http://www.cisco.com/warp/public/779/largent/learn/technologies/CiscoAssure.html`

"Cisco Service Management System,"
`http://www.cisco.com/warp/public/779/servpro/solutions/csm/`

"Cisco Service Management System—Statement of Direction,"
`http://www.cisco.com/warp/public/cc/cisco/mkt/servprod/sms/tech/csms_sd.htm`

"Cisco Service Management—A White Paper,"
`http://www.cisco.com/warp/public/cc/cisco/mkt/servprod/sms/tech/csm_wp.htm`

For information on 3Com's directory-enabled networking initiative, see

"3Com's Framework for Policy-Based Networking,"
`http://www.3com.com/technology/tech_net/white_papers/500681.html`

"Directory-Enabled Networks and 3Com's Framework for Policy-Powered Networking,"
`http://www.3com.com/technology/tech_net/white_papers/500665.html`

For information on Nortel Network's directory-enabled networking initiative, see

"A Policy-Based Approach to Application-Optimized Networking,"
`http://www.nortelnetworks.com/solutions/collateral/policynote.pdf`

For information on Cabletron's directory-enabled networking initiative, see

"Cabletron and Novell Collaborate to Bring Directory-Enabled Networking to the Enterprise,"
`http://www.cabletron.com/ournews/1999/mar/3-22.html`

"Cabletron Unveils Next Steps in Standards-Based Directory Enabled Networking Initiative,"
`http://www.cabletron.com/ournews/1999/apr/4-5.html`

For information on Check Point's directory-enabled networking initiative, see

"Check Point Software Technologies Ltd.'S Meta IP Delivers Next Generation IP Address Management Services for the Enterprise,"
`http://www.checkpoint.com/press/1998/metaip101998.html`

"Check Point Software Technologies and Microsoft Expand Strategic Partnership,"
`http://www.checkpoint.com/press/1998/microsoft0511.html`

For information on Fore System's directory-enabled networking initiative, see

"FORE Systems Introduces Industry's Most Advanced Directory-Enabled Networking Solution,"
`http://www.fore.com/press/current/PR901_27.html`

"Fore Adds Directory Agent For Enterprise-Wide Policy Networking,"
`http://www.internetwk.com/news0199/news012199-8.htm`

"Policy Networking Gets a Little More Gravitas—Fore Adds Directory Agent For Enterprisewide Policy Networking,"
`http://www.techweb.com/se/directlink.cgi?INW19990125S0022`

"Directory Enabled Networking (DEN) Demo, presented at the May 1999 Networld+Interop." This URL, though active during N+I, has now been moved.
`http://www.fore.com/solutions/dendemo/`

For information on Lucent's directory-enabled networking initiative, see

"Lucent and Novell Work Jointly to Accelerate Development and Adoption of Directory-Enabled Networking Standards,"
`http://www.lucent.com/press/1098/981019.nsc.html`

"Lucent Technologies and Novell to Present Directory-Enabled Networking Seminar Program Across Europe,"
`http://www.lucent.com/press/0399/990326.nsa.html`

"QIP Enterprise 5.0 Product Brief,"
`http://www.lucent.com/dns/products/qip_b_ldap.html`

"CajunView Suite Product Brief,"
`http://www.lannet.com/site/products/cajunview/cviewds.htm`

For information on Newbridge Network's directory-enabled policy management applications, see

"The Newbridge Affiliate Strategy,"
`http://prodweb.newbridge.com/affiliates/index_main.html`

For information on Novell's directory-enabled initiatives, see

"Keynote Address from Christopher Stone, Sr. Vice President, Strategy and Business Development," for Novell's BrainShare '99 Conference in March 22, 1999,
`http://www.novell.com/pressroom/presskit/brainshare99/stone_keynote.html`

"CIO Monthly Forum," April 1999
`http://www.novell.com/corp/cio/`

"NDS 8 Reviewer's Guide,"
`http://www.novell.com/products/nds/ndsv8_rg.html`

"Nortel Networks and Novell Team to Deliver Directory-Enabled Networking to Enterprise Networks and the Internet,"
`http://www.novell.com/press/archive/1998/11/pr98142.html`

"Novell and Cisco—Announcing NDS Interoperability with Cisco Hardware,"
`http://www.novell.com/lead_stories/98/nov18/`

For information on Ukiah Software's directory-enabled policy management applications, see

"NetRoad Policy Management Presentation,"
`http://www.ukiahsoft.com/NetRoad%20APS%20presentation/sld016.htm`

13

The Future of Directory- and Policy-Enabled Networks

The purpose of this chapter is to first briefly review what we have learned about DEN and policy-based networking, and then to describe the future directions of directory- and policy-enabled networks. This chapter emphasizes anticipated developments in policy-enabled networking.

Why DEN Is so Important

DEN represents a new network management paradigm. Not only does it leverage existing investments in directory and other repository technologies, it ushers in a new way of thinking about network management. Instead of focusing on individual device configuration and management, DEN emphasizes the greater whole (for example, an autonomous system, network, or some other type of system) as a means for providing a set of *services* that can be used.

This reflects the move toward Intelligent Networks. Administrators are overwhelmed in the growing complexity of application needs and networks. Throwing bandwidth at this combination doesn't work, because the root of the problem is the *mix of network traffic and different services required by that mix.*

The real advantage that DEN and policy-based networking offer is binding clients of the network to services the network provides. This means that both the needs of the clients of the network and the capabilities of the network must be well known, easily accessible, and represented in a standard format in order to accomplish this.

Users, printers, file servers, and other important network resources are already described in the directory. Describing network elements and services in the directory centralizes the knowledge, encourages standardized access and representation of information, and capitalizes on the existing investment that the customer has in the directory.

There are several compelling reasons for using DEN along with a centralized repository. Arguably, the most important of these is that it serves as the foundation for policy-enabled networking.

Policy-based networking enables the sharing and reuse of policy information. This can be used for many things; in this book, we have been concerned primarily with its application to controlling in a standard way configuration of network devices and services. This can be accomplished because the network, its components, and the services that are provided by the network can also be described in a standard way. This has three principal benefits:

- Different users and applications can now share and reuse this information.

- Management applications can now use a uniform interface for controlling the network, even though it is made up of heterogeneous devices that have different capabilities and interfaces.

- Network administrators can define common configurations for particular types of network elements, as well as network elements that play a particular role in the network, without worrying about the specific type and model of the network element.

These are all very powerful benefits. The first enables applications that have completely different interfaces and APIs to exchange and share data. For example, a vendor can describe its devices in a DEN-compliant format and then ship them to another vendor who can read and reuse them. Cisco and Tivoli demonstrated this by shipping low-level configuration and modeling descriptions of Cisco devices to the Tivoli TME network management tool. The advantage is that this information can be examined using the Tivoli GUI, which makes a compelling, seamless experience for the network manager using TME. This is in spite of the very different GUIs and APIs that Cisco and Tivoli use.

An example of the second was given in the section "Cisco's Policy-Based Architecture" in Chapter 11, when CiscoAssure was discussed. CiscoAssure was used to abstract the particular capabilities and configuration methods of the devices that it controls and present information describing those devices to the administrator in a common format. This simplifies the job for the administrator and ensures consistent configuration.

The third is very powerful, but in a more subtle way. It is the first step toward viewing the network as a set of configurable objects in the system. This is behind some of the recent work in the DMTF Networks Working Group, as well as the IETF Policy Framework Working Group.

Another compelling reason is the opportunity to increase the security of the network. By containing information for network devices and services, common authentication and authorization methods can be performed for groups of devices and network resources. The directory is a very good repository for organizational information (for example, group definitions) and for security information (for example, public key storage).

The use of the directory in applications that administer or configure the network is a powerful configuration management paradigm. It is a way to manage the *network*, as opposed to individual systems or devices *in* the network. It is, therefore, inherently different than SNMP and other similar protocols, and better suited than these protocols to the task of expressing and distributing policy and other information that needs to be shared and reused. This does not mean that the directory will replace SNMP *per se*; while it could be used to implement the instrumentation of individual systems, that is not its current target. Rather, it targets defining the outcome of system configurations ("VoIP should get a certain kind of service in my network"), which individual systems will have to interpret locally ("VoIP traffic is marked with the (differentiated services) PHB of 111000 and should be admitted using RSVP and placed into the EF (Expedited Forwarding) queue on each interface"). SNMP then becomes a way to monitor and do certain kinds of configuration, while the directory manages certain other aspects of configuration, and manual configuration is required perhaps for yet other kinds.

Directions in Policy-Based Networking

Policy-based networking shows great promise. However, it is still in its infancy. This means that it needs to be carefully applied to problems until it is better understood, and not viewed as a panacea.

There is worry that policy-based networking is too complicated. This is because people get overwhelmed by the enormous potential differences that need to be controlled: differences in capabilities of network devices, differences in how network devices are controlled, and so on.

This is why object-oriented design is so important. Through the principle of abstraction, a policy-based system can project a view that organizes information and functions that are tailored to the application-specific needs of a given set of users. As was shown in the previous chapter, a Policy Server does not, and should not, have to show a screen that forces the user to look at MIB information or type low-level commands using a Telnet interface. Rather, much greater benefit is gained by abstracting the low-level configuration of devices into a higher-level form that can be understood by network managers. In addition, this enables the same policies and tools to be applied to different devices that serve the same function.

One way of obtaining large benefits from a more simplistic design approach is to apply policy-based networking to a pre-provisioned network. That is, divide the network into some number of paths, each of which is pre-provisioned to supply some level of traffic conditioning. Use policy-based networking to control the actual provisioning of each path by classifying each interface of each network element into one or more of several categories (called "roles") and then applying the given policy to each role. This ensures that network interfaces that have the same function will be provisioned the same way. Note that this avoids having to manually configure each individual device and repetitively set the same commands. It also avoids having to learn the differences in provisioning different types of devices (for example, one wants Telnet/CLI, and another wants COPS) as well as when to use what type of mechanism (for example, the different types of queuing mechanisms that devices support).

In this respect, the most obvious near-term use for policy-based networking is in differentiating traffic. This takes two forms. The first is to protect mission-critical traffic from other types of traffic that consume network resources that are needed by mission-critical traffic. The second is to differentiate traffic according to a set of agreed-upon service levels and apply the conditioning represented by a particular service level to the traffic flowing through a device.

A little farther downstream, companies will move toward incorporating various forms of multimedia into their existing set of applications. These could include video-conferencing applications, distance learning, and a number of other applications. This means that, at a fundamental level, the types of traffic that must be shared and given appropriate service become more complicated. Not only has the number of traffic types increased, but the demands that each application has on the network has grown in volume and complexity. The management of this environment cannot be performed without a comprehensive strategy that abstracts these differences and requirements into policies.

In addition, many corporations are reluctant to deploy multimedia applications of any type because they do not know how the increased traffic patterns and demands of these new applications will affect their existing applications. This ends up being a complicated problem with a large number of facets. In such cases, one must try to reduce the number of factors that contribute to the problem. Policy-based networking can be used to aggregate devices and traffic types. This enables policies to be defined that are installed against these device and network service aggregates, simplifying the entire system.

Policies can also be used to secure access to these new capabilities, as well as to ensure that proper authentication, authorization, accounting, and auditing is performed. This combination can be used to restrict the introduction of new services to a well-defined, known subset of employees (or subscribers of a service), so that the effects of these new services can be carefully monitored and controlled.

In the future, corporations will be ready to migrate from individual networks that carry a specific type of traffic to a converged network that accommodates data, voice, and video on the same line.

The conflicting requirements that result from continually adding additional forms of disparate traffic is precisely why policy-based networking is so important. New, additional requirements from new applications usually expect a certain level of QoS that conflicts with one or more existing provisioned services. With complex types of traffic intermingled in the network, some centralized and easily administered means for managing and allotting network resources must be installed. Such policies must instead rely on the intelligence that is distributed throughout the network as well as the intelligence that is embedded in the clients that are using the network.

IETF Update

The IETF has several working groups that are deeply involved in defining and using policy to control network services. The following is a chronological account of the working groups that were formed to solve this problem, and some views as to their progress and future.

The Integrated Services Model

The Integrated Services Working Group (IntServ) was the Internet community's first attempt to analyze the issues and define a solution to provide QoS to applications using the Internet. IntServ defined a guaranteed service that was aimed at supporting the needs of real-time applications that had specific latency and jitter requirements. This service provides firm bounds on end-to-end datagram queueing delays, and is documented in RFC 2212.

It then defined a controlled load service that provides a non-real-time service that is insensitive to congestion. It uses admission control to assure that this service is received even when the network element is overloaded. This is documented in RFC 2211. This then led to RSVP.

The RSVP Working Group was formed to design the Resource reSerVation Protocol as a means to reserve services in the network. The acceptance of these requests results in better network service to some flows, possibly at the expense of service to traditional best-effort flows. This is an explicit signaling mechanism.

This model has a number of strengths. Perhaps its most obvious strength is that it is designed to provide absolute service guarantees. Support for unicast or multicast, along with the ability to detect lost connections and deallocate resources as a response to that, are additional strengths.

However, IntServ has a number of weaknesses. The most important of these is that it requires each network device participating in the reservation to maintain state. While this may be practical for a small number of long-lived flows, it does not do well when confronted with a large number of short-lived flows.

Furthermore, while RSVP works well over IP, Layer 2 networks vary greatly in their characteristics and QoS capabilities. Therefore, the IETF formed the Integrated Services over Specific Link Layers (ISSLL) Working Group to map RSVP QoS requirements to different types of layer two networks.

The Resource Allocation Protocol (RAP) Working Group was formed to establish a scalable policy control model for RSVP. Two additional sub-goals are to facilitate the enforcing and reporting of operational policy constraints. Toward this end, RSVP message formats contain a placeholder for policy data elements, which may contain information relevant to the network's decision to grant a reservation request.

The Differentiated Services Model

The Differentiated Services Working Group (DiffServ) was formed primarily to address the scaling concerns of the Integrated Services Model. It is built around the notion of defining relatively simple and coarse methods of providing differentiated classes of service for Internet traffic. The DiffServ approach centers around changing the semantics of the type of service (ToS) byte in the IPv4 ToS octet (or the IPv6 Traffic Class octet) header. A new, 6-bit field is defined to specify QoS semantics. This is done by defining a set of bit patterns that signify that the traffic to which that packet belong should receive a particular *per-hop behavior*, or forwarding treatment, at each network node.

The DiffServ Working Group has standardized a common layout to be used for both octets, called the "DS field." This, along with an attendant architecture, is defined in RFC 2474 and RFC 2475, respectively. The DiffServ Working Group will also standardize a small number of specific per-hop behaviors, and recommend a particular bit pattern or "code point" of the DS field for each one.

This addresses the scaling problems found in the Integrated Services Model by aggregating traffic into classes, each with a different set of QoS requirements and treatments. By eliminating explicit signaling of QoS requirements between the source and the destination, setup costs and resource utilization are reduced significantly. On the other hand, aggregating traffic makes the exact characteristics of the service delivered somewhat unpredictable. This is why DiffServ does not specify a specific *guarantee* of service, but rather a relative ordering among the different traffic aggregations, such that one aggregate consistently gets better or worse traffic treatment relative to other aggregates.

The Policy Framework Working Group

The previous groups were concerned with protocols and low-level mechanisms to provide network QoS. However, there was no relation between these and policies (much less business rules) to control the configuration of network devices. The Policy Framework Working Group (PFWG) was formed in order to specify the linkage between high-level business rules and low-level device configurations that could provide the services specified by those high-level business rules.

More formally, the IETF recognized a need to represent, manage, and share policies and policy information in a vendor-independent, interoperable, scalable manner. The goal of the PFWG is to demonstrate the design and implementation of an architecture, Information Model, and schema that can be used for general policy purposes. To demonstrate this, the PFWG will work with other IETF Working Groups to demonstrate an end-to-end policy mapping for signaled and provisioned QoS. Thus, there are four main work items in the PFWG:

- Define an overall framework that will meet these needs.

- Define an Information Model that describes the base objects that represent policy in a generic way, as well as specific objects that represent signaled and provisioned QoS.

- Define a schema, suitable for implementation in a directory that uses LDAP as its access protocol, that can represent the core Information Model; define another schema that can represent the QoS Information Model.

- Show that the core Information Model and schema, along with the QoS Information Model and schema, can be combined with appropriate work from the Differentiated Services Working Group and the RSVP Admission Policy Working Group; the object of this combination is to prove that policy, when specified at a high-level, can still be used to configure network devices.

The framework is a high-level architecture that identifies the major functional components in a policy system, the interfaces that enable each component to talk to the other components in the system, and the data flow within the system. Its purpose is to define how policy can be defined, managed, distributed, and communicated between administrators and network devices. The Information Model provides a repository- and technology-independent description of the objects used to construct policies and policy information, and how they relate with other objects in a system. Finally, the schema maps the data defined in the Information Model to a specific target implementation, in this case, a directory that uses LDAP as its access protocol.

The work being done in the PFWG has been shown to be applicable to a wide variety of other IETF Working Groups. Therefore, the Information Model was purposely split into a "core" Information Model which was applicable to all domains, and a "QoS" Information Model that was specifically targeted at signaled (RSVP) and provisioned (Differentiated Services) QoS. Similarly, the resulting LDAP schemata were split into one that was derived from the "core" Information Model, and one that was derived from the "QoS" Information Model. The QoS Information Model and schema will provide an example to other IETF Working Groups in showing how to derive domain-specific information and models from the core Information Model and schema.

The IP Security Policy Working Group

The PFWG defined a general framework for expressing the composition and storage of policy. It is currently defining a refinement of these general constructs to model network QoS.

However, there is a need to control access to network resources in a scalable, secured, and reliable fashion. Administrative entities may need to be able to securely discover and negotiate access control information for entities along the path of the communication. They may also need to impose policy constraints on these entities, as well as other security-related work.

To address these problems, the IP Security Policy (IPSP) Working Group was formed. It is concerned with developing security policies that can also work with the core Policy Model developed in the PFWG.

Policy in Other Working Groups

DHCP, AAA, and other working groups are considering the adoption of the core Policy Model. This is because a policy-based approach offers a more flexible means for modeling configuration and state. However, nothing firm has been decided at this time, other than it is a goal for these different policies to work together with each other. This will likely be added as a charter item to the PFWG.

Rechartering of PFWG, DiffServ, and RAP

The PFWG, along with the Differentiated Services Working Group and the Resource Allocation Protocol Working Group, are currently being rechartered to work more closely together.

The reason for this is that these working groups all have overlapping goals. For example, the PFWG is charged with developing a generalized framework (based on CIM) that supports the definition, modification, management, storage, and retrieval of policy information. The proof of concept is to be the QoS schema.

However, there is a large gulf of information between the QoS schema defined in the PFWG and that in the Differentiated Services Working Group. This has resulted in the rechartering of the DiffServ Working Group, which is working on developing a MIB for representing differentiated services as well as the development of a PIB (Policy Information Base). The PIB is very similar to a MIB and serves as a bridge between the data model represented by a MIB and the Information Model represented in the QoS schema. Similarly, the PFWG is being rechartered to work on items that align it more closely with other working groups. DiffServ, RAP, and IPSP have already been identified.

However, there's still a problem: How does configuration information actually get downloaded from a Policy Decision Point (PDP) to a Policy Enforcement Point (PEP)? The RAP Working Group will be rechartered to finish the development of extensions to COPS that are necessary for downloading configuration information from a PDP to a PEP.

Thus, with the inclusion of the PIB, we have a structured and extensible way to represent information at different levels of abstraction. The Information Model defines the characteristics of and relationships between objects that represent policies and policy information. A schema binds this to a specific repository implementation. A PIB conveys the information in a schema, plus additional information describing the state of the network and other data not suitable for storage in a directory, in a form understandable by a network element. This form enables the policy to actually control the behavior of the network element. Finally, a MIB allows the network manager to read the configuration of the device (as well as change it directly, if necessary) to see what effect the new policy-driven configuration is having on traffic.

DMTF Update

The DMTF has produced a robust and extensible Information Model in the CIM 2.2 release. However, there are a number of working groups that are getting ready to propose additional Common Models that build on the CIM Core Model. This section briefly addresses this work.

Policy

The Policy (also known as service level agreement, or SLA) Working Group is chartered with extending the CIM to allow the definition and association of policies, rules, and expressions that enable communications with and management of CIM data and services. The work will use the core Information Model and schema defined in the IETF PFWG as its basis. It will then generalize this work so that it can be used by other Common Models, as well as enhance it to serve as the foundation for representing policies for information other than network QoS. This work should first appear in the CIM 2.3 release (due by the end of 1999) and progress forward from there.

The Information Model of the QoS schema developed in the IETF PFWG will be worked on by the Networks Working Group of the DMTF. This is because the networking subject matter expertise is in that group, not the SLA Working Group. This will evolve into a QoS sub-model in the Network Common Model and has a good chance of making the CIM 2.3 release.

The LDAP-compatible schema will be merged into the DEN effort (which is guided by the Networks Working Group). The SLA and the Networks Working Groups will work together to integrate these schemata into DEN.

Users and Security

The User Working Group has started to define objects, relationships, and access methods required to represent Security Principles. A *Security Principle* is an entity that can refer to a user, consumer, organization, or groups of one or more of these. The User Working Group will also model basic security mechanisms (for example, X.509 certificates, Kerberos tickets, and so forth) and the concept of an "account." This is because security needs to be tightly integrated into the concept of a Security Principle. All these objects will be defined in the User Common Model, which uses the concepts of the CIM Core Model and extends them to model users, security objects, and security relationships.

Database

The Database Working Group will produce a new Common Model that represents Relational Databases as an extension of the CIM Core Model. As such, it seeks to describe the general management characteristics of relational databases, not the characteristics of any particular relational database implementation.

The first version of the database model will define the basic concepts of a relational database system, including storage management, the catalog, users, transactions, and security. More advanced concepts, such as replication, data movement and transformation, and OLAP, will be addressed in the next version of the model.

Summary

This chapter reviewed the fundamental motivation for using DEN, as well as how DEN serves as part of the foundation of policy-based networking. This was defined as a symbiotic relationship, as modeling policies extended the underlying Information Model of DEN.

The possible applications of policy-based networking were then described. A roadmap for its anticipated development was discussed. This roadmap showed that policy-based networking will focus initially on traffic differentiation, moving subsequently to enabling multimedia applications and finally, assisting in the implementation of converged data-voice-video networks.

A brief status of the applicable IETF working groups and their rechartering based around policy-based networking was discussed. The reader is encouraged to track the Policy Framework, Differentiated Services, and Resource Allocation Protocol Working Groups closely.

Finally, a brief update was provided that describes several new DMTF Working Groups and their charters.

Recommended Further Study and References

The home pages of the IETF Working Groups that were described in this chapter are

Differentiated Services:
`http://www.ietf.org/html.charters/diffserv-charter.html`

Integrated Services:
`http://www.ietf.org/html.charters/intserv-charter.html`

Integrated Services Over Specific Link Layers:
`http://www.ietf.org/html.charters/issll-charter.html`

Policy Framework Working Group:
`http://www.ietf.org/html.charters/policy-charter.html`

RSVP:
`http://www.ietf.org/html.charters/rsvp-charter.html`

RSVP Admission Policy:
`http://www.ietf.org/html.charters/rap-charter.html`

Index

The *Macmillan Technology Series* is a comprehensive and authoritative set of guides to the most important computing standards of today. Each title in this series is aimed at bringing computing professionals closer to the scientists and engineers behind the technological implementations that will change tomorrow's innovations in computing.

Currently available titles in the *Macmillan Technology Series* include:

Gigabit Ethernet Networking, **by David G. Cunningham, Ph.D., and William G. Lane, Ph.D. (ISBN: 1-57870-062-0)**

Written by key contributors to the Gigabit Ethernet standard, *Gigabit Ethernet Networking* provides network engineers and architects both the necessary context of the technology and advanced knowledge of its deployment. This book offers critical information to enable readers to make cost-effective decisions about how to design and implement their particular network to meet current traffic loads and to ensure scalability with future growth.

DSL: Simulation Techniques and Standards Development for Digital Subscriber Line Systems, **by Walter Chen (ISBN: 1-57870-017-5)**

The only book on the market that deals with xDSL technologies at this level, *DSL: Simulation Techniques and Standards Development for Digital Subscriber Line Systems* is ideal for computing professionals who are looking for new high-speed communications technology, who must understand the dynamics of xDSL communications to create compliant applications, or who simply want to better understand this new wave of technology.

ADSL/VDSL Principles, **by Dr. Dennis J. Rauschmayer (ISBN: 1-57870-015-9)**

ADSL/VDSL Principles provides the communications and networking engineer with practical explanations, technical detail, and in-depth insight needed to fully implement ADSL and VDSL. This book covers topics that are essential to the successful implementation of these technologies.

LDAP: Programming Directory-Enabled Applications with Lightweight Directory Access Protocol, **by Tim Howes and Mark Smith (ISBN: 1-57870-000-0)**

This book is the essential resource for programmers, software engineers, and network administrators who need to understand and implement LDAP to keep software applications compliant. If you design or program software for network computing or are interested in directory services, *LDAP* is an essential resource to help you understand the LDAP API; to learn how to write LDAP programs; to understand how to LDAP-enable an existing application; and to learn how to use a set of command-line LDAP tools to search and update directory information.

Upcoming titles in the *Macmillan Technology Series* include:

Supporting Service Level Agreements on an IP Network, by Dinesh Verma (ISBN: 1-57870-146-5)

Service level agreements (SLAs), which allow network service providers to contract with their customers for different levels of quality of service, are becoming increasingly popular. *Supporting Service Level Agreements on an IP Network* describes methods and techniques that can be used to ensure that the requirements of SLAs are met. This essential guide covers SLA support on traditional best-effort IP networks, as well as support of SLAs using the latest service differentiation techniques under discussion in the IETF and other standards organizations. *Supporting Service Level Agreements on an IP Network* provides information services managers and engineers with critical, practical insight into the procedures required to fulfill their service level agreements.

Virtual Private Networks, by David Bovee (ISBN: 1-57870-120-1)

The technologies involved in creating virtual private networks (VPNs) are still evolving and developing. A VPN can have a significant effect on reducing overall networking costs because it utilizes the free resource of the Internet instead of relying on expensive T-1 or telephone connections. *Virtual Private Networks* provides the detailed technical information that network architects need to decide how to optimally build their VPN to meet the needs of their organization and networking environment.

Directory Enabled Networking, by John Strassner (ISBN: 1-57870-140-6)

Directory enabled networking (DEN) is a rapidly developing industry and standards effort in the Desktop Management Task Force (DMTF). DEN allows network architects and engineers to manage their networks through centralized control and provisioning, which yields significant reductions in cost of ownership. DEN is also a fundamental technology for policy-based networking, which is receiving a lot of attention in the networking industry. The author, John Strassner, is the creator of the DEN specification as well as the chair of the DMTF DEN working group. *Directory Enabled Networking* is a critical resource for network architects and engineers to consider how to optimally utilize this technology in their networking environments.

***Understanding the Public Key Infrastructure*, by Carlisle Adams and Steve Lloyd (ISBN: 1-57870-166-x)**

Public Key Infrastructure (PKI) is a new technology critical for securing data and communication in both enterprise and Internet environments. *Understanding the Public Key Infrastructure* provides network architects and implementers with essential information for deploying and enhancing critical business services. The authors, Carlisle Adams and Steve Lloyd, have been extensively involved with the design, standardization, and real-world deployment of PKIs. *Understanding the Public Key Infrastructure* presents unique expertise on PKI techology not available in any other source.

***SNMP Agents*, by Bob Natale (ISBN: 1-57870-110-4)**

Because SNMP is the dominant network management tool in the market, SNMP agents are included in every device that is expected to be connected to a network. Author Bob Natale, Chair of IETF Extensible SNMP Agent Working Group and the WinSNMP Industry Forum, provides critical information for network architects and engineers to manage their networks with this powerful technology. *SNMP Agents* is an essential resource for creating and implementing SNMP agents that perform optimally in a particular network environment.

***Intrusion Detection*, by Rebecca Gurley Bace (ISBN: 1-57870-185-6)**

Intrusion detection is a critical new area of technology within network security. An intrusion detection system serves as a system alert for unauthorized access for networks and systems connected to the Internet. This comprehensive guide to topics in intrusion detection covers the foundations of intrusion detection and system audit. *Intrusion Detection* provides a wealth of information, ranging from commercial intrusion detection products to design considerations. Author Rebecca Bace is one of the founders of the field of intrusion detection, and is a nationally recognized expert.

The *Macmillan Network Architecture and Development Series* is a comprehensive set of guides that provides computing professionals with the unique insight of leading experts in today's networking technologies. Each volume explores a technology or set of technologies that is needed to build and maintain the optimal network environment for any particular organization or situation.

Currently available titles in the *Macmillan Network Architecture and Development Series* include:

Wide Area High Speed Networks, by Dr. Sidnie Feit (ISBN: 1-57870-114-7)

Conventional telephony, ISDN networks, ATM networks, packet-switched networks, and Internet data technologies coexist today in a complex tapestry of networks. This book clearly explains each technology, describes how they interoperate, and puts their various uses and advantages into perspective. *Wide Area High Speed Networks* is an authoritative resource that will enable networking designers and implementors to determine which technologies to use in their networks and for which roles.

Switched, Fast, and Gigabit Ethernet, by Sean Riley and Robert A. Breyer (ISBN: 1-57870-073-6)

Switched, Fast, and Gigabit Ethernet, Third Edition is the one and only solution needed to understand and fully implement this entire range of Ethernet innovations. Acting both as an overview of current technologies and hardware requirements as well as a hands-on, comprehensive tutorial for deploying and managing Switched, Fast, and Gigabit Ethernets, this guide covers the most prominent present and future challenges network administrators face.

Understanding and Deploying LDAP Directory Services, by Tim Howes, Mark Smith, and Gordon Goode (ISBN: 1-57870-070-1)

This comprehensive tutorial provides the reader with a thorough treatment of LDAP directory services. Designed to meet multiple needs, the first part of the book presents a general overview of the subject matter. The next three sections cover detailed instructions for design, deployment, and integration of directory services. The text is full of practical implementation advice and real-world deployment examples to help the reader choose the path that makes the most sense for the specific organization.

Designing Addressing Architectures for Routing and Switching, by Howard C. Berkowitz (ISBN: 1-57870-059-0)

Designing Addressing Architectures for Routing and Switching provides a systematic methodology for planning the wide area and local area network streets on which users and servers live. It guides the network designer in developing rational systems that are flexible and that maintain a high level of service. Intended for people who are, or want to be, responsible for building large networks, this book offers a system and taxonomy for building networks that meet user requirements. It includes practical examples, configuration guides, case studies, tips, and warnings.

Wireless LANs: Implementing Interoperable Networks, by Jim Geier (ISBN: 1-57870-081-7)

This book provides both a context for understanding how an enterprise can benefit from the application of wireless technology and the proven tools for efficiently implementing a wireless LAN. Based on the most recent developments in the field, _Wireless LANs: Implementing Interoperable Networks_ gives network engineers vital information on planning, configuring, and supporting wireless networks.

Upcoming titles in the _Macmillan Network Architecture and Development Series_ include:

Local Area High Speed Networks, by Dr. Sidnie Feit (ISBN: 1-57870-113-9)

With Web intranets driving bandwidth needs increasingly higher, the technologies being deployed in local area networks are changing rapidly. For example, inexpensive Ethernet network interface cards and switches are now commonly available. Many networking professionals are interested in evaluating these new technologies for implementation. _Local Area High Speed Networks_ provides real-world implementation expertise for these technologies, including traces, so that users can realistically compare and decide how to optimally deploy them in their network environment. This comprehensive guide covers Ethernet technologies, virtual LANs, and routing and switching technologies.

The DHCP Handbook, by Ralph Droms and Ted Lemon (ISBN: 1-57870-137-6)

The DHCP Handbook provides network architects and administrators with an authoritative overview of the Dynamic Host Configuration Protocol, as well as expert information on how to set up and manage a DHCP server. This book will show networking professionals already working with DHCP systems how to take full advantage of the technology to solve their management and address assignment problems. An essential resource, _The DHCP Handbook_ provides the reader with critical information and expertise from author Ralph Droms, the chair of the IETF Dynamic Host Configuration (DHC) working group on automated network configuration, and author Ted Lemon, who wrote the ISC DHCP server code.

Designing Routing and Switching Architectures for Enterprise Networks,
by Howard Berkowitz (ISBN: 1-57870-060-4)

A critical resource for network architects and engineers, *Designing Routing and Switching Architectures for Enterprise Networks* teaches the reader how to select the optimal switches and routers for his or her network environment, and it guides the reader on effective deployment. This book provides the unique insight and experience of real-world network design from Howard Berkowitz, an experienced network designer, developer, and contributor to the standards process.